RUGBY LEAGUE 1998

DAVID MIDDLETON

Harper*Sports*
An imprint of HarperCollins*Publishers*

Harper*Sports*
An imprint of HarperCollins*Publishers*, Australia

First published in Australia in 1998
by HarperCollins*Publishers* Pty Limited
ACN 009 913 517
A member of HarperCollins*Publishers* (Australia) Pty Limited Group
http://www.harpercollins.com.au

Copyright © David Middleton 1998

This book is copyright.
Apart from any fair dealing for the purposes of private study, research, criticism or review, as permitted under the Copyright Act, no part may be reproduced by any process without written permission.
Inquiries should be addressed to the publishers.

HarperCollins*Publishers*
25 Ryde Road, Pymble, Sydney NSW 2073, Australia
31 View Road, Glenfield, Auckland 10, New Zealand
77–85 Fulham Palace Road, London W6 8JB, United Kingdom
Hazelton Lanes, 55 Avenue Road, Suite 2900, Toronto, Ontario M5R 3L2
and 1995 Markham Road, Scarborough, Ontario M1B 5M8, Canada
10 East 53rd Street, New York NY 10032, USA

ISBN 0 7322 6424 3

Typesetting and design: Brevier Design
Printed in Australia by Griffin Press Pty Ltd on 79gsm Bulky Paperback
Club emblems and Australian Rugby League logos are the copyright of the ARL and may not be reproduced.

9 8 7 6 5 4 3 2 1
01 00 99 98

About the Author
David Middleton has been the editor of the official NSW Rugby League Yearbook since the first in the current series was released, in early 1988 (*Rugby League 1998* is eleventh in the series). He is recognised as Australia's leading rugby league historian and statistician. Middleton was a feature writer with *Rugby League Week* for nine years, before leaving the magazine in early 1993 to establish his own rugby league information agency, *League Information Servies*. David will be part of 2UE's top rating Continuous Call rugby league coverage during 1998.

Photographs
The photographs in *Rugby League 1998* were provided by Clifford White, who can be contacted in Sydney on (02) 9982 6363.

All information in this book is correct as at 31 January, 1998

Contents

Introduction by *David Middleton* 2

FEATURES

Paul Harragon Interview 4
Newcastle's Rugby League Roots 11
The Premiership Coaches ... From Halloway to Reilly 15
Players of the Year 19
Team of the Year 24
Roll of Honour 25
1997 in Review 27
Vale 46

OPTUS CUP

Round 1	50	Round 12	72
Round 2	52	Round 13	74
Round 3	54	Round 14	76
Round 4	56	Round 15	78
Round 5	58	Round 16	80
Round 6	60	Round 17	82
Round 7	62	Round 18	84
Round 8	64	Round 19	86
Round 9	66	Round 20	88
Round 10	68	Round 21	90
Round 11	70	Round 22	92

Competition Tables 94
Minor Qualifying Finals 97
Major Qualifying Finals 100
Preliminary Finals 103
Grand Final 105
Second Grade 107
Award Winners 1997 109

ARL CLUBS

Balmain	112	Parramatta	124
Gold Coast	114	St George	126
Illawarra	116	South Queensland ...	128
Manly-Warringah	118	South Sydney	130
Newcastle	120	Sydney City	132
North Sydney	122	Western Suburbs	134

Coca-Cola World Sevens 136
City v Country 138
State of Origin 139
Australia v Rest of the World......................... 143

SUPER LEAGUE — TELSTRA CUP

Round 1	144	Round 10	157
Round 2	145	Round 11	158
Round 3	147	Round 12	160
Round 4	148	Round 13	161
Round 5	150	Round 14	163
Round 6	151	Round 15	164
Round 7	153	Round 16	166
Round 8	154	Round 17	167
Round 9	156	Round 18	168

Competition Tables 170
Finals.. 172
Grand Final 174
Super League World Nines 175
Super League Tri-Series 176
Super League World Club Challenge 179
Australia–New Zealand Tests 186
Australia–Great Britain Super League Series 187

SUPER LEAGUE CLUBS

Adelaide	189	Cronulla	197
Auckland	190	Hunter	199
Brisbane	192	North Queensland	201
Canberra	194	Penrith..............	203
Canterbury...........	196	Perth	204

RECORDS

Australian Scoreboard................................ 206
ARL Premiership Records............................. 215
Club-by-Club Records 224
Extinct Clubs 251
City v Country 1927–1997 261
New South Wales v Queensland 1908–1997.............. 263
Australian Test Results 1908–1997................... 281
Australian Internationals 1908–1997................. 286

1998 PREMIERSHIP DRAW **299**

The NSW Rugby League 1997

DIRECTORS AND MANAGEMENT

Chairman: K.R.Arthurson A.M. (resigned Feb 28, 1997). W.Lockwood (appointed Mar 6, 1997).
General Manager: J.R.Quayle (resigned Dec 20, 1996). N.Whittaker (appointed Feb 1, 1997).
Directors: T.J.Bellew O.A.M. (retired Dec 20, 1996), D.J.Barnhill, R.A.Beattie, D.Cortese (appointed Feb 24, 1997), D.W.Fitzgerald, R.Millward, N.Politis (appointed Dec 6, 1996), M.Buckling (elected Dec 6, 1996, resigned Jun 24, 1997), D.Leckie (appointed Dec 9, 1996, resigned Jan 20, 1997).

MEMBERS OF THE LEAGUE 1997

Patrons: J.N.Argent O.B.E. O.A.M. Ed., K.R.Arthurson A.M.
Chairman: K.R.Arthurson (resigned Feb 28, 1997), W.Lockwood (appointed Mar 6, 1997).
Vice-Presidents: E.H.Cox, C.Love, R.A.Dunn O.A.M., R.J.Ibbitson, B.Kurtz, W.Monaghan, R.S.O'Donnell, J.J.O'Toole O.A.M. M.B.E., J.B.Riordan, D.Robinson.

Delegates

Balmain: D.Munk, J.Chalk
Gold Coast: P.Broughton, T.Bellew O.A.M.
Illawarra: B.Millward, I.Kirk
Manly: F.Stanton, R.Hudson
Newcastle: I.Bonnette, M.Hill
Newtown: A.Reid, F.Farrington
North Sydney: B.Saunders, R.Beattie
Parramatta: D.Fitzgerald, A.Overton
South Queensland: E.Laakso, D.Knight
South Sydney: D.Bampton, L.Bell
St George: B.Johnston, The Hon D.McClelland A.C.
Sydney City: B.Gurr, N.Politis
Western Suburbs: M.Bullock, R.Watson
Country Rugby League: D.Barnhill, V.Byrne, R.Lanesbury, W.Kimberley
Referees Association: L.Matthews, D.Wintin

Committees

Australian Rugby League Directors
J.Quayle (resigned Dec 20, 1996), N.Whittaker (appointed Feb 1, 1997), T.J.Bellew, D.Barnhill, W.Lockwood, D.Fitzgerald, B.Millward (alternate)

Marketing, Promotions and Sponsorship Committee
R.Beattie (Chairman), J.Quayle (resigned Dec 20, 1996), N.Whittaker (appointed Feb 1, 1997), T.Connaghan, J.Davis-Slade, J.Thorpe, R.Tate, G.Willoughby, G.Foster (resigned Jan 14, 1997), I.Ross (appointed Feb 17, 1997)

Top Marketing Group
R.Beattie (Chairman), I.Ross, N.Whittaker, J.Wright, M.Melhuish, P.Metzner, M.Crawford, R.Scrimshaw, S.Cameron, T.Barnett, R.Winten, A.Hammell

National Premiership Council
D.Fitzgerald, N.Whittaker, B.Saunders, D.Munk, B.Millward, I.Bonnette, F.Stanton, E.Laakso, P.Broughton, D.Bampton, B.Johnston, B.Gurr, M.Bullock, P.Cross, P.Harrison

NSWRL Coaching Council Members
W.Sullivan, J.Hayes, P.Kelly, G.Ross, S.Browne, S.Hood, K.Holman, I.Laycock, W.Portlock, T.Baitieri, M.Aldous, P.Corcoran, M.Meredith

Finance Committee
D.Cortese (Chairman), J.Quayle (resigned Dec 20, 1996), N.Whittaker (appointed Feb 1, 1997), W.Kimberley, J.Jones, C.Turner, A.David (resigned Dec 9, 1996), S.Costigan A.O. (appointed Aug 18, 1997)

Coaching and Development Policy Committee
D.Barnhill (Chairman), M.Meredith, W.Smiles, M.Doyle (resigned July 1997), P.O'Dwyer, W.Young, D.Bampton, B.Saunders, G.Tiernan, M.Carr, B.Wallace

Appeals Committee
E.Cox, W.Monaghan, R.O'Donnell

Boundaries Committee
E.Cox, R.Ibbitson, B.Kurtz, W.Monaghan

Judiciary Committee
A.Sullivan Q.C. (Chairman), R.Coote, D.Brooks, M.Bolt, K.Boustead

Judiciary Appeals Board
The Hon Sir Laurence Street A.C. K.C.M.G., Two Vice-Presidents

Metropolitan Selection Committee
D.Furner (Chairman), M.Falla, J.Hayes, K.Holman, B.McCarthy, J.Raper, C.Renilson, I.Walsh, J.Sattler

New South Wales Selection Committee
D.Furner (Chairman), E.Lumsden, J.Raper, M.Falla (Deputy)

Australian Selection Committee Representatives
D.Furner (Chairman), A.Beetson, L.Geeves, E.Lumsden, J.Raper, A.Smith

Referees Advisory Board
B.Bolton, J.Connor, M.Dunn, M.Edwards, P.Elliss, P.Filmer, M.Gerber, J.Griffith, M.Hourigan, K.Jeffes, I.McCall, R.Pearce, K.Roberts, M.Ryan, D.Spagarino, T.Stafford, M.Tomsett, D.Wintin, J.Yard

Metropolitan Cup Policy Committee
T.J.Bellew (Chairman), J.Coates (Convenor), T.Williams (Assistant Convenor), S.McIlveen, T.Melcalfe, G.Staines, W.Smith, A.Reid, D.Mooney, R.Gibbons, R.Nalder, K.Aggett

Metropolitan Cup Judiciary Committee
G.Glass (Chairman), R.Aboud (Alternate Chairman), R.Sigsworth, One Vice-President

Salary Payments Committee
D.Cortese (Chairman), two invited members *(Note: This committee was not required to meet during 1997)*

Drugs Judiciary Tribunal
The Hon Sir Laurence Street A.C. K.C.M.G. (Chairman), M.Cleary, Dr T.James, Dr W.Monaghan (alternate)

Introduction

By DAVID MIDDLETON

After a thousand days and a billion dollars, an end to hostilities in Rugby League's destructive civil war was finally called in December 1997.

The warring parties had all but bled themselves dry. Even Super League's parent company, worldwide media giant News Corporation, refused to pour more good money for bad in their bid to wrest control of the game from its traditional managers, the Australian Rugby League.

For their part, the ARL appeared well ahead in the short term. However, they too were aware of the dangers of continuing to "go it alone" without long-term funding guarantees. So the demands of the dollar which began the regrettable saga on April Fool's Day, 1995, dictated its conclusion. Thankfully, the rival organisations reached their compromise before Rugby League's vital signs had ebbed to a flat-line.

While the fallout from the battle is expected to be felt for a long time there is some cause for optimism. Long-suffering supporters can prepare for a united competition of 20 teams in 1998, a representative season in which all-comers are considered and a final series in which the best teams in the country are pitted against each other.

It will be a far cry from 1997, the most divisive year in the game's 90 years in Australia. Two competitions inevitably diluted the enthusiasm of supporters and the acrimony and propaganda that proliferated in sections of the media turned many more away. The casualties of war have been considerable. Tens of thousands of supporters have been 'lost', careers have suffered and entire footballing entities have been laid to waste. Rugby League in Western Australia is perhaps the most significant victim.

An expansion team of the ARL in 1995, the Western Reds became an early target of Super League, who viewed a national competition as a central component of its plans. But instead of this becoming a genuine investment in the future of the code in the west, Super League abandoned ship in 1997, because the geographically-isolated franchise could not pay its way. Instead of celebrating 50 years in Perth in 1998, the Western Australian Rugby League is now facing an uphill battle for its survival.

The Hunter Mariners, a team which performed with remarkable results in the face of some mountainous obstacles in 1997, were another to meet their doom. Located in the middle of the staunchest ARL stronghold in the country, the Mariners were living on borrowed time from the outset.

The Mariners were the odd team out when the warring parties struck their deal for a 20-team competition. On the ARL side, the South Queensland Crushers ended their short premiership tenure by drowning in a sea of debt. At the start of the 1995 season, the Crushers shaped as a viable and potentially successful alternative to the Brisbane Broncos, but the ravages of the ARL-Super League conflict were felt severely in Brisbane. In 1997, the Crushers' crowds dropped alarmingly — a situation equally attributable to the conflict as to the team's moderate performances. Then an attempt to merge the Crushers with South-East

Queensland's third team, the improved Gold Coast Chargers, proved a miserable failure.

Just as 1997 had its negative aspects, there were some positives as well. Standing out like a blazing beacon was Newcastle's epic grand final win over Manly. Achieved in the final six seconds of the game, the Knights scored one of the game's most remarkable victories. They were urged on by an army of loyal Newcastle supporters, but the Knights also benefited from an anti-Manly sentiment that intensified as a result of some of the Sea Eagles' on-field antics. The game in Australia has not previously witnessed the scenes of jubilation that followed the Knights' win. A civic reception was watched by over 100,000 people and old-timers in Newcastle rated the celebrations bigger than those that followed World War II.

As part of its comprehensive coverage of the game as it was played in Australia in 1997, *Rugby League 1998* includes coverage of both ARL and Super League competitions. It is important, from an historical perspective, that the records and results of Super League's one and only season be recorded in this Yearbook. The traditional competition, which completed its 90th season in 1997, is again covered in full.

The recording of players' records in view of the single season of Super League presents its own difficulties. Just as the international records of World Series Cricket representatives are not included in official Test cricket records, players who appeared in Super League's Australian teams in 1997 are not included in the comprehensive list of Australian internationals which appears at the back of the Yearbook. In the club records section, only the records of players competing in ARL premiership matches are included, although all record-breaking performances by Super League players are noted.

A major feature of *Rugby League 1998* is an in-depth interview with Newcastle captain Paul Harragon, who discusses the events surrounding the Knights' premiership victory and some interesting revelations about his own career. As well, we identify some of the men who shaped the history of the game in Newcastle. And there is a detailed look at the men who have coached at first-grade level down the years and a surprising discovery of the most successful coach in premiership history.

Also included are all the regular features of past Rugby League Yearbooks, including the five Players of the Year, the Team of the Year and the extensive Year in Review section.

The challenges facing the new National Rugby League Championship in 1998 are among the most important to have been confronted by the sport in this country. It will be a difficult year with the 20 teams fighting for 16 licenses in 1999 and 14 by the year 2000.

Clearly, inner-Sydney clubs such as Balmain and South Sydney will be under the greatest threat to survive. Discussions over the fate of these clubs and possible mergers for the 1999 season are expected to dominate the media throughout 1998. However, finally, there now appears a clear direction for the game's future. How the game evolves from here will be unpalatable to some, but for Rugby League to again prosper in Australia it is time for the tough decisions to be made.

INTRODUCTION

RUGBY LEAGUE 1998 Interview:

Paul Harragon

Paul Harragon's finest season in Rugby League was almost over before it began. A series of excruciating migraine headaches struck down the Newcastle captain in the 1997 pre-season, threatening his very future. In this revealing interview with Rugby League 1998, *the man known as 'The Chief' openly discusses this personal crisis, along with a range of issues relating to the Newcastle Knights and their incredible premiership victory. Harragon also reveals that he will walk away from the game after just two more seasons.*

A foundation player with the Newcastle Knights, Harragon has been an integral member of the team throughout the 1990s. In 1997 he achieved the ultimate honour in premiership football when he led the Knights to their epic grand final win over Manly. This was the pinnacle of a season of remarkable personal achievement for the Newcastle captain, who led Country Origin to a convincing win over City, helped spearhead New South Wales' State of Origin victory over Queensland and also played in the one-off Test for Australia against the Rest of the World.

Here Harragon discusses in detail the events surrounding Newcastle's miracle grand final win, of the emotion-charged build-up, the game itself and its incredible aftermath. To kick-off the interview, Rugby League 1998 *asked Harragon to rate his top three magic moments of 1997.*

Paul Harragon: I think Darren Albert would have to be involved in one or two of them. That try-saving tackle he made on Matt Seers (in the Newcastle-Norths preliminary final) was one. If he didn't make that tackle we mightn't have got through. I enjoyed the start of the grand final — just to be there after all the build-up — and, of course, the final six seconds.

Rugby League 1998: For 40 minutes the grand final seemed to follow the same script as the major qualifying final against Manly. The same score at halftime, a Manly try right before the break ... At what point did you feel the tide begin to turn?

PH: In the first half it seemed to be the same old story, except for the good start we had. We tried to work them over physically, but it was the same old go, they went down our right-hand edge because their outside backs are a fair bit more mature and experienced. Whenever they play us they raid us down the edge and they come up with the goods every time. Basically with two quick shifts of the ball they came up with two tries and it looked like the same deal again.

But even though that happened and we made a few bad mistakes, at half-time we weren't concerned about the score. We talked about a few different incidents, about what was going on and how we were going to work it out. Everyone was cool and calm, we weren't worried about coming from behind, we were just concerned about doing the job. We came back out and concentrated on what we had to do. They didn't score another point. The essence was we just wanted it more.

To get back to your question — the turnaround — with 12 minutes to go they had two sets of six on our line and we held them out. If they had scored then there's no way in the world we could have come back. We held them out and that was crucial for us to be given the chance to possibly win. I think when Hoppo (Manly winger, John Hopoate) didn't kick the ball out on the sixth tackle it was the break we needed that gave us the chance to win.

RL98: For all that's been said about the amazing support you had from the people of Newcastle that day, and of course before that day, is it something you are conscious of when you're on the field?

PH: As with all sports you're a little bit conscious of what's around you when you first run out, but when you get into the moment you can't hear too much. But, honestly, towards the end I could really feel, more than hear, the crowd lifting us up. When it got close towards the end I could actually feel them driving us home. I had resigned myself to extra-time. We had missed a couple of kicks and we weren't working in the right direction for another one, but we weren't out on our feet. We were actually a bit more pumped up and feeling better with ourselves. And the pressure mounted on Manly. They were supposed to be leading comfortably and win well and every second we were a chance of catching them the pressure built on them. They were the ones out on their feet and I think that was a direct effect of the crowd.

RL98: How did the grand final hype compare with your expectations?

PH: When we had got close before, and made the semi-finals, the joint was jumping and we imagined that making the grand final would be a huge deal. At the start of the week it was a little bit slow. There was the red-and-blue house, red-and-blue pies and red-and-blue beer, but as the week went on it became absolute hysteria. For the days before the game the buzz was more than I thought it would be and then, after we won, it was like a dream. We did a parade of Newcastle by car and streets that I'd been through 1000 times were like I'd never seen them before. There were thousands of people everywhere. It was crazy!

RL98: The Newcastle Knights have made a lot of people very happy in 1997. Have you become aware of any effects that will be felt in the longer term?

PH: The weekend of the grand final and the following Tuesday are part of history. They were great, thank you very much, but I think the whole thing has manifested itself into something much bigger. One thing that has been gauged is consumer confidence and they say that has gone right up. Something I have noticed since the grand final is when I've been to Sydney or somewhere else outside Newcastle, people come up to me and say they're from Hamilton, or wherever, and they're really proud to come from Newcastle. I suppose people have always been proud, but there's always been a bit of a stigma with BHP and the rest of it. But we've got Mark Richards, silverchair, The Screaming Jets and now a championship footy side.

RL98: Have you noticed any differences in Newcastle itself. Is it possible to be recognised any more than you already are?

PH: I don't think so. But the thing is it has been unparalleled as far as celebrations go in anything that has happened in Newcastle. And not only sport. Even an old Digger, who came up to us on the

Tuesday when there were 100,000 people in Civic Park, said the size of the celebration and the feeling of goodwill was bigger than the celebrations and the dancing in the streets that followed World War II. So nothing matches it as far as celebrations go in this town. You can't get much bigger.

RL98: You weren't supposed to win the grand final. You had lost on 11 previous occasions to Manly and you had no players in your side who had played in a grand final. How did you deal with that. Did you talk about those issues or did you ignore them?

PH: We were confronted with them every time we did an interview. The journos got onto those facts and gave us a bit of a hiding with them, but it's irrelevant. If you're going to do something special you need a reason.

I was prepared to tell the boys, 'Everyone is already proud of us — we've made the grand final — and really we're in a no-lose situation. Manly have all the pressure so let's enjoy ourselves, but let's make sure we don't get overawed.' That's what I was going to say, but as the week went on and we left on the Saturday, the feeling began to grow inside us that we could win. The swell began to build and when we left home on the bus there were about 15,000 people waving to us and wishing us well and the energy we felt was electrifying. It was emotion. I don't cry, I'm as tinny as they get, but when there were just so many people on either side of the bus guiding us through, I was welling up. And then as we got up the road, I reckon for the next 30 kilometres, they were everywhere — old blokes, young people — they were just willing us on. I thought then, 'Something special is going to happen.'

It rolled on, all the way to Gosford there were people on the side of the road. And I remember another key to it came from something 'Gus' Gould had told us about Penrith, who've got a lot of similarities to us. They won the grand final (in 1991) as underdogs and the towns are reasonably similar as far as unemployment goes. Anyway, they had a meeting the night before their grand final. They went around asking each player what it meant to them and sometimes, it might sound a bit corny, but when you're coming up to a big game or something important, blokes tend to open up. Roycey Simmons, the elder statesman, said, 'the big fella can take me tomorrow, if we win this, nothing else matters.' It worked for Roycey — two tries and man of the match in the grand final.

With that in the back of my mind I called the blokes up to my room for a bit of a meeting and a few of the younger guys said, 'Another meeting?' But we went up there and started ... and MG (Marc Glanville) cried his eyes out. It was a magic moment and again there was this electric energy. I think everyone sensed then that it was going to happen for us. When you make your mind up to do something, nothing can stop you. That's why we never got too worried when we were behind. After that meeting, I think it was all over.

RL98: The focus in the media leading up to the grand final was on Andrew Johns and his punctured lung. Was it a concern for the players or did you know more than everyone else did?

PH: He was always going to be sweet. If anything, at that end of the year, freshness is everything — mentally and physically. He had been lying in bed for three or four days. He was fresh as a daisy, mentally keen and with a fire in the belly. And when he came to training he was sprinting around like a madman, so he actually lifted us. What seemed like a negative to the punters was actually a positive for us.

RL98: How much work did you put into trying to influence the Johns boys to stay in Newcastle, rather than sign with another club for 1998?

PH: I was involved a little bit, but as I've said before, they know how we all feel about them, they know how important they are, but it's their decision. 'Joey' (Andrew Johns) was always going to stay, he'd made his intentions clear. He was happy to stay if he could get the money he felt he deserved. Matty was a little different. He had to sum a few things up. I was never too worried because I always felt they wanted to stay, but again, it was something they had to decide for themselves.

RL98: Have we seen the best of the Johns brothers yet?

PH: They're going pretty good, aren't they? Joey is an uncanny, eccentric, freakish type of player and I think he's going to be pretty special. Matty is a hard worker, always stays later at training, likes working with the kids. He's magic at calling our moves and he anticipates well and he throws a beautiful ball. So they're great for the club, but to answer your question I'd have to say no. Early in their careers, they had some trouble with their composure, which was brought on by frustration. But this aspect of their game has been improving all the time. That said, I still reckon the best is yet to come.

RL98: How do you guard against a premiership 'hangover'?

PH: Again, we've looked to the past, and because Penrith had the similarities going into the grand final, they would have the same similarities after. Penrith's year fell apart in tragic circumstances when Ben Alexander died and that was the reason why they didn't go so good. Our reason could have been that Adam Muir is gone, Marc Glanville is gone, but the players are aware that there can be no excuses.

We've had a bit of a plan. We only had six weeks off after the grand final so we were still pretty fit. We aim to start the season with a real impact and hopefully stay in the top three or four all year. We want to give ourselves a 'no-pressure zone'. If we drop a game or two we're still going to be third or fourth and people will say we're still on track, but if we drop to sixth or seventh, the pressure's going to come down on us, it will get worse and worse, we'll be trying harder and harder but we won't be able to recover. So the 'no-pressure zone' is the go.

RL98: Going back to the initial days of the ARL/Super League war, in 1995 — is there any part that you played in the conflict that you would have changed?

PH: Yes. 1995 for me was a very frustrating year. I heard a lot of footballers say that the Super League thing affected their game in 1996. Well it really affected mine in '95. Coming up to the State of Origin series, I was doing a lot of running around, going to Sydney, to Melbourne for promotions and that sort of thing, for the ARL. What was happening at the time was so big that I believed it was the right thing to put myself out for the sake of the game.

Then they picked what everyone said was a second-rate Queensland side and at the same time I had been strongly touted as the captain of the New South Wales team. They named the NSW side and I wasn't captain and I copped that, but I admit that I thought to myself this is not going to be the same, that we're going to win easily. I had been going away a lot for the ARL and not training properly. I got myself into a rut and it put me right out. We got beaten 3-0 and not in a million

PAUL HARRAGON

lifetimes would I have thought that would have happened — which I guess is the beauty of Rugby League. But it just seemed to me that the game I was protecting and had put myself out for had bitten me on the bum. I got brushed for the first Test. And I have to say I was filthy, ropeable. So, yes, if I had my time over again, I'd do things differently.

It doesn't matter what you do or what you think you're doing is right, at the end of the day, you've still got to play good football. If you're playing good football, no-one can annoy you too much. You have to look after your own bed first then you can look after everyone else's. It's not morally correct, but first of all you're a sportsman and you've got to play good footy. That's the number one. It was a harsh lesson to learn.

RL98: What about from the club's point of view. Should negotiations have been handled differently there?

PH: Oh yes. One day it will all come out. It was a sham. Newcastle's administration had been eroded away by Super League and most of the players had spoken with Super League. It came to a bit of a D-Day and the ARL were desperate to talk to the players, just to get their point across. The administration gave us some wrong information and it looked like we weren't going to get the chance to talk to the ARL. A lot of blokes were about to sign and that's when I was talking to Bozo (Bob Fulton). He just said, 'Get the players together and get them down here (to Sydney).' That's when I organised the bus, got the boys on, and we drove to Sydney. All we did was listen, have a bit of a yarn and come back, no one signed or anything.

There was a bit of trouble then. They (Super League) got on to the Johns brothers and they were about to sign, so the next night, Phil Gould came up. There was a lot of conjecture, it was a very, very hard situation, because all the (Knights) administration was Super League and later left to go to Super League and they were making things pretty difficult. But, at the end of the day, everything worked out fine. All the boys made the right decision. They had all the information in front of them. This new game was going to build a new grandstand for us, make us a new ground, but somehow it didn't sit with everyone. We based the decision on what we felt was right. For most blokes, the money was pretty similar, so that wasn't an issue.

RL98: It would be an understatement to say you were happy with the way it all turned out?

PH: It broke for us on the Sunday night. I was on the phone until about three o'clock, talking to Super League, talking to the ARL, I went to Sydney at about seven or eight in the morning, spoke to Ken Cowley and young Lachlan and David Smith. There was the money, talk of a new grandstand, media work. I thought, 'Wow, this is pretty special stuff.' It's going to be hard to tell the ARL. But as soon as I sat down with the ARL and got both bits of information in front of me, it was staring at me as plain as day what was morally the right way to go. Thank heavens the ARL wasn't that far behind Super League, so that made it that much easier as well.

RL98: Personally, you were in a fair bit of bother at the start of 1997 with migraines. How bad were they and did they threaten your career?

PH: Yeah, they did. We went away to Coffs Harbour to play Manly in a trial. The day before the match I came down with this mad headache and the doctor thought it was hyperventilation. Anyway, it was the maddest headache I'd ever had. It made me dizzy, I got pins and needles in my arms, I was cramping up. I didn't know what it was. It was like a seizure. Anyway I had about seven of those in about three weeks — really severe and really often. The final straw was the first game of the year. I got a bit of a bump on the melon against St George and it triggered one of these off. I was out there on the oval and I had everything going on me. I had bad memory loss and the rest of it. So I went to see the specialist in Newcastle and he thought four or five weeks off, minimum. I got onto some good medication which stopped it all.

But if I'd had another concussion afterwards it would have really made me stop and think. You can't go through that all the time. But I never had another problem. I came back, there were no bumps, no knockouts. I'd been really doughy for a long while after it started, but my sharpness came back. It was fine.

RL98: You're 30 in 1998. Have you thought about how much time you've got left in the game?

PH: Yeah, I've got two years left to go. I've got a season at 29 and a season at 30 and that's it. Those two years will be enough for me. I know some blokes who are still going strong at 35, but with me, I think, I'll be doing it a bit too tough physically by then. You know, with the knees and the back, it'll be just too hard work. And even though I might be feeling okay and be capable of playing another year and earning better than a good wage, two more years will just be nice.

RL98: What challenges have you got left?

PH: From the Knights' point of view, I reckon Newcastle have got the potential to build a bit of a dynasty, like Canberra did and the Broncos did. I know it might sound a little bit far-fetched, but I thought the grand final was a bit far-fetched at the start of the year, too. I think the amount of Rugby League that's played here and with the juniors coming through that we can start a bit of a dynasty. Financially, we have to get a bit better and I know that the current administration is working on ways to do that.

I reckon we can instil that Liverpool 'do-or-die' soccer fervour — something special. Over the next few years I think it would be good to get a bit of tradition up and running. It would be good to win another one (premiership) but you don't play all year just for the little goal at the end. It's the journey along the way. You have to keep a really high standard.

RL98: Presumably you will still be in Newcastle in two years time. Have you set yourself for a career in the media?

PH: No. I feel a bit like a kid who's just leaving school and doesn't know what he's going to do. Two years is a long time. I have a few business interests with my brother, I've signed a six-year deal with Channel Nine and when I finish football I'll renegotiate which direction I go in there. I reckon I'll do a combination of about three things. I'll have some involvement in football, there's the media and I'll be able to spend more time with my family.

RL98: How would you describe your relationship with Mark Carroll?

PH: 'Spud' (Carroll) and I are from two completely different planes. I've ended up from wing, centre, lock, second row to the front row, whereas Spud's always been a front row, possibly a second row. I was always two off the ruck, running off someone, while Spud's always played a more traditional role, not too much off-loading, just going forward, hit the deck, quick play-the-balls, bit of intimidation. But over the last couple of years, because you get a bit bigger, a bit slower, I've come from wider out. When you're a front-rower, sometimes when you're in your own half you've got to hit the deck, get the quick play-the-balls and get the team up and running and rolling. Other times when you're in their half you look to unload a bit, and all the way you keep it tight in defence, a bit of intimidation to make sure you're on top. Honesty around the rucks. A little bit of leadership, organise what's going on.

When it comes to intimidation, that's a part of the game. If the other bloke is trying to intimidate the side, well you've got to put a stop to it. As far as my relationship with Spud goes, I respect him as a competitor. In the grand final he just kept trying and trying and trying. Even in the last six seconds he tried to get Darren Albert. He's really honest. You know he'll eat 17 bananas before a game and have the right amount of Sustagen, he'll do everything to the tee and he always lifts when we have a clash but that's really it. On the field we go as hard as we can, but off the field, when we're in a representative side, for instance, I'll end up speaking to Spud more times than anyone else. There's no problem.

RL98: On the other side of it, there was some bad blood between the Knights and Manly late in the year — accusations of spitting in the semi-final and the Nik Kosef 'torpedo' tackle on Matthew Johns. Is that likely to continue?

PH: There has always been genuine feeling between the clubs since the start. Rather than being a personal attack, it's an impersonal thing between two identities. To chop our boys knees out is highly illegal. But Nik (Kosef) is a friend of mine, so I see it as an impersonal thing. To say 'Butts' (Tony Butterfield) was spitting and that type of thing, well they did a couple of things that were probably worse than that. So I was disappointed at them blowing up. And the reason they were blowing up was because Nik got a week. We thought they were crying a little bit over spilt milk, but it all added to the build-up of the grand final.

RL98: What about next time you meet?

PH: Yeah, it will be on again. All the old stuff will be dredged up. Buttsy's not happy. Tezza's (Terry Hill) been going around saying he spits and so forth.

RL98: Will there be any scores to settle?

PH: No, there's not time. When we played the grand final, the last thing I was thinking about was settling old scores from two weeks ago. It's enough to go in thinking about your job.

RL98: Has the game's future been on your mind during the off-season. Do you discuss it much with your team-mates?

PH: It's got nothing to do with us, it's out of our hands, which is a shame. We can only play what's in front of us.

That's why it's unfair to criticise a lot of kids, on both sides, who have played for Australia in the last two or three years, particularly this year, who wouldn't have played for Australia had all of this not happened. You can only play what's in front of you, you can do no more.

If you win a grand final or represent your country, you've only done the best you could, there should be no criticism. People say the game's wrecked and can't be fixed but that's the biggest load of hogwash I know.

They (News Limited) could have picked a lot of other sports in the first place. They didn't, because Rugby League is the Greatest Game of All. If one grand final could do so much to turn it around, imagine in two years time when the game's put all of this behind it. It will be where it should be — the number one sport in Australia.

I truly believe that.

Newcastle's Rugby League Roots

Amid the bitter division that has rocked Rugby League since 1995, it has been the stronghold of Newcastle that has kept the ship above the waves. In fact, the people of this famous NSW city, who were recognised by the former chairman of the Australian Rugby League, Ken Arthurson, when he dedicated his 1997 autobiography, *Arko: My Game*, to them, may well go down as the saviours of the Greatest Game of All.

In his book, Arthurson explained how the support and the true loyalty of Newcastle folk kept him and his ARL colleagues going when the conflict had wearied them to the point of exhaustion. Arthurson was acutely aware how strong are the ties that bind Novocastrians. Strands that have been reinforced through natural disaster, industrial unrest and crippling unemployment are not easily broken.

The role of Newcastle and its people in the Rugby League conflict of 1995-97 can never be underestimated. They were passionate supporters of the ARL cause. They protested the loudest at News Limited's incursions and never gave anyone cause to doubt where their loyalties lay.

Newcastle's passion for Rugby League has a distinguished history. When, in 1997, the Knights celebrated their 10th anniversary in the ARL competition with their maiden premiership victory, it came not only on the 200th anniversary of the settlement of the city, but also in the 90th year of Rugby League in Newcastle ...

It is an oft-forgotten fact that a Newcastle team competed in the first two seasons of the NSWRL premiership, in 1908 and 1909.

Early overtures to Newcastle's rugby league enthusiasts by the game's Australian founders had fallen on deaf ears. A stirring speech by NSWRL chairman Henry Hoyle failed to impress a gathering at Pike's Rooms in Bolton Street on February 8, 1908, but by April 11, *The Arrow* newspaper reported that Newcastle would be fielding a team in the new competition run by the NSWRL.

The players who joined the Newcastle League team were former Rugby Union players, who abandoned the local competition that had been in existence since before the turn of the century. They were known in Newcastle as the 'Rugby League Rebels' and travelled to Sydney each weekend in 1908 to meet the eight Sydney-based clubs.

Newcastle's first match was played against Glebe at Wentworth Park on April 20, 1908. Wearing hooped jerseys of red and white, the team was: J.Smith; W.Bailey, E.McGuinness, A.Coleman, G.Hardy; R.Lawson, E.Patfield; J.Bartley, S.Carpenter, C.Croft, A.Nicholson, P.Kay, A.Richards.

Bill 'Jerry' Bailey scored all his team's points with a try and a goal. Newcastle lost the match 8-5. In the following weeks, the Rebels beat Cumberland 37-0 and Wests 24-2 to stamp themselves as one of the more powerful sides in the competition. By the end of the program of nine matches, Newcastle had won four and lost five to narrowly miss the final series. Winger Bailey proved one of the stars for the Rebels, scoring nine tries and gaining selection on the first tour of England with the Kangaroos.

Jerry Bailey was one of the prime

movers behind the establishment of the Newcastle team in 1908 and later the South Newcastle club in a local district competition. A barber by profession, Bailey possessed great speed, had an ability to kick goals from difficult angles and often beat tackles by diving over his opponent. Retiring from football in 1916, he became a prominent administrator and was a leader of a breakaway movement in Newcastle after a dispute with the NSWRL. The NSWRL formed its own Newcastle competition with teams loyal to the establishment, and rival competitions operated in 1917 and 1918. When the two competitions eventually came together, Bailey was president. A coach to many aspiring Newcastle youngsters, Bailey was a life member of the Newcastle Rugby League. He died in 1952.

Newcastle's other original Kangaroo was forward Patrick Walsh. Born in the heart of Newcastle, at Cook's Hill, in 1879, Walsh distinguished himself as a Rugby Union international, playing three Tests against the British Lions in 1904, before switching to League in 1908. Despite being surprisingly left out of the originally selected squad of Kangaroos, Walsh joined the tour late, and quickly established himself as an integral member of the team. He played in all three Tests. At the end of the tour he signed with Huddersfield, where he played for three seasons.

Returning to Australia, Walsh enlisted in the AIF in 1915 and was posted to the Australian Light Horse Regiment. He served for almost seven weeks on Gallipoli before serving with the Regiment in Palestine and the Sinai. *The London Gazette* of June 14, 1918, announced that: 'Corporal P.B. Walsh had been mentioned in despatches by General Sir E.H.H. Allenby for distinguished and gallant service and devotion to duty.'

Walsh returned to Australia in 1920 and, although the aftermath of war service affected his health, remained one of the most popular sportsmen in the Newcastle district. He outlived his Newcastle Kangaroo team-mate by a year, dying in 1953.

The Newcastle Rebels' first captain was Stan Carpenter, another League player who served with distinction in the first World War. Carpenter gained fame for acts of great heroism in the Gallipoli campaign, such as when, with Lance Corporal E.A. Roberts, he made four journeys with a stretcher in the face of enemy fire to rescue wounded soldiers at a place called Fisherman's Hut.

The Newcastle side of 1909 featured many of the same players from the 1908 season. The year was significant for two reasons. Sydney teams travelled to Newcastle for the first time and Newcastle qualified for the semi-finals.

Easts were the first side to venture north, beating the local team 18-16 on May 29. Newcastle downed Wests 34-0, with Bailey scoring three tries, on June 26 and then the Rebels defeated eventual premiers South Sydney 5-0 on August 7. A week later, Souths reversed the result at Sydney's Agricultural Ground, to thrash Newcastle 20-0 in a semi-final.

One of the newcomers in 1909 was rugged front-rower Joe Shakespeare, a player with a remarkable sporting background. In his 1966 book, *The Saga of The Western Men*, author Bob Power describes Shakespeare's story as having 'a real Dick Whittington background'. As Power explained, Shakespeare's boxing preparation took place under the handling of James Williams at a place known as 'Dog and Rat' ...

'At that time residents of this now fine residential area frowned on the name given to the locality, which suggested a lower social strata than the more posh areas of New Lambton and New Lambton Heights. Its naming came from the days when the Geordie miners of Lambton indulged in their favourite sporting activity. Scouring the nearby hills they would catch large kangaroo rats and turn on an allcomers coursing event. The starting points were the bottom end of Lambton Park or on the flat near the present Griffiths Road boundary between Lambton and Waratah. Here would gather the most motley collection of dog breed for miles around to line up and join in the chase. Like the ringkeeper at the two-up school, the Geordie promoters had a job to keep the excited spectators in check as the barking hounds strained at the leash in anticipation of the rat being released. With short sticks in their hand they drew lines on the ground as a warning to keep clear of the starting point, and at the same time they yelled in loud voices: 'Stand back, stand back, let dog see rat, let dog see rat.' With order restored the starter would give the signal and away went the quarry to invariably head for the thick scrubland on the flat where East Lambton Park now stands, with fox terriers, whippets, beagle hounds and nondescript breeds following in full chase — and so the name Dog and Rat was coined.

'From this isolated lonely area came (Shakespeare) and apart from his football prowess young Joe was to make the name of Dog and Rat famous down the years in the boxing world. Following a succession of victories against local talent he went on to fight the great Coalfields pugilist Billy McNabb three times for a win and two defeats. On 27th September, 1913, he was to meet the idol of Maitland, 18-year-old Les Darcy. The result of that encounter is now past history. Joe Shakespeare was defeated on a technical knockout in seven rounds, but in defeat he will always be recalled as the Dog and Rat boy who fought the mighty Darcy. In later years he became the Mayor of Cessnock and a distinguished citizen in the district.'

The success of the Newcastle Rebels in the NSWRL competition enticed many former Rugby players to switch to the new code. This, and an industrial upheaval in the mining industry, led to the establishment of a four-team club competition in Newcastle in 1910. A large number of players were employed in Hunter district coal mines and widespread resentment was generated against officials of the Union, many of whom were also associated in the ownership of local mines, where free labour had been introduced. This practice angered the miners, who took exception to playing Rugby Union under the banner of their industrial enemies. Bob Power wrote: 'It was regarded as anti-union to even fraternise with the players of the Rugby Union code.'

With many players and supporters switching to Rugby League for the beginning of the 1910 season, it was decided to stage a four-team club competition in order to meet the demand. The first round of fixtures was set down for Saturday, May 7, 1910, however the death of King Edward VII forced the postponement until May 14. Club sides South, North, Central and West entered senior and junior teams to compete for the Potter Shield.

Daniel 'Laddo' Davies was only a schoolboy when the Potter Shield kicked off in 1910, however in the coming years he was to have a profound effect on the game in Newcastle. He was, in every sense, a seminal figure in the development of the code in the Coalfields city.

As his name would suggest, Dan Davies was of Welsh ancestry, a five-eighth of remarkable ability who cut a dashing figure on the football field. He would arrive at a game wearing below-the-knee knickers and carrying his football gear in a big black handkerchief. His faithful companion was a tan-and-white beagle hound, Banjo, and in his home town of Lambton, Davies was a genuine footballing hero. After scoring the winning try for Western Suburbs in the final of the Potter Shield in 1916 his popularity soared and he soon came under the eye of Sydney talent scouts.

Officials from Glebe enticed him to play for their club in 1917 and Davies subsequently headed for Sydney, moving in with a relative at Annandale. Despite a residential qualification rule being in vogue at the time, Glebe officials condoned Davies' residence outside their boundary without question. But problems were ahead when Glebe met Annandale early in the 1917 season.

Davies played strongly in Glebe's convincing 26-5 win, scoring a brilliant try and a landing a penalty goal. Aware of Davies' residential status and embarrassed at the drubbing they received, Annandale officials fired in a protest to the NSWRL. Glebe officials assured Davies everything would be all right and prepared a declaration on Davies' behalf, which Davies duly signed.

The NSWRL's ruling was a stunner. President James Joynton Smith took the two points off Glebe and suspended Davies for life.

Davies returned to his home town, but with the League's all-embracing suspension hanging over his head, he appeared destined to remain on the sidelines. However, he hadn't counted on the loyalty of Newcastle league officials and supporters who worked tirelessly to have the suspension lifted.

The matter came to a head in Newcastle later in the 1917 season, when West were drawn to play North. West's captain Freddie Bell indicated his team would not take the field unless Davies was allowed to take his place in their side. After a conference of officials, Davies was permitted to play, but later the Newcastle Referees' Association informed the NSWRL that a disqualified player had taken part in a match.

After an exhaustive inquiry, all of the League's Northern Branch officials, with the exception of East Newcastle's delegates, were suspended from office. West, North, South and Central clubs soon broke away from the NSWRL to form their own competition. They were labelled 'Bolsheviks' and suspended for life by the NSWRL. Meanwhile, East Newcastle and parts of South and North clubs remained loyal to the NSWRL and were dubbed the 'Lilywhites'. For two years separate competitions were played before the two warring parties came together to form the Newcastle Rugby League. All players, including Davies, were reinstated and allowed to resume playing for their respective clubs.

These were the formative years of the game in Newcastle, with great football men such as Jerry Bailey, Pat Walsh, Stan Carpenter, Joe Shakespeare and Laddo Davies its central figures. Newcastle Rugby League continued and continues to be a stronghold of the game, with a production line of champions that has been the envy of every football-playing district in the land.

Over 50 Newcastle products have represented Australia, and among them have been nine Test captains. Players such as Clive Churchill, Brian Carlson, Johnny Graves, Les Johns, Herb Narvo, Noel Pidding, Wally Prigg, and today's champions, Paul Harragon, Robbie O'Davis and Matthew and Andrew Johns, have been among the brightest stars in the game.

There could have been no more fitting reward for the 'steel' city's immense contribution to the game over 90 years than their premiership victory in 1997.

The Premiership Coaches
... From Halloway to Reilly

The role of the coach has altered dramatically over the past 90 years. At one time 'coach' was merely a fancy title given to the player who led the team on its limited training run. More importantly, in those days he was the team captain, who had full control of tactics and approach both on and off the field. However, as the game became more scientific and more time was devoted to the preparation of teams for premiership matches, the role of the coach gradually evolved.

For at least the first decade of the game in Australia, the coach, as a specialist position, did not exist. But by the late teens and early 1920s, former internationals such as Chris McKivat, Bill Kelly, 'Ricketty' Johnston and Ray Norman had developed a new vocation as 'off-field' coaches. The more traditional role of 'captain-coach' was gradually phased out, but even in the modern day, captain-coaches have taken charge of teams both on and off the playing arena. The most recent was Wally Lewis, who was in control of the Gold Coast's fortunes in a captain-coach capacity in 1992.

St George enjoyed resounding success with captain-coaches during their undefeated run of 11 premierships from 1956-66. In that period, 10 of their titles were won with captain-coaches. These days, however, the demands of the game dictate that the role of the coach is a full-time job. It is also one with a parlous future. Jack Gibson would say 'there are only two types of coaches, those who have been sacked and those who are about to be sacked'.

Rugby League 1998 presents a list of club coaches for all premiership clubs and for clubs which have previously competed in the premiership competition. While this list is easily the most comprehensive ever published, because of the slow evolution of the specialist coach, the lists for some of the longer established clubs are incomplete.

Auckland
Frank Endacott (1997), John Monie (1995-97).

Balmain
Wayne Pearce (1994-97), Alan Jones (1991-93), Warren Ryan (1988-90), Bill Anderson (1987), Frank Stanton (1981-86), Dennis Tutty (1980), Ron Willey (1977-79), Paul Broughton (1975-76), Alan Mason (1974), Leo Nosworthy (1969-73), Keith Barnes (1967-68), Harry Bath (1961-66), John O'Toole (1958-60), Sid Ryan (1957), N.G. 'Latchem' Robinson (1930, 1944-47, 1954-56), Arthur Patton (1952-53), Jim Duckworth (1951), Athol Smith (1948-50), Bill Kelly (1914-15, 1938-43), Harold Matthews (1937), Joe 'Chimpy' Busch (1935-36), George Robinson (1933-34), Charles 'Chook' Fraser (1921-25, 1932), Reg Latta (1929, 1931), Cec 'Dick' Fifield (1930), Alf 'Son' Fraser (1925-29), Arthur 'Pony' Halloway (1916-20), Robert Graves (1908-13).

Brisbane
Wayne Bennett (1988-97).

Canberra
Mal Meninga (1997), Tim Sheens (1988-96), Wayne Bennett (1987), Don Furner (1982-87).

Canterbury
Chris Anderson (1990-97), Phil Gould (1988-89), Warren Ryan (1984-87), Ted Glossop (1978-83), Malcolm Clift (1973-77), Bob Hagan (1971-72), Kevin Ryan (1967-70), Roger Pearman (1966), Eddie Burns (1960-62, 1965), Clive Churchill (1963-64),

THE PREMIERSHIP COACHES   15

Cec Cooper (1958-59), Col Geelan (1957), Vic Hey (1955-56), Vic Bulgin (1951), Alby Why (1950-52), Henry Porter (1949), Arthur 'Pony' Halloway (1948), Ross McKinnon (1946-47), Bill Kelly (1945), Cec 'Dick' Fifield (1944), Ron Bailey (1941, 1944), Roy Kirkaldy (1943), Jerry Brien (1939, 1942), Alan Brady (1940), Jimmy Craig (1938), George Mason (1937), Frank Burge (1936), Tedda Courtney (1935).

Cronulla
Johnny Lang (1994-97), Arthur Beetson (1992-93), Allan Fitzgibbon (1988-91), Jack Gibson (1985-87), Terry Fearnley (1983-84), Greg Pierce (1981-82), Tommy Bishop (1970-73, 1980), Norm Provan (1978-79), Ted Glossop (1977), Johnny Raper (1975-76), Noel Thornton (1974), Ken Kearney (1967-69).

Gold Coast
Phil Economidis (1996-97), John Harvey (1994-95), Wally Lewis (1992-93), Malcolm Clift (1991), Bob McCarthy (1988-90).

Illawarra
Andrew Farrar (1997), Allan McMahon (1996), Allan Fitzgibbon (1982-83, 1995), Graham Murray (1991-95), Ron Hilditch (1989-90), Terry Fearnley (1988), Brian Smith (1984-87).

Manly
Bob Fulton (1983-88, 1993-97), Graham Lowe (1990-92), Alan Thompson (1989), Ray Ritchie (1981-82), Allan Thomson (1980), Frank Stanton (1975-79), Ron Willey (1962, 1970-74), George Hunter (1968-69), Wally O'Connell (1966-67), Russ Pepperell (1964-65), Tony Paskins (1963), Ken Arthurson (1957-61), Pat Devery (1955-56), Ray Norman (1954), Roy Bull (1953), Wally O'Connell (1950-52), George Mullins (1949), Ray Stehr (1947-48), Harold Johnston (1947).

Newcastle
Malcolm Reilly (1995-97), David Waite (1991-94), Allan McMahon (1988-91).

North Queensland
Tim Sheens (1997), Graham Lowe (1996), Grant Bell (1995).

Norths
Peter Louis (1993-97), Steve Martin (1990-92), Frank Stanton (1987-89), Brian Norton (1985-86), Greg Hawick (1960, 1985), John 'Chow' Hayes (1983-84), Ron Willey (1980-82), Tom Bishop (1979), Bill Hamilton (1977-78), Noel Kelly (1973-76), Merv Hicks (1971-72), Roy Francis (1969-70), Col Greenwood (1968), Billy Wilson (1967), Fred Griffiths (1963-66), Bob Sullivan (1961-62), Ross McKinnon (1959), Trevor Allan (1957-58), Bruce Ryan (1956), Rex Harrison (1954-55), Ross McKinnon (1952-53), Laurie Doran (1951), Frank Hyde (1943-44, 1950), Harry McKinnon (1949), Cliff Pearce (1947-48), Harry 'Acka' Forbes (1946), Jack O'Reilly (1942), Roy Thompson (1941), Arthur 'Pony' Halloway (1941), Bob 'Botsy' Williams (1939), Laurie Ward (1937), Frank Burge (1935), Arthur Edwards (1933), Tom Wright (1931), Chris McKivat (1921-22).

Parramatta
Brian Smith (1997), Ron Hilditch (1994-96), Mick Cronin (1990-93), John Monie (1984-89), Jack Gibson (1981-83), John Peard (1980), Terry Fearnley (1976-79), Norm Provan (1975), Dave Bolton (1973-74), Ian Walsh (1971-72), Ron Lynch (1970), Ian Johnston (1968-69), Brian Hambly (1967), Ken Thornett (1965-66), Ken Kearney (1962-64), Ron Boden (1961), Jack Rayner (1958-60), Ken Slattery (1957), Cec 'Dick' Fifield (1956), Johnny Slade (1955), Charlie Gill (1954), Vic Hey (1948-53), Frank McMillan (1947).

Penrith
Royce Simmons (1994-97), Phil Gould (1990-94), Ron Willey (1988-89), Tim Sheens (1985-87), John Peard (1982-83), Len Stacker (1979-81), Don Parish (1977-78), Barry Harris (1975-76), Mick Stephenson (1975), Jack Clare (1974), Leo Trevena (1967, 1973), Bob Boland (1968-72).

St George
David Waite (1996-97), Brian Smith (1991-95), Craig Young (1989-90), Ted Glossop (1988), Roy Masters (1982-87), Harry Bath (1977-81), Graeme Langlands (1972-76), Jack Gibson (1970-71), Johnny Raper (1969), Norm Provan (1962-65, 1968), Ian Walsh (1966-67), Ken Kearney (1954-55, 1957-61), Norm Tipping (1956), Johnny Hawke (1951-52), Jim Duckworth (1948-50), Doug McRitchie (1947), Arthur 'Snowy' Justice (1936, 1947), Charlie Lynch (1947),

Herb Narvo (1946), Bill Kelly (1944), Neville Smith (1939-41, 1943), Len Kelly (1942), Norm Pope (1938), Frank Burge (1927-30, 1937), Peter Burge (1937), Eddie Root (1936), Albert 'Ricketty' Johnston (1933-35), H. 'Mick' Kadwell (1931-32), Herb Gilbert (1921-24).

South Sydney
Ken Shine (1994-97), Bob McCarthy (1975, 1994), Frank Curry (1991-93), George Piggins (1986-90), Ron Willey (1983-85), Bill Anderson (1980-82), Jack Gibson (1978-79), John O'Neill (1977), Johnny King (1976), Clive Churchill (1958, 1967-75), Bernie Purcell (1964-66), Denis Donoghue (1959-63), Jack Rayner (1950-55), Dave Watson (1947-49), Arthur Hennessy (1918, 1946), Eric Lewis (1945), Alf 'Smacker' Blair (1927, 1944), Jim Tait (1941-43), Charlie Lynch (1928-34, 1937-40), Dave Watson (1935-36), Howard Hallett (1925-26), Owen McCarthy (1924), John Rosewell (1913).

Sydney City
Phil Gould (1995-97), Arthur Beetson (1977-78, 1985-88, 1994), Mark Murray (1991-94), Hugh McGahan (1990), Russell Fairfax (1989-90), Laurie Freier (1983-84), Bob Fulton (1979-82), Jack Gibson (1967-68, 1974-76), Tony Paskins (1973), Don Furner (1970-72), Louis Neumann (1969), Bert Holcroft (1965-66), Nat Silcock (1964), Dick Dunn (1960-63), Terry Fearnley (1961), Dave Brown (1940, 1943, 1957-59), Frank O'Connor (1955-56), Ferris Ashton (1954), Col Donohoe (1953), Ernie Norman (1950-52), Ray Stehr (1939, 1941, 1946, 1949), Percy Williams (1940), Arthur 'Pony' Halloway (1930-31, 1933-38, 1945), Joe Pearce (1942, 1944), Frank Burgo (1932), George Boddington (1929), Ray Norman (1922-23).

Western Suburbs
Tommy Raudonikis (1995-97), Wayne Ellis (1994), Warren Ryan (1991-94), John Bailey (1988-90), Laurie Freier (1988), Steve Ghosn (1986-87), Ken Gentle (1984-85), Len Stacker (1983), Terry Fearnley (1982), Roy Masters (1978-81), Keith Holman (1954-55, 1977), Don Parish (1972-76), Ron Watson (1970-71), Noel Kelly (1966-69), Ken Kearney (1965), Jack Fitzgerald (1961-64), Dudley Beger (1960), Vic Hey (1958-59), Jack Walsh (1946, 1956-57), Peter McLean (1953), Tom McMahon (1952), Jeff Smith (1948, 1950-51), Col Maxwell (1949), Frank Burge (1947), Frank McMillan (1931, 1936, 1945), Henry Bolewski (1944), Paddy Bugden (1944), Alf Blair (1943), A.McGuinness (1942), Les Mead (1941), Merv Gray (1940), Jim Craig (1929-30, 1932, 1939), Cec 'Dick' Fifield (1938), Jerry Brien (1937), Bill Brogan (1933), Chris McKivat (1928), Clarrie Prentice (1927), Albert 'Ricketty' Johnston (1924).

Extinct clubs

Glebe
Jack Hickey (1924).

Hunter Mariners
Graham Murray (1997)

Newtown
Brian Moore (1983), Warren Ryan (1979-82), Johnny Raper (1978), Paul Broughton (1977-78), Clarrie Jeffreys (1974-76), Jack Gibson (1973), Harry Bath (1969-71), Dick Poole (1955-58, 1966-68), Allan Ellis (1962-65), Charles 'Chicka' Cahill (1959-61), Col Geelan (1954), Frank Johnson (1952-53), Frank Farrell (1946-51), Arthur Folwell (1942-44), Percy Williams (1941), Frank Burge (1940), Charles 'Boxer' Russell (1933), Albert 'Ricketty' Johnston (1923, 1925-26), Bill Farnsworth (1924), Arthur 'Pony' Halloway (1923).

South Queensland
Steve Bleakley (1997), Bob Lindner (1995-96).

University
Bill Kelly (1923-24).

Western Reds
Dean Lance (1997), Peter Mulholland (1995-96).

- No coaches are documented for extinct clubs Annandale, Cumberland or Newcastle (1908-09).
- Coaches details relate to first grade NSWRL/ARL premiership positions, with the exception of 1997 Super League postings.

THE PREMIERSHIP COACHES

Premiership coaches 1908-97

Arthur 'Pony' Halloway has been dead for almost 40 years and his deeds as a football tactician all but forgotten, yet he is the man who has masterminded more premiership victories than any other coach. An original Kangaroo in 1908-09, Halloway devised four premiership wins in five years for Balmain as a player-coach (1916-17-19-20) and then four for Eastern Suburbs (1935-36-37-45) in an off-field capacity. With eight premiership titles, Halloway is clearly coaching's highest achiever, ahead of post-WWII coaches Jack Rayner, Ken Kearney and Jack Gibson, each of whom captured five titles.

Apart from his long playing career with Glebe, Eastern Suburbs and Balmain, Halloway coached Easts for 10 seasons in the 1930s and '40s and also had stints with Newtown (1923), Norths (1941) and Canterbury (1948). A list of premiership-winning coaches follows.

1997 Malcolm Reilly *(Newcastle)*
1996 Bob Fulton *(Manly)*
1995 Chris Anderson *(Canterbury)*
1994 Tim Sheens *(Canberra)*
1993 Wayne Bennett *(Brisbane)*
1992 Wayne Bennett *(Brisbane)*
1991 Phil Gould *(Penrith)*
1990 Tim Sheens *(Canberra)*
1989 Tim Sheens *(Canberra)*
1988 Phil Gould *(Canterbury)*
1987 Bob Fulton *(Manly)*
1986 John Monie *(Parramatta)*
1985 Warren Ryan *(Canterbury)*
1984 Warren Ryan *(Canterbury)*
1983 Jack Gibson *(Parramatta)*
1982 Jack Gibson *(Parramatta)*
1981 Jack Gibson *(Parramatta)*
1980 Ted Glossop *(Canterbury)*
1979 Harry Bath *(St George)*
1978 Frank Stanton *(Manly)*
1977 Harry Bath *(St George)*
1976 Frank Stanton *(Manly)*
1975 Jack Gibson *(Easts)*
1974 Jack Gibson *(Easts)*
1973 Ron Willey *(Manly)*
1972 Ron Willey *(Manly)*
1971 Clive Churchill *(Souths)*
1970 Clive Churchill *(Souths)*
1969 Leo Nosworthy *(Balmain)*
1968 Clive Churchill *(Souths)*
1967 Clive Churchill *(Souths)*
1966 Ian Walsh *(St George)*
1965 Norm Provan *(St George)*
1964 Norm Provan *(St George)*
1963 Norm Provan *(St George)*
1962 Norm Provan *(St George)*
1961 Ken Kearney *(St George)*
1960 Ken Kearney *(St George)*
1959 Ken Kearney *(St George)*
1958 Ken Kearney *(St George)*
1957 Ken Kearney *(St George)*
1956 Norm Tipping *(St George)*
1955 Jack Rayner *(Souths)*
1954 Jack Rayner *(Souths)*
1953 Jack Rayner *(Souths)*
1952 Tom McMahon *(Wests)*
1951 Jack Rayner *(Souths)*
1950 Jack Rayner *(Souths)*
1949 Jim Duckworth *(St George)*
1948 Jeff Smith *(Wests)*
1947 N. 'Latchem' Robinson *(Balmain)*
1946 N. 'Latchem' Robinson *(Balmain)*
1945 A. 'Pony' Halloway *(Easts)*
1944 N. 'Latchem' Robinson *(Balmain)*
1943 Arthur Folwell *(Newtown)*
1942 Jerry Brien *(Canterbury)*
1941 Neville Smith *(St George)*
1940 Dave Brown *(Easts)*
1939 Bill Kelly *(Balmain)*
1938 Jimmy Craig *(Canterbury)*
1937 A. 'Pony' Halloway *(Easts)*
1936 A. 'Pony' Halloway *(Easts)*
1935 A. 'Pony' Halloway *(Easts)*
1934 Frank McMillan *(Wests)*
1933 C. 'Boxer' Russell *(Newtown)*
1932 Charlie Lynch *(Souths)*
1931 Charlie Lynch *(Souths)*
1930 Jimmy Craig *(Wests)*
1929 Charlie Lynch *(Souths)*
1928 Charlie Lynch *(Souths)*
1927 A. 'Smacker' Blair *(Souths)*
1926 Howard Hallett *(Souths)*
1925 Howard Hallett *(Souths)*
1924 C. 'Chook' Fraser *(Balmain)*
1923 Ray Norman *(Easts)*
1922 Chris McKivat *(Norths)*
1921 Chris McKivat *(Norths)*
1920 A. 'Pony' Halloway *(Balmain)*
1919 A. 'Pony' Halloway *(Balmain)*
1918 Arthur Hennessy *(Souths)*
1917 A. 'Pony' Halloway *(Balmain)*
1916 A. 'Pony' Halloway *(Balmain)*
1915 Bill Kelly *(Balmain)*
1914 Howard Hallett *(Souths)*
1913 Dally Messenger *(Easts)*
1912 Dally Messenger *(Easts)*
1911 Dally Messenger *(Easts)*
1910 C. Boxer Russell *(Newtown)*
1909 Arthur Hennessy *(Souths)*
1908 Arthur Hennessy *(Souths)*

RUGBY LEAGUE 1998

PLAYERS OF THE YEAR

BRAD FITTLER

The key to Brad Fittler's brilliant year in 1997 was a greater involvement at club level. So often the pragmatist who would pick and choose the moments he would inject himself into a game, the 25-year-old added a new dimension to his football — and Sydney City were the direct beneficiaries. Alternating for much of the season between five-eighth and lock forward, Fittler had a firm grip on the controls of the Roosters' ship and it was no coincidence that the club enjoyed their best season in a decade.

A long-term groin injury had forced Fittler to spend the majority of the 1996 season fulfilling an organising role, and the loss of his line-breaking abilities was one of the factors in the Roosters' sudden exit from that year's final series.

The injury was repaired with two bouts of off-season surgery, leaving the Test skipper fit to lead Sydney City's most serious assault on a premiership title since the 1980s. Under the watchful eye of coach and confidante Phil Gould, Fittler helped the Roosters negotiate the early rounds of the competition without halfback and playmaker Adrian Lam, who was recovering from a shoulder operation. Lam returned in time to take his place in Queensland's State of Origin side, where he was named captain for the first time. But just as Lam and Fittler were about to create a slice of history as opposing State of Origin captains from the same premiership club, Fittler broke his thumb in the Round-10 match against St George. The injury forced him to miss the entire Origin series, costing him the opportunity to lead the Blues to back-to-back victories over the Maroons.

It was the first time injury had ruled Fittler out of a representative match since he made his State of Origin debut in 1990. He missed four matches for the Roosters, who developed the staggers in his absence. From the time of his injury on May 9, the Roosters did not win another game until July 26.

But it was Fittler's brilliance, combined with the mercurial skills of fullback Andrew Walker, that led the Roosters out of the wilderness, in the Round-17 clash against Illawarra. From that point, the pair dominated in man-of-the-match stakes as the Roosters embarked on an eight-match winning streak. Fittler's form was top shelf. His running game took pressure off his team-mates and his skill in off-loading the ball and creating space for support runners was uncanny.

Fittler's vintage season was recognised in early September when he was named the inaugural winner of the Nokia Provan-Summons Medal, as the best player in the ARL competition. It was an honour that Fittler was delighted to accept.

'It's one thing for people to say you are a great player but you can't accept that until you win this award,' Fittler said after receiving the medal.

Of course, people have been saying Fittler is a great player since he first represented NSW and Australia as an 18-year-old in 1990. Earlier in 1997, Fittler was rated the player most wanted by a majority of coaches in ARL and

Super League competitions in a newspaper survey. A staggering 75 per cent of the 22 coaches surveyed rated Fittler the player they would target if he was on the open market. Fittler also received endorsement as the best player in the game from his peers, in *Rugby League Week's* annual poll of 100 players, drawn equally from ARL and Super League camps.

There was yet another new side to Brad Fittler in 1997 — that of outspoken media commentator. Refusing to be silenced on any issue, Fittler espoused his views on subjects as diverse as jersey design, the success of the State of Origin series, referee 'bashing' and the newspaper coverage of the game. Some of his comments raised the hackles of ARL officialdom, but Fittler was determined that his views be expressed without fear or favour.

This is a single-minded approach that continues to drive Fittler to great heights as one of the game's paramount performers.

PAUL HARRAGON

Early on, 1997 was shaping as anything but Paul Harragon's best season in Rugby League. A six-week stint on the sidelines followed a series of paralysing migraines that at one point threatened his career. The blinding headaches began in the pre-season and continued into the premiership proper until he was directed by doctors to stand down indefinitely. The cause of the headaches was a mystery and checks by neurosurgeons revealed no underlying problem.

By late September, though, medical concerns were light years away when Harragon triumphed with his Newcastle team-mates in one of the game's greatest grand finals.

Harragon, who turned 29 a month after the grand final, had made a full recovery from the migraines in time to take his place in the season's representative matches. Returning to football in the Round-7 clash with Manly at Brookvale, Harragon was later selected as Country captain and led his team to a 17-4 victory over City at Marathon Stadium. He was tipped as a likely New South Wales captain once Brad Fittler was ruled out with a broken thumb, but in similar circumstances to 1995, Harragon was overlooked, this time for Manly's Geoff Toovey.

In the first match of the series, Harragon equalled Fittler's record of 16 consecutive Origin appearances for New South Wales and passed the mark in Melbourne two weeks later ... on the night the Blues wrapped up the series. For Harragon, an integral part of the NSW team since 1992, it was his fifth series victory.

Harragon and NSW front-row partner Mark Carroll also teamed up in the Australian side which played the one-off Test against the Rest of the World in July. The two formed a strong alliance in representative football, providing a fearsome spearhead for New South Wales and Australia, but when it came to club football there were no greater rivals. Confrontations between the pair became a feature of Newcastle-Manly matches. Their brutal body contact was described as 'a human train crash' and gates swelled just to see these two warriors come together. They were at it again in the grand final, battering each other with one shuddering jolt after another.

Until that point, Carroll's Manly side invariably had the better of Harragon's Knights. In 11 consecutive matches, including three in 1997, Manly finished in front on the scoreboard. But once the Knights qualified for the grand final, Harragon knew the tide was about to turn. His considerable leadership skills drew the tight-knit Newcastle club even closer. He boosted the Knights' belief in their own ability and he convinced them that Manly's previous dominance and their superior experience in big-match football could be overcome.

Harragon was a pillar of strength in the decider, leading the Knights' opening onslaught and exhorting his team-mates to go the distance. When Darren Albert completed the Newcastle fairytale six seconds from fulltime, there were few who enjoyed the moment more than the man they call 'The Chief'. In 10 years of top-grade football, Harragon had spilled as much blood as anyone, had endured his share of the hard times and had worked his heart out to give his club and his district credibility as a Rugby League force.

When Paul Harragon eventually looks back on his career in Rugby League, the year 1997 is a certainty to take pride of place.

ROBBIE O'DAVIS

Robbie O'Davis led his opponents on a merry dance in 1997. The Newcastle Knights' fullback, who plays his football with a rare and refreshing spirit of joyfulness, was the *nonpareil* star of the Australian Rugby League. His efforts for Queensland and Newcastle were of the highest order. Voted the Queensland players' player of the State of Origin series and the Clive Churchill Medal winner as the man of the match in the grand final, O'Davis experienced a season beyond his wildest dreams.

Confident and outgoing, O'Davis was a key member of the Knights' premiership assault from the outset of the 1997 season. With the Johns brothers and skipper Paul Harragon missing through injury at the start of the year, O'Davis was suddenly thrust into a senior role.

Only 24 at the time (he turned 25 early in September), O'Davis rose to the occasion, displaying more maturity and consistency in his game, traits which helped keep the Knights' season on the boil while his higher-profile team-mates were sidelined.

The absence of Super League players made his selection at fullback in the Queensland State of Origin side a formality. He was close to Queensland's best player in the first two matches and was narrowly shaded by team-mate Gary Larson for man-of-the-match honours in the third match, won 18-12 by Queensland at the Sydney Football Stadium. The image of O'Davis withstanding intense pressure from New South Wales chasers to take a bomb as the fulltime siren sounded in the third match typified his courageous efforts.

Such displays produced a new nickname 'Robbie O'Save-us', and led Queensland coach Paul Vautin to name O'Davis as the leading player in the game: 'I think he's just about the best player in the competition at the moment,' Vautin commented during the Origin series. 'He's so confident, he can make a break, he defends and under the high ball, there's no drama at all.'

O'Davis' confidence in picking up a rolling ball, his poise under the high-ball, his evasive kick-returns and his remarkable last-ditch defence were features of his play in 1997. But so too was his celebration of a try. The 'jig of joy', a move O'Davis adapted from the movie 'The Last Boy Scout', became his trademark. Rather than a display of 'muggairism', O'Davis' actions were a refreshing expression of personality and colour in a sport that often takes itself too seriously.

O'Davis had cause to celebrate twice during the grand final. Once when he stood up Terry Hill to score in the 34th minute and the second when he lunged forward and placed the ball on the line, six minutes from fulltime. His second try, converted simply by Andrew Johns, levelled the scores at 16-all and set up Darren Albert's grandstand finish.

O'Davis' two-try effort was a first

PLAYERS OF THE YEAR

for a fullback in a grand final and so too was his Clive Churchill Medal.

'I'm living in a dream,' he told reporters in the emotional aftermath to the grand final. 'Everything I wanted to achieve in life I have done in 12 months. I married a great lady, we had a baby and I won a grand final.'

Life couldn't have been sweeter for Rugby League's dancing fullback.

JOHN SIMON

Twelve months after languishing in reserve grade at Sydney City, John Simon reclaimed his reputation as one of the game's finest all-round halfbacks with a career-best season at Parramatta. It was a mighty turnaround by the 25-year-old Illawarra junior, who accepted a big-money offer to join the Roosters for three years at the end of the 1995 season. But his failure to oust incumbent halfback Adrian Lam led to a long spell in reserve grade and a request for a release from the final two seasons of his contract.

The Roosters acceded, freeing Simon to join the wealth of talent at Parramatta. In all probability he will not make a wiser move in his football career.

Simon came under the eye of new Eels coach Brian Smith, himself a former halfback and one of the most astute coaching minds in Rugby League. Smith placed great faith in Simon's ability as a playmaker, and stuck solid to him when the Eels slumped to five consecutive losses early in the season. There were calls for Simon to be dumped in favour of second grade halfback Chris Lawler, but Smith would hear none of it. Smith was certain the major problem was the wealth of ball-playing talent, with senior men such as Dean Pay, Jason Smith, Jim Dymock and Simon all intent on getting their hands on the football.

It took a meeting of the senior men to decide that Simon was the player to call the shots and a season which began as a disaster for the Eels soon took on a far more positive look. Simon's confidence-level rose as he marshalled the men around him. His long-kicking game tied down the opposition and his pinpoint bombs led to countless tries.

The wins began to mount for Parramatta. They turned a disastrous 1-5 win-loss record into a 12-5 result after 17 rounds. After Simon masterminded the Eels' best win of the season, against Manly at Brookvale, coach Smith declared his halfback 'just about the smartest footballer I've ever coached'. Smith labelled Simon 'Radar', after the *MASH* character who would carry out his colonel's orders while they were still thoughts in the colonel's mind.

Simon made a welcome return to the representative arena in 1997, helping Country to a 17-4 win over City and then playing a mighty role in New South Wales' series victory over Queensland. He was among the Blues' best in the first game, after coming from the bench to replace an injured Andrew Johns, and then he kicked the crucial field goal in Melbourne which broke a 14-all deadlock and wrapped up the series for New South Wales. A continuation of his good form at club level led to his selection for Australia in the one-off Test against the Rest of the World in July.

By September, Parramatta had qualified in third place for their first final series since 1986, but Simon's efforts to lift the Eels to higher honours were thwarted by a massive injury toll in the first semi-final against Newcastle.

Simon's outstanding season was officially recognised with his second placing in the Nokia Provan-Summons Medal.

GEOFF TOOVEY

Geoff Toovey's reputation for toughness was already established well before the 1997 season, yet his ability to maintain high standards while playing with injury earned wider recognition than ever. Manly and Australian coach Bob Fulton describes him as one of the toughest players ever to play Rugby League. 'Week in, week out he performs at the highest level — and often with injuries,' Fulton said during the '97 season.

During 1997, Toovey battled a succession of injuries, yet remained one of the most important players in the ARL competition. He was a centrepiece of Manly's minor premiership win and their third grand final appearance in three years. He was among New South Wales' best players in the State of Origin series and played a leading hand in Australia's one-off victory over the Rest of the World in July. Toovey's ability to play on through injury was never better typified than in the grand final when he overcame a bout of concussion from a questionable Paul Harragon tackle and an eye injury caused by the straying boot of Newcastle centre Adam MacDougall to be the best player on the losing side. In fact, Toovey may even have won back-to-back Clive Churchill Medals but for the superb display of Knights' fullback Robbie O'Davis.

After a personal best season in 1996, in which he captained Manly to a premiership, spearheaded NSW to a 3-0 State of Origin series win and captained Australia in a Test against Papua New Guinea, Toovey began '97 under an injury cloud. Off-season surgery to repair a double hernia left him short of condition early in the year, but there was never any sign that he was anything but 100 per cent fit.

The recurrence of a neck injury, a rib cartilage injury suffered in the Rest of the World Test and his grand final woes would have put most players out of football, yet Toovey battled through all 25 matches for the Sea Eagles, three State of Origin games and a Test for Australia against the Rest of the World, displaying peak form throughout.

Testaments to Toovey's toughness featured prominently in the press throughout the year. Parramatta and Australian warhorse Ray Price said: 'Toovey is as courageous as any player I've ever seen. And I've seen plenty.'

Former Balmain and Australian front-rower Steve Roach remarked: 'He's pound for pound the toughest player I've ever seen.'

Manly, NSW and Australian teammate Mark Carroll commented: 'I admire Toovey a hell of a lot because he's a little bloke who has been bashing giants for a long time.'

And Cronulla's veteran front-rower Les Davidson added: 'In terms of genuine toughness, he is the man. He made a huge impression on me by backing up a week after fracturing his eye socket to lead Manly to a grand final win (in 1996).'

Toovey was forced to play a more versatile role for the Sea Eagles in 1997 following the arrival of former South Sydney halfback Craig Field. Unchallenged in the halfback role for almost a decade at Manly, Toovey shifted between half, five-eighth and hooker at various stages of the season. His success in the hooking role at representative level was carried into the club arena and Toovey often bamboozled his opponents with the timing of his dummy-half runs and provided considerable momentum for his running forwards.

Toovey played his 200th grade game for Manly in 1997 and will close in on 200 first-grade games early in the 1998 season.

Coach Fulton paid Toovey even more glowing praise late in the year when he declared his star halfback was a 'natural' to one day assume the coaching reins at Manly. In the meantime, Toovey will be doing his utmost to ensure Manly remain among the leading teams in the competition.

Injury or no injury.

PLAYERS OF THE YEAR

RUGBY LEAGUE 1998

TEAM OF THE YEAR

Fullback:	ROBBIE O'DAVIS *(Newcastle)*
Wingers:	DARREN ALBERT *(Newcastle)*, JACK ELSEGOOD *(Sydney City)*
Centres:	CRAIG INNES *(Manly)*, TERRY HILL *(Manly)*
Five-eighth:	BRAD FITTLER *(Sydney City)*
Halfback:	JOHN SIMON *(Parramatta)*
Props:	PAUL HARRAGON *(Newcastle)*, MARK CARROLL *(Manly)*
Hooker:	GEOFF TOOVEY *(Manly)*
Second-rowers:	ADAM MUIR *(Newcastle)*, LUKE RICKETSON *(Sydney City)*
Lock:	NIK KOSEF *(Manly)*

Grand finalists Newcastle and Manly dominate places in *Rugby League 1998's* Team of the Year, a reflection on the outstanding success achieved by both in 1997.

The Sea Eagles, who led the minor premiership from go to whoa, have five players in the top 13, while the Knights, who came from behind to score their maiden grand final victory, supply four players. The remaining four are drawn from Sydney City and Parramatta.

Our five players of the year have all won places in the top 13, with Geoff Toovey winning the hooker's role and Parramatta's John Simon claiming the halfback position.

After spending the majority of the 1996 season in reserve grade with Sydney City, Simon's switch to Parramatta may turn out to be the best move he ever makes. With a vast array of talent around him, Simon took charge and directed his team-mates superbly. The former Illawarra junior kicked a decisive field goal which helped New South Wales secure the State of Origin series in the second game at the Melbourne Cricket Ground and won a place in Australia's Test squad for the one-off match against the Rest of the World in Brisbane.

The wing berths are taken by two players with little experience in the representative arena. Newcastle's Darren Albert was a surprising omission from the NSW State of Origin side after a strong display for Country in their win over City, but his form for the Knights was of a high standard throughout the season. His two magic moments — a crucial tackle on North Sydney fullback Matt Seers in the preliminary final and the try, six seconds from fulltime in the grand final — were highlights to savour for a lifetime.

Elsegood joined Sydney City in less than ideal circumstances, after the NSW Industrial Court ruled his Super League contract with Canterbury invalid. However, he put his troubles behind him to perform consistently for the Roosters and finished the season with 12 tries.

Manly trio Geoff Toovey, Craig Innes and Mark Carroll and Test captain Brad Fittler are the only players to retain their places in the Team of the Year from the 1996 season.

Toovey was an inspirational and at times heroic performer for Manly — his effort on a losing side in the grand final was magnificent. His developing role as a dummy-half runner at both club and representative level earn him a position in the Team of the Year at hooker.

Innes confirmed his standing as one of the finest centres in the game with a second season of consistent form for the Sea Eagles, while his centre partner Terry Hill wins a place on the strength of his week-to-week form and a rich harvest of 22 tries from 23 matches.

Carroll's wholehearted style at all levels of the game ensured he held onto a front row position, while his Newcastle adversary Paul Harragon makes his first appearance in the Team of the Year after leading his club to their maiden premiership win.

Fittler retains his place for the sixth consecutive season, appearing for only the second time at five-eighth, where he played periodically in 1997. The Test captain missed the State of Origin series through injury but played a leading role in the Roosters' charge to the finals.

The back-rowers are all newcomers to the Team of the Year. Newcastle's Adam Muir and Sydney City's Luke Ricketson form a formidable second row, while Manly's representative forward Nik Kosef takes the No. 13 position. The back-rowers beat a hotly contested field which included Steve Menzies and Daniel Gartner (Manly); Gary Larson, David Fairleigh and Billy Moore (Norths); and Jim Dymock and Jason Smith (Parramatta). Ricketson, the only non-international player among the contenders earned his place through an enormously high defensive workrate and his tireless support play.

The fullback spot was a no-contest. Newcastle's Robbie O'Davis outplayed Test fullback Tim Brasher on a number of occasions throughout the year and was in dazzling form as the Knights played their way through a tough finals program to claim the Optus Cup.

ROLL OF HONOUR

1987-88

Players of the Year: Hugh McGahan (Easts), Michael O'Connor (Manly), Wayne Pearce (Balmain), Dale Shearer (Manly), Peter Sterling (Parramatta).
Team of the Year: Gary Belcher (Canberra); Dale Shearer (Manly), Michael O'Connor (Manly), Peter Jackson (Canberra), Steve Morris (Easts); Cliff Lyons (Manly), Peter Sterling (Parramatta); Ian Roberts (Souths), Royce Simmons (Penrith), Peter Tunks (Canterbury), Les Davidson (Souths), Hugh McGahan (Easts), Wayne Pearce (Balmain).

1988-89

Players of the Year: Ben Elias (Balmain), Garry Jack (Balmain), Allan Langer (Brisbane), Wally Lewis (Brisbane), Gavin Miller (Cronulla).
Team of the Year: Garry Jack (Balmain); John Ferguson (Canberra), Michael O'Connor (Manly), Peter Jackson (Canberra), Andrew Ettingshausen (Cronulla); Wally Lewis (Brisbane), Allan Langer (Brisbane); Paul Dunn (Canterbury), Ben Elias (Balmain), Sam Backo (Canberra), Paul Sironen (Balmain), Gavin Miller (Cronulla), Wayne Pearce (Balmain).

1989-90

Players of the Year: Gary Belcher (Canberra), Bradley Clyde (Canberra), Mal Meninga (Canberra), Gavin Miller (Cronulla), Kerrod Walters (Brisbane).
Team of the Year: Gary Belcher (Canberra); Michael Hancock (Brisbane), Tony Currie (Brisbane), Mal Meninga (Canberra), John Ferguson (Canberra); Phil Blake (Souths), Ricky Stuart (Canberra); Steve Roach (Balmain), Kerrod Walters (Brisbane), Glenn Lazarus (Canberra), Paul Sironen (Balmain), Gavin Miller (Cronulla), Bradley Clyde (Canberra).

1990-91

Players of the Year: Gary Belcher (Canberra), Glenn Lazarus (Canberra), Cliff Lyons (Manly), Mal Meninga (Canberra), Peter Sterling (Parramatta).
Team of the Year: Gary Belcher (Canberra); Michael Hancock (Brisbane), Mal Meninga (Canberra), Andrew Ettingshausen (Cronulla), John Ferguson (Canberra);

Cliff Lyons (Manly), Peter Sterling (Parramatta); Steve Roach (Balmain), Ben Elias (Balmain), Glenn Lazarus (Canberra), Paul Sironen (Balmain), John Cartwright (Penrith), Bob Lindner (Wests).

1991-92

Players of the Year: Greg Alexander (Penrith), Bradley Clyde (Canberra), Allan Langer (Brisbane), Ewan McGrady (Canterbury), Mal Meninga (Canberra).
Team of the Year: Michael Potter (St George); Rod Wishart (Illawarra), Mal Meninga (Canberra), Andrew Ettingshausen (Cronulla), Willie Carne (Brisbane); Peter Jackson (Norths), Allan Langer (Brisbane); Craig Salvatori (Easts), Steve Walters (Canberra), Martin Bella (Manly), David Gillespie (Wests), Mark Geyer (Penrith), Bradley Clyde (Canberra).

1992-93

Players of the Year: Gary Freeman (Easts), Allan Langer (Brisbane), Glenn Lazarus (Brisbane), Steve Renouf (Brisbane), Steve Walters (Canberra).
Team of the Year: Michael Potter (St George); Willie Carne (Brisbane), Steve Renouf (Brisbane), Paul McGregor (Illawarra), Michael Hancock (Brisbane); Brad Fittler (Penrith), Allan Langer (Brisbane); Glenn Lazarus (Brisbane), Steve Walters (Canberra), Mark Sargent (Newcastle), John Cartwright (Penrith), Trevor Gillmeister (Brisbane), Bradley Clyde (Canberra).

1993-94

Players of the Year: Mark Coyne (St George), Brad Mackay (St George), Ricky Stuart (Canberra), Kerrod Walters (Brisbane), Steve Walters (Canberra).
Team of the Year: Michael Potter (St George); Willie Carne (Brisbane), Mark Coyne (St George), Brad Fittler (Penrith), Noa Nadruku (Canberra); Kevin Walters (Brisbane), Ricky Stuart (Canberra); Ian Roberts (Manly), Steve Walters (Canberra), Glenn Lazarus (Brisbane), Bob Lindner (Illawarra), Paul Sironen (Balmain), Brad Mackay (St George).

1994-95

Players of the Year: Bradley Clyde (Canberra), Greg Florimo (Norths), Brett Mullins (Canberra), Dean Pay (Canterbury), Ricky Stuart (Canberra).
Team of the Year: Brett Mullins (Canberra); Rod Wishart (Illawarra), Steve Renouf (Brisbane), Ruben Wiki (Canberra), Sean Hoppe (Norths); Greg Florimo (Norths), Ricky Stuart (Canberra); John Lomax (Canberra), Steve Walters (Canberra), Ian Roberts (Manly), Dean Pay (Canterbury), Bradley Clyde (Canberra), Brad Fittler (Penrith).

1995-96

Players of the Year: Laurie Daley (Canberra), Brad Fittler (Penrith), Andrew Johns (Newcastle), Gary Larson (Norths), Steve Menzies (Manly).
Team of the Year: Tim Brasher (Sydney Tigers); Rod Wishart (Illawarra), Steve Renouf (Brisbane), Terry Hill (Manly), Sean Hoppe (Auckland); Laurie Daley (Canberra), Andrew Johns (Newcastle); David Gillespie (Manly), Steve Walters (Canberra), Mark Carroll (Manly), Steve Menzies (Manly), Gary Larson (Norths), Brad Fittler (Penrith).

1996-97

Players of the Year: Tim Brasher (Sydney Tigers), Laurie Daley (Canberra), Daniel Gartner (Manly), Allan Langer (Brisbane), Geoff Toovey (Manly).
Team of the Year: Tim Brasher (Sydney Tigers); Rod Wishart (Illawarra), Craig Innes (Manly), Andrew Ettingshausen (Cronulla), Brett Dallas (Norths); Laurie Daley (Canberra), Geoff Toovey (Manly); Mark Carroll (Manly), Jim Serdaris (Manly), Glenn Lazarus (Brisbane), Daniel Gartner (Manly), David Fairleigh (Norths), Brad Fittler (Sydney City).

1997-98

Players of the Year: Brad Fittler (Sydney City), Paul Harragon (Newcastle), Robbie O'Davis (Newcastle), John Simon (Parramatta), Geoff Toovey (Manly).
Team of the Year: Robbie O'Davis (Newcastle); Darren Albert (Newcastle), Craig Innes (Manly), Terry Hill (Manly), Jack Elsegood (Sydney City); Brad Fittler (Sydney City), John Simon (Parramatta); Paul Harragon (Newcastle), Geoff Toovey (Manly), Mark Carroll (Manly), Adam Muir (Newcastle), Luke Ricketson (Sydney City), Nik Kosef (Manly).

1997 IN REVIEW

JANUARY

January 1: North Sydney captain Jason Taylor and several team-mates are involved in an ugly incident at a one-day cricket match at the SCG. Norths officials launch an investigation into allegations that players threw cups of urine over patrons during a Mexican wave. The incident attracts national attention of the most negative kind.

January 5: ARL chairman Ken Arthurson says North Sydney should consider sacking any players found guilty of misbehaviour.

January 6: Jason Taylor retains his role as North Sydney captain.

January 10: Newcastle second-rower Adam Muir signs a four-year deal with North Sydney, beginning in 1998.

January 17: Super League secure free-to-air rights with Channel Nine, leaving the Nine network to televise both ARL and Super League competitions in 1997. The move prompts ARL chief executive Neil Whittaker to admit that the ARL's season draw may have to be modified. The *Daily Telegraph* hails the move as a major coup for Super League in its battle against the ARL. Super League CEO John Ribot predicts a flood of ARL players would switch camps in 1998. Channel Nine chief executive David Leckie resigns from the board of the ARL.

January 20: The Canberra Raiders restructure their board of directors, and announce Department of Defence Secretary Tony Ayers as the new club chairman, replacing club founder Les McIntyre. Raiders' CEO Kevin Neil says the club is considering a public float.

January 22: ARL chairman Ken Arthurson announces his resignation from the NSWRL and ARL boards, effective from February 28. Leading ARL executive Greg Mitchell also announces his resignation ... ABC Radio secures the national rights to broadcast Super League games.

January 25: Canterbury allow winger Hazem El Masri to play in the Lebanese team assembled for the ARL World Sevens.

January 26: The *Sun-Herald* reveals that Manly and Sydney City have again been targeted by Super League.

January 28: Neil Whittaker begins his new career as chief executive of the Australian Rugby League.

January 29: Former Test winger Willie Carne becomes the first leading Australian Rugby League player to switch to Rugby Union when he confirms a two-year deal with the Queensland Rugby Union ... John McDonald is named interim chairman of the Australian Rugby League ... Optus Vision executive Ian Ross is seconded by the ARL to take over as marketing manager until the end of the season. He replaces Graeme Foster, who resigned earlier in the month due to illness.

January 30: The *Sydney Morning Herald* reveals that Channel Nine has switched its Monday Night Football timeslot from 8.30pm to 9.30pm because of the success of Australian drama series *Water Rats*.

January 31: The Herald discloses that the ARL Friday Night Football fixture will also be televised at 9.30pm in 1997 ... Super League's World Nines begins in Townsville ... Super League's International Board chairman Maurice Lindsay announces that business interests are prepared to invest $60 million into an eight-team competition in Japan.

FEBRUARY

February 1: Super League officials are embarrassed by a bungle with their high-tech video refereeing system during a World Nines match in Townsville.

February 2: Reacting to persistent media rumours linking Manly to Super League, Cronulla chairman Peter Gow says Cronulla fans will have nothing to do with the ARL premiers. "We don't like 'em, we don't trust them and we don't want 'em," he said ... Controversial Sydney media personality Ray Hadley announces he has quit Channel Nine's *Footy Show* ... The Australian Super League side is beaten by New Zealand in a quarter-final of the World Nines. The Kiwis win the Nines for the second consecutive year.

February 3: New Zealand RL president Graham Carden announces he will not stand for re-election in March.

February 4: Super League is officially launched in Australia by Canberra's Laurie Daley.

1997 YEAR IN REVIEW

February 5: The NSW Industrial Court begins hearing a case involving five Penrith players, Brisbane recruit Anthony Mundine and Canterbury's Rod Silva. The players were challenging the validity of ARL loyalty contracts ... John Lang is appointed the Australian Super League coach under a selection system which rewards the leading premiership coach from the previous season with the top job ... Ken Cowley is appointed chairman of Super League.

February 6: Manly and Sydney City officials rubbish speculation linking them to Super League and guarantee the Australian Rugby League they have no interest in the rebel competition.

February 9: Two North Sydney players are fined $5000 each following an inquiry into incidents at the New Years Day cricket match at the SCG. The club insists Jason Taylor was not one of the players fined ... Parramatta win their first trophy in more than a decade when they take out the World Sevens competition and claim $65,000 in prize money.

February 10: The *Australian Financial Review* suggests a merger between the ARL and Super League could be deemed illegal under the Trade Practices Act.

February 11: ARL and Queensland selector Des Morris defects to Super League.

February 12: Super League's new judiciary system is unveiled. The feature of the new judiciary is a points system which ranks various grades of offence.

February 13: Wayne Bennett is named coach of the Queensland Tri-series team ... ARL captain Brad Fittler endorses a Super Bowl match between the winners of the ARL and Super League competitions ... Manly release second-rower Solomon Haumono from the final year of his contract, clearing him to join Super League club Canterbury in 1997.

February 15: A crowd of over 10,000 turn out for the Charity Shield match between St George and Souths at the Sydney Football Stadium. Saints continue their domination of the annual match, winning 26–18.

February 16: The *Sun-Herald* reports that Manly and Sydney City have formally committed themselves to Super League.

February 17: Strained relations between the Newcastle Knights and the Hunter Mariners deteriorate further with both camps threatening legal action against each other over comments aired in the media ... The *Sydney Morning Herald* reports that Super League CEO John Ribot has invited Victorian Premier Jeff Kennett to bid for the Super League grand final ... Balmain call for an inquiry into an incident in which Newcastle hooker Brett Clements is cleared of an apparent spear tackle of Tigers' lock Glenn Morrison ... Reports of a merger between the financially troubled South Queensland Crushers and the Gold Coast Chargers surface.

February 18: The ARL apply for an injunction in the NSW Supreme Court to prevent Jack Elsegood and John Cross, both of whom had signed ARL loyalty contracts, from turning out for Super League clubs Canterbury and Penrith ... The South Queensland Crushers announce their intention to fight on without the on-going financial backing of Kerry Packer's PBL.

February 19: The London Broncos announce that British millionaire Richard Branson is to buy a 20 per cent stake in the club ... North Queensland coach Tim Sheens is named as coach of the NSW Tri-Series team ... Super League boss Ian Frykberg says there will be only one competition in 1998 and that it will be Super League, with the probable addition of two ARL clubs.

February 20: The *Daily Telegraph* reveals that Super League is considering relocating the Perth Reds to Melbourne in 1998 ... The South Queensland Crushers face a player exodus after officials reveal the club will withhold match payments of up to $10,000 until the end of the season ... The ARL's National Premiership Committee recommend the re-introduction of a salary cap in conjunction with a point-index system in 1998.

February 21: The North Sydney club receives more bad publicity following an alleged incident between several players and a number of elderly lawn bowlers in a suburban car park.

February 22: Newcastle lock Marc Glanville is sent off for a spear tackle on Manly prop Mark Carroll in a fiery trial match at Coffs Harbour ... Auckland chief executive

Ian Robson succumbs to pressure from the Warriors' board by announcing his resignation.

February 23: Former Kangaroos Geoff Gerard and Chris Mortimer are appointed selectors of the NSW Tri-series team.

February 24: An unusual alliance is formed when Parramatta Leagues Club is announced as the major sponsor of the Parramatta Rugby Union side ... The ARL's 1997 competition is launched at a function at Sydney's Town Hall.

February 25: Super League announce a $1 million sponsorship of their referees by Sony Computer Entertainment.

February 26. The Perth Reds announce that chief executive Brad Mellen would be standing down from his position ... The ARL refuse an offer from John Cross and Jack Elsegood to repay the $150,000 they each received for signing loyalty payments.

February 27: The NSW Supreme Court grants the ARL's application for an interlocutory injunction to restrain Jack Elsegood and John Cross from playing with Super League clubs in 1997.

February 28: Outgoing ARL chairman Ken Arthurson has his final day in office ... Telstra is named as naming rights sponsor for Super League in 1997.

MARCH

March 1: After two years of hype, volumes of legal documents and acres of newsprint, the Super League competition finally gets under way with a curious crowd of 42,000 watching the Brisbane Broncos clash with the Auckland Warriors at ANZ Stadium. Competition favourites, the Broncos dominate the match, winning 14–2.

March 3: Super League referee Bill Harrigan is critical of the breakaway competition's "wired for sound" innovation, which broadcasts every comment made by the referee. The innovation receives a lukewarm response from television viewers ... The ARL approve eight rule changes which were trialled during the pre-season Country Carnival ... North Queensland forward Tyran Smith is the first player to be cited by Super League's judiciary.

March 5: The *Newcastle Herald* reports that Knights' prop Glenn Grief will be sidelined for the season after a life-threatening blood clot in his chest followed a major knee reconstruction ... The ARL announce they will not go ahead with the video refereeing system because of concern over delays arriving at decisions ... ARL chief executive Neil Whittaker moves to strengthen the rules banning spear tackles.

March 6: The NSWRL Board elect Warren Lockwood unopposed as chairman, replacing Ken Arthurson ... The South Queensland Crushers announce AV Jennings as major sponsor for 1997 ... Parramatta announce a major sponsorship deal with sports wear company Asics.

March 7: A bumper crowd of 25,114 turn out for the ARL's season opener between Parramatta and Norths at Parramatta Stadium. Recovering from extensive brain surgery, former Parramatta forward Adam Ritson greets the crowd ... The Canberra Raiders confirm a multi-million dollar sponsorship deal with Ansett.

March 10: ARL and Super League officials admit augmenting attendances by giving away thousands of tickets to opening round matches.

March 11: Banned Super League recruit John Cross returns to the Illawarra Steelers ... Super League appoint former Auckland chief executive Ian Robson as general manager of marketing, replacing Gary Pearse, who resigned a week earlier ... Super League CEO John Ribot says there is a strong chance that Super League would establish a club in Melbourne in 1998 ... Auckland chairman Gerald Ryan launches a stinging broadside against referees saying "I know blind people aged 106 at the bottom of the South Island that could referee better than some of the Australians."

March 12: Newcastle captain Paul Harragon is sidelined for a month because of continuing migraine attacks ... Super League asks clothing manufacturer Nike to improve the numbering on its jumpers following complaints by spectators and television viewers.

March 14: Banned by the courts from playing with Super League, Jack Elsegood signs a one-year deal with Sydney City. Under the terms of his Super League contract, Super League is forced to pay Elsegood $190,000 to play for the Roosters. Elsegood is immediately rushed into first grade at the expense of Darren Junee.

March 16: The South Queensland Crushers score a staggering 23–6 upset victory over big-spenders Parramatta ... Stand-in Canberra skipper Laurie Daley blames his team's poor attitude for their fourth successive defeat and not new coach Mal Meninga.

March 17: An incident in a weekend match in which North Sydney's Chris Caruana allegedly racially vilified Newcastle's Owen Craigie leads the ARL to develop a policy aimed at stamping out racial and religious taunts on the field. Caruana is fined and relegated from the Bears' starting lineup.

March 19: Super League dump advertising agency Young and Rubicam in favour of an agency headed by Siimon Reynolds ... Quentin Pongia becomes the first player suspended by the Super League judiciary when he is found guilty of a reckless tackle ... The ARL announces that clubs face fines of $20,000 if players are found guilty of racial abuse ... St George's Football Club board appoint Doug McClelland as their new chairman, succeeding Warren Lockwood.

March 21: ARL boss Neil Whittaker admits the ARL will not consider establishing a team in Melbourne in 1998 unless it is guaranteed immediate success.

March 22: St George's Nathan Brown stars in his team's 20–8 defeat of Illawarra, leading Steelers' coach Andrew Farrar to describe the young hooker as "Dally M, Churchill, Gasnier and Wally Lewis all in one" ... Speculation intensifies that John Monie's days as Auckland coach are numbered ... The *Sunday Telegraph* reports that newly-appointed New Zealand chairman Gerald Ryan wants to review the NZRL's agreement with Super League and is prepared to talk with ARL CEO Neil Whittaker.

March 24: South Queensland fullback Clinton Schifcofske admits to a positive drug test for anabolic steroids ... Canberra's woeful start to the season continues with a 24–8 loss to Brisbane at ANZ Stadium.

March 25: The NZRL confirm they will not consider playing Test matches against the Australian Rugby League's national team.

March 27: The ARL announce the establishment of a new major player of the year award to replace the Rothmans Medal, outlawed by Federal Government legislation. The Nokia Provan-Summons Medal is to be judged by media as well as referees ... In his weekly *Sydney Morning Herald* column, Sydney City coach Phil Gould is highly critical of the Super League competition, questioning its passion, credibility and substance.

March 30: After four successive defeats, Mal Meninga's Canberra Raiders break through for their first win of the Super League season, beating newcomers the Hunter Mariners 18–12.

APRIL

April 2: *Rugby League Week* describes Parramatta as $9 million duds after the Eels slumped to their third consecutive loss.

April 3: Perth's Mark Geyer considers quitting the game after he is suspended for 10 weeks by the Super League judiciary after being found guilty of eye-gouging and reckless tackle charges.

April 4: Manly produce a memorable win over Sydney City at Brookvale Oval. Trailing 18–0 after 18 minutes, the Sea Eagles storm back to win the match 34–24. Roosters coach Phil Gould is furious with Manly's tactics, which he says, were deliberately aimed at "taking out" the player kicking the ball ... Mark Geyer reveals his suspension will cost him $200,000 ... Two spectators are burned by fireworks at a Super League match at Penrith.

April 5: Super League judiciary commissioner Jim Hall says changes to the controversial new system will be considered ... The ARL confirms that Phil Gould has quit as coach of the Sydney Origin team, citing personal reasons.

April 7: Manly second-rower Steve Menzies escapes censure by the ARL judiciary by sneaking through a loophole in the spear tackle rule. The League's efforts to close the loophole had yet to be implemented.

April 8: The *Australian* reports that Super League is giving away thousands of free tickets in a bid to boost the attendance at the opening Tri-Series match between New South Wales and Queensland at the Sydney Football Stadium. The ARL insist there will be no such giveaways for the State of Origin series ... John McDonald is officially installed as non-executive chairman of the Australian Rugby League.

April 9: In a *Canberra Times* article headed "Football boring: Stuart", Ricky Stuart claims Super League's insistence on speeding up the play-the-ball area may have backfired and created a "very boring" brand of football ... Super League chief executives vote for tougher judiciary penalties after a series of lenient sentences.

April 11: The *Sydney Morning Herald* declares that Super League's Tri-Series competition is in trouble with no sponsor named and reports of ticket giveaways ranging from 4,000 to 17,000 for the opening match. An official crowd of 26,731 is announced for the Tri-Series opener, won 38–10 by NSW.

April 13: The *Sun-Herald* reports that Norths and Manly have held secret merger talks ... Balmain back Michael Gillett accuses referee Paul McBlane of grabbing his jumper during a match against St George at Kogarah Oval and Tigers' coach Wayne Pearce storms into the referees' room after fulltime.

April 14: Norths coach Peter Louis is appointed coach of the Sydney Origin side.

April 15: Referee Paul McBlane is dumped to second grade over the jersey-grabbing incident at Kogarah.

April 16: AFL officials are angered at reports that fans queued up outside the Sydney Cricket Ground to watch the Swans were "ambushed" by offers of free tickets to the Super League Tri-Series match next door at the Sydney Football Stadium ... The *Sydney Morning Herald* accuses Super League of "hijacking the Anzac spirit" by paying $20,000 to gain the support of the RSL to promote their Anzac Day Test match between Australia and New Zealand ... An all-in brawl in a Commonwealth Bank Cup schoolboys game between Camp Hill and Clairvaux MacKillop College leads to the abandonment of the competition's sponsorship by the Commonwealth Bank. Twenty players are handed suspensions ranging from one week to 12 months.

April 17: Four Adelaide Rams players are disciplined by the club after being charged by police following a fight outside an Adelaide strip club ... The ARL's 12 clubs commit themselves to the 1998 Optus Cup and a $5 million salary cap ... Phil Gould announces he will stand down as NSW Origin coach after five seasons at the helm of the Blues.

April 18: Super League judiciary chairman Ian Callinan QC rejects Mark Geyer's bid to appeal against his eye-gouging ban.

April 20: Newcastle coach Malcolm Reilly claims that Manly are "beatable" despite his team's 22–8 loss at Brookvale Oval ... Balmain hooker Darren Senter is the surprise selection in the first ARL representative teams of 1997.

April 23: Perth captain Mark Geyer drops planned Supreme Court action to overturn his suspension for eye-gouging ... Canberra lock Bradley Clyde tarnishes his perfect record when he receives a one-week suspension for a grade three dangerous tackle ... All 12 ARL clubs sign a document pledging loyalty to each other and the establishment ... Tom Raudonikis is elected coach of the NSW State of Origin side.

April 25: A moderate crowd of 23,829 turn out to watch Australian Super League's inaugural Test match, won 34–22 by Australia over New Zealand ... On a wet night in Newcastle, 9,164 spectators watch Country Origin down City Origin 17–4 at Marathon Stadium.

April 26: South Queensland fullback Clinton Schifcofske returns to football after his reprimand which followed a positive drugs test.

April 27: A *Sunday Telegraph* survey reveals Brad Fittler is the player who would be at the top of the shopping list of 75 per cent of ARL and Super League coaches were he on the open market ... Wests end Manly's undefeated start to the season with a 19–16 win at Campbelltown.

April 29: John Monie is sacked as coach of the Auckland Warriors and immediately replaced by reserve grade coach Frank Endacott ... North Sydney coach Peter Louis escapes a $10,000 fine but is reprimanded for his comments criticising match officials after his team's controversial Round 7 loss to Balmain.

April 30: The ARL releases details of its points index system to be introduced in 1998.

MAY

May 1: The ARL announce a three-year sponsorship of the State of Origin series with Coca-Cola. The deal is worth a reported $2 million ... The *Courier-Mail* reports crowds in Brisbane are down 45 per cent since

1995 ... The Parramatta club is fined $5000 after coach Brian Smith's public criticism of referee Sean Hampstead following the Round 7 match against Illawarra.

May 2: The NSWRL seconds Frank Stanton from Manly to fill the role as business development manager.

May 4: Manly and Illawarra fight out a thrilling 34–all draw at Steelers Stadium, equalling the record for the highest scoring draw in premiership history.

May 5: St George re-sign hooker Nathan Brown for five years in a deal worth a reported $500,000 a season ... A meeting between ARL and Education Department officials resolves to introduce a new code of conduct to NSW schools to cut the level of violence at school sports matches ... Sydney City coach Phil Gould is reappointed until the end of the 1999 season.

May 6: New Zealand chairman Gerald Ryan calls for an Oceania team to replace the New Zealand team as the third side in Super League's Tri-Series competition ... Super League-aligned New Zealand deputy chairman David Lange says the ARL has a superior competition. "For whatever reason, the arrival of Super League hasn't enhanced the product. It's Australian rival is playing better, harder, more competitive football." ... NSW treasurer Michael Egan announces a 33 per cent tax increase on poker machine revenue from NSW licensed clubs, a decision which could have dire ramifications on player payments.

May 7: After days of speculation, troubled fullback Julian O'Neill is sacked by the Perth Reds over a number of off-field incidents.

May 8: A Parramatta magistrate jails a player for three months for shoulder-charging a referee during an A-Grade match in the Penrith Junior League ... Australian coach Peter Mulholland is sacked as coach of Euro Super League club Paris-St Germain.

May 9: Queensland down New Zealand 26–12 in Auckland in the second match in Super League's Tri-Series competition ... The NSWRL announce a change to the NSW State of Origin jersey following a merchandising deal with Canterbury sportswear company.

May 10: The ARL comes under fire from the Australian Family Association over a State of Origin advertisement which appeared in two magazines, stating: "State of Origin 97 — right arms, eye teeth and left nuts are no guarantee of a ticket".

May 11: Torrential rain forces the postponement of the Round 10 match between Newcastle and Souths at Marathon Stadium.

May 13: NSW captain Brad Fittler criticises the Blues' new jersey and says it should never have been changed ... Auckland Warriors coach Frank Endacott is appointed head coach of the club until the end of the 1999 season ... Tooheys returns as sponsor of the NSW State of Origin team after earlier announcing it would discontinue its sponsorship.

May 14: An apparently wrong decision costs New Zealand a place in the Tri-Series final. NSW down the Kiwis 20–15 before a moderate crowd at Bruce Stadium ... Former Great Britain captain Garry Schofield is charged with threatening to kill his estranged wife.

May 15: Julian O'Neill signs a two-year $400,000 contract with South Sydney ... The touch judge at the centre of Super League's Tri-Series bungle is demoted to reserve grade ... New Zealand team manager Laurie Stubbing infuriates Super League by claiming the no-try decision was part of a marketing plot to ensure NSW met Queensland in the Tri-Series final at ANZ Stadium.

May 16: Super League decide to play their grand final at ANZ Stadium in Brisbane ... Super League CEO John Ribot says there is a 90 per cent chance of a single competition in 1998.

May 18: North Sydney and Manly officials disagree over the possibility of a merger between the clubs in a single competition in 1998. Manly coach Bob Fulton says a merger is possible, however Norths' chief executive Bob Saunders described the proposal as "unlikely".

May 19: NSW defeat Queensland 23–22 in a period of sudden-death extra-time in the Tri-series final at ANZ Stadium ... Illawarra's Queensland front-rower Craig Smith is fined $5000 after being found guilty by the judiciary of a high tackle, clearing him to play in the opening State of Origin match ... Geoff Toovey is named captain of the NSW State of Origin side and Adrian Lam the

Queensland leader when teams for the opening match of the 1997 series are announced.

May 21: The *Daily Telegraph* reports that Super League boss Ian Frykberg and ARL chief executive Neil Whittaker have met to discuss a compromise in the game's civil war ... Parramatta coach Brian Smith predicts that English clubs will "struggle to keep up" in Super League's World Club Challenge competition ... Super League announce it will include a team from Melbourne in the 1998 competition ... More than 900 officials, players and supporters from both sides of the game's divide honour former Parramatta prop Adam Ritson at a benefit night in Sydney.

May 22: Victorian Premier Jeff Kennett casts doubt on Super League's ability to set up a team in Melbourne by 1998.

May 23: Aussie Home Loans agree to a three-year deal to sponsor the ARL's national schoolboy competition ... Sydney-based Super League clubs agree in principle to open merger talks with ARL clubs.

May 24: Super League chief executive John Ribot denies he has quit his job to take over as the head of a new Melbourne Super League team.

May 25: The *Sun-Herald* reports that State of Origin players have been forced to accept a 33 per cent pay cut for the 1997 series .. News Limited papers confirm John Ribot has quit as Super League CEO to head up the Melbourne franchise.

May 28: A crowd of 28,222 watch NSW defeat Queensland 8–6 in the State of Origin opener at Suncorp Stadium ... Malcolm Reilly is appointed coach of the Rest of the World team to play Australia in a one-off Test in Brisbane on July 11 ... NSW Tri-Series match-winner Noel Goldthorpe is dropped from the Hunter Mariners' starting lineup and stripped of the club's captaincy.

May 29: Balmain fullback Tim Brasher is given permission to negotiate with rival clubs ... Television ratings figures for the opening Origin match indicate a considerable viewer preference for the ARL over Super League's Tri-series.

May 30: A proposal for a one-off Test against an ARL Australian team is tabled at a board meeting of the New Zealand Rugby League.

JUNE

June 1: Balmain's Test fullback Tim Brasher tells the *Sun-Herald* he was "ripped off" by receiving an ARL loyalty payment of "only" $300,000 ... The *Sunday Telegraph* reports that Gold Coast coach Phil Economidis has received offers from two Sydney clubs.

June 2: Crowd violence rears its ugly head at a Rugby League match when an estimated 2000 people become involved in a riot at Belmore Sports Ground after a Super League match between Canterbury and Penrith. Two men were arrested, a policeman was injured and a touch judge was threatened by a man who ran onto the field ... Julian O'Neill is selected in the Queensland State of Origin side after just one-and-a-half games for South Sydney.

June 3: The Canberra Raiders deny a report that star halfback Ricky Stuart is to be sacked by the club at the end of the season ... A young police officer reveals he drew his revolver when confronted by a knife-wielding youth during the riot at Belmore Sports Ground ... Queensland coach Paul Vautin says he will resign if the Maroons lose the State of Origin series.

June 4: Before a ball is kicked in Super League's ambitious World Club Challenge competition, marketing manager Ian Robson says the competition would be reviewed at the end of the season, because of the high cost of running the event, reported to be around $5 million.

June 6: Illawarra prop Scott Cram is cleared of spinal damage after being flown to hospital by helicopter following an injury in the Round 13 match against Balmain.

June 8: Despite heated denials by officials, the *Sun-Herald* reports that Julian O'Neill missed training for the Queensland State of Origin side ... Super League's worst fears are realised when Canberra whitewash Halifax 70–6 — one of a series of lopsided scores in the opening round of the World Club Challenge.

June 9: Optus Communications chief executive Ziggy Switkowski resigns and is replaced by Englishman Peter Howell-Davies.

June 11: News Limited's *Daily Telegraph* chooses the day of the second State of Origin match to renew speculation about a proposed merger between Manly and North

1997 IN REVIEW

Sydney. "Manly and North Sydney are close to agreeing to an historic merger with the full blessing of the ARL," reports chief writer Peter Frilingos beneath the banner headline "Wedding Bells"... *Rugby League Week*'s annual players' poll again installs Brad Fittler as the number one player in the game. Of the 100 players polled (50 ARL and 50 Super League), 53 said the ARL had a stronger competition, 27 said Super League was stronger, while 20 rated the competitions of equal strength ... A crowd of just 25,015 turn out at the Melbourne Cricket Ground to watch NSW wrap up the State of Origin series with a 15-14 win over Queensland. Blues coach Tom Raudonikis chooses to leave hooker Aaron Raper on the bench.

June 12: Neither ARL or Super League officials are able to give a guarantee that they will establish a team in Melbourne in 1998 ... St George extend the contract of coach David Waite until the end of 2000 ... Former New Zealand coach Graham Lowe says a syndicate in which he is involved could be ready to make an offer to buy the Auckland Warriors soon ... ARL selector John Raper says his son Aaron should have played in the State of Origin match at the MCG.

June 15: The *Sunday Telegraph* declares that the fate of South Sydney coach Ken Shine is all but sealed after football manager Frank Cookson reveals the club will place advertisements for his position in the coming weeks ... Newcastle winger Darren Albert and Norths hooker Mark Soden suffer signs of hypothermia after another Marathon Stadium match is deluged by rain. The smallest crowd in the Knights' history (6281) watch the match played in 13 degree temperatures on a day in which 46mm of rain fell in Newcastle ... ARL chief executive Neil Whittaker confirms he has been involved in talks between rival pay-television operators aimed at ending the Super League war.

June 16: After another weekend of thrashings, the *Daily Telegraph* claims the World Club Challenge has turned into a "$6m nightmare" ... The ARL judiciary suspends NSW centre Paul McGregor until June 26 after his citing in the second State of Origin match ... Nineteen-year-old Illawarra five-eighth Trent Barrett is the surprise choice to replace Jim Dymock for NSW in the final Origin match.

June 17: Super League's judicial system cops further criticism when Brisbane's Gorden Tallis escapes with nothing more than a warning letter after a brutal attack on Wigan forward Terry O'Connor ... Pay TV operator Optus says it will continue to honour its $120 million funding package to the ARL, but stops short of drawing up an official agreement.

June 18: The English Rugby League appoints former international Joe Lydon to conduct a commission into the playing standards of its clubs in response to the dominance of Australian clubs during the early rounds of the World Club Challenge.

June 19: Super League offer the ARL control of the game in a combined competition, as long as Super League retains control of the finances ... ARL clubs recommend that plans to establish a club in Melbourne in 1998 be postponed for 12 months.

June 20: Super League says there is "a prospect" of ARL clubs switching allegiances at the end of the 1997 season if there was no compromise in the game ... Sydney editor-publisher Bill Mordey relinquishes control of the game's official magazine *Big League*, after 20 years, citing declining sales.

June 22: The *Sunday Telegraph* reports that League legend Graeme Langlands has joined the Canberra Raiders as a recruitment officer ... It is revealed that Super League intend to abandon its controversial jersey-numbering system in 1998 in response to months of protest from supporters.

June 23: Western Suburbs centre Brandon Pearson is released from his contract after a falling out with club officials and coach Tom Raudonikis ... Perth Reds chairman Stephen Edwards says his club's position is safe, despite mounting debts and the club's poor form in the early rounds of the World Club Challenge. "We have had it on the highest authority that our position in either Super League or in a united competition — and in Perth — is secure next year," Edwards said. "Those assurances have come from Ken Cowley and Ian Frykberg." ... Brisbane football manager Chris Johns quits the club to take up the position as chief executive of Super League's new Melbourne franchise ... The *Daily Telegraph* reports that Canterbury

Bankstown Leagues Club will lodge an application to build a $150 million sporting development at Liverpool's Woodward Park ... Super League warns the ARL that three more of its clubs are poised to defect unless a compromise is reached in time for 1998.

June 24: John Ribot formally announces his resignation as chief executive of Super League in order to become proprietor of the new Melbourne franchise.

June 25: Queensland salvage some pride with an 18–12 win in the final State of Origin match before a highly credible crowd of 33,241 at the Sydney Football Stadium.

June 26: Sydney City and North Sydney resist the "urge to merge" by announcing their intention to continue to stand alone in the event of a joint competition with Super League ... Super League announce the appointment of a new chief executive, Colin Sanders, former CEO of the Royal Agricultural Society of NSW.

June 27: The *Sydney Morning Herald* reports that the ARL will explore the possibility of forming a partnership with News Limited in order to share financial control of a merged competition ... The Perth Reds extend the contract of coach Dean Lance until the end of 2000 ... ARL chief executive Neil Whittaker places a July 30 deadline on compromise talks with Super League ... Queenslanders Jamie Goddard (fighting) and Wayne Bartrim (high tackle) and NSW halfback Andrew Johns (fighting) are suspended for two matches after incidents arising from the third State of Origin match.

June 29: The *Sun-Herald* runs an alarmingly frank interview with Perth wildman Mark Geyer, who claims Chris Quinn, the Adelaide player who accused him of eye-gouging: "is the man I most hate in the world. I'd be lying if I said I didn't want to kill the bloke" ... Super League boss Ian Frykberg confirms the 22–team World Club Challenge format will be scrapped in 1998 ... Sydney City sign Brandon Pearson ahead of the June 30 player signing deadline ... North Sydney respond emphatically to thoughts of a merger with Manly by thrashing their northside rivals by the record score of 41–8 at North Sydney Oval ... Mark Geyer is placed on report in his first match back from a 10-match suspension.

JULY

July 1: South Sydney president George Piggins indicates his club will consider legal action against Optus Vision if the communications carrier withdraws its funding of ARL clubs ... Sydney City halfback Adrian Lam is named captain of the Rest of the World team ... Controversial Perth forward Mark Geyer is suspended for three weeks for a high tackle.

July 2: North Sydney ace Greg Florimo scores a rare rating of 10 out of 10 in *Rugby League Week* after his vintage performance against Manly ... ARL chief executive Neil Whittaker says he is disappointed at a premature announcement by Super League on a joint ARL-Super League initiative to impose a moratorium on player signings until the end of August.

July 3: The *Sydney Morning Herald* reports that North Sydney have held secret negotiations to explore a move to the Central Coast, fearing that their only alternative in a joint competition is to merge with neighbours Manly ... New Zealand international Tyran Smith is released from his contract with the North Queensland Cowboys ... Super League boss Ian Frykberg questions the commitment of ARL clubs to the peace process after they fail to agree to a moratorium on player signings ... Parramatta chief executive Denis Fitzgerald confirms his club has held merger discussions with Balmain.

July 4: The ARL announces its clubs have agreed to a moratorium on player signings until the end of August.

July 5: Tyran Smith signs with the Hunter Mariners for the rest of the 1997 season ... Troubled Rabbitoh Julian O'Neill is sacked from first grade for missing a South Sydney training session.

July 6: The *Sun-Herald* reports that former Gold Coast and Canberra halfback Jason Gregory has received an out-of-court settlement in the vicinity of $250,000 for a tackle that ended his career five years ago ... The *Sunday Telegraph* reveals that former Sydney City, Manly and Gold Coast tough man Ron Gibbs has joined the Country Rugby League's refereeing ranks ... St George say they will "fight to the bitter end" to avoid merging with another club.

July 7: The *Australian* reports that the New

1997 IN REVIEW

Zealand Rugby League is preparing to sue former chairman Graham Carden for $1.35 million.

July 8: An AAP report suggests that the Brisbane Broncos face a financial loss of $1 million in 1997, but still expect to be the most successful off-field performer of the season ... Australian coach Bob Fulton calls for a united tour of New Zealand and England at the end of the season if a compromise is reached between the ARL and Super League.

July 9: The powerful South Sydney Junior Leagues Club threatens to withdraw its annual $3.5 million contribution to the sport if the Rabbitohs are treated badly in the peace-making process ... Super League boss Ian Frykberg and ARL chief executive Neil Whittaker tentatively agree to an internal draft in the event of a united competition in 1998.

July 10: Gold Coast and South Queensland officials agree to investigate any opportunities for a joint venture between them for the 1998 season.

July 11: It is reported that a police inquiry has been launched into the affairs of Euro Super League club Paris-St Germain following allegations that the Paris players — largely Australian — have been using six-month visas instead of work permits. The report says European Super League chief executive Maurice Lindsay is to be questioned by police over the affair ... Australia beat the Rest of the World 28–8 in a high-quality game at Suncorp Stadium. Rival coaches Bob Fulton and Malcolm Reilly agree that the Rest of the World team would beat either of Super League's Great Britain or New Zealand teams ... Parramatta chief executive Denis Fitzgerald urges all Sydney-based clubs to investigate the possibility of joint ventures for 1998.

July 13: Leading player manager George Mimis predicts that up to 20 League stars would jump ship to Rugby Union within 12 months ... Brisbane captain Allan Langer and Canberra five-eighth Laurie Daley call for a united Australian team to tour Great Britain if a compromise is reached between Super League and the ARL.

July 14: A crowd of just 13,067 turn out for the match billed as Super League's "grand final preview" at Bruce Stadium. The Broncos score a decisive 19–4 victory ... Wests chief executive Martin Bullock scotches talk of a possible merger with Canterbury ... The ARL produces a blueprint for a 16-team competition in 1998 and plans to reduce the number of teams to 14 in 1999.

July 15: The president of the National Tax Accountants Association, Ray Reagan, says the tax office is gearing to target more than 700 players in AFL, Soccer, Rugby League and Rugby Union ... Super League formulate their own proposal for a united competition in 1998 with just 12 teams, including only four in Sydney.

July 16: A four-man consortium, including former New Zealand coach Graham Lowe, table a $4 million bid for ownership of the Auckland Warriors ... Super League boss Ian Frykberg says a Super Bowl-style end-of-season game against the ARL premiers is a must, regardless of the outcome of compromise talks with the ARL.

July 17: AAP reports that Super League crowds have plummeted 45 per cent since the start of the World Club Challenge competition ... Another AAP report says Super League players believe Parramatta, Sydney City and Manly will join their competition if compromise talks come to nothing ... The Auckland Rugby League reject a $NZ4 million offer to buy the Warriors.

July 18: The *Sydney Morning Herald* reports that a Super Bowl contest has been pencilled in for October 25 at the Sydney Football Stadium ... The ARL announce a formal renewal of its $120 million funding agreement with Optus Communications until 2000 ... Canberra Raiders chief executive Kevin Neil reveals his club will consider a relocation from Bruce Stadium if it cannot negotiate a reduction in rent from the ACT Government.

July 19: Sydney City coach Phil Gould says he would like to see the ARL "go it alone" following Optus' renewal of their funding guarantee. "And I'd tell Super League to go to hell." ... The ARL extends its deadline in negotiations with Super League until early August.

July 20: Ian Frykberg says Super League will not budge on the critical issue of control of the game unless the ARL can commit long-term finance to a dual-funding proposal

... Parramatta win their 10th consecutive match with a high-quality 28–22 defeat of Newcastle at Parramatta Stadium ... ARL chief executive Neil Whittaker says the structure of the 1998 competition would have to be finalised by October 1 if the game was to regain the public's confidence.

July 21: Former Balmain player Ian McCann wins an out-of-court settlement of more than $75,000 over injuries sustained in a tackle by Mario Fenech in 1992 ... ARL boss Neil Whittaker urges Illawarra to explore merger options for involvement in a unified competition in 1998 ... Frank Stanton returns to his role of Manly-Warringah chief executive following the completion of his secondment to the ARL.

July 22: Super League decides to give a home ground advantage to the higher-placed team during the breakaway competition's inaugural final series ... Canberra are knocked out of the World Club Challenge after a shock 38–18 loss to the London Broncos ... State of Origin referee Kelvin Jeffes becomes the third representative referee dropped by the ARL in 1997.

July 23: Super League supremo Ian Frykberg says a Melbourne side will not be included in any national competition unless it can prove to be self-supporting.

July 24: Brisbane's *Courier-Mail* reports the ARL wants to shift a semi-final clash from Brisbane back to Sydney following poor attendances at Suncorp Stadium in 1997 ... Ian Frykberg and Neil Whittaker agree that the central problem of how a united competition could be run and financed is achievable with a single board of directors running the game in Australia.

July 25: Parramatta extend their winning run to 11 consecutive matches with a 17–10 win over Manly at Brookvale Oval. The result places them one victory short of their club record, set in 1964 and equalled in 1977. Manly coach Bob Fulton calls for video replays to be used during the final series after a number of contentious decisions during the match ... An agreement is reached to merge pay-TV operators Australis and Foxtel, a move which would substantially weaken Optus Vision's position in the pay-TV marketplace.

July 27: The *Sunday Mail* reports that the Brisbane Broncos are considering a return to Suncorp Stadium under a $70 million plan by Sports Minister Mick Veivers that would increase the ground's capacity to 56,000 ... The *Sunday Telegraph* reveals that top secret merger talks have been held between arch-rivals St George and Cronulla.

July 28: Auckland lawyer Jennifer Haydock is named the new chief executive of the New Zealand Rugby League, becoming the first woman to hold the position with the NZRL ... North Sydney's plans to relocate to the Central Coast receive a setback when the move is opposed by the Central Coast Rugby League.

July 29: Canberra coach Mal Meninga and second-rower David Furner are pictured in Sydney's *Daily Telegraph* wearing women's clothing during the fourth Ashes Cricket Test at Headingley. London's *Daily Mirror* accuses a Canberra player of trying to steal Glenn McGrath's bat after the team was admitted to the Australian dressing-room ... The ARL warns the English Rugby Football League it risks a massive damages bill if it continues to promote Australia's Tests against Great Britain in late 1997 as matches involving "The Kangaroos".

July 30: *Rugby League Week* reports that the Perth Reds have sacked 20 senior players, fuelling speculation that the club is to be swallowed up by the new Melbourne franchise ... Former Australian referee Greg McCallum confirms he is resigning as director of referees in Great Britain and will return home by the end of the year.

July 31: South Sydney chairman George Piggins says any Super League club that wishes to return to the ARL would be welcomed ... The ARL confirms it has switched the September 12 qualifying semi-final from Brisbane's Suncorp Stadium to Parramatta Stadium ... New Zealand chairman Gerald Ryan renews threats that the Kiwis may break ranks with Super League by playing a Test against the ARL.

AUGUST

August 1: St George great Norm Provan attacks the ARL's decision to downgrade the Giltinan Shield from a premiership trophy to the reward for the competition's minor premiers ... Manly produce their best defensive effort of the season to deny

Newcastle 14–12 in front of a crowd of over 25,000 at Marathon Stadium ... ARL chief executive Neil Whittaker extends an open invitation to Optus and Foxtel to attend the next round of peace talks with Super League.

August 3: The *Sun-Herald* reports that Channel Nine will revert to the 8.30pm Rugby League timeslot once the ARL and Super League begin their final series ... Parramatta's winning run comes to an end at the hands of Illawarra, who score a shock 28–24 win at Parramatta Stadium ... North Sydney celebrate "Flo Day" at North Sydney Oval to commemorate Greg Florimo's 250th first grade appearance ... The ARL stand firm in their opposition to the introduction of video referees during the final series despite renewed calls from leading coaches Phil Gould and Bob Fulton.

August 4: *The Canberra* Times reports that the Raiders have sought and received written references from the Australian cricket team to defend them from accusations of embarrassing off-field behaviour during their World Club Challenge tour of England ... South Sydney skipper Darrell Trindall is suspended for the remainder of the season after being found guilty of a high tackle charge ... Penrith win their sixth consecutive World Club Challenge match but it appears their opponents, St Helens will be the ones to qualify for the quarter finals despite losing all six of their preliminary games in the farcical international Super League competition ... ARL captains back the call for the use of the video referee during the final series.

August 5: The Players' Union meet with the ARL to formulate a policy ensuring player managers obtain official accreditation.

August 6: The *Sydney Morning Herald* reveals that Super League has failed to live up to the predictions it made available during the 1995 Federal Court case ... ARL and Super League officials agree in principle to a proposal for peace.

August 7: South Sydney president George Piggins warns the ARL it cannot afford to turn its back on any Establishment club if it wants total support for a peace deal with Super League.

August 8: The NSWRL celebrates its 90th anniversary ... The *Sydney Morning Herald* reveals the proposed united competition would be called Super League and its chief executive would be appointed by News Limited.

August 9: *The Australian* reports that representatives of ARL clubs would rather prolong the two-competition scenario than play in a competition called Super League.

August 10: Balmain captain Paul Sironen confirms he will play another season with the club ... A series of radio and television polls show an overwhelming opposition to the name Super League being used for a united competition ... As the call for the implementation of video referees becomes deafening, the ARL finds an unlikely ally in the guise of Super League referees' boss Graham Annesley. Annesley says it would be difficult to introduce the new technology in time for the final series.

August 12: AAP reports of "growing indications" that ARL and Super League bosses could be prepared to accept a united 20-team competition in 1998 ... North Queensland hooker Jason Death donates $10,000 to charity and avoids punishment from the Cowboys after he stripped in a Leeds hotel during the World Club Challenge.

August 13: The Country Rugby League asks for financial compensation for affected parties before it considers supporting North Sydney's bid to relocate to the Central Coast.

August 14: Country club Aberdeen take legal action to stop the Group 21 grand final between Denman and Muswellbrook because of a bitter dispute over player registration ... The likelihood of a 20-team competition in 1998 increases when Super League boss Ian Frykberg says a transition period may be necessary in the interests of peace.

August 15: North Queensland coach Tim Sheens calls for a player draft to be included in plans for a single competition in 1998 ... Super League coaches and players vote to abandon a proposed Super Bowl contest for 1997.

August 16: Brisbane Broncos coach Wayne Bennett likens the ARL's seven-team finals format as "an exhibition down sideshow alley, where everybody gets a stuffed prize".

August 17: A crowd of 13,845 turns out for the South Queensland–St George clash at Suncorp Stadium after the gates are thrown open by Crushers' officials ... Manly veteran Cliff Lyons announces he will have another season with the Sea Eagles.

August 18: South Sydney announce the appointment of former international Steve Martin to a two-year contract to coach the club ... Peace talks between the ARL and Super League break down after the boss of the breakaway league, Ian Frykberg, says demands placed on the peace process by Optus Vision were unacceptable.

August 22: ARL chief executive Neil Whittaker says he would welcome inquiries from Super League clubs worried about their futures if rival competitions continued in 1998 ... Brisbane's *Courier-Mail* names Peter Sterling as the most complete halfback of the past 20 years ... The Newcastle Knights announce a plan to take over the debt-ridden Cardiff Workers Club.

August 24: The *Sun-Herald* reveals that Canterbury coach Chris Anderson is interested in coaching the new Melbourne franchise, despite months of denials ... The Gold Coast are reported to have turned their backs on the proposed merger with the South Queensland Crushers, announcing their intention to stand alone in 1998 ... Newcastle Knights winger Darren Albert tells the *Sunday Telegraph* he wants out of his two-year deal with Super League's Hunter Mariners.

August 26: The ARL threatens to take action against Sydney City after coach Phil Gould names virtually the entire second grade side for the final round "dead rubber" clash with North Sydney ... The ARL announces a $500,000 deal with retail giant Harvey Norman to sponsor the ARL's final series ... The Industrial Relations Commission brings down the first award that will guarantee ARL first grade players a minimum wage of $36,100 a season.

August 27: *Rugby League Week* reports that a fan has left South Sydney $200,000 in his will ... Yet another off-field indiscretion sees Hadouken Julian O'Neill dropped from the starting lineup to play Manly and fined around $10,000 ... Canberra sign boom Auckland Rugby Union centre Lesley Vainikolo ... Sydney City back down on plans to rest 14 players from the Round 22 clash with North Sydney after intervention from ARL boss Neil Whittaker.

August 28: An *Inside Sport* article claims 15 Perth players were involved in the use of steroids from late 1994 to early 1995 ... The debt-ridden South Queensland Crushers are effectively finished as a top grade entity after ARL officials opt to push ahead with a merger with the Gold Coast Chargers. Players are told their club will not be a part of any competition in 1998.

August 29: A stockbroking firm estimates the ARL-Super League war has cost the Nine Network $20 million, most of it in lost advertising revenue ... The South Queensland Crushers and the Gold Coast Chargers agree to become the first clubs to merge in the 89-year history of the code.

August 30: The *Sydney Morning Herald* speculates that Parramatta and Balmain will be the next clubs to merge ... Balmain's bid for the semi-finals is brought undone by a hot Newcastle Knights, who win 34–10 at Marathon Stadium.

August 31: Paul Langmack becomes only the third player to play 300 first grade games on the day his Wests team are thrashed 39–18 by South Queensland in the Crushers' final premiership match. The Crushers' victory allows their proposed merger partners Gold Coast to sneak past Wests and qualify for the finals for the first time ... The moratorium on player signings officially expires.

SEPTEMBER

September 1: Former international Willie Carne announces his retirement from football after just one season of Rugby Union.

September 2: Canterbury chief executive Bob Hagan leads the call for Super League to abandon Monday Night Football in 1998 following disappointing crowd figures ... Former ARL chairman Ken Arthurson targets Super League and its leading identities for a roasting in his biography, *Arko*, launched in Sydney ... The Newcastle Knights sign a lucrative sponsorship deal with Impulse Airlines, worth a reported $1.5 million over three years.

September 3: John Ribot says he is preparing for an 11-team Super League competition in 1998 with Melbourne making its debut and the Perth Reds remaining in place ... Illawarra re-sign Craig Smith on a new three-year deal.

September 4: The ARL wins a NSW

1997 IN REVIEW

Supreme Court case which binds Illawarra's John Cross and Sydney City's Jack Elsegood to ARL loyalty contracts, strengthening the Establishment's bargaining position in its fight with Super League ... The *Daily Telegraph* reports that English league chief Maurice Lindsay has been asked to explain how he spent $220,000 on personal expenses over the past two years ... Canterbury coach Chris Anderson quits the club to link with Super League's new Melbourne franchise.

September 5: The Gold Coast Chargers cause a boilover with their 25–14 defeat of Illawarra in the first of the season's ARL semi-finals ... ARL chief executive Neil Whittaker reveals that Super League want the proposed new company that is to run the game in 1998 to absorb Super League's debt for 1997.

September 6: The television replay of Super League's major semi-final between Brisbane and Cronulla is delayed because of coverage of the funeral of Diana, Princess of Wales ... Sydney City scores a 33–21 win over Norths in extra-time in the second ARL qualifying semi-final.

September 7: The *Sun-Herald* reports that Tooheys will drop its long-standing naming rights sponsorship of the NSW State of Origin team ... Outgoing Canterbury coach Chris Anderson admits a factional fight within the club was responsible for his departure ... Super League clubs complain that a deal between Canberra and Auckland which saw classy young centre Lesley Vainikolo swapped for Raiders' veteran Quentin Pongia has breached Super League's transfer rules ... Newcastle advance to a showdown with minor premiers Manly after their 28–20 win over Parramatta ... The ARL decide against shifting the Gold Coast–Sydney City semi-final back to its originally scheduled venue at Suncorp Stadium, despite average crowds at the opening weekend of semi-final matches in Sydney.

September 9: The *Sydney Morning Herald* reports that Ken Cowley has flown to England to investigate at first-hand the crisis in the British game ... Sydney City captain Brad Fittler wins the inaugural Nokia Provan-Summons Medal in a ceremony in Sydney. Illawarra's Scott Cram is named rookie of the year and Gold Coast's Phil Economidis the coach of the year ... Parramatta call 20-year-old rookie Dennis Moran into their team to play North Sydney in an elimination semi-final.

September 10: Veteran utility player Des Hasler announces his retirement, at the age of 36 ... The *Sydney Morning Herald* reveals crowds for the first weekend of the finals (ARL and Super League) have slumped 63 per cent on 1993 figures ... Steve Folkes is confirmed as Canterbury coach for 1998 ... Super League chief executive Colin Sanders hits out at NSW Sports Minister Gabrielle Harrison for describing herself as an ARL fan.

September 11: International fullback Tim Brasher fails to meet a deadline to sign a three-year $1.5 million contract offered by Balmain ... Perth halfback Matthew Rodwell signs with St George ... The release of News Corporation's annual report for 1997 reveals Super League's losses have topped $237 million to the end of June. ARL CEO Neil Whittaker says it would be impossible for a united competition to absorb Super League's debt.

September 12: Sydney City end the fairytale run of the Gold Coast with a 32–10 win in an elimination semi-final at Parramatta Stadium ... Australian Rugby Union chief executive John O'Neill claims the troubles experienced by Rugby League since 1995 may eventually lead to a unification of the Rugby codes.

September 13: The *Sydney Morning Herald* reveals that two players who tested positive to steroids in the past year had been merely reprimanded by the ARL ... Erindale College becomes the first ACT school to win the game's premier national schoolboy title when they down Parramatta Marist 26–12 in the final of the Aussie Home Loans Cup ... North Sydney get back on track for their first grand final appearance since 1943 with a 24–14 win over Parramatta in the second elimination semi-final.

September 14: The *Sun Herald* warns that Western Suburbs' decision to sack 19 players as well as reserve grade coach Jason Alchin could affect the club's ability to recruit players for 1998 ... The *Sunday Telegraph* claims that the Brisbane Broncos are under enormous pressure to retain their star players because of a belief among Super League officials that the Broncos are too strong for the good of the competition ... Manly down Newcastle 27–12 in a fiery semi-final at the Sydney Football Stadium. Afterwards, an angry Gary Johns, the father of Newcastle's Johns brothers confronts ARL boss Neil Whittaker furious at a "torpedo-style" tackle by Manly's Nik Kosef on Matthew Johns ... Six days before the Super League grand final, Brisbane centre Anthony Mundine admits he is considering quitting the club at the end of the season.

September 15: Manly lock Nik Kosef is suspended for one match for performing an illegal "torpedo tackle" on Newcastle five-eighth Matthew Johns ... The ARL throw out six complaints from the Manly club relating to Newcastle players ... Canberra confirm Super League's worst-kept secret that prop Quentin Pongia has been released from the final year of his contract.

September 16: Brisbane's *Courier-Mail* reports that Queensland businessman Barry Maranta has sold his controlling interest in the London Broncos to British tycoon Richard Branson ... The *Sydney Morning Herald* reports that England's switch to a summer season has not resulted in new pay television subscribers, despite an outlay of more than £30 million ... Matthew Johns fires back at comments made by Manly chief executive Frank Stanton at Nik Kosef's judiciary hearing that Johns had feigned injury after the illegal tackle by Kosef in the qualifying semi-final.

September 17: Super League announce their new Melbourne franchise is to be known as "Melbourne Storm".

September 18: Laurie Daley is named Super League's player of the year. The ARL initiates legal action against the English Rugby League over income from the 1995 Centenary World Cup.

September 19: The *Daily Telegraph* reports that the Hunter Mariners have been forced to employ full-time security guards after vandals threw large rocks through the club's front doors and windows ... South Queensland coach Steve Bleakley is told his services are no longer required, minimising his chances of landing a position with the proposed South Queensland–Gold Coast merger ... Super League officials agree to cancel the proposed Test between Australia and France in November ... Hunter Mariners' chairman Jeff McCloy resigns.

September 20: Clive Churchill is rated the greatest Australian player in the game's history in a *Courier-Mail* series ... Newcastle qualify for their first grand final after downing North Sydney 17–12 in the first preliminary final at the Sydney Football Stadium ... Brisbane score a dominating 26–8 win over Cronulla before a record crowd of 58,912 in the Super League grand final at ANZ Stadium.

September 21: The Canberra Raiders claim they are owed $3000 by Owen Craigie from a cash advance they gave the Newcastle centre in 1994 ... A field goal three minutes from fulltime by Manly halfback Craig Field gives the Sea Eagles a one-point win over Sydney City in the second preliminary final.

September 22: Manly hooker Jim Serdaris is ruled out of the grand final after copping a one-match suspension for performing a dangerous throw on Sydney City opposite Simon Bonetti in the preliminary final ... David Manson is appointed to referee his second grand final ... Newcastle halfback Andrew Johns undergoes surgery to repair a perforated lung, but vows to play in the grand final.

September 23: The ARL announces it will form a new company to run the game in 1998 and invites Super League and its clubs to join the company.

September 24: AAP reports that 12 players who were cut from Western Suburbs are taking legal action against the club claiming unfair dismissal ... Manly and Australian team doctor Nathan Gibbs warns that Andrew Johns could risk death if he plays in the grand final with a punctured lung ... South Queensland Crushers players are told their club's joint venture with the Gold Coast Chargers is "not a foregone conclusion" ... The *Daily Telegraph* captures the grand final fever in Newcastle with a back page photograph of a New Lambton house painted red and blue.

September 25: The *Daily Telegraph* reports that Newcastle coach Malcolm Reilly will become the first foreign coach in almost 60 years to lead a team to a premiership victory if the Knights beat Manly in the grand final

... Former Manly, Souths and Norths first-grader Wayne Chisholm is charged with 30 drug offences after being arrested during a major police operation on the Gold Coast ... Newcastle skipper Paul Harragon is awarded the Ken Stephen Memorial Award for community involvement at the ARL's official grand final breakfast in Sydney ... Andrew Johns is cleared by a cardio-thoracic specialist to play in the grand final ... Balmain's popular development manager George Thompson dies after a long illness ... Sydney Football Stadium management bans Rocky, Newcastle's horse mascot, from appearing at the grand final.

September 26: New Zealand upset the Australian Super League side 30–12 in a Test match in Auckland.

September 27: Former ARL chairman and Manly stalwart Ken Arthurson tells AAP: "If ever Manly have to get beat then I hope it's Newcastle that do it."

September 28: The *Sun-Herald* reports that News Limited is poised to agree on a two-conference, 20–team competition in 1998, with regular crossovers, joint representative sides and an end-of-season Super Bowl ... Newcastle perform one of Rugby League's greatest fairytale victories. A try to winger Darren Albert inside the last 10 seconds breaks a 16–all deadlock. The Knights' 22–16 win over Manly creates scenes of hysteria unprecedented in the game's history. Thousands of supporters line the Knights' route back to Newcastle and an estimated 25,000 Novocastrians greet the team on arrival. Robbie O'Davis becomes the first fullback to win the Clive Churchill Medal. Manly coach Bob Fulton applauds the Knights' effort.

September 29: Newcastle centre Adam MacDougall is cited for stomping Manly captain Geoff Toovey during the grand final ... Prime Minister John Howard says that Newcastle's triumph in the grand final is a marvellous tonic for an area that had been dogged by unemployment woes.

September 30: Television ratings figures for the grand final reveal that the grand final averaged 1,048,777 viewers in Sydney, compared with an average of 461,500 for the AFL grand final ... A crowd estimated at 50,000 celebrate with the Knights at a ticker-tape parade through the streets of Newcastle.

OCTOBER

October 1: News Limited's executive director of sport Ian Frykberg says his company is ready to give the ARL a guarantee that a united competition would not be held liable for the $300 million set-up costs for Super League ... The *Daily Telegraph* reports that journeyman fullback Robbie Ross is set to become the Melbourne Storm's first signing ... *Rugby League Week* reports that the New Zealand Rugby League have no faith in the future of Super League's Tri-Series concept ... Super League officially announce that the Perth Reds would be disbanded because of mounting debts.

October 2: Super League players Anthony Mundine, Phil Adamson and Carl Macnamara are directed to return to Australian Rugby League clubs by the New South Wales Industrial Court, although the ARL contracts of Steve Carter, Robbie Beckett, Danny Farrar and Rod Silva are set aside. ARL officials are angered at Super League's reaction to the verdict after they claim victory on the basis that Justice Hill found all the contracts to be unfair. ARL CEO Neil Whittaker accuses Super League of "clutching at straws".

October 3: Auckland thump Bradford 62–14 in a quarter final of Super League's World Club Challenge ... In England, the Hunter Mariners overcome Wigan 22–18 at Central Park.

October 4: Steve Renouf scores five tries as Brisbane coast past St Helens 66–12 in another lopsided World Club Challenge quarter final.

October 5: The last British club is eliminated from the World Club Challenge when Cronulla thrash the London Broncos 40–16 in London.

October 7: Rupert Murdoch and his son Lachlan express confidence that there would be one competition in Australia in 1998.

October 8: St George sign Anthony Mundine to a three-year $2 million contract ... Newcastle centre Adam MacDougall is suspended for three matches for stomping on Manly captain Geoff Toovey during the grand final. His suspension rules him out of two competition matches, any pre-season matches and the World Sevens ... Parramatta tell hooker Aaron Raper he is no longer required.

October 10: Brisbane advance to the final of the World Club Challenge with a 22–16 defeat of Auckland at ANZ Stadium.

October 11: The *Sydney Morning Herald* reports that South Sydney has released 30 players and then signed Sydney City front-rower Terry Hermansson ... The Hunter Mariners advance to the World Club Challenge final with a shock 22–18 defeat of Cronulla at Shark Park.

October 12: The *Sun-Herald* reveals that Cronulla is on the verge of sacking their best forward, Kiwi Tawera Nikau ... The *Sunday Telegraph* says that 250 players face the sack as 20 clubs prepare to operate on a $4 million salary cap in a unified competition ... English chairman Maurice Lindsay accuses British players of "not putting their bodies on the line when it mattered" in Super League's ill-fated World Club Challenge. In a lengthy article in the *Sunday Telegraph*, Lindsay attempts to justify the $200,000 expense bill he ran up over two years.

October 13: Parramatta sign goalkicking former South Queensland fullback Clinton Schifcofske ... Manly give international front-rower Mark Carroll permission to negotiate with rival clubs.

October 15: AAP reports that North Sydney have all but deferred the club's proposed relocation to the Central Coast until 1999 after being assured a place in a 20-team united competition.

October 14: Gold Coast re-sign halfback Wes Patten for a further two seasons ... Western Suburbs prevent prop Harvey Howard from representing the Great Britain side in the November Test series against the Australian Super League side.

October 15: Balmain confirm the signing of Manly fullback Shannon Novin.

October 16: The ARL announce tough new penalties for drug users ... The Gold Coast City Council confirms it has been negotiating with Super League over the relocation of the Hunter Mariners to the tourist strip.

October 17: Brisbane claim a further $1 million in prizemoney after thrashing the Hunter Mariners 36–12 in the final of the World Club Challenge ... The Melbourne Storm confirm the signing of former Perth players Rodney Howe and Robbie Kearns ... Penrith youngster Craig Gower signs a four-year contract with the Panthers worth $1.8 million.

October 18: The *Sunday Telegraph* reports that Sydney Rugby Union club Randwick and the South Sydney Rabbitohs have entered merger talks.

October 20: Ricky Stuart is replaced as Canberra captain by Laurie Daley. Stuart claims a feud with chief executive Kevin Neil is behind the decision and threatens to leave the club.

October 22: An ACT magistrate acquits Canberra winger Noa Nadruku of two charges of assault because he was "too drunk" to form an intent. In an 11-hour drinking binge, Nadruku drank 14 schooners and six stubbies of beer and half a bottle of wine before assaulting two women outside a Canberra nightclub. The decision to acquit him sparks national outrage.

October 24: Matthew and Andrew Johns end months of speculation over their playing futures by re-signing with Newcastle for three years in a deal estimated to have cost $3 million ... Noa Nadruku is sacked by the Canberra Raiders because of his misconduct.

October 26: The *Sun-Herald* reports that peace talks between the ARL and Super League have taken a turn for the worse and Lachlan Murdoch tells Super League clubs to prepare for two competitions again in 1998.

October 28: The ARL's special appeals committee reject Adam MacDougall's bid to have his case re-heard after he was suspended for stomping Manly's Geoff Toovey in the grand final.

October 29: The Melbourne Storm confirm the signing of 31-year-old Brisbane Broncos front-rower Glenn Lazarus.

October 30: The *Sydney Morning Herald* reports that Rugby League recorded the highest number of positive drug tests — 13 — among the 47 sports screened by the Australian Sports Drug Agency during the past year.

October 31: The proposed merger between the South Queensland Crushers and the Gold Coast Chargers is officially abandoned, with the Chargers to continue in their own right.

NOVEMBER

November 1: The Australian Super League side down Great Britain 38–14 in the first Test at Wembley.

November 2: The *Sun-Herald* reports that Australian Super League players have been forced to take a pay-cut because of "belt-tightening at Super League" ... In an article in the *Sunday Telegraph*, Super League boss Ian Frykberg reportedly has stepped in to settle a long-running dispute between Ricky Stuart and the Canberra Raiders.

November 4: Paris-St Germain are dumped from the Euro Super League competition for 12 months because of poor performance on the field.

November 5: Noa Nadruku signs a three-year deal with North Queensland ... Talented 18-year-old Ryan Cross signs with Sydney City.

November 6: Police discover the body of former international Peter Jackson in a motel room at Engadine in Sydney. A manic-depressive, the much-loved 33-year-old died from an apparent drug overdose.

November 7: A fight over the services of Balmain lock Glenn Morrison looms after the Tigers and North Sydney both believe they have the 21-year-old under contract ...

November 8: Great Britain square the Test series with the Australian Super League side with a 20–12 win at Old Trafford.

November 9: The *Sun-Herald* reports that Monday Night Football is set to be scrapped by Super League in 1998 ... Balmain threaten to sue lock Glenn Morrison after he allegedly walked out on the club mid-contract.

November 10: Newcastle grand final lock Marc Glanville escapes conviction for assaulting a woman at a hotel, a magistrate finding she was a "pest".

November 12: Super League's world board chairman Maurice Lindsay offers to stand down if it will help bring about peace in the conflict between the ARL and Super League.

November 14: Laurie Daley tells the *Sydney Morning Herald* he regrets some of the things he said during the Super League split. "It was a bad thing, what happened, and I can only hope it never happens again," he says ... Norths sign NSW Rugby Union's rookie of the year, Joel Wilson ... Super League's World Board chairman Maurice Lindsay calls for an end to extended international tours. "I think we should restructure what was an old-fashioned system," Lindsay says.

November 16: The *Sunday Telegraph* reports that former Penrith and Perth second-rower Peter Shiels has signed with the Newcastle Knights for two seasons ... The National Basketball League announce that a consortium headed by Canterbury Leagues Club has won the Sydney's second NBL franchise ... Australia's Super League side claims the Test series over Great Britain with a 37–20 third Test win at Elland Road.

November 21: Tim Brasher signs a two-year deal with South Sydney worth a reported $450,000 a year.

November 22: Bob Fulton offers to stand down as national coach if it will hasten a compromise between the ARL and Super League.

November 24: Compromise talks continue between ARL CEO Neil Whittaker and Super League boss Ian Frykberg.

November 25: The ARL announce a policy of naming players who test positive to performance-enhancing drugs ... It is announced that the New South Wales State of Origin side will revert to its traditional all-blue strip in 1998.

November 26: Melbourne announce the signing of New Zealand Test lock Tawera Nikau ... Parramatta reinstate winger Ian Herron, six weeks after he was cut by the club.

November 28: The Federal Government decides that premier Rugby League games will be seen on free-to-air television in 1998.

November 30: The Sunday press reveals that the ARL World Sevens competition has become a victim of the ARL-Super League conflict ... The *Sunday Telegraph* reports that Canberra's Brett Mullins has been reprimanded by Super League CEO Colin Sanders after an alleged hotel brawl in England during the Super League Test series.

DECEMBER

December 2: The *Sydney Morning Herald* reports that a peace settlement in the ARL-Super League war is expected within a week.

December 3: Hunter Mariners halfback Noel Goldthorpe signs with the Adelaide Rams ...

The London Times reveals that only two European Super League clubs have been found to be profitable in a damning independent survey conducted by accountancy firm KPMG ... North Sydney Leagues Club members vote to proceed with plans to amalgamate with the Seagulls Leagues Club at Tweed Heads.

December 5: Newcastle chairman Michael Hill replaces North Sydney's Ray Beattie on the NSWRL Board. The NSWRL announce a loss of $4,539,693 for the year at their AGM.

December 6: The *Daily Telegraph* reports that League peace will be announced "next week".

December 8: The *Telegraph* says that clubs will be offered large financial incentives to merge to create a single 14-team competition in 1999 ... North Sydney football club members vote overwhelmingly to relocate the club to the Central Coast by 1999. The move had 87 per cent approval.

December 9: John McDonald is re-elected chairman of the Australian Rugby League at the League's annual general meeting, after retiring member Tom Bellew "crossed the floor" to vote for the Queenslander. Illawarra chief executive Bob Millward is appointed to replace Bellew. The League announce a loss of $2,826,939 for the year.

December 10: The NSWRL seek legal advice to overturn the ARL board elections after their attempt to oust chairman John McDonald failed.

December 11: Olympics Minister Michael Knight announces a $20 million upgrade of Campbelltown Sports Ground. Work is due to begin at the end of 1998 ... Further ructions are felt on the ARL Board where NSW Country Rugby League general manager David Barnhill is replaced by Sydney City chairman Nick Politis.

December 14: The *Sunday Telegraph* reports that several top-line Parramatta players have been involved in an ugly brawl in a Parramatta hotel ... Canberra star Brett Mullins reveals he has agreed to undergo an alcohol awareness program ... ARL player of the year Brad Fittler is left out of *Open Rugby's* World XIII.

December 16: Gold Coast chief executive Paul Broughton announces his retirement at the club's annual general meeting. His involvement in the game spanned 45 years.

December 19: A series of the most important meetings in the history of Rugby League in Australia take place at the Sydney Football Stadium. The end of the ARL-Super League war, which spanned almost 1000 days, comes after the 40-man NSWRL general committee vote 36-4 in favour of a peace deal devised by ARL chief executive Neil Whittaker and Super League boss Ian Frykberg. The terms of the deal result in plans for a 20-team competition in 1998, a 16-team competition in 1999 and a 14-team competition in 2000. The deal is contingent on a further $16.5 million in funding for the 11 ARL clubs.

December 21: South Sydney president George Piggins says the ARL has "caved in to Rupert" (Murdoch), by paying too high a price for peace ... Leading player manager Sam Ayoub says a $3m salary cap, planned for 1998, is too low for clubs ... The ARL rule young lock Glenn Morrison must return to Balmain after a contractual dispute between Morrison, Balmain and North Sydney. The case is likely to end in the courts.

December 22: South Sydney manager Frank Cookson suggests the compromise between the ARL and Super League involved a 12-team competition after 2000.

December 23: ARL premiers Newcastle are listed on the second line of betting for the 1998 premiership behind Manly and Brisbane by bookmakers CentreBet.

December 24: The ARL secures the final funding of $16.5 million from Optus and Channel Nine to enable its 11 teams to enter the National competition on an equal financial footing with the nine Super League clubs.

December 28: The *Sun-Herald* announces Sydney City prop Jason Lowrie has accepted less money to return to the club for 1998 ... The *Sunday Telegraph* says that Super League's leading officials have decided to support Neil Whittaker as the man to lead the National competition in 1998.

December 31: Super League's Hunter Mariners are disbanded after merger talks with the Gold Coast Chargers break down.

VALE

ARTHUR DREW
(1924–April 28, 1997)

A long-serving administrator with the Parramatta club, Arthur William Drew died in April, aged 82.

Drew was an original director of the Parramatta Leagues club in 1959 and held the position for more than 20 years.

He was president of the Parramatta club when it won premierships in 1982 and 1983.

TOM BROCK
(1929–April 30, 1997)

Thomas George Brock was an unsung hero of Rugby League, one of the many back-room men who volunteer thousands of hours of service to the game they love.

Brock, who died in April, was an 'old-style' league enthusiast — an historian, archivist, life member and supporter — whose first love was the South Sydney Rabbitohs. Brock had collected a virtual museum of South Sydney paraphernalia, material dating from the birth of the club in 1908 right up to the present day.

He was actively involved in the South Sydney schools carnival for over 30 years and in more recent times had assembled a display of historical Rabbitohs' memorabilia for South Sydney Leagues Club.

Three months after his death, Souths' officials were overwhelmed by Brock's generosity — he left the club $200,000 in his will.

NEVILLE SMITH
(1916–August 5, 1997)

Neville Bussey Smith, who led St George to its maiden premiership victory in 1941, died in August at the age of 81.

Smith was appointed Saints' youngest captain-coach in 1939, after joining the club via Bathurst and Brisbane. He was working in a flour mill in Bathurst in the late Depression years, when fears of getting dust on his lungs led to a move north to Queensland. He played three seasons with Valleys and represented Queensland in 1938.

A dashing second-rower and goalkicker, Smith reluctantly accepted an offer from Saints in 1939, and preceded to lift the club from the premiership cellar (they were equal last in 1938). In 1939 they made the semi-finals, in 1940 Saints won the Club Championship for the first time, and in 1941 Smith led the club to its first premiership win.

During his time at St George he also played six times for New South Wales and captained the state against Queensland in 1940, but like many players of his era, Smith missed the opportunity of representing Australia because of World War II.

He maintained close links with the game following his retirement in 1946 and was Australian chairman of selectors in the 1960s.

Dr KEVIN HOBBS
(1928–August 29, 1997)

Dr Kevin Hobbs, who died at Bribie Island in August after a long illness, was the first doctor to introduce a drug testing program for Rugby League in Queensland.

He also carried out extensive tests on training and playing sport in the tropics. In the early 1970s, he initiated a live-in training camp at Lang Park for the Queensland side.

He also ran a successful sports medicine practice in the Brisbane suburb of Kelvin Grove.

GEORGE THOMPSON
(1938–September 25, 1997)

George Thompson was one of the game's most popular officials. The development manager of the Balmain Tigers, Thompson died in September of a stroke after a long battle with cancer.

He was described by close friend and Gold Coast chief executive Paul Broughton as 'one of the finest people I've ever known in sport'. Thompson's popularity was underlined by the large crowd of mourners at his funeral. The Balmain club staged a tribute dinner in his honour late in the year.

DENIS JACKWITZ
(1926–October 18, 1997)

A tough and resourceful hooker, Denis Keith Jackwitz, who died of cancer in October, played six times for Queensland in the 1950s after learning his football in Ipswich.

In his early days in Ipswich, Jackwitz packed between Dud Beattie and Gary Parcell, both of whom later became internationals. Jackwitz represented Queensland in six matches in 1955 and 1956 when he partnered internationals Duncan Hall and Brian Davies in a formidable front row.

PETER JACKSON
(1964–November 5, 1997)

The Rugby League world was saddened in November by the tragic death of former international Peter Jackson. A father of three young children, Jackson was found dead in a motel room from an apparent drug overdose. He had been undergoing treatment for manic depression.

Jackson first made a name for himself as a strong and classy centre with Souths in Brisbane. After making his debut for Queensland in State of Origin in 1986, he headed to Canberra to link up with former Souths Brisbane team-mates Mal Meninga and Gary Belcher, along with coach Wayne Bennett. He played in the 1987 grand final for the Raiders, and in 1988 made his Test debut in the 100th Test between Australia and Great Britain, which was also the first Test played at the Sydney Football Stadium. In a memorable debut, Jackson scored two tries in Australia's 17-6 victory.

He left Canberra at the end of 1988 to spend two seasons with the Brisbane Broncos, before playing out his career with North Sydney. By the time he hung up his boots in 1993, Jackson had played 17 State of Origin matches for Queensland and nine Tests for Australia.

He later forged a successful career in the media, on radio 2UE and on television with Channel Nine, where he made regular appearances on 'The Midday Show' with Kerri-Anne Kennerley. He also wrote a number of magazine columns.

Over 600 mourners attended his funeral at his home town of Stanwell Park, south of Sydney. Jackson is survived by wife Siobhan and children Lucy, Jimmy and Ned.

The following tribute was delivered by former team-mate Gary Belcher at Jackson's memorial service.

'Dear Jacko,
Sorry I didn't get to say goodbye, but you've left me with so many great memories that I'm finding it hard to get upset.
If there is a God, I bet he's already had a few laughs, thanks to you. And I'm sure that when St Peter quizzed you at the Pearly Gates you would have told him your old favourite about being a member of the Queensland Police Force — the best police force that money could buy!

VALE

Mate, I just couldn't keep up with you. From our first big night out after you stormed into Souths as an 18-year-old, I realised that you alone could burn the candle at both ends and be none the worse for wear the next day. Or so it seemed. Remember when you turned up at Davies Park in 1983, a skinny, gangly, pimply-faced 18-year-old who acted 16 but played like 25. Bob McCarthy knew you were something special and threw you straight into the centres with Mal, and into my jersey! Thanks, mate. I wouldn't have made it as a centre.

I loved your one-arm-around-the-corner passes; your wild hugs and yells when we scored; your one sock down around your ankles; the way you mixed with players from every grade. I don't know how we had any fun before you came along.

The night Karlene and I announced our engagement, you grabbed the microphone and sang 'You Are So Beautiful'. You couldn't sing like Joe Cocker, but you looked a lot like him three or four hours later!

And what about the '85 grand final. What a day for a whole team to play their best footy. Within an hour we were half-tanked and totally hoarse. And you never did sing the team song, you just yelled it, non-stop. Maybe the only time you've been more responsible than me was after the match, when in all the excitement, I forgot Karlene, and you brought her back to the club, although it did take an unusually long time. Remember the pub crawl. While we were bagging Mick Jakl about the stud in his ear, you decided you wanted one. So you grabbed Mick's stud and tried to push its blunt end through your ear lobe. That didn't work so you made me do it! There was obvious pain, but that's never been a problem for you, Jacko.

You screamed and hollered and partied on.

I was wrapped when you came to Canberra in '87 to join Mal and me. We'd been there a year and the place certainly needed an injection of life and talent. You gave Canberra a Peter Jackson enema. There were already some party animals down there, but none had the same mix of ability and passion that you gave to every team you played in.

We made out Test debuts together in 1988, with you in the centres and me on the bench. During the national anthem, I had a tear in my eye, but you were crying openly. Your highs were always higher, Peter, and your lows lower. Your two tries gave me almost as big a buzz as it gave you. I hope people outside your team-mates realise just how good you were.

They talk about Wally and Fatty and Gilly being Blues-haters, and I know how it feels to want to beat those lairs from down south. But you were right up there with the best when it came to State of Origin passion. Wally hadn't ever missed an Origin match until you filled in for him in '88. So many people doubted Queensland could win without him. But not the players. We knew how deep you could dig if you wanted something bad enough. And, of course, you had no doubt either. We won, so you told Wally he'd want to play well next time, because the last bloke who wore the No. 6 for Queensland had a blinder!

I was shattered when Wayne Bennett left Canberra at the end of 1987 and you obviously felt betrayed. But, of course, you understood and forgave him in time to join the Broncos yourself in 1989. I was shattered again. Here we were, so close to winning a premiership, and my closest footy mate, who shared that three-way understanding with Mal and myself, was leaving. I knew you partly regretted it, too. Especially when we beat Balmain and you should have been there. What about your phone call on the morning of the grand final, already half-cut, when you made me promise to say g'day to you when we won. You had more confidence in me, sometimes, than I ever did. Thanks for the pep talks, intentional or not. How many times did I have a shocker and you'd say, 'Badge, just run the ball, everything else will happen.' I needed to hear it and you were always there to help.

What happened back in Brissie, Jacko? Injuries? Did you mix with the wrong crowd? Expectations too high?

Remember that State of Origin game you missed, but you still had to party with us.

We ended up wrestling outside Triple M at about 3am, before you took us into the boardroom for free drinks. We went home at 4am because busso for training was at 8am. But that wasn't enough for you. You came back to the Travelodge, bashed on my door until Bobby Lindner woke up and then you threatened to break it down if we didn't let you in. We heard you walk away and thought you were leaving, but you sprinted back and smashed through the door. Your defence to 'Tosser' Turner was that it was my fault for not letting you in. So you then became the first player ever kicked out of an Origin camp ... and you weren't even in the team.

Then there was the 1989 New Zealand tour. I can't remember much about our three wins over the Kiwis, but I'll never forget when we locked big Sam in the bus toilet until he finally burst out 20 minutes later screaming,

'I'm claustrophobic!' And even the Canterbury players swear that you do a better Peter Moore impersonation than the Bullfrog himself. Matey!

Gee, you were great for North Sydney. Laurie Daley reminds me so much of you, mate, the way he puts his heart and soul into every play. If the Bears couldn't win with you playing, it's hard to see them getting up without you.

I was always such a dork compared to you, Jacko. Even when it wasn't quite funny, you'd make everyone laugh with your wide-mouthed roar and a big slap on your leg. Remember back at Souths when you had Kenny Rachs' four-year-old son pointing at himself after a shower and saying 'Whang-dang-go'. If anyone else did it — not funny. Coming from you — hilarious.

I couldn't keep up with you, Action, so I gave up long ago. Mal could, Eddie Muller could, Cement and Kevie could, Mick McLean and, of course, Siobhan as well. Laurie in his younger days got top marks in his 'Jacko's party hard and play even harder' apprenticeship. Des Byrne tried to keep up, but you had youth on your side back then, mate.

So what happened? How could it get so bad? For someone with so many friends, who was loved by nearly everyone he met, why couldn't we help? I know it's too late now, but I wish I could have said goodbye. I wish we could just play one more game together, you throwing long balls, Mal running into space, me there to finish off your great work. The hugs at the end, a few beers, some belly laughs and then goodbye!

I love you Jacko. It'll never be the same without you.

Badge'

OPTUS CUP ROUND 1
MARCH 7, 8, 9

Return of the Blue-and-Gold

Parramatta's army of fans made a welcome return to Parramatta Stadium for the season opener against North Sydney, and were rewarded with a 10-8 result after a thrilling exhibition of football.

The Eels' biggest home crowd in a decade watched their team defend superbly during a heart-stopping final 10 minutes, during which they held only a slender two-point lead. Goalkicking decided the match — an irony considering that a kicker of the calibre of Jason Taylor was on the losing side. The leading goalkicker of 1996 missed his two attempts at goal after both sides had scored two tries.

Parramatta centre Jarrod McCracken was particularly damaging for the winners, leading new coach Brian Smith to claim he had recaptured his best form. 'He's got that menace back in his eyes and he pulled off some terrific defence for us,' Smith said.

There was a sparkle in the football at Leichhardt Oval 24 hours later, when Balmain returned to their spiritual home after a two-year absence to meet 1996 premiers Manly. A bumper crowd of 18,247 watched the home side go close to an upset victory before Manly hooker Jim Serdaris burrowed through from dummy half to snatch the lead, 17 minutes from fulltime. The crowd were treated to some scintillating play, none better than the individual try scored by fullback Tim Brasher shortly before halftime.

The game was assured of a tight finish when Manly winger Danny Moore was sin-binned six minutes before the final whistle. Balmain continued to hammer the Manly line, but were unable to find a way through, and the Sea Eagles hung on to win 14-10.

Gold Coast made a perfect start to the new season with a 24-16 win over Wests at Campbelltown. It was the first time a Gold Coast side had beaten Wests in 12 premiership meetings. And it was also a red-letter day for winger Shane Russell, who crossed for a club record four tries in his first match for the Chargers.

A rain-soaked Marathon Stadium meant Newcastle's clash with St George was never going to be an attractive spectacle, but the Knights emerged with an 11-6 win over the 1996 grand finalists. Newcastle winger Darren Albert scored the only two tries of the match, while Saints lock Wayne Bartrim kept his side in the running with three penalty goals. A 79th-minute field goal to Robbie O'Davis — the first in his senior career — gave the home side an important buffer. Leo Dynevor made a solid debut as Andrew Johns' halfback replacement.

Illawarra handed South Sydney a nine-try 50-10 thumping at WIN Stadium, signalling a depressing winter ahead for Rabbitoh coach Ken Shine. Souths' defence was woeful, giving Paul McGregor, teenage five-eighth Trent Barrett and lock Brett Rodwell *carte blanche* to attack. Winger Rod Wishart equalled his club record of 22 points for the third time.

South Queensland began strongly against Sydney City at the Sydney Football Stadium, and led 8-0 midway through the first half, but a drop in intensity allowed the Roosters to dominate. At this point, coach Phil Gould teamed Andrew Walker and Brad Fittler at half and five-eighth and the Roosters' attack blossomed. The Roosters led 18-10 at halftime and piled on a further 16 unanswered points in the second half.

ROUND 1 — RESULTS

Parramatta 10 (C.King, S.Whereat tries; J.Simon goal) defeated **Norths** 8 (B.Moore, C.Caruana tries) at Parramatta Stadium, Friday night, March 7.

Scrums: Norths 13–12. Penalties: Parramatta 8–6. Crowd: 25,114. Referee: David Manson. Halftime: Norths 8–6. Goalkickers: Simon (Parramatta) 1/1, Herron (Parramatta) 0/1, Taylor (Norths) 0/2. Seconds: Parramatta 32–20. Under-20s: Parramatta 30–0.
PARRAMATTA: Riolo; Barnes, McCracken, Woods, Whereat; Kelly, Simon; Johnston, Campbell, King, Pay (c), Jason Smith, Dymock. Interchange: Bell, Herron, Lovell, Morgan.
NORTHS: Seers; Pethybridge, Ikin, Caruana, Roy; Buettner, Taylor (c); Stuart, Soden, Trindall, Larson, Fairleigh, Florimo. Interchange: Reber, Moore, Fritz, Loyshon.

Gold Coast 24 (S.Russell 4, J.Goddard tries; B.Hurst, G.Mackay goals) defeated **Wests** 16 (B.Pearson 2, A.Willis tries; A.Leeds 2 goals) at Campbelltown Sports Ground, Saturday, March 8.

Scrums: Wests 7–6. Penalties: Wests 11–7. Crowd: 6490. Referee: Paul Simpkins. Halftime: Gold Coast 14–6. Goalkickers: Hurst (Gold Coast) 1/4, Mackay (Gold Coast) 1/2, Leeds (Wests) 2/4. Seconds: Wests 26–4. Under-20s: Wests 32–24.
GOLD COAST: King, Suluvale, Mackay (c), Nicol, Russell; Zahra, Orr; Bella, Goddard, Driscoll, Durheim, Hurst, Schloss. Interchange: Whittaker, Sattler, Patten, Anderson.
WESTS: Leeds; D.Willis, Ken McGuinness, Pearson, Laing; A.Willis, Hasler; Howard, Mescia, J.Smith, Kennedy, Dunn, Langmack (c). Interchange: Skandalis, Wallis, Millard, Georgallis.

Manly 14 (T.Hill 2, J.Serdaris tries; C.Innes goal) defeated **Balmain** 10 (D.Senter, T.Brasher tries; Brasher goal) at Leichhardt Oval, Saturday night, March 8.

Scrums: Balmain 9–4. Penalties: Manly 10–8. Crowd: 18,247. Referee: Kelvin Jeffes. Halftime: Balmain 8–4. Goalkickers: Innes (Manly) 1/2, Field (Manly) 0/2, Brasher (Balmain) 1/3. Seconds: Balmain 12–10. Under-20s: Balmain 22–20.
MANLY: Hancock; Moore, Innes, Hill, Hopoate; Toovey (c), Field; Gillespie, Serdaris, Carroll, Menzies, Gartner, Kosef. Interchange: Tierney, Hunter, Weepu, Johnson.
BALMAIN: Brasher; Langaloa, Kennedy, Donaghey, Edwards; Hanley, Gillett; Walker, Senter, Sironen (c), Stimson, O'Neil, Morrison. Interchange: Starr, Smith, Freer, Nable.
Sin bin: Moore (Manly).

Sydney City 34 (C.Rigon 2, I.Cleary, S.Gourley, M.Sing, J.Sinclair, M.Miles tries; Cleary 3 goals) defeated **South Queensland** 10 (J.Wendt, J.Hudson tries; C.Schifcofske goal) at Sydney Football Stadium, Sunday, March 9.

Scrums: Sydney City 7–4. Penalties: Sydney City 7–6. Crowd: 8475. Referee: Matt Hewitt. Halftime: Sydney City 18–10. Goalkickers: Cleary (Sydney City) 3/7, Schifcofske (South Queensland) 1/3. Seconds: South Qld 26–20. Under-20s: Sydney City 16–14.
SYDNEY CITY: Cleary, Junee, Sing, Shearer, Miles; Walker, Wood; Lowrie, Bonetti, Hermansson, Ricketson, Gourley, Fittler (c). Interchange: Troy, Rigon, Logan, Sinclair.
SOUTH QUEENSLAND: Schifcofske; Hudson, Toshack, Eagar, Wendt; Watson, Pezet; Jones, Teevan (c), O'Brien, Protheroe, Retchless, Wilson. Interchange: Couper, Tookey, Smith, Antonik.

Newcastle 11 (D.Albert 2 tries; R.O'Davis goal; O'Davis field goal) defeated **St George** 6 (W.Bartrim 3 goals) at Marathon Stadium, Sunday, March 9.

Scrums: Newcastle 6–5. Penalties: Newcastle 11–10. Crowd: 9389. Referee: Eddie Ward. Halftime: Newcastle 6–2. Goalkickers: O'Davis (Newcastle) 1/3, Bartrim (St George) 3/3. Seconds: St George 22–8. Under-20s: St George 20–4.
NEWCASTLE: O'Davis; Albert, Grogan, Craigie, MacDougall; M.Johns, Dynevor; Butterfield, Jackson, Harragon (c), Richards, Muir, Glanville. Interchange: Peden, Gidley, Fletcher.
ST GEORGE: D.Smith; Bell, Coyne (c), Lenihan, Brunker; Hardy, Kusto; Hearn, Brown, Ward, Thompson, Treacy, Bartrim. Interchange: Pearson, Tangata-Toa, Kenward, Blacklock.

Illawarra 50 (B.Rodwell 3, R.Wishart 2, W.Clifford 2, B.Mackay, S.Timmins tries; Wishart 7 goals) defeated **Souths** 10 (M.Manning try; Manning 3 goals) at WIN Stadium, Sunday, March 9.

Scrums: Illawarra 5–4. Penalties: Illawarra 11–7. Crowd: 7697. Referee: Paul McBlane. Halftime: Illawarra 20–10. Goalkickers: Wishart (Illawarra) 7/9, Manning (Souths) 3/3. Seconds: Illawarra 24–8. Under-20s: Illawarra 22–14.
ILLAWARRA: Reeves; Wishart, Timmins, McGregor (c), Clifford; Barrett, Air; Bradstreet, Callaway, Smith, Bristow, Mackay, Rodwell. Interchange: Cram, Tunbridge, David, Hart.
SOUTHS: O'Meara; Hogan, Wilson, Manning, O'Koefe; Simon, Trindall (c); Rubin, Donato, Parsons, Ostini, Tassell, Burns. Interchange: Penna, Sutton, O'Donnell, McLeod.
Sin bin: Tassell (Souths).

STANDINGS: Illawarra 2, Sydney City 2, Gold Coast 2, Newcastle 2, Manly 2, Parramatta 2, Norths 0, Balmain 0, St George 0, Wests 0, South Queensland 0, Souths 0.

OPTUS CUP ROUND 2
MARCH 14, 15, 16

Manly survive Saints comeback

Manly and St George kicked off Round 2 before a big crowd at Kogarah Oval with a display of football rated far more exciting than their 1996 grand final showdown.

Ground officials were forced to throw open the gates moments before the start of the match to prevent a stampede. The official crowd of 16,706 threw their support behind St George's second-half comeback after Manly had raced to a 16-0 lead at the break. Winger Mark Bell sparked the revival when he sprinted the length of the field after taking an intercept. Then Adrian Brunker crossed twice in quick time, reducing the deficit to four points. In the end, poor goalkicking by Wayne Bartrim (one from four) cost Saints victory. Best for Manly was halfback Craig Field, who scored two tries. In two matches for his new club he had already added a new dimension to their attack.

Manly front-rower Neil Tierney was sent from the field five minutes from fulltime for punching St George captain Mark Coyne.

Western Suburbs' plan to turn on the aggression against Sydney City backfired in every way in a poor advertisement for the game at the Sydney Football Stadium. The Magpies lost the match 18-6 and then lost two key players for a total of six weeks: the judiciary suspended Harvey Howard for four weeks and Damian Kennedy for two.

Referee Eddie Ward struggled to keep a rein on emotions in the game, and at one stage he issued a general caution to the Western Suburbs team. His failure to dismiss Howard for a blatantly foul tackle on Roosters' captain Brad Fittler ultimately led to his relegation from first grade.

The early loss of five-eighth architect Matthew Johns proved costly for Newcastle, who fell 34-20 to Norths in a topsy-turvy game at North Sydney Oval. Johns was sent from the field for a high tackle after just five minutes. Despite this advantage, Norths struggled to gain the upper hand and midway through the second half, they led by just two points.

For the second successive week, Balmain squandered a halftime lead, this time falling 18-10 to a gutsy Illawarra after going to the break up 10-0.

A superb solo try to centre William 'Bubba' Kennedy put the Tigers in a position to win the match, but the game eventually turned just after halftime, with a 60-metre burst by Illawarra winger Rod Wishart, scooping up a loose ball. Opposite winger Wayne Clifford scored twice more for the Steelers and Wishart's three goals gave the visitors a safe margin.

The defensive intensity of Parramatta's 10-8 first-round win over Norths was not apparent when they were swamped 23-6 by 1996 wooden-spooners South Queensland at Suncorp Stadium. It was a stunning reversal for the Eels, who were accused of having things 'too easy' in life by their coach Brian Smith. It was a memorable day for the troubled Brisbane club, the crowd of 9,523 giving the Crushers a standing ovation after they won in all three grades.

A meagre crowd — little more than 4,000 — watched South Sydney scrape home with a 26-16 win over the Gold Coast in a lacklustre affair at the Sydney Football Stadium. The Rabbitohs scored five tries to three and finished the stronger after the Chargers took the lead eight minutes from fulltime.

ROUND 2 — RESULTS

Manly 18 (C.Field 2, J.Serdaris tries; Field 3 goals) defeated **St George** 14 (A.Brunker 2, M.Bell tries; W.Bartrim goal) at Kogarah Oval, Friday night, March 14.

Scrums: 6–all. Penalties: St George 10–8. Crowd: 16,706. Referee: Paul McBlane. Halftime: Manly 16–0. Goalkickers: Field (Manly) 3/4, Bartrim (St George) 1/4. Seconds: Manly 26–14. Under-20s: St George 16–14.
MANLY: Hancock; Moore, Innes, Hill, Hopoate; Toovey (c), Field; Gillespie, Serdaris, Carroll, Menzies, Gartner, Kosef. Interchange: Tierney, Fulton, Weepu, Hunter.
ST GEORGE: Raper; Bell, Coyne (c), Lenihan, Brunker; Kenward, Kusto; Hearn, Brown, Ward, Thompson, Treacy, Bartrim. Interchange: Pearson, D.Smith, B.Smith, Clinch.
Sent off: Tierney (Manly), 75 min. **Charge:** Striking. **Sentence:** One week.

Sydney City 18 (D.Shearer, J.Elsegood tries; I.Cleary 5 goals) defeated **Wests** 6 (Ken McGuinness try; A.Leeds goal) at Sydney Football Stadium, Saturday, March 15.

Scrums: 4–all. Penalties: Sydney City 12–8. Crowd: 10,105. Referee: Eddie Ward. Halftime: Sydney City 14–0. Goalkickers: Cleary (Sydney City) 5/7, Leeds (Wests) 1/4. Seconds: Sydney City 26–20. Under-20s: Sydney City 24–4.
SYDNEY CITY: Cleary; Miles, Sing, Sinclair, Elsegood; Fittler (c), Shearer; Lowrie, Bonetti, Hermansson, Gourley, Ellis, Ricketson. Interchange: Rigon, Troy, Wood, Junee.
WESTS: Leeds; Laing, Ken McGuinness, Pearson, D.Willis; Georgallis, Newton; Howard, Mescia, J.Smith, Kennedy, Langmack (c), Hasler. Interchange: Millard, Yates, Skandalis, Kevin McGuinness.
Sent off: Kennedy (Wests), 11 min. **Charge:** High tackle. **Sentence:** Two weeks. **Cited:** Howard (Wests). **Charge:** High tackle. **Sentence:** Four weeks.

Illawarra 18 (W.Clifford 2, R.Wishart tries; Wishart 3 goals) defeated **Balmain** 10 (W.Kennedy try; C.Freer 2, M.Withers goals) at Leichhardt Oval, Saturday night, March 15.

Scrums: Balmain 7–5. Penalties: Balmain 11–0. Crowd: 8211. Referee: David Manson. Halftime: Balmain 10–0. Goalkickers: Wishart (Illawarra) 3/4, Freer (Balmain) 2/3, Withers (Balmain) 1/1. Seconds: Balmain 30–16. Under-20s: Balmain 26–20.
ILLAWARRA: Reeves; Wishart, Timmins, McGregor (c), Clifford; Barrett, Air; Bradstreet, Callaway, Smith, Bristow, Mackay, Rodwell. Interchange: Tunbridge, Cram, David, J.Cross.
BALMAIN: Brasher; Langaloa, Kennedy, Donaghey, Edwards; Freer, Gillett; Walker, Senter, Sironen (c), Stimson, Smith, Hanley. Interchange: Starr, Bosse, Withers, Wilson.

Norths 34 (J.Taylor 2, M.Seers, D.Fairleigh, B.Ikin, N.Roy tries; Taylor 5 goals) defeated **Newcastle** 20 (R.O'Davis, A.MacDougall, L.Dynevor tries; O'Davis 4 goals) at North Sydney Oval, Sunday, March 16.

Scrums: Newcastle 7–6. Penalties: Newcastle 10–5. Crowd: 10,109. Referee: Paul Simpkins. Halftime: Norths 16–12. Goalkickers: Taylor (Norths) 5/6, O'Davis (Newcastle) 4/5. Seconds: Newcastle 19–4. Under-20s: Norths 17–4.
NORTHS: Seers; Pethybridge, Ikin, Caruana, Roy; Buettner, Taylor (c); Larson, Reber, Trindall, Moore, Fairleigh, Florimo. Interchange: Stuart, Fritz, Hall, Leyshon.
NEWCASTLE: O'Davis; Albert, Grogan, Craigie, MacDougall; M.Johns (c), Dynevor; Butterfield, Jackson, Richards, Peden, Muir, Glanville. Interchange: Fletcher, Gidley, Conley, Moodie.
Sent off: Johns (Newcastle) 5 min. **Charge:** High tackle. **Sentence:** One week.

Souths 26 (D.McLeod 2, M.Manning, M.Hogan, M.Moore tries; Manning 3 goals) defeated **Gold Coast** 16 (J.Schloss, S.Russell, W.Patten tries; G.Mackay 2 goals) at Sydney Football Stadium, Sunday, March 16.

Scrums: 8–all. Penalties: 6–all. Crowd: 4404. Referee: Matt Hewitt. Halftime: 10–all. Goalkickers: Manning (Souths) 3/6, Mackay (Gold Coast) 2/3. Seconds: Gold Coast 15–14. Under-20s: Souths 34–6.
SOUTHS: O'Meara; Moore, Hogan, Manning, Crotty; Simon, Trindall (c); Driscoll, Skelly, Rubin, Quinn, Burns, Sutton. Interchange: McLeod, Ostini, Tassell, White.
GOLD COAST: King; Suluvale, Mackay (c), Nicol, Russell; Zahra, Orr; Bella, Goddard, Driscoll, Sattler, Hurst, Schloss. Interchange: Patten, Whittaker, Nahi, Fox.

South Queensland 23 (M.Protheroe, M.Tookey, A.Bella, M.Eagar tries; C.Schifcofske 3 goals; C.Wilson field goal) defeated **Parramatta** 6 (K.Lovell try; I.Herron goal) at Suncorp Stadium, Sunday, March 16.

Scrums: South Queensland 11–7. Penalties: Parramatta 8–5. Crowd: 9523. Referee: Kelvin Jeffes. Halftime: South Queensland 6–2. Goalkickers: Schifcofske (South Queensland) 3/4, Herron (Parramatta) 1/2. Seconds: South Queensland 16–11. Under-20s: South Queensland 16–12.
SOUTH QUEENSLAND: Schifcofske; Doyle, Toshack, Eagar, Wendt; Watson, Pezet; Jones, Teevan (c), O'Brien, Protheroe, Retchless, Wilson. Interchange: Couper, Tookey, Smith, Bella.
PARRAMATTA: Riolo; Herron, McCracken, Woods, Whereat; Kelly, Simon; Johnston, Campbell, King, Pay (c), Jason Smith, Dymock. Interchange: Bell, Barnes, Lovell, Morgan.

STANDINGS: Illawarra 4, Sydney City 4, Manly 4, Norths 2, Gold Coast 2, South Queensland 2, Newcastle 2, Parramatta 2, Souths 2, St George 0, Balmain 0, Wests 0.

OPTUS CUP ROUND 3
MARCH 21, 22, 23

One try in 80 minutes, but ...

Eighty minutes of football at Parramatta Stadium produced only one try, but the consensus among the crowd of 17,254 was that a truly remarkable contest had been played out before them. Sydney City took the honours, 8-2, over a Parramatta side that was anything but disgraced.

For the first 45 minutes, play seesawed from one end of the field to the other, with neither side able to find a way through unrelenting defensive cordons. The only try of the match was scored by Darren Junee after 58 minutes, from a towering Andrew Walker bomb.

Rival coaches Phil Gould (Sydney City) and Brian Smith (Parramatta) spoke in glowing terms of the spectacle: 'When you've got people chasing across field and grabbing blokes in full flight, front-rowers coming across and knocking wingers into touch and a fullback running the ball into touch with four blokes bearing down on him, that's what football is all about. It was one of the best wins I've ever been associated with,' said Gould.

'I thought our defence was phenomenal,' said Smith. 'I gave them a lot of praise at halftime because I thought they defended outstandingly and, to be fair, they (Sydney City) weren't able to get across our line tonight. They didn't carry the ball over, it was off a kick.'

Manly paid a heavy price for a gripping 12-8 win over Norths in the local derby at Brookvale Oval.

The Sea Eagles lost front-line forwards David Gillespie and Jim Serdaris with knee injuries during the second half of the match, as the team was fighting to repel a determined North Sydney. Chasing their first win at Brookvale since 1990, the Bears trailed 12-6 at halftime, and despite repeatedly playing their way into sound attacking positions, their follow-through was poor.

St George hooker Nathan Brown turned in a masterful performance as Saints climbed from the competition cellar with a 20-8 win over Illawarra at WIN Stadium. Slotted into a playmaking role by Saints coach David Waite, Brown orchestrated Saints' attack with precision and was the key factor in his team's three-tries-to-one victory.

South Sydney showed their win over the Gold Coast was no fluke when they scored a commanding 17-8 win over Wests at the Sydney Football Stadium. Souths scored two first-half tries (Driscoll, McLeod) to lead 10-2 at the break, and when rookie winger Matt Hogan crossed midway through the second half, the points were safe.

Keen to prove a point to his former coach Wayne Pearce, Gold Coast halfback Wes Patten was the stand-out player in the Chargers' emphatic 26-6 defeat of Balmain at Carrara Stadium.

Patten scored one long-distance try and set up another as the Chargers raced to a match-winning 20-6 lead at halftime.

Newcastle equalled the club's record-winning margin and punished an inept South Queensland — 44-0 — at Marathon Stadium. International second-rower Adam Muir opened the scoring after just three minutes with the first of three power-laden tries. By halftime the Knights led 22-0. Halfback Leo Dynevor controlled play superbly at halfback and combined beautifully with teenage five-eighth Matthew Gidley to keep the scoreboard ticking over.

ROUND 3 — RESULTS

Manly 12 (D.Gartner, C.Innes tries; C.Field 2 goals) defeated **Norths** 8 (W.Leyshon try; J.Taylor 2 goals) at Brookvale Oval, Friday night, March 21.

Scrums: Norths 8–6. Penalties: Norths 5–3. Crowd: 18,539. Referee: David Manson. Halftime: Manly 12–6. Goalkickers: Field (Manly) 2/3, Taylor (Norths) 2/3. Seconds: Norths 38–26. Under-20s: Manly 22–10.
MANLY: Hancock; Moore, Innes, Hill, Hopoate; Toovey (c), Field; Gillespie, Serdaris, Carroll, Menzies, Gartner, Kosef. Interchange: Weepu, Fulton, Lyons.
NORTHS: Seers; Pethybridge, Caruana, Florimo, Roy; Buettner, Taylor (c); Stuart, Reber, Trindall, Larson, Fairleigh, Moore. Interchange: Fritz, Hall, Leyshon, Williams.

St George 20 (D.Wagon, J.Lenihan, S.Kenward tries; W.Bartrim 4 goals) defeated **Illawarra** 8 (G.Air try; R.Wishart 2 goals) at WIN Stadium, Saturday, March 22.

Scrums: Illawarra 9–8. Penalties: 7–all. Crowd: 8661. Referee: Paul Simpkins. Halftime: St George 18–4. Goalkickers: Bartrim (St George) 4/5, Wishart (Illawarra) 2/3. Seconds: Illawarra 16–10. Under-20s: Illawarra 8–6.
ST GEORGE: D.Smith; Wagon, Coyne (c), Lenihan, Brunker; Kenward, Clinch; Hearn, Brown, Ward, Thompson, Treacy, Bartrim. Interchange: Pearson, B.Smith, Kusto.
ILLAWARRA: Reeves; Wishart, Timmins, McGregor (c), Clifford; Barrett, Air; Bradstreet, Callaway, Smith, Bristow, Mackay, Rodwell. Interchange: Tunbridge, Cram, David, J.Cross.
Cited: Hearn (St George). **Charge:** High tackle. **Sentence:** Exonerated.

Sydney City 8 (D.Junee try, I.Cleary 2 goals) defeated **Parramatta** 2 (J.Simon goal) at Parramatta Stadium, Saturday night, March 22.

Scrums: 9–all. Penalties: Parramatta 11–8. Crowd: 17,254. Referee: Paul McBlane. Halftime: 0–all. Goalkickers: Cleary (Sydney City) 2/3, Simon (Parramatta) 1/2. Seconds: Parramatta 26–16. Under-20s: Sydney City 20–6.
SYDNEY CITY: Junee (c); Elsegood, Sing, Cleary, Miles; Shearer, Wood; Lowrie, Bonetti, Hermansson, Ricketson, Gourley, Rigon. Interchange: Walker, Troy, Barnhill, Sinclair.
PARRAMATTA: Riolo; Herron, McCracken, Woods, Whereat; Kelly, Simon; Johnston, Raper, King, Pay (c), Jason Smith, Dymock. Interchange: Lovell, Campbell, Bell, Barnes.
Sin bin: Cleary (Sydney City).

Gold Coast 26 (A.King, J.Schloss, W.Patten, G.Mackay, C.Orr tries; Mackay 2, W.Anderson goals) defeated **Balmain** 6 (J.Bostock try; T.Brasher goal) at Carrara Stadium, Saturday night, March 22.

Scrums: Gold Coast 8–4. Penalties: Balmain 11–4. Crowd: 9851. Referee: Sean Hampstead. Halftime: Gold Coast 20–6. Goalkickers: Mackay (Gold Coast) 2/4, Anderson (Gold Coast) 1/1, Brasher (Balmain) 1/2. Seconds: Gold Coast 14–12. Under-20s: 14–all.
GOLD COAST: King; Suluvale, Mackay (c), Nicol, Russell; Zahra, Patten; Bella, Goddard, Driscoll, Durheim, Hurst, Schloss. Interchange: Anderson, Orr, Sattler, Whittaker.
BALMAIN: Brasher (c); Langaloa, Kennedy, Donaghey, Bostock; Hanley, Gillett; Walker, Senter, Starr, Stimson, Smith, Morrison. Interchange: Webber, Nable, Wilson, Bayssari.

Souths 17 (D.McLeod, M.Hogan, P.Driscoll tries; M.Manning 2 goals; D.Trindall field goal) defeated **Wests** 8 (A.Doyle try; A.Leeds, W.Newton goals) at Sydney Football Stadium, Sunday, March 23.

Scrums: Wests 8–6. Penalties: Wests 14–6. Crowd: 5108. Referee: Kelvin Jeffes. Halftime: Souths 10–2. Goalkickers: Manning (Souths) 2/3, Skelly (Souths) 0/1, Leeds (Wests) 1/1, Newton (Wests) 1/1. Seconds: 26–all. Under-20s: 16–all.
SOUTHS: O'Meara; Moore, McLeod, Manning, Hogan; Simon, Trindall (c); Rubin, Skelly, Driscoll, Burns, Quinn, Sutton. Interchange: Wilson, Ostini, Tassell.
WESTS: Leeds; D.Willis, Ken McGuinness, Pearson, Laing; Georgallis, Newton; Skandalis, Mescia, J.Smith, Millard, Langmack (c), Hasler. Interchange: Yates, Dunn, Doyle, Kevin McGuinness.
Cited: Millard (Wests). **Charge:** Dangerous tackle. **Sentence:** Exonerated.

Newcastle 44 (A.Muir 3, L.Dynevor 2, O.Craigie, D.Albert, M.Gidley tries; Dynevor 5, R.O'Davis goals) defeated **South Queensland** 0, at Marathon Stadium, Sunday, March 23.

Scrums: South Queensland 12–7. Penalties: 6–all. Crowd: 15,114. Referee: Matt Hewitt. Halftime: Newcastle 22–0. Goalkickers: Dynevor (Newcastle) 5/6, O'Davis (Newcastle) 1/3. Seconds: South Queensland 22–10. Under-20s: Newcastle 10–6.
NEWCASTLE: O'Davis; Albert, Grogan, Craigie, MacDougall; Gidley, Dynevor; Richards, Jackson, Butterfield (c), Muir, Peden, Glanville. Interchange: Fletcher, Conley, Moodie, Duderus.
SOUTH QUEENSLAND: Hubbard; Hudson, Toshack, Eagar, Wendt; Watson, Pezet; O'Brien, Teevan (c), Jones, Protheroe, Retchless, Wilson. Interchange: Couper, Tookey, A.Bella, Hamilton.

STANDINGS: Sydney City 6, Manly 6, Illawarra 4, Newcastle 4, Gold Coast 4, Souths 4, Norths 2, St George 2, Parramatta 2, South Queensland 2, Wests 0, Balmain 0.

OPTUS CUP ROUND 4
MARCH 27, 28, 29, 30

Knights' best in two years

Newcastle produced their best attacking display in two seasons to score a 28-16 win over Sydney City in the Good Friday clash at the Sydney Football Stadium. The Knights exhibited superb ball control in outscoring the Roosters five tries to two. Halfback Leo Dynevor continued his rapid rise to prominence with two slashing tries and four goals, adding to his 18 points against the Crushers five days earlier. Dynevor, the 23-year-old replacement for injured half Andrew Johns, was mentioned as a possible Queensland State of Origin halfback, so impressive was his display.

With audacious passes invariably finding their mark, the Knights fired brilliantly in the first half to establish a match-winning 22-6 lead at the break.

Celebrating 10 years at Campbelltown Sports Ground, Western Suburbs broke through for their first win of the 1997 Optus Cup, with a well-executed 25-16 defeat of Parramatta.

The Magpies astutely detected that the Eels were vulnerable under the high ball, and their air attack won them three tries. After three successive losses, Wests finally rediscovered the spirit that took them to the finals in 1996, and fought on well after the scores were locked at 12-all at halftime. Magpie captain Paul Langmack claimed that a night on the town just two days before the match had had the desired effect, and that the team was now back on track.

Illawarra centre Shaun Timmins played an unhappy part in history after duffing a kick from near the posts that would have given his team a last-minute victory over Norths at North Sydney Oval. The Steelers inexplicably squandered a 14-4 halftime lead and looked headed for defeat with Norths leading 18-14 as the clock counted down. But in the shadows of fulltime, Illawarra replacement winger Brendan Hauville scorched across for a try which levelled the scores.

Timmins failed to convert the try, and the Steelers were forced to settle for an 18-all draw. In a first for the ARL competition, all three grades were drawn.

Balmain became the last team for 1997 to break their duck when they downed South Sydney 22-16 in front of a healthy crowd — more than 11,000 — at Leichhardt Oval. The Tigers bounced back from a disappointing display against the Gold Coast to finish on top of a spirited Rabbitohs side in a tough and competitive match. Balmain winger James Langaloa came of age as a first-grader with three slashing tries, while centre William 'Bubba' Kennedy scored a long-distance four-pointer. Souths looked a strong chance to make it three wins in a row before halfback and captain Darrell Trindall was forced from the field with knee trouble late in the match.

The impact of veteran five-eighth Cliff Lyons was all the spark Manly needed to deliver a 36-16 win over South Queensland at Suncorp Stadium. The Sea Eagles trailed 2-0 before Lyons was injected into the game midway through the first half. Lyons laid on tries for Craig Innes and Terry Hill before scoring a third himself. Centre Terry Hill finished the match with a hat-trick of tries for the Sea Eagles.

St George emerged with the two premiership points in a scrappy clash with the Gold Coast Chargers at Kogarah Oval. Saints won the match 18-12 after leading 16-0 at the break.

ROUND 4 — RESULTS

Wests 25 (P.Langmack, D.Hasler, A.Laing, Ken McGuinness tries; A.Leeds 4 goals; Leeds field goal) defeated **Parramatta** 14 (D.Riolo, J.McCracken tries; J.Simon 3 goals) at Campbelltown Sports Ground, Thursday night, March 27.

Scrums: Wests 5–4. Penalties: Parramatta 11–10. Crowd: 11,592. Referee: Matt Hewitt. Halftime: 12–all. Goalkickers: Leeds (Wests) 4/5, Simon (Parramatta) 3/4. Seconds: Parramatta 19–10. Under-20s: Parramatta 20–8.
WESTS: Leeds; D.Willis, Ken McGuinness, Pearson, Laing; A.Willis, Georgallis; Skandalis, Mescia, Millard, Dunn, J.Smith, Langmack (c). Interchange: Hasler, Yates, Doyle, Kevin McGuinness.
PARRAMATTA: Riolo; Barnes, McCracken, Woods, Whereat; Bell, Simon; Johnston, Raper, Pay (c), Lovell, Jason Smith, Dymock. Interchange: Kelly, Campbell, Morgan, Collins.

Newcastle 28 (L.Dynevor 2, B.Grogan, L.Jackson, J.Moodie tries; Dynevor 4 goals) defeated **Sydney City** 16 (J.Elsegood, A.Walker, S.Gourley, I.Cleary 2 goals) at Sydney Football Stadium, Friday night, March 27.

Scrums: Sydney City 7–5. Penalties: 6–all. Crowd: 17,353. Referee: Kelvin Jeffes. Halftime: Newcastle 22–6. Goalkickers: Dynevor (Newcastle) 4/6, Cleary (Sydney City) 2/5. Seconds: Newcastle 18–8. Under-20s: Sydney City 52–28.
NEWCASTLE: O'Davis; Albert, Grogan, Craigie, MacDougall; M.Johns (c), Dynevor; Butterfield, Jackson, Richards, Peden, Muir, Glanville. Interchange: Conley, Moodie, Gidley, Fletcher.
SYDNEY CITY: Junee; Elsegood, Sing, Cleary, Miles; Shearer, Walker; Lowrie, Bonetti, Hermansson, Ricketson, Gourley, Fittler (c). Interchange: Barnhill, Rigon, Sinclair, Troy.
Sin bin: Richards (Newcastle), Ricketson (Sydney City).

Norths 18 (C.Caruana, M.Seers, J.Taylor tries; Taylor 3 goals) drew with **Illawarra** 18 (B.Reeves, W.Clifford, D.Callaway, B.Hauville tries; R.Wishart goal) at North Sydney Oval, Saturday, March 28.

Scrums: Norths 10–9. Penalties: Norths 8–2. Crowd: 8319. Referee: Paul McBlane. Halftime: Illawarra 14–4. Goalkickers: Taylor (Norths) 3/4, Wishart (Illawarra) 1/3, Timmins (Illawarra) 0/1. Seconds: 18–all. Under-20s: 12–all.
NORTHS: Seers; Hall, Ikin, Caruana, Roy; Buettner, Taylor (c); Stuart, Reber, Trindall, Leyshon, Florimo, Moore. Interchange: Williams, Fritz, Horder.
ILLAWARRA: Reeves; Wishart, Timmins, McGregor (c), Clifford; Barrett, Robinson; Bradstreet, Callaway, Smith, Cram, Mackay, Rodwell. Interchange: Tunbridge, J.Cross, Bristow, Hauville.
Sin bin: Reeves (Illawarra).

Manly 36 (T.Hill 3, C.Hancock 2, C.Innes, C.Lyons tries; C.Field 3, Innes goals) defeated **South Queensland** 16 (A.Hamilton, T.Pezet tries; Pezot 4 goals) at Suncorp Stadium, Saturday night, March 28.

Scrums: Manly 8–6. Penalties: Manly 9–6. Crowd: 9147. Referee: Sean Hampstead. Halftime: Manly 12–4. Goalkickers: Field (Manly) 3/6, Innes (Manly) 1/1, Pezet (South Queensland) 4/4. Seconds: South Queensland 20–14. Under-20s: South Queensland 22–20.
MANLY: Hancock; Moore, Innes, Hill, Hopoate; Toovey (c), Field; Tierney, Fulton, Weepu, Menzies, Gartner, Kosef. Interchange: Lyons, Hunter, Johnson, Guberina.
SOUTH QUEENSLAND: Hubbard; Hudson, Roedder, Eagar, Wendt; Watson, Pezet; O'Brien, Teevan (c), Jones, Retchless, Bella, Wilson. Interchange: Hamilton, Tookey, Antonik, Saunders.

St George 18 (L.Murphy, B.Smith, B.Kusto tries; W.Bartrim 3 goals) defeated **Gold Coast** 12 (G.Mackay, J.Nicol tries; Mackay, D.Anderson goals) at Kogarah Oval, Sunday, March 29.

Scrums: St George 11–10. Penalties: St George 10–5. Crowd: 6052. Referee: David Manson. Halftime: St George 16–0. Goalkickers: Bartrim (St George) 3/5, Mackay (Gold Coast) 1/1, Anderson (Gold Coast) 1/1. Seconds: Gold Coast 24–14. Under-20s: Gold Coast 18–16.
ST GEORGE: D.Smith; Murphy, Coyne (c), Lenihan, Brunker; Kenward, Clinch; Hearn, Brown, Ward, Thompson, Treacy, Bartrim. Interchange: Pearson, B.Smith, Kusto, Hardy.
GOLD COAST: King; Suluvale, Mackay (c), Nicol, Russell; Zahra, Patten; Bella, Goddard, Driscoll, Durheim, Hurst, Schloss. Interchange: Anderson, Orr, Sattler, Whittaker.
Sin bin: Zahra (Gold Coast).

Balmain 22 (J.Langaloa 3, W.Kennedy tries; T.Brasher 3 goals) defeated **Souths** 16 (D.Trindall 2, D.McLeod tries; M.Manning 2 goals) at Leichhardt Oval, Sunday, March 29.

Scrums: Souths 5–4. Penalties: Souths 8–7. Crowd: 11,319. Referee: Paul Simpkins. Halftime: Balmain 14–10. Goalkickers: Brasher (Balmain) 3/6, Manning (Souths) 2/4. Seconds: Balmain 30–10. Under-20s: Balmain 18–14.
BALMAIN: Brasher; Langaloa, Kennedy, A.Milford, Bostock, Hanley, Jolly; Starr, Senter, Sironen (c), Stimson, O'Neil, Morrison. Interchange: Walker, Bayssari, Gillett, Smith.
SOUTHS: O'Meara; Moore, McLeod, Manning, Hogan; Simon, Trindall (c); Rubin, Skelly, Driscoll, Burns, Quinn, Sutton. Interchange: Wilson, Ostini, White.
Sin bin: Hanley (Balmain), O'Meara (Souths).

STANDINGS: Manly 8, Newcastle 6, Sydney City 6, Illawarra 5, Gold Coast 4, St George 4, Souths 4, Norths 3, Wests 2, Balmain 2, Parramatta 2, South Queensland 2.

ROUND 4

OPTUS CUP ROUND 5
APRIL 4, 5, 6

A game for the ages

A crowd of over 18,000, plus a huge television audience, savoured a game for the ages at Brookvale Oval. Manly's 34-24 win over Sydney City had all the hallmarks of a classic. An opening onslaught by the Roosters had the premiers 18 points down after just 18 minutes of play but, displaying all the qualities that had taken them to premiership honours in 1996, the Sea Eagles fought back. They trailed 18-16 at halftime and hit the front for the first time 15 minutes from the end, with a try from Craig Innes.

The game was jam-packed with incident and controversy. Roosters fullback Darren Junee had his leg broken in the eighth minute, Manly captain Geoff Toovey was taken from the field with his neck in a brace, Manly forward Daniel Gartner left the field with a shoulder injury, Sydney City captain Brad Fittler hurt his knee and Rooster David Barnhill underwent surgery after almost severing his ear in a head clash. Barnhill and Manly second-rower Steve Menzies were placed on report and Roosters coach Phil Gould complained about Manly's controversial 'torpedo-style' tackling technique (which led to Fittler's injury). Manly coach Bob Fulton compared the intensity of the match to State of Origin football, and even beaten coach Gould agreed it was a great game.

St George lock Wayne Bartrim had a field day as St George cruised to a 34-4 win over a disappointing South Sydney at the Sydney Football Stadium. Running with greater freedom than in previous matches, Bartrim scored a hat-trick of tries and kicked five goals for a personal best tally of 22 points for the match.

Parramatta slumped to a new low at Marathon Stadium as Newcastle scored a commanding 29-10 victory. A crowd of over 20,000 watched their team maintain the irresistible form that brought them their strong win over premiership hot shots Sydney City a week earlier. The Knights scored five tries to two against a Parramatta side that stumbled and fumbled its way to a fourth consecutive defeat. With halves Leo Dynevor and Matthew Gidley in charge, the Knights stormed to a 28-10 lead 10 minutes after halftime.

North Sydney were lucky to escape with a win when they made the trek to Gold Coast's Carrara Stadium, but thanks to a superb sideline conversion by captain Jason Taylor, the Bears got out of trouble.

The improving Gold Coast troubled Norths from the outset, and were leading 16-6, with only 15 minutes left on the clock, before the Bears staged their rearguard action. Tries to Michael Buettner and Chris Caruana levelled the score before Taylor's booming conversion.

Balmain produced their strongest defensive performance in several years to score a 28-0 shut-out of Wests before an enthusiastic crowd at Leichhardt Oval. The Tigers scored three tries in each half and did not allow Wests a clean break all afternoon. 'That is a tough task when you are in front by a large margin, because quite often the intensity drops off,' said a delighted coach Wayne Pearce.

Illawarra coach Andrew Farrar suggested the crowd of 6,144 who turned out to watch the Steelers beat South Queensland 14-6 should be entitled to their money back after one of the poorest quality games seen in Wollongong. The win meant that the Steelers led the club championship for the first time in their history — one of the few redeeming features of the day.

ROUND 5 — RESULTS

Manly 34 (A.Hunter 2, T.Hill, D.Gartner, D.Moore, C.Innes tries; C.Field 5 goals) defeated **Sydney City** 24 (A.Walker, D.Shearer, L.Ricketson, I.Cleary tries; Cleary 4 goals) at Brookvale Oval, Friday night, April 4.

Scrums: Sydney City 12–5. Penalties: Manly 6–4. Crowd: 18,185. Referee: David Manson. Halftime: Sydney City 18–16. Goalkickers: Field (Manly) 5/6, Cleary (Sydney City) 4/4. Seconds: Sydney City 22–20. Under-20s: Sydney City 28–10.
MANLY: Hancock; Moore, Innes, Hill, Hopoate; Toovey (c), Field; Tierney, Fulton, Carroll, Menzies, Gartner, Kosef. Interchange: Hunter, Colella, Weepu, Lyons.
SYDNEY CITY: Junee; Elsegood, Cleary, Shearer, Miles; Fittler (c), Walker, Lowrie, Garlick, Hermansson, Barnhill, Gourley, Ricketson. Interchange: Troy, Rigon, Gaffey, Sing.
Cited: Menzies (Manly). **Charge:** Dangerous throw. **Sentence:** Exonerated. Barnhill (Sydney City). **Charge:** Striking, high tackle. **Sentence:** Exonerated.

St George 34 (W.Bartrim 3, N.Brown 2, J.Ainscough tries; Bartrim 5 goals) defeated **Souths** 4 (D.McLeod try) at Sydney Football Stadium, Saturday, April 5.

Scrums: Souths 10–9. Penalties: Souths 7–5. Crowd: 7200. Referee: Kelvin Jeffes. Halftime: St George 18–0. Goalkickers: Bartrim (St George) 5/7, Manning (Souths) 0/2. Seconds: Souths 18–10. Under-20s: Souths 12–10.
ST GEORGE: D.Smith; Bell, Coyne (c), Ainscough, Brunker, Hardy, Clinch; Hearn, Brown, Ward, Thompson, Treacy, Bartrim. Interchange: Pearson, B.Smith, Kenward, Saukuru.
SOUTHS: O'Meara; Moore, McLeod, Manning, Hogan; Wilson, Penna; Rubin, Skelly (c), Driscoll, Burns, Ostini, Sutton. Interchange: Simon, Parsons, White.
Sin bin: Hearn (St George).

Norths 20 (B.Ikin, M.Buettner, C.Caruana tries; J.Taylor 4 goals) defeated **Gold Coast** 16 (S.Russell, W.Patten, C.Nahi tries; D.Anderson 2 goals) at Carrara Stadium, Saturday night, April 5.

Scrums: Norths 6–5. Penalties: Gold Coast 7–4. Crowd: 9280. Referee: Paul Cimpkins. Halftime: Norths 6–4. Goalkickers: Taylor (Norths) 4/4, Anderson (Gold Coast) 2/3, Mackay (Gold Coast) 0/2. Seconds: Gold Coast 34–18. Under-20s: Gold Coast 23–20.
NORTHS: Seers, Pethybridge, Ikin, Florimo, Roy; Buettner, Taylor (c); Stuart, Soden, Trindall, Larson, Fairleigh, Moore. Interchange: Caruana, Hall, Leyshon, Pomery.
GOLD COAST: McKelleher; Dwyer, Mackay (c), Nicol, Russell, Orr, Patten; Hella, Goddard, Driscoll, Durheim, Hurst, Schloss. Interchange: Anderson, Butler, Nahi, Goodrich.

Newcastle 29 (A.Muir, M.Glanville, D.Albert, B.Peden, L.Dynevor tries; Dynevor 4 goals; Glanville field goal) defeated **Parramatta** 10 (S.Collins, I.Herron tries; Herron goal) at Marathon Stadium, Sunday, April 6.

Scrums: Newcastle 10–8. Penalties: Newcastle 9–8. Crowd: 21,225. Referee: Paul McBlane. Halftime: Newcastle 16–6. Goalkickers: Dynevor (Newcastle) 4/6, Herron (Parramatta) 1/2. Seconds: Parramatta 18–8. Under-20s: Parramatta 28–8.
NEWCASTLE: O'Davis; Albert, Grogan, Craigie, Moodie; Gidley, Dynevor, Butterfield (c), Jackson, Richards, Peden, Muir, Glanville. Interchange: Fletcher, M.Johns, Conley, Clements.
PARRAMATTA: Collins; Herron, McCracken, Woods, Carige; Bell, Simon; Johnston, Raper, Pay (c), Horsnell, Jason Smith, Dymock. Interchange: Lovell, Morgan, Campbell, Kelly.

Illawarra 14 (A.Bristow, S.Timmins, T.Barrett tries; D.Bradstreet goal) defeated **South Queensland** 6 (J.Hudson try; Hudson goal) at WIN Stadium, Sunday, April 6.

Scrums: South Queensland 15–13. Penalties: South Queensland 9–5. Crowd: 6144. Referee: Matt Hewitt. Halftime: Illawarra 4–0. Goalkickers: Bradstreet (Illawarra) 1/1, Reeves (Illawarra) 0/2, Hudson (South Queensland) 1/2. Seconds: Illawarra 22–14. Under-20s: Illawarra 19–6.
ILLAWARRA: Reeves; Hauville, Timmins, McGregor (c), Clifford; Barrett, Air; Bradstreet, Robinson, Smith, Cram, Mackay, J.Cross. Interchange: Bristow, Tunbridge, David, Hart.
SOUTH QUEENSLAND: Hubbard; Hudson, Roedder, Saunders, Wendt; Cairns, Antonik; O'Brien, Teevan (c), Jones, A.Bella, Retchless, Hamilton. Interchange: Tookey, Cruckshank, Mooney, Carmichael.

Balmain 28 (M.Withers, M.Gillett, J.Langaloa, G.Morrison, G.Donaghey, T.Brasher tries; Withers 2 goals) defeated **Wests** 0, at Leichhardt Oval, Sunday, April 6.

Scrums: 12–all. Penalties: Wests 9–5. Crowd: 9079. Referee: Sean Hampstead. Halftime: Balmain 14–0. Goalkickers: Withers (Balmain) 2/6. Seconds: Wests 19–18. Under-20s: Balmain 16–14.
BALMAIN: Brasher; Langaloa, Kennedy, Donaghey, Withers; Hanley, Jolly; Walker, Senter, Sironen (c), Stimson, O'Neil, Morrison. Interchange: Starr, Smith, Gillett, Webber.
WESTS: Leeds; D.Willis, Ken McGuinness, Pearson, Laing; A.Willis, Georgallis; Skandalis, Mescia, J.Smith, Dunn, Kennedy, Langmack (c). Interchange: Millard, Hasler, Yates, Kevin McGuinness.
Sin bin: Kennedy (Wests), Walker (Balmain).

STANDINGS: Manly 10, Newcastle 8, Illawarra 7, St George 6, Sydney City 6, Norths 5, Gold Coast 4, Balmain 4, Souths 4, Wests 2, Parramatta 2, South Queensland 2.

OPTUS CUP ROUND 6
APRIL 11, 12, 13

Eels stumble again

Parramatta regained some much-needed self-respect before a 20,000-strong crowd at Parramatta Stadium, but for the fifth week in a row they went home without the points, going down 18-8 to Manly in a bruising encounter.

The Eels sported a new look, thanks to a one-off sponsorship deal with a confectionery company, but a change in uniform could not change the club's fortunes. After trailing by four points at halftime, a dummy-half try to second-rower Dean Pay levelled the scores soon after the resumption, but a dubious try to prop Neil Tierney gave Manly a lead they would not relinquish. The sin-binning of second-rower Jarrod McCracken in the 70th minute was the final straw for the Eels. While he was cooling his heels for a professional foul, Craig Field and Cliff Lyons combined for the try that clinched the result.

Illawarra five-eighth Trent Barrett scored a points victory over a less-than-fully-fit Brad Fittler, as the Steelers maintained their place among the front-runners with a 26-20 upset at the Sydney Football Stadium.

The 19-year-old Barrett led Illawarra's attack with polished style, and took the visitors to a 16-0 lead after just 19 minutes. With Fittler doing his utmost, despite his painful knee injury, the Roosters pulled up to 16-12 at halftime, but Illawarra went right on with the job in the second half.

Halfback and captain Jason Taylor became the most prolific pointscorer in the history of the North Sydney club with an 18-point haul against a hapless South Sydney at Bear Park. Norths won the match 34-14, but Taylor's record was the talking point afterwards. His tally took him to 695 points, eclipsing the 39-year-old record of 1950s fullback Allen Arkey.

Goalkicking was the difference in a hard-fought match between Newcastle and Wests at Campbelltown — won 8-4 on the boot of Newcastle halfback Leo Dynevor. Both sides scored one try, but Dynevor's two goals from two attempts got his team home for its fifth win from six matches. The game was spoiled by a spate of dropped balls from both sides, but neither coach was unhappy with the teams' strong all-round defensive effort. 'It was a pretty credible effort, but one missed tackle and we lost a ball game,' lamented Magpies coach Tom Raudonikis.

Referee Paul McBlane was in the hot seat after St George beat Balmain 16-10 in a day of controversy at Kogarah Oval. St George defended stoutly after Balmain levelled the scores at 10-all midway through the second half, and halfback Gavin Clinch finally produced the match-winning try.

Normally subdued Balmain coach Wayne Pearce made a beeline for the referees' room at fulltime. He was convinced that a number of McBlane's decisions had had a direct bearing on the outcome of the match. An on-field incident, in which McBlane was found to have manhandled Balmain replacement Michael Gillett, eventually led to McBlane's demotion to second grade.

The Gold Coast had to overcome an 8-1 penalty account against them before downing South Queensland 22-14 at Suncorp Stadium. The Chargers led early, then fell behind early in the second half, but two late tries gave them their third win of the season.

ROUND 6 — RESULTS

Newcastle 8 (M.Gidley try; L.Dynevor 2 goals) defeated **Wests** 4 (D.Willis try) at Campbelltown Sports Ground, Friday night, April 11.

Scrums: Wests 11–4. Penalties: 7–all. Crowd: 11,185. Referee: Sean Hampstead. Halftime: Newcastle 2–0. Goalkickers: Dynevor (Newcastle) 2/2, Leeds (Wests) 0/2. Seconds: Newcastle 6–0. Under-20s: Wests 26–18.
NEWCASTLE: O'Davis; Albert, Cochrane, Craigie, Moodie; Gidley, Dynevor; Butterfield (c), Jackson, Richards, Peden, Muir, Glanville. Interchange: Fletcher, O'Doherty, Conley.
WESTS: Leeds; D.Willis, Ken McGuinness, Pearson, Laing; Kevin McGuinness, Georgallis; Skandalis, Mescia, Dunn, J.Smith, Millard, Langmack (c). Interchange: Harris, Doyle, Hasler.

Norths 34 (J.Taylor, M.Buettner, B.Ikin, D.Hall, M.Seers tries; Taylor 7 goals) defeated **Souths** 14 (M.Moore 2, P.Quinn tries; C.Skelly goal) at North Sydney Oval, Saturday, April 12.

Scrums: 6–all. Penalties: Norths 6–5. Crowd: 7158. Referee: Matt Hewitt. Halftime: Norths 16–6. Goalkickers: Taylor (Norths) 7/8, Skelly (Souths) 1/3. Seconds: Norths 32–16. Under-20s: Souths 12–10.
NORTHS: Seers; Hall, Ikin, Florimo, Roy; Buettner, Taylor (c); Stuart, Soden, Trindall, Larson, Fairleigh, Moore. Interchange: Caruana, Williams, Leyshon, Pethybridge.
SOUTHS: O'Meara; Moore, McLeod, Howlett, Hogan; Simon, Trindall (c); Francis, Skelly, Parsons, Ostini, Quinn, Burns. Interchange: Sutton, Driscoll, Amos, Tassell.
Sin bin: O'Meara (Souths).

Manly 18 (D.Gartner, N.Tierney, C.Lyons tries; C.Field 3 goals) defeated **Parramatta** 8 (D.Pay try; I.Herron 2 goals) at Parramatta Stadium, Saturday night, April 12.

Scrums: Manly 5–4. Penalties: 8–all. Crowd: 20,202. Referee: Kelvin Jeffes. Halftime: Manly 8–4. Goalkickers: Field (Manly) 3/4, Herron (Parramatta) 2/4. Seconds: Parramatta 26–16. Under-20s: Parramatta 26–25.
MANLY: Hancock; Moore, Innes, Hill, Hunter, Toovey (c); Field; Tierney, Fulton, Carroll, Menzies, Hopoate, Gartner. Interchange: Lyons, Weepu, Colella.
PARRAMATTA: Riolo; Herron, Carige, Kelly, Whereat; Dymock, Simon; Johnston, Brown, Pay (c), McCracken, Spence, Jason Smith. Interchange: Morgan, Campbell, Collins, Bell.
Sin bin: McCracken (Parramatta).

St George 16 (J.Ainscough, C.Clinch tries; W.Bartrim 4 goals) defeated **Balmain** 10 (W.Kennedy, J.Langaloa tries; M.Withers goal) at Kogarah Oval, Sunday, April 13.

Scrums: Balmain 6–4. Penalties: St George 12–6. Crowd: 8291. Referee: Paul McBlane. Halftime: St George 10–4. Goalkickers: Bartrim (St George) 4/5, Withers (Balmain) 1/3. Seconds: St George 8–6. Under-20s: Balmain 26–22.
ST GEORGE: D.Smith; Bell, Coyne (c), Ainscough, Brunker; Kenward, Clinch; Hearn, Brown, Ward, Thompson, Treacy, Bartrim. Interchange: Pearson, B.Smith, Hardy.
BALMAIN: Brasher; Langaloa, Kennedy, Donaghey, Withers; Hanley, Jolly; Walker, Senter, Sironen (c), Stimson, O'Neil, Morrison. Interchange: Starr, Smith, Gillett, Webber.

Illawarra 26 (T.Barrett 2, B.Reeves 2, J.Cross tries; D.Bradstreet 2, Reeves goals) defeated **Sydney City** 20 (I.Cleary, A.Walker, S.Rigon tries; Cleary 4 goals) at Sydney Football Stadium, Sunday April, 13.

Scrums: 5–all. Penalties: Sydney City 8–4. Crowd: 7600. Referee: Paul Simpkins. Halftime: Illawarra 16–12. Goalkickers: Bradstreet (Illawarra) 2/3, Reeves (Illawarra) 1/2, Cleary (Sydney City) 4/4. Seconds: Sydney City 18–14. Under-20s: Sydney City 26–16.
ILLAWARRA: Reeves; Hauville, Timmins, McGregor (c), Clifford; Barrett, Air; Bradstreet, Robinson, Smith, Cram, Mackay, J.Cross. Interchange: Bristow, Tunbridge, David, Hart.
SYDNEY CITY: Cleary; Elsegood, Sing, Shearer, Clarke; Walker, Fittler (c); Lowrie, Bonetti, Hermansson, Barnhill, Gourley, Ricketson. Interchange: Troy, Rigon, Mostyn, Duckworth.

Gold Coast 22 (D.Anderson, B.Hurst, B.Plowman, M.Dwyer tries; Anderson 2, G.Mackay goals) defeated **South Queensland** 14 (M.Toshack, M.Eagar, P.Hubbard tries; J.Hudson goal) at Suncorp Stadium, Sunday, April 13.

Scrums: 5–all. Penalties: South Queensland 8–1. Crowd: 5290. Referee: Sean Hampstead. Halftime: Gold Coast 12–8. Goalkickers: Anderson (Gold Coast) 2/3, Mackay (Gold Coast) 1/1, Hudson (South Queensland) 1/3. Seconds: South Queensland 13–12. Under-20s: Gold Coast 22–16.
GOLD COAST: McKelleher; Dwyer, Mackay (c), Anderson, Russell; Orr, Patten; Bella, Goddard, Driscoll, Durheim, Hurst, Schloss. Interchange: Sattler, Nahi, Plowman, Currie.
SOUTH QUEENSLAND: Hubbard; Hudson, Toshack, Eagar, Wendt; Cairns, Antonik; O'Brien, Teevan (c), Jones, Hamilton, Retchless, Saunders. Interchange: A.Bella, Tookey, Protheroe, Nutley.
Sin bin: Goddard (Gold Coast), Hudson (South Queensland).

STANDINGS: Manly 12, Newcastle 10, Illawarra 9, St George 8, Norths 7, Gold Coast 6, Sydney City 6, Balmain 4, Souths 4, Wests 2, Parramatta 2, South Queensland 2.

OPTUS CUP ROUND 7
APRIL 18, 19, 20

Manly go four clear

Manly jumped four points clear at the top of the table with a decisive 22-8 victory over Newcastle at Brookvale Oval in a match marred by the Sea Eagles' handling errors and sledging tactics.

Manly took no time in placing their stamp on the match, scoring two tries in the opening 10 minutes. By the 29th minute they led 18-0, and despite a try to Knights winger Jason Moodie just before halftime, the Knights never looked like making a match of it.

Manly winger John Hopoate and halfback Craig Field unleashed a barrage of abuse aimed particularly at Knights youngsters Matthew Gidley and Darren Albert, while forward giant Billy Weepu and Newcastle hooker Lee Jackson were involved in a scuffle in the tunnel after both were sin-binned for fighting late in the match. There were also claims that Manly players had abused referee Paul Simpkins and his touch judges when decisions went against them. One of the few highlights of the match for Newcastle was a tackle by Knights lock Marc Glanville on Manly halfback Craig Field.

After their 9-7 win over North Sydney at Leichhardt Oval, Balmain coach Wayne Pearce claimed his side had come of age.

After a frustrating loss to St George a week earlier, Pearce was delighted with the way his charges fought back and also with the way they responded to Norths' lift in intensity midway through the match. The Tigers led 6-2 at halftime but Norths hit back to lead 7-6, thanks to the boot of Jason Taylor. A field goal to improved five-eighth Michael Gillett, and a late penalty goal to winger Michael Withers, secured the Tigers a quality victory. Norths' coach Peter Louis was livid afterwards and risked a $10,000 fine for his criticism of match officials.

Parramatta ended a demoralising six-week run of losses with a 23-16 defeat of Illawarra in trying circumstances at WIN Stadium. Led by the boot of halfback and former Steeler John Simon, Parramatta led 12-2 after just 12 minutes and kept Illawarra at arm's length for the remainder of the match. Eels' coach Brian Smith was fuming at a number of refereeing rulings, particularly ref Sean Hampstead's decision to send fullback Paul Carige off for a high tackle midway through the second half.

Wests bounced back from successive losses to Balmain and Newcastle to score a slick 24-8 win over St George at Kogarah Oval. The Magpies' return to form coincided with the return from suspension of English front-rower Harvey Howard, whose added thrust helped his pack dominate Saints' six. Wests led by four points at halftime, but outscored Saints 12-0 in the second term.

Sydney City and the Gold Coast turned on a 58-point thriller at Carrara Stadium — the Roosters deservedly took the match 34-24. The Chargers led 18-12 at halftime, but the Roosters, inspired by Fittler, finished far stronger.

A dressing down by captain Darrell Trindall provided South Sydney with the necessary incentive to overcome a 12-man South Queensland side at the Sydney Football Stadium. The Crushers led Souths 20-6 after 49 minutes, despite losing forward Danny Nutley, sent from the field for a high tackle midway through the first half. Trindall's inspiration helped Souths storm back into the game and emerge with a 24-20 result.

ROUND 7 — RESULTS

Balmain 9 (M.Gillett try; M.Withers 2 goals; Gillett field goal) defeated **North Sydney** 7 (J.Taylor 3 goals; Taylor field goal) at Leichhardt Oval, Friday night, April 18.

Scrums: Balmain 7–3. Penalties: 6–all. Crowd: 12,613. Referee: David Manson. Halftime: Balmain 6–4. Goalkickers: Withers (Balmain) 2/3, Taylor (North Sydney) 3/4. Seconds: Balmain 24–4. Under-20s: Balmain 16–6.

BALMAIN: Brasher; L.Milford, Kennedy, Webber, Withers; Gillett, Jolly; Walker, Senter, Sironen (c), Stimson, O'Neil, Morrison. Interchange: Starr, Smith, McPherson, Bayssari.

NORTHS: Seers; Roy, Florimo, Ikin, Hall; Buettner, Taylor (c); Stuart, Soden, Trindall, Larson, Fairleigh, Moore. Interchange: Caruana, Pethybridge, Williams, Fritz.

Sin bin: Florimo (Norths).

Wests 24 (B.Pearson, D.Willis, A.Laing, A.Leeds tries; Leeds 4 goals) defeated **St George** 8 (A.Brunker try; W.Bartrim 2 goals) at Kogarah, Saturday, April 19.

Scrums: St George 9–6. Penalties: St George 13–4. Crowd: 5434. Referee: Matt Hewitt. Halftime: Wests 12–8. Goalkickers: Leeds (Wests) 4/7, Bartrim (St George) 2/2. Seconds: St George 32–14. Under-20s: Wests 18–10.

WESTS: Leeds; D.Willis, Ken McGuinness, Pearson, Laing; Kevin McGuinness, Georgallis; Howard, Mescia, Skandalis, Millard, Dunn, Langmack (c). Interchange: J.Smith, Kennedy, Hasler, Doyle.

ST GEORGE: Raper; Bell, Coyne (c), Ainscough, Brunker; Hardy, Clinch; Hearn, Brown, Ward, Thompson, Treacy, Bartrim. Interchange: Pearson, B.Smith, Lenihan, Tangata-Toa.

Parramatta 23 (S.Kelly 2, S.Whereat, J.Bell tries; I.Herron 3 goals; J.Simon field goal) defeated **Illawarra** 16 (W.Robinson, W.Clifford, A.Bristow tries; D.Bradstreet, B.Reeves goals) at WIN Stadium, Saturday night, April 19.

Scrums: Illawarra 7–5. Penalties: Illawarra 7–4. Crowd: 11,992. Referee: Sean Hampstead. Halftime: Parramatta 20–8. Goalkickers: Herron (Parramatta) 3/5, Bradstreet (Illawarra) 1/3, Reeves (Illawarra) 1/1. Seconds: Parramatta 16–8. Under-20s: Illawarra 22–6.

PARRAMATTA: Riolo; Herron, Kelly, Carige, Whereat; Bell, Simon; Johnston, Brown, Morgan, Horsnell, McCracken (c), Dymock. Interchange: Campbell, Koina, Collins, Lovell.

ILLAWARRA: Reeves, Hauville, Timmins, McGregor (c), Clifford, Barrett, Air; Bradstreet, Robinson, Smith, Cram, Mackay, J.Cross. Interchange: Bristow, David, Tunbridge, Seru.

Sent off: Carige (Parramatta), 62 min. **Charge:** High tackle. **Sentence:** Exonerated. **Cited:** Cram. **Charge:** Dangerous throw. **Sentence:** Exonerated.

Sydney City 34 (A.Walker 2, M.Sing 2, S.Rigon, B.Fittler tries; I.Cleary 5 goals) defeated **Gold Coast** 24 (G.Mackay, J.Goddard, B.Plowman, W.Patten tries; B.Hurst 4 goals) at Carrara Stadium, Saturday night, April 19.

Scrums: Sydney City 8–4. Penalties: Gold Coast 10–9. Crowd: 9211. Referee: Eddie Ward. Halftime: Gold Coast 18–12. Goalkickers: Cleary (Sydney City) 5/6, Hurst (Gold Coast) 4/5. Seconds: Gold Coast 13–0. Under-20s: Sydney City 34–10.

SYDNEY CITY: Mostyn; Elsegood, Sing, Rigon, Cleary; Walker, Wood; Lowrie, Garlick, Hermansson, Ricketson, Gourley, Fittler (c). Interchange: Troy, Shearer, Gaffey, Duckworth.

GOLD COAST: King; Dwyer, Mackay (c), Currie, Bai; Orr, Patten; Bella, Goddard, Driscoll, Durheim, Hurst, Schloss. Interchange: Sattler, Nahi, Plowman, O'Reilly.

Sin bin: Goddard (Gold Coast), Patten (Gold Coast), Garlick (Sydney City).

Manly 22 (J.Hopoate, S.Menzies, A.Hunter, C.Hancock tries; C.Field 3 goals) defeated **Newcastle** 8 (J.Moodie, R.O'Davis tries) at Brookvale Oval, Sunday April 20.

Scrums: Newcastle 7–4. Penalties: Manly 8–6. Crowd: 15,487. Referee: Paul Simpkins. Halftime: Manly 18–4. Goalkickers: Field (Manly) 3/4, Dynevor (Newcastle) 0/2. Seconds: Newcastle 18–12. Under-20s: Manly 32–18.

MANLY: Hancock; Moore, Innes, Hill, Hopoate; Lyons, Field; Tierney, Toovey (c), Carroll, Menzies, Gartner, Kosef. Interchange: Weepu, Hunter, Johnson.

NEWCASTLE: O'Davis; Albert, MacDougall, Craigie, Moodie; Gidley, Dynevor; Butterfield (c), Jackson, Richards, Peden, Muir, Glanville. Interchange: Harragon, Fletcher, Clements, Conley.

Sin bin: Weepu (Manly), Jackson (Newcastle).

Cited: Muir (Newcastle). **Charge:** Dangerous throw. **Sentence:** One week.

Souths 24 (D.Trindall 2, D.Burns, D.McLeod tries; C.Skelly 4 goals) defeated **South Queensland** 20 (J.Hudson, M.Toshack, A.Hamilton, M.Tookey tries; Hudson, N.Antonik goals) at Sydney Football Stadium, Sunday April 20.

Scrums: Souths 8–6. Penalties: South Queensland 10–7. Crowd: 4353. Referee: Kelvin Jeffes. Halftime: South Queensland 14–6. Goalkickers: Skelly (Souths) 4/5, Hudson (South Queensland) 1/5, Antonik (South Queensland) 1/1. Seconds: Souths 24–10. Under-20s: Souths 14–10.

SOUTHS: O'Meara; Moore, McLeod, Howlett, Amos; Penna, Trindall (c); Rubin, Skelly, Parsons, Ostini, Quinn, Burns. Interchange: Driscoll, Francis, Simon, Wilson.

SOUTH QUEENSLAND: Hubbard; Hudson, Toshack, Eagar, Wendt; Cairns, Antonik; Tookey, Teevan (c), Jones, Hamilton, Retchless, Saunders. Interchange: Wilson, Nutley, Woodward, Protheroe.

Sent off: Nutley (South Queensland), 23 min. **Charge:** High tackle. **Sentence:** Two weeks.

STANDINGS: Manly 14, Newcastle 10, Illawarra 9, St George 8, Sydney City 8, Norths 7, Gold Coast 6, Balmain 6, Souths 6, Wests 4, Parramatta 4, South Queensland 2.

OPTUS CUP ROUND 8
APRIL 26, 27

Hasler inspires mighty Magpies

Manly's undefeated start to the 1997 season came to an end at Campbelltown Stadium where a Western Suburbs side, inspired by former Sea Eagle Des Hasler, ground out a 19-16 victory. With nine players backing up from the City-Country game two days earlier, Manly were clearly below their best, with a spate of handling errors disrupting their momentum. In fact, despite being in touch for the entire distance, Manly never led at any stage of the game. Wests captain Paul Langmack provided some dazzling moments for the parochial home crowd, particularly with his acrobatic role in a Ciriaco Mescia try in the 28th minute.

Both sides scored three tries, but Wests fullback Andrew Leeds gave his side the winning edge with three goals from five attempts, plus a field goal. Manly's concerns after the game surrounded injuries suffered by second-rower Daniel Gartner (broken thumb), David Gillespie (knee injury) and Nik Kosef (ribs).

It took a lethargic Newcastle Knights almost an hour to gain the upper hand against Illawarra in a mediocre display at Marathon Stadium.

With five Newcastle players appearing in their second game in three days, the Knights looked vulnerable in the first half, and Illawarra centre Paul McGregor was allowed to dictate terms. The match turned on a try scored by Knights centre Owen Craigie midway through the second half.

North Sydney erased the painful memories of their preliminary final loss to St George in September 1996 with a massive 54-14 win at North Sydney Oval. The Bears dominated from the outset, scoring the first of their nine tries after just five minutes. At halftime the Bears led 24-4, and although Saints hit back with a try just after the resumption, it was merely a hiccup in the North Sydney procession. Jason Taylor equalled the club record he shares with legendary winger Harold Horder by scoring 26 points.

Parramatta's graph continued in an upward direction with a 28-10 win over the Gold Coast at Parramatta Stadium. Led again by halfback John Simon, the Eels posted five tries to two and always looked to have the measure of the Chargers. Simon's kicking, passing and running game was impeccable, and strong support from no-frills forwards Peter Johnston and Justin Morgan played its part in the morale-boosting victory.

Halfback Adrian Lam made a successful return from off-season surgery as the Sydney City Roosters mauled neighbours South Sydney 42-0 at the Sydney Football Stadium. The star for the Roosters was skipper Brad Fittler, backing up just 24 hours after captaining the City side against Country. Fittler scored two tries and had a hand in two others, and was then rewarded by coach Phil Gould with an early shower 15 minutes from fulltime. Gould described the match as a turning point for the club — there had been some indifferent form in recent matches.

Balmain made it four wins from five matches, but failed to impress in a dour 18-16 win over the South Queensland Crushers. The kicking game of five-eighth Michael Gillett was pivotal to the Tigers' victory: three of the Tigers' four tries came from his boot. After a neck-and-neck tussle, Balmain kicked eight points clear with a Michael Withers try in the 65th minute, and the hapless Crushers could not bridge the gap.

ROUND 8 — RESULTS

Balmain 18 (M.Withers 2, C.McPherson, G.Morrison tries; Withers goal) defeated **South Queensland** 16 (J.Hudson, S.Retchless, M.Tookey tries; C.Schifcofske 2 goals) at Suncorp Stadium, Saturday, April 26.

Scrums: Balmain 6–4. Penalties: South Queensland 11–6. Crowd: 5998. Referee: Mark Oaten. Halftime: Balmain 8–4. Goalkickers: Withers (Balmain) 1/4, Schifcofske (South Queensland) 2/3. Seconds: Balmain 34–20. Under-20s: South Queensland 20–12.
BALMAIN: Brasher; L.Milford, Kennedy, Webber, Withers; Gillett, Jolly; Starr, Senter, Sironen (c), Stimson, O'Neil, Morrison. Interchange: McPherson, Walker, Smith, Edwards.
SOUTH QUEENSLAND: Hubbard; Hudson, Eagar, Carmichael, Schifcofske; Cairns, Antonik; Tookey, Teevan (c), Jones, Hamilton, Retchless, Wilson. Interchange: Saunders, Woodward, Protheroe, A.Bella.

Sydney City 42 (J.Elsegood 3, B.Fittler 2, R.Miles, M.Sing, N.Gaffey tries; I.Cleary 5 goals) defeated **Souths** 0, at Sydney Football Stadium, Saturday night, April 26.

Scrums: Souths 5–4. Penalties: Souths 6–5. Crowd: 9123. Referee: Sean Hampstead. Halftime: Sydney City 22–0. Goalkickers: Cleary (Sydney City) 5/8. Seconds: Sydney City 22–14. Under-20s: Souths 11–8.
SYDNEY CITY: Cleary; Elsegood, Sing, Rigon, Miles; Walker, Lam; Lowrie, Garlick, Hermansson, Ricketson, Gourley, Fittler (c). Interchange: Troy, Wood, Shearer, Gaffey.
SOUTHS: O'Meara; Moore, McLeod, Howlett, Waugh; Murray, Trindall (c); Ostini, Skelly, Parsons, Gillard, Quinn, Burns. Interchange: Francis, Stimson, Simon, Amos.

Norths 54 (G.Larson 2, N.Roy 2, J.Taylor 2, B.Ikin, D.Hall, C.Caruana tries; Taylor 9 goals) defeated **St George** 14 (L.Thompson, G.Clinch, D.Smith tries; W.Bartrim goal) at North Sydney Oval, Sunday, April 27.

Scrums: St George 8–4. Penalties: St George 9–6. Crowd: 12,629. Referee: Paul Simpkins. Halftime: Norths 24–4. Goalkickers: Taylor (Norths) 9/10, Bartrim (St George) 1/3. Seconds: St George 29–10. Under-20s: Norths 18–8.
NORTHS: Seers; Hall, Ikin, Buettner, Roy; Florimo, Taylor (c); Stuart, Soden, Trindall, Larson, Fairleigh, Moore. Interchange: Caruana, Leyshon, Williams, Reber.
ST GEORGE: D.Smith; Bell, Coyne (c), Ainscough, Brunker; Hardy, Clinch; Hearn, Brown, Pearson, Thompson, Treacy, Bartrim. Interchange: Ward, D.Smith, Raper, Lenihan.
Sin bin: Coyne (St George).

Wests 19 (C.Mescia, A.Leeds, Ken McGuinness tries; Leeds 3 goals; Leeds field goal) defeated **Manly** 16 (T.Hill, S.Menzies, C.Lyons tries; C.Field 2 goals) at Campbelltown Sports Ground, Sunday, April 27.

Scrums: Wests 11–8. Penalties: Manly 11–10. Crowd: 10,231. Referee: Eddie Ward. Halftime: 4–all. Goalkickers: Leeds (Wests) 3/5, Field (Manly) 2/3. Seconds: Manly 13–10. Under-20s: Manly 40–22.
WESTS: Leeds; D.Willis, Ken McGuinness, Pearson, Laing; Doyle, Georgallis; Howard, Mescia, Skandalis, Millard, Dunn, Langmack (c). Interchange: J.Smith, Hasler, Kevin McGuinness, Donovan.
MANLY: Hancock; Moore, Innes, Hill, Hopoate; Toovey (c), Field; Tierney, Fulton, Carroll, Menzies, Gartner, Kosef. Interchange: Gillespie, Lyons, Weepu, Hunter.
Cited: Hill (Manly). **Charge:** Dangerous throw. **Sentence:** Exonerated. Hancock (Manly). **Charge:** Dangerous throw. **Sentence:** Exonerated.

Newcastle 20 (J.Moodie, O.Craigie, M.Gidley, R.O'Davis tries; O'Davis 2 goals) defeated **Illawarra** 4 (G.Air try) at Marathon Stadium, Sunday, April 27.

Scrums: Newcastle 12–8. Penalties: Newcastle 9–7. Crowd: 12,582. Referee: Kelvin Jeffes. Halftime: Newcastle 6–4. Goalkickers: O'Davis (Newcastle) 2/3, Dynevor (Newcastle) 0/2, Reeves (Illawarra) 0/1. Seconds: Newcastle 30–14. Under-20s: Illawarra 30–20.
NEWCASTLE: O'Davis; Albert, Cochrane, Craigie, Moodie; Gidley, Dynevor; Butterfield (c), Jackson, Richards, Peden, Muir, Glanville. Interchange: Fletcher, Harragon, Conley, Clements.
ILLAWARRA: Reeves; Seru, Timmins, McGregor (c), Clifford; Barrett, Air; Cram, Robinson, Smith, Bradstreet, Mackay, J.Cross. Interchange: Bristow, David, Rodwell, Tunbridge.

Parramatta 28 (J.Simon, P.Johnston, J.McCracken, S.Collins, S.Whereat tries; I.Herron 4 goals) defeated **Gold Coast** 10 (T.O'Reilly, C.Bowen tries; B.Hurst goal) at Parramatta Stadium, Sunday, April 27.

Scrums: Gold Coast 7–5. Penalties: Parramatta 8–4. Crowd: 10,093. Referee: Matt Hewitt. Halftime: Parramatta 24–6. Goalkickers: Herron (Parramatta) 4/5, Hurst (Gold Coast) 1/2. Seconds: Parramatta 36–0. Under-20s: Parramatta 42–2.
PARRAMATTA: Riolo; Herron, Kelly, Carige, Whereat; Bell, Simon; Johnston, Campbell, Morgan, Horsnell, McCracken (c), Dymock. Interchange: Collins, Pay, Brown, Lovell.
GOLD COAST: McKelleher; Dwyer, Mackay, Bai, Anderson; O'Reilly, Patten; Bella, Goddard, Driscoll, Sattler, Hurst, Schloss. Interchange: Bowen, Nahi, Plowman, Des Clark.
Cited: Anderson (Gold Coast). **Charge:** Dangerous throw. **Sentence:** Two weeks.

STANDINGS: Manly 14, Newcastle 12, Sydney City 10, Norths 9, Illawarra 9, Balmain 8, St George 8, Gold Coast 6, Wests 6, Parramatta 6, Souths 6, South Queensland 2.

OPTUS CUP ROUND 9
MAY 2, 3, 4

Twelve-try epic in Wollongong

It was the day WIN Stadium rained tries. In a match that proved to be a wonderfully absorbing contest, there were 12 tries in all, many of them highly spectacular efforts. When referee David Manson signalled fulltime, Manly and Illawarra had equalled a longstanding premiership record for the highest-scoring draw — 34-all. For the Sea Eagles it was something of a Houdini act. Down by 12 points with just six minutes left on the clock, the premiers conjured two late converted tries to draw level. They were aided first by the dismissal of teenage Illawarra five-eighth Trent Barrett, who was sent off in the 66th minute for a high tackle on Steve Menzies, and then by the sin-binning of replacement forward David Cox three minutes later.

Early in the match, Manly looked capable of winning in a canter, after scoring 12 points in even time. But by halftime, the Steelers had fought back to level at 18-all. Three Illawarra tries in the early stages of the second half gave the home side an apparently unassailable lead, but then Barrett and Cox were dismissed, giving Manly the opportunity to storm home.

North Sydney continued a purple patch of form with a slick 20-6 defeat of Western Suburbs in the Friday night match at North Sydney Oval. After a dogged opening, Norths took control midway through the first half, and a disappointing Wests did not get another look in.

The Bears led 8-6 at halftime and scored two second-half tries (Seers, Taylor) to cruise to victory. Seers' try was the highlight of the match. From a standing start, the diminutive fullback accelerated through the Magpie defence and raced 30 metres to score.

Balmain had nothing to show for 80 minutes of grind against Sydney City, going down 18-14 in a tough showdown at Leichhardt Oval.

The Tigers led 10-0 early after two tries and a conversion to improving winger Michael Withers, but Wayne Pearce's men then committed the cardinal sin of conceding tries on either side of halftime, and this proved a killer for them. First Brad Fittler and Luke Ricketson combined for a Ben Duckworth try a minute before the break, and then Shane Rigon won the race for a Ricketson kick-through five minutes after the resumption and levelled the scores. An Ivan Cleary try six minutes later gave Sydney City a six-point lead from which they were never headed.

The rapidly improving Gold Coast Chargers made the Newcastle Knights look decidedly second-rate in a 32-24 result in wet conditions at Carrara Stadium. The score was not an accurate reflection of the trend of the match. Gold Coast led 32-6 before the Knights ran in three late tries.

At the Sydney Football Stadium, in another high-scoring event, Parramatta struggled for the full distance to put South Sydney away. The Eels ultimately had the class, and won the match 32-26, but not before the Rabbitohs produced one of their grittier efforts of the season.

St George were guilty of committing almost every fundamental error in the book before escaping with a 32-22 win over the South Queensland Crushers at Kogarah Oval. Saints were their own worst enemies; the Crushers led from the 18th to the 72nd minute before two late tries to hooker Nathan Brown allowed Saints to emerge with the two points.

ROUND 9 — RESULTS

Norths 20 (B.Dallas, M.Seers, J.Taylor tries; Taylor 4 goals) defeated **Wests** 6 (D.Willis try; A.Leeds goal) at North Sydney Oval, Friday night, May 2.

Scrums: Norths 11–6. Penalties: 8–7. Crowd: 13,554. Referee: Kelvin Jeffes. Halftime: Norths 8–6. Goalkickers: Taylor (Norths) 4/6, Leeds (Wests) 1/1. Seconds: Norths 20–10. Under-20s: Norths 17–10.
NORTHS: Seers; Dallas, Ikin, Buettner, Roy; Florimo, Taylor (c); Stuart, Soden, Trindall, Larson, Fairleigh, Moore. Interchange: Caruana, Williams, Leyshon, Hall.
WESTS: Leeds; D.Willis, Ken McGuinness, Pearson, Laing; Doyle, Georgallis; Howard, Mescia, Skandalis, Dunn, Millard, Langmack (c). Interchange: Kevin McGuinness, Kennedy, Hasler, J.Smith.
Cited: Larson (Norths). **Charge:** Dangerous throw. **Sentence:** Two weeks.

Parramatta 32 (S.Whereat 2, I.Horron, J.Smith, S.Collins tries; Herron 6 goals) defeated **Souths** 26 (B.O'Meara, S.Donato, D.Trindall, P.Stimson, M.Moore tries; Trindall 3 goals) at Sydney Football Stadium, Saturday, May 3.

Scrums: Souths 7–5. Penalties: 9–all. Crowd: 6219. Referee: Eddie Ward. Halftime: Parramatta 18–16. Goalkickers: Herron (Parramatta) 6/7, Trindall (Souths) 3/5. Seconds: Parramatta 28–6. Under-20s: Parramatta 21–8.
PARRAMATTA: Riolo; Herron, Kelly, Carige, Whereat; Bell, J.Simon; Johnston, Brown, Morgan, Horsnell, McCracken (c), Dymock. Interchange: Pay, Smith, Campbell, Collins.
SOUTHS: O'Meara; Moore, Wilson, Howlett, Waugh; Murray, Trindall (c); Ostini, Donato, Stimson, Sutton, Slattery, Burns. Interchange: Gillard, Driscoll, C.Simon, Quinn.

Gold Coast 32 (J.Schloss 3, A.King, W.Patten, T.O'Reilly tries; B.Hurst 3, G.Mackay goals) defeated **Newcastle** 24 (J.Moodie 2, E.Cochrane, M.Hughes tries; L.Dynevor 4 goals) at Carrara Stadium, Saturday night, May 3.

Scrums: Gold Coast 4–2. Penalties: Newcastle 6–4. Crowd: 4900. Referee: Sean Hampstead. Halftime: Gold Coast 24–6. Goalkickers: Hurst (Gold Coast) 3/5, Mackay (Gold Coast) 1/1, Dynevor (Newcastle) 4/4. Seconds: Gold Coast 10–6. Under-20s: Gold Coast 24–18.
GOLD COAST: King; Dwyer, Mackay (c), McKelleher, Bai; O'Reilly, Patten; Des Clark, Goddard, Driscoll, Sattler, Hurst, Schloss. Interchange: Nahi, Parsons, Plowman, Orr.
NEWCASTLE: O'Davis; Albert, Moodie, Craigie, Cochrane; Gidley, Dynevor; Butterfield (c), Jackson, Richards, Peden, Muir, Glanville. Interchange: Harragon, Hughes, Fletcher, Conley.

Sydney City 18 (B.Duckworth, S.Higon, I.Cleary tries; Cleary 3 goals) defeated **Balmain** 14 (M.Withers 2, J.Webber tries; Withers goal) at Leichhardt Oval, Sunday, May 4.

Scrums: Sydney City 6–4. Penalties: 8–all. Crowd: 11,953. Referee: Paul Simpkins. Halftime: Balmain 10–4. Goalkickers: Cleary (Sydney City) 3/5, Withers (Balmain) 1/4. Seconds: Sydney City 28–24. Under-20s: Balmain 26–12.
BALMAIN: Brasher; L.Milford, Kennedy, Webber, Withers; Gillett, Jolly; Starr, Senter, Sironen (c), Stimson, O'Neil, Morrison. Interchange: Walker, Smith, McPherson, A.Milford.
SYDNEY CITY: Cleary; Elsegood, Sing, Rigon, Clarke; Walker, Lam; Lowrie, Garlick, Hermansson, Ricketson, Gourley, Fittler (c). Interchange: Logan, Duckworth, Wood, Gaffey.

Illawarra 34 (B.Mackay, T.Barnett, J.Cross, B.Reeves, S.Cram, S.Timmins tries; D.Bradstreet 3, Reeves 2 goals) drew with **Manly** 34 (C.Innes 3, T.Hill 2, D.Moore tries; C.Field 5 goals) at WIN Stadium, Sunday, May 4.

Scrums: 4–all. Penalties: Manly 6–4. Crowd: 9835. Referee: David Manson. Halftime: 18–all. Goalkickers: Bradstreet (Illawarra) 3/4, Reeves (Illawarra) 2/3, Field (Manly) 5/6. Seconds: Manly 42–10. Under-20s: Manly 8–6.
ILLAWARRA: Reeves; Seru, Rodwell, Timmins, Clifford; Barrett, Air; Smith, Robinson, Bradstreet, Bristow, Mackay, J.Cross (c). Interchange: Cram, David, Cox, Purcell.
MANLY: Hancock; Moore, Innes, Hill, Hopoate; Toovey (c); Field, Carroll, Fulton, Tierney, Menzies, Serdaris, Kosef. Interchange: Gillespie, Lyons, Weepu.
Sin bin: Cox (Illawarra), Serdaris (Manly).
Sent off: Barrett (Illawarra), 66 min. **Charge:** High tackle. **Sentence:** Two weeks.

St George 32 (M.Bell 3, N.Brown 2, M.Coyne tries; W.Bartrim 4 goals) defeated **South Queensland** 22 (M.Eagar, C.Schifcofske, C.Wilson, A.Hamilton tries; Schifcofske 3 goals) at Kogarah Oval, Sunday, May 4.

Scrums: St George 7–5. Penalties: South Queensland 7–6. Crowd: 5003. Referee: Matt Hewitt. Halftime: South Queensland 14–10. Goalkickers: Bartrim (St George) 4/7, Schifcofske (Crushers) 3/6. Seconds: St George 30–10. Under-20s: St George 22–18.
ST GEORGE: D.Smith; Bell, Coyne (c), Ainscough, Brunker, Konward, Kusto, Hearn, Brown, Ward, D.Smith, Treacy, Bartrim. Interchange: Pearson, Lenihan, Saukuru, Tangata-Toa.
SOUTH QUEENSLAND: Hubbard; Hudson, Toshack, Eagar, Schifcofske; Cairns, Antonik; O'Brien, Teevan (c), Retchless, Hamilton, Protheroe, Wilson. Interchange: Bickerstaff, Tookey, Couper.
Sin bin: B.Smith (St George).

> **STANDINGS:** Manly 15, Sydney City 12, Newcastle 12, Norths 11, Illawarra 10, St George 10, Balmain 8, Gold Coast 8, Parramatta 8, Wests 6, Souths 6, South Queensland 2.

ROUND 9   67

OPTUS CUP ROUND 10

MAY 9, 10, 11, JULY 13

Roosters' warm winter night

The first icy blast of winter livened up supporters of Sydney City and St George at the Sydney Football Stadium, but by fulltime of this Round 10 clash it was the Roosters who had warmed their fans with a steady-as-she-goes 22-8 victory. With front-line forwards Terry Hermansson and Jason Lowrie ploughing through the rucks, the Roosters always looked the better side, although Saints showed plenty of courage to hang in until the late stages. Halfback Adrian Lam continued his strong comeback from a shoulder operation with another man of the match award, and looked ready to take on an important role for Queensland's State of Origin side.

The crushing blow for Saints came 12 minutes from fulltime when centre Jacin Sinclair snatched a rebound from an Ivan Cleary penalty attempt and crossed unopposed next to the posts.

A 26-all draw with the Gold Coast Chargers on a day of abysmal weather left premiers Manly without a winning result for three weeks. The salvaging of one point turned out to be a blessing for Manly, though, despite the fact that they scored six tries to the Chargers' four.

The Gold Coast troubled Manly from the outset, led for almost the entire match, and looked to be headed for their first win at Brookvale Oval when they held a 26-18 lead three minutes from fulltime.

Skilful Parramatta forward Jason Smith bounced back to his best as the Eels continued their winning surge with a 25-14 defeat of Balmain in pouring rain at Parramatta Stadium. Balmain led 8-6 at halftime, but the sin-binning of Test fullback Tim Brasher and injuries to key forwards Paul Sironen and Darren Senter were critical to the outcome. With Smith in control, the Eels raced to a 20-8 lead midway through the second half, and headed towards their fourth successive win.

A strong southerly wind and driving rain made conditions difficult at WIN Stadium, where Wests crafted a 6-2 win over Illawarra in a tough Saturday night match. The first half was scoreless and the only try of the game was scored in the 58th minute by 36-year-old Des Hasler, when he burrowed beneath the Illawarra defence.

The South Queensland Crushers paid heavily for an appalling lapse in concentration late in the first half of their 36-22 loss to North Sydney at Suncorp Stadium.

Leading 8-2 after half an hour of their best football of the season, the Crushers collapsed to trail 20-8 at halftime. Halfback Jason Taylor spearheaded Norths' fightback and played a hand in four of his team's six tries as well as landing six goals from seven attempts.

* Newcastle's Round 10 clash with South Sydney was postponed after Marathon Stadium was deluged by rain on May 11, but when the match was eventually played two months later, as part of the split Round 16, conditions were little better. A record low Marathon Stadium crowd of 6,177 braved cold and rain to watch halfback Andrew Johns inspire the Knights' 30-0 victory. Coming off the bench after playing for Australia against the Rest of the World 48 hours earlier, Johns was in dazzling touch.

ROUND 10 — RESULTS

Sydney City 22 (A.Walker, J.Elsegood, J.Sinclair, A.Lam tries; I.Cleary 3 goals) defeated **St George** 8 (W.Bartrim try; Bartrim 2 goals) at Sydney Football Stadium, Friday night, May 9.

Scrums: 6–all. Penalties: Sydney City 7–5. Crowd: 9238. Referee: David Manson. Halftime: Sydney City 12–6. Goalkickers: Cleary (Sydney City) 3/6, Bartrim (St George) 2/2. Seconds: St George 20–10. Under-20s: Sydney City 18–16.
SYDNEY CITY: Cleary; Elsegood, Sinclair, Sing, Bourke; Walker, Lam; Bourke, Garlick, Lowrie, Gourley, Ricketson, Fittler (c). Interchange: Wood, Barnhill, Duckworth, Logan.
ST GEORGE: D.Smith; Bell, Coyne (c), Ainscough, Brunker; Kenward, Kusto; Ward, Brown, Hearn, Tangata-Toa, Treacy, Bartrim. Interchange: Lenihan, Pearson, B.Smith.
Cited: Gourley (Sydney City). **Charge:** High tackle. **Sentence:** Two weeks.

Norths 36 (J.Stuart, B.Dallas, N.Roy, M.Soden, W.Leyshon, D.Hall tries; J.Taylor 6 goals) defeated **South Queensland** 22 (J.Hudson 2, M.Bickerstaff, M.Toshack tries; C.Schifcofske 3 goals) at Suncorp Stadium, Saturday May 10.

Scrums: Norths 7–4. Penalties: South Queensland 5–2. Crowd: 5447. Referee: Eddie Ward. Halftime: Norths 20–8. Goalkickers: Taylor (Norths) 6/7, Schifcofske (South Qld) 3/5. Seconds: 16–all. Under-20s: Norths 16–14.
NORTHS: Seers; Dallas, Ikin, Buettner, Roy; Florimo, Taylor (c); Stuart, Soden, Trindall, Williams, Fairleigh, Moore. Interchange: Caruana, Hall, Leyshon, Pomery.
SOUTH QUEENSLAND: Hubbard; Hudson, Toshack, Eagar, Schifcofske; Saunders, Antonik; O'Brien, Teevan (c), Retchless, Bickerstaff, Protheroe, Wilson. Interchange: Couper, Tookey, Sologinkin, Watson.
Sin bin: Hall (Norths).

Wests 6 (D.Hasler try; A.Leeds goal) defeated **Illawarra** 2 (D.Bradstreet goal) at WIN Stadium, Saturday night, May 10.

Scrums: Wests 6–5. Penalties: Illawarra 10–7. Crowd: 5546. Referee: Sean Hampstead. Halftime: 0–all. Goalkickers: Leeds (Wests) 1/3, Bradstreet (Illawarra) 1/3. Seconds: Illawarra 16–12. Under-20s: Wests 14–8.
WESTS: Leeds; P.Smith, Ken McGuinness, Donovan, Laing; Kevin McGuinness, Georgallis; Howard, Hasler, Skandalis, Dunn, Kennedy, Langmack (c). Interchange: Doyle, J.Smith, Millard, Taylor.
ILLAWARRA: Reeves; Seru, Timmins, Rodwell, Clifford; Purcell, Air; Bradstreet, Robinson, Smith, David, Bristow, J.Cross (c). Interchange: Cram, Cox, Hart, Hooper.
Sin bin: Leeds (Wests), Reeves (Illawarra).

Parramatta 25 (J.Bell, J.Simon, S.Kelly, J.Dymock tries; Simon 3, I.Herron goals; Simon field goal) defeated **Balmain** 14 (J.Webber, W.Kennedy tries; M.Withers 3 goals) at Parramatta Stadium, Saturday night, May 10.

Scrums: Parramatta 8–7. Penalties: Balmain 8–6. Crowd: 11,150. Referee: Paul Simpkins. Halftime: Balmain 8–6. Goalkickers: Simon (Parramatta) 3/4, Herron (Parramatta) 1/3, Withers (Balmain) 3/3. Seconds: Balmain 30–16. Under-20s: Balmain 32–14.
PARRAMATTA: Riolo; Herron, Kelly, Carige, Whereat; Bell, Simon; Johnston, Raper, Pay (c), Jason Smith, Horsnell, Dymock. Interchange: Morgan, Koina, Collins, Barnes.
BALMAIN: Brasher; L.Milford, Kennedy, Webber, Withers; Gillett, Jolly; Starr, Senter, Sironen (c), Stimson, Smith, Morrison. Interchange: McPherson, A.Milford, O'Neil.
Cited: Johnston (Parramatta). **Charge:** Two dangerous tackles. **Sentence:** Exonerated.

Manly 26 (C.Innes 2, C.Hancock, A.Hunter, S.Menzies, C.Lyons tries; C.Field goal) drew with **Gold Coast** 26 (G.Mackay, J.Schloss, J.McKelleher, J.Nicol tries; B.Hurst 5 goals) at Brookvale Oval, Sunday, May 11.

Scrums: Manly 7–6. Penalties: 11–all. Crowd: 2506. Referee: Kelvin Jeffes. Halftime: Gold Coast 14–10. Goalkickers: Field (Manly) 1/6, Hurst (Gold Coast) 5/6, Orr (Gold Coast) 0/1. Seconds: Manly 20–6. Under-20s: Gold Coast 22–8.
MANLY: Hancock; Moore, Innes, Hill, Hunter, Toovey (c); Field, Tierney, Serdaris, Carroll, Menzies, Hopoate, Kosef. Interchange: Gillespie, Lyons, Fulton.
GOLD COAST: King; Dwyer, Mackay (c), McKelleher, Bai; O'Reilly, Patten; Des Clark, Goddard, Driscoll, Sattler, Hurst, Schloss. Interchange: Parsons, Orr, Nicol, Smith.
Sin bin: Tierney (Manly).

Newcastle 30 (R.O'Davis 2, B.Peden 2, O.Craigie tries; A.Johns 5 goals) defeated **South Sydney** 0, at Marathon Stadium, Sunday, July 13 (postponed from Sunday, May 11).

Scrums: South 7–6. Penalties: Newcastle 8–6. Crowd: 6177. Referee: Sean Hampstead. Halftime: Newcastle 6–0. Goalkickers: A.Johns (Newcastle) 5/6. Seconds: Souths 14–4. Under-20s: Souths 26–16.
NEWCASTLE: O'Davis; Albert, Hughes, Craigie, Cochrane; M.Johns, Dynevor; Butterfield, Clements, Harragon (c), Peden, Muir, Glanville. Interchange: A.Johns, Fletcher, Conley, Jackson.
SOUTH SYDNEY: O'Meara; Moore, Murray, Howlett, Orford; O'Neill, Trindall (c); Parsons, Donato, Ostini, Burns, Glassle, Gillard. Interchange: Slattery, Penna, Francis, Peters.
Sin bin: Trindall (Souths).

STANDINGS: Manly 16, Sydney City 14, Norths 13, Newcastle 12*, Illawarra 10, St George 10, Parramatta 10, Gold Coast 9, Balmain 8, Wests 8, Souths 6*, South Queensland 2. * Newcastle and Souths did not play until July 13. These standings do not include the Knights' two points from that match.

ROUND 10

OPTUS CUP ROUND 11
MAY 16, 17, 18

Norths move to second

North Sydney snatched a 19-18 win from Sydney City in a high-energy duel before a healthy crowd at North Sydney Oval. After running up a 14-4 lead just before halftime, the Bears appeared headed for disaster when second-rower Danny Williams was sent to the sin bin early in the second half for holding down Roosters prop Terry Hermansson. Sydney City responded quickly with a try to centre Peter Clarke, and they scored again through Matt Sing, even though Norths were back to 13 men.

The Bears' fortunes changed when the Roosters lost Ivan Cleary and Terry Hermansson — Cleary to the sin bin for a professional foul, and Hermansson off for a high tackle. With 13 playing 11, Norths took little time to gain an advantage. A try to second-rower David Fairleigh levelled the scores seven minutes from fulltime, and halfback Jason Taylor succeeded with his second attempt at field goal two minutes from the end.

The return of the Johns brothers provided a reversal of fortunes for the Newcastle Knights, who scored a valuable 26-18 win over Balmain at Leichhardt Oval to stay in touch with the leading group of teams. Halfback Andrew Johns was playing his first game since injuring his ankle pre-season, while Matthew was back after a five-week lay-off with an injured thigh. Coach Malcolm Reilly used the pair in stages as they battled to regain match fitness, but their periodic presence was enough to inspire their team to victory. Winger Darren Albert and fullback Robbie O'Davis were among the Knights' best, with O'Davis escaping the clutches of Test fullback Tim Brasher to score a crucial try.

Parramatta's winning run continued with a 17-10 win over St George, despite a night of heavy rain and a field of mud at Kogarah Oval. On the eve of State of Origin selection, Eels' lock Jim Dymock produced his best form, contributing some clever ballwork along with a kicking game that kept St George guessing all night. With John Simon calling the shots at halfback, and Dymock working his magic on the fringe of the rucks, Parramatta had begun to achieve the balance that had been missing since the arrival of $9 million worth of talent during the preceding 12 months.

Illawarra sank further into the mire with an 11-10 loss to the Gold Coast on a wet and dismal night at Carrara Stadium.

A late field goal to Gold Coast second-rower Brendan Hurst gave the home side a well-deserved victory.

South Sydney caused Manly a few early problems at the Sydney Football Stadium before a late surge saw the premiers claim a 30-16 victory.

Souths scored three tries to lead 16-8 at halftime, but the second half was all Manly. Winger Andrew Hunter put the Sea Eagles within striking distance soon after the resumption, then second-rower Steve Menzies crossed for a hat-trick (50 min, 66 min and 79 min) to leave the Rabbitohs reeling. New recruit Julian O'Neill came off the bench in his first appearance for South Sydney.

Western Suburbs skipper Paul Langmack overcame a heavy knock early in his team's clash with South Queensland to play a leading role in their 32-12 victory. Wests led 14-4 at the break, but powered home with three tries in the final 30 minutes.

ROUND 11 — RESULTS

Parramatta 17 (N.Barnes, S.Whereat, J.Smith tries; J.Simon 2 goals; Simon field goal) defeated **St George** 10 (M.Coyne, A.Brunker tries; W.Bartrim goal) at Kogarah Oval, Friday night, May 16.

Scrums: Parramatta 9–7. Penalties: Parramatta 9–8. Crowd: 5504. Referee: Kelvin Jeffes. Halftime: Parramatta 13–0. Goalkickers: Simon (Parramatta) 2/6, Bartrim (St George) 1/2. Seconds: St George 20–6. Under-20s: Parramatta 13–6.
PARRAMATTA: Collins; Barnes, Kelly, Carige, Whereat; Bell, Simon; Johnston, Raper, Pay (c), Jason Smith, Horsnell, Dymock. Interchange: Riolo, Morgan, Lovell, Campbell.
ST GEORGE: D.Smith; Bell, Coyne (c), Ainscough, Brunker; Kenward, Kusto; Hearn, Brown, Ward, Tangata-Toa, Treacy, Bartrim. Interchange: Pearson, Hardy, Rameka, Clinch.

Newcastle 26 (D.Albert 2, J.Moodie, R.O'Davis, L.Dynevor tries; A.Johns 2, Dynevor goals) defeated **Balmain** 18 (M.Gillett, J.Webber, S.Jolly tries; T.Brasher 2, M.Withers goals) at Leichhardt Oval, Saturday, May 17.

Scrums: 5–all. Penalties: Balmain 7–5. Crowd: 5323. Referee: Eddie Ward. Halftime 10–all. Goalkickers: Johns (Newcastle) 2/3, Dynevor (Newcastle) 1/3, Brasher (Balmain) 2/2, Withers (Balmain) 1/3. Seconds: Balmain 14–12. Under-20s: 24–all.
NEWCASTLE: O'Davis; Albert, Gidley, Craigie, Moodie; M.Johns, Dynevor; Butterfield, Jackson, Harragon (c), Richards, Muir, Glanville. Interchange A.Johns, Fletcher, Peden, O'Doherty.
BALMAIN: Brasher; L.Milford, Kennedy, Webber, Withers; Gillett, Jolly; Starr, Senter, Sironen (c), Stimson, Smith, Morrison. Interchange: Walker, O'Neil, A.Milford.
Cited: Muir (Newcastle). **Charge:** Dangerous throw. **Sentence:** Exonerated.

Gold Coast 11 (J.Goddard, G.Mackay tries; B.Hurst goal; Hurst field goal) defeated **Illawarra** 10 (S.Timmins, W.Robinson tries; R.Wishart goal) at Carrara Stadium, Saturday night, May 17.

Scrums: Illawarra 6–4. Penalties: Gold Coast 9–2. Crowd: 5813. Referee: David Manson. Halftime: Gold Coast 6–4. Goalkickers: Hurst (Gold Coast) 1/3, Wishart (Illawarra) 1/2. Seconds: Gold Coast 13–8. Under-20s: Gold Coast 00 £0.
GOLD COAST: King; Dwyer, Mackay (c), McKelleher, Bai; O'Reilly, Patten; Des Clark, Goddard, Driscoll, Sattler, Hurst, Schloss. Interchange: Nahi, Parsons, Orr, Nicol.
ILLAWARRA: Seru; Wishart, McGregor (c), Rodwell, Olifford; Timmins, Robinson, Cram, J.Cross, Smith, Bristow, Bradstreet, Hart. Interchange: Reeves, Cox, David, M.Cross.
Cited: David (Illawarra). **Charge:** Careless high tackle. **Sentence:** Six weeks. **Cited:** Smith (Illawarra). **Charge:** High tackle. **Sentence:** $5000 fine.

Norths 19 (N.Roy, M.Seers, D.Fairleigh tries; J.Taylor 3 goals; Taylor field goal) defeated **Sydney City** 18 (G.Bourke, P.Clarke, M.Sing tries; I.Cleary 3 goals) at North Sydney Oval, Sunday, May 18.

Scrums: Sydney City 9–5. Penalties: Sydney City 9–8. Crowd: 14,644. Referee: Paul Simpkins. Halftime: Norths 14–6. Goalkickers: Taylor (Norths) 3/5, Cleary (Sydney City) 3/5. Seconds: Sydney City 16–12. Under-20s: Sydney City 14–10.
NORTHS: Seers; Dallas, Caruana, Buettner, Roy; Florimo, Taylor (c); Stuart, Soden, Trindall, Williams, Fairleigh, Moore. Interchange: Ikin, Hall, Leyshon, Pomery.
SYDNEY CITY: Cleary; Elsegood, Sing, Clarke, Bourke; Walker, Lam; Lowrie, Garlick (c); Hermansson, Ricketson, Barnhill, Duckworth. Interchange: Wood, Logan, Sinclair, Troy.
Sin bin: Williams (Norths), Cleary (Sydney City).
Sent off: Hermansson (Sydney City) 75 min. **Charge:** Striking. **Sentence:** Exonerated.

Wests 32 (Ken McGuinness 2, Kevin McGuinness, B.Dunn, D.Hasler, D.Willis tries; A.Leeds 4 goals) defeated **South Queensland** 12 (M.Eagar, D.Watson, C.Schifcofske tries) at Campbelltown Sports Ground, Sunday, May 18.

Scrums: Wests 6–5. Penalties: Wests 9–7. Crowd: 5732. Referee: Matt Hewitt. Halftime: Wests 14–4. Goalkickers: Leeds (Wests) 4/7, Schifcofske (South Queensland) 0/3. Seconds: South Queensland 28–6. Under-20s: Wests 22–10.
WESTS: Leeds; D.Willis, Ken McGuinness, Kevin McGuinness, Laing; Doyle, Georgallis; Howard, Hasler, Skandalis, Dunn, Kennedy, Langmack (c). Interchange: Millard, J.Smith, Hodgson.
SOUTH QUEENSLAND: Watson; Hudson, Toshack, Eagar, Schifcofske; Saunders, Antonik; O'Brien, Teevan (c), Retchless, Bickerstaff, Protheroe, Wilson. Interchange: Sologinkin, Nutley, Moule.

Manly 30 (S.Menzies 3, T.Hill, A.Hunter, J.Hopoate tries; C.Innes 2, C.Field goals) defeated **Souths** 16 (P.Howlett, M.Ostini, S.Donato tries; D.Trindall 2 goals) at Sydney Football Stadium, Sunday, May 18.

Scrums: Manly 8–6. Penalties: Manly 8–7. Crowd: 6020. Referee: Sean Hampstead. Halftime: Souths 16–8. Goalkickers: Innes (Manly) 2/3, Field (Manly) 1/3, Trindall (Souths) 2/2, O'Neill (Souths) 0/1. Seconds: Souths 20–10. Under-21s: Souths 21–20.
MANLY: Hancock; Moore, Innes, Hill, Hunter; Toovey (c); Field; Gillespie, Serdaris, Carroll, Menzies, Hopoate, Kosef. Interchange: Lyons, Fulton, Tierney.
SOUTHS: Amos; O'Keefe, Howlett, O'Meara, Moore; Murray, Trindall (c); Ostini, Donato, Stimson, Quinn, Slattery, Burns. Interchange: O'Neill, Driscoll, Sutton, Simon.
Sin bin: Stimson (Souths).

STANDINGS: Manly 18, Norths 15, Sydney City 14, Newcastle 14*, Parramatta 12, Gold Coast 11, Illawarra 10, Wests 10, St George 10, Balmain 8, Souths 6*, South Queensland 2. * Newcastle and Souths had a match in hand.

OPTUS CUP ROUND 12
MAY 23, 24, 25, 30, 31, JUNE 1

Tigers recall glory days

On one of the most dramatic afternoons of the 1997 season, Balmain produced a display reminiscent of the Tigers of the late 1980s to end Manly's longstanding undefeated record at Brookvale Oval. Manly were beaten on home soil for the first time since 1995. The Tigers reversed their first-round 14-10 loss to Manly and recorded their first win at Brookvale since 1984. They led 12-0 at halftime and turned in an outstanding second-half defensive effort as Manly's troops rallied.

With a two-week build-up to the match because of the split round, Balmain began at maximum intensity and were able to penetrate the Manly defence for two first-half tries (Kennedy and Langaloa). Manly had six players backing up after the first State of Origin match and had difficulty matching the Tigers' enthusiasm.

Referee Paul Simpkins battled hard to keep a lid on simmering emotions and he ended up sin-binning Cliff Lyons and Tim Brasher for fighting, Ellery Hanley for a professional foul and John Hopoate for dissent. Balmain players James Langaloa and William 'Bubba' Kennedy were reported for lifting in a tackle, and Manly's Scott Fulton for a high tackle. In another dramatic moment, Manly's giant forward Billy Weepu had to be assisted from the field when he slammed his head into the turf after a legitimate three-man Balmain tackle.

At Kogarah Oval, St George and Newcastle produced one of the more entertaining games of the season, which finished in a narrow 20-18 victory to Saints.

St George scored four tries to three and hung on to win after Knights' winger Darren Albert scored his second try late in the match. The game was guaranteed to carry plenty of feeling with former Knights Ainscough, Brunker, Tangata-Toa and Treacy, as well as coach David Waite, all plotting against their former club.

With five players backing up 48 hours after the first State of Origin match, Parramatta's winning surge continued with an impressive 25-14 win over Norths at North Sydney Oval.

Origin star John Simon was again involved in everything for Parramatta. With a try, a hand in two others, two goals and a field goal, his contribution was immense.

South Queensland broke through for their first win since Round 2 with a 28-14 upset defeat of Sydney City at Suncorp Stadium. The star for the Crushers was winger Clinton Schifcofske, the player who voluntarily stood down earlier in the season after admitting taking steroids.

At the Sydney Football Stadium, Moghseen Jadwat endured a baptism of fire in his debut as a first-grade referee when a questionable pass resulted in an Illawarra try and a 28-all draw with South Sydney. A pass from Illawarra replacement Chris Leikvoll which led to a try to winger Wayne Clifford looked to be forward, and the small but parochial South Sydney crowd were livid.

Western Suburbs veterans Des Hasler and Paul Langmack helped the Magpies into the top seven for the first time in 1997 when they led a 26-10 defeat of the Gold Coast at Carrara Stadium. Chargers' coach Phil Economidis produced one of the best quotes of the season when asked if there were any positives to emerge from the match. 'I'm positive a few of my blokes won't be there next week,' he quipped.

ROUND 12 — RESULTS

South Queensland 28 (C.Schifcofske 2, A.Moule, M.Protheroe, M.Bickerstaff tries; Schifcofske 4 goals) defeated **Sydney City** 14 (I.Cleary, S.Logan tries; I.Cleary 3 goals) at Suncorp Stadium, Friday night, May 23.

Scrums: Sydney City 7–5. Penalties: South Queensland 5–4. Crowd: 5518. Referee: Sean Hampstead. Halftime: South Queensland 12–6. Goalkickers: Schifcofske (South Queensland) 4/5, Cleary (Sydney City) 3/3. Seconds: South Queensland 13–6. Under-20s: South Queensland 23–18.
SOUTH QUEENSLAND: Watson; Hudson, Toshack, Eagar, Schifcofske; Moule, Antonik; O'Brien, Teevan (c), Retchless, Bickerstaff, Protheroe, Wilson. Interchange: Saunders, Nutley, Sologinkin, Tookey.
SYDNEY CITY: Cleary; Elsegood, Rigon, Gaffey, Bourke; Walker, Wood; Lowrie, Garlick (c), Hermansson, Ricketson, Barnhill, Duckworth. Interchange: Troy, Shearer, Logan, Sinclair.
Sin bin: Antonik (South Queensland).
Cited. Nutley (South Queensland). **Charge:** Striking. **Sentence:** Four weeks.

Wests 26 (D.Hasler, S.Millard, A.Doyle, J.Skandalis tries; A.Leeds 5 goals) defeated **Gold Coast** 10 (T.O'Reilly, S.Sattler tries; G.Mackay goal) at Campbelltown Sports Ground, Saturday, May 24.

Scrums: Gold Coast 8–6. Penalties: Gold Coast 10–6. Crowd: 5978. Referee: Eddie Ward. Halftime: Wests 14–6. Goalkickers: Leeds (Wests) 5/5, Mackay (Gold Coast) 1/2. Seconds: Gold Coast 19–12. Under-20s: 24–all.
WESTS: Leeds; D.Willis, Kevin McGuinness, Pearson, Laing; Doyle, Georgallis; J.Smith, Mescia, Howard, Kennedy, Dunn, Langmack (c). Interchange: Skandalis, Millard, Hodgson, Hasler.
GOLD COAST: King; Mackay (c), McKelleher, Nicol, Bai; O'Reilly, Patten; Des Clark, Orr, Parsons, Sattler, Hurst, Nahi. Interchange: Durheim, Whittaker, Blackett, Napoli.

Souths 28 (D.Trindall, P.Sutton, C.Simon, P.Howlett, M.Moore tries; J.O'Neill 4 goals) drew with **Illawarra** 28 (D.Bradstreet, B.Reeves, D.Cox, W.Robinson, W.Clifford tries; Bradstreet 2, Reeves 2 goals) at Sydney Football Stadium, Sunday, May 25.

Scrums: Illawarra 6–5. Penalties: Illawarra 5–4. Crowd: 4271. Referee: Mohseen Jadwat. Halftime: Illawarra 18–12. Goalkickers: O'Neill (Souths) 4/7, Bradstreet (Illawarra) 2/2, Reeves (Illawarra) 2/4. Seconds: Illawarra 26–16. Under-20s: Souths 22–10.
SOUTHS: McLeod; Moore, Murray, Howlett, O'Keefe; O'Neill, Trindall (c); Ostini, Donato, Stimson, Francis, Slattery, Burns. Interchange: Driscoll, Simon, Sutton, Orford.
ILLAWARRA: Reeves; Seru, Rodwell, Timmins, Clifford; Barrett, Robinson; Cram, J.Cross (c), Bradstreet, Bristow, Hart, Mackay. Interchange: Cox, Tunbridge, Lainey, Leikvoll.

Parramatta 25 (S.Whereat 2, S.Kelly, J.Simon, N.Barnes tries; Simon 2 goals; Simon field goal) defeated **Norths** 14 (B.Dallas, C.Caruana, M.Buettner tries; J.Taylor goal) at North Sydney Oval, Friday night, May 30.

Scrums: Parramatta 9–7. Penalties: Norths 5–3. Crowd: 13,281. Referee: David Manson. Halftime: Parramatta 13–6. Goalkickers: Simon (Parramatta) 2/5, Taylor (Norths) 1/4. Seconds: Norths 30–14. Under-20s: Parramatta 18–10.
PARRAMATTA: Carige; Navale, Kelly, Barnes, Whereat; Bell, Simon; Johnston, Raper, Pay (c), McCracken, Jason Smith, Dymock. Interchange: Campbell, Morgan, Horsnell, Lovell.
NORTHS: Seers; Dallas, Ikin, Buettner, Roy; Florimo, Taylor (c); Stuart, Soden, Trindall, Larson, Fairleigh, Moore. Interchange: Caruana, Hall, Leyshon, Williams.

Balmain 14 (W.Kennedy, J.Langaloa tries; M.Withers 3 goals) defeated **Manly** 10 (G.Toovey, J.Serdaris tries; C.Field goal) at Brookvale Oval, Saturday, May 31.

Scrums: 6–all. Penalties: Balmain 13–10. Crowd: 6068. Referee: Paul Simpkins. Halftime: Balmain 12–0. Goalkickers: Withers (Balmain) 3/6, Field (Manly) 1/2, Nevin (Manly) 0/1. Seconds: Manly 20–12. Under-20s: Manly 24–18.
BALMAIN: Brasher; Langaloa, Kennedy, Webber, Withers; Gillett, Jolly; Starr, Senter, Sironen (c), Stimson, Hanley, Morrison. Interchange: Walker, O'Neil, Smith, Nable.
MANLY: Nevin; Hancock, Innes, Hill, Hunter; Toovey (c); Field; Gillespie, Serdaris, Carroll, Menzies, Hopoate, Kosef. Interchange: Tierney, Weepu, Fulton, Lyons.
Sin bin: Hanley (Balmain), Brasher (Balmain), Hopoate (Manly), Lyons (Manly).
Cited: Langaloa (Balmain). **Charge:** Dangerous throw. **Sentence:** Two weeks. **Cited:** Kennedy (Balmain). **Charge:** Dangerous throw: **Sentence:** Exonerated.
Cited: Fulton (Manly). **Charge:** High tackle. **Sentence:** Exonerated.

St George 20 (M.Coyne, A.Brunker, W.Bartrim, C.Ward tries; Bartrim 2 goals) defeated **Newcastle** 18 (D.Albert 2, O.Craigie tries; L.Dynevor 3 goals) at Kogarah Oval, Sunday, June 1.

Scrums: St George 10–5. Penalties: St George 9–5. Crowd: 6125. Referee: Matt Hewitt. Halftime: Newcastle 10–6. Goalkickers: Bartrim (St George) 2/3, Clinch (St George) 0/1, Dynevor (Newcastle) 3/4. Seconds: St George 22–6. Under-20s: St George 18–16.
ST GEORGE: D.Smith; Bell, Coyne (c), Ainscough, Brunker; Hardy, Clinch; Pearson, Brown, Ward, Tangata-Toa, Treacy, Bartrim. Interchange: Thompson, Felsch, Lenihan, Kenward.
NEWCASTLE: O'Davis; Albert, Gidley, Craigie, Moodie; M.Johns, Dynevor; Butterfield, Jackson, Harragon (c), Peden, Muir, Fletcher. Interchange: Conley, Clements, Hughes, O'Doherty.

STANDINGS: Manly 19, Norths 15, Newcastle 14*, Sydney City 14, Parramatta 14, Wests 12, St George 12, Illawarra 11, Gold Coast 11, Balmain 10, Souths 7*, South Queensland 4. * Newcastle and Souths had a match in hand.

OPTUS CUP ROUND 13
JUNE 6, 7, 8, 13, 14, 15

Bears master Arctic winds

Two players were treated for hypothermia after some of the worst weather conditions ever experienced in a premiership match descended on the luckless Newcastle Knights at Marathon Stadium. Newcastle winger Darren Albert suffered dizziness and disorientation and Norths hooker Mark Soden also suffered symptoms of hypothermia in a match played in driving rain and an icy-cold southerly wind. North Sydney, though, proved themselves the masters of wet-weather football with a dominating 26-6 victory.

A crowd of 6,281 braved the Arctic conditions, but any joy Knights supporters had hoped to derive from the day was shortlived after a second-minute try to veteran front-rower Tony Butterfield and the conversion by Leo Dynevor. From that point, Norths dominated territory and possession and, in the appalling conditons, their halftime lead of 18-6 was a match-winning one. Knights officials estimated the weather cost the club $80,000 in lost gate receipts.

Manly winger John Hopoate turned in one of his most devastating performances to score a hat-trick of tries and help his team to a 28-4 defeat of St George at Brookvale Oval. The big Tongan winger had been much criticised for his on-field antics, but for the majority of this match, Hopoate let his football do the talking. Manly's Origin contingent showed few ill-effects from 80 minutes of football only 48 hours earlier, and Bob Fulton agreed that the team's defence was back at its best.

Western Suburbs helped coach Tom Raudonikis cap the finest week of his coaching career with a 24-18 win over Sydney City just three days after Raudonikis had helped steer NSW to a series victory over Queensland in his first season as Blues coach. Trailing 18-10 midway through the second half, Wests looked down and out until veteran Des Hasler came up with two tries to spark his team to life. A late try to centre Kevin McGuinness put a seal on the Magpies' best win of the season.

Illawarra rookie Scott Cram sent a giant scare through WIN Stadium when he had to be air-lifted to hospital suffering suspected spinal damage midway through his team's clash with Balmain.

News that the 20-year-old had been cleared of any serious damage eased some of the Steelers' pain after their 18-6 defeat. The winning point of the match for Balmain came in a two-minute period midway through the first half. A 95-metre try to 'Bubba' Kennedy, and another to winger Laloa Milford, gave the Tigers a 12-0 lead which they protected until late in the match. Trent Barrett scored, reducing Balmain's lead to six, but a late try to Adam Starr wrapped up the result for the Tigers.

Parramatta coach Brian Smith was forced to field virtually an entire second grade side against South Queensland at Parramatta Stadium, but any fears he may have harboured that his side's hard-earned six-match winning streak was in jeopardy were quickly dispelled. The Eels won 52-10.

Gold Coast continued their brave bid for a historic semi-final berth with a commanding 28-4 defeat of South Sydney at Carrara Stadium. Without State of Origin forwards Jamie Goddard and Jeremy Schloss, the Chargers were still able to dominate up front.

ROUND 13 — RESULTS

Balmain 18 (L.Milford, W.Kennedy, A.Starr tries; M.Withers 3 goals) defeated **Illawarra** 6 (T.Barrett try; D.Bradstreet goal) at WIN Stadium, Friday night, June 6.

Scrums: Balmain 7–5. Penalties: 7–all. Crowd: 8184. Referee: Matt Hewitt. Halftime: Balmain 12–0. Goalkickers: Withers (Balmain) 3/3, Bradstreet (Illawarra) 1/1. Seconds: Illawarra 27–20. Under-20s: Illawarra 26–10.

BALMAIN: Withers; Scott, Kennedy, Webber, L.Milford; Gillett, Jolly; Starr, Senter, Sironen (c), Stimson, O'Neil, Smith. Interchange: Walker, Rudd, St Clair, Donaghey.
ILLAWARRA: Reeves; Seru, Rodwell, Timmins, Clifford; Barrett, Robinson; Cram, Callaway, Bradstreet, Hart, Mackay, J.Cross (c). Interchange: Cox, Bristow, Leikvoll, Air.

Gold Coast 28 (G.Mackay 2, M.Bai, W.Patten, S.Russell tries; B.Hurst 4 goals) defeated **Souths** 4 (J.Orford try) at Carrara Stadium, Saturday, June 7.

Scrums: 7–all. Penalties: Gold Coast 6–3. Crowd: 5316. Referee: Paul Simpkins. Halftime: Gold Coast 12–0. Goalkickers: Hurst 4/5 (Gold Coast) Mackay (Gold Coast) 0/1, Trindall (South Sydney) 0/1. Seconds: Souths 20–10. Under-20s: Souths 32–30.

GOLD COAST: King; Bai, Nicol, Mackay (c), Russell; Orr, Patten; Des Clark, Dave Clark, Driscoll, Sattler, Nahi, Hurst. Interchange: Parsons, Durheim, O'Reilly, McKelleher.
SOUTHS: O'Meara; Moore, Murray, Howlett, Orford; Simon, Trindall (c); Ostini, Donato, Stimson, Francis, Slattery, Burns. Interchange: Driscoll, Sutton, Penna, Slockee.

Parramatta 52 (J.McCracken 2, N.Barnes 2, A.Frew, P.Carige, J.Morgan, J.Bell, B.Horsnell, K.Lovell tries; C.Lawler 6 goals) defeated **South Queensland** 10 (S.Retchless, J.Hudson tries; C.Schifcofske goal) at Parramatta Stadium, Sunday, June 8.

Scrums: Parramatta 6–5. Penalties: Parramatta 7–6. Crowd: 10,009. Referee: Sean Hampstead. Halftime: Parramatta 32–6. Goalkickers: Lawler (Parramatta) 6/10, Schifcofske (Crushers) 1/2. Seconds: South Queensland 17–16. Under-20s: Parramatta 25–24.

PARRAMATTA: Carige; Navale, Barnes, McCracken (c), Frew; Bell, Lawler; Johnston, Brown, Lovell, Campbell, Morgan, Horsnell. Interchange: Cayless, Keina, Jamie Smith, Douglas.
SOUTH QUEENSLAND: Watson; Hudson, Toshack, Eagar, Schifcofske; Moule, Antonik; Jones, Teevan (c), Retchless, Bickerstaff, Protheroe, Wilson. Interchange: Saunders, Sologinkin, Cruckshank, Pezet.

Manly 28 (J.Hopoate 3, C.Hancock, C.Field, C.Lyons tries; C.Innes 2 goals) defeated **St George** 4 (A.Brunker try) at Brookvale Oval, Friday night, June 13.

Scrums: Manly 7–6. Penalties: Manly 6–5. Crowd: 10,083. Referee: Kelvin Jeffes. Halftime: Manly 10–4. Goalkickers: Innes (Manly) 2/3, Field (Manly) 0/3, Lyons (Manly) 0/1, Bartrim (St George) 0/1. Seconds: St George 20–16. Under-20s: Manly 30–4.

MANLY: Hancock; Moore, Innes, Hill, Hopoate; Toovey (c), Field; Tierney, Serdaris, Carroll, Menzies, Gartner, Kosef. Interchange: Fulton, Nevin, Gillespie, Lyons.
ST GEORGE: D.Smith; Bell, Coyne (c), Ainscough, Brunker; Hardy, Clinch; Pearson, Brown, Ward, Tangata-Toa, Treacy, Bartrim. Interchange: Felsch, Thompson, Kenward, Lenihan.

Wests 24 (B.Hodgson 2, D.Hasler 2, Kevin McGuinness tries; A.Leeds 2 goals) defeated **Sydney City** 18 (A.Walker 2, B. Duckworth tries; I.Cleary 3 goals) at Campbelltown Sports Ground, Saturday, June 14.

Scrums: Sydney City 8–7. Penalties: Wests 6–4. Crowd: 6832. Referee: David Manson. Halftime: Sydney City 12–10. Goalkickers: Leeds (Wests) 2/5, Cleary (Sydney City) 3/3. Seconds: Sydney City 28–8. Under-20s: Wests 32–26.

WESTS: Leeds; D.Willis, Ken McGuinness, Kevin McGuinness, Hodgson; Doyle, Georgallis; Howard, Mescia, J.Smith, Dunn, Millard, Langmack (c). Interchange: Skandalis, Kennedy, Hasler, Capovilla.
SYDNEY CITY: Cleary; Elsegood, Sing, Clarke, Bourke; Walker, Lam (c); Lowrie, Garlick, Hermansson, Barnhill, Gourley, Ricketson. Interchange: Troy, Rigon, Duckworth, Wood.

Norths 26 (C.Caruana 2, B.Moore, N.Roy tries; J.Taylor 5 goals) defeated **Newcastle** 6 (T.Butterfield try; L.Dynevor goal) at Marathon Stadium, Sunday, June 15.

Scrums: Newcastle 8–7. Penalties: Newcastle 8–5. Crowd: 6281. Referee: Eddie Ward. Halftime: Norths 18–6. Goalkickers: Taylor (Norths) 5/5, Dynevor (Newcastle) 1/1. Seconds: Norths 12–10. Under-20s: Newcastle 17–10.

NORTHS: Seers, Dallas, Ikin, Caruana, Roy; Buettner, Taylor (c); Stuart, Soden, Trindall, Fairleigh, Florimo, Moore. Interchange: Pomery, Larson, Williams, McLean.
NEWCASTLE: O'Davis; Albert, Gidley, Craigie, Moodie; M.Johns, Dynevor; Butterfield, Jackson, Harragon (c), Peden, Muir, Glanville. Interchange: Fletcher, Conley, Smailes, Hughes.

STANDINGS: Manly 20, Norths 17, Parramatta 16, Sydney City 14, Newcastle 14*, Wests 14, Gold Coast 13, Balmain 12, St George 12, Illawarra 11, Souths 7*, South Queensland 4. * Newcastle and Souths had a match in hand.

OPTUS CUP ROUND 14
JUNE 20, 21, 22, JULY 27, 28, 29

Greg Florimo's finest day

North Sydney supporters invaded the field to congratulate their heroes after the Bears beat Manly 41-8, inflicting their biggest-ever defeat on their northside neighbours.

Speculation that Norths would merge with Manly in a rationalised competition in 1998 was a particularly sensitive issue among Norths players and fans, with the majority dead set against such a move. Such talk gave the Bears special motivation against the Sea Eagles, and they produced one of their best performances.

Leading the way was five-eighth Greg Florimo, who played what many regarded as the finest match of his career. Florimo scored a try (his first of the season) and had a hand in three others as the Bears converted a 14-4 lead at halftime into a 41-8 landslide.

After their undefeated start to the season, Manly, with half their side involved in representative football, had won just two of their previous seven games.

Parramatta made it eight wins in a row with a strong 18-6 defeat of Sydney City at the Sydney Football Stadium. The two premiership contenders slugged it out for the first 40 minutes before the Eels began to dominate in the second half with a display of class and character.

Second-rower Jarrod McCracken led the way with some tremendous defensive work and a number of strong breaks in attack. The loss was the Roosters' fourth in succession. They missed injured State of Origin centre Matt Sing, and Brad Fittler struggled for condition in his return from a broken thumb.

The rise and rise of the Gold Coast continued at Leichhardt Oval when the Chargers scored their second win of the year over Balmain. The Chargers won 22-20 after leading 22-12 early in the second half. Two tries to Papua New Guinea Test player Tom O'Reilly put the Chargers in the box seat soon after halftime, and the team withstood a strong fightback by Balmain late in the match. An on-field complaint by Balmain hooker Darren Senter to referee Matt Hewitt that he had been bitten was not included in Hewitt's match report, but ARL chief executive Neil Whittaker arranged the citing of Gold Coast second-rower Chris Nahi anyway.

The Newcastle Knights did enough to beat last-placed South Queensland 24-6 at Suncorp Stadium, but fell short of convincing anyone they were genuine premiership contenders. The Knights lacked direction in their attack and their kicking game was below its best — a factor caused primarily by the continued absence of halfback and playmaker Andrew Johns. After missing a large slice of the season through injury, Johns was now sidelined for two weeks after a suspension in the final State of Origin match. Fullback Robbie O'Davis picked up another players' player award for the Knights.

It took 78 minutes for Illawarra to assert their superiority on the scoreboard, despite outplaying St George for the majority of their clash at Kogarah Oval. Centre Brett Rodwell scored the winning try two minutes from fulltime, leading coach Andrew Farrar to label his team 'Cardiac Kids'.

A try 60 seconds from fulltime to rookie prop Matt Parsons gave South Sydney a richly deserved 20-16 win over Wests at Campbelltown Sports Ground. Halfback and skipper Darrell Trindall laid on three of Souths' four tries.

ROUND 14 — RESULTS

Souths 20 (J.Orford 2, D.Penna, M.Parsons tries; D.Trindall 2 goals) defeated **Wests** 16 (J.Skandalis, Kevin McGuinness tries; A.Leeds 4 goals) at Campbelltown Sports Ground, Friday night, June 20.

Scrums: 4–all. Penalties: 6–all. Crowd: 7937. Referee: Sean Hampstead. Halftime: Souths 10–8. Goalkickers: Trindall (Souths) 2/5, Leeds (Wests) 4/5. Seconds: Wests 14–8. Under-20s: Wests 28–24.
SOUTHS: O'Meara; Moore, Penna, Howlett, Orford; Murray, Trindall (c); Parsons, Donato, Ostini, Francis, Glassie, Burns. Interchange: Stimson, Slattery, Gillard, Simon.
WESTS: Leeds; Lomanimako, D.Willis, Kevin McGuinness, Hodgson; Doyle, Georgallis; Howard, Mescia, Skandalis, Millard, Kennedy, Langmack (c). Interchange: J.Smith, Dunn, Hasler, A.Willis.
Sin bin: Simon (Souths).

Gold Coast 22 (T.O'Reilly 2, Dave Clark, W.Patten tries; B.Hurst 3 goals) defeated **Balmain** 20 (M.Gillett 2, W.Kennedy tries; M.Withers 4 goals) at Leichhardt Oval, Saturday, June 21.

Scrums: Balmain 5–4. Penalties: Balmain 14–7. Crowd: 5752. Referee: Matt Hewitt. Halftime: 12–all. Goalkickers: Hurst (Gold Coast) 3/4, Withers (Balmain) 4/5. Seconds: Balmain 22–15. Under-20s: Balmain 18–16.
GOLD COAST: King; Bai, Mackay (c), Nicol, Russell; Orr, Patten; Parsons, Dave Clark, Plowman, Sattler, Nahi, Hurst. Interchange: Durheim, O'Reilly, Bella, McKelleher.
BALMAIN: Withers; Donaghey, Kennedy, Webber, L.Milford; Gillett, Jolly; Starr, Senter, Sironen (c), Stimson, O'Neil, Smith. Interchange: Morrison, Walker, St Clair.
Cited: Nahi (Gold Coast). **Charge:** Biting. **Sentence:** Exonerated.

Illawarra 12 (B.Rodwell 2, G.Air tries) defeated **St George** 10 (C.Ward, M.Bell tries; S.Price goal) at Kogarah Oval, Sunday, June 22.

Scrums: Illawarra 7–6. Penalties: Illawarra 9–7. Crowd: 7257. Referee: Paul Simpkins. Halftime: Illawarra 8–4. Goalkickers: Reeves (Illawarra) 0/2, Bradstreet (Illawarra) 0/2, Price (St George) 1/2, Clinch (St George) 0/2. Seconds: St George 20–18. Under-20s: St George 24–14.
ILLAWARRA: Reeves; Britten, Rodwell, Timmins, Clifford; Air, Robinson; Cram, Callaway, Bradstreet, Hart, Mackay, J.Cross (c). Interchange: Leikvoll, Lamey, Cox.
ST GEORGE: Raper; Bell, Wagon, Lenihan, Brunker; Kenward, Clinch; Pearson, Brown (c), Ward, Rameka, Thompson, Hardy. Interchange: Felsch, B.Smith, Price, Murphy.
Cited: Raper (St George). **Charge:** Abusing referee. **Sentence:** Two weeks.

Parramatta 18 (J.McCracken, S.Kelly tries; I.Herron 5 goals) defeated **Sydney City** 6 (P.Clarke try; I.Cleary goal) at Sydney Football Stadium, Friday night, June 27.

Scrums: Sydney City 5–3. Penalties: Sydney City 6–4. Crowd: 8917. Referee: Kelvin Jeffes. Halftime: Sydney City 6–4. Goalkickers: Herron (Parramatta) 5/5, Cleary (Sydney City) 1/2. Seconds: Parramatta 22–20. Under-20s: Parramatta 30–10.
PARRAMATTA: Carige; Herron, Barnes, Kelly, Navale; Bell, Simon; Johnston, Raper, Pay (c), Morgan, McCracken, Jason Smith. Interchange: Collins, Lovell, Campbell, Koina.
SYDNEY CITY: Cleary; Elsegood, Fittler (c), Walker, Miles; Hayden, Lam; Lowrie, Bonetti, Hermansson, Barnhill, Gourley, Ricketson. Interchange: Wood, Logan, Clarke, Rigon.
Cited: Pay (Parramatta). **Charge:** Dangerous throw. **Sentence:** Exonerated. **Cited:** Gourley (Sydney City). **Charge:** High tackle. **Sentence:** Two weeks.

Newcastle 24 (R.O'Davis, T.Fletcher, M.Johns, O.Craigie tries; L.Dynevor 4 goals) defeated **South Queensland** 6 (M.Protheroe try; C.Schifcofske goal) at Suncorp Stadium, Saturday, June 28.

Scrums: South Queensland 10–9. Penalties: South Queensland 10–7. Crowd: 4769. Referee: Eddie Ward. Halftime: Newcastle 20–2. Goalkickers: Dynevor (Newcastle) 4/4, Schifcofske (South Queensland) 1/2. Seconds: South Queensland 22–8. Under-20s: Newcastle 34–26.
NEWCASTLE: O'Davis; Albert, Gidley, Craigie, Moodie; M.Johns, Dynevor; Butterfield, Jackson, Harragon (c), Peden, Muir, Glanville. Interchange: Fletcher, Conley, Smailes, Hughes.
SOUTH QUEENSLAND: Watson; Hudson, Toshack, Eagar, Schifcofske; Moule, Antonik; O'Brien, Teevan (c), Retchless, Bickerstaff, Protheroe, Wilson. Interchange: Sologinkin, Saunders, Jones, Tookey.
Cited: Watson (South Queensland). **Charge:** Striking. **Sentence:** Two weeks.

Norths 41 (B.Dallas 2, B.Moore, D.Williams, D.Fairleigh, G.Florimo, C.Caruana tries; J.Taylor 6 goals, Taylor field goal) defeated **Manly** 8 (J.Hopoate, S.Menzies tries) at North Sydney Oval, Sunday, June 29.

Scrums: Manly 5–2. Penalties: Norths 4–3. Crowd: 14,615. Referee: David Manson. Halftime: Norths 14–4. Goalkickers: Taylor (Norths) 6/9, Field (Manly) 0/2. Seconds: Norths 18–12. Under-20s: Norths 18–10.
NORTHS: Seers; Dallas, McLean, Caruana, Roy; Florimo, Taylor (c); Stuart, Soden, Trindall, Fairleigh, Larson, Moore. Interchange: Pomery, Williams, Hall, Reber.
MANLY: Hancock; Hopoate, Innes, Moore, Hunter; Toovey (c), Field; Gillespie, Serdaris, Carroll, Menzies, Gartner, Kosef. Interchange: Fulton, Lyons, Tierney, Nevin.
Sin bin: Field (Manly).

STANDINGS: Manly 20, Norths 19, Parramatta 18, Newcastle 16*, Gold Coast 15, Sydney City 14, Wests 14, Illawarra 13, Balmain 12, St George 12, Souths 9*, South Queensland 4. * Newcastle and Souths had a match in hand.

OPTUS CUP ROUND 15
JULY 4, 5, 6

Rooster heroics in Newcastle

Sydney City salvaged a 14-all draw against Newcastle in remarkable circumstances at Marathon Stadium. On another slippery Marathon surface, Newcastle looked to have had the match won when halfback Leo Dynevor and centre Owen Craigie combined for Dynevor to score in the 75th minute. But they couldn't hang on.

Down 14-8 with only a minute to play, Roosters' captain Brad Fittler chipped over the Newcastle line. Andrew Walker took the ball on his fingertips and kicked into the Newcastle in-goal. Leading the chase for Sydney City was second-rower Luke Ricketson, who had completed 43 tackles and 25 hit-ups during the match. Ricketson touched down, leaving fullback Ivan Cleary with a high-pressure conversion attempt to snatch the draw. He made no mistake, so after four straight losses, the Roosters had at last claimed another premiership point.

A week after one of their best-ever wins, North Sydney slumped to a 15-8 loss against Illawarra at WIN Stadium. A superb second-half defensive effort by the Steelers kept their line intact as Norths tried valiantly to find a way through. So good was the Steelers' defence, though, that Norths were forced into repeated errors. Illawarra led 9-8 at halftime, but despite frustrating the Bears throughout the final 40 minutes, they could not put a seal on the match until two minutes from the end, when skipper Paul McGregor touched down after a long pass from five-eighth Trent Barrett. The win lifted Illawarra back into the top seven.

Gold Coast captain Graham Mackay was sent off after 29 minutes of his team's clash with St George, but that was no barrier to the Chargers, and they went on to win 22-14 before a five-figure crowd in wet conditions at Carrara Stadium.

The Gold Coast led 12-4 when Mackay was sent off for striking St George winger Mark Bell. They advanced their lead to 18-4 soon after halftime, following a try to replacement John McKelleher. The Chargers' victory was their eighth for the season, making them the most successful Gold Coast team in 10 years in the ARL competition. Coach Phil Economidis described the win as the most courageous in the club's history.

Parramatta equalled their best winning run in 20 years with a courageous 20-18 win over Western Suburbs at Parramatta Stadium. The Eels confirmed themselves as serious premiership contenders after fighting their way back from a 12-4 deficit midway through the first half.

Five-eighth Jason Bell sparked the Eels with a series of long bursts, while Fijian winger Eparama Navale came off the bench to score a hat-trick of tries. A bumper Saturday afternoon crowd of 15,372 watched the match.

The sin-binning of Souths' five-eighth Scott Murray proved critical to the outcome of the Rabbitohs' clash with Balmain at the Sydney Football Stadium. Souths led 2-0 when Murray was marched for a professional foul. By the time he returned, the Tigers led 12-2, and from that point they never looked like losing. The Tigers won 16-2, reigniting their finals charge.

Manly centre Terry Hill scored four tries as the Sea Eagles responded to their record loss to North Sydney with a 46-12 demolition of South Queensland in miserable conditions at Brookvale Oval. Manly ran in 30 second-half points.

ROUND 15 — RESULTS

Newcastle 14 (R.O'Davis, L.Dynevor tries; Dynevor 3 goals) drew with **Sydney City** 14 (J.Elsegood, L.Ricketson tries; I.Cleary 3 goals) at Marathon Stadium, Friday night, July 4.

Scrums: Newcastle 6–5. Penalties: Newcastle 7–5. Crowd: 6562. Referee: David Manson. Halftime: Sydney City 8–0. Goalkickers: Dynevor (Newcastle) 3/4, Cleary (Sydney City) 3/4. Seconds: Newcastle 26–0. Under-20s: Newcastle 16–14.
NEWCASTLE: O'Davis; Albert, Gidley, Craigie, Hughes; M.Johns, Dynevor; Butterfield, Jackson, Harragon (c), Peden, Muir, Glanville. Interchange: Fletcher, Smailes, Conley, Cochrane.
SYDNEY CITY: Cleary; Elsegood, Sing, Pearson, Miles; Fittler (c), Lam; Lowrie, Garlick, Hermansson, Barnhill, Ricketson, Rigon. Interchange: Troy, Bonetti, Walker, Hayden.
Sin bin: Harragon (Newcastle).

Parramatta 20 (E.Navale 3, K.Lovell S.Collins tries) defeated **Wests** 18 (A.Doyle, P.Langmack, D.Kennedy tries; A.Leeds 3 goals) at Parramatta Stadium, Saturday, July 5.

Scrums: Wests 8–6. Penalties: Parramatta 6–4. Crowd: 15,372. Referee: Matt Hewitt. Halftime: Wests 12–8. Goalkickers: Simon (Parramatta) 0/5, Herron (Parramatta) 0/1, Leeds (Wests) 3/4. Seconds: Parramatta 30–14. Under-20s: Wests 35–32.
PARRAMATTA: Carige; Herron, Barnes, Kelly, Collins; Bell, Simon; Lovell, Raper, Pay (c), Morgan, McCracken, Jason Smith. Interchange: Navale, Campbell, Pettet, Horsnell.
WESTS: Leeds; Willis, Ken McGuinness, Kevin McGuinness, Hodgson; Doyle, Georgallis; Howard, Mescia, Skandalis, Dunn, Kennedy, Langmack (c). Interchange: Capovilla, Hasler, Millard.

Gold Coast 22 (M.Bai, M.Bella, J.McKelleher, S.Russell tries; B.Hurst 3 goals) defeated **St George** 14 (A.Brunker, D.Rameka, D.Wagon tries; S.Price goal) at Carrara Stadium, Saturday night, July 5.

Scrums: St George 6–5. Penalties: Gold Coast 9–5. Crowd: 10,738. Referee: Kelvin Jeffes. Halftime: Gold Coast 14–4. Goalkickers: Hurst (Gold Coast) 3/6, Price (St George) 1/3, Thompson (St George) 0/1. Seconds: Gold Coast 24–18. Under-20s: St George 24–10.
GOLD COAST: King; Bai, Mackay (c), Nicol, Russell; O'Reilly, Patten; Parsons, Dave Clark, Driscoll, Sattler, Hurst, Nahi. Interchange: Durheim, Bella, Des Clark, McKelleher.
ST GEORGE: Ainscough; Bell, Coyne (c), Wagon, Brunker; Price, Clinch; Pearson, Brown, Felsch, Ward, Thompson, Hardy. Interchange: Lenihan, B.Smith, Kenward, Rameka.
Sent off: Mackay (Gold Coast), 29 min. **Charge:** Striking. **Sentence:** Caution. **Cited:** Bell (St George). **Charge:** Striking. **Sentence:** Exonerated. **Cited:** Coyne (St George). **Charge:** Dangerous tackle. **Sentence:** Exonerated.

Illawarra 15 (T.Barrett, P.McGregor tries; G.Air 2, D.Moon goals; Barrett field goal) defeated **Norths** 8 (B.Dallas try; J.Taylor 2 goals) at WIN Stadium, Sunday, July 6.

Scrums: 8–all. Penalties: 6–all. Crowd: 7219. Referee: Eddie Ward. Halftime: Illawarra 9–8. Goalkickers: Air (Illawarra) 2/3, Moon (Illawarra) 1/1, Taylor (North Sydney) 2/3. Seconds: Illawarra 16–14. Under-20s: Norths 8–4.
ILLAWARRA: Rodwell; Moon, Timmins, McGregor (c), Clifford; Barrett, Air; Cram, Callaway, Smith, Hart, Mackay, J.Cross. Interchange: Cox, Lamey, Seru, Leikvoll.
NORTHS: Seers; Dallas, Ikin, Caruana, Roy; Florimo, Taylor (c); Stuart, Soden, Trindall, Larson, Fairleigh, Moore. Interchange: Williams, Pomery, Reber, Hall.

Manly 46 (T.Hill 4, J.Hopoate 2, C.Hancock 2 D.Moore, S.Menzies tries; A.Hunter 3 goals) defeated **South Queensland** 12 (A.Moule, N.Sologinkin tries; C.Schifcofske 2 goals) at Brookvale Oval, Sunday, July 6.

Scrums: South Queensland 4–2. Penalties: South Queensland 8–7. Crowd: 5055. Referee: Sean Hampstead. Halftime: Manly 16–6. Goalkickers: Hunter (Manly) 3/6, Innes (Manly) 0/2, Friend (Manly) 0/2, Schifcofske (Crushers) 2/2. Seconds: Manly 22–6. Under-20s: Manly 34–18.
MANLY: Hancock; Moore, Innes, Hill, Hopoate; Toovey (c), Field; Gillespie, Serdaris, Carroll, Menzies, Gartner, Kosef. Interchange: Hunter, Tierney, Fulton, Lyons.
SOUTH QUEENSLAND: Schifcofske; Hudson, Toshack, Eagar, Wendt; Moule, Teevan (c); O'Brien, Antonik, Retchless, Sologinkin, Protheroe, Wilson. Interchange: Saunders, Bickerstaff, Couper, Hubbard.

Balmain 16 (M.Withers, G.Morrison tries; Withers 4 goals) defeated **Souths** 2 (D.Trindall goal) at Sydney Football Stadium, Sunday, July 6.

Scrums: Balmain 12–6. Penalties: Balmain 9–6. Crowd: 6528. Referee: Paul Simpkins. Halftime: 2–all. Goalkickers: Withers (Balmain) 4/6, Trindall (Souths) 1/1. Seconds: Balmain 38–10. Under-20s: Souths 32–10.
BALMAIN: Brasher; Withers, Kennedy, Webber, Langaloa; Gillett, Nable; Walker, Senter, Sironen (c), Stimson, Smith, Morrison. Interchange: Starr, O'Neil, St Clair, Donaghey.
SOUTHS: O'Meara; Moore, Penna, Howlett, Orford; Murray, Trindall (c); Parsons, Donato, Ostini, Francis, Glassie, Burns. Interchange: Stimson, Slattery, Gillard, Simon.
Sin bin: Murray (Souths).

STANDINGS: Manly 22, Parramatta 20, Norths 19, Newcastle 17*, Gold Coast 17, Sydney City 15, Illawarra 15, Balmain 14, Wests 14, St George 12, Souths 9*, South Queensland 4. * Newcastle and Souths had a match in hand.

ROUND 15

OPTUS CUP ROUND 16
JULY 12, 18, 19, 20

Manly find their steel

Rival front-rowers Terry Hermansson (Sydney City) and Mark Carroll (Manly) were sent off for head-butting as Manly rediscovered their defensive steel in a 21-12 win at the Sydney Football Stadium. Hermansson and Carroll were sent off by referee Eddie Ward in the 25th minute, after a scrum erupted. To that point, the Roosters dominated territory and possession, but almost immediately after the pair was marched, Manly scored twice (Hopoate and Menzies), to lead 8-0. The Roosters responded before halftime with a try to halfback Adrian Lam and they assumed the lead only minutes after the resumption when centre Brandon Pearson scored after intercepting a Cliff Lyons pass.

Lyons atoned for his mistake, though, when he dummied and strolled through a hole in the Roosters' defence to set up a 14-12 lead after 48 minutes. A late try to Terry Hill and a field goal to Craig Field gave the Sea Eagles a nine-point winning margin.

A crowd of over 20,000 watched one of the most captivating games of the season at Parramatta Stadium, when Parramatta outplayed Newcastle to win 28-22 and complete their 10th successive victory. Newcastle dominated the first half and led 16-10 at the break, but a departure from their smart play of the first period opened the door for Parramatta, who quickly turned a six-point deficit into a 28-18 lead. A late try to captain Paul Harragon gave the Knights a slim chance of claiming a draw, but with the crowd behind them, the Eels hung on.

The Gold Coast went close to a remarkable comeback victory after scoring five tries in 22 minutes before falling 34-28 to Norths at North Sydney Oval. Centre Ben Ikin scored his third try for Norths a minute after halftime, opening up a 30-4 lead, but with a glut of possession, the Chargers stormed back into the match. They scored tries in the 45th, 52nd, 56th, 60th and 67th minutes, cutting Norths' lead to two points. Five-eighth Chris Orr was tackled into touch a metre from Norths' line, killing what could have been the match-winning try.

Western Suburbs' McGuinness brothers scored two tries apiece to steer the Magpies to a 20-10 win over Balmain at Campbelltown, keeping alive their hopes of a finals berth.

After a torrid first half the scores were locked at 10-all. After the break the Magpies skipped to a 14-10 lead, then Balmain had an apparently legitimate try disallowed when hooker Darren Senter was held up over the line.

St George and South Sydney turned on a thriller at Kogarah Oval, before the Saints emerged with a 29-28 victory.

The first half was all St George. They scored five tries to lead 24-6 at the break and looked like rattling up a cricket score, but their early control disappeared in the second term. Throwing caution to the wind, Souths stormed back into the game, with Darrell Trindall in fine touch. The Rabbitohs drew to 28-22 before Saints' Jamie Ainscough kicked a crucial field goal.

South Queensland offered resistance for 40 minutes, but there was no stopping a determined Illawarra, who ran out 34-8 winners at Suncorp Stadium. Illawarra led just 6-4 at the break and were lucky not to be trailing after a questionable decision to disallow a Crushers' try.

ROUND 16 — RESULTS

Wests 20 (Ken McGuinness 2, Kevin McGuinness 2 tries; A.Leeds 2 goals) defeated **Balmain** 10 (W.Kennedy, L.Milford tries; M.Withers goal) at Campbelltown Sports Ground, Saturday, July 12.

Scrums: Balmain 9-7. Penalties: Wests 10-4. Crowd: 6718. Referee: Kelvin Jeffes. Halftime: 10-all. Goalkickers: Leeds (Wests) 2/4, Withers (Balmain) 1/3. Seconds: Balmain 30-17. Under-20s: Balmain 22-4.

WESTS: Leeds; D.Willis, Ken McGuinness, Kevin McGuinness, Hodgson; Doyle, Georgallis; Howard, Hasler, Capovilla, Dunn, Kennedy, Langmack (c). Interchange: McMenemy, Taylor, Millard.

BALMAIN: Withers; L.Milford, Kennedy, Donaghey, Langaloa; Gillett, Nable; Walker, Senter, Sironen (c), Stimson, Hanley, Morrison. Interchange: Starr, O'Neill, Smith, Scott.

Sin bin: Hasler (Wests).

Manly 21 (J.Hopoate, C.Lyons, S.Menzies, I.Hill tries; C.Field, A.Hunter goals; Field field goal) defeated **Sydney City** 12 (A.Lam, B.Pearson tries; I.Cleary 2 goals) at Sydney Football Stadium, Friday night, July 18.

Scrums: Sydney City 6-3. Penalties: Manly 10-4. Crowd: 12,385. Referee: Eddie Ward. Halftime: Manly 8-6. Goalkickers: Field (Manly) 1/3, Hunter (Manly) 1/2, Cleary (Sydney City) 2/2. Seconds: Manly 24-6. Under-20s: Manly 19-12.

MANLY: Hancock; Hunter, Innes, Hill, Hopoate; Lyons, Toovey (c); Gillespie, Serdaris, Carroll, Menzies, Gartner, Kosef. Interchange: Field, Tierney, Fulton, Moore.

SYDNEY CITY: Walker; Miles, Cleary, Pearson, Elsegood; Fittler (c), Lam; Lowrie, Garlick, Hermansson, Barnhill, Ricketson, Rigon. Interchange: Sing, Troy, Hayden, Bonetti.

Sent off: Hermansson (Sydney City) 25 min. **Charge:** Headbutting. **Sentence:** Exonerated. **Sent off:** Carroll (Manly) 25 min. **Charge:** Headbutting. **Sentence:** Exonerated.

Illawarra 34 (P.McGregor 2, A.Hart, S.Timmins, G.Air, B.Mackay tries; D.Moon 5 goals) defeated **South Queensland** 8 (C.Wilson, A.Moule tries) at Suncorp Stadium, Saturday, July 19.

Scrums: Illawarra 7-3. Penalties: South Queensland 9-4. Crowd: 2364. Referee: Paul Simpkins. Halftime: Illawarra 6-4. Goalkickers: Moon (Illawarra) 5/6, Schifcofske (South Queensland) 0/2. Seconds: South Queensland 34-14. Under-20s: South Queensland 32-14.

ILLAWARRA: Rodwell; Moon, Timmins, McGregor (c), Clifford; Barrett, Air; Cram, Callaway, Smith, Hart, Mackay, J.Cross. Interchange: Cox, Bradstreet, Lamey, Reeves.

SOUTH QUEENSLAND: Schifcofske; Hudson, Toshack, Eagar, Wendt; Saunders, Teevan (c); O'Brien, Antonin, Retchless, Bickerstaff, Protheroe, Wilson. Interchange: Sologinkin, Couper, Moule, Davis.

Norths 34 (B.Ikin 2, D.Fairleigh, B.Dallas, D.Hall tries; J.Taylor 5 goals) defeated **Gold Coast** 28 (M.Bai, J.Nicol, B.Hurst, S.Parsons, A.King, K.Blackett tries; Hurst 2 goals) at North Sydney Oval, Sunday, July 20.

Scrums: Norths 7-5. Penalties: Norths 9-8. Crowd: 8371. Referee: Matt Hewitt. Halftime: Norths 26-4. Goalkickers: Taylor (Norths) 5/7, Hurst (Gold Coast) 2/6. Seconds: Gold Coast 26-20. Under-20s: Norths 22-8.

NORTHS: Seers; Dallas, Ikin, Caruana, Roy; Florimo, Taylor (c); Stuart, Soden, Trindall, Larson, Fairleigh, Moore. Interchange: Pomery, Reber, Hall, Williams.

GOLD COAST: King; Bai, Mackay (c), Nicol, Russell; Orr, Patten; Parsons, Dave Clark, Driscoll, Sattler, Nahi, Hurst. Interchange: Des Clark, Bella, Durheim, Blackett.

Sin bin: Des Clark (Gold Coast).

St George 29 (A.Brunker 3, D.Wagon 2, L.Murphy tries; S.Price 2 goals; J.Ainscough field goal) defeated **Souths** 28 (P.Howlett 2, D.Penna, D.O'Keefe, P.Stimson tries; J.O'Neill 4 goals) at Kogarah Oval, Sunday July 20.

Scrums: Souths 6-2. Penalties: 8-all. Crowd: 6883. Referee: Paul McBlane. Halftime: St George 24-6. Goalkickers: Price (St George) 2/6, O'Neill (Souths) 4/6. Seconds: Souths 16-14. Under-20s: St George 30-12.

ST GEORGE: Ainscough; Murphy, Coyne (c), Wagon, Brunker; Price, Kusto; Ward, Brown, Pearson, Treacy, Thompson, Tangata-Toa. Interchange: Felsch, Rameka, B.Smith, Lenihan.

SOUTHS: Wood; Moore, Penna, Howlett, O'Keefe; O'Neill, Trindall (c); Parsons, Murray, Ostini, Burns, Moseley, White. Interchange: Stimson, Gillard, Simon, Francis.

Sin bin: Brown (St George).

Parramatta 28 (P.Carige 2, S.Whereat, J.Bell, J.Simon, J.McCracken tries; Simon 2 goals) defeated **Newcastle** 22 (O.Craigie, M.Hughes, D.Smailes, P.Harragon tries; A.Johns 3 goals), at Marathon Stadium, Sunday, July 20.

Scrums: Parramatta 10-6. Penalties: 3-all. Crowd: 20,148. Referee: David Manson. Halftime: Newcastle 16-10. Goalkickers: Simon (Parramatta) 2/6, A.Johns (Newcastle) 3/5. Seconds: Parramatta 20-14. Under-20s: Parramatta 40-26.

PARRAMATTA: Carige; Navale, Barnes, Kelly, Whereat; Bell, Simon; Lovell, Raper, Pay (c), Morgan, McCracken, Dymock. Interchange: Campbell, Pettet, Collins, Horsnell.

NEWCASTLE: O'Davis; Albert, Hughes, Craigie, Cochrane; M.Johns, A.Johns; Harragon (c), Jackson, Butterfield, Peden, Muir, Glanville. Interchange: Fletcher, Smailes, Conley, Dynevor.

STANDINGS: Manly 24, Parramatta 22, Norths 21, Newcastle 19, Illawarra 17, Gold Coast 17, Wests 16, Sydney City 15, Balmain 14, St George 14, Souths 9, South Queensland 4.

OPTUS CUP ROUND 17

JULY 25, 26, 27

Eels win 11th-straight

Parramatta joined Manly at the top of the premiership ladder after a magnificent 17-10 win over the Sea Eagles at Brookvale Oval. The win was the 11th in succession for the Eels and capped a remarkable rise up the table: after seven rounds, Parramatta had been placed equal last. The inspiration for the victory was halfback John Simon, who contributed a try, a goal and three field goals.

Parramatta coach Brian Smith described Simon as possibly the smartest player he has ever coached after watching the 25-year-old engineer the three-tries-to-two win. 'He seems to know what you are thinking before you decide to do it,' Smith said.

A crowd of over 22,000 watched the titanic struggle, which was not decided until the final minutes. Manly halfback Geoff Toovey played a brilliant game for a losing side, scoring a superb solo try which reduced the leeway to one point midway through the second half.

Injuries to Manly fullback Craig Hancock (broken ankle) and Parramatta centre Stuart Kelly (fractured jaw) would rule them out for the rest of the season.

On the same night that Simon was weaving his magic for Parramatta, another halfback was doing likewise for his team at Marathon Stadium. Andrew Johns turned in a similarly dominating performance as the Knights crushed Western Suburbs 42-18. Johns was in irresistible touch, his silky skills mesmerising Wests in an eight-try rout. Winger Darren Albert and centre Owen Craigie capitalised on Johns' superb service, both players scoring a hat-trick of tries.

The win lifted Newcastle to within three points of the competition lead and, conversely, made Western Suburbs' job of reaching the final seven considerably more difficult.

Sydney City scored their first win in seven matches with a 34-12 win over Illawarra, rejuvenating their premiership hopes. With their season riding on the result, the Roosters produced the goods and always looked in control of a disappointing Illawarra outfit, who also needed to win. Sydney City's key men, captain Brad Fittler and halfback Adrian Lam, delivered at the right time and were heavily involved in most of their team's six tries.

The Gold Coast continued their rapid rise to prominence with a dominating 40-18 win over South Queensland at Carrara Stadium. Halfback Wes Patten was at his elusive best for the Chargers, scoring three tries himself and playing a hand in several others. The Chargers raced to a 28-2 lead after an hour, but the sin-binning of Queensland hooker Jamie Goddard sparked a mini-resurgence for the Crushers, who then scored two tries in the space of two minutes.

North Sydney scored six tries, overwhelming South Sydney 40-8 in a one-sided contest at the Sydney Football Stadium. The Bears showed few of the lapses that almost cost them victory over the Gold Coast a week earlier and went on with the job well after leading 20-8 at halftime.

Balmain made more of their opportunities than St George, and scored a 10-4 victory in a gruelling clash at Leichhardt Oval. There was no score in the first half, but two tries in 10 minutes after the break to the Tigers (Gillett and Kennedy) set up a vital win.

ROUND 17 — RESULTS

Parramatta 17 (J.McCracken, J.Simon, N.Barnes tries; Simon goal; Simon 3 field goals) defeated **Manly** 10 (T.Hill, G.Toovey tries; C.Field goal) at Brookvale Oval, Friday night, July 25.

Scrums: Manly 7–1. Penalties: Manly 10–6. Crowd: 22,746. Referee: David Manson. Halftime: 4–all. Goalkickers: Simon (Parramatta) 1/3, Field (Manly) 1/1, Hunter (Manly) 0/2. Seconds: Manly 22–14. Under-20s: Parramatta 10–6.
PARRAMATTA: Carige; Navale, Barnes, Kelly, Whereat; Bell, Simon; Horsnell, Raper, Pay (c), Morgan, McCracken, Dymock. Interchange: Lovell, Jason Smith, Campbell, Collins.
MANLY: Hancock; Hunter, Innes, Hill, Hopoate; Lyons, Toovey (c); Gillespie, Serdaris, Carroll, Menzies, Gartner, Kosef. Interchange: Field, Fulton, Tierney, Moore.

Newcastle 42 (D.Albert 3, O.Craigie 3, M.Glanville, A.Muir tries; A.Johns 5 goals) defeated **Wests** 18 (D.Willis, D.Kennedy, Ken McGuinness tries; A.Leeds 3 goals) at Marathon Stadium, Friday night, July 25.

Scrums: Newcastle 9–5. Penalties: Newcastle 5–4. Crowd: 17,197. Referee: Matt Hewitt. Halftime: Newcastle 20–6. Goalkickers: Johns (Newcastle) 5/8, Leeds (Wests) 3/3. Seconds: Newcastle 34–16. Under-20s: Wests 22–16.
NEWCASTLE: O'Davis; Albert, Hughes, Craigie, Cochrane; M.Johns, A.Johns; Butterfield, Clements, Harragon (c), Peden, Muir, Glanville. Interchange: Conley, Richards, Smailes, Grogan.
WESTS: Leeds; D.Willis, Ken McGuinness, Kevin McGuinness, Hodgson; Doyle, Georgallis; Howard, Hasler, Skandalis, Dunn, Kennedy, Langmack (c). Interchange: Capovilla, McMenemy, Laing, A.Willis.
Sin bin: McMenemy (Wests).

Sydney City 34 (M.Sing 2, B.Pearson 2, J.Elsegood, A.Hayden tries; I.Cleary 5 goals) defeated **Illawarra** 12 (W.Clifford, P.McGregor tries; D.Moon 2 goals) at WIN Stadium, Saturday, July 26.

Scrums: Sydney City 6–5. Penalties: Illawarra 9–5. Crowd: 8241. Referee: Paul McBlane. Halftime: Sydney City 12–2. Goalkickers: Cleary (Sydney City) 5/7, Moon (Illawarra) 2/6. Seconds: Illawarra 36–16. Under-20s: Illawarra 40–4.
SYDNEY CITY: Walker, Elsegood, Cleary, Pearson, Sing; Hayden, Lam; Lowrie, Bonetti, Barnhill, Gourley, Ricketson, Fittler (c). Interchange: Hermansson, Rigon, Miles, Fletcher.
ILLAWARRA: Rodwell; Moon, Timmins, McGregor (c), Clifford; Barrett, Air; Cram, Callaway, Smith, Hart, Lamoy, Mackay. Interchange: Leikvoll, Cox, Tunbridge, Purcell.
Sin bin: Rigon (Sydney City).

Balmain 10 (M.Gillett, W.Kennedy tries; T.Brasher goal) defeated **St George** 4 (L.Murphy try) at Leichhardt Oval, Saturday night, July 26.

Scrums: Balmain 6–4. Penalties: Balmain 11–9. Crowd: 8099. Referee: Eddie Ward. Halftime: 0–all. Goalkickers: Brasher (Balmain) 1/2, Withers (Balmain) 0/1, Dartim (St George) 0/1. Seconds: St George 12–8. Under-20s: St George 14–12.
BALMAIN: Brasher; Langaloa, Kennedy, Withers, L.Milford; Gillett, Nable; Walker, Senter, Sironen (c), Stimson, Smith, Morrison. Interchange: Starr, O'Neil, Hanley, Donaghey.
ST GEORGE: Ainscough; Murphy, Coyne (c), Wagon, Brunker; Price, Kusto; Pearson, Brown, Ward, Treacy, Thompson, Bartrim. Interchange: Felsch, Rameka, Tangata-Toa.

Norths 40 (B.Dallas 2, P.Stringer 2, M.Seers, J.Taylor tries; Taylor 8 goals) defeated **Souths** 8 (D.O'Keefe, J.Orford tries) at Sydney Football Stadium, Sunday, July 27.

Scrums: 7–all. Penalties: Norths 8–5. Crowd: 5074. Referee: Sean Hampstead. Halftime: Norths 20–8. Goalkickers: Taylor (Norths) 8/8, Barnes (Souths) 0/2, O'Neill (Souths) 0/1. Seconds: Souths 24–12. Under-20s: Norths 34–18.
NORTHS: Seers; Dallas, Ikin, Caruana, Roy; Florimo, Taylor (c); Pomery, Soden, Trindall, Larson, Fairleigh, Moore. Interchange: Hall, Reber, Williams, Stringer.
SOUTHS: Wood; Orford, Moore, Howlett, O'Keefe; O'Neill, Trindall (c); Parsons, Murray, Ostini, Gillard, Moseley, Burns. Interchange: Stimson, White, Barnes, Francis.
Sin bin: O'Neill (Souths), Trindall (Souths).

Gold Coast 40 (W.Patten 3, M.Bai, J.Nicol, B.Hurst, A.King tries; Hurst 3, G.Mackay 3 goals) defeated **South Queensland** 18 (C.Wilson, T.Pezet, C.Teevan tries; C.Schifcofske 3 goals) at Carrara Stadium, Sunday, July 27.

Scrums: South Queensland 8–6. Penalties: South Queensland 6–5. Crowd: 8392. Referee: Tony Maksoud. Halftime: Gold Coast 10–2. Goalkickers: Hurst (Gold Coast) 3/3, Mackay (Gold Coast) 3/4, Schifcofske (South Queensland) 3/4. Seconds: South Queensland 28–14. Under-20s: South Queensland 20–10.
GOLD COAST: King; Bai, Mackay (c), Nicol, Anderson; Orr, Patten; Parsons, Goddard, Driscoll, Sattler, Hurst, Schloss. Interchange: Des Clark, Nahi, Blackett, O'Reilly.
SOUTH QUEENSLAND: Schifcofske; Hudson, Toshack, Moule, Wendt; Watson, Teevan (c); O'Brien, Antonik, Couper, Protheroe, Rotohloss, Wilson. Interchange: Sologinkin, Bickerstaff, Nutley, Pezet.
Sin bin: Goddard (Gold Coast).

STANDINGS: Manly 24, Parramatta 24, Norths 23, Newcastle 21, Gold Coast 19, Sydney City 17, Illawarra 17, Balmain 16, Wests 16, St George 14, Souths 9, South Queensland 4.

OPTUS CUP ROUND 18
AUGUST 1, 2, 3

Knights claim moral victory

Manly's defence returned to its brilliant best after weathering a barrage from Newcastle in a gripping encounter at Marathon Stadium.

The Sea Eagles' 14-12 win sent a warning to every team vying for the premiership that they would have to come up with something extraordinary to beat the premiers in the defensive frame of mind they were in at Newcastle. The Knights dominated possession and field position throughout the second half, but the pickings were slim indeed.

The superb short kicking game of brothers Matthew and Andrew Johns made sure that Manly spent long periods defending their own line, but apart from a try to Brett Grogan midway through the second half, the Sea Eagles kept their line intact. The only other Newcastle try (in the third minute) came from a Matthew Johns kick. However, replays clearly showed that winger Evan Cochrane dropped the ball before forcing it.

Despite the result, Newcastle coach Malcolm Reilly believed his side had claimed a 'moral' victory. 'They got the two points, but quite frankly, I thought we outplayed them,' he said.

Parramatta's bid to equal a club record 12 consecutive wins was foiled by Illawarra in a fast and furious contest at Parramatta Stadium.

The Steelers, who were the first victims of Parramatta's winning run, ended it with a 28-24 win. They claimed the result with a Paul McGregor-inspired comeback from 24-14 down midway through the second half. Tries to McGregor and replacement Adam Bristow levelled the scores four minutes from fulltime, then five-eighth Trent Barrett produced an extraordinary effort to claim victory two minutes from the end.

Barrett chipped into Parramatta's in-goal, stepped outside the field of play and then dived back into the in-goal area.

North Sydney's Brett Dallas scored a classic winger's try to sink Balmain's hopes as the Bears chalked up a 22-14 win. Balmain looked impressive as they scored two tries to lead 10-2 after half an hour, but then Norths captain Jason Taylor kicked a penalty goal, then scored and converted his own try, and the scores were level shortly before halftime. Dallas's try came right on the halftime siren. Receiving a long pass from Taylor, Dallas got outside his opposite, James Langaloa, stepped past fullback Tim Brasher and pinned his ears back in a wonderful arcing run to the tryline. A healthy crowd of 18,854 turned out to celebrate Greg Florimo's 250th first-grade game.

Reluctant fullback Andrew Walker was the star turn in Sydney City's 28-12 defeat of the Gold Coast at the Sydney Football Stadium, a win which elevated the Roosters into fifth position on a congested ladder.

St George's semi-finals hopes were all but washed up after Western Suburbs scored a commanding 26-6 win at Campbelltown Sports Ground. Magpie fullback Andrew Leeds celebrated his 100th first-grade game as his team punished St George for their poor ball control.

A field goal to lock Craig Wilson gave the South Queensland Crushers their third win of the season in the bottom-of-the-table clash with South Sydney at Suncorp Stadium. The Crushers led 16-6 before Souths levelled with two tries midway through the second half.

ROUND 18 — RESULTS

Manly 14 (S.Nevin, J.Hopoate tries; Nevin 3 goals) defeated **Newcastle** 12 (E.Cochrane, B.Grogan tries; A.Johns 2 goals) at Marathon Stadium, Friday night, August 1.

Scrums: Newcastle 6–3. Penalties: Manly 7–4. Crowd: 25,077. Referee: Eddie Ward. Halftime: Manly 8–6. Goalkickers: Nevin (Manly) 3/3, Johns (Newcastle) 2/2. Seconds: Manly 24–22. Under-20s: Manly 20–10.
MANLY: Nevin; Moore, Innes, Hill, Hopoate; Lyons, Toovey (c); Tierney, Serdaris, Carroll, Menzies, Gartner, Kosef. Interchange: Gillespie, Field, Fulton, Hunter.
NEWCASTLE: O'Davis; Albert, Hughes, Craigie, Cochrane; M.Johns, A.Johns; Butterfield, Clements, Harragon (c), Peden, Muir, Glanville. Interchange: Richards, Grogan, Fletcher, Conley.

Sydney City 28 (B.Pearson 2, M.Sing 2, B.Fittler tries; I.Cleary 4 goals) defeated **Gold Coast** 12 (J.Nicol, C.Nahi tries; B.Hurst 2 goals) at Sydney Football Stadium, Saturday, August 2.

Scrums: Gold Coast 6–5. Penalties: Sydney City 8–5. Crowd: 4780. Referee: David Manson. Halftime: Sydney City 10–8. Goalkickers: Cleary (Sydney City) 4/5, Hurst (Gold Coast) 2/2, Mackay (Gold Coast) 0/1. Seconds: Sydney City 46–8. Under-20s: Sydney City 46–10.
SYDNEY CITY: Walker; Elsegood, Cleary, Pearson, Sing; Hayden, Lam; Lowrie, Bonetti, Barnhill, Gourley, Ricketson, Fittler (c). Interchange: Hermansson, Fletcher, Miles, Rigon.
GOLD COAST: King; Bai, Mackay (c), Nicol, McKelleher; Orr, Patten; Des Clark, Goddard, Driscoll, Sattler, Hurst, Schloss. Interchange: Nahi, Bella, O'Reilly, Blackett.

Wests 26 (Ken McGuinness, Kevin McGuinness, B.Dunn, A.Doyle tries; B.Hodgson 5 goals) defeated **St George** 6 (J.Ainscough try; W.Bartrim goal) at Campbelltown Sports Ground, Saturday night, August 2.

Scrums: Wests 8–5. Penalties: 8–all. Crowd: 9152. Referee: Paul McBlane. Halftime: 6–all. Goalkickers: Hodgson (Wests) 5/6, Leeds (Wests) 0/2, Bartrim (St George) 1/2. Seconds: St George 18–6. Under-20s: St George 19–10.
WESTS: Leeds; D.Willis, Ken McGuinness, Laing, Hodgson; Doyle, Georgallis; Howard, Kevin McGuinness, Skandalis, Millard, Kennedy, Langmack (c). Interchange: Capovilla, Dunn, A.Willis, McMenemy.
ST GEORGE: Ainscough; Murphy, Coyne (c), Wagon D.Smith; Price, Kusto; Pearson, Brown, Ward, Tangata-Toa, Thompson, Bartrim. Interchange: B.Smith, Rameka, Raper, Felsch.

South Queensland 17 (C.Schifcofske, M.Toshack, S.Retchless tries; Schifcofske 2 goals; C.Wilson field goal) defeated **Souths** 16 (J.Orford, D.Penna, D.O'Keefe tries; J.O'Neill 2 goals) at Suncorp Stadium, Sunday, August 3.

Scrums: Souths 11–10. Penalties: South Queensland 8–4. Crowd: 3545. Referee: Tony Maksoud. Halftime: South Queensland 10–6. Goalkickers: Schifcofske (South Queensland) 2/3, O'Neill (Souths) 2/3. Seconds: Souths 22–18. Under-20s: Souths 26–18.
SOUTH QUEENSLAND: Schifcofske; Hudson, Toshack, Eagar, Doyle; Watson, Teevan (c); O'Brien, Antonik, Jones, Bickerstaff, Retchless, Wilson. Interchange: Pezet, Protheroe, Sologinkin, Nutley.
SOUTHS: O'Neill; Orford, Penna, Simon, O'Keefe; Murray, Trindall (c); Parsons, Williams, McEwen, White, Slattery, Burns. Interchange: Rubin, Donato, Wilson, Wood.

Sent off: Trindall (Souths), 72 min. **Charge:** High tackle. **Sentence:** Six weeks.

Norths 22 (J.Taylor, B.Dallas, M.Seers tries; Taylor 5 goals) defeated **Balmain** 14 (T.Brasher, L.Milford, P.Sironen tries; M.Withers goal) at North Sydney Oval, Sunday, August 3.

Scrums: Balmain 13–8. Penalties: Norths 5–4. Crowd: 18,854. Referee: Sean Hampstead. Halftime: Norths 16–10. Goalkickers: Taylor (Norths) 5/6, Withers (Balmain) 1/3. Seconds: Balmain 22–6. Under-20s: Balmain 40–4.
NORTHS: Seers; Dallas, Ikin, Caruana, Roy; Florimo, Taylor (c); Pomery, Soden, Trindall, Larson, Fairleigh, Moore. Interchange: Hall, Buettner, Williams, Stuart.
BALMAIN: Brasher; Langaloa, Kennedy, Withers, L.Milford; Gillett, Nable; Walker, Senter, Sironen (c), Stimson, Smith, Morrison. Interchange: Starr, O'Neil, Donaghey, Hanley.

Sin bin: Brasher (Balmain).

Illawarra 28 (W.Clifford 2, B.Rodwell, P.McGregor, A.Bristow, T.Barrett tries; D.Bradstreet 2 goals) defeated **Parramatta** 24 (S.Whereat, S.Collins, A.Raper, J.Bell, E.Navale tries; J.Simon 2 goals) at Parramatta Stadium, Sunday, August 3.

Scrums: Parramatta 3–2. Penalties: Parramatta 8–6. Crowd: 15,419. Referee: Matt Hewitt. Halftime: Parramatta 14–10. Goalkickers: Bradstreet (Illawarra) 2/3, Reeves (Illawarra) 0/2, Timmins (Illawarra) 0/1, Simon (Parramatta) 2/5. Seconds: Parramatta 34–4. Under-20s: Illawarra 26–20.
ILLAWARRA: Reeves; Seru, Rodwell, McGregor (c), Clifford; Timmins, Barrett; Cram, Callaway, Smith, Hart, Lamey, Mackay. Interchange: Leikvoll, Bradstreet, Bristow, Hauville.
PARRAMATTA: Carige; Navale, Barnes, McCracken, Whereat, Dell, Simon, Horsnell, Raper, Pay (c), Morgan, Jason Smith, Dymock. Interchange: Collins, Lovell, Campbell, Jamie Smith.

STANDINGS: Manly 26, Norths 25, Parramatta 24, Newcastle 21, Sydney City 19, Illawarra 19, Gold Coast 19, Wests 18, Balmain 16, St George 14, Souths 9, South Queensland 6.

OPTUS CUP ROUND 19
AUGUST 8, 9, 10

Saints gain revenge

Despite being in 10th place on the ladder, St George coach David Waite was still talking semi-finals after his side surprised North Sydney 22-14 at Kogarah Oval. Saints played with more enthusiasm than they had showed for much of the 1997 season, and Waite believed it was possible for his charges to win their final three matches (against South Queensland, Sydney City and Parramatta) and sneak into the top seven with 22 points.

Rookie winger Lee Murphy had his best game in first grade, with three tries for the Saints. He capitalised on an untidy game by Norths fullback Matt Seers, who had great difficulty handling the high ball. The Bears had several chances to win the match, but all the close decisions went against them.

Parramatta returned to the winners' circle with a comfortable but unimpressive 18-8 victory over the Gold Coast at Carrara Stadium. In front of their biggest crowd of the season, the Chargers offered little resistance, and Parramatta had the match well in their keeping when they led 14-0 at halftime.

The Chargers scored late tries through Jamie Goddard and Marcus Bai, but the sparkle that had been the trademark of the side in 1997 was nowhere to be seen.

The Newcastle Knights were accused of conceding penalties to halt the momentum of the Illawarra Steelers at WIN Stadium. Deliberate ploy or not, it proved effective, as the Knights ran up a 22-12 victory to register their first win in Wollongong since 1993.

The Knights were penalised 15-6 by referee Paul McBlane, and second-rower Adam Muir was lucky to escape being sin-binned after conceding four penalties. The Steelers fought back well to trail 14-12 — after being behind 14-2 at one stage of the first half — when winger Wayne Clifford finished a wonderful team try in the 52nd minute. Minutes later, their good work was undone when Knights hooker Brett Clements burrowed across the line from close to the ruck.

Sydney City bombed five tries but still managed to overwhelm South Sydney 40-20 in the local derby at the Sydney Football Stadium. Fullback Andrew Walker was again the guiding light, with a superb attacking display. He scored one try and set up another two, while halfback Adrian Lam scored two tries and had a hand in another three. Souths did well to cut the Roosters' early 22-2 lead to 22-14 at halftime, but the second half became a red, white and blue cakewalk. Youngster Willie Peters impressed in his top-grade debut for South Sydney.

Premiership favourites Manly made Western Suburbs look second rate in a 48-14 whitewash at Brookvale Oval. Without captain Paul Langmack, the Magpies were in trouble from the outset against a Manly side intent on a payback for their first-round 19-16 loss at Campbelltown. At halftime the Sea Eagles led 34-0, and although the Magpies regained some credibility by sharing the scoring 14-all in the second term, it was a forgettable day for the black and whites.

Balmain made heavy weather of their 32-14 defeat of South Queensland at Leichhardt Oval, despite a 20-0 lead at halftime. The Tigers went to sleep after the resumption, allowing the Crushers a sniff at 20-14, before late tries to Laloa Milford and Tim Brasher sealed an important win.

ROUND 19 — RESULTS

St George 22 (L.Murphy 3, L.Felsch tries; W.Bartrim 3 goals) defeated **Norths** 14 (C.Caruana, M.Buettner, G.Florimo tries; J.Taylor goal) at Kogarah Oval, Friday night, August 8.

Scrums: 5–all. Penalties: Norths 8–6. Crowd: 5007. Referee: Matt Hewitt. Halftime: St George 10–4. Goalkickers: Bartrim (St George) 3/4, Taylor (Norths) 1/4. Seconds: St George 26–22. Under-20s: Norths 36–16.
ST GEORGE: Raper; Murphy, Coyne (c), Wagon, D.Smith; Price, Clinch; Pearson, Brown, Ward, Tangata-Toa, Thompson, Bartrim. Interchange: Felsch, B.Smith, Lenihan, Henare.
NORTHS: Seers; Dallas, Ikin, Caruana, Roy; Buettner, Taylor (c); Stuart, Soden, Trindall, Larson, Fairleigh, Florimo. Interchange: Hall, Pomery, Williams.
Sin bin: Murphy (St George).

Sydney City 40 (A.Lam 2, J.Elsegood, A.Walker, R.Allan, B.Pearson, M.Sing tries; I.Cleary 6 goals) defeated **Souths** 20 (D.Penna 2, D.Burns tries; J.O'Neill 4 goals) at Sydney Football Stadium, Saturday, August 9.

Scrums: Sydney City 8–7. Penalties: Souths 7–6. Crowd: 4720. Referee: Kelvin Jeffes. Halftime: Sydney City 22–14. Goalkickers: Cleary (Sydney City) 6/7, O'Neill (Souths) 4/4. Seconds: Sydney City 20–10. Under-20s: Sydney City 26–8.
SYDNEY CITY: Walker; Elsegood, Cleary, Pearson, Sing; Allan, Lam; Barnhill, Bonetti, Hermansson, Gourley, Ricketson, Fittler (c). Interchange: Rigon, Fletcher, Hood, Miles.
SOUTHS: O'Neill (c); Orford, Wood, Wilson, O'Keefe; Murray, Peters; Parsons, Williams, Ostini, White, McNicholas, Burns. Interchange: McEwen, Penna, Slattery, Francis.

Parramatta 18 (N.Barnes, J.Morgan, E.Navale tries; J.Simon 3 goals) defeated **Gold Coast** 8 (J.Goddard, M.Bai tries) at Carrara Stadium, Saturday night, August 9.

Scrums: 6–all. Penalties: Gold Coast 12–9. Crowd: 13,182. Referee: Sean Hampstead. Halftime: Parramatta 14–0. Goalkickers: Simon (Parramatta) 3/6, Hurst (Gold Coast) 0/2. Seconds: Parramatta 18–16. Under-20s: Gold Coast 38–24.
PARRAMATTA: Carige; Navale, Barnes, McCracken, Collins; Bell, Simon; Horsnell, Raper, Pay (c), Morgan, Jason Smith, Dymock. Interchange: Campbell, Lovell, Jamie Smith, Wyer.
GOLD COAST: King; Bai, Mackay (c), Nicol, McKelleher, Orr, Patten; Bella, Goddard, Driscoll, Sattler, Hurst, Nahi. Interchange: Schloss, Parsons, Blackett, O'Reilly.
Sin bin: Orr (Gold Coast), Horsnell (Parramatta).

Manly 48 (T.Hill 3, S.Menzies 2, S.Nevin, J.Serdaris, C.Innes, A.Colella tries; Nevin 6 goals) defeated **Wests** 14 (Kevin McGuinness 2, Ken McGuinness tries; B.Hodgson goal) at Brookvale Oval, Sunday, August 10.

Scrums: Manly 6–3. Penalties: Manly 6–4. Crowd: 12,631. Referee: David Manson. Halftime: Manly 34–0. Goalkickers: Nevin (Manly) 6/9, Hodgson (Wests) 1/3. Seconds: Manly 42–12. Under-20s: Manly 38–16.
MANLY: Nevin; Moore, Innes, Hill, Hopoate; Lyons, Toovey (c); Tierney, Serdaris, Carroll, Colella, Menzies, Kosef. Interchange: Hunter, Fulton, Gillespie, Field.
WESTS: Leeds; D.Willis, Ken McGuinness, A.Willis, Hodgson; Doyle, Georgallis; Howard, Kevin McGuinness, Skandalis, Kennedy, Millard, Hasler (c). Interchange: Capovilla, Dunn, Mescia, McMenemy.

Newcastle 22 (R.O'Davis, D.Albert, B.Clements tries; A.Johns 5 goals) defeated **Illawarra** 12 (D.Bradstreet, W.Clifford tries; B.Reeves 2 goals) at WIN Stadium, Sunday, August 10.

Scrums: Newcastle 5–2. Penalties: Illawarra 15–6. Crowd: 10,038. Referee: Paul McBlane. Halftime: Newcastle 14–6. Goalkickers: Johns (Newcastle) 5/6, Reeves (Illawarra) 2/2, Bradstreet (Illawarra) 0/1. Seconds: Illawarra 20–12. Under-20s: Illawarra 36–8.
NEWCASTLE: O'Davis; Albert, Craigie, Grogan, Hughes; M.Johns, A.Johns; Butterfield, Clements, Harragon (c), Muir, Peden, Glanville. Interchange: Richards, Fletcher, Conley, Cochrane.
ILLAWARRA: Reeves, Seru, Timmins, Rodwell, Clifford; McGregor (c), Barrett; Cram, Callaway, Smith, Hart, Lamey, Mackay. Interchange: Bristow, Bradstreet, Hauville, Leikvoll.

Balmain 32 (W.Kennedy, D.Senter, A.Nable, J.Langaloa, L.Milford, T.Brasher tries; M.Withers 4 goals) defeated **South Queensland** 14 (J.Hudson, T.Pezet, B.Doyle tries; C.Schifcofske goal) at Leichhardt Oval, Sunday, August 10.

Scrums: South Queensland 6–4. Penalties: South Queensland 9–4. Crowd: 5101. Referee: Eddie Ward. Halftime: Balmain 20–0. Goalkickers: Withers (Balmain) 4/6, Schifcofske (South Queensland) 1/3. Seconds: Balmain 27–16. Under-20s: 26–all.
BALMAIN: Brasher; Langaloa, Kennedy, Withers, L.Milford; Gillett, Nable; Walker, Senter, Sironen (c), O'Neil, Smith, Morrison. Interchange: Hanley, Starr, Rudd, Donaghey.
SOUTH QUEENSLAND: Schifcofske; Hudson, Toshack, Eagar, Doyle; Watson, Pezet; Couper, Antonik, Jones, Protheroe, Retchless, Wilson (c). Interchange: Nutley, Sologinkin, A.Bella, Thorburn.

STANDINGS: Manly 28, Parramatta 26, Norths 25, Newcastle 23, Sydney City 21, Illawarra 19, Gold Coast 19, Balmain 18, Wests 18, St George 16, Souths 9, South Queensland 6.

OPTUS CUP ROUND 20
AUGUST 15, 16, 17

Wests revive finals hopes

A week after suffering their most humiliating defeat of the season, Western Suburbs reignited their hopes of reaching the finals with an 18-10 win over a 12-man North Sydney side at Campbelltown Sports Ground.

The Bears lost front-rower Josh Stuart, sent from the field after 15 minutes for a high tackle on Wests' replacement forward Shayne McMenemy, and despite leading 6-0 at halftime, they were always going to have to battle to hold off an enthusiastic Magpie outfit.

The turning point came a few minutes after halftime, when the Magpies won a scrum against the feed 25 metres out from the North Sydney line. Three rucks later, winger Brett Hodgson crossed for Wests' first try. They hit the lead when centre Kevin McGuinness scored midway through the second half. Then fullback Andrew Leeds kicked a field goal, putting his side in the comfort zone. Centre Ben Ikin scored for Norths eight minutes from fulltime, but the Magpies wrapped it up with a try to hooker Ciriaco Mescia four minutes from the whistle.

Manly continued their drive towards a third consecutive grand final appearance with an emphatic 30-14 defeat of Illawarra at Brookvale Oval.

There was never much doubt that Manly would take the two points on offer, despite Illawarra tries on either side of halftime (Barrett and Seru). Winger Danny Moore scored the first of his three tries after 10 minutes, and Manly were never headed after that point.

Newcastle moved into a share of third place on the Optus Cup ladder with a 44-18 win over the Gold Coast at Marathon Stadium. The Knights gained a measure of revenge over their shock 32-24 Round 9 loss at Carrara, but for a team with serious premiership aspirations, there was little to savour in the victory. The Knights were at times brilliant as they rattled up eight tries, but at other times their defensive commitment went out the window — they conceded four tries.

Balmain gave Sydney City an early taste of semi-final intensity in a torrid workout at the Sydney Football Stadium. With Andrew Walker producing another magical kicking display, the Roosters emerged with an 18-10 victory, continuing their surge towards a top three finish. Walker's spiralling bombs caused Balmain's fullback Tim Brasher no end of problems, and by the end of the day the Test star's confidence was shattered. The Roosters paid a heavy price for their win, however, with goalkicking centre Ivan Cleary breaking his thumb and five-eighth Adam Hayden fracturing an ankle.

A thumping second-half performance by Parramatta brought a smile to the face of coach Brian Smith as he watched his team score a 36-18 win over South Sydney at Parramatta Stadium.

The Eels trailed 12-8 at halftime, but ran in five second-half tries to signal a dramatic return to form. Winger Russell Wyer made a successful return to first grade after almost 12 months recovering from knee and shoulder surgery, while prop Peter Johnston also made a successful comeback from injury.

St George continued to push for a berth in the top seven when they scored a 14-0 shutout of the South Queensland Crushers at Suncorp Stadium. A crowd of 13,845 watched the match after the gates were thrown open to the public.

ROUND 20 — RESULTS

Wests 19 (B.Hodgson, Kevin McGuinness, C.Mescia tries; A.Leeds 3 goals; Leeds field goal) defeated **Norths** 10 (M.Buettner, B.Ikin tries; J.Taylor goal) at Campbelltown Sports Ground, Friday night, August 15.

Scrums: Wests 7–5. Penalties: Wests 10–5. Crowd: 10,219. Referee: Paul McBlane. Halftime: Norths 6–0. Goalkickers: Leeds (Wests) 3/4, Taylor (Norths) 1/2. Seconds: Norths 34–16. Under-20s: Norths 32–18.
WESTS: Leeds; D.Willis, Ken McGuinness, Kevin McGuinness, Hodgson; A.Willis, Georgallis; Skandalis, Mescia, Millard, Dunn, Kennedy, Langmack (c). Interchange: Capovilla, Hasler, McMenemy, Dowse.
NORTHS: Seers; Dallas, Buettner, Caruana, Roy; Florimo, Taylor (c); Stuart, Soden, Trindall, Larson, Fairleigh, Williams. Interchange: Hall, Pomery, Ikin, Reber.
Sin bin: Taylor (Norths).
Sent off: Stuart (Norths), 15 min. **Charge:** High tackle. **Sentence:** Three weeks. **Cited:** Kennedy (Wests). **Charge:** High tackle. **Sentence:** Exonerated.

Sydney City 18 (A.Hayden, A.Walker, N.Gaffey tries; I.Cleary 3 goals) defeated **Balmain** 10 (W.Kennedy 2 tries; M.Withers goal) at Sydney Football Stadium, Saturday, August 16.

Scrums: Sydney City 8–3. Penalties: 8–all. Crowd: 7183. Referee: Matt Hewitt. Halftime: Sydney City 12–4. Goalkickers: Cleary (Sydney City) 3/3, Withers (Balmain) 1/2. Seconds: Balmain 30–20. Under-20s: Balmain 20–16.
SYDNEY CITY: Walker; Elsegood, Cleary, Pearson, Sing; Hayden, Lam; Bonetti, Hermansson, Gourley, Ricketson, Fittler (c). Interchange: Rigon, Gaffey, Clarke, Garlick.
BALMAIN: Brasher; Langaloa, Kennedy, Withers, L.Milford; Gillett, Nable; Sironen (c), Senter, Walker, Stimson, O'Neil, Morrison. Interchange: Smith, Rudd, Donaghey, Hanley.

Parramatta 36 (N.Barnes, J.Simon, J.Morgan, T.Campbell, E.Navale, S.Collins tries; Simon 5, R.Wyer goals) defeated **Souths** 18 (B.O'Meara, W.Peters tries; J.O'Neill 5 goals) at Parramatta Stadium, Saturday night, August 16.

Scrums: 6–all. Penalties: Parramatta 13–10. Crowd: 11,301. Referee: Eddie Ward. Halftime: Souths 12–8. Goalkickers: Simon (Parramatta) 5/7, Wyer (Parramatta) 1/1, O'Neill (Souths) 5/5. Seconds: Parramatta 26–4. Under-20s: Souths 24–10.
PARRAMATTA: Carige; Whereat, Barnes, Wyer, Collins; Bell, Simon; Johnston, Campbell, Morgan, Jason Smith, McCracken (c), Dymock. Interchange: Navale, Horsnell, Jamie Smith, Lovell.
SOUTHS: O'Meara, Orford, Penna, Murray, O'Keefe; O'Neill (c), Peters; Parsons, Williams, Ostini, Slattery, Burns, Wilson. Interchange: McEwen, Rubin, White, Barnes.
Sin bin: Parsons (Souths).

Newcastle 44 (A.Muir 2, W.Richards, M.Hughes, B.Grogan, R.O'Davis, D.Albert, T.Butterfield tries; A.Johns 6 goals) defeated **Gold Coast** 18 (G.Mackay, W.Patten, T.O'Reilly, J.Goddard tries; B.Hurst goal) at Marathon Stadium, Sunday, August 17.

Scrums: Newcastle 10–2. Penalties: Newcastle 5–2. Crowd: 15,063. Referee: David Manson. Halftime: Newcastle 22–10. Goalkickers: Johns (Newcastle) 6/9, Hurst (Gold Coast) 1/2, Mackay (Gold Coast) 0/2. Seconds: Newcastle 36–14. Under-20s: Newcastle 34–14.
NEWCASTLE: O'Davis; Albert, Grogan, Craigie, Hughes; M.Johns, A.Johns; Harragon (c), Clements, Butterfield, Muir, Peden, Richards. Interchange: Conley, Fletcher, Crowe.
GOLD COAST: King; Bai, Mackay (c), Nicol, McKelleher; O'Reilly, Patten; Driscoll, Goddard, Parsons, Hurst, Sattler, Schloss. Interchange: Bella, Maher, Nahi, Blackett.

Manly 30 (D.Moore 3, A.Colella, C.Lyons, T.Hill tries; S.Nevin 3 goals) defeated **Illawarra** 14 (T.Barrett, F.Seru, W.Clifford tries; D.Moon goal) at Brookvale Oval, Sunday, August 17.

Scrums: Illawarra 11–8. Penalties: Manly 10–5. Crowd: 11,167. Referee: Kelvin Jeffes. Halftime: Manly 10–6. Goalkickers: Nevin (Manly) 3/7, Moon (Illawarra) 1/3. Seconds: Illawarra 26–12. Under-20s: Manly 34–4.
MANLY: Nevin; Moore, Innes, Hill, Hopoate; Lyons, Toovey (c); Tierney, Serdaris, Carroll, Menzies, Colella, Kosef. Interchange: Gillespie, Field.
ILLAWARRA: Moon; Seru, McGregor (c), Rodwell, Clifford; Barrett, Robinson; Cram, Callaway, Smith, Hart, Lamey, Mackay. Interchange: Bristow, Bradstreet, Leikvoll, J.Cross.

St George 14 (M.Bell, J.Lenihan, C.Pearson tries; W.Bartrim goal) defeated **South Queensland** 0, at Suncorp Stadium, Sunday, August 17.

Scrums: St George 8–2. Penalties: South Queensland 9–5. Crowd: 13,845 (free admission). Referee: Sean Hampstead. Halftime: St George 4–0. Goalkickers: Bartrim (St George) 1/2, Price (St George) 0/1. Seconds: South Queensland 13–12. Under-20s: St George 26–22.
ST GEORGE: D.Smith; Murphy, Coyne (c), Wagon, Bell; Price, Clinch; Pearson, Brown, Ward, Tangata-Toa, Thompson, Bartrim. Interchange: Felsch, Lenihan, Brunker, Hearn.
SOUTH QUEENSLAND: Schifcofske; Hudson, Toshack, Eagar, Doyle; Moule, Teevan (c); O'Brien, Antonik, Nutley, Bickerstaff, Retchless, Wilson. Interchange: Pezet, Tookey, Protheroe, A.Bella.

STANDINGS: Manly 30, Parramatta 28, Norths 25, Newcastle 25, Sydney City 20, Wests 20, Illawarra 19, Gold Coast 19, Balmain 18, St George 18, Souths 9, South Queensland 6.

ROUND 20

OPTUS CUP ROUND 21
AUGUST 22, 23, 24

Balmain's best in a decade

Balmain produced one of their finest performances of the 1990s to crush Parramatta 26-6 at Leichhardt Oval.

The match was in the balance at halftime when the Tigers led just 8-6, but tries to second-rower Mark Stimson and centre Greg Donaghey put Balmain in the box seat soon after the resumption. Balmain's defence swarmed and menaced Parramatta's attack for the full 80 minutes. It was breached only once, when prop Peter Johnston scored for the Eels in the 32nd minute. Fullback Tim Brasher described it as the best defensive effort he had seen, and coach Wayne Pearce declared it the best defence he had witnessed in his time at the club.

After leading 18-6 at the 57-minute mark, Balmain rammed home their advantage, with veteran Ellery Hanley sprinting 60 metres to score.

Winger Michael Withers added the icing to the cake with a try four minutes from fulltime. On a memorable night, in front of over 18,000 fans, Balmain scored wins in all three grades against the leaders of the club championship.

The Gold Coast took a giant leap towards a historic semi-finals berth with a 25-10 defeat of competition favourites Manly at Carrara Stadium.

The crowd of 15,872 cheered wildly as the Chargers produced their best win of the season and their first victory over Manly since 1989.

Hot and cold halfback Wes Patten was definitely hot on this occasion, and 33-year-old front-rower Martin Bella played a memorable farewell game at 'home', with a powerful display.

Sydney City secured a semi-final berth and St George bowed out of the reckoning as the Roosters ground out a 20-16 victory in a tense match at Kogarah Oval.

Saints were ruing a controversial no-try ruling, against winger Damien Smith 12 minutes from fulltime, which could have made all the difference to the result. The Roosters led 14-10 at the time and the try could have given St George the lead. Instead, Sydney City took advantage of the let-off and took the ball to the opposite end of the field, where halfback Adrian Lam delivered an exquisite pass to fullback Andrew Walker, who sealed the result with his second try. Minutes earlier Lam had been replaced by coach Phil Gould and given a dressing down for taking too many wrong options in attack.

Illawarra played themselves into a strong position to challenge for a semi-final place with a comprehensive 34-10 win over Western Suburbs at Campbelltown.

Both sides had everything to play for, but it was Illawarra who displayed the greater determination, despite playing in hostile territory. Wests trailed 14-10 at halftime, but instead of lifting their tackling effort in the second half, the Magpies' defence fell to pieces.

Newcastle took 40 minutes to find their feet against South Sydney, but then they ran up a 26-8 win and took another step towards a top three finish. Souths led 2-0 at halftime after a scrappy first 40 minutes, but when Knights centre Owen Craigie scored after eight minutes of the second term, the floodgates opened.

North Sydney ran in eight tries to thump South Queensland 42-8 at North Sydney Oval. The Bears took time to gather momentum, but once they found their feet, it was a one-way procession.

ROUND 21 — RESULTS

Balmain 26 (M.Withers 2, L.Milford, G.Donaghey, M.Stimson, E.Hanley tries; Withers goal) defeated **Parramatta** 6 (P.Johnston try; I.Herron goal) at Leichhardt Oval, Friday night, August 22.

Scrums: Balmain 6–4. Penalties: Balmain 8–7. Crowd: 18,203. Referee: Paul McBlane. Halftime: Balmain 8–6. Goalkickers: Withers (Balmain) 1/4, Brasher (Balmain) 0/3, Herron (Parramatta) 1/1, Simon (Parramatta) 0/1. Seconds: Balmain 22–12. Under-20s: Balmain 16–2.
BALMAIN: Brasher; Donaghey, Kennedy, Withers, L.Milford; Gillett, Nable; Walker, Senter, Sironen (c), Stimson, O'Neil, Morrison. Interchange: Starr, Langaloa, Rudd, Hanley.
PARRAMATTA: Riolo; Herron, Wyer, Barnes, Navale; Bell, Simon; Pay (c), Raper, Morgan, McCracken, Jason Smith, Dymock. Interchange: Collins, Campbell, Horsnell, Johnston.

Sydney City 20 (A.Walker 2, J.Elsegood, D.Miles tries; Walker 2 goals) defeated **St George** 16 (D.Smith, A.Brunker, S.Price tries; W.Bartrim 2 goals) at Kogarah Oval, Saturday, August 23.

Scrums: Sydney City 7–6. Penalties: Sydney City 9–6. Crowd: 7178. Referee: Kelvin Jeffes. Halftime: Sydney City 8–6. Goalkickers: Walker (Sydney City) 2/5, Bartrim (St George) 2/4. Seconds: Sydney City 44–20. Under-20s: Sydney City 48–4.
SYDNEY CITY: Walker; Elsegood, Sing, Pearson, Miles; Fittler (c), Lam; Barnhill, Bonetti, Hermansson, Gourley, Ricketson, Gaffey. Interchange: Rigon, Garlick, Clarke, Allan.
ST GEORGE: Murphy; D.Smith, Coyne (c), Wagon, Brunker; Price, Clinch; Pearson, Brown, Ward, Tangata-Toa, Thompson, Bartrim. Interchange: Treacy, Felsch, Ainscough.

Gold Coast 25 (C.Nahi, A.King, T.O'Reilly, S.Sattler tries; B.Hurst 4 goals; Hurst field goal) defeated **Manly** 10 (S.Menzies, J.Hopoate tries; S.Nevin goal) at Carrara Stadium, Saturday night, August 23.

Scrums: Manly 9–5. Penalties: Manly 9–5. Crowd: 15,872. Referee: Matt Hewitt. Halftime: Gold Coast 14–6. Goalkickers: Hurst (Gold Coast) 4/5, Nevin (Manly) 1/2. Seconds: Gold Coast 14–10. Under-20s: Manly 28–14.
GOLD COAST: King; Bai, Mackay (c), Nicol, Plowman; O'Reilly, Patten; Bella, Goddard, Parsons, Sattler, Hurst, Schloss. Interchange: Nahi, Maher, Blackett, McKelleher.
MANLY: Nevin; Moore, Innes, Hill, Hopoate; Lyons, Toovey (c); Tierney, Serdaris, Carroll, Menzies, Colella, Kosef. Interchange: Field, Fulton, Gillespie, Weepu.

Norths 42 (B.Moore 2, N.Roy 2, M.Buettner 2, P.Stringer, M.Seers tries; J.Taylor 5 goals) defeated **South Queensland** 8 (T.Pezet try; C.Schifcofske 2 goals) at North Sydney Oval, Sunday August 24.

Scrums: South Queensland 7–3. Penalties: Norths 9–6. Crowd: 7308. Referee: Eddie Ward. Halftime: Norths 16–8. Goalkickers: Taylor (Norths) 5/8, Schifcofske (South Queensland) 2/2. Seconds: Norths 36–10. Under-20s: South Queensland 31–18.
NORTHS: Seers; Dallas, Ikin, Buettner, Roy; Florimo, Taylor (c); Pomery, Caruana, Trindall, Larson, Fairleigh, Moore. Interchange: Hall, Stringer, Williams, Reber.
SOUTH QUEENSLAND: Schifcofske; Hudson, Toshack, Eagar, Doyle; Pezet, Teevan (c); R.Bella, Antonik, Nutley, Bickerstaff, Retchless, Wilson. Interchange: Protheroe, Tookey, Saunders, A.Bella.

Newcastle 26 (D.Albert 2, O.Craigie, B.Peden, A.MacDougall tries; L.Dynevor 3 goals) defeated **Souths** 8 (B.Williams try; J.O'Neill 2 goals) at Sydney Football Stadium, Sunday, August 24.

Scrums: Souths 4–3. Penalties: Souths 9–6. Crowd: 4260. Referee: Sean Hampstead. Halftime: Souths 2–0. Goalkickers: Dynevor (Newcastle) 3/5, O'Neill (Souths) 2/2. Seconds: Souths 26–20. Under-20s: Souths 30–28.
NEWCASTLE: O'Davis; Albert, Craigie, Grogan, Hughes; M.Johns, Dynevor; Butterfield, Clements, Harragon (c), Richards, Fletcher, Peden. Interchange: MacDougall, Conley, Smailes, Crowe.
SOUTHS: O'Meara; Orford, Penna, Simon, O'Keefe; O'Neill (c), Murray; Rubin, Williams, Ostini, Slattery, Burns, Wilson. Interchange: Parsons, Francis, White, Howlett.
Sin bin: Murray (Souths), Smailes (Newcastle).

Illawarra 34 (T.Barrett 3, S.Timmins 2, C.Leikvoll, W.Clifford tries; D.Moon 3 goals) defeated **Wests** 10 (Ken McGuinness, S.Georgallis tries; A.Leeds goal) at Campbelltown Sports Ground, Sunday, August 24.

Scrums: Illawarra 6–5. Penalties: Wests 8–4. Crowd: 8534. Referee: David Manson. Halftime: Illawarra 14–10. Goalkickers: Moon (Illawarra) 3/7, Leeds (Wests) 1/2. Seconds: Wests 18–16. Under-20s: Illawarra 14–4.
ILLAWARRA: Moon; Seru, Timmins, Rodwell, Clifford; J.Cross (c), Barrett; Cram, Callaway, Smith, Bradstreet, Lamey, Mackay. Interchange: Bristow, Leikvoll, McGregor, Robinson.
WESTS: Leeds; D.Willis, Ken McGuinness, Kevin McGuinness, Hodgeon; A.Willis, Georgallis; Howard, Mescia, Millard, Dunn, Kennedy, Langmack (c). Interchange: Hasler, McMenemy, Capovilla, J.Smith.

STANDINGS: Manly 30, Parramatta 28, Norths 27, Newcastle 27, Sydney City 25, Illawarra 21, Gold Coast 21, Balmain 20, Wests 20, St George 18, Souths 9, South Queensland 6.

OPTUS CUP ROUND 22
AUGUST 29, 30, 31

Knights too powerful

Newcastle sounded an ominous warning to their premiership rivals with a thumping 34-10 win over Balmain at Marathon Stadium.

The loss ended Balmain's brave bid for a semi-finals spot, but elevated the Knights to a place in the top three. Newcastle led 14-4 at halftime, although Balmain had the chance to fight their way back when it appeared that winger James Langaloa had scored a length-of-the-field intercept try soon after the resumption. Referee David Manson remained unmoved near the Balmain posts, however, awarding the Knights an offside penalty. So instead of looking at a 14-10 score, Balmain trailed 16-4 when Andrew Johns landed the penalty goal. From that point on, the Knights ran riot.

The Tigers chose their most important match of the year to suffer their heaviest defeat. They went into the game as the best defensive team in the competition, but the magnitude of the loss meant they handed that mantle to the Knights.

A spare parts Sydney City outfit scored a remarkable 29-20 victory over North Sydney at the Sydney Football Stadium and then started their preparations for meeting the same team at the same place in a qualifying semi-final six days later.

The Roosters went through the most disrupted preparation imaginable as they took on the Bears in what was effectively a 'dead rubber', but put it all over the Bears, who appeared to be developing a case of the staggers at the business end of the season.

Sydney City went into the match without Andrew Walker, Matt Sing, Jack Elsegood, Luke Ricketson, Scott Gourley, Jason Lowrie, Ivan Cleary, Adam Hayden, Sean Garlick and Robert Miles, but their replacements stood tall.

Test centre Paul McGregor produced his best performance of the season to spearhead Illawarra's 28-6 defeat of the Gold Coast at WIN Stadium and steer his team to its first finals berth since 1992. McGregor was in devastating touch, and the Chargers had no answer to his strength and skill. By halftime the Steelers were on their way to a top seven berth, with a lead of 20-0. The loss left the Chargers with an anxious wait to find out whether or not they would also qualify for the top seven. Ironically, the South Queensland Crushers did the right thing by their proposed merger partners by downing Western Suburbs 39-18 at Suncorp Stadium. The Crushers' win in their final match meant Gold Coast advanced to the finals at the expense of the Magpies.

It was a humiliating exit for Wests, and captain Paul Langmack, who was playing his 300th first-grade match. The Magpies only had to beat the competition wooden spooners to secure a semi-final position, but they never looked like winning. They trailed 12-0 after seven minutes, and the day never brightened.

The absence of a top-line goalkicker cost Parramatta a premiership point and placed their top-three berth in jeopardy after a 12-all draw with St George at Parramatta Stadium. The Eels scored three tries to one, but they missed with all three shots at goal.

Manly officially wrapped up the minor premiership with a 36-18 defeat of South Sydney at Brookvale Oval. The Sea Eagles trailed 18-16 at halftime, but four second-half tries saw them cruise to an effortless win.

ROUND 22 — RESULTS

Parramatta 12 (E.Navale, P.Carige, S.Collins tries) drew with **St George** 12 (L.Murphy try; W.Bartrim 4 goals) at Parramatta Stadium, Friday night, August 29.

Scrums: St George 11–6. Penalties: Parramatta 12–11. Crowd: 16,055. Referee: Eddie Ward. Halftime: 8–all. Goalkickers: Simon (Parramatta) 0/2, Wyer (Parramatta) 0/1, Bartrim (St George) 4/5. Seconds: Parramatta 28–4. Under-20s: St George 43–22.
PARRAMATTA: Carige; Collins, Wyer, Barnes, Navale; Bell, Simon; Pay (c), Raper, Horsnell, Jason Smith, Morgan, Dymock. Interchange: Pettet, Lovell, Riolo, Campbell.
ST GEORGE: Murphy; Lenihan, Wagon, Ainscough, B.Smith; Price, Clinch; Pearson, Brown (c), Ward, Tangata-Toa, Thompson, Bartrim. Interchange: Hearn, D.Smith, Perkins, Henare.
Sin bin: Murphy (St George).

Newcastle 34 (D.Albert 2, M.Hughes, A.Johns, A.MacDougall, W.Richards tries; A.Johns 5 goals) defeated **Balmain** 10 (A.Nable 2 tries; M.Withers goal) at Marathon Stadium, Saturday, August 30.

Scrums: Balmain 9–5. Penalties: Newcastle 4–2. Crowd: 22,157. Referee: David Manson. Halftime: Newcastle 14–4. Goalkickers: Johns (Newcastle) 5/7, Withers (Balmain) 1/2. Seconds: Newcastle 18–12. Under-20s: Newcastle 18–17.
NEWCASTLE: O'Davis; Albert, Hughes, Craigie, MacDougall; M.Johns, A.Johns; Butterfield, Clements, Harragon (c), Peden, Muir, Glanville. Interchange: Richards, Fletcher, Crowe, Gidley.
BALMAIN: Brasher; Donaghey, Kennedy, Withers, L.Milford; Gillett, Nable; Starr, Senter, Sironen (c), Stimson, O'Neil, Morrison. Interchange: Rudd, Langaloa, Hanley, McPherson.

Illawarra 28 (J.Cross, P.McGregor, D.Callaway, W.Clifford tries; D.Moon 6 goals) defeated **Gold Coast** 6 (B.Plowman try; G.Mackay goal) at WIN Stadium, Saturday night, August 30.

Scrums: 9–all. Penalties: Illawarra 9–6. Crowd: 12,089. Referee: Paul McBlane. Halftime: Illawarra 20–0. Goalkickers: Moon (Illawarra) 6/7, Mackay (Gold Coast) 1/1. Seconds: Illawarra 24–0. Under-20s: Illawarra 48–12.
ILLAWARRA: Moon; Seru, Timmins, Rodwell, Clifford; McGregor (c), Barrett; Cram, Callaway, Smith, J.Cross, Lamey, Mackay. Interchange: Hart, Leikvoll, Reeves, Bradstreet.
GOLD COAST: King; Bai, Mackay (c), Nicol, Plowman; O'Reilly, Patten; Bella, Goddard, Parsons, Sattler, Hurst, Schloss. Interchange: Driscoll, Nahi, McKelleher, Orr.

Sydney City 29 (G.Bourke, C.Halliday, A.Lam, S.Rigon, N.Wood tries; B.Pearson 3, R.Allan goals; B.Fittler field goal) defeated **Norths** 20 (M.Buettner, M.Reber, D.Hall tries; J.Taylor 4 goals) at Sydney Football Stadium, Sunday, August 31.

Scrums: Sydney City 6–3. Penalties: Sydney City 12–11. Crowd: 8569. Referee: Matt Hewitt. Halftime: 14–all. Goalkickers: Pearson (Sydney City) 3/5, Allan (Sydney City) 1/1, Taylor (Norths) 4/4. Seconds: Norths 40–14. Under-20s: Norths 22–14.
SYDNEY CITY: Shearer; Bourke, Clarke, Pearson, Halliday; Fittler (c), Lam; Barnhill, Bonetti, Hermansson, Logan, Fletcher, Gaffey. Interchange: Hood, Rigon, Wood, Allan.
NORTHS: Seers; Dallas, Caruana, Buettner, Roy; Florimo, Taylor (c); Pomery, Reber, Trindall, Larson, Fairleigh, Moore. Interchange: Hall, Williams, Pethybridge, Stringer.
Sin bin: Seers (Norths).

Manly 36 (A.Hunter 2, D.Gartner, C.Innes, J.Hopoate, G.Toovey, D.Moore tries; S.Nevin 4 goals) defeated **Souths** 18 (D.Penna, T.Barnes, T.Slattery, D.O'Keefe tries; Barnes goal) at Brookvale Oval, Sunday, August 31.

Scrums: Souths 9–6. Penalties: Souths 7–6. Crowd: 7514 Referee: Paul Simpkins. Halftime: Souths 18–16. Goalkickers: Nevin (Manly) 4/7, Barnes (Souths) 1/4. Seconds: Manly 24–10. Under-20s: Manly 30–24.
MANLY: Nevin; Hunter, Moore, Innes, Hopoate; Lyons, Toovey (c); Tierney, Serdaris, Carroll, Menzies, Gartner, Kosef. Interchange: Fulton, Field, Gillespie, Durdevic.
SOUTHS: O'Meara; Waugh, Penna, Simon, O'Keefe; Barnes, Murray; Rubin, Williams, Ostini, Slattery, Francis, Burns (c). Interchange: White, McNicholas, O'Neill, Wilson.

South Queensland 39 (M.Toshack, J.Jones, J.Hudson, M.Protheroe, C.Schifcofske, M.Eagar tries; Schifcofske 7 goals; C.Wilson field goal) defeated **Wests** 18 (B.Hickman, A.Leeds, J.Skandalis tries; Leeds 3 goals) at Suncorp Stadium, Sunday, August 31.

Scrums: Wests 9–7. Penalties: 8–all. Crowd: 11,588 (free admission). Referee: Kelvin Jeffes. Halftime: South Queensland 19–6. Goalkickers: Schifcofske (South Queensland) 7/8, Leeds (Wests) 3/3. Seconds: South Queensland 36–6. Under-20s: South Queensland 25–12.
SOUTH QUEENSLAND: Schifcofske; Hudson, Toshack, Eagar, Smith; Watson, Pezet; O'Brien, Teevan (c), Jones, Protheroe, Retchless, Wilson. Interchange: Nutley, Moule, A.Bella, Tookey.
WESTS: Leeds; D.Willis, Ken McGuinness, Kevin McGuinness, Hickman, Georgallis, Hasler; Howard, Mescia, Skandalis, Smith, Kennedy, Langmack (c). Interchange: McMenemy, Capovilla, A.Willis.
Sin bin: McMenemy (Wests), Eagar (South Queensland).

FINAL STANDINGS

Manly	32	Gold Coast	21
Newcastle	29	Balmain	20
Parramatta	29	Wests	20
Norths	27	St George	19
Sydney City	27	Souths	9
Illawarra	23	South Queensland	8

ARL OPTUS CUP 1997

FIRST GRADE

	P	W	L	D	F	A	Pts
Manly	22	15	5	2	521	366	32
Newcastle	22	14	7	1	512	320	29
Parramatta	22	14	7	1	431	359	29
Norths	22	13	8	1	529	341	27
Sydney City	22	13	8	1	487	366	27
Illawarra	22	10	9	3	423	376	23
Gold Coast	22	10	11	1	438	466	21
Balmain	22	10	12	-	339	340	20
Wests	22	10	12	-	355	424	20
St George	22	9	12	1	331	392	19
Souths	22	4	17	1	323	630	9
South Qld	22	4	18	-	321	630	8

SECOND GRADE

	P	W	L	D	F	A	Pts
Parramatta	22	15	7	-	468	317	30
Balmain	22	14	8	-	485	330	28
St George	22	13	9	-	395	351	26
South Qld	22	12	9	1	401	389	25
Illawarra	22	11	10	1	393	413	23
Manly	22	11	11	-	439	356	22
Sydney City	22	11	11	-	413	437	22
Gold Coast	22	11	11	-	311	421	22
Norths	22	9	11	2	436	430	20
Souths	22	9	12	1	336	441	19
Newcastle	22	9	13	-	345	326	18
Wests	22	4	17	1	292	503	9

UNDER-20s

	P	W	L	D	F	A	Pts
Balmain	22	13	6	3	441	362	29
Souths	22	13	8	1	434	411	27
Manly	22	13	9	-	492	361	26
Sydney City	22	12	10	-	476	375	24
Parramatta	22	12	10	-	451	375	24
Illawarra	22	11	10	1	417	346	23
Norths	22	11	10	1	350	359	23
St George	22	11	11	-	354	399	22
Wests	22	9	11	2	391	473	20
South Qld	22	8	13	1	417	428	17
Gold Coast	22	7	13	2	381	574	16
Newcastle	22	6	15	1	391	532	13

CLUB CHAMPIONSHIP

	First Grade	Second Grade	Under-20s	Total
Parramatta	116	90	48	254
Manly	128	66	52	246
Balmain	80	84	58	222
Sydney City	108	66	48	222
Norths	108	60	46	214
Illawarra	92	69	46	207
St George	76	78	44	198
Newcastle	116	54	26	196
Gold Coast	84	66	32	182
Souths	36	57	54	147
Wests	80	27	40	147
South Qld	32	75	34	141

* First grade points are multiplied by four, second grade by three, Under-20s by two

TOP POINTSCORERS
(After 22 premiership rounds)

Player	Tries	Goals	FG	Points
Jason Taylor (Norths)	9	89	3	217
Ivan Cleary (Sydney City)	5	69	-	158
Andrew Leeds (Wests)	3	47	3	109
Wayne Bartrim (St George)	5	43	-	106
Michael Withers (Balmain)	8	35	-	102
Leo Dynevor (Newcastle)	8	34	-	100
Clinton Schifcofske (South Qld)	6	35	-	94
Brendan Hurst (Gold Coast)	3	37	2	88
John Simon (Parramatta)	6	25	7	81
Terry Hill (Manly)	20	-	-	80
Craig Field (Manly)	3	31	1	75
Andrew Johns (Newcastle)	1	33	-	70
Darren Albert (Newcastle)	17	-	-	68
Graham Mackay (Gold Coast)	8	13	-	58
Robbie O'Davis (Newcastle)	10	8	1	57
Wayne Clifford (Illawarra)	14	-	-	56
Ian Herron (Parramatta)	2	24	-	56
Craig Innes (Manly)	10	6	-	52
Andrew Walker (Sydney City)	12	2	-	52
John Hopoate (Manly)	12	-	-	48
William Kennedy (Balmain)	12	-	-	48
Steve Menzies (Manly)	12	-	-	48
Wes Patten (Gold Coast)	12	-	-	48

TOP TRY SCORERS
(After 22 premiership rounds)

Player	Tries	Player	Tries
Terry Hill *(Manly)*	20	Brett Dallas *(Norths)*	10
Darren Albert *(Newcastle)*	17	Jack Elsegood *(Sydney City)*	10
Wayne Clifford *(Illawarra)*	14	Craig Innes *(Manly)*	10
John Hopoate *(Manly)*	12	Robbie O'Davis *(Newcastle)*	10
William Kennedy *(Balmain)*	12	Matt Sing *(Sydney City)*	10
Steve Menzies *(Manly)*	12	Shane Whereat *(Parramatta)*	10
Wes Patten *(Gold Coast)*	12	Chris Caruana *(Norths)*	9
Andrew Walker *(Sydney City)*	12	Jason Hudson *(South Qld)*	9
Trent Barrett *(Illawarra)*	11	Kevin McGuinness *(Wests)*	9
Adrian Brunker *(St George)*	11	Brandon Pearson (Wests, Sydney City)	9
Ken McGuinness *(Wests)*	11	Jason Taylor *(Norths)*	9
Owen Craigie *(Newcastle)*	10		

TOP GOALKICKERS
(After 22 premiership rounds)

Player	Goals	Attempts
Jason Taylor *(Norths)*	89	119
Ivan Cleary *(Sydney City)*	69	96
Andrew Leeds *(Wests)*	47	77
Wayne Bartrim *(St George)*	43	68
Brendan Hurst *(Gold Coast)*	37	60
Clinton Schifcofske *(South Qld)*	35	55
Michael Withers *(Balmain)*	35	70
Leo Dynevor *(Newcastle)*	34	51
Andrew Johns *(Newcastle)*	33	46
Craig Field *(Manly)*	31	60
John Simon *(Parramatta)*	25	57
Ian Herron *(Parramatta)*	24	36
Julian O'Neill *(Souths)*	21	29
Dean Moon *(Illawarra)*	18	30
Shannon Nevin *(Manly)*	17	29
Rod Wishart *(Illawarra)*	14	21
Darren Bradstreet *(Illawarra)*	13	23
Graham Mackay *(Gold Coast)*	13	25
Matt Manning *(Souths)*	10	17

HARVEY NORMAN FINALS SERIES

MINOR QUALIFYING FINALS — SEPTEMBER 5, 6, 7

Chargers' turnaround stuns the Steelers

Game 1 (6th v 7th)
Gold Coast 25, Illawarra 14

Less than one week after being humbled 28-6 by Illawarra, the Gold Coast performed a 33-point turnaround and defeated the Steelers 25-14 in the elimination minor qualifying final.

Many thought that merely qualifying for the finals would be reward enough for Phil Economidis' Chargers, who had already achieved a record season, but someone forgot to tell that to the players. The Chargers based their game plan on a simple rule — shut down Illawarra captain Paul McGregor, the man who had destroyed them six nights earlier at WIN Stadium.

It took the Gold Coast 62 minutes to score in Wollongong, but only two at Parramatta Stadium, when centre Jason Nicol crossed for the opening try. The scent of an upset was in the air at halftime when the Gold Coast led 14-4. Illawarra's best player, 19-year-old Trent Barrett, put his team back in the hunt when he scored 10 minutes into the second session, but it was the handling mistakes that virtually handed the match to the Chargers on a platter.

Industrious back-rower Scott Sattler extended Gold Coast's lead to 20-8 after 56 minutes, but their attempts to put the game beyond Illawarra's reach were foiled when rookie front-rower Scott Cram reduced the Chargers' lead to 20-14, 10 minutes before fulltime.

Halfback Wes Patten's field goal, three minutes before the end, finally extinguished the Steelers' season, before replacement John McKelleher rubbed salt into Illawarra's wounds with a 78th minute try.

Soon-to-retire Gold Coast veteran Martin Bella extended his career by another game with a vigorous effort in the front row, while hooker Jamie Goddard was dynamic at dummy-half and Patten was a constant threat to the Illawarra defence.

Fears that the Chargers would be without Goddard and replacement forward Clayton Maher for their second semi-final after the pair was reported for a dangerous tackle on Illawarra's John Cross were eased when they were found to have no case to answer.

Gold Coast 25 (J.Nicol, J.Schloss, G.Mackay, S.Sattler, J.McKelleher tries; Mackay 2 goals; W.Patten field goal) defeated **Illawarra** 14 (F.Seru, T.Barrett, S.Cram tries; D.Bradstreet goal) at Parramatta Stadium, Friday night, September 5.

Scrums: Gold Coast 9-6. Penalties: Illawarra 9-5. Crowd: 8197. Referee: David Manson. Halftime: Gold Coast 14-4. Goalkickers: Mackay (Gold Coast) 2/3, Anderson (Gold Coast) 0/2, Bradstreet (Illawarra) 1/1, Moon (Illawarra) 0/2.

GOLD COAST: King; Bai, Mackay (c), Nicol, Anderson; O'Reilly, Patten; Bella, Goddard, Parsons, Sattler, Des Clark, Schloss. Interchange: Nahi, McKelleher, Maher, Plowman.

ILLAWARRA: Moon; Seru, Timmins, Rodwell, Clifford; McGregor (c), Barrett; Cram, Callaway, Smith, J.Cross, Lamey, Mackay. Interchange: Hart, Leikvoll, Bradstreet, Reeves.

MINOR QUALIFYING FINALS

Game 2 (4th v 5th)
Sydney City 33, Norths 21

A wobbly field goal to halfback Adrian Lam was the catalyst for Sydney City's 33-21 win (in extra time) over North Sydney in a thrilling and memorable second minor qualifying final at the Sydney Football Stadium.

Lam's field goal, with only a few seconds of regular time remaining, levelled the scores at 15-all, forcing the match into overtime. The Roosters trailed 13-0 after 40 minutes, so their hard-earned second-half fightback gave them the ascendancy going into the extra 20-minute period.

They dominated the extra time, scoring three tries to one to advance to a meeting with the Gold Coast in the second week of qualifying finals.

The cool head of coach Phil Gould was an important factor in the Roosters' victory. He calmed his players at halftime and convinced them they had not played badly in the first half and that Norths would be hard-pressed to play as well for the second 40 minutes: 'Trust me, you can do it,' Gould told them.

He also had special words for fullback Andrew Walker, who had been pressured into several errors by a buoyant North Sydney defence during the first half. 'You have won more games for us than you have lost this year and you will continue to do so,' he told him. 'I'm on your side.'

A master at tapping into the mood of his team, Gould's words hit their mark: Walker and his team-mates rolled up their sleeves in the second period and refused to be beaten. They were first to score in the second half, through an Ivan Cleary penalty, and then Walker scored two tries to level the scores at 14-all, with eight minutes of regular time remaining.

Jason Taylor kicked his third field goal for Norths five minutes from fulltime, and when Lam could not sight Walker or captain Brad Fittler, the intended kickers, he opted to shoot for goal himself. The ball wobbled across the bar to level the scores at 15-all, much to the dismay of the Bears.

It was a telling psychological blow for Norths, who had to endure another 20 minutes of toil when they believed they had the match safely under wraps. Roosters hooker Sean Garlick broke the deadlock two minutes after the restart, and Ivan Cleary put the result beyond doubt with a try three minutes later.

Norths' room was a sombre sight after the match, but they tried their best to remain positive. A second chance awaited them a week later.

'It was a fantastic game of football and it was a huge improvement from us,' praised coach Peter Louis. 'It is always disappointing to lose, but I am sure we can come back.'

The result meant that Sydney City would now face the Gold Coast Chargers in one knockout semi-final, while Norths would oppose the loser of the Newcastle-Parramatta playoff scheduled for the following day.

Sydney City 33 (A.Walker 2, A.Lam, I.Cleary, S.Garlick tries; Cleary 6 goals; Lam field goal) defeated **Norths** 21 (B.Ikin, B.Dallas, C.Caruana tries; J.Taylor 3 goals; Taylor 3 field goals), in extra-time after scores were tied 15-all at end of 80 minutes, at the Sydney Football Stadium, Saturday, September 6. Scrums: 5-all. Penalties: Sydney City 9-6. Crowd: 11,332. Referee: Kelvin Jeffes. Halftime: Norths 13-0. Goalkickers: Cleary (Sydney City) 6/7, Taylor (Norths) 3/4.

SYDNEY CITY: Walker; Elsegood, Cleary, Pearson, Sing; Fittler (c), Lam; Barnhill, Bonetti, Hermansson, Gourley, Ricketson, Gaffey. Interchange: Garlick, Rigon, Fletcher, Wood.

NORTHS: Seers; Dallas, Hall, Buettner, Roy; Ikin, Taylor (c); Pomery, Soden, Trindall, Larson, Florimo, Moore. Interchange: Caruana, Williams, Reber, Stringer.

Sin bin: Seers (Norths).

Game 3 (2nd v 3rd)
Newcastle 28, Parramatta 20

Newcastle advanced to a meeting with minor premiers Manly after beating Parramatta 28-20 in one of the most gruelling semi-final matches on record.

Parramatta coach Brian Smith spent much of the second half rotating his interchange players and desperately trying to determine who was fit to return to the battle. He said there were at least three players who should not have been on the field in the latter stages of the match and Jason Bell, Paul Carige, Dean Pay and Ian Herron were all unable to finish the game.

The toll was no less serious for the Knights. Fullback Robbie O'Davis was put out of the game with concussion and centre Matthew Gidley was carted off with a broken leg. There were concerns that a rib injury to halfback Andrew Johns would rule him out of the clash with the Sea Eagles.

The injuries added drama to an enthralling contest. The match began on a disastrous note for the Knights, when Andrew Johns' kick-off sailed dead in-goal on the full. Parramatta took full advantage of the early field position to race in three tries in 18 minutes, to lead 18-0.

But as quickly as their big lead was established, it was slashed, as the Knights responded in kind. A double to winger Adam MacDougall and one to second-rower Adam Muir reduced the margin to 18-16 five minutes before halftime. O'Davis suffered a nasty head knock just before the break when he successfully tackled runaway Parramatta centre Nathan Barnes just short of the tryline. A try at that point could have tilted the balance of the match.

Parramatta moved to a four-point lead with a 47th minute penalty goal to Ian Herron, but just eight minutes later Andrew Johns put his stamp on the match with a try that left the Eels demoralised.

Taking the ball 15 metres from the Parramatta line, Johns stepped inside Dean Pay, beneath a John Simon tackle, past Troy Campbell and Justin Morgan and then stepped off his right foot to beat Russell Wyer and score, levelling the scores at 20-all. Johns damaged his ribs when he was tackled heavily as he scored and was in too much pain to attempt the conversion.

Up stepped second-rower Bill Peden, who, unfortunately for Newcastle, missed the simple attempt. Soon after, centre Owen Craigie kicked an angled penalty goal to give the Knights the lead for the first time in the match. Four minutes later referee Paul McBlane awarded a questionable try to replacement back Brett Grogan. The decision squared the ledger after a similarly doubtful ruling had allowed Jason Bell a try in the first half, but the calls for video assistance were again raised after the match.

Newcastle 28 (A.MacDougall 2, A.Muir, A.Johns, B.Grogan tries; A.Johns 3, O.Craigie goals) defeated **Parramatta** 20 (N.Barnes, J.Bell, I.Herron tries; Herron 4 goals) at the Sydney Football Stadium, Sunday, September 7.

Scrums: Newcastle 9-7. Penalties: Parramatta 5-4. Crowd: 17,849. Referee: Paul McBlane. Halftime: Parramatta 18-16. Goalkickers: Johns (Newcastle) 3/4, Craigie (Newcastle) 1/1, Peden (Newcastle) 0/1, Herron (Parramatta) 4/5.

NEWCASTLE: O'Davis; Albert, Gidley, Craigie, MacDougall; M.Johns, A.Johns; Butterfield, Clements, Harragon (c), Peden, Muir, Glanville. Interchange: Richards, Fletcher, Grogan, Hughes.

PARRAMATTA: Carige; Herron, Lovell, Barnes, Navale; Bell, Simon; Pay (c), Raper, Morgan, Jason Smith, McCracken, Dymock. Interchange: Campbell, Horsnell, Wyer, Pettet.

MINOR QUALIFYING FINALS

HARVEY NORMAN FINALS SERIES
MAJOR QUALIFYING FINALS — SEPTEMBER 12, 13, 14

The end of the Gold Coast fairytale

Game 1
Sydney City 32, Gold Coast 10

Hot favourites Sydney City ended the Gold Coast Chargers' fairytale run with a 32-10 win in the first major qualifying final at Parramatta Stadium.

The match was a contest for almost an hour — until the sin-binning of Chargers' captain Graham Mackay. Mackay had remonstrated with referee Paul McBlane as the teams left the field at halftime. When he again launched a verbal assault on McBlane after a decision went against the Chargers in the 54th minute, McBlane had no hesitation in sending him to the sin bin. While the former international was off the field, the Roosters scored three tries, killing off the Chargers' challenge.

With skipper Brad Fittler calling the shots, Sydney City started confidently, and it was Fittler who was first to score, after just six minutes. The Chargers responded with a try to centre Jason Nicol a few minutes later, but by halftime the Roosters had cleared out to 16-4.

Gold Coast prop Des Clark barged over three minutes after the resumption to make a game of it, but the loss of Mackay ended any faint hope the Chargers had that they could spring a major upset.

Tries to Matt Sing, Nathan Wood and Ivan Cleary took the Roosters from 16-10 to 30-10. The reality of the match was that even if Mackay had not been sin-binned, it was doubtful that the Chargers could have won.

Fullback Andrew Walker continued his outstanding late season form to play a starring role in the Roosters' win, with Fittler and Lam contributing heavily. The down side to the victory was the loss of penetrative centre Brandon Pearson, whose broken arm would rule him out for the rest of the season.

The loss ended a record season for the Chargers and their coach-of-the-year, Phil Economidis. He was philosophical after the match: 'We've exceeded all expectations, but the fairytale's over; 'Gus' Gould ripped out the last couple of pages. It didn't finish the way we wanted it to,' Economidis said.

The match marked the end of the career of veteran front-rower Martin Bella.

Sydney City 32 (I.Cleary 2, B.Fittler, A.Walker, M.Sing, N.Wood tries; Cleary 4 goals) defeated **Gold Coast** 10 (J.Nicol, Des Clark tries; D.Anderson goal) at Parramatta Stadium, Friday night, September 12.

Scrums: Sydney City 7-4. Penalties: Sydney City 8-6. Crowd: 10,466. Referee: Paul McBlane. Halftime: Sydney City 16-4. Goalkickers: Cleary (Sydney City) 4/8, Anderson (Gold Coast) 1/2, Mackay (Gold Coast) 0/1.

SYDNEY CITY: Walker; Miles, Cleary, Pearson, Sing; Fittler (c), Lam; Barnhill, Bonetti, Hermansson, Gourley, Ricketson, Gaffey. Interchange: Garlick, Rigon, Fletcher, Wood.

GOLD COAST: King; Bai, Mackay (c), Nicol, Anderson; O'Reilly, Patten; Bella, Goddard, Parsons, Sattler, Des Clark, Schloss. Interchange: Nahi, Maher, Plowman, Driscoll.

Sin bin: Mackay (Gold Coast).

Game 2
Norths 24, Parramatta 14

Parramatta's mounting injury worries took their toll in the major qualifying final against Norths at the Sydney Football Stadium, and the Eels' season ended with a 24-14 loss.

After their torrid battle with Newcastle a week earlier, the Eels struggled to field a fit 13, and managed only 25 minutes of ballwork in the lead-up to the match.

Predictably, Parramatta put everything into their opening assault. They led 10-0 after 12 minutes and 14-6 at halftime, but they could not hold out a determined North Sydney, who showed few ill-effects after their 100-minute loss to Sydney City seven days earlier.

The second half was all Norths. They scored 18 unanswered points as the Eels grew wearier by the minute. Pivotal to the Bears' win was the injection into the match of interchange player Chris Caruana. His fierce attitude was infectious, and he helped the Bears rediscover their fight.

Early tries to wingers Ian Herron and Shane Whereat gave Parramatta fans cause for optimism, but signs that the Eels' luck was not in emerged in the 19th minute, when a kick by Matt Seers was touched in-flight by a Parramatta defender and Bears centre Michael Buettner was able to scoop up the ball 20 metres upfield.

Buettner charged into open space and then sent an inside ball to winger Brett Dallas, who scored a try, totally against the run of play.

Parramatta responded with a strong try to lock Jim Dymock six minutes before halftime, and the Eels' hopes were high when they led by eight points at the break.

Their lead could have been extended to 14 points soon after the resumption but for a disallowed try to second-rower Justin Morgan. Referee David Manson ruled a pass from Jason Smith to Morgan was forward. This was the pivotal moment of the match.

Caruana left the bench to replace Mark Reber at hooker, and a succession of strong dummy-half bursts provided Norths with vital momentum. David Hall scored after 56 minutes, Caruana backed up a break by captain Jason Taylor to score soon after, and 15 minutes from fulltime, Caruana's reverse pass sent Taylor across for the try that sealed the win.

Parramatta's season ended with two losses, but their best year since 1986 did not deserve to be judged on those two matches.

The absence of five-eighth Jason Bell (broken leg) caused a significant disruption to the Eels' backline, and several other players, including key men Dean Pay and Jason Smith, carried injuries into the match.

For the fourth time in the 1990s, Norths had qualified for the preliminary final and a tilt at their first grand final since 1943.

Norths 24 (D.Hall, B.Dallas, C.Caruana, J.Taylor tries; Taylor 4 goals) defeated **Parramatta** 14 (I.Herron, J.Dymock, S.Whereat tries; Herron goal) at the Sydney Football Stadium, Saturday, September 13. Scrums: Norths 12-6. Penalties: Parramatta 3-0. Crowd: 17,025. Referee: David Manson. Halftime: Parramatta 14-6. Goalkickers: Taylor (Norths) 4/4, Herron (Parramatta) 1/3.

NORTHS: Seers; Dallas, Ikin, Buettner, Roy; Florimo, Taylor (c), Pomery, Reber, Trindall, Larson, Fairleigh, Moore. Interchange: Hall, Caruana, Williams, Stuart.

PARRAMATTA: Riolo; Herron, Lovell, Barnes, Whereat; Jason Smith, Simon; Pay (c), Moran, Johnston, Morgan, McCracken, Dymock. Interchange: Wyer, Horsnell, Pettet, Raper.

MAJOR QUALIFYING FINALS

Game 3
Manly 27, Newcastle 12

The newspaper headline said it all: 'Not bad for a dead rubber'. This referred to the fact that the result of the Manly-Newcastle major qualifying final had little bearing on the outcome of the final series. The words captured the mood of the fans after another maximum intensity qualifying final.

Two clubs with a growing rivalry ripped into each other at full throttle. There was no thought of self-preservation, even though, under the seven-team final series system, the winner and the loser would both have to front up again a week later, the winner to meet the in-form Sydney City and the loser to face North Sydney.

It was Manly who took the match 27-12, but not before an epic struggle. The Knights did not rate the loss a psychological blow to their premiership hopes. Newcastle went into the match without key men halfback Andrew Johns and fullback Robbie O'Davis, both of whom were expected to be fit should the Knights qualify for a rematch with the Sea Eagles in the grand final.

The game was not without its controversy. A 'torpedo-style' tackle by Manly's Nik Kosef on Newcastle five-eighth Matthew Johns provoked an angry response from the Knights and led to Johns' father confronting ARL chief executive Neil Whittaker after the match. Kosef was cited by the ARL's video review committee and later suspended for one week by the judiciary.

Manly took the early running, and for the second week in a row, Newcastle found themselves in catch-up mode early in the match. Against Parramatta the Knights had trailed 18-0 early in the match, and this time they were down 12-0 after 10 minutes following a 25-metre burst to the tryline by Manly lock Anthony Colella and a try to centre Terry Hill. The Knights hit back quickly, though, when centre Owen Craigie scored and halfback Leo Dynevor landed two goals.

The Sea Eagles landed a telling blow when winger John Hopoate powered through the tackle of winger Darren Albert to score a minute before halftime. The Knights were first to score after the resumption, however, with Matthew Johns diving on a loose ball in Manly's in-goal. It wasn't until the final 17 minutes that the Sea Eagles took control of a Newcastle side that was running short on fit troops.

Hopoate and Hill both completed try doubles and Craig Field added a field goal to clinch the win three minutes from fulltime.

The long-running battle between Mark Carroll and Paul Harragon continued, with Harragon taking the points on this occasion after Carroll knocked himself flat in a first-half exchange.

Manly 27 (T.Hill 2, J.Hopoate 2, A.Colella tries; S.Nevin 3 goals; C.Field field goal) defeated **Newcastle** 12 (O.Craigie, M.Johns tries; L.Dynevor 2 goals) at the Sydney Football Stadium, Sunday, September 14.

Scrums: Manly 5-3. Penalties: 6-all. Crowd: 26,531. Referee: Kelvin Jeffes. Halftime: Manly 16-8. Goalkickers: Nevin (Manly) 3/5, Dynevor (Newcastle) 2/3.

MANLY: Nevin; Moore, Innes, Hill, Hopoate; Kosef, Toovey (c); Gillespie, Serdaris, Carroll, Menzies, Gartner, Colella. Interchange: Fulton, Lyons, Tierney, Field.

NEWCASTLE: Hughes; Albert, Grogan, Craigie, MacDougall; M.Johns, Dynevor; Butterfield, Clements, Harragon (c), Peden, Muir, Glanville. Interchange: Richards, Fletcher, Jackson, Cochrane.

Cited: Kosef (Manly). **Charge:** Dangerous tackle. **Sentence:** One week.

HARVEY NORMAN FINALS SERIES

PRELIMINARY FINALS — SEPTEMBER 20, 21

Matthew Johns kicks Newcastle into the grand final

Game 1
Newcastle 17, Norths 12

A 36-metre Matthew Johns field goal two minutes from fulltime thrust Newcastle into the club's first grand final with a 17-12 defeat of the luckless North Sydney Bears. Just when this preliminary final was headed for extra time, Johns found his mark, breaking a 12-all deadlock and consigning the Bears to another off-season of heartache. The Bears took a short kick-off but their attempt to snatch an unlikely victory backfired when Owen Craigie raced away to score in the dying seconds.

The Knights' win was built on a strong first-half effort, in which they led 12-4, and a powerful defence that was able to limit the Bears to two tries after halftime. Tries to fullback Robbie O'Davis and hooker Bill Peden were both the result of Andrew Johns kicks that were spilled by Bears halfback and captain Jason Taylor.

To his credit, Taylor landed two penalty goals to keep his side in the hunt, and helped inspire a strong second-half fightback. But it was five-eighth Greg Florimo who was responsible for both North Sydney tries, the first from a magical over-the-shoulder pass to winger Nigel Roy and the second from a decisive pass which found a runaway Michael Buettner.

Ironically, Taylor, statistically the best kicker in the Optus Cup, missed both conversion attempts, either of which could have seen the Bears advance to the grand final. Twice the Knights pulled off try-saving tackles that could have changed the outcome of the match. First, centre Owen Craigie combined with Robbie O'Davis to fell Norths second-rower David Fairleigh close to the tryline, and three minutes later Darren Albert pulled off the most memorable tackle of the 1997 final series with a scything effort on tryline-bound Norths fullback Matt Seers, who had run 70 metres.

For the fourth time in seven years, Norths were left to lament an exit from the competition one week before the grand final. 'Don't ask me why, but it happens to us all the time,' said coach Peter Louis. 'Fundamental errors put us behind the eight-ball. It was a semi-final, it was hard to come back, but to our credit, we did.'

Newcastle 17 (R.O'Davis, O.Craigie, B.Peden tries; A.Johns 2 goals; M.Johns field goal) defeated **Norths** 12 (M.Buettner, N.Roy tries; J.Taylor 2 goals) at the Sydney Football Stadium, Saturday September 20.

Scrums: Norths 8-4. Penalties: Norths 10-5. Crowd: 22,510. Referee: Kelvin Jeffes. Halftime: Newcastle 12-4. Goalkickers: Johns (Newcastle) 2/2, Dynevor (Newcastle) 0/1, Taylor (Norths) 2/5.

NEWCASTLE: O'Davis; Albert, MacDougall, Craigie, Hughes; M.Johns, A.Johns; Butterfield, Peden, Harragon (c), Richards, Muir, Glanville. Interchange: Fletcher, Crowe, Dynevor, Dunley.

NORTHS: Seers; Dallas, Ikin, Buettner, Roy; Florimo, Taylor (c); Stuart, Reber, Trindall, Larson, Williams, Moore. Interchange: Fairleigh, Hall, Caruana, Pomery.

PRELIMINARY FINALS

Game 2
Manly 17, Sydney City 16

Sydney City scored three tries to Manly's two, but it was the defending premiers who won through to a grand final showdown with the Newcastle Knights after a heart-stopping 17-16 win in the second preliminary final.

Sea Eagles' halfback Craig Field potted a field goal three minutes from fulltime to break a 16-all deadlock after it appeared certain the match would be decided in extra-time.

The game was a thriller from start to finish. It featured teeth-rattling defence, breathtaking attacking movements and moments of high drama and controversy.

The Roosters scored the only try of the first half after Manly winger Danny Moore spilled a kick and it bounced into the waiting arms of Jack Elsegood, who scored in the 30th minute. The Tricolours went to the break with a 6-4 lead after fullback Shannon Nevin had landed two penalty goals for Manly. The Sea Eagles went into overdrive after halftime; an Anthony Colella break led to a Craig Innes try in the 45th minute and then Steve Menzies scored the try of the game after early work from Moore and Terry Hill in a movement which covered 80 metres.

Down 16-6, Sydney City refused to concede, and responded with tries to Elsegood (67 min) and second-rower Scott Gourley (73 min), which levelled the scores.

Manly enjoyed all the field position in the latter stages of the match and Field's one-pointer came after two unsuccessful attempts by Nevin. The Roosters were unable to play themselves into a position to try one of their own.

A significant handling error by hooker Sean Garlick proved particularly costly for the Roosters. Instead of working themselves into position for the drop goal, Sydney City handed possession to Manly and they were then able to work themselves deep inside Sydney City's ARL Clubs territory.

Field's one-point came with two minutes and 51 seconds left on the clock, and provided extra gratification for the 24-year-old who left South Sydney at the end of the 1996 season with the hope of playing in a grand final.

Manly's victory was soured by referee David Manson's reporting of Manly forwards Jim Serdaris and Neil Tierney for a dangerous throw on Roosters' replacement hooker Simon Bonetti. Although Tierney escaped censure, Serdaris was called before the judiciary and handed a one-week suspension, ruling him out of the grand final.

Boom youngster Anthony Colella turned in another outstanding performance for the Sea Eagles, and Geoff Toovey, Mark Carroll, Steve Menzies, Daniel Gartner and match-winner Field also played mighty roles in the victory, which put the Sea Eagles into their third consecutive grand final.

The result gave the ARL the grand final they so desperately hoped for. Manly and Newcastle prepared for the grudge match of the decade.

Manly 17 (C.Innes, S.Menzies tries; S.Nevin 4 goals; C.Field field goal) defeated **Sydney City** 16 (J.Elsegood 2, S.Gourley tries; I.Cleary 2 goals) at the Sydney Football Stadium, Sunday September 21.
Scrums: Sydney City 7-3. Penalties: 5-all. Crowd: 30,794. Referee: David Manson. Halftime: Manly 8-6. Goalkickers: Nevin (Manly) 4/5, Cleary (Sydney City) 2/3.
MANLY: Nevin; Moore, Innes, Hill, Hopoate; Toovey (c), Field; Gillespie, Serdaris, Carroll, Menzies, Gartner, Colella. Interchange: Lyons, Tierney.
SYDNEY CITY: Walker; Elsegood, Cleary, Rigon, Sing; Fittler (c), Lam; Barnhill, Garlick, Hermansson, Gourley, Ricketson, Gaffey. Interchange: Bonetti, Fletcher, Wood, Shearer.
Cited: Serdaris (Manly). **Charge**: Dangerous throw. **Sentence**: One week.

HARVEY NORMAN FINALS SERIES
GRAND FINAL — SEPTEMBER 28

A great day for The Greatest Game

Newcastle 22, Manly 16

The Newcastle Knights achieved one of the greatest fairytale victories in the long history of grand finals and, in doing so, gave the game of Rugby League the shot in the arm it so desperately needed.

The Knights' remarkable 22-16 win over Manly was achieved with only six seconds to spare before the match was to go into extra-time. A player with the audacity to go for broke, when almost every indicator suggested he do otherwise, came up with the match-winning play that brought delirium to a city and high emotion to even the most hardened supporters of the game.

Halfback Andrew Johns, who had been hospitalised earlier in the week with a perforated lung, darted out of dummy-half to the short side, dummied and gave 21-year-old winger Darren Albert open passage to the line. The record crowd erupted with unprecedented scenes of hysteria.

In pure football terms, the Knights went into the match as rank outsiders. Not one member of their squad had played a grand final, and they were up against the defending premiers, who had tasted both success and failure at grand final time in the past two seasons.

Manly had beaten Newcastle at their last 11 meetings. Not since 1992 had the Knights finished on top. For 40 minutes the script was a familiar one. Mark Carroll and Paul Harragon hurled themselves into each other with a series of bone-rattling charges and Manly scored three first-half tries (Hopoate, Innes and Nevin) to one (O'Davis) to lead 16-8 at the break — the same halftime score as two weeks earlier, when the Sea Eagles went on to win a major qualifying final 27-12.

The second half was dramatically different. The Knights inched to within six points with an Andrew Johns penalty goal in the 57th minute, and the pro-Newcastle crowd began to find their voice. Although there were noticeable signs of fatigue on both sides, the Knights remained willing. Repeated errors thwarted their attempts to work play down Manly's end of the field and the game became a war of attrition that the more experienced Sea Eagles looked destined to win.

At times the Knights looked out on their feet. Albert threw a pass from dummy-half that bobbled dangerously in-goal before being forced dead. The goal-line drop-out meant further pressure, which the Knights surely could not survive.

But, miraculously, they held on. Replacement forward Troy Fletcher made a long surge down centre-field and soon after that fullback Robbie O'Davis danced and jinked and with fullback Shannon Nevin and prop Mark Carroll hanging off him, managed to plant the ball on the line for a try. Andrew Johns converted, tying the scores at 16-all with five minutes left on the clock.

The final five minutes became a frantic grab for territory and the opportunity

GRAND FINAL 105

to shoot for field goal. Cliff Lyons had already missed once when he attempted to give Manly a seven-point buffer, but the flow of the game had altered.

Newcastle five-eighth Matthew Johns failed with two attempts, one which fell short and the other which agonisingly hit the upright and bounced away. With 30 seconds remaining, Andrew Johns made an attempt from out wide, but the kick was charged down. The Knights regained possession and it was from the next ruck that Johns dared to be different and sent Albert on his never-to-be-forgotten dash for the line.

Two-try hero Robbie O'Davis was judged man of the match. He became the first fullback to claim the Clive Churchill Medal and the first fullback to score two tries in a grand final.

While O'Davis was a worthy man of the match, there was no better performer on the Manly side than Geoff Toovey. Concussed in the first half when attempting to tackle Adam MacDougall, then struck in the face by the same player in the second half, Toovey returned to play a heroic role for the Sea Eagles.

Team-mate Craig Field also displayed great courage in returning to the field after badly injuring an ankle in the first 20 minutes of the game.

Beaten coach Bob Fulton sensed the tide turning late in the game. 'It was a fairytale come true. It seemed to be fate towards the end,' Fulton said. 'I'd say we were probably the better side on the day but they did everything they had to do. It's a credit to them, a credit to their coach and a credit to their district. If Manly weren't involved, there's no better club or group of people that I would like to see win it.'

Victorious coach Malcolm Reilly became the first foreign coach to win a premiership since New Zealander Bill Kelly took Balmain to the 1939 title. 'I'm just ecstatic. I've never been involved in a game that has had such a dramatic finish,' he said.

On the 200th anniversary of the founding of the city of Newcastle and the 10th anniversary of Newcastle's readmission to the major premiership competition, the Newcastle Knights entered Rugby League history.

Newcastle 22 (R.O'Davis 2, D.Albert tries; A.Johns 5 goals) defeated **Manly** 16 (J.Hopoate, C.Innes, S.Nevin tries; Nevin 2 goals) at the Sydney Football Stadium, Sunday, September 28.

Scrums: Newcastle 7-3. Penalties: Manly 7-4. Crowd: 42,482 (ground record). Referee: David Manson. Touch judges: Phil Cooley, Col White. In-goal judges: Paul Macinante, Tom Peet. Halftime: Manly 16-8. Goalkickers: Johns (Newcastle) 5/6, Nevin (Manly) 2/4. **Cited:** MacDougall (Newcastle). **Charge:** Striking. **Sentence:** Suspended for the 1998 pre-season plus two premiership games.

NEWCASTLE
1. Robbie O'Davis
2. Darren Albert
3. Adam MacDougall
4. Owen Craigie
5. Mark Hughes
6. Matthew Johns
7. Andrew Johns
8. Tony Butterfield
9. Bill Peden
10. Paul Harragon (c)
11. Wayne Richards
12. Adam Muir
13. Marc Glanville
Interchange
15. Troy Fletcher
16. Scott Conley
18. Lee Jackson
19. Steve Crowe

MANLY
1. Shannon Nevin
2. Danny Moore
3. Craig Innes
4. Terry Hill
5. John Hopoate
6. Geoff Toovey (c)
7. Craig Field
17. David Gillespie
15. Anthony Colella
10. Mark Carroll
11. Steve Menzies
12. Daniel Gartner
13. Nik Kosef
Interchange
8. Neil Tierney
9. Cliff Lyons
14. Scott Fulton
16. Andrew Hunter

BY THE CLOCK

Min.		
10	Hopoate try, Nevin goal	Manly 6-0
25	Innes try	Manly 10-0
30	A.Johns goal	Manly 10-2
34	O'Davis try, A.Johns goal	Manly 10-8
38	Nevin try, Nevin goal	Manly 16-8
57	A.Johns goal	Manly 16-10
75	O'Davis try, A.Johns goal	16-all
80	Albert try, A.Johns goal	Newcastle 22-16

CLIVE CHURCHILL MEDAL WINNER
Robbie O'Davis (Newcastle)

SECOND GRADE

LOWER GRADES FINALS SERIES

Parra's fourth seconds title

Unwanted halfback Chris Lawler spearheaded Parramatta to their first title in any grade since 1988 when they downed Balmain 26-16 in the second grade grand final. Lawler had been controversially overlooked by Eels' first-grade coach Brian Smith for all but one match of the 1997 season, despite the halfback's skills as a playmaker and goalkicker. Lawler played a major role in the Eels' 10-point victory over Balmain and his sweetly-timed pass to winger Steve Collins helped seal the win late in the match.

Parramatta had been beaten three times by Balmain during the season, but won the game that mattered most. They led 16-4 at halftime, and 18-4 soon after, but Balmain rallied to trail 22-16 with seven minutes remaining after a strong try to forward Chris St Clair.

Lawler's runaround with fullback David Riolo and his neat pass to a flying Collins wrapped up the premiership win three minutes from fulltime. After the match Lawler told reporters he would not be with the Eels in 1998. 'I'm still not certain what I'll be doing next year but I won't be at Parramatta,' Lawler said. 'That's the club's decision, not mine.'

The win gave Parramatta their fourth second (reserve) grade title, and followed their previous title win in 1979.

MINOR QUALIFYING FINALS

Manly 24 (Albert Torrens 2, Brett Warton, Nathan Black, Brent Byrne, Shayne Dunley tries) defeated **Sydney City** 22 (Greg Bourke, Ben MacDougall, Richie Allan, Matthew Relf tries; Bourke 2, Allan goals), September 5.
Sth Queensland 16 (Ryan Russell, Robert Bella, Heath Cruckshank tries; Scott Thorburn 2 goals) defeated **Illawarra** 10 (Paul Rossi, Andrew Purcell tries; Craig Fitzgibbon goal), September 6.
Balmain 22 (Lee Hennessey, Craig Freer, Chris St Clair tries; Freer 5 goals) defeated **St George** 18 (Lawrence Raleigh, Darren Remeka, Jamie Owens tries; Ben Kusto 3 goals), September 7.

MAJOR QUALIFYING FINALS

Sth Queensland 32 (Paul Hubbard, David Myles, Heath Cruckshank, Michael Davis, Tim Donovan tries; Myles 4, Scott Thorburn 2 goals) defeated **Manly** 16 (Albert Torrens, Alf Duncan, Shayne Dunley tries; Duncan 2 goals), September 12.
St George 24 (Damien Smith, Troy Perkins, Jamie Owens, Joel Caine, Jamie Kennedy tries; Caine 2 goals) defeated **Illawarra** 10 (Luke Patten try; Craig Fitzgibbon 3 goals), September 13.
Balmain 22 (Josh Bostock, Jamy Forbes, Chris St Clair, David Bayssari tries; Bayssari 3 goals) defeated **Parramatta** 17 (Eparama Navale 2, Daniel Brown tries; Chris Lawler 2 goals; Lawler field goal), September 14.

PRELIMINARY FINALS

Parramatta 24 (Andrew Frew 2, Scott Davey 2 tries; Chris Lawler 4 goals) defeated **St George** 10 (Ben Kusto 2, Nathan Blacklock tries; Jamie Owens 2 goals), September 20.
Balmain 12 (Chris St Clair, Steven Jolly tries; Craig Freer 2 goals) defeated **South Queensland** 8 (Jeremy Smith, David Myles tries), September 21.

GRAND FINAL

Parramatta 26 (A.Frew, S.Davey, S.Collins, D.Moran, S.Crouch tries; C.Lawler 3 goals) defeated **Balmain** 16 (L.Hennessey, D.Bayssari, C.St Clair tries; C.Freer 2 goals), September 28. Referee: Kelvin Jeffes. Scrums: 8-all. Penalties: Balmain 6-2. Goalkickers: Lawler (Parramatta) 3/6, Freer (Balmain) 2/3. Halftime: Parramatta 16-4.

PARRAMATTA: David Riolo; Andrew Frew, Greig Harland, Scott Davey, Steve Collins; Dennis Moran, Chris Lawler; Chris King, Daniel Brown, Nathan Cayless, Darren Pettet (c), Steve Crouch, Nathan Koina. Interchange: Troy Campbell, Craig Baker, Michael Vella, Leon Douglas. Coach: Peter Sharp.

BALMAIN: Gary Edwards; Lee Hennessey, Marshall Scott, Josh Bostock, Greg Donaghey; David Bayssari, Craig Freer; Adam Starr, Chris St Clair, Bernard Wilson (c), Asa Milford, Jody Rudd, Chris McPherson. Interchange: Jamy Forbes, Todd Batson, Tia Liavaa, Steven Jolly. Coach: Dan Stains.

UNDER-20s

A year after finishing with the wooden spoon, Balmain capped a remarkable turnaround to claim the under-20s premiership after a hard-fought 13-12 win over Sydney City in the grand final.

A try to former North Queensland forward Andrew Meads helped the Tigers to a 12-6 lead midway through the second half, after the scores had been locked at 6-all at halftime. They increased their lead with a late field goal to captain and five-eighth Anthony Golder. Golder's one point proved crucial because a converted try to Roosters' winger Chad Halliday just 90 seconds from fulltime cut Balmain's lead to 13-12.

The win was especially sweet for Balmain centre Jamin Hall and prop Michael Worboys, who had been released by Sydney City at the end of the 1996 season. The victory gave Balmain their first win in any grade since they took out the reserve grade title in 1984.

Nine members of the Tigers' grand final side played in the club's 1996 President's Cup outfit that finished a distant last.

MINOR QUALIFYING FINALS

Norths 28 (David Cook 2, Wes Tillott 2, Erin Wignell, David Hicks tries; Wade Kelly 2 goals) defeated **Illawarra** 12 (Mark Simon, Andrew Bobbin, Trent Burns tries), September 5.

Parramatta 22 (Dennis Moran, Trent Tavoletti, Chris Smith, Ian Hindmarsh tries; Moran 3 goals) defeated **Sydney City** 14 (Justin Brooker 2, Ronald Prince tries; Damien Mostyn goal), September 6.

Souths 21 (Shane Rothery, Tere Glassie, Robert Simms tries; Troy Barnes 4 goals; Barnes field goal) defeated **Manly** 20 (Chris West, Todd Eadie, Dallas Waters, Toby Green tries; Waters 2 goals), September 7.

MAJOR QUALIFYING FINALS

Parramatta 26 (John Wilson, Morgan Quinlan, Simon Gwynne, Andrew McFarland, Michael Vella tries; Adam Toro 3 goals) defeated **Norths** 16 (David Cook, Nick Shaw, Jamie Fitzgerald tries; Wade Kelly 2 goals), September 12.

Sydney City 18 (Justin Brooker, Chad Halliday, Justin Smith tries; Smith 3 goals) defeated **Manly** 16 (Leigh Krilich, Toby Green, Luke Faul tries; Dallas Waters 2 goals), September 13.

Balmain 34 (Jamin Hall, Luke Barrell, John Kaho, Blake Comerford, Andrew Meads, Troy Wozniak, Mark Schrantz tries; Hall 3 goals) defeated **Souths** 14 (Troy Barnes, Tere Glassie tries; Barnes 3 goals), September 14.

PRELIMINARY FINALS

Sydney City 42 (Paul Khoury 2, Justin Brooker, Ronald Prince, Matthew Relf, Trent Robinson, Justin Smith tries; Smith 7 goals) defeated **Souths** 10 (Troy Barnes, Shane Rothery tries; Barnes goal), September 20.

Balmain 16 (Jamin Hall 2, Michael Worboys tries; Hall 2 goals) defeated **Parramatta** 14 (John Wilson, Luke O'Connor tries; Adam Toro 3 goals), September 21.

GRAND FINAL

Balmain 13 (R.Chehade, A.Meads tries; J.Hall 2 goals; A.Golder field goal) defeated **Sydney City** 12 (C.Halliday, A.Large tries; J.Smith 2 goals), September 28.

Referee: Paul McBlane. Halftime: 6-all.

BALMAIN: Luke Haylen; Rabie Chehade, Jamin Hall, Luke Barrell, John Kaho; Anthony Golder (c), Blake Comerford; Michael Worboys, Martin Cook, David Wright, Troy Wozniak, Steve Valentish, Andrew Meads. Interchange: Troy Guyatt, Jon Olsen, James Webster, Mark Schrantz. Coach: Peter Camroux.

SYDNEY CITY: Justin Brooker; Anthony Minichiello, Chad Halliday, Ben MacDougall, Damien Mostyn; Justin Smith, Paul Khoury (c); Trent Robinson, Matthew Relf, Peter Cusack, Andrew Lomu, Hayes Lauder, Jay Croke. Interchange: Brendan Currie, Andrew Roberts, Ronald Prince, Andrew Large. Coach: Arthur Kitinas.

AWARD WINNERS 1997

Following the forced abandonment of the Rothmans Medal presentation because of anti-tobacco legislation, a new award was introduced in 1997 by the ARL and supported by the Nokia telecommunications company. The Nokia Provan-Summons Medal replaced the Rothmans Medal and was named in honour of Norm Provan and Arthur Summons, whose images appeared in the famous 'Gladiators' photograph, snapped by *Sun-Herald* photographer John O'Gready after the 1963 grand final, and which adorn the Optus Cup trophy.

For the first time, the media was included in the voting process, which previously had been the sole domain of officiating referees. The awards ceremony, staged in Sydney's ANA Hotel in September, also comprised presentations to the coach of the year, the rookie of the year and the State of Origin player of the series.

NOKIA PROVAN-SUMMONS MEDAL

Sydney City and Australian Test captain Brad Fittler confirmed his status as the leading player in the game when he was awarded the inaugural Provan-Summons Medal. Fittler won the award ahead of Parramatta's John Simon and 1996 winner Jason Taylor of North Sydney.

The 25-year-old Test five-eighth missed four games during the season through injury, however he polled enough points during the 18 games he did play to take out his first major individual award. Fittler told the large gathering at the presentation ceremony that he was honoured to win the award. 'It's one thing for people to say you are a great player but you can't accept that until you win this award,' he said.

Fittler did not appear on the leader's board after the first five rounds of the season, but had moved into a share of the lead by Round 10. He was equal sixth after 15 rounds, and by Round 20 he had moved to third place behind Simon and Taylor. He stormed home in the final two rounds of the season to score nine points out of a possible 12.

Fittler was the first Sydney City player to win the competition's official Best and Fairest award since Mike Eden in 1983.

Major Points for 1997

40	Brad Fittler (Sydney City)
35	John Simon (Parramatta)
34	Jason Taylor (Norths)
32	Robbie O'Davis (Newcastle)
30	Jason Bell (Parramatta)
28	Wes Patten (Gold Coast)
26	Greg Florimo (Norths), Brendan Hurst (Gold Coast), Brad Mackay (Illawarra), Steve Menzies (Manly), Colin Ward (St George)
24	Andrew Walker (Sydney City)
23	Daniel Gartner (Manly), Nik Kosef (Manly)
20	Jim Dymock (Parramatta), Michael Gillett (Balmain), Adrian Lam (Sydney City), Mark Soden (North Sydney)
19	Tony Butterfield (Newcastle)
18	Paul Harragon (Newcastle), Jeremy Schloss (Gold Coast)
17	Leo Dynevor (Newcastle), Craig Innes (Manly)
16	Tim Brasher (Balmain), Billy Moore (Norths), Darren Senter (Balmain)
15	Dean Pay (Parramatta)
14	Nathan Brown (St George), Darren Burns (Souths), Paul Langmack (Wests), Matt Seers (Norths)
13	David Fairleigh (Norths), Terry Hermansson (Sydney City), William Kennedy (Balmain), Cliff Lyons (Manly), Glenn Morrison (Balmain), Lance Thompson (St George)
12	Darren Albert (Newcastle), Craig Field (Manly), Andrew Leeds (Wests), Justin Morgan (Parramatta), Craig Wilson (South Queensland)
11	Dean Callaway (Illawarra), Terry Hill

(Manly), Kevin McGuinness (Wests),
Luke Ricketson (Sydney City),
Will Robinson (Illawarra), Jason Smith
(Parramatta), Mark Stimson (Balmain)
10 Bill Dunn (Wests), Jason Hudson
(South Queensland)
9 Brett Clements (Newcastle),
Jarrod McCracken (Parramatta),
Brendan Reeves (Illawarra),
Steve Trindall (Norths)
8 Mark Carroll (Manly), Owen Craigie
(Newcastle), Peter Driscoll (Souths)
7 Simon Bonetti (Sydney City),
Troy Campbell (Parramatta), Adam Doyle
(Wests), Andrew King (Gold Coast),
Ciriaco Mescia (Wests), Matt Parsons
(Souths), Troy Pezet (South Queensland), Shane Russell (Gold Coast),
Jim Serdaris (Manly), Paul Sironen
(Balmain), Hudson Smith (Balmain),
Adam Starr (Balmain), Craig Teevan
(South Queensland)

Best and Fairest Medal winners

1968 Terry Hughes (Cronulla)
1969 Denis Pittard (Souths)
1970 Kevin Junee (Easts)
1971 Denis Pittard (Souths)
1972 Tom Raudonikis (Wests)
1973 Ken Maddison (Cronulla)
1974 Graham Eadie (Manly)
1975 Steve Rogers (Cronulla)
1976 Ray Higgs (Parramatta)
1977 Mick Cronin (Parramatta)
1978 Mick Cronin (Parramatta)
1979 Ray Price (Parramatta)
1980 Geoff Bugden (Newtown)
1981 Kevin Hastings (Easts)
1982 Greg Brentnall (Canterbury)
1983 Michael Eden (Easts)
1984 Terry Lamb (Canterbury)
1985 Wayne Pearce (Balmain)
1986 Mal Cochrane (Manly)
1987 Peter Sterling (Parramatta)
1988 Barry Russell (Cronulla)
1980 Gavin Miller (Cronulla) and Mark
Sargent (Newcastle)
1990 Peter Sterling (Parramatta)
1991 Ewan McGrady (Canterbury)
1992 Allan Langer (Brisbane)
1993 Ricky Stuart (Canberra)
1994 David Fairleigh (Norths)
1995 Paul Green (Cronulla)
1996 Jason Taylor (Norths)
1997 Brad Fittler (Sydney City)
(Rothmans Medal 1968-96,
Nokia Provan-Summons Medal 1997)

ROOKIE OF THE YEAR

Illawarra front-rower Scott Cram capped an outstanding first season in top-grade football when he was named the ARL's Rookie of the Year.

A product of the Western Suburbs club in Wollongong, Cram cemented a first-grade berth early in the season, quickly impressing with his honesty and willingness for hard work. But his playing future hung in the balance one night in June after he was airlifted to hospital by helicopter suffering suspected spinal damage. Doctors cleared him of serious injury, enabling him to resume with the Steelers as they made their march to the finals.

Rookie of the Year winners

1992 Matthew Rodwell (Newcastle)
1993 Jack Elsegood (Manly)
1994 Matt Seers (Norths)
1995 John Hopoate (Manly)
1996 Ben Kennedy (Canberra)
1997 Scott Cram (Illawarra)
(Norwich Rising Star 1992-96, ARL Rookie of the Year 1997)

COACH OF THE YEAR

No-one was surprised when affable Gold Coast coach Phil Economidis was named Coach of the Year for 1997. The Chargers enjoyed by far the most successful season of any Gold Coast team over the past decade and Economidis played no small part.

Written off as finals prospects at the start of the season, the Chargers were moulded into a competitive unit by Economidis, who plotted upset victories over most of the leading teams in the competition. That he achieved his results on a restricted budget and with limited playing resources made him a stand-out for the award.

STATE OF ORIGIN PLAYER OF THE SERIES

Queensland halfback Adrian Lam was a surprised winner of the ARL's award for the player of the State of Origin series. Not because the Queensland side he captained lost the series two games to one, but Lam thought one of his team-mates deserved the honour.

'My team-mate Robbie O'Davis had a great series so I'm a bit surprised to get the award, especially because the series didn't go how we wanted it to,' he said.

Lam was a strong performer in his first series as Queensland captain and played an inspiring role in the final match at the Sydney Football Stadium, won 18-12 by the Maroons.

DALLY M AWARDS

The Dally M awards, conducted by the News Limited organisation since 1980, were discontinued in 1997 because of the staging of separate ARL and Super League competitions.

Previous winners are listed below.

Dally M Player-of-the-Year winners

1980	Robert Laurie (Souths)
1981	Steve Rogers (Cronulla)
1982	Ray Price (Parramatta)
1983	Terry Lamb (Wests)
1984	Michael Potter (Canterbury)
1985	Greg Alexander (Penrith)
1986	Peter Sterling (Parramatta)
1987	Peter Sterling (Parramatta)
1988	Gavin Miller (Cronulla)
1980	Gavin Miller (Cronulla)
1990	Cliff Lyons (Manly)
1991	Michael Potter (St George)
1992	Gary Freeman (Easts)
1993	Ricky Stuart (Canberra)
1994	Cliff Lyons (Manly)
1995	Laurie Daley (Canberra)
1996	Allan Langer (Brisbane)

CLIVE CHURCHILL MEDAL

History has an uncanny sense of symmetry and it was never more so than when Robbie O'Davis captured the Clive Churchill Medal as man of the match in the 1997 grand final. The award itself is named after a diminutive and gallant fullback, who was born and bred in the city of Newcastle.

O'Davis may not have been born there, but his slashing two-try effort against Manly in the 1997 decider assures him of favoured son status in the Newcastle district for the rest of his days. O'Davis had his own claims on history as the first fullback to win the Medal.

'If I get hit by a bus tomorrow, I will die a very happy man,' an elated O'Davis told a massive television audience seconds after the award was announced on grand final day.

Clive Churchill Medal Winners

1986	Peter Sterling (Parramatta)
1987	Cliff Lyons (Manly)
1988	Paul Dunn (Canterbury)
1980	Bradley Clyde (Canberra)
1990	Ricky Stuart (Canberra)
1991	Bradley Clyde (Canberra)
1992	Allan Langer (Brisbane)
1993	Brad Mackay (St George)
1994	David Furner (Canberra)
1995	Jim Dymock (Bulldogs)
1996	Geoff Toovey (Manly)
1997	Robbie O'Davis (Newcastle)

OTHER MAJOR AWARDS

Rugby League Week **Player of the Year:** Brad Fittler (Sydney City)

Runners-up: Craig Smith (Illawarra), Jamie Goddard (Gold Coast)

Super League Player of the Year (Telstra Medal): Laurie Daley (Canberra)

Super League Coach of the Year: Wayne Bennett (Brisbane)

AWARD WINNERS 1997

THE CLUBS

Balmain

Balmain's best season since 1990 still could not ease the disappointment of missing out on the finals for the seventh successive year.

The Tigers were formidable opponents in almost every game they played in 1997. Their defence was among the best in the competition, and they were semi-final possibilities until the final match of the regular season.

Their failure to take the extra step was cause for much frustration in Tiger Town. If narrow losses to grand finalists Manly in the opening match of the season (10-14), Sydney City in Round 9 (14-18) or Gold Coast in Round 14 (20-22) had been reversed, Balmain would have been certain qualifiers.

Instead, they went into their final round match against Newcastle at Marathon Stadium needing to win to keep their finals hopes alive. The Tigers met a hot opposition that day, a team showing the kind of form that would take them to premiership honours a month later. Balmain's 34-10 loss was their biggest defeat of the season.

A week earlier, the Tigers had produced their best win of the season — 26-6 against Parramatta at Leichhardt Oval. The Eels were just a week away from clinching the club championship, but in a tremendous display of depth, the Tigers won all three grades that night, before a bumper crowd of 18,203.

The quality of that performance was almost equalled by a 14-10 win over Manly at Brookvale Oval and a 28-0 defeat of Wests at Leichhardt in Round 5. Manly had not been beaten at home since 1995, but Balmain's display of class and aggression that day showed they could match any team in the competition.

The Tigers' return to their 'spiritual' home of Leichhardt Oval was a significant boost to the club in every way. Two seasons in the 'wilderness' at

PLAYERS RECORDS 1997

Player	App	Int	T	G	FG	Pts
David Bayssari	-	3	-	-	-	0
Stephen Bosse	-	1	-	-	-	0
Josh Bostock	2	-	1	-	-	4
Tim Brasher	19	-	4	8	-	32
Greg Donaghey	9	6	2	-	-	8
Gary Edwards	2	1	-	-	-	0
Craig Freer	1	1	-	2	-	4
Michael Gillett	19	3	6	-	1	25
Ellery Hanley	8	6	1	-	-	4
Steven Jolly	11	-	1	-	-	4
William Kennedy	22	-	12	-	-	48
James Langaloa	13	2	7	-	-	28
Chris McPherson	-	5	1	-	-	4
Asa Milford	1	3	-	-	-	0
Laloa Milford	14	-	5	-	-	20
Glenn Morrison	19	1	3	-	-	12
Adam Nable	8	3	3	-	-	12
Mark O'Neil	13	7	-	-	-	0
Jody Rudd	-	5	-	-	-	0
Marshall Scott	1	1	-	-	-	0
Darren Senter	22	-	2	-	-	8
Paul Sironen	21	-	1	-	-	4
Hudson Smith	10	10	-	-	-	0
Chris St Clair	-	3	-	-	-	0
Adam Starr	10	11	1	-	-	4
Mark Stimson	21	-	1	-	-	4
Shane Walker	13	7	-	-	-	0
Jason Webber	9	3	3	-	-	12
Bernard Wilson	-	2	-	-	-	0
Michael Withers	18	1	8	35	-	102
30 players	22		62	45	1	339

CAPTAINCY: Sironen 21, Brasher 1

Parramatta Stadium had not attracted the fans and had done nothing for performances on the field. The turnaround began on the opening night of their '97 campaign. A crowd of 18,247 turned out to watch Balmain take on defending premiers Manly and, although disappointed by the narrow 14-10 defeat, they could not have been more pleased with the spirit and determination of Wayne Pearce's charges.

Encouraging crowds continued to watch Balmain at Leichhardt, creating an atmosphere to which the Tigers responded on the field. Crowds averaged 10,355, a 63 per cent improvement on their average at Parramatta Stadium in 1996 and the best figures at Leichhardt since the grand final year of 1989.

The downside to the season was the unseemly delay in contract negotiations with fullback Tim Brasher. The club could not strike a deal with the Test fullback, despite talks which stretched the full length of the season. It distracted attention from the club's improvement on the field and did little to enhance the image of the club or the game. Ultimately, the club stood its ground, and when Brasher failed to meet a deadline on a new contract, they ceased negotiations.

Brasher's departure for South Sydney meant the Tigers could afford two or three additional quality players. The arrival of Manly grand final fullback Shannon Nevin could prove especially valuable, not only as a fullback replacement for Brasher. A former Australian Junior Kangaroo captain, Nevin is also a competent goalkicker, an area in which the Tigers have struggled for several seasons.

Balmain's kickers, led by winger Michael Withers, landed only 50 per cent of their attempts at goal in 1997.

Club captain Paul Sironen agreed to another season with the Tigers in 1998 and, given a clear run with injuries, could overtake Garry Jack's record 244 first-grade games with the club. Sironen's experience will continue to combine well with the emerging talents of Michael Gillett, Mark Stimson, Darren Senter, Adam Nable and William 'Bubba' Kennedy, all of whom enjoyed outstanding seasons in 1997.

Young centre Jason Webber impressed in his first season in first grade until sidelined with injury. He should return a better player in 1998.

Balmain performed exceptionally in the lower grades, Peter Camroux's under-20s winning the premiership, and Dan Stains' second grade bowing out only in the grand final. The emergence of these two sides was due in no small part to the development work of George Thompson, who sadly passed away in September.

Despite the uncertainty that has gripped Rugby League, Balmain strengthened their position in 1997 by concentrating on two of life's most basic tenets — hard work and discipline.

MATCH RECORDS 1997

Played	Ground	Result	Score
Manly	Leichhardt	Lost	10-14
Illawarra	Leichhardt	Lost	10-18
Gold Coast	Carrara	Lost	6-26
Souths	Leichhardt	Won	22-16
Wests	Leichhardt	Won	28-0
St George	Kogarah	Lost	10-16
Norths	Leichhardt	Won	9-7
South Qld	Suncorp	Won	18-16
Sydney City	Leichhardt	Lost	14-18
Parramatta	Parramatta	Lost	14-25
Newcastle	Leichhardt	Lost	18-26
Manly	Brookvale	Won	14-10
Illawarra	WIN	Won	18-6
Gold Coast	Leichhardt	Lost	20-22
Souths	Stadium	Won	16-2
Wests	Campbelltown	Lost	10-20
St George	Leichhardt	Won	10-4
Norths	North Sydney	Lost	14-22
South Qld	Leichhardt	Won	32-14
Sydney City	Stadium	Lost	10-18
Parramatta	Leichhardt	Won	26-6
Newcastle	Marathon	Lost	10-34

Played 22: won 10, lost 12, for 339, against 340

THE CLUBS

Gold Coast

The performance of the Gold Coast Chargers under coach Phil Economidis in 1997 was like a breath of fresh air in the most disturbing and divided season in the game's history.

Apparently finished as a Rugby League entity at the end of 1995, the 'new' Gold Coast rose from the ashes of eight failed seasons at Tweed Heads to establish a new base at Carrara, and with a tougher, more competitive outlook, achieved success beyond any reasonable expectation.

The signs were there in 1996 that Economidis had that special ingredient that defines a quality football coach, but without a stable of stars like those of the higher-profile clubs, results were modest. Even with the competition split down the middle, no-one rated Economidis' team a hope of matching skills with the established Sydney clubs.

They were made to take notice on the first Saturday of the 1997 season. The Chargers scored their first-ever win over Western Suburbs, and new winger Shane Russell crossed for a club-record four tries. In a golden period for the club in May and June, the Chargers won five and drew one of seven matches.

Among their scalps were eventual premiers Newcastle, whom they beat 32-24 at Carrara, and semi-finalists Illawarra (11-10 at Carrara). They were unlucky not to beat Manly for the first time at Brookvale Oval, instead settling for a 26-all draw.

Later in the season they broke through for their first win over Manly since 1989 when they thumped the defending premiers 25-10 before 15,872 fans at Carrara.

The fairytale charge looked certain to end, though, when they were humbled 28-6 by Illawarra in the Round 22 match at WIN Stadium.

PLAYERS RECORDS 1997

Player	App	Int	T	G	FG	Pts
Darren Anderson	5	4	1	7	-	18
Marcus Bai	18	-	5	-	-	20
Martin Bella	13	5	1	-	-	4
Keith Blackett	-	7	1	-	-	4
Craig Bowen	-	1	1	-	-	4
Dave Clark	4	-	1	-	-	4
Des Clark	8	4	1	-	-	4
Kris Currie	1	1	-	-	-	0
Damien Driscoll	18	2	-	-	-	0
Tony Durheim	6	5	-	-	-	0
Matthew Dwyer	7	-	1	-	-	4
Jared Fox	-	1	-	-	-	0
Jamie Goddard	19	-	5	-	-	20
Michael Goodrich	-	1	-	-	-	0
Brendan Hurst	22	-	3	37	2	88
Andrew King	21	-	5	-	-	20
Graham Mackay	24	-	9	15	-	66
Clayton Maher	-	4	-	-	-	0
John McKelleher	10	6	3	-	-	12
Chris Nahi	6	14	3	-	-	12
Frank Napoli	-	1	-	-	-	0
Jason Nicol	18	2	7	-	-	28
Tom O'Reilly	11	6	6	-	-	24
Chris Orr	12	6	1	-	-	4
Stephen Parsons	10	5	1	-	-	4
Wes Patten	22	2	12	-	1	49
Brett Plowman	3	6	3	-	-	12
Shane Russell	10	-	8	-	-	32
Scott Sattler	18	6	3	-	-	12
Jeremy Schloss	18	1	7	-	-	28
Hamish Smith	-	1	-	-	-	0
Henry Suluvale	4	-	-	-	-	0
Gavin Whittaker	-	5	-	-	-	0
Scott Zahra	4	-	-	-	-	0
34 players	24		88	59	3	473

CAPTAINCY: Mackay 24

Incredibly, the South Queensland Crushers, playing their last-ever match, managed to knock Western Suburbs out of the running and give the Chargers an 11th hour reprieve. The Chargers scraped into the finals in seventh position, meaning they would confront Illawarra for the second week running in the first elimination semi-final.

To most pundits, the Gold Coast were mere cannon fodder for Paul McGregor and the Steelers, who made such light work of their match in Wollongong. But the Gold Coast were determined to make something of their opportunity at Parramatta Stadium. They began brilliantly, with a Jason Nicol try in the opening minutes. The Chargers barely gave Illawarra a sniff, and at fulltime, the Gold Coast were up 25-14, giving them a semi-final win at their first attempt.

The dream run ended a week later at the hands of Sydney City, but not even defeat at Parramatta Stadium could dampen celebrations for a record year. Predictably, Economidis was named coach of the year at the ARL's Nokia awards. His common-sense approach to coaching and his down-to-earth style earned him many admirers.

The acquisition of halfback Wes Patten from Balmain was one of the club's most important purchases. The 23-year-old had failed to establish himself as a top-grader with the Tigers, but the Chargers were prepared to give him the chance. He did not disappoint, providing the spark the club had lacked. He finished the year with 12 tries and, significantly, played two of his best games against Balmain — matches both won by the Chargers.

Fullback Andrew Kling was named Chargers' player of the year and 23-year-old front-rower Steve Parsons the rookie of the year. Both returned to the Coast in 1997 after stints in British football. Hooker Jamie Goddard and lock Jeremy Schloss played their way into Queensland's State of Origin side, while five-eighth Tom O'Reilly, winger Marcus Bai and back-rower Chris Nahi all represented the Rest of the World in the one-off Test against Australia.

Veteran Martin Bella ended his career on a high note with a number of storming late-season efforts. Coach Economidis took full advantage of the unlimited interchange rule to use the 33-year-old Bella in short, effective bursts.

Home crowds showed a significant increase on 1996 figures. The average crowd at Carrara, 8,958, was up 24 per cent. The increase in local support, plus the better-than expected results on the field, convinced club officials that the Chargers should strive to remain a separate entity in the game.

Discussions with the financially embattled South Queensland Crushers to form the game's first joint venture were aborted late in the year.

MATCH RECORDS 1997

Played	Ground	Result	Score
Wests	Campbelltown	Won	24-16
Souths	Stadium	Lost	16-26
Balmain	Carrara	Won	26-6
St George	Kogarah	Lost	12-18
Norths	Carrara	Lost	16-20
South Qld	Suncorp	Won	22-14
Sydney City	Carrara	Lost	24-34
Parramatta	Parramatta	Lost	10-28
Newcastle	Carrara	Won	32-24
Manly	Brookvale	Drew	26-all
Illawarra	Carrara	Won	11-10
Wests	Carrara	Lost	10-26
Souths	Carrara	Won	28-4
Balmain	Leichhardt	Won	22-20
St George	Carrara	Won	22-14
Norths	North Sydney	Lost	28-34
South Qld	Carrara	Won	40-18
Sydney City	Stadium	Lost	12-28
Parramatta	Carrara	Lost	8-18
Newcastle	Marathon	Lost	18-44
Manly	Carrara	Won	25-10
Illawarra	WIN	Lost	6-28
ILLAWARRA	PARRAMATTA	WON	25-14
SYDNEY CITY	PARRAMATTA	LOST	10-32

Played 24: won 11, lost 12, drew 1, for 473, against 512

THE CLUBS

Illawarra

Illawarra experienced a season of solid improvement in 1997 under the strong and positive leadership of coach Andrew Farrar.

The Steelers rallied well after the bitterly disappointing years of 1995 and 1996 to qualify for the finals for only the second time in the club's history. Ultimately, though, the club fell short of expectations when they were bundled out of the final series by the Gold Coast in the first elimination semi-final.

The uncompromising style which was a trademark of Farrar's playing career quickly became evident in his coaching methods, and there were encouraging results early in the season. The Steelers won four and drew one of their first six matches to be placed third on the ladder.

Injuries and representative requirements took their toll, though, as the Steelers slumped to two draws and five losses from their next seven matches. They recovered with a series of strong performances late in the season, including a 15-8 defeat of Norths a week after the Bears had humbled Manly by a record score, a 28-24 win over Parramatta, which ended the Eels' 10-match winning streak, and important wins over Wests (34-10) and Gold Coast (28-6) when a semi-final berth was on the line.

Captain Paul McGregor carried the Steelers' hopes during 1997 and for much of the year he did not disappoint. At times he was back to his devastating best and showed the way to an inexperienced backline that was crying out for leadership.

Unsettling for McGregor and the rest of the Steelers were doubts over the Test centre's future with the club. It appeared that Illawarra would not have the funds to retain McGregor, and many supporters were becoming resigned to losing him — until he came to an agreement with management late in the year.

Test winger Rod Wishart played just

PLAYERS RECORDS 1997

Player	App	Int	T	G	FG	Pts
Glen Air	13	1	4	2	-	20
Trent Barrett	20	-	12	-	1	49
Darren Bradstreet	15	6	2	14	-	36
Adam Bristow	7	10	3	-	-	12
Jonathan Britten	1	-	-	-	-	0
Dean Callaway	15	-	2	-	-	8
Wayne Clifford	23	-	14	-	-	56
David Cox	-	9	1	-	-	4
Scott Cram	18	5	2	-	-	8
John Cross	15	4	3	-	-	12
Michael Cross	-	1	-	-	-	0
Maea David	1	9	-	-	-	0
Andrew Hart	10	6	1	-	-	4
Brendon Hauville	3	3	1	-	-	4
Jason Hooper	-	1	-	-	-	0
Terry Lamey	7	4	-	-	-	0
Chris Leikvoll	-	11	1	-	-	4
Brad Mackay	21	-	3	-	-	12
Paul McGregor	17	1	6	-	-	24
Dean Moon	6	1	-	18	-	36
Andrew Purcell	1	2	-	-	-	0
Brendon Reeves	16	4	5	8	-	36
Will Robinson	12	1	3	-	-	12
Brett Rodwell	19	1	6	-	-	24
Fili Seru	12	2	2	-	-	8
Craig Smith	20	-	-	-	-	0
Shaun Timmins	22	-	7	-	-	28
Brendon Tunbridge	-	10	-	-	-	0
Rod Wishart	5	-	3	14	-	40
30 players	23		81	56	1	437

CAPTAINCY: McGregor 17, J.Cross 6

five matches before the recurrence of a shoulder injury forced him to undergo surgery and sit out the season. The injury cost Wishart the chance of becoming the first Steeler to score 1,000 first-grade points. At the time of his injury he had amassed 986 points. Wishart's loss made it even more important for McGregor to lead from the front. Nineteen-year-old five-eighth Trent Barrett benefitted greatly from McGregor's presence; so much so that he was selected to play for NSW in the final State of Origin match.

Barrett undoubtedly would have led the voting in rookie of the year calculations but for a two-week suspension served for a high tackle on Manly's Steve Menzies in Round 9.

Barrett, a youngster from Temora, in the NSW Riverina, showed great maturity in his first full season in first grade, developed some outstanding ball skills and growing in confidence with each appearance.

As Barrett was ineligible for the rookie of the year award, the title went to a team-mate, front-rower Scott Cram. A local junior, Cram established himself in first grade early in the season and went on to appear in every match. He survived a major scare in the Round 13 game against Balmain at WIN Stadium, when he was airlifted to hospital with suspected spinal injuries. Cleared by orthopaedic specialists, Cram was fit to take his place in the Steelers' lineup for their next match.

Cram and Barrett were two members of an exciting crop of players who had their first real taste of first grade in 1997. Keen to blood as many talented youngsters as possible, coach Farrar introduced players such as Terry Lamey, Andrew Hart, Chris Leikvoll, Brendon Tunbridge and Adam Bristow to first grade.

MATCH RECORDS 1997

Played	Ground	Result	Score
Souths	WIN	Won	50-10
Balmain	Leichhardt	Won	18-10
St George	WIN	Lost	8-20
Norths	North Sydney	Drew	18-all
Sth Queensland	WIN	Won	14-6
Sydney City	Stadium	Won	26-20
Parramatta	WIN	Lost	16-23
Newcastle	Marathon	Lost	4-20
Manly	WIN	Drew	34-all
Wests	WIN	Lost	2-6
Gold Coast	Carrara	Lost	10-11
Souths	Stadium	Drew	28-all
Balmain	WIN	Lost	6-18
St George	Kogarah	Won	12-10
Norths	WIN	Won	15-8
Sth Queensland	Suncorp	Won	34-8
Sydney City	WIN	Lost	12-34
Parramatta	Parramatta	Won	28-24
Newcastle	WIN	Lost	12-22
Manly	Brookvale	Lost	14-30
Wests	Campbelltown	Won	34-10
Gold Coast	WIN	Won	28-6
GOLD COAST	PARRAMATTA	LOST	14-25

Played 23: won 10, lost 10, drew 3, for 437, against 401

The performance of the Steelers' lower grades was a feature of the season, and for the first time in the club's history, all three grades qualified for the finals.

Player of the year went to New Zealand-born prop Craig Smith. Virtually unheralded at the start of the season, Smith survived a visit to the judiciary to take his place in the Queensland State of Origin side, and later represented the Rest of the World against Australia.

The retention of McGregor was a priority for Steelers' management, who were otherwise relatively inactive in the player market; the only signficant new blood to arrive at the club in 1998 will be former Norths and South Queensland lock Craig Wilson.

The club's bright start to the 1997 season led to an increase in home crowds from 7,450 in 1996 to 8,695 in 1997.

ILLAWARRA

THE CLUBS

Manly-Warringah

For the second time in three seasons, Manly were left to contemplate a heartbreaking grand final loss after having proved themselves the best team in the competition during the regular season.

The Sea Eagles had everything in their favour going into the grand final — they had beaten Newcastle at their previous 11 meetings, and they were a team with vast grand final experience confronting a team of grand final novices.

That they led Newcastle by six points with five minutes to play and somehow managed to lose by six was bewildering for a side that had built its reputation on its defence.

However, the fact was that Manly's 1997 defensive record was not in the same league as their tight defence of 1996. The Sea Eagles of 1997 conceded 72 tries in their 25 games — an average of 2.9 tries per game. In 1996, Manly allowed just 34 tries — 1.4 per game.

There were a number of factors at work in the decline of the Sea Eagles' defence. The departure of fullback Matthew Ridge and second-rower Owen Cunningham had a significant impact. Ridge was missed for his talk and Cunningham for his workrate.

The other factor was a change in emphasis by referees on the ruck rule. Super League players and coaches decided that the way to speed up the game was to make play-the-balls lightning fast. The ARL tried to strike a balance between an existing rule that was being exploited by defending players lying on top of the tackled player for as long as they possibly could and Super League's new system (which, until sanity prevailed, was in danger of allowing the game to turn into touch football).

The upshot was that Manly's defenders were forced to retreat faster. Their opponents could build greater momentum, and tries flowed.

The gap between Manly and the rest of the field narrowed dramatically in 1997. During the season, the Sea Eagles were beaten by Balmain and Wests, two teams that missed the seven-team finals

PLAYERS RECORDS 1997

Player	App	Int	T	G	FG	Pts
Mark Carroll	24	-	-	-	-	0
Anthony Colella	6	2	3	-	-	12
Dragan Durdevic	-	1	-	-	-	0
Craig Field	17	8	3	31	3	77
Scott Fulton	5	16	-	-	-	0
Daniel Gartner	18	-	4	-	-	16
David Gillespie	12	9	-	-	-	0
Matt Guberina	-	1	-	-	-	0
Craig Hancock	17	-	7	-	-	28
Terry Hill	23	-	22	-	-	88
John Hopoate	25	-	15	-	-	60
Andrew Hunter	8	8	7	4	-	36
Craig Innes	25	-	12	6	-	60

Player	App	Int	T	G	FG	Pts
Robert Johnson	-	2	-	-	-	0
Nik Kosef	23	-	-	-	-	0
Cliff Lyons	8	15	7	-	-	28
Steve Menzies	25	-	13	-	-	52
Danny Moore	22	2	7	-	-	28
Shannon Nevin	9	2	3	26	-	64
Jim Serdaris	19	-	4	-	-	16
Neil Tierney	13	11	1	-	-	4
Geoff Toovey	25	-	3	-	-	12
Billy Weepu	1	10	-	-	-	0
23 players	25		111	67	3	581

CAPTAINCY: Toovey 25

series, they drew (34-all) with sixth-placed Illawarra, they had a draw (26-all) and a loss to the Gold Coast, who finished the minor rounds in seventh place, and they were beaten by a record score by North Sydney (41-8).

But for all of that, Manly were comfortable minor premiers for the third consecutive season. They won their first seven games and were never headed on the competition ladder. They recorded a number of magnificent victories, particularly against Sydney City (34-24 at Brookvale) and Newcastle (14-12 at Marathon).

The Sea Eagles dominated the ARL's representative teams. Ten players were involved in the City-Country match at Newcastle, seven players figured in the State of Origin series, and six played in the Australia-Rest of the World Test.

The team was again inspired by the efforts of halfback Geoff Toovey. His heroic grand final performance on a beaten side typified his toughness and character. His coach, Bob Fulton, would not swap him for any other halfback in Rugby League. So effective is his leadership that Fulton branded the 28-year-old a natural to become a future first-grade coach.

Around him, centres Terry Hill and Craig Innes formed a formidable partnership, scoring 34 tries between them; Hill topped the ARL lists with 22. Utility back Craig Field exhibited some wonderful attacking skills, and 22-year-old second-rower Anthony Colella proved to be the discovery of the 1997 finals series.

Once again, the back row of Steve Menzies, Daniel Gartner and Nik Kosef excelled, with Menzies again up among the leading tryscorers, with 13 for the season.

The Sea Eagles were rocked by the loss of fullback Craig Hancock with a fractured leg in the Round 17 loss to Parramatta, and one-week suspensions which ruled Nik Kosef out of the preliminary final against Sydney City and Jim Serdaris out of the grand final.

Manly struggled in the area of goalkicking, achieving only 54 per cent success in 1997, compared with 74 per cent in 1996.

The arrival of former Canberra winger Luke Phillips, who scored 122 points for North Queensland in 1997, may redress that concern.

The club farewelled Test prop Mark Carroll (London), winger Danny Moore (Wigan), centre Craig Innes (Leeds), international stalwart David Gillespie (retired), fullback Shannon Nevin (Balmain) and former Junior Kiwi representatives Billy Weepu and Robert Johnson (both released).

Crowds at home fell marginally on 1996 averages.

MATCH RECORDS 1997

Played	Ground	Result	Score
Balmain	Leichhardt	Won	14-10
St George	Kogarah	Won	18-14
Norths	Brookvale	Won	12-8
South Qld	Suncorp	Won	36-16
Sydney City	Brookvale	Won	34-24
Parramatta	Parramatta	Won	18-8
Newcastle	Brookvale	Won	22-8
Wests	Campbelltown	Lost	16-19
Illawarra	WIN	Drew	34-all
Gold Coast	Brookvale	Drew	26-all
Souths	Stadium	Won	30-16
Balmain	Brookvale	Lost	10-14
St George	Brookvale	Won	28-4
Norths	North Sydney	Lost	8-41
South Qld	Brookvale	Won	46-12
Sydney City	Stadium	Won	21-12
Parramatta	Brookvale	Lost	10-17
Newcastle	Marathon	Won	14-12
Wests	Brookvale	Won	48-14
Illawarra	Brookvale	Won	30-14
Gold Coast	Carrara	Lost	10-25
Souths	Brookvale	Won	36-18
NEWCASTLE	STADIUM	WON	27-12
SYDNEY CITY	STADIUM	WON	17-16
NEWCASTLE	STADIUM	LOST	16-22

Played 25: won 17, lost 6, drew 2, for 581, against 416

MANLY-WARRINGAH

THE CLUBS

Newcastle

The Newcastle Knights' first act in defending the premiership won so gallantly in September was to create a 'no-pressure zone'. The Knights have looked back at previous premiership winners and how they have defended their crowns to establish strategies of their own for 1998. They figure the first six weeks is the key to a successful year. If they stumble at the first hurdle, then the pressure could crush them.

Of course this is all new territory for the Knights, who won their first premiership title in the most dramatic circumstances against Manly. The victory produced scenes of hysteria and emotion never before witnessed in the game in Australia.

The springboard to victory came late in the season. Although among the front-running teams for the entire home-and-away series, it took a 34-10 pasting of Balmain in the final round at Marathon Stadium to establish the Knights as genuine premiership material. Until that point, Balmain had the best defensive record in the league, but that was laid bare by the Knights, who turned in a sizzling performance.

There were other superb displays during the year as well — a 28-16 win against Sydney City at the Sydney Football Stadium and a 29-10 win over Parramatta at Marathon among them — but the timing of the win, and the Knights' complete domination of the Tigers, cast the die for the weeks ahead.

Newcastle played four finals series matches of unequalled intensity. They outlasted Parramatta 28-20 in a match in which there were barely 26 fit players left standing, were beaten 27-12 by Manly in a rugged and spiteful qualifying final, survived a nail-biting preliminary final with North Sydney and then overcame Manly in the final six seconds of the grand final.

It took a team of great character to go the distance. Led superbly by Paul Harragon, the Knights had the support

PLAYERS RECORDS 1997

Player	App	Int	T	G	FG	Pts
Darren Albert	26	-	18	-	-	72
Danny Buderus	-	1	-	-	-	0
Anthony Butterfield	26	-	2	-	-	8
Brett Clements	9	4	1	-	-	4
Evan Cochrane	7	3	2	-	-	8
Scott Conley	-	21	-	-	-	0
Owen Craigie	26	-	12	1	-	50
Stephen Crowe	-	5	-	-	-	0
Leo Dynevor	17	2	8	36	-	104
Troy Fletcher	2	23	1	-	-	4
Matthew Gidley	12	4	3	-	-	12
Marc Glanville	23	-	2	-	1	9
Brett Grogan	9	3	4	-	-	16
Paul Harragon	18	3	1	-	-	4
Mark Hughes	12	5	4	-	-	16
Lee Jackson	15	3	1	-	-	4
Andrew Johns	9	2	2	43	-	94
Matthew Johns	20	1	2	-	1	9
Adam MacDougall	10	1	5	-	-	20
Jason Moodie	9	3	6	-	-	24
Adam Muir	25	-	8	-	-	32
Robbie O'Davis	25	-	13	8	1	69
Jarrod O'Doherty	-	3	-	-	-	0
Bill Peden	24	2	5	-	-	20
Wayne Richards	14	6	2	-	-	8
Daniel Smailes	-	6	1	-	-	4
26 players	26		103	88	3	591

CAPTAINCY: Harragon 18, Butterfield 6, M.Johns 2

of a city steeped in league tradition behind them. Harragon overcame a worrying period early in the season when a series of migraines threatened his playing future.

Halfback Andrew Johns also spent a long period sidelined with an ankle injury sustained in a pre-season match. He appeared in just 11 matches for the Knights in 1997, but his contribution to the grand final victory can never be underestimated — he created the winning grand final try for Darren Albert with a play few others would have dared.

Fullback Robbie O'Davis was consistently the best player for the Knights in 1997. Classy and confident, O'Davis outplayed Test fullback Tim Brasher during the State of Origin series and was a deserving winner of the Clive Churchill Medal. Muir, Harragon, front-rower Tony Butterfield and utility forward Bill Peden were also wonderful contributors during the year.

The future of Johns brothers Matthew and Andrew was a source of constant speculation throughout the season. For a time it appeared a squeeze on finances, exacerbated by a procession of home matches affected by rain, would force the pair to seek new clubs. Matthew appeared the more likely to seek a challenge elsewhere, but by October the club was able to re-sign the pair for a further three years.

The rain was the only down side to the Knights' record year. Five games were seriously affected by the weather and, for the first time in Newcastle's 10 seasons in the premiership, a match was postponed (Round 10 against South Sydney). Officials estimated the weather cost the club $200,000 in lost gate receipts. The rain was largely to blame for an 18 per cent drop in home attendances. Yet despite this, the Knights topped 20,000 fans three times during the season.

MATCH RECORDS 1997

Played	Ground	Result	Score
St George	Marathon	Won	11-6
Norths	North Sydney	Lost	20-24
South Qld	Marathon	Won	44-0
Sydney City	Stadium	Won	28-16
Parramatta	Marathon	Won	29-10
Wests	Campbelltown	Won	8-4
Manly	Brookvale	Lost	8-22
Illawarra	Marathon	Won	20-4
Gold Coast	Carrara	Lost	24-32
Balmain	Leichhardt	Won	26-18
St George	Kogarah	Lost	18-20
Norths	Marathon	Lost	6-26
South Qld	Suncorp	Won	24-6
Sydney City	Marathon	Drew	14-all
Souths	Marathon	Won	30-0
Parramatta	Parramatta	Lost	22-28
Wests	Marathon	Won	42-18
Manly	Marathon	Lost	12-14
Illawarra	WIN	Won	22-12
Gold Coast	Marathon	Won	44-18
Souths	Stadium	Won	26-8
Balmain	Marathon	Won	34-10
PARRAMATTA	STADIUM	WON	28-20
MANLY	STADIUM	LOST	12-27
NORTHS	STADIUM	WON	17-12
MANLY	STADIUM	WON	22-16

Played 26: won 17, lost 8, drew 1, for 591, against 395

The nucleus of Newcastle's grand final-winning side will remain in 1998, but missing will be foundation lock forward Marc Glanville and second-rower Adam Muir. Also missing will be fringe first-graders Leo Dynevor, Scott Conley and Scott Coxon. The Knights have strengthened their pack with the signing of Perth forward Peter Shiels.

The retention of the majority of their stars and the mature performances of emerging talents such as Owen Craigie, Mark Hughes, Matthew Gidley, Jason Moodie and Troy Fletcher, gives the Knights and their army of supporters hope that the club can remain one of the front-running teams for many years to come.

NEWCASTLE

THE CLUBS

North Sydney

For the fourth time in the 1990s, North Sydney stumbled at the final hurdle. A heartbreaking loss in the preliminary final against Newcastle followed similar exits in the 1991, 1994 and 1996 finals series.

There were times during the year when the Bears seemed to have finally turned the corner. Record victories over Manly (41-8) and St George (54-14) had many pundits predicting that Norths' 54-year grand final drought would be broken at last.

And it was a near thing. In a key moment of their preliminary final against Newcastle, Norths fullback Matt Seers headed for the tryline, only to be cut down centimetres short by Newcastle flyer Darren Albert. In a match that was decided by a field goal in the final two minutes, a try to the Bears at that time may have changed history. And captain Jason Taylor, who had broken a number of records during the year with his prolific pointscoring, failed with two relatively easy shots at goal, either of which could have made all the difference.

Norths' apparently endless disappointments forced a number of players to look for new challenges in 1998. Long-serving players Chris Caruana and David Hall headed to Souths, utility forward Danny Williams joined Melbourne and prop Brenton Pomery signed with Wests.

For a number of those remaining, age is catching up. Greg Florimo turned 30 midway through the 1997 season, Gary Larson will be 31 when the 1998 season kicks off, and hooker Mark Soden will be 30 late in 1998. It would appear that if the current North Sydney outfit is to figure in a grand final, it will need to be sooner, rather than later.

The make-up of the Bears' top team will be essentially the same in 1998, but thrown into the mix is Newcastle's Test back-rower Adam Muir and Balmain lock Glenn Morrison. They will vie with Billy Moore, David Fairleigh and Gary Larson for one of three back row spots, with Larson likely to shift to the front row on a permanent basis.

PLAYERS RECORDS 1997

Player	App	Int	T	G	FG	Pts
Michael Buettner	20	1	9	-	-	36
Chris Caruana	15	10	11	-	-	44
Brett Dallas	17	-	12	-	-	48
David Fairleigh	22	1	4	-	-	16
Greg Florimo	25	-	2	-	-	8
Darren Fritz	-	5	-	-	-	0
David Hall	5	19	6	-	-	24
Wade Horder	-	1	-	-	-	0
Ben Ikin	20	2	9	-	-	36
Gary Larson	21	1	2	-	-	8
William Leyshon	1	10	2	-	-	8
Willie McLean	1	1	-	-	-	0
Billy Moore	22	1	4	-	-	16
Scott Pethybridge	4	3	-	-	-	0
Brenton Pomery	6	10	-	-	-	0
Mark Reber	6	9	1	-	-	4
Nigel Roy	25	-	9	-	-	36
Matt Seers	25	-	8	-	-	32
Mark Soden	18	-	1	-	-	4
Paul Stringer	-	4	3	-	-	12
Josh Stuart	18	3	1	-	-	4
Jason Taylor	25	-	10	98	6	242
Steve Trindall	25	-	-	-	-	0
Danny Williams	4	18	1	-	-	4
24 players	25		95	98	6	582

CAPTAINCY: Taylor 25.

The Bears will field one of the most accomplished teams in the competition. Their strongest possible lineup comprises seven internationals and 10 State of Origin representatives. Norths have all the elements of a successful team, but getting the job done has not been their strong suit.

After landmark victories over Manly and St George, the Bears' form faltered badly in the final weeks of the 1997 season. In fact, they managed to win only two of their last seven matches.

In their first semi-final, they led Sydney City 13-0 before losing in extra-time, and after a 24-14 defeat of an injury-hit Parramatta in the major qualifying final, the Bears were pipped by the Knights in the match that could have put them into a grand final against neighbours and arch-rivals Manly.

It was suggestions of a future merger with Manly that helped produce the Bears' biggest-ever win over the Sea Eagles in June. Five-eighth Greg Florimo turned in one of the finest games of his career that day as Norths and their fans gave a crystal-clear indication of their views on a northside merger.

The future of the club was a burning topic of conversation throughout the season. With only one possible alternative to an amalgamation of northern Sydney clubs, Bears' management set about exploring the option of a relocation to the Central Coast. This move is a proposition that looks likely to go ahead in 1999, with the Bears to establish a new base at Gosford's Grahame Park.

The future of coach Peter Louis, the longest-serving first-grade coach in the history of the North Sydney club, was the subject of speculation after the narrow loss to Sydney City, but he sought and received a vote of confidence from management and will enter his sixth season as top-grade coach in 1998.

Halfback and captain Jason Taylor continued to set the standard when it came to pointscoring. In 1997 he became the highest scorer in the history of the Bears, eclipsing the record of 1950s fullback Allen Arkey. For the second time he broke his own club record for most points in a season, finishing the year with 242.

And Taylor was close to a landmark in another area. By the end of the 1997 season he had played 97 top grade games for Norths without missing one since he joined the club in 1994.

Five-eighth Greg Florimo played his 250th first-grade match during the season and Gary Larson closed in on 200 top-grade games.

Home crowds averaged 11,173 in 1997, a small increase on 1996 figures.

MATCH RECORDS 1997

Played	Ground	Result	Score
Parramatta	Parramatta	Lost	8-10
Newcastle	North Sydney	Won	34-20
Manly	Brookvale	Lost	8-12
Illawarra	North Sydney	Drew	18-all
Gold Coast	Carrara	Won	20-16
Souths	North Sydney	Won	34-14
Balmain	Leichhardt	Lost	7-9
St George	North Sydney	Won	54-14
Wests	North Sydney	Won	20-6
South Qld	Suncorp	Won	36-22
Sydney City	North Sydney	Won	19-18
Parramatta	North Sydney	Lost	14-25
Newcastle	Marathon	Won	26-6
Manly	North Sydney	Won	41-8
Illawarra	WIN	Lost	8-15
Gold Coast	North Sydney	Won	34-28
Souths	Stadium	Won	40-8
Balmain	North Sydney	Won	22-14
St George	Kogarah	Lost	14-22
Wests	Campbelltown	Lost	10-19
South Qld	North Sydney	Won	42-8
Sydney City	Stadium	Lost	20-29
SYDNEY CITY	STADIUM	LOST	21-33
PARRAMATTA	STADIUM	WON	24-14
NEWCASTLE	STADIUM	LOST	12-17

Played 25: won 14, lost 10, drew 1, for 586, for 405

THE CLUBS

Parramatta

The Parramatta Eels emerged in 1997 from a decade in the wilderness, and re-established themselves as a genuine premiership force.

The Eels achieved respectability after a stunning 10-game winning streak and a brave fight in two semi-finals, despite a crippling injury toll. It was the first time since their premiership year of 1986 that the club had qualified for the finals, and even though their exit from the competition was premature, it was anything but a failure.

In his first season with the club, coach Brian Smith transformed a disjointed outfit into premiership contenders after discovering how best to blend the array of talent at his fingertips. Smith had to cope with plenty of pressure early in his tenure. A five-match losing sequence at the start of the season had his team branded '$9 million flops'.

Losses to the South Queensland Crushers (23-6), Wests (25-14) and Newcastle (29-10) left the critics circling like vultures. The team turned the corner after an improved effort against long-time rivals Manly, and finally got back on the winners' list with victory over Illawarra at Wollongong. The momentum built as the Eels negotiated the representative season without defeat.

By the end of July, the Eels were in sight of a club record-equalling 11 consecutive wins. Win number 10 saw them topple defending premiers Manly 17-10 at Brookvale Oval. With halfback John Simon in command, the Eels joined Manly at the top of the Optus Cup ladder. Ironically, when they embarked on their winning run, the Eels were equal last.

The win at Brookvale was the last in that memorable run, though. A week later they were surprised by Illawarra at Parramatta Stadium and although they

PLAYERS RECORDS 1997

Player	App	Int	T	G	FG	Pts
Nathan Barnes	16	3	8	-	-	32
Jason Bell	19	4	6	-	-	24
Daniel Brown	4	1	-	-	-	0
Troy Campbell	5	17	1	-	-	4
Paul Carige	18	-	-	4	-	-	16
Nathan Cayless	-	1	-	-	-	0
Steven Collins	6	11	7	-	-	28
Leon Douglas	-	1	-	-	-	0
Jim Dymock	21	-	2	-	-	8
Andrew Frew	1	-	1	-	-	4
Ian Herron	13	1	4	29	-	74
Brett Horsnell	11	7	1	-	-	4
Peter Johnston	16	1	2	-	-	8
Stuart Kelly	14	2	5	-	-	20
Chris King	3	-	1	-	-	4
Nathan Koina	-	4	-	-	-	0
Chris Lawler	1	-	-	6	-	12
Karl Lovell	6	14	3	-	-	12
Jarrod McCracken	21	-	7	-	-	28
Dennis Moran	1	-	-	-	-	0
Justin Morgan	15	8	3	-	-	12
Eparama Navale	10	2	7	-	-	28
Dean Pay	19	2	1	-	-	4
Darren Pettet	-	5	-	-	-	0
Aaron Raper	15	1	1	-	-	4
David Riolo	11	2	1	-	-	4
John Simon	23	-	6	25	7	81
Jamie Smith	-	4	-	-	-	0
Jason Smith	18	2	2	-	-	8
Matt Spence	1	-	-	-	-	0
Shane Whereat	16	-	11	-	-	44
David Woods	5	-	-	-	-	0
Russell Wyer	3	3	-	1	-	2
33 players	24		84	61	7	465

CAPTAINCY: Pay 19, McCracken 5

PLAYERS OF THE YEAR

Clifford White

Robbie O'Davis (Newcastle, Queensland and Australia).

PLAYERS OF THE YEAR

Geoff Toovey (Manly, NSW and Australia).

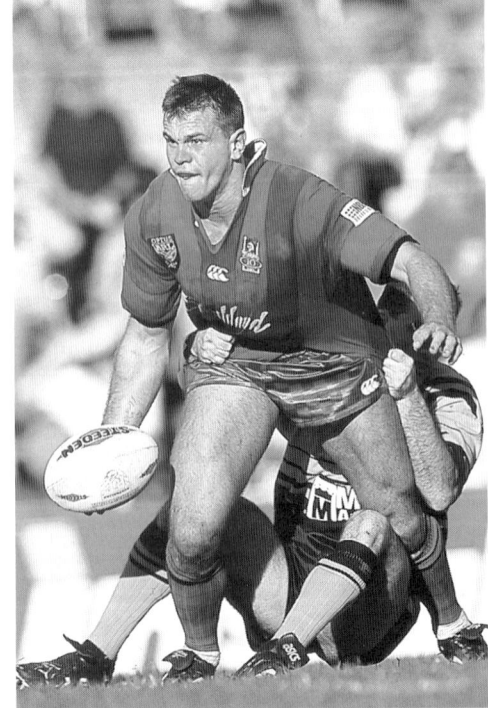

Paul Harragon (Newcastle, NSW and Australia).

PLAYERS OF THE YEAR

Above: John Simon (Parramatta, NSW and Australia).

Right: Brad Fittler (Sydney City, NSW and Australia).

Clifford White

Above: Grand Final day '97 ... Manly's Mark Carroll (left) meets Paul Harragon.

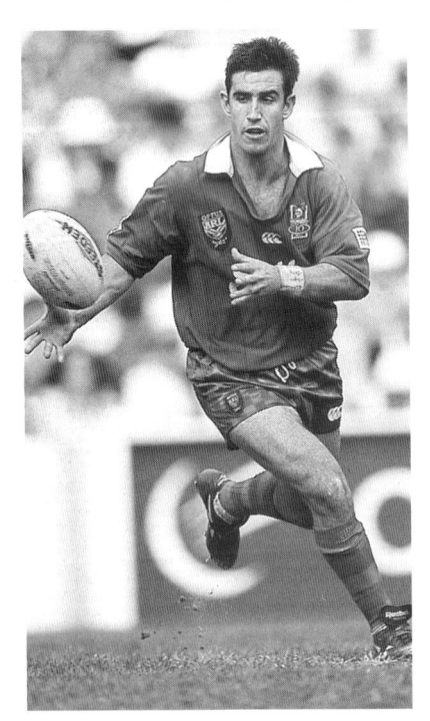

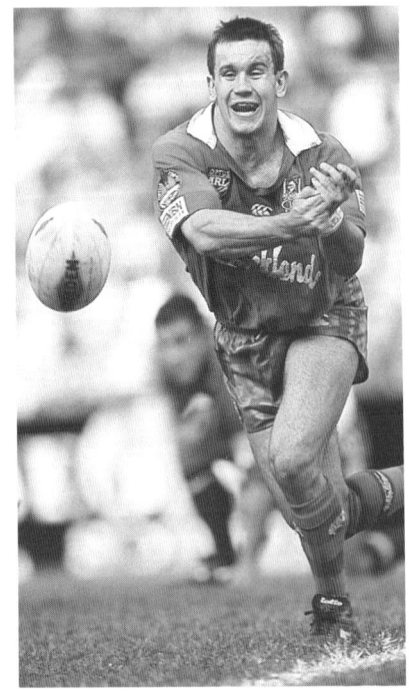

The Knights' amazing double act ... Andrew Johns (left) and his brother, Matthew.

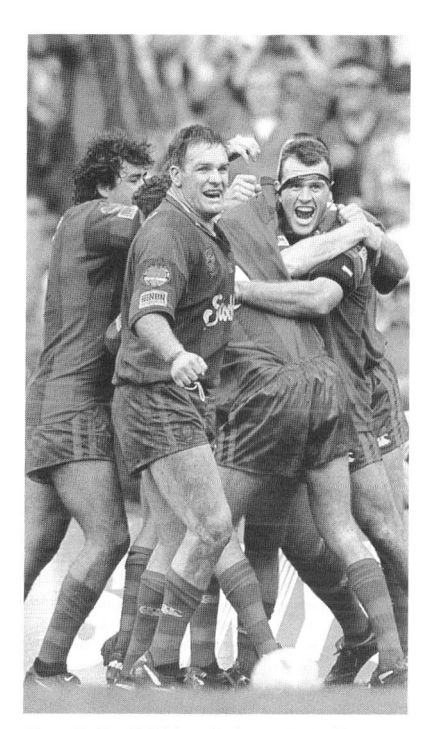

Tony Butterfield (centre) reacts to Darren Albert's premiership-winning try.

Paul Harragon shows Knights fans what it's all about!

Manly skipper Geoff Toovey upends Adam MacDougall in the Grand Final.

Clifford White

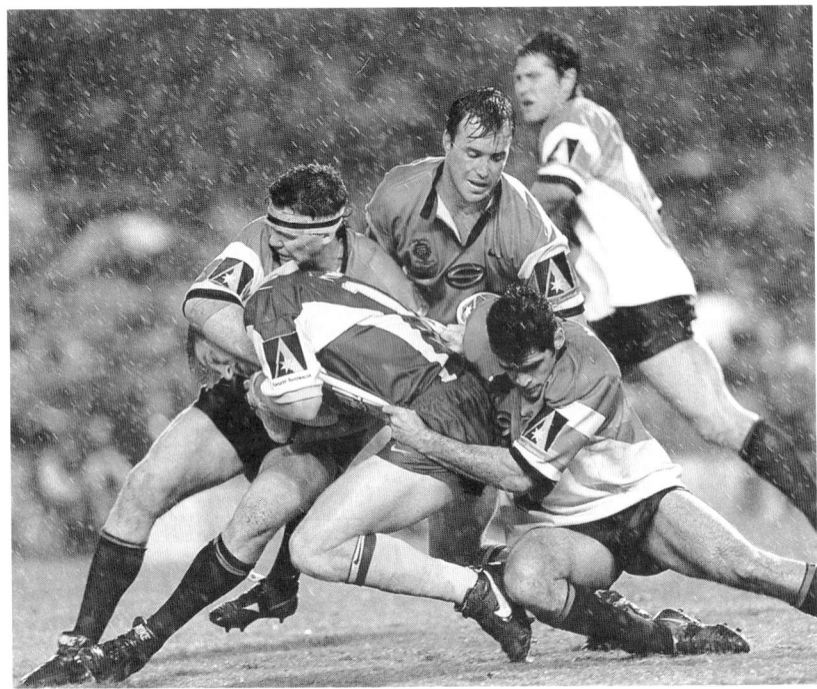

Brisbane's most improved forward, Brad Thorn, charges at the Cronulla forwards during the Super League Grand Final.

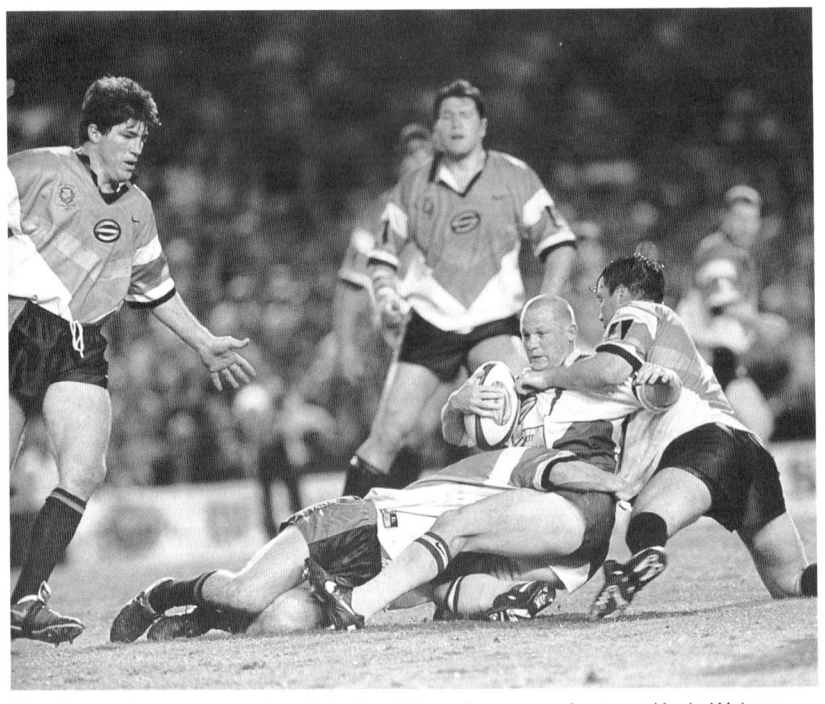

The Broncos' success owed much to the skills and courage of veteran Kevin Walters.

Super League's player of the year, Laurie Daley (Canberra, NSW and Australia).

Clifford White

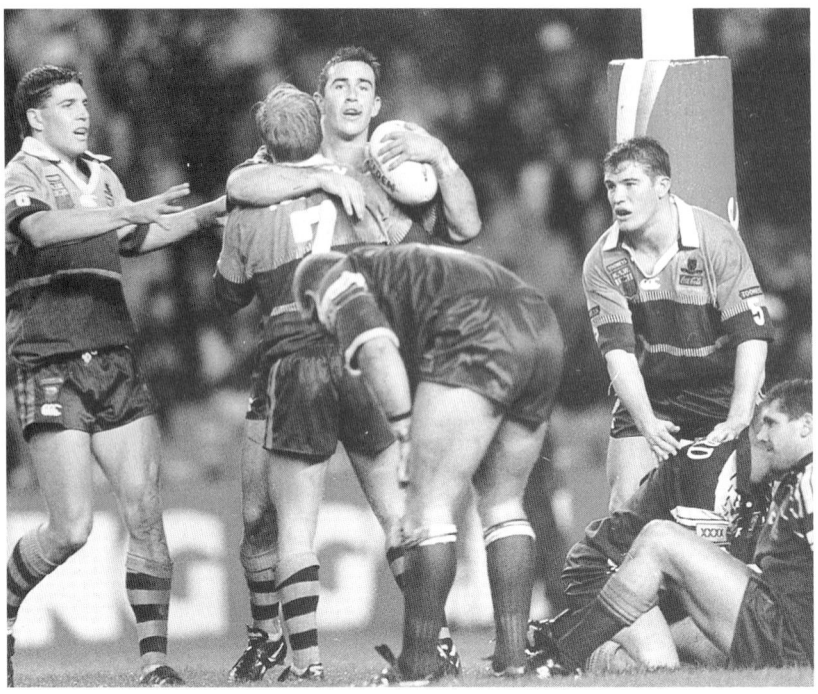

NSW's captain Geoff Toovey (No. 7) celebrates Andrew Johns' try in the final game of the '97 series. Queensland won the match, but the Blues won the series 2-1.

NSW's Bradley Clyde takes a spectacular mark during the dramatic Tri-Series final.

recovered to beat the Gold Coast and South Sydney, the irresistible form of earlier in the season had evaporated.

They were humbled 26-6 by Balmain at Leichhardt Oval, and drew 12-all with St George in the final round at home, to finish third on the ladder. The unimpressive run-up to the finals was exacerbated by an injury crisis that was beginning to bite. A brutal first semi-final against Newcastle was the beginning of the end. By fulltime, the Eels had a mammoth injury toll that cost them virtually any hope of beating North Sydney in a major qualifying final.

Parramatta's season ended two weeks before the grand final when they went down 24-14 to the Bears. With a spare parts team, the Eels stood little chance, and despite leading 14-6 at halftime, the lack of fit troops soon told.

A number of Eels enjoyed their best season in years. Halfback John Simon had arguably his best year in Rugby League, representing NSW and Australia and finishing second in voting for the inaugural Provan-Summons Medal. Simon took charge of the team from his position one off the ruck and controlled play superbly with his long and short kicking game and strong playmaking instincts.

Outside him, Jason Bell thrived on Simon's service and sparked his team's backline with an impressive array of attacking skills. Former Canterbury foursome Jim Dymock, Jarrod McCracken, Dean Pay and Jason Smith provided great value for the club and were instrumental in the charge to the finals.

The outstanding results of 1997 did not stop coach Smith from wielding the axe at the end of the year. The likelihood of a salary cap and a points index system being introduced for the 1998 season forced the club to release a large number of players, including international hooker Aaron Raper, Chris Lawler, David Woods, Peter Johnston,

MATCH RECORDS 1997

Played	Ground	Result	Score
Norths	Parramatta	Won	10-8
South Qld	Suncorp	Lost	6-23
Sydney City	Parramatta	Lost	2-8
Wests	Campbelltown	Lost	14-25
Newcastle	Marathon	Lost	10-29
Manly	Parramatta	Lost	8-18
Illawarra	WIN	Won	23-16
Gold Coast	Parramatta	Won	28-10
Souths	Stadium	Won	32-26
Balmain	Parramatta	Won	25-14
St George	Kogarah	Won	17-10
Norths	North Sydney	Won	25-14
South Qld	Parramatta	Won	52-10
Sydney City	Stadium	Won	18-6
Wests	Parramatta	Won	20-18
Newcastle	Parramatta	Won	28-22
Manly	Brookvale	Won	17-10
Illawarra	Parramatta	Lost	24-28
Gold Coast	Carrara	Won	18-8
Souths	Parramatta	Won	36-18
Balmain	Leichhardt	Lost	6-26
St George	Parramatta	Drew	12-all
NEWCASTLE	STADIUM	LOST	20-28
NORTHS	STADIUM	LOST	14-24

Played 24: won 14, lost 9, drew 1, for 465, against 411

Russell Wyer, Steve Collins, Ian Herron, Troy Campbell, Chris King, Daniel Brown and Brett Horsnell.

The only newcomers are South Queensland trio Mark Tookey, Troy Pezet and Clinton Schifcofske, and South Sydney utility back David Penna. Schifcofske will be welcomed particularly for his goalkicking — the Eels achieved only 54 per cent success with the boot in 1997.

Other highlights of 1997 for Parramatta included the second grade premiership, victory in the World Sevens competition in February and the club championship pennant, won by the club for the first time since 1986.

The outstanding results of 1997 helped Parramatta enjoy the best home crowd averages in the ARL competition. An average of 15,647 watched their 11 home games — the club's best figures since 1986 and a massive 41 per cent increase on 1996.

THE CLUBS

St George

The loss of 11 players of first-grade standard was a blow from which St George could not recover in 1997. The ravages of Super League and the departure of players to rival ARL clubs cut a swathe through the Saints ranks, and after qualifying for the grand final in 1996, it was little surprise that the club finished out of semi-final contention just one year later.

Stars of the calibre of Noel Goldthorpe, Anthony Mundine, Troy Stone, David Barnhill, Jason Stevens, Scott Gourley and Kevin Campion are not easily replaced, and despite a modest recruitment program, Saints were unable to compete on a level-footing with the competition's leading teams.

International back Jamie Ainscough and second-rower Darren Treacy joined the club from Newcastle and State of Origin front-rower Tony Hearn arrived from South Queensland. The trio strengthened their new club but could not plug all the gaps.

The season started promisingly for coach David Waite. Saints won four of their first six matches to occupy fourth place on the ladder before a mid-season slump saw them crash from finals reckoning. Their effort in winning just three of their next 12 matches was a bitter disappointment for supporters, who had become accustomed to more positive results. Among the poor results was a humiliating 54-14 loss to Norths, two defeats by Western Suburbs and a thrashing at the hands of Manly at Brookvale Oval.

Saints finished the year on a high note, with two wins and a draw from their final four matches. They exacted some revenge on Norths with a 22-14 win at Kogarah in Round 19, and drew 12-all with Parramatta in their last hit-out of the season, when there was nothing at stake.

Midway through the year St George scored a 20-18 win over ultimate premiers Newcastle, a gratifying result

PLAYERS RECORDS 1997

Player	App	Int	T	G	FG	Pts
Jamie Ainscough	14	1	3	-	1	13
Wayne Bartrim	19	-	5	43	-	106
Mark Bell	14	-	6	-	-	24
Nathan Blacklock	-	1	-	-	-	0
Nathan Brown	22	-	4	-	-	16
Adrian Brunker	18	1	11	-	-	44
Gavin Clinch	14	2	2	-	-	8
Mark Coyne	20	-	3	-	-	12
Luke Felsch	2	8	1	-	-	4
Jeff Hardy	8	3	-	-	-	0
Tony Hearn	11	2	-	-	-	0
Robert Henare	-	2	-	-	-	0
Shane Kenward	8	5	1	-	-	4
Ben Kusto	8	2	1	-	-	4
Jim Lenihan	6	10	2	-	-	8
Lee Murphy	8	1	7	-	-	28
Corey Pearson	11	11	1	-	-	4
Troy Perkins	-	1	-	-	-	0
Steven Price	8	1	1	4	-	12
Darren Rameka	1	5	1	-	-	4
Dean Raper	4	2	-	-	-	0
Colin Saukuru	-	2	-	-	-	0
Brad Smith	2	13	1	-	-	4
Damien Smith	15	2	2	-	-	8
Andrew Tangata-Toa	10	4	-	-	-	0
Lance Thompson	17	2	1	-	-	4
Darren Treacy	15	1	-	-	-	0
Daniel Wagon	10	-	4	-	-	16
Colin Ward	21	1	2	-	-	8
29 players	22		59	47	1	331

CAPTAINCY: Coyne 20, Brown 2

considering the high proportion of former Newcastle players in Saints' ranks.

They will add another next season with the signing of former Knights' and Perth halfback Matthew Rodwell. The rookie of the year in 1992, Rodwell has since had three 'lost' seasons in the west, and is determined to make up for lost time with his new club in 1998.

The most encouraging signing was that of prodigal son Anthony Mundine. A player capable of freakish deeds on the football field, Mundine returns after a season with the Brisbane Broncos, where he never truly settled. His decision to return to Saints was hastened by an Industrial Court ruling which upheld the ARL loyalty contract he had signed before agreeing to terms with the Broncos. Saints went all out to snare his signature, such is their confidence in his abilities.

His partnership with Rodwell, a gifted and intelligent footballer, could be the key to a turnaround in Saints' fortunes. Coach Waite alternated between Gavin Clinch and Ben Kusto in the vital halfback position in 1997, but neither was able to fully grasp the opportunity.

Gifted hooker Nathan Brown was slotted into a playmaking role at first receiver, but it was a stop-gap measure that had only limited success. The combination of Mundine and Rodwell should allow Brown to return to dummy-half, a role in which he has achieved much success over the past five years.

On the positive side for Saints in '97 was the 'discovery' of youngsters such as Lee Murphy, Daniel Wagon and Steven Price, who coped well with the step up to first grade. St George's most consistent player was front-rower Colin Ward, who played in all 22 matches and worked tirelessly to carry the ball across the advantage line. Young second-rower Lance Thompson also performed strongly, while lock Wayne Bartrim was in great form early in the season.

Another boost to Saints in 1998 is the signing of one of the country's brightest schoolboy prospects, Daniel Heckenberg, from Western Suburbs. A graduate of St Gregory's College, Campbelltown, Heckenberg represented Sydney Under-18s and the Australian Schoolboys in 1997.

Saints' decline from grand finalists in 1996 to finish ahead of only Souths and the South Queensland Crushers in 1997 had a predictable effect on crowds attending matches at Kogarah Oval. The average of only 7,224 was a 36 per cent drop on '96 and the worst average crowd figures for the club since 1988.

MATCH RECORDS 1997

Played	Ground	Result	Score
Newcastle	Marathon	Lost	6-11
Manly	Kogarah	Lost	14-18
Illawarra	WIN	Won	20-8
Gold Coast	Kogarah	Won	18-12
Souths	Stadium	Won	34-4
Balmain	Kogarah	Won	16-10
Wests	Kogarah	Lost	8-24
Norths	North Sydney	Lost	14-54
South Qld	Kogarah	Won	32-22
Sydney City	Stadium	Lost	8-22
Parramatta	Kogarah	Lost	10-17
Newcastle	Kogarah	Won	20-18
Manly	Brookvale	Lost	4-28
Illawarra	Kogarah	Lost	10-12
Gold Coast	Carrara	Lost	14-22
Souths	Kogarah	Won	29-28
Balmain	Leichhardt	Lost	4-10
Wests	Campbelltown	Lost	6-26
Norths	Kogarah	Won	22-14
South Qld	Suncorp	Won	14-0
Sydney City	Kogarah	Lost	16-20
Parramatta	Parramatta	Drew	12-all

Played 22: won 9, lost 12, drew 1, for 331, against 392

THE CLUBS

South Queensland

The South Queensland Crushers arrived on the scene in 1995 amid much fanfare as the second premiership team in Brisbane and a genuine rival for the high-flying Brisbane Broncos.

But on the last day of August, 1997, the Crushers were finished. Victims of the ARL-Super League war that had drained much of the lifeblood from the sport, South Queensland played its final game.

Nowhere were the ravages of war more keenly felt than in Brisbane. Not even the Broncos were exempt from its effects: their crowds fell from an average of over 43,000 in 1993 to less than 20,000 in the space of just four seasons.

For a fledgling team like the Crushers, the effects were magnified. Their support in 1995 was remarkable. Average crowds of more than 21,000 watched their games at Suncorp Stadium, despite results that were, at best, moderate. A year later, their figures had dropped to little more than 13,000, and in 1997 crowds averaged just over 7,000 per game. If it had not been for two 'free days' late in the season, when officials threw open the gates, their average would have been further eroded.

Millions of dollars were spent in investments for the future of the Crushers and millions more were spent in rescue packages when it became evident that the club could not pay its players, let alone meet its other commitments.

The club was living on borrowed time throughout the 1997 season, in which results went from bad to worse. Late in the season it was announced that the only option left was to enter into merger discussions with the Gold Coast Chargers.

The Crushers even helped their

PLAYERS RECORDS 1997

Player	App	Int	T	G	FG	Pts
Nathan Antonik	17	2	-	1	-	2
Anthony Bella	3	6	1	-	-	4
Robert Bella	-	3	-	-	-	0
Matthew Bickerstaff	9	3	2	-	-	8
Shane Cairns	5	-	-	-	-	0
Kerry Carmichael	1	1	-	-	-	0
David Couper	2	7	-	-	-	0
Heath Cruckshank	-	2	-	-	-	0
Michael Davis	-	1	-	-	-	0
Brian Doyle	4	1	1	-	-	4
Michael Eagar	20	-	5	-	-	20
Andrew Hamilton	5	2	3	-	-	12
Paul Hubbard	8	1	1	-	-	4
Jason Hudson	21	-	9	3	-	42
John Jones	12	1	1	-	-	4
Phil Mooney	-	1	-	-	-	0
Aaron Moule	7	2	3	-	-	12
Danny Nutley	2	6	-	-	-	0
Clinton O'Brien	17	-	-	-	-	0
Troy Pezet	7	4	4	4	-	24
Mark Protheroe	14	6	4	-	-	16
Steele Retchless	22	-	3	-	-	12
Ben Roedder	2	-	-	-	-	0
Don Saunders	6	7	-	-	-	0
Clinton Schifcofske	17	-	6	35	-	94
Jeremy Smith	1	2	-	-	-	0
Nathan Sologinkin	1	9	1	-	-	4
Craig Teevan	21	-	1	-	-	4
Scott Thorburn	-	1	-	-	-	0
Mark Tookey	2	13	3	-	-	12
Matt Toshack	19	-	5	-	-	20
Dave Watson	12	1	1	-	-	4
Jason Wendt	10	-	1	-	-	4
Craig Wilson	19	1	3	-	3	15
Paul Woodward	-	2	-	-	-	0
35 players	22		58	43	3	321

CAPTAINCY: Teevan 21, Wilson 1

proposed 'partners' win a place in the final series when they defeated Wests 39-18 in the last game of the season. But not long after the grand final, the discussions were shelved when Gold Coast declared that the merged entity could not be saddled with the Crushers' massive debt.

The last-round win over Wests was one of just four by the Crushers in their final season. They began their home campaign brilliantly when they downed the big-spending Parramatta 23-6. But the rot set in almost immediately, with a 44-0 drubbing at the hands of Newcastle. This match marked the beginning of a nine match losing streak. The Crushers slipped to last position after four rounds and remained in the same position for the rest of the season. They caught Sydney City on the hop during the split rounds for the State of Origin series, winning 28-14, they beat Souths late in the season, and finished with their record-breaking defeat of Wests.

The win over the Magpies was laced with irony. The 21-point margin was the Crushers' biggest win in their short history. Fullback Clinton Schifcofske broke records for most goals in a match (seven) and most points in a match (18). The win cost Wests a place in the finals and guaranteed a place for the Gold Coast who, at the time, were to combine with the Crushers in a merged team in 1998.

Relatively few of the Crushers' players had secured contracts with rival clubs by late in 1997. Clinton Schifcofske, Mark Tookey and Troy Pezet signed with Parramatta; Aaron Moule with Melbourne; Craig Wilson with Illawarra; Clinton O'Brien, Scott Thorburn and Phil Mooney with the Gold Coast; and Steele Retchless with the London Broncos, but many more remained without a club.

Front-rower Retchless stood out as the Crushers' best player throughout 1997. The former Bronco forward played all 22 matches and was the Crushers' main 'go-forward' player. He received good support from Clinton O'Brien, who played State of Origin during the year, while backs Schifcofske and Jason Hudson also performed brightly.

Schifcofske will go into the history books as the top pointscorer for the Crushers. His 94 points for the season was a record, as was his career tally of 108. Hudson finished the year as the club's top tryscorer with 11.

For coach Steve Bleakley, helping to make the Crushers a competitive unit was one of the toughest challenges in Rugby League in 1997. At times he appeared to be making progress, but with only limited resources at his disposal, his task was a near-impossible one.

MATCH RECORDS 1997

Played	Ground	Result	Score
Sydney City	Stadium	Lost	10-34
Parramatta	Suncorp	Won	23-6
Newcastle	Marathon	Lost	0-44
Manly	Suncorp	Lost	16-36
Illawarra	WIN	Lost	6-14
Gold Coast	Suncorp	Lost	14-22
Souths	Stadium	Lost	20-24
Balmain	Suncorp	Lost	16-18
St George	Kogarah	Lost	22-32
Norths	Suncorp	Lost	22-36
Wests	Campbelltown	Lost	12-32
Sydney City	Suncorp	Won	28-14
Parramatta	Parramatta	Lost	10-52
Newcastle	Suncorp	Lost	6-24
Manly	Brookvale	Lost	12-46
Illawarra	Suncorp	Lost	8-34
Gold Coast	Carrara	Lost	18-40
Souths	Suncorp	Won	17-16
Balmain	Leichhardt	Lost	14-32
St George	Suncorp	Lost	0-14
Norths	North Sydney	Lost	8-42
Wests	Suncorp	Won	39-18

Played 22: won 4, lost 18, for 321, against 630

SOUTH QUEENSLAND

THE CLUBS

South Sydney

The light is brightening at the end of South Sydney's long tunnel. Hope has returned to a club that has struggled to remain competitive for the better part of the 1990s.

The appointment of new coach Steve Martin is perhaps the most important decision Rabbitoh officials have ever made. They are banking on Martin producing the goods in the same way he did when he joined North Sydney in 1990. Along with former club president David Hill, Martin was responsible for reversing the fortunes of the Bears who, at the time, were perennial battlers.

The signing of Martin was the first act in a shift in culture at South Sydney. For the first time in their modern history, the Rabbitohs have entered the player market in an aggressive fashion. Headed by Balmain's Test fullback Tim Brasher, the club's list of acquisitions also includes Chris Caruana and David Hall from Norths, Terry Hermansson and Sean Garlick from Sydney City and Jeremy Schloss from Gold Coast.

The experience and talent drawn to the club should result in an immediate transformation of the Rabbitohs, who have finished no higher than ninth since 1990. Combined with the existing talent such as Darren Burns, Darrell Trindall, Julian O'Neill and young halfback Willie Peters, the newcomers will provide Martin with a solid base from which to launch the Rabbitohs' 1998 campaign.

It will be a vital season in every respect for Souths, whose support and

PLAYERS RECORDS 1997

Player	App	Int	T	G	FG	Pts
Dean Amos	2	2	-	-	-	0
Troy Barnes	1	2	1	1	-	6
Darren Burns	22	-	2	-	-	8
Chris Crotty	1	-	-	-	-	0
Shannon Donato	8	1	2	-	-	8
Peter Driscoll	4	6	1	-	-	4
Michael Francis	6	7	-	-	-	0
Brett Gillard	3	4	-	-	-	0
Tere Glassie	3	-	-	-	-	0
Michael Hogan	6	-	2	-	-	8
Phil Howlett	12	1	4	-	-	16
Matt Manning	5	-	2	10	-	28
Adam McEwen	1	2	-	-	-	0
Donald McLeod	7	2	6	-	-	24
Paul McNicholas	1	1	-	-	-	0
Marty Moore	16	-	5	-	-	20
Tate Moseley	2	-	-	-	-	0
Scott Murray	15	-	-	-	-	0
Damian O'Donnell	-	1	-	-	-	0
Danny O'Keefe	10	-	4	-	-	16
Brendan O'Meara	17	-	2	-	-	8
Julian O'Neill	8	2	-	21	-	42
Jeff Orford	9	1	5	-	-	20

Player	App	Int	T	G	FG	Pts
Michael Ostini	18	3	1	-	-	4
Matthew Parsons	12	2	1	-	-	4
David Penna	9	4	6	-	-	24
Willie Peters	2	1	1	-	-	4
Paul Quinn	7	1	1	-	-	4
Ian Rubin	8	2	-	-	-	0
Craig Simon	9	9	1	-	-	4
Cole Skelly	7	-	-	5	-	10
Troy Slattery	8	4	1	-	-	4
Jack Slockee	-	1	-	-	-	0
Peter Stimson	4	5	2	-	-	8
Paul Sutton	5	5	1	-	-	4
Jason Tassell	1	3	-	-	-	0
Darrell Trindall	17	-	6	8	1	41
Nigel Waugh	3	-	-	-	-	0
Aaron White	3	7	-	-	-	0
Bart Williams	5	-	1	-	-	4
Shane Wilson	6	5	-	-	-	0
Garth Wood	3	1	-	-	-	0
42 players	22		58	45	1	323

CAPTAINCY: Trindall 17, O'Neill 3, Burns 1, Skelly 1

results have been deteriorating steadily. In fact, in 1997 Souths recorded their worst crowd figures in more than 40 years. They averaged less than 5,500 to their home matches at the Sydney Football Stadium, with a high of only 7,200 for the clash with St George in April.

Unless performances and crowds improve significantly in 1998, the Rabbitohs are likely to face some unpalatable decisions — to merge, fold or accept a place in a minor competition.

Martin began his official duties by clearing out the players he considered were not of first-grade standard. Among the 30 players handed their notice were Peter Driscoll, Shane Wilson, Marty Moore, Jeff Orford, Peter Stimson, Jason Tassell and Craig Simon.

Departing coach Ken Shine sifted through 42 players in 1997 as he strived to build a winning combination, but positive results were few and far between. Souths won just four matches (and drew one) to finish ahead of only the South Queensland Crushers.

Souths' year began well, with wins over the Gold Coast and Wests in the first three rounds. But after defeating the Crushers 24-20 in April, the side managed only one more win all season. They finished the year with nine consecutive losses. Any hopes Shine harboured of remaining with the club for a fifth season disappeared in this period.

In his first season with the Rabbitohs, former Wests lock Darren Burns enjoyed a tremendous year. Despite playing more often than not in a losing team, Burns never stopped trying and was rewarded with the club's captaincy in the final match of the season.

The Rabbitohs' hopes were invariably pinned on evasive halfback Darrell Trindall. His ad-lib style unsettled the most organised defensive patterns, but too often he became an easy mark because his support was missing. A high tackle earned Trindall

MATCH RECORDS 1997

Played	Ground	Result	Score
Illawarra	WIN	Lost	10-50
Gold Coast	Stadium	Won	26-16
Wests	Stadium	Won	17-8
Balmain	Leichhardt	Lost	16-22
St George	Stadium	Lost	4-34
Norths	North Sydney	Lost	14-34
South Qld	Stadium	Won	24-20
Sydney City	Stadium	Lost	0-42
Parramatta	Stadium	Lost	26-32
Manly	Stadium	Lost	16-30
Illawarra	Stadium	Drew	28-all
Gold Coast	Carrara	Lost	4-28
Wests	Campbelltown	Won	20-16
Balmain	Stadium	Lost	2-16
Newcastle	Marathon	Lost	0-30
St George	Kogarah	Lost	28-29
Norths	Stadium	Lost	8-40
South Qld	Sunoorp	Lost	16-17
Sydney City	Stadium	Lost	20-40
Parramatta	Parramatta	Lost	18-36
Newcastle	Stadium	Lost	8-26
Manly	Brookvale	Lost	18-36

Played 22: won 4, lost 17, drew 1, for 323, against 630

a six-week suspension late in the season.

Troubled Queenslander Julian O'Neill arrived at the club in June after his celebrated falling out with Super League club Perth, but despite some further lapses in discipline, he represented Queensland in two State of Origin matches and was solid at the back for his new club.

Souths' other representative player in 1997 was centre Phil Howlett, who played in the one-off Test match for Rest of the World against Australia.

There should be a different look about South Sydney in 1998. Their new coach is a strict disciplinarian who will not tolerate anything less than 100 per cent professionalism. It will take a lot to turn the Rabbitohs into a competteive force, but under Steve Martin's watchful eye, don't rule out a dramatically improved Red and Green outfit. And if they do manage to string together some wins, the crowds will be back in their thousands.

SOUTH SYDNEY

THE CLUBS

Sydney City

A strong off-season build-up had the pundits predicting that Sydney City would fight out the 1997 grand final with Manly.

History shows that the Roosters failed to make the premiership decider, but it would be a harsh critic who would suggest their season was a flop. Their much-anticipated clash with Manly occurred one week early in a preliminary final. The Roosters competed superbly, but in the end, a last-gasp field goal by Manly utility Craig Field denied them a place in the grand final.

The loss to Manly was the final chapter in a season of rich achievement for coach Phil Gould and the Roosters. The club enjoyed their most successful season in a decade, played a number of captivating matches, and played well enough to suggest they can make an even more serious bid for premiership honours in 1998.

The Roosters were never out of the top seven in 1997, despite the fact that they failed to win a match during a six-week slump in the middle of the season. They emerged from this horror stretch to win their last six matches before the finals. With the form on the board, the Roosters entered the finals series with confidence. They were trailing Norths 13-0 in the first qualifying final, but recovered, forcing the match into extra-time with an Adrian Lam field goal in the final seconds of regular time, before claiming the match 33-21.

A week later they had little trouble knocking the high-achieving Gold Coast side out of the premiership race, but against Manly, as well as they competed, they could not land the knockout blow.

It was one of three losses to the Sea Eagles in 1997. The clash between the clubs at Brookvale was one of the high

PLAYERS RECORDS 1997

Player	App	Int	T	G	FG	Pts	Player	App	Int	T	G	FG	Pts
Richie Allan	1	2	1	1	-	6	Darren Junee	4	1	1	-	-	4
David Barnhill	17	3	-	-	-	0	Adrian Lam	17	-	6	-	1	25
Simon Bonetti	14	3	-	-	-	0	Scott Logan	1	6	1	-	-	4
Greg Bourke	5	-	2	-	-	8	Jason Lowrie	18	-	-	-	-	0
Peter Clarke	5	3	2	-	-	8	Robert Miles	11	3	3	-	-	12
Ivan Cleary	23	-	8	81	-	194	Damien Mostyn	1	1	-	-	-	0
Ben Duckworth	2	5	2	-	-	8	Brandon Pearson	10	-	6	3	-	30
Peter Ellis	1	-	-	-	-	0	Luke Ricketson	24	-	2	-	-	8
Jack Elsegood	22	-	12	-	-	48	Shane Rigon	8	15	6	-	-	24
Brad Fittler	21	-	5	-	1	21	Dale Shearer	7	4	2	-	-	8
Bryan Fletcher	1	6	-	-	-	0	Jacin Sinclair	2	5	2	-	-	8
Nigel Gaffey	6	5	2	-	-	8	Matt Sing	20	2	11	-	-	44
Sean Garlick	11	4	1	-	-	4	Julian Troy	-	13	-	-	-	0
Scott Gourley	20	-	3	-	-	12	Andrew Walker	21	2	15	2	-	64
Chad Halliday	1	-	1	-	-	4	Nathan Wood	4	11	2	-	-	8
Adam Hayden	4	2	2	-	-	8	33 players	25		98	87	2	568
Terry Hermansson	23	2	-	-	-	0							
Dallas Hood	-	2	-	-	-	0							

CAPTAINCY: Fittler 21, Garlick 2, Junee 1, Lam 1

points of the ARL season. Sydney City led 18-0 before Manly prevailed 34-24 in a game of brilliant end-to-end action. Back at the SFS, Manly prevailed 21-12 in another tense clash.

In the first month of the competition, the Roosters downed Parramatta 8-2 at Parramatta Stadium in a game that received high praise from both the winning and the losing coach, and a week later they figured in another thriller, this time at the Sydney Football Stadium, in which they went down 28-16 to Newcastle.

The Roosters based their season on a powerful defensive game that was led by front rowers Terry Hermansson and Jason Lowrie, along with David Barnhill and the outstanding Luke Ricketson. One of their key men in attack was halfback Adrian Lam, who returned from off-season shoulder surgery to show further improvement as a playmaker.

Captain Brad Fittler experienced arguably his finest season at club level, producing his best form consistently and taking out the inaugural Nokia Provan-Summons Medal as the ARL's official player of the year. A broken thumb cost him the opportunity of leading New South Wales to another State of Origin series win, but the lay-off left him fresh to help plot the Roosters' course to the finals.

And Andrew Walker developed into a fullback of remarkable ability. Reluctant to shift from five-eighth to the last line of defence, Walker excelled as an attacking player from broken play and his ability to kick spiralling 'up-and-unders' bewildered many an opponent. After a match against Balmain, Tigers coach Wayne Pearce labelled Walker a better exponent of the 'bomb' than former international Johnny Peard, who was so successful with the ploy at Parramatta in the late 1970s.

MATCH RECORDS 1997

Played	Ground	Result	Score
South Qld	Stadium	Won	34-10
Wests	Stadium	Won	18-6
Parramatta	Parramatta	Won	8-2
Newcastle	Stadium	Lost	16-28
Manly	Brookvale	Lost	24-34
Illawarra	Stadium	Lost	20-26
Gold Coast	Carrara	Won	34-24
Souths	Stadium	Won	42-0
Balmain	Leichhardt	Won	18-14
St George	Stadium	Won	22-8
Norths	North Sydney	Lost	18-19
South Qld	Suncorp	Lost	14-28
Wests	Campbelltown	Lost	18-24
Parramatta	Stadium	Lost	6-18
Newcastle	Marathon	Drew	14-all
Manly	Stadium	Lost	12-21
Illawarra	WIN	Won	34-12
Gold Coast	Stadium	Won	28-12
Souths	Stadium	Won	40-20
Balmain	Stadium	Won	18-10
St George	Kogarah	Won	20-16
Norths	Stadium	Won	29-20
NORTHS	STADIUM	WON	33-21
GOLD COAST	PARRAMATTA	WON	32-10
MANLY	STADIUM	LOST	16-17

Played 25: won 15, lost 9, drew 1, for 568, against 414

In his first season in first grade, former Griffith hooker Simon Bonetti showed maturity and is expected to take on the top-grade hooking role on a fulltime basis following the departure of Sean Garlick to South Sydney.

Season crowds averaged few more than 9,000 per match, a sizeable drop on 1996 figures. The loss of Monday night televised football affected the Roosters' crowds. Monday Night Football was a highly popular innovation during the latter half of the 1996 season and the Roosters enjoyed some bumper crowds, albeit boosted by ticket giveaways. Despite the Roosters' good results, the crowd average was one of the club's lowest figures of the 1990s. Four Saturday afternoon matches at the Football Stadium did not help their cause.

SYDNEY CITY

THE CLUBS

Western Suburbs

The Magpies' early exit from the 1997 premiership ranks as one of the club's most disappointing recent efforts.

With three weeks remaining before the finals, Tommy Raudonikis' team produced one of their typically gritty efforts to upset Norths 19-10 at Campbelltown Sports Ground, helping themselves to sixth position on the ladder.

In their two remaining matches, they were to face Illawarra at Campbelltown and South Queensland at Suncorp Stadium. A win in either game would have been enough to secure the Magpies a place in the finals.

Against Illawarra, and playing before their home crowd for the last time in 1997, the Magpies conceded seven tries in a 34-10 loss. A week later, with captain Paul Langmack celebrating the magical milestone of 300 first-grade games, the Magpies capitulated again, falling to the Crushers in an embarrassingly lopsided 39-18 result.

That loss cost Wests a place in the finals, a situation that had been unthinkable only two weeks earlier. The Magpies, though, should never have allowed themselves to be in a position where their finals hopes rested on those last two games. The truth was that Wests' season finished as poorly as it began.

The 1996 quarter-finalists won only one of their first six matches, placing them behind the eight-ball from the outset. Six wins from their next seven matches put them back into the finals picture, until a lack of consistency in the latter stages of the season cost them a top seven place.

Raudonikis and Wests' officials acted quickly after the disaster of 1997, axing more than a dozen players. The departures included established first-graders Bill Dunn, James Smith, Adam Doyle, Andrew Willis, Shane Millard, Darren Capovilla and Paul Smith. The sackings sent a shock wave through the

PLAYERS RECORDS 1997

Player	App	Int	T	G	FG	Pts
Darren Capovilla	1	7	-	-	-	0
Adam Donovan	1	1	-	-	-	0
Gary Dowse	-	1	-	-	-	0
Adam Doyle	11	5	4	-	-	16
Bill Dunn	16	4	2	-	-	8
Steve Georgallis	21	1	1	-	-	4
Chad Harris	-	1	-	-	-	0
Des Hasler	9	12	6	-	-	24
Brett Hickman	1	-	1	-	-	4
Brett Hodgson	9	2	3	6	-	24
Harvey Howard	17	-	-	-	-	0
Damian Kennedy	15	3	2	-	-	8
Aseri Laing	13	1	2	-	-	8
Paul Langmack	21	-	2	-	-	8
Andrew Leeds	22	-	3	47	3	109
SLomanimako	1	-	-	-	-	0
Ken McGuinness	20	-	11	-	-	44
Kevin McGuinness	15	6	9	-	-	36
Shayne McMenemy	-	7	-	-	-	0
Ciriaco Mescia	16	1	2	-	-	8
Shane Millard	12	8	1	-	-	4
Willie Newton	2	-	-	1	-	2
Brandon Pearson	10	-	3	-	-	12
John Skandalis	16	4	3	-	-	12
Jim Smith	9	7	-	-	-	0
Paul Smith	1	-	-	-	-	0
Brett Taylor	-	2	-	-	-	0
Shaun Walliss	-	1	-	-	-	0
Andrew Willis	6	4	1	-	-	4
Darren Willis	21	-	5	-	-	20
Chris Yates	-	4	-	-	-	0
31 players	22		61	54	3	355

CAPTAINCY: Langmack 21, Hasler 1

Campbelltown club, but only time will tell if the Raudonikis 'rocket' had the desired effect on those remaining with the club.

There was clearly a lack of application at Wests in 1997. The playing personnel had changed little after the encouraging results of 1996, but the on-field performances had stagnated.

The frustrating aspect of the season for Raudonikis was the knowledge that the club had the ability to compete against every team in the competition. During the year they recorded wins against Manly, Illawarra, Gold Coast, Sydney City, Norths and Parramatta, leaving premiers Newcastle as the only final series team they did not beat at some point of the season.

On the other side of the coin, the Magpies lost four games to teams who failed to reach the finals. A win against any one of those would have been enough to win a place in the top seven.

The Magpies' best win of the year came in Round 8 when they pipped the previously undefeated Manly 19-16 at Campbelltown. Former Sea Eagles' stalwart Des Hasler helped inspire the win against his old club and was cheered from the ground after the nail-biting victory.

The leading performer for Wests was undoubtedly centre Ken McGuinness, who graduated to State of Origin selection during the season. His combination with younger brother Kevin was a feature of the Magpies' year. The pair were involved in a memorable match against Balmain when they each scored two tries in a 20-10 win.

Fullback Andrew Leeds again delivered sterling service to the club. Along with halfback Steve Georgallis, Leeds played all 22 matches and joined former fullback John Dorahy as the fourth-highest pointscorer in the Magpies' history.

MATCH RECORDS 1997

Played	Ground	Result	Score
Gold Coast	Campbelltown	Lost	16-24
Sydney City	Stadium	Lost	6-18
Souths	Stadium	Lost	8-17
Parramatta	Campbelltown	Won	25-14
Balmain	Leichhardt	Lost	0-28
Newcastle	Campbelltown	Lost	4-8
St George	Kogarah	Won	24-8
Manly	Campbelltown	Won	19-16
Norths	North Sydney	Lost	6-20
Illawarra	WIN	Won	6-2
South Qld	Campbelltown	Won	32-12
Gold Coast	Carrara	Won	26-10
Sydney City	Campbelltown	Won	24-18
Souths	Campbelltown	Lost	16-20
Parramatta	Parramatta	Lost	18-20
Balmain	Campbelltown	Won	20-10
Newcastle	Marathon	Lost	18-42
St George	Campbelltown	Won	26-6
Manly	Brookvale	Lost	14-48
Norths	Campbelltown	Won	19-10
Illawarra	Campbelltown	Lost	10-34
South Qld	Suncorp	Lost	18-39

Played 22: won 10, lost 12, for 355, against 424

Captain Langmack also figured prominently. He played his 300th first-grade game in the final match of the season and is likely to slip past Geoff Gerard to move into second place behind Terry Lamb on the all-time appearance list next season. His ball-playing skills and on-field leadership continue to be important weapons for the Magpies.

And veteran Des Hasler was a popular and reliable performer in his final season in the game. After 16 seasons of first grade, the 36-year-old former international announced his retirement in October.

Crowds at Campbelltown averaged 8,602 in 1997, an increase of 21 per cent on 1996 figures and the club's best figures since 1992.

The Magpies have added Newcastle pair Leo Dynevor and Scott Coxon along with front-rower Brenton Pomery from Norths, to their playing roster for 1998.

WESTERN SUBURBS

COCA-COLA WORLD SEVENS
FEBRUARY 8, 9

Brian Smith's perfect start

Success-starved Parramatta took out their first top-grade title of any description since 1986 with a decisive 32-22 defeat of North Sydney in the final of the 1997 Coca-Cola World Sevens. This was the perfect start for new coach Brian Smith, who had taken on the top job after a successful stint with British club Bradford.

Teams representing Italy and Lebanon participated in the World Sevens for the first time. The Lebanese team, coached by former Western Suburbs coach Steve Ghosn, were well-supported and performed strongly to advance to the quarter-finals of the main draw. Super League club Canterbury granted special permission for winger Hazem El Masri to play for the Lebanese side in the Sevens.

Right from the beginning of the '97 Sevens, the Eels displayed early signs of developing into one of the top sides of the season, after a bitterly disappointing 1996 in which a huge recruitment drive brought precious little in return. They downed Balmain and South Queensland in their two group matches, enabling them to compete for the main competition prize and a $65,000 winners' purse.

The Eels defeated Lebanon 22-10 in a quarter-final, before a hard-fought 24-12 win over Western Suburbs in a semi-final. The turning point in the Eels' Sevens campaign came in this match when forward Troy Campbell knocked the ball from the grip of Magpies' centre Ken McGuinness as the Wests player prepared to touch down for what would have been a crucial try.

This win set up a showdown with 1996 Sevens runners-up North Sydney. Parramatta started powerfully in the final, scoring three converted tries to lead 18-10 at halftime. They took a near unbeatable lead minutes after the resumption when a Ben Ikin fumble led to a try to Nathan Barnes and a 24-10 lead. Norths scored twice in the second half through Gary Larson, but the Eels clearly had their measure.

Campbell was named player of the series, and he was well supported by Jim Dymock, Jason Smith, Nathan Barnes, Stuart Kelly and Chris Lawler.

Balmain also tasted a rare success with victory in the Trophy division. Goalkicking proved the difference in the Tigers' 22-16 defeat of 1996 Sevens champions Newcastle in the final. St George took out the Plate division with an 18-8 win over the South Queensland Crushers in the final.

Hard-hit by the split in the game, crowds for the two-day tournament totalled 29,561, a 20 per cent fall on 1996 figures.

COCA-COLA WORLD SEVENS RESULTS

Group 1
NRL Fiji defeated American Samoa 22-18, Tonga defeated NRL Fiji 16-14, Tonga defeated American Samoa 16-12.
Group 2
Newcastle defeated Souths 20-18, Souths defeated St George 28-16, St George defeated Newcastle 26-22.
Group 3
Aboriginal Dream Team defeated Papua New Guinea 26-10, New Zealand defeated Papua New Guinea 32-18, Aboriginal Dream Team

defeated New Zealand 16-14.

Group 4
Norths defeated Sydney City 16-6, Sydney City defeated Gold Coast 22-18, Norths defeated Gold Coast 22-20.

Group 5
Italy defeated Japan 34-4, Italy defeated USA 20-0, USA defeated Japan 18-14.

Group 6
Illawarra defeated Manly 14-10, Wests defeated Illawarra 26-12, Wests defeated Manly 18-12.

Group 7
Lebanon defeated Melbourne 24-4, Lebanon defeated NSW Country 16-14, NSW Country defeated Melbourne 16-12.

Group 8
Balmain defeated South Queensland 20-16, Parramatta defeated Balmain 18-4, Parramatta defeated South Queensland 16-10.

The winners of each group advanced to the Cup Championship finals, the second-placed teams played the Trophy division and the third-placed teams contested the Plate.

PLATE QUARTER-FINALS
St George defeated American Samoa 44-14, Gold Coast defeated Papua New Guinea 32-4, Manly defeated Japan 42-4, South Queensland defeated Melbourne 36-10.

PLATE SEMI-FINALS
St George defeated Gold Coast 18-16, South Queensland defeated Manly 16-14.

PLATE FINAL
St George defeated South Queensland 18-8. Prizemoney: St George $5,000.

TROPHY QUARTER-FINALS
Newcastle defeated NRL Fiji 34-16, Sydney City defeated New Zealand 22-10, Illawarra defeated USA 18-6, Balmain defeated NSW Country 26-12.

TROPHY SEMI-FINALS
Newcastle defeated Sydney City 34-22, Balmain defeated Illawarra 18-10.

TROPHY FINAL
Balmain defeated Newcastle 22-16. Prizemoney: Balmain $6,000.

CUP QUARTER-FINALS
Souths defeated Tonga 20-10, Norths defeated Aboriginal Dream Team 12-8, Wests defeated Italy 38-12, Parramatta defeated Lebanon 22-10.

CUP SEMI-FINALS
Norths defeated Souths 24-18, Parramatta defeated Wests 24-12.

CUP FINAL
Parramatta 32 (J.Smith 2, J.Dymock, T.Campbell, N.Barnes, S.Kelly tries; C.Lawler 3, Kelly goals) defeated **North Sydney** 22 (G.Florimo 2, G.Larson 2 tries; J.Taylor 3 goals).

PARRAMATTA: Nathan Barnes, Shane Whereat, Stuart Kelly, Jarrod McCracken (c), Jim Dymock, Chris Lawler, Jason Bell, Chris King, Troy Campbell, Jason Smith.

NORTHS: Matt Seers, Brett Dallas, Michael Buettner, Ben Ikin, Greg Florimo, Chris Caruana, Jason Taylor (c), David Fairleigh, Mark Soden, Gary Larson.

Referee: David Manson.

Prizemoney: Parramatta $65,000. Norths $30,000.

Player of the tournament: Troy Campbell (Parramatta).

Most points: Ben Kusto (St George) 28, Terry Hill (Manly) 28.

Most tries: Terry Hill (Manly) 7.

Crowds: Saturday 14,445. Sunday 15,116. Total 29,561.

Competing teams (24), Balmain, Gold Coast, Illawarra, Manly, Newcastle, North Sydney, Parramatta, St George, South Queensland, South Sydney, Sydney City, Western Suburbs, American Samoa, Aboriginal Dream Team, Italy, Japan, Lebanon, Melbourne, New Zealand, NRL Fiji, NSW Country, Papua New Guinea, Tonga, USA.

All group matches were played at Sydney Football Stadium on Saturday, February 8. All quarter finals, semi-finals and finals were played at SFS on Sunday, February 9.

SEVENS WINNERS

1988	Souths	1993	Easts
1989	Balmain	1994	Manly
1990	Manly	1995	Manly
1991	Newcastle	1996	Newcastle
1992	Wigan	1997	Parramatta

SEVENS RECORDS

Most tries in one match: 4 Mark Ross (Gold Coast) v Cronulla, 1988, Martin Offiah (Wigan) v Brisbane, 1992, Noa Nadruku (Fiji) v Wests, 1993.

Most tries in tournament: 10 Martin Offiah (Wigan), 1992.

Most points in one match: 26 Phil Blake (Souths) v Penrith, 1988 (3 tries, 7 goals).

Most points in tournament: 62 Phil Blake (Souths), 1988 (8 tries, 15 goals).

Highest aggregate score: 66 points — Souths 46, Penrith 20, 1988; Newcastle 48, Norths 18, 1996 (Cup final).

Biggest winning margin: 56 points — New Zealand 56, Canada 0, 1996.

Record tournament crowds: 82,008, 1994.

COCA-COLA WORLD SEVENS

CITY v COUNTRY

Country triumph ... again!

Country 17, City 4

For the first time in 35 years, Country won back-to-back victories over City — a 17-4 win at Marathon Stadium added to their 18-16 triumph in 1996.

Inspired by captain Paul Harragon, the Country side out-muscled their City counterparts on a wet Marathon Stadium field, and finished the game with three tries to one.

Harragon had completed only 30 minutes play in seven weeks and was expected to play only a small part in the match, but he was fired up from the outset and revisited his stormy relationship with Manly's Mark Carroll in several thunderous confrontations.

Attacking play was at a premium because of the slippery conditions and the heavy rain which began to fall midway through the first half. It took 30 minutes for the first points to be posted. Country centre Paul McGregor slid across for a try after he, lock Nik Kosef and veteran front-rower David Gillespie provided the lead-up in a high-quality movement. Halfback John Simon converted from out wide to give Country a 6-0 lead.

City replied shortly before halftime with a solo try to captain Brad Fittler, which Craig Field failed to convert. Country went to the break leading 6-4.

City were forced to make last-ditch tackles on McGregor and Newcastle winger Darren Albert soon after the resumption. A tough defensive grind ensued, with Country gradually gaining the ascendancy.

Country fullback Matt Seers scored the try that broke the nexus midway through the second half. A Harragon burst put Country into tryscoring position, and from the next ruck a Harragon pass found Seers, who skirted past his opposite, Balmain's Tim Brasher, to score between the posts.

Enjoying an outstanding senior representative debut, Newcastle five-eighth Matthew Gidley put the match out of City's reach four minutes from fulltime with a 35-metre field goal, then just two minutes from fulltime, replacement William 'Bubba' Kennedy scored for Country to open up a 13-point margin.

Country Origin 17 (P.McGregor, M.Seers, W.Kennedy tries; J.Simon 2 goals; M.Gidley field goal) defeated **City Origin** 4 (B.Fittler try) at Marathon Stadium, Friday night, April 25.

Scrums: Country 8-7. Penalties: 6-all. Crowd: 9164. Referee: David Manson. Halftime: Country 6-4. Goalkickers: Simon (Country) 2/3, Field (City) 0/1.

COUNTRY ORIGIN: Matt Seers (Norths); Darren Albert (Newcastle), Brandon Pearson (Wests), Paul McGregor (Illawarra), Darren Willis (Wests); Matthew Gidley (Newcastle), John Simon (Parramatta); Paul Harragon (Newcastle – c), Ciriaco Mescia (Wests), David Gillespie (Manly), Marc Glanville (Newcastle), Scott Gourley (Sydney City), Nik Kosef (Manly). Interchange: Bill Dunn (Wests), Glenn Morrison (Balmain), Wayne Richards (Newcastle), William Kennedy (Balmain). Coach: Tom Raudonikis.

CITY ORIGIN: Tim Brasher (Balmain); Craig Hancock (Manly), Terry Hill (Manly), Michael Buettner (Norths), John Hopoate (Manly); Brad Fittler (Sydney City – c), Geoff Toovey (Manly); Mark Carroll (Manly), Darren Senter (Balmain), Colin Ward (St George), Daniel Gartner (Manly), Steve Menzies (Manly), Jim Dymock (Parramatta). Interchange: Craig Field (Manly), Josh Stuart (Norths), Luke Ricketson (Sydney City), Shane Rigon (Sydney City). Coach: Peter Louis.

STATE OF ORIGIN

NSW take stirring series

MATCH NO. 1
NSW 8, Queensland 6
Suncorp Stadium, May 28

New South Wales went one up in the 1997 series with an 8-6 victory over Queensland in a typically intense Origin clash at Suncorp Stadium.

Both sides scored one try, but it was the Blues' ability to hang in after building an 8-0 lead before halftime that saw them take first blood.

New South Wales centre Paul McGregor scored the Blues' only try in the 31st minute after a trademark sidestep caught the Queensland defence napping. Earlier, McGregor had been forced from the field with a pinched nerve in his neck which left him with no feeling in his left arm. Blues doctor Nathan Gibbs at first ruled McGregor out for the rest of the game, but after the injury was manipulated, McGregor was cleared to return to the fray.

The big Illawarra centre wasn't the ony casualty for New South Wales as the tough physical contest took its toll. Hooker Andrew Johns was assisted from the field with a suspected broken leg and Rod Wishart was forced off with a dislocated shoulder.

Down 8-0 at halftime, Queensland responded superbly in the second half and attacked New South Wales' line in waves. It was a credit to the Blues' defence that, despite Queensland's dominance of possession, they forced their way through only once in the second half.

Twelve minutes from fulltime, Adrian Lam, making his debut as Queensland captain, showed remarkable strength to carry Tim Brasher and Steve Menzies across the line with him. Wayne Bartrim converted to set up an absorbing finish.

A controversial decision by referee Kelvin Jeffes not to restart the tackle count, after it appeared that Brasher had got a hand to a Jason Smith bomb six minutes from fulltime, was hotly disputed by Queensland coach Paul Vautin, and although replays were inconclusive, Jeffes stood by his decision.

Man of the match, NSW captain Geoff Toovey, took charge of the final stages of the game with a series of pressure-relieving bursts from dummy-half. Replacement John Simon and Queenslanders Robbie O'Davis and Adrian Lam were also contenders for man of the match.

Queensland coach Paul Vautin lamented his team's poor kicking game in the first half of the match, a factor, he said, which cost the team dearly: 'Our options in the first half were terrible. Some of the grubber kicks were shockers. It was awful just to watch it. A couple of times we kicked on the fourth tackle and I certainly didn't coach them to do that.'

After four consecutive losses, Vautin was now fighting for his position as Queensland coach. Despite the loss, he remained confident after his team's improved second-half performance. The Maroons' kicking game picked up and they kept their mistakes to a bare minimum. Vautin attributed the rejuvenation to a more settled Adrian Lam, who, he said, had worried too much about the team and not his own game in the first half.

'Adrian became a halfback as well as a captain in the second half,' Vautin said. 'I remember in my first game as Queensland captain the same thing happened to me and I worried too much about the team instead of my own game.'

The crowd of 28,222 was the smallest to attend an Origin game since a sell-out crowd of 26,500 went to Olympic Park, Melbourne, in 1990. 'The game deserved a sell-out,' said ARL chief executive Neil Whittaker. 'And it would have been sold out if circumstances had been different,' he said, referring to the game's damaging split.

New South Wales 8 (P.McGregor try; A.Johns, R.Wishart goals) defeated **Queensland** 6 (A.Lam try; W.Bartrim goal) at Suncorp Stadium, Wednesday night, May 28.

Scrums: Queensland 8-5. Penalties: NSW 6-5. Crowd: 28,222. Referee: Kelvin Jeffes. Halftime: NSW 8-0. Goalkickers: Johns (NSW) 1/2, Wishart (NSW) 1/1, Bartrim (Queensland) 1/1. Man of the match: Geoff Toovey (NSW).

NEW SOUTH WALES: Tim Brasher; Rod Wishart, Terry Hill, Paul McGregor, Jamie Ainscough; Jim Dymock, Geoff Toovey (c); Paul Harragon, Andrew Johns, Mark Carroll, Steve Menzies, Adam Muir, Nik Kosef. Interchange: David Fairleigh, Dean Pay, John Simon, Ken McGuinness. Coach Tom Raudonikis.

QUEENSLAND: Robbie O'Davis; Brett Dallas, Matt Sing, Mark Coyne, Danny Moore; Ben Ikin, Adrian Lam (c); Neil Tierney, Jamie Goddard, Craig Smith, Gary Larson, Billy Moore, Wayne Bartrim. Interchange: Jason Smith, Jeremy Schloss, Tony Hearn, Stuart Kelly. Coach: Paul Vautin.

MATCH NO. 2
NSW 15, Queensland 14
Melbourne Cricket Ground, June 11

A John Simon field goal wrapped up the Blues' fifth State of Origin series win in six years as New South Wales pipped Queensland 15-14 in Game 2 at the Melbourne Cricket Ground.

In the most attractive big match played in Melbourne, the Blues led 14-0 early in the first half, before Queensland staged a courageous fightback.

The Maroons had the chance to snatch the game in the final minutes, but a penalty attempt by Julian O'Neill, in his return to State of Origin football, swung wide. Man of the match Paul McGregor was placed on report and later cited for a tackle on Queensland winger Matt Sing which gave O'Neill the late grab for victory.

'All I could think about was the fact I had lost the game for us,' said McGregor. 'I wasn't worried about myself. I was shattered and I was praying Jules would miss as he lined up the kick.'

As they did in Brisbane, New South Wales began strongly, racing in three tries to lead 14-0 after half an hour. In his first game in the Blues' starting line-up, Wests winger Ken McGuinness scored first from a McGregor flick pass. Lock Nik Kosef scored soon after a dropped ball by Queensland winger Brett Dallas, then five-eighth Jim Dymock supported McGregor and McGuinness to score the third try in the 27th minute.

The Blues held an iron grip on the match and a landslide victory looked imminent until Queensland caught New South Wales short on the left side of the field. Sing took a short pass from lock Billy Moore to open Queensland's scoring after 34 minutes.

Two minutes before halftime the Maroons were in again, when captain Adrian Lam selectively passed to fullback Robbie O'Davis, who scored close to the posts, giving O'Neill a comfortable conversion. Five minutes after the resumption the Maroons levelled, when Dallas slipped away from a Jamie Ainscough tackle to score after he had accepted a pass from Jason Smith.

There was no further score until Simon landed his field goal from 26 metres out, 11 minutes from fulltime.

O'Davis had the opportunity to level at 15-all four minutes later, but his field goal attempt was wayward. The Maroons' only other chance came with O'Neill's unsuccessful penalty attempt, five minutes from fulltime.

Queensland coach Paul Vautin, who reversed a pre-match vow to stand down from his position if Queensland lost the match, was proud of the way his troops fought back. 'How can I walk away after tonight?' he said. 'I was so proud of the way they came back. If you can be happy with a loss then I'm ecstatic.'

Both sides underwent late changes to their starting lineups, with NSW coach Tom Raudonikis opting to start with John Simon at halfback and Geoff Toovey at hooker, with Aaron Raper reverting to the fresh reserves bench. Raper spent 80 minutes warming the bench, a decision which led to an angry outburst by State selector (and Raper's father) Johnny Raper. Vautin, meanwhile, shifted Jamie Goddard to the reserves bench and promoted Wayne Bartrim to start the match at hooker.

The crowd of 25,105 was considered satisfactory, given the circumstances of the game in 1997, but was nonetheless the lowest State of Origin crowd since 1988.

The win gave New South Wales their fifth successive win, their best effort ever in Origin football. Blues prop Paul Harragon claimed a milestone with his 17th consecutive State of Origin appearance — a record for NSW — while the match itself claimed a first with all 12 premiership clubs represented.

New South Wales 15 (K.McGuinness, N.Kosef, J.Dymock tries; J.Simon goal; Simon field goal) defeated **Queensland** 14 (M.Sing, R.O'Davis, B.Dallas tries; J.O'Neill goal) at Melbourne Cricket Ground, Wednesday night, June 11.
Scrums: NSW 8-6. Penalties: Queensland 6-5. Crowd: 25,105. Referee: David Manson. Halftime: NSW 14-10. Goalkickers: Simon (NSW) 1/3, O'Neill (Queensland) 1/4, Bartrim (Queensland) 0/1. Man of the match: Paul McGregor (NSW)
NEW SOUTH WALES: Tim Brasher; Ken McGuinness, Paul McGregor, Terry Hill, Jamie Ainscough; Jim Dymock, John Simon; Paul Harragon, Geoff Toovey (c), Mark Carroll, Steve Menzies, Adam Muir, Nik Kosef. Interchange: David Fairleigh, Dean Pay, Matt Seers. Aaron Raper did not play. Coach: Tom Raudonikis.
QUEENSLAND: Robbie O'Davis; Brett Dallas, Stuart Kelly, Mark Coyne, Matt Sing; Ben Ikin, Adrian Lam (c); Neil Tierney, Wayne Bartrim, Craig Smith, Gary Larson, Jason Smith, Billy Moore. Interchange: Jamie Goddard, Jeremy Schloss, Clinton O'Brien, Julian O'Neill. Coach: Paul Vautin.
Cited: McGregor (NSW). **Charge:** Careless high tackle. **Sentence:** Suspended until June 26.

MATCH NO. 3
Queensland 18, NSW 12
Sydney Football Stadium, June 25

Queensland produced their best performance of the 1997 series to upset New South Wales 18-12 in the final State of Origin match at the Sydney Football Stadium.

The Maroons played with courage to salvage pride and respect before a bumper crowd of 33,241, who turned out in wet conditions to watch the dead rubber.

The Maroons defied the trend of the opening two matches by getting off to a flyer. Five-eighth Ben Ikin scored a stunning individual try after just four minutes, and centre Julian O'Neill scored from an Ikin pass and converted his own try after 13 minutes, to establish a 12-0 lead. A lone penalty goal to New South Wales replacement John Simon was the Blues' only score of the first half.

Referee Eddie Ward disallowed two New South Wales tries before halftime. Second-rower Steve Menzies was ruled to have been held up over the line, and fullback Tim Brasher lost the ball as he attempted to drag in a high-bouncing

Andrew Johns kick soon after. The woes continued for New South Wales shortly after the start of the second half when Mark Coyne scored from an Adrian Lam chip-kick. The Blues responded with tries to Jamie Ainscough (59 min) and Andrew Johns (75 min), but the home side never looked like winners.

They had a couple of opportunities to salvage a draw in the final five minutes and with 10 seconds to play Simon hoisted a bomb, which was taken consummately by Robbie O'Davis, one of the Maroons' best players of the series.

Tension between the sides exploded in the eighth minute when front-rowers Mark Carroll and Craig Smith reeled out of a scrum exchanging punches. Hookers Jamie Goddard and Andrew Johns also stood toe-to-toe, leading to an all-in skirmish. When order was finally restored, Goddard and Johns were sent to the sin bin by referee Ward and placed on report. Suffering concussion, Smith left the field soon after and did not return.

Queensland coach Paul Vautin called for the ARL to cite Carroll over the incident, leading NSW officials to consider citing a number of Maroons. Queensland forward Wayne Bartrim was also placed on report for a high tackle on 19-year-old NSW five-eighth Trent Barrett later in the match.

The Maroons endured a crippling injury toll, and at one point Vautin had run out of reserves. Ikin was knocked unconscious when he attempted a tackle on North Sydney team-mate Michael Buettner in the first half and was taken to hospital. Winger Matt Sing (ankle) and Smith (concussion) suffered injuries that prevented their return, and Smith's front-row partner Clinton O'Brien spent 20 minutes off the field recovering from a knock to the head.

'I said to the fellas that tonight was probably the greatest win in the 17-year history of Origin football,' Paul Vautin said. Vautin likened the Maroons' performance to one by the 1989 Queensland side which beat NSW despite being reduced by injury to 12 men.

Blues' coach Tom Raudonikis accepted defeat gracefully. 'There were some heads down when the boys came in the dressing rooms,' Raudonikis said, 'but I said to my blokes, "Come on, we won the series. They (Queensland) were too good tonight. But who cares? We won the series, we had a super game of rugby league tonight".'

The sequel to the match was played out at a special ARL judiciary hearing where Andrew Johns, Jamie Goddard and Wayne Bartrim were each handed a two-match suspension.

Queensland 18 (B.Ikin, J.O'Neill, M.Coyne tries; O'Neill 3 goals) defeated **New South Wales** 12 (J.Ainscough, A.Johns tries; J.Simon, Johns goals) at the Sydney Football Stadium, Wednesday night, June 25. Scrums: NSW 9-6. Penalties: Queensland 8-7. Crowd: 33,241. Referee: Eddie Ward. Halftime: Queensland 12-2. Goalkickers: O'Neill (Queensland) 3/4, Johns (NSW) 1/2, Simon (NSW) 1/1. Man of the match: Gary Larson (Queensland).

QUEENSLAND: Robbie O'Davis; Brett Dallas, Mark Coyne, Julian O'Neill, Matt Sing; Ben Ikin, Adrian Lam (c); Clinton O'Brien, Jamie Goddard, Neil Tierney, Gary Larson, Jason Smith, Billy Moore. Interchange: Stuart Kelly, Jeremy Schloss, Craig Smith, Wayne Bartrim. Coach: Paul Vautin.

NEW SOUTH WALES: Tim Brasher; Ken McGuinness, Jamie Ainscough, Terry Hill, Matt Seers; Trent Barrett, Geoff Toovey (c); Mark Carroll, Andrew Johns, Paul Harragon, Adam Muir, Steven Menzies, Nik Kosef. Interchange: John Simon, Michael Buettner, Dean Pay, David Fairleigh. Coach: Tom Raudonikis.

Sin bin: Goddard (Queensland), Johns (NSW). **Cited:** Goddard (Queensland). **Charge:** Fighting. **Sentence:** Two matches. **Cited:** Johns (NSW). **Charge:** Fighting. **Sentence:** Two matches. **Cited:** Bartrim (Queensland). **Charge:** High tackle. **Sentence:** Two matches.

AUSTRALIA v REST OF THE WORLD

Small crowd see Aussies win

ONE-OFF TEST
Australia 28, Rest of the World 8, Suncorp Stadium

The ARL's only international match of the season deserved a bigger crowd than the 14,927 which turned up to Suncorp Stadium to watch Australia down a Rest of the World side 28-8.

The match hung in the balance for over an hour before the overwhelming favourites overran their opposition, who were made up of ARL-contracted players representing Great Britain, New Zealand, Papua New Guinea and Tonga.

Coached by Newcastle's high-profile mentor Malcolm Reilly, the Rest dominated possession in the first half and scored two tries to one to lead 8-6 at halftime. St George forward Darren Rameka scored first after halfback and captain Adrian Lam showed some stunning footwork. Australia hit back to claim a 6-4 lead with a converted try to fullback Tim Brasher, but on the stroke of halftime, Parramatta's Jarrod McCracken scooped up a loose ball for the Rest of the World to take a two-point lead.

With an even share of possession in the second-half, the world champion Australian side clicked into gear, scoring four second-half tries and claiming a comfortable victory. The pick of the tries was the second scored by Brasher off a miraculous Robbie O'Davis pass, four minutes into the second term.

It was little surprise that the Australian side began slowly, with five players choked up with the 'flu. Winger Brett Dallas withdrew from the side 90 minutes before kick-off, while halfback Geoff Toovey arrived at the ground only an hour before kick-off after returning to Sydney for the birth of his first child.

After the match, rival coaches Fulton and Reilly agreed that the Rest of the World team would beat both New Zealand and Great Britain.

Best players for the Rest of the World were Wigan pair Gary Connolly and Jason Robinson, captain Adrian Lam and back-rowers Jarrod McCracken and Andrew Tangata-Toa.

Australia 28 (T.Brasher 2, T.Hill, S.Menzies, M.Sing tries; A.Johns 3, J.Simon goals) defeated **Rest of the World** 8 (D.Rameka, J.McCracken tries) at Suncorp Stadium, Friday night, July 11, 1997.

Scrums: Australia 8-5. Penalties: Rest of the World 5-4. Crowd: 14,927. Referee: David Manson. Halftime: Rest of the World 8-6. Goalkickers: Johns (Australia) 3/4, Simon (Australia) 1/1, Innes (Rest) 0/2. Man of the match: Paul Harragon (Australia).

AUSTRALIA: Tim Brasher; Mark Coyne, Paul McGregor, Terry Hill, Robbie O'Davis; Brad Fittler (c), Geoff Toovey; Paul Harragon, Andrew Johns, Mark Carroll, Steve Menzies, Gary Larson, Billy Moore. Interchange: Matt Sing, John Simon, Nik Kosef, Dean Pay. Coach: Bob Fulton.

REST OF THE WORLD: Gary Connolly (Great Britain); Jason Robinson (Great Britain), Craig Innes (New Zealand), Phil Howlett (Tonga), Marcus Bai (Papua New Guinea); Thomas O'Reilly (Papua New Guinea), Adrian Lam (Papua New Guinea) (c); Jason Lowrie (New Zealand), Lee Jackson (Great Britain), Terry Hermansson (New Zealand), Darren Rameka (New Zealand), Jarrod McCracken (New Zealand), Andrew Tangata-Toa (Tonga). Interchange: Craig Smith (New Zealand), Harvey Howard (Great Britain), Chris Nahi (New Zealand), Willie McLean (New Zealand). Coach: Malcolm Reilly.

RUGBY LEAGUE 1998

Super League — The 1997 Season

TELSTRA CUP ROUND 1
MARCH 1, 2, 3

A jittery opening night

A curious crowd of 42,361 ventured to Brisbane's ANZ Stadium for the opening night of Super League, keen to see if the football lived up to the hype.

It was a lot to ask, considering the months of promotional hoopla on top of two years of headlines and speculation. As it turned out, the Brisbane Broncos drew first blood with a 14-2 victory over the Auckland Warriors, but some opening night nerves, combined with a football that was as slippery as a cake of soap, detracted from the spectacle.

When they controlled the ball, the Broncos looked far more competent in attack than an Auckland side that lacked penetration and organisation.

Mal Meninga's coaching career kicked off on the worst possible note when Canberra were trounced 26-4 by Cronulla at the Sydney Football Stadium. Favoured by many to win the inaugural Super League premiership, the Raiders were humbled by a sparkling opening onslaught by Cronulla which netted 20 points in the first 23 minutes. Canberra never recovered.

North Queensland kicked off their season with a 24-16 win over newcomers Adelaide in wet conditions at Stockland Stadium. Adelaide's 16-4 lead at halftime should have been enough to win the match, but a lack of ball control let the Cowboys back into it. In a rare footballing occurrence, brothers Kerrod Walters (Adelaide) and Steve Walters (North Queensland) captained the rival sides.

In his first match back at Penrith after a three-year absence, Greg Alexander sparked the Panthers' 30-20 win over Perth with a decisive first-half try.

At Breakers Stadium, the Hunter Mariners were in with a great chance of winning their first competition match against Canterbury before a try two minutes from fulltime to Bulldogs fullback Rod Silva.

ROUND 1 — RESULTS

Brisbane 14 (M.Hancock, S.Renouf, B.Thorn tries; D.Lockyer goal) defeated **Auckland** 2 (M.Ridge goal) at ANZ Stadium, Saturday night, March 1.
Scrums: Brisbane 15–11. Penalties: Brisbane 7–4. Crowd: 42,361. Referee: Bill Harrigan. Halftime: Brisbane 8–2. Goalkickers: Lockyer (Brisbane) 1/3, Ridge (Auckland) 1/1. Reserves: Auckland 13–12.
BRISBANE: Lockyer; Hancock, Mundine, Renouf, Sailor; Walters; Langer (c); Gee, Driscoll, Lazarus, Ryan, Tallis, Smith. Replacements; Thorn, Webcke, Carroll, Plath.
AUCKLAND: Ridge (c); Hoppe, T.Ropati, Ellis, A.Swann;

Ngamu, Jones; Young, Eru, Vagana, Betts, Kearney, L.Swann. Replacements: Malam, Horo, I.Ropati.

North Queensland 24 (S.Walters 2, T.Smith, L.Phillips tries; Phillips 4 goals) defeated **Adelaide** 16 (K.Walters, B.Galea tries; K.Wrigley 4 goals) at Stockland Stadium, Saturday night, March 1.

Scrums: 9–all. Penalties: 6–all. Crowd: 17,738. Referee: Brian Grant. Halftime: Adelaide 16–4. Goalkickers: Phillips (Cowboys) 4/5, Wrigley (Adelaide) 4/4.
NORTH QUEENSLAND: Mahon; Phillips, Tabuai, Warren, Mercy; A.Dunemann, Ferris; Lomax, Walters (c), Locke, Smith, Roberts, Cunningham. Replacements: Death, Jones, I.Dunemann, Cope.
ADELAIDE: Maguire; Simonds, Kiri, Paiyo, Tamani; Wrigley, Topper; Hick, Walters (c), McKenzie, Boughton, Galea, Blair. Replacements: Campion, Quinn, Stone, Mamando.
Cited: Smith (North Queensland). **Charge:** Grade 2 careless high tackle. **Sentence:** 95 demerit points.

Canterbury 20 (M.Ryan 2, D.Halligan, R.Silva tries; Halligan 2 goals) defeated **Hunter** 16 (P.Marquet, N.Goldthorpe tries; N.Zisti 4 goals) at Breakers Stadium, Sunday, March 2.

Scrums: Canterbury 15–10. Penalties: Hunter 6–4. Crowd: 6579. Referee: Stephen Clark. Halftime: Canterbury 14–10. Goalkickers: Halligan (Canterbury) 2/4, Zisti (Hunter) 4/4. Reserves: Canterbury 38–22.
CANTERBURY: Silva; Halligan, Ryan, Timu, El Masri; Norton, Polla-Mounter; Newton, Hetherington, Britt, Gillies (c), Haumono, Reardon. Replacements: Smith, Relf.
HUNTER: Ross; Beauchamp, Zisti, Godden, Thompson; Hill, Goldthorpe; Maddison, McCormack, Dooley, Marquet, T.Iro (c), Piccinelli. Replacements: Stone, Poching.
Sin bin: Smith (Canterbury).

Penrith 30 (P.Jorgensen, S.Domic, R.Girdler, S.Carter, G.Alexander tries; Girdler 5 goals) defeated **Perth** 20 (G.Fleming 2, J.Grieve, R.Kearns tries; D.Chapman 2 goals) at Penrith Football Stadium, Sunday, March 2.

Scrums: Penrith 10–5. Penalties: Perth 8–7. Crowd: 8398. Referee: Tim Mander. Halftime: Penrith 12–8. Goalkickers: Girdler (Penrith) 5/6, Chapman (Perth) 2/2, Ryan (Perth) 0/2. Reserves: Perth 40–12.
PENRITH: Jorgensen; Williams, Domic, Girdler, Thompson; Carter (c), Alexander; Macnamara, Gower, Johnson, Gall, M.Adamson, Brown. Replacements: P.Adamson, Boyd, Falcon.
PERTH: Fleming; Daylight, Bell, Dever, Ryan; Wilson, Chapman; Howe, Fuller, Kearns, Shiels, Mark Geyer (c), Fritz. Replacements: Grieve, Green.

Cronulla 26 (M.Rogers 2, A.Ettingshausen, R.Barnett, G.Bell tries; Rogers 3 goals) defeated **Canberra** 4 (D.Booby try) at Sydney Football Stadium, Monday night, March 3.

Scrums: 10 all. Penalties: Cronulla 6–3. Crowd: 22,683. Referee: Graham Annesley. Halftime: Cronulla 22–0. Goalkickers: Rogers (Cronulla) 3/6, Furner (Canberra) 0/1. Reserves: Cronulla 18–6.
CRONULLA: Peachey; Barnett, Bell, Ettingshausen (c), Rogers; Healey, Green; Davidson, Treister, Lee, Ryan, Long, Nikau. Replacements: McKenna, Strauss, Dykes, Stevens.
CANBERRA: Nagas; Booby, Wiki, Boyle, Nadruku; Daley, Stuart (c); Pongia, Woolford, Davico, Hetherington, Furner, Clyde. Replacements: Kennedy, Westley, Burnham, Gaffa.

STANDINGS: Cronulla 2, Brisbane 2, Penrith 2, North Queensland 2, Canterbury 2, Hunter 0, Adelaide 0, Perth 0, Auckland 0, Canberra 0.

TELSTRA CUP ROUND 2
MARCH 7, 8, 9, 10

Thriller at Belmore

A Mitch Healey field goal gave Cronulla a 13-12 win over Canterbury in a hard-fought Monday night clash at Belmore Sports Ground.

Canterbury began solidly, with a powerhouse try to Solomon Haumono. Daryl Halligan's conversion and two penalty goals opened up an 8-0 lead after 18 minutes. Cronulla responded with a try to veteran Les Davidson after winger Mat Rogers stole the ball from Halligan in a one-on-one tackle.

Halligan's boot kept the Bulldogs in touch, but the 12-all impasse was broken by Healey's field goal in the 69th minute, securing a rare victory for Cronulla at Belmore.

Talented 18-year-old Panther Craig Gower helped kill off the Canberra Raiders in the nation's capital with a brilliant two-try display. Penrith won the match 33-20 after leading 13-6 at halftime. Raiders' coach Mal Meninga accused his players of 'attitude problems', and five-eighth Laurie Daley admitted complacency contributed to the loss.

Brisbane were a class above the Adelaide Rams in a 28-12 romp at ANZ Stadium. The Broncos lost interest after leading 24-6 at halftime, but were never under any threat. Wendell Sailor completed a hat-trick of tries for Brisbane, including one which covered 70 metres.

The Perth Reds scored an important away victory (22-20) over the North Queensland Cowboys at Stockland Stadium. A defensive lapse by rookie Cowboys winger Jim Ahmat allowed Greg Fleming to score the match-winner for the Reds in the 74th minute.

Auckland overcame a 10-0 deficit to register their first premiership points with an 18-14 win over the Hunter Mariners at Ericsson Stadium.

After two rounds of Super League football, three teams — Brisbane, Cronulla and the surprising Panthers — remained undefeated.

ROUND 2 — RESULTS

Perth 22 (G.Fleming 2, D.Fritz, J.Doyle tries; C.Ryan 3 goals) defeated **North Queensland** 20 (J.Ferris, I.Roberts, J.Ahmat tries; L.Phillips 4 goals) at Stockland Stadium, Friday night, March 7.

Scrums: North Queensland 9–7. Penalties: North Queensland 7–3. Crowd: 15,745. Referee: Tim Mander. Halftime: Perth 14–12. Goalkickers: Ryan (Perth) 3/3, O'Neill (Perth) 0/2, Phillips (North Queensland) 4/5. Reserves: Perth 21–14.
PERTH: Fleming; Ryan, Bell, Dever, Daylight; Wilson, Rodwell (c); Kearns, Fuller, Howe, Grieve, Shiels, Fritz. Interchange: Doyle, O'Neill, Green, Higgins.
NORTH QUEENSLAND: Mahon; Phillips, Shipway, Cope, Ahmat; A.Dunemann, Ferris; Lomax, Walters (c), Locke, Smith, Roberts, Cunningham. Interchange: Tabuai, Cressbrook, Jones, Ketchell.

Auckland 18 (S.Hoppe 2, S.Eru tries; M.Ridge 3 goals) defeated **Hunter Mariners** 14 (P.Marquet, G.Thompson, T.Iro tries; N.Zisti goal) at Ericsson Stadium, Saturday night, March 8.

Scrums: 8–all. Penalties: Auckland 8–7. Crowd: 20,300. Referee: Brian Grant. Halftime: Auckland 12–10. Goalkickers: Ridge (Auckland) 3/3, Zisti (Mariners) 1/3. Reserves: Auckland 24–12.
AUCKLAND: Ridge (c); Hoppe, T.Ropati, A.Swann, Ellis; Ngamu, Jones; Vagana, Eru, Horo, Betts, Kearney, L.Swann. Interchange: Young, Malam.
HUNTER: Ross; Thompson, Godden, Zisti, Beauchamp; Hill, Goldthorpe; Stone, McCormack, Maddison, T.Iro (c); Marquet, Piccinelli. Interchange: Poching, Dooley, Dorreen, Brann.

Penrith 33 (C.Gower 2, S.Carter 2, P.Jorgensen, A.Hinson tries; G.Alexander 4 goals; Alexander field goal) defeated **Canberra** 20 (N.Nadruku, L.Priddis, D.Booby, B.Kennedy tries; D.Furner 2 goals) at Bruce Stadium, Sunday, March 9.

Scrums: Canberra 6–5. Penalties: Canberra 7–6. Crowd: 10,849. Referee: Graham Annesley. Halftime: Penrith 13–6. Goalkickers: Alexander (Penrith) 4/7, Furner (Canberra) 2/4. Reserves: Penrith 22–20.
PENRITH: Jorgensen; Williams, Hinson, Domic, Thompson; Carter (c), Alexander; Johnson, Gower, Macnamara, Gall, M.Adamson, Brown. Interchange: P.Adamson, Falcon.
CANBERRA: Booby; Gaffa, Wiki, Burnham, Nadruku; Daley, Stuart (c); Davico, Woolford, Pongia, Hetherington, Furner, Clyde. Interchange: Westley, Kennedy, Priddis.
Sin bin: Pongia (Canberra).

Brisbane 28 (W.Sailor 3, S.Renouf, D.Lockyer, K.Walters tries; Lockyer 2 goals) defeated **Adelaide** 12 (R.Maybon, M.McKenzie tries; K.Wrigley 2 goals) at ANZ Stadium, Sunday, March 9.

Scrums: Brisbane 11–8. Penalties: Adelaide 8–5. Crowd: 16,279. Referee: Stephen Clark. Halftime: Brisbane 24–6. Goalkickers: Lockyer (Brisbane) 2/6, Wrigley (Adelaide) 2/2.
BRISBANE: Lockyer; Hancock, Renouf, Carroll, Sailor; Walters, Langer (c); Webcke, Driscoll, Lazarus, Thorn, Tallis, Smith. Interchange: Plath, S. Walker, Gee, Ryan.
ADELAIDE: Maybon; Simonds, Paiyo, Kiri, Tamani; Wrigley, Topper; Campion, S. Walters (c), Hick, Pierce, Boughton, Blair. Interchange: McKenzie, Quinn, Mamando, Schifilliti.

Cronulla 13 (L.Davidson, C.McKenna tries; M.Rogers 2 goals; M.Healey field goal) defeated **Canterbury** 12 (S.Haumono try; D.Halligan 4 goals) at Belmore Sports Ground, Monday night, March 10.

Scrums: 8–all. Penalties: Canterbury 8–6. Crowd: 14,490. Referee: Bill Harrigan. Halftime: Cronulla 12–10. Goalkickers: Rogers (Cronulla) 2/2, Halligan (Canterbury) 4/5. Reserves: Canterbury 24–6.
CRONULLA: Peachey; Barnett, Ettingshausen (c), Bell, Rogers; Healey, Green; Davidson, Treister, Strauss, Ryan, Long, Nikau. Interchange: McKenna, Pierce, Dykes, Richardson.
CANTERBURY: Silva; El Masri, Timu, Ryan, Halligan; Norton, Polla-Mounter; Newton, Hetherington, Britt, Haumono, Gillies (c), Reardon. Interchange: Smith, Relf, Marteene, Berrigan.

STANDINGS: Brisbane 4, Cronulla 4, Penrith 4, North Queensland 2, Canterbury 2, Perth 2, Auckland 2, Hunter 0, Adelaide 0, Canberra 0.

TELSTRA CUP ROUND 3
MARCH 14, 15, 16, 17

Canberra stay winless

Canberra sank further into the abyss with a dismal defensive display, allowing Canterbury to overrun them 38-26 at Belmore Sports Ground.

The Raiders were never in it. They lacked the intensity of the Bulldogs, who went to the halftime break leading 22-10. The points continued to flow in the second half as Canberra's defence wilted.

Afterwards, stand-in skipper Laurie Daley told the media that 'we played like a bunch of sheilas' and that any deficiencies in the Raiders' operation were the responsibility of the players and not of new coach Mal Meninga.

Super League's video referee innovation came in for criticism after a dubious decision resulted in a try to Cronulla prop Danny Lee during the Sharks' 34-8 defeat of the Auckland Warriors.

Video referee Noel Bissett ruled that Auckland fullback Matthew Ridge failed to force the ball cleanly in-goal before Lee 'scored' the try late in the game. Repeated replays of the incident indicated Bissett almost certainly came up with the wrong decision. Fortunately, the ruling did not have a bearing on the outcome of the match.

Three second-half tries allowed Brisbane to remain undefeated when they scored a 26-16 victory over Perth at the WACA. The Broncos looked to be in some trouble with a lacklustre first-half effort, but they regrouped well after coach Wayne Bennett pointed out some shortcomings during the break.

The North Queensland Cowboys paid a high-price for their massive error count with a 19-12 loss to Penrith at Stockland Stadium. The Cowboys committed 16 handling errors to the Panthers' five.

An Adelaide Oval crowd of 27,435 watched the Rams score their first competition victory with a 10-8 win over the Hunter Mariners. Both sides scored one try, but the Rams held the upper hand for virtually the entire match.

ROUND 3 — RESULTS

Adelaide 10 (C.Blair try; K.Wrigley 3 goals) defeated **Hunter Mariners** 8 (G.Thompson try; N.Zisti 2 goals) at Adelaide Oval, Friday night, March 14.

Scrums: Hunter 7–4. Penalties: Hunter 7–5. Crowd: 27,435. Referee: Brian Grant. Halftime: Adelaide 10–2. Goalkickers: Wrigley (Adelaide) 3/4, Zisti (Hunter) 2/2.
ADELAIDE: Maybon; Tamani, Wrigley, Quinn, Simonds; Schifilliti, Stone; Campion, Walters (c), Corvo, Pierce, Boughton, Blair. Interchange: Mamando, Paiyo, Galea, Hick.
HUNTER: Ross; Thompson, Godden, Zisti, Beauchamp; Hill, Goldthorpe; Stone, McCormack, Maddison, T.Iro (c), Marquet, Picchelli. Interchange: Puching, Brann, Dooley, Swain.

Penrith 19 (A.Hinson 2, S.Domic tries; R.Girdler 3 goals; G.Alexander field goal) defeated **North Queensland** 12 (L.Phillips, K.Warren tries; Phillips 2 goals) at Stockland Stadium, Saturday night, March 15.

Scrums: North Queensland 15–8. Penalties: North Queensland 9–5. Crowd: 18,003. Referee: Tim Mander. Halftime: Penrith 14–6. Goalkickers: Girdler (Penrith) 3/4, Phillips (North Queensland) 2/3. Reserves: North Queensland 34–18.
PENRITH: Jorgensen; Hinson, Thompson, Domic, Williams; Girdler, Alexander (c); Johnson, Gower, Macnamara, Gall, M.Adamson, Brown. Interchange: P.Adamson, Falcon, Drew, Hicks.
NORTH QUEENSLAND: Mahon; Phillips, Shipway, Cope, Ahmat; A.Dunemann, Ferris; Jones, Walters (c), Lomax, Roberts, Smith, Cunningham. Interchange: Locke, Death, Ketchell, Warren.

Canterbury 38 (M.Ryan 2, S.Marteene, S.Gillies, T.Norton, J.Hetherington tries; D.Halligan 7 goals) defeated **Canberra** 20 (N.Nadruku 2, B.Clyde,

B.Hetherington, T.Payten tries; C.O'Neall 2, D.Furner goals) at Belmore Sports Ground, Sunday, March 16.

Scrums: Canterbury 11–4. Penalties: Canterbury 12–10. Crowd: 9025. Referee: Bill Harrigan. Halftime: Canterbury 24–10. Goalkickers: Halligan (Canterbury) 7/8, O'Neall (Canberra) 2/3, Furner (Canberra) 1/2. Reserves: Canberra 24–20.

CANTERBURY: Ryan; El Masri, Timu, Marteene, Halligan; Norton, Polla-Mounter; Britt, Hetherington, Newton, Haumono, Gillies (c), Reardon. Interchange: Relf, Smith, Schraader.

CANBERRA: Nadruku; McNamara, Wiki, Burnham, O'Neill; Daley (c), Woolford; Pongia, Priddis, Davico, Hetherington, Furner, Clyde. Interchange: Westley, Kennedy, Payten.

Sin bin: Furner (Canberra).

Cited: Pongia (Canberra). **Charge:** Grade 2 reckless high tackle. **Sentence:** Four weeks.

Brisbane 26 (A.Langer, D.Lockyer, D.Smith, W.Sailor tries; Lockyer 5 goals) defeated **Perth** 16 (C.Ryan, S.Wilson, P.Bell tries; J.O'Neill 2 goals) at the WACA Ground, Sunday, March 16.

Scrums: Perth 8–6. Penalties: Brisbane 11–6. Crowd: 11,109. Referee: Steve Clark. Halftime: Perth 16–10. Goalkickers: Lockyer (Brisbane) 5/6, O'Neill (Perth) 2/3. Reserves: Brisbane 28–10.

BRISBANE: Lockyer; Devere, Hancock, Renouf, Sailor; Walters, Langer (c); Lazarus, Driscoll, Gee, Ryan, Thorn, Smith. Interchange: Tallis, Scott, Plath, B.Walker.

PERTH: O'Neill; Ryan, Bell, Fleming, Daylight; Wilson, Rodwell; Kearns, Fuller, Howe, Geyer (c), Shiels, Fritz. Interchange: Grieve, Green, Higgins, Dever.

Cronulla 34 (G.Bell 2, D.Lee, D.Peachey, D.Treister tries; M.Rogers 7 goals) defeated **Auckland** 8 (D.Betts try; M.Ridge 2 goals) at Shark Park, Monday night, March 17.

Scrums: Cronulla 7–1. Penalties: Cronulla 7–4. Crowd: 16,860. Referee: Graham Annesley. Halftime: Cronulla 10–6. Goalkickers: Rogers (Cronulla) 7/7, Ridge (Auckland) 2/2. Reserves: Cronulla 25–12.

CRONULLA: Peachey; Barnett, Ettingshausen (c), Bell, Rogers, Healey, Green; Lee, Treister, Davidson, Ryan, Long, Nikau. Interchange: Strauss, Stevens, Dykes.

AUCKLAND: Ridge (c); Ellis, T. Ropati, A.Swann, Hoppe; Ngamu, Jones; Young, Eru, Horo, Betts, Kearney, L.Swann. Interchange: Malam, Vagana, Buckingham.

STANDINGS: Cronulla 6, Brisbane 6, Penrith 6, Canterbury 4, North Queensland 2, Perth 2, Adelaide 2, Auckland 2, Hunter 0, Canberra 0.

TELSTRA CUP ROUND 4
MARCH 21, 22, 23, 24

Broncos add to Mal's woes

Brisbane coach Wayne Bennett contributed to the woes of his former prodigy Mal Meninga when the Broncos thumped Canberra 24-8 at ANZ Stadium.

The Raiders slumped to outright last on the competition ladder with their fourth consecutive loss. Brisbane led from the ninth minute, when Wendell Sailor scored the opening try, and from that point they were never threatened by an opposition that lacked ball control and any sting in their defence.

Fundamental errors by the Raiders led to two of the Broncos' four tries.

Perth fullback Julian O'Neill experienced one of his best days in football with a stunning 26-point contribution to the Reds' 34-6 win over Canterbury at Perth Oval. O'Neill scored four tries and landed five goals in a brilliant individual display. The Reds led 18-6 at the break and stormed home with 14 unanswered points in the second half.

Penrith's favourite son, Greg Alexander, celebrated his 200th first-grade game with a wonderful display as the Panthers thrashed Cronulla 38-10 at Penrith Football Stadium. Cronulla started the match with a 90-metre runaway try to winger Brett Howland, but the tide turned quickly and Penrith went to halftime leading 20-6.

At Breakers Stadium, the Hunter Mariners broke through for their first competition victory when they demolished the North Queensland Cowboys 38-10. It was 10-all at halftime, but in an incredible 13-minute period, from the 49th to the 62nd minute, the Mariners scored five tries and four conversions.

The Adelaide Rams sprang a major surprise with a 16-12 defeat of a grossly disappointing Auckland Warriors outfit at Ericsson Stadium. The Warriors missed fullback Matthew Ridge, who withdrew only four hours before kick-off.

ROUND 4 — RESULTS

Adelaide 16 (C.Blair, W.Simonds tries; K.Wrigley 3, L.Williamson goals) defeated **Auckland** 12 (S.Jones, T.Tuimavave tries; M.Ellis 2 goals) at Ericsson Stadium, Friday night, March 21.

Scrums: Adelaide 6–5. Penalties: Auckland 11–8. Crowd: 13,000. Referee: Tim Mander. Halftime: Auckland 10–8. Goalkickers: Wrigley (Adelaide) 3/5, Williamson (Adelaide) 1/1, Ellis (Auckland) 2/5.
ADELAIDE: Quinn; Simonds, Kiri, Williamson, Tamani; Wrigley, Stone; Corvo, Schifilliti (c), Campion, Pierce, Boughton, Blair. Interchange: Paiyo, Mamando, Galea.
AUCKLAND: Blake; Hoppe, T. Ropati, A.Swann, Ellis; Ngamu, Jones; Horo, Eru, Young, Betts, Kearney (c), L.Swann. Interchange: Vagana, Tuimavave, Buckingham.
Cited: Young (Auckland). **Charge:** Grade 2 striking. **Sentence:** One week.

Hunter 38 (J.Carlaw 2, G.Thompson, N.Piccinelli, T.Maddison, K.Beauchamp, N.Zisti tries; Zisti 5 goals) defeated **North Queensland** 10 (L.Phillips, K.Warren tries; Phillips goal) at Breakers Stadium, Saturday night, March 22.

Scrums: North Queensland 9–3. Penalties: Hunter 6–5. Crowd: 6090. Referee: Brian Grant. Halftime: 10–all. Goalkickers: Zisti (Hunter) 5/8, Phillips (North Queensland) 1/3. Reserves: Hunter 28–16.
HUNTER: Ross; Thompson, Zisti, Carlaw, Beauchamp; Hill, Goldthorpe (c); Maddison, Swain, Stone, T.Iro, Marquet, Piccinelli. Interchange: Brann, Miles, Collins, Dorreen.
NORTH QUEENSLAND: Mahon; Phillips, Cope, Shipway, Bowman; Doyle, Ferris; Roberts, Walters (c), Lomax, Tabuai, Jones, Cunningham. Interchange: Warren, Smith, Cressbrook, Death.

Penrith 38 (D.Brown 2, P.Jorgensen, A.Hinson, R.Girdler, J.Williams tries; Girdler 7 goals) defeated **Cronulla** 10 (B.Howland 2 tries; M.Healey goal) at Penrith Football Stadium, Sunday, March 23.

Scrums: 7–all. Penalties: Cronulla 8–3. Crowd: 8138. Referee: Steve Clark. Halftime: Penrith 20–6. Goalkickers: Girdler (Penrith) 7/7, Healey (Cronulla) 1/3. Reserves: Cronulla 26–16.

PENRITH: Jorgensen; Williams, Thompson, Domic, Hinson; Girdler, Alexander (c); Johnson, Gower, Macnamara, Edwards, M.Adamson, Brown. Interchange: Waddell, Falcon, Drew, Hicks.
CRONULLA: Peachey; Barnett, Bell, Ettingshausen (c), Howland; Healey, Green; Davidson, Treister, Lee, Ryan, Long, Nikau. Interchange: Stevens, McKenna, Sammut, Dykes.

Perth 34 (J.O'Neill 4, E.Edgar, M.Geyer tries; O'Neill 5 goals) defeated **Canterbury** 6 (R.Relf try; D.Halligan goal) at Perth Oval, Sunday, March 23.

Scrums: Canterbury 13–6. Penalties: 5–all. Crowd: 7135. Referee: Graham Annesley. Halftime: Perth 18–6. Goalkickers: O'Neill (Perth) 5/8, Halligan (Canterbury) 1/2. Reserves: Canterbury 28–14.
PERTH: O'Neill; Edgar, Bell, Fleming, Daylight; Wilson, Rodwell; Fuller, Howe, Mark Geyer (c), Shiels, Fritz. Interchange: Grieve, Green, Higgins, Dever.
CANTERBURY: Ryan; El Masri, Marteene, Timu, Halligan; Norton, Polla-Mounter; Newton, Hetherington, Britt, Gillies (c), Haumono, Reardon. Interchange: Relf, Smith, Price, Schraader.
Sin bin: Gillies (Canterbury).

Brisbane 24 (W.Sailor, G.Tallis, A.Langer, M.Hancock tries; D.Lockyer 4 goals) defeated **Canberra** 8 (D.Westley, B.Kennedy tries) at ANZ Stadium, Monday night, March 24.

Scrums: Canberra 10–7. Penalties: Brisbane 8–3. Crowd: 26,103. Referee: Bill Harrigan. Halftime: Brisbane 12–4. Goalkickers: Lockyer (Brisbane) 4/5, Furner (Canberra) 0/2. Reserves: Brisbane 38–6.
BRISBANE: Lockyer; Hancock, Carroll, Renouf, Sailor; Kevin Walters, Langer (c); Gee, Driscoll, Lazarus, Ryan, Tallis, Smith. Interchange: Thorn, Plath, Scott.
CANBERRA: Nagas; O'Neall, Wiki, Nadruku, McNamara; Daley (c), Burnham; Hetherington, Woolford, Westley, Furner, Kennedy, Clyde. Interchange: Davico, Lea, Payten, Priddis.

STANDINGS: Ponrith 8, Brisbane 8, Cronulla 6, Perth 4, Canterbury 4, Adelaide 4, Hunter 2, North Queensland 2, Auckland 2, Canberra 0.

TELSTRA CUP ROUND 4

TELSTRA CUP ROUND 5
MARCH 27, 29, 30, 31

Brisbane's fifth straight

Brisbane came through their toughest test of the early rounds of the 1997 season with their undefeated record intact after downing Cronulla 14-12 at ANZ Stadium.

In the most intensely fought match of the new competition, the Broncos twice came from behind to take the match. They trailed 6-2 early and 12-8 at halftime, after Cronulla winger Mat Rogers scored all his team's points with two converted tries.

Lock Darren Smith crossed for the winning try midway through the second half when he swivelled out of the tackles of Andrew Ettingshausen and David Peachey.

North Queensland overcame the dismissal of captain Steve Walters to score a morale-boosting 16-14 win over Canterbury at Belmore Sports Ground. The Cowboys trailed 14-12 when Walters was sent off for kneeing Canterbury forward Robert Relf. Down to 12 men, the Cowboys scored the winning try, through centre Paul Bowman, six minutes from fulltime. In a fiery match, four players were later cited and suspended by the Super League judiciary.

Perth captain Mark Geyer again landed in hot water after he was reported for a reckless tackle and eye-gouging in the Reds' 18-16 win over Adelaide at Adelaide Oval. Geyer was in devastating form, but another judiciary appearance would mean a long spell on the sidelines.

With Matthew Ridge and Stephen Kearney tending injuries, the Auckland Warriors scored a 16-14 win over Penrith at Ericsson Stadium. The Panthers' cause was damaged by the dismissal of prop Gordon Falcon, sent off for fighting eight minutes after halftime.

Canberra broke through for their first win of the season when they downed the Hunter Mariners 18-12 at Bruce Stadium.

ROUND 5 — RESULTS

Perth 18 (M.Daylight, S.Wilson, J.O'Neill tries; O'Neill 2 goals; O'Neill, M.Fuller field goals) defeated **Adelaide** 16 (C.Quinn, K.Wrigley tries; Wrigley 4 goals) at Adelaide Oval, Thursday night, March 27.

Scrums: Adelaide 7–6. Penalties: Adelaide 12–5. Crowd: 16,294. Referee: Brian Grant. Halftime: Perth 12–4. Goalkickers: O'Neill (Perth) 2/3, Wrigley (Adelaide) 4/4.
PERTH: O'Neill; Daylight, Bell, Dever, Ryan; Wilson, Rodwell; Howe, Fuller, Kearns, Shiels, Mark Geyer (c), Fritz. Interchange: Green, Grieve, Horan, Higgins.
ADELAIDE: Quinn; Simonds, Wrigley, Williamson, Tamani; Schifilliti, Stone; Corvo, Walters (c), Campion, Pierce, Boughton, Blair. Interchange: Mamando, Paiyo, Cann, McKenzie.
Cited: Blair (Adelaide). **Charge:** Grade 3 dangerous throw.**Sentence:** Two weeks. Geyer (Perth).**Charges:** Grade 4 reckless tackle and gouging. **Sentence:** 10 weeks.

Auckland 16 (T.Ropati, S.Hoppe, D.Betts tries; M.Ridge, M.Ellis goals) defeated **Penrith** 14 (R.Girdler, B.Drew tries; Girdler 3 goals) at Ericsson Stadium, Saturday night, March 29.

Scrums: Auckland 7–5. Penalties: Penrith 7–6. Crowd: 19,400. Referee: Bill Harrigan. Halftime: Auckland 8–2. Goalkickers: Ridge (Auckland) 1/2, Ellis (Auckland) 1/3, Ngamu (Auckland) 0/1, Girdler (Penrith) 3/3. Reserves: Auckland 26–22.
AUCKLAND: Ridge (c); Hoppe, T.Ropati, A.Swann, Ellis; Ngamu, Jones; Horo, Eru, Malam, Betts, Kearney, Tuimavave. Interchange: Henare, Vagana, Endacott, I.Ropati.
PENRITH: Jorgensen; Williams, Thompson, Domic, Hinson; Girdler, Alexander (c); Macnamara, Gower, Johnson, Falcon, M.Adamson, Brown. Interchange: Petersen, Drew, Waddell, MacGillivray.
Sent off: Falcon (Penrith). **Charge:** Contrary conduct (fighting). **Sentence:** One week.

Canberra 18 (D.Furner, C.O'Neall, B.Kennedy tries; Furner 3 goals) defeated **Hunter Mariners** 12 (T.Miles, K.Beauchamp tries; N.Zisti 2 goals)

150   *RUGBY LEAGUE 1998*

at Bruce Stadium, Sunday, March 30.

Scrums: Hunter 9–7. Penalties: Canberra 7–4. Crowd: 15,650. Referee: Tim Mander. Goalkickers: Furner (Canberra) 3/5, Zisti (Hunter) 2/2, Swain (Hunter) 0/1. Reserves: Hunter 40–6.
CANBERRA: Nagas; O'Neall, Wiki, Nadruku, McNamara; Daley (c), Burnham; Hetherington, Priddis, Davico, Kennedy, Furner, Clyde. Interchange: Westley, Paten, Woolford.
HUNTER: Ross; Beauchamp, Carlaw, Zisti, Thompson; Hill, Goldthorpe (c); Stone, Swain, Maddison, Marquet, T.Iro, Piccinelli. Interchange: Brann, Miles, B.Kimmorley.

North Queensland 16 (S.Mahon, M.Shipway, P.Bowman tries; L.Phillips 2 goals) defeated **Canterbury** 14 (M.Ryan 2 tries; D.Halligan 3 goals) at Belmore Sports Ground, Monday, March 31.

Scrums: North Queensland 12–6. Penalties: North Queensland 13–5. Crowd: 9830. Referee: Stephen Clark. Halftime: North Queensland 12–6. Goalkickers: Phillips (North Queensland) 2/3, Halligan (Canterbury) 3/3. Reserves: Canterbury 14–12.
NORTH QUEENSLAND: Mahon; Phillips, Shipway, Bowman, Cope; Doyle, Ferris; Locke, Walters (c), Lomax, Jones, Roberts, Cunningham. Interchange: A. Dunemann, Cressbrook, Smith.
CANTERBURY: Ryan; El Masri, Marteene, Timu, Halligan; Norton, Polla-Mounter; Newton, Hetherington, Britt, Relf, Gillies (c), Reardon. Interchange: Smith, Price.

Sent off: Walters (North Queensland), 66 min. **Charge:** Grade 3 striking. **Sentence:** One week.
Cited: Jones (North Queensland). **Charge:** Grade 2 striking. **Sentence:** One week. Britt (Canterbury). **Charge:** Grade 4 reckless tackle. **Sentence:** Two weeks. Lomax (North Queensland). **Charge:** Grade 3 careless high tackle. **Sentence:** Three weeks. Polla-Mounter (Canterbury). **Charge:** Grade 1 striking. **Sentence:** One week.

Brisbane 14 (K.Walters, D.Smith tries; D.Lockyer 3 goals) defeated **Cronulla** 12 (M.Rogers 2 tries; Rogers 2 goals) at ANZ Stadium, Monday night, March 31.

Scrums: 7–all. Penalties: Brisbane 4–0. Crowd: 17,294. Referee: Graham Annesley. Halftime: Cronulla 12–8. Goalkickers: Lockyer (Brisbane) 3/3, Rogers (Cronulla) 2/2. Reserves: Cronulla 32–12.
BRISBANE: Lockyer; Devere, Renouf, Carroll, Sailor; Walters, Langer (c); Lazarus, Plath, Gee, Thorn, Tallis, Smith. Interchange: Ryan, Webcke, Driscoll.
CRONULLA: Peachey; Rogers, Ettingshausen (c), Bell, Barnett; Healey, Green; Stevens, Treister, Lee, Long, Ryan, Nikau. Interchange: Strauss, McKenna, Pierce, Dykes.

STANDINGS: Brisbane 10, Penrith 8, Cronulla 6, Perth 6, Canterbury 4, Adelaide 4, North Queensland 4, Auckland 4, Hunter 2, Canberra 2.

TELSTRA CUP ROUND 6
APRIL 4, 5, 6, 7

Warriors stun the Raiders

A week after their first win of the season, Canberra's semi-final hopes nosedived again, with a 31-24 loss to the Auckland Warriors at Bruce Stadium.

Making matters worse for the Raiders was an ankle ligament injury suffered by lock Bradley Clyde, adding to an already crippling injury situation. The Raiders' effort was patchy, mixing some slick attacking play with periods of poor defence and flagging intensity. A Marc Ellis field goal in the 66th minute gave the Warriors a 25-24 lead and a try a minute from fulltime to replacement forward Bryan Henare secured the points for Auckland.

Cronulla bounced back from two successive defeats to down the Perth Reds 20-6 at the WACA. The Sharks won the match with a second-string forward pack after injuries cut a swathe through the side. Perth coach Dean Lance accused his side of complacency after wins over Canterbury and Adelaide.

Four players were carried from the field and two sent to the sin bin in Brisbane's 42-16 defeat of North Queensland at Stockland Stadium. The Broncos' undefeated record was never threatened, despite an improved and frenetic opening from the Cowboys. Brisbane's Darren Lockyer and Cowboys trio Luke Phillips, Jason Ferris and Tyran Smith all left the field on stretchers.

At Penrith, the Panthers hung on to defeat the Hunter Mariners 36-24 after leading 22-8 early in the second half.

Ryan Girdler landed eight goals for the Panthers from as many attempts.

Canterbury and Adelaide took part in a tryscoring frenzy at Belmore; the Bulldogs finished with a flourish to win 34-22. Few could have predicted that after six rounds Canberra would be propping up the Super League ladder. Or that Penrith would be the Broncos' closest challengers.

ROUND 6 — RESULTS

Penrith 36 (J.Williams 2, G.Alexander, P.Adamson, M.Adamson tries; R.Girdler 8 goals) defeated **Hunter** 24 (R.Ross 2, W.Poching, N.Zisti tries; Zisti 4 goals) at Penrith Football Stadium, Friday night, April 4.

Scrums: Hunter 10–7. Penalties: Hunter 12–8. Crowd: 8926. Referee: Steve Clark. Halftime: Penrith 16–8. Goalkickers: Girdler (Penrith) 8/8, Zisti (Hunter) 4/7. Reserves: Hunter 20–10.
PENRITH: Jorgensen; Williams, Domic, Thompson, Hinson; Girdler, Alexander (c); Macnamara, Gower, Waddell, MacGillivray, M.Adamson, Brown. Interchange: P.Adamson, Boyd, Johnson, Petersen.
HUNTER: Ross; Beauchamp, Carlaw, Zisti, Thompson; Hill, Goldthorpe; Stone, Swain, Maddison, Marquet, T.Iro (c), Piccinelli. Interchange: Miles, Brann, Doherty.

Brisbane 42 (T.Carroll 2, S.Renouf 2, P.Ryan 2, D.Smith, M.Devere tries; D.Lockyer 4, Devere goals) defeated **North Queensland** 16 (J.Death 2, R.Cressbrook tries; J.Doyle 2 goals) at Stockland Stadium, Saturday night, April 5.

Scrums: Brisbane 10–4. Penalties: Brisbane 11–6. Crowd: 30,122 (ground record). Halftime: Brisbane 22–4. Goalkickers: Lockyer (Brisbane) 4/6, Devere (Brisbane) 1/1, Doyle (North Queensland) 2/2. Reserves: North Queensland 16–6.
BRISBANE: Lockyer; Devere, Renouf, Carroll, Sailor; Walters, Langer (c); Lazarus, Driscoll, Gee, Thorn, Tallis, Smith. Interchange: Webcke, Ryan, Plath, B. Walker.
NORTH QUEENSLAND: Mahon; Phillips, Shipway, Bowman, Cope; Doyle, Ferris; Locke, Death, Roberts (c), Smith, Galea, Cunningham. Interchange: Scott, Ketchell, Cressbrook, A.Dunemann.
Sin bin: Sailor (Brisbane), Galea (North Queensland).

Cronulla 20 (N.Graham, C.McKenna, G.Bell, D.Peachey tries; M.Rogers 2 goals) defeated **Perth** 6 (P.Shiels try; J.O'Neill goal) at the WACA, Sunday, April 6.

Scrums: Perth 12–6. Penalties: Perth 7–4. Crowd: 9200. Referee: Brian Grant. Halftime: Cronulla 12–4. Goalkickers: Rogers (Cronulla) 2/4, O'Neill (Perth) 1/2. Reserves: Perth 32–16.
CRONULLA: Peachey; Rogers, Ettingshausen (c), Bell, Barnett; Healey, Green; Strauss, Treister, Pierce, McKenna, Ryan, Nikau. Interchange: Graham, Forrester, Richardson, Fisher.
PERTH: O'Neill; Daylight, Mather, Bell, Ryan; Wilson, Rodwell (c); Howe, Fuller, Kearns, Higgins, Shiels, Fritz. Interchange: Green, Doyle, Horan, Chapman.

Canterbury 34 (S.Haumono 2, S.Marteene, S.Price, S.Gillies, R.Silva tries; D.Halligan 5 goals) defeated **Adelaide** 22 (B.Mamando 2, J.Tamani, W.Simonds tries; L.Williamson 3 goals) at Belmore Sports Ground, Sunday, April 6.

Scrums: Canterbury 3–2. Penalties: 8–all.. Crowd: 7234. Referee: Graham Annesley. Halftime: Adelaide 16–14. Goalkickers: Halligan (Canterbury) 5/8, Williamson (Adelaide) 3/4.
CANTERBURY: Ryan; El Masri, Marteene, Timu, Halligan; Norton, McRae; Newton, Hetherington, Haumono, Price, Gillies (c), Hughes. Interchange: Relf, Ward, Silva, Berrigan.
ADELAIDE: Maybon; Simonds, Quinn, Williamson, Tamani, Schifiliti, Stone; McKenzie, Walters (c), Corvo, Campion, Pierce, Boughton. Interchange: Mamando, Galea, Hick, Cann.

Auckland 31 (S.Kearney, I.Ropati, S.Hoppe, S.Jones, B.Henare tries; M.Ellis 5 goals; Ellis field goal) defeated **Canberra** 24 (L.Daley 2, D.Furner, G.McNamara, S.Woolford tries; Furner 2 goals) at Bruce Stadium, Monday night, April 7.

Scrums: Canberra 7–2. Penalties: 8–all. Crowd: 15,061. Referee: Tim Mander. Halftime: 14–all. Goalkickers: Ellis (Auckland) 5/6, Furner (Canberra) 2/5, O'Neall (Canberra) 0/1. Reserves: 24–all.
AUCKLAND: Ellis; I.Ropati, T.Ropati, A.Swann, Hoppe; Ngamu, Jones; Horo, Eru, Young, Kearney (c), Betts, Tuimavave. Interchange: Vagana, Henare.
CANBERRA: Nagas; O'Neall, Mullins, Wiki, McNamara; Daley, Stuart (c); Hetherington, Priddis, Davico, Kennedy, Furner, Clyde. Interchange: Westley, Burnham, Woolford, Payten.

STANDINGS: Brisbane 12, Penrith 10, Cronulla 8, Perth 6, Canterbury 6, Auckland 6, Adelaide 4, North Queensland 4, Hunter 2, Canberra 2.

TELSTRA CUP ROUND 7
APRIL 12, 13, 14

Bulldogs test new rulebook

Canterbury admitted testing Super League's new ruck rules with a dominant defensive display in their 16-6 win over Cronulla at a windswept Shark Park.

The Bulldogs conceded 12 penalties, but succeeded in closing Cronulla out of the game with their slowing tactics. Canterbury scored three tries to nil in their best effort of the season.

Cronulla had six players backing up from the opening Tri-series match, and lacked any spark in their play. Canterbury led 12-4 at halftime and defied the Sharks despite running against a blustery southerly wind in the second half. Referee Bill Harrigan was forced to call a halt before the fulltime siren when fans invaded the pitch.

Canberra gained revenge for their Round 2 loss to Penrith to score a 30-20 victory in the return match at Penrith Football Stadium. A crucial tackle by halfback Ricky Stuart on Penrith lock Darren Brown late in the match saved the day for the Raiders.

Undefeated Brisbane scored a solid 20-10 win over Adelaide at Adelaide Oval, despite having six players backing up from Queensland's loss in the first Tri-series match, and two others missing through injury. Two of the Broncos' tries were scored after captain Allan Langer opted to run the ball on the fifth tackle.

The Hunter Mariners scored four tries to two in their 18-10 win over Auckland at Breakers Stadium. The Mariners skipped to an early 8-0 lead and held the Warriors at bay for the rest of the match.

North Queensland were unlucky to lose 6-4 to Perth at the WACA after the Reds scored their only points of the match four minutes before fulltime. Perth centre Paul Bell scored the only try of the game.

ROUND 7 — RESULTS

Hunter 18 (N.Piccinelli 2, J.Carlaw 2 tries; N.Zisti goal) defeated **Auckland** 10 (S.Hoppe, I.Ropati tries; M.Ellis goal) at Breakers Stadium, Saturday night, April 12

Scrums: 8–all. Penalties. Auckland 7–4. Crowd: 7710. Referee: Tim Mander. Halftime: Hunter 8–0. Goalkickers: Zisti (Hunter) 1/3, Goldthorpe (Hunter) 0/1, Ellis (Auckland) 1/1, Ridge (Auckland) 0/1. Reserves. Auckland 2 1–4.
HUNTER: Ross; Beauchamp, Carlaw, Zisti, Thompson; Hill, Goldthorpe (c); Stone, McCormack, Brann, Marquet, Piccinelli, Swain. Interchange: Doherty, Poching, Godden.
AUCKLAND: Ridge (c); Hoppe, A.Swann, T.Hopati, Ellis; Ngamu, Jones; Young, Eru, Horo, Betts, Kearney, Tuimavave. Interchange: Vagana, Henare, I.Ropati.

Perth 6 (P.Bell try, J.O'Neill goal) defeated **North Queensland** 4 (J.Doyle 2 goals) at WACA, Saturday night, April 12.

Scrums: Perth 11–7. Penalties: Perth 13–9. Crowd: 9701. Referee: Steve Clark. Halftime: North Queensland 4–0. Goalkickers: O'Neill (Perth) 1/1, Doyle (North Queensland) 2/4. Reserves: Perth 50–6.
PERTH: O'Neill; Daylight, Bell, Fleming, Ryan; Wilson, Rodwell (c); Kearns, Fuller, Howe, Shiels, Grieve, Fritz. Interchange. Green, Higgins, Horan, Chapman.
NORTH QUEENSLAND: Mahon; Miller, Shipway, Bowman, Loomans; Doyle, I.Dunemann, Buttigieg, Walters (c); Roberts, Jones, Ryan, Cunningham. Interchange: Scott, Murphy, Warwick, Death.
Cited: Bowman (North Queensland). **Charge:** Grade 3 dangerous throw. **Sentence:** Three weeks.

Brisbane 20 (A.Langer, D.Smith, M.Devere, P.Lee tries; D.Lockyer 2 goals) defeated **Adelaide** 10 (W.Simonds, A.Pierce tries; K.Wrigley goal) at Adelaide Oval, Sunday, April 13.

Scrums: Brisbane 6–4. Penalties: Adelaide 9–5. Crowd: 17,633. Referee: Brian Grant. Halftime: Brisbane 14–4. Goalkickers: Lockyer (Brisbane) 2/4, Wrigley (Adelaide) 1/4.
BRISBANE: Lockyer; Devere, Smith, Carroll, Sailor;

Walters, Langer (c); Lazarus, Driscoll, Gee, Thorn, Lee, Ryan. Interchange: Webcke, Plath, S. Walker, Lee.

ADELAIDE: Maybon; Simonds, Quinn, Wrigley, Tamani; Schifilliti, Stone; McKenzie, Walters (c), Corvo, Campion, Galea, Pierce. Interchange: Mamando, Hick, Cann, Maguire.

Canberra 30 (B.Kennedy 3, L.Priddis, R.Lightning tries; D.Furner 3, Lightning, M.O'Neall goals) defeated **Penrith** 20 (C.Gower 2, J.Williams tries; R.Girdler 4 goals) at Penrith Football Stadium, Sunday, April 14.

Scrums: Canberra 8–7. Penalties: Penrith 7–5. Crowd: 7134. Referee: Graham Annesley. Halftime: 14–all. Goalkickers: Furner (Canberra) 3/4, Lightning (Canberra) 1/1, O'Neall (Canberra) 1/1, Girdler (Penrith) 4/4. Reserves: Penrith 50–12.

CANBERRA: Nagas; Lightning, Mullins, Wiki, McNamara; Daley, Stuart (c); Davico, Priddis, Westley, Hetherington, Furner, Kennedy. Interchange: Woolford, Burnham, Payten, O'Neall.

PENRITH: Jorgensen; Williams, Thompson, Domic, Hinson; Girdler, Casey; Macnamara, Gower, Johnson, MacGillivray, M.Adamson, Brown (c). Interchange: P.Adamson, Petersen, Boyd.

Canterbury 16 (H.El Masri 2, M.Ryan tries; D.Halligan 2 goals) defeated **Cronulla** 6 (M.Rogers 3 goals) at Shark Park, Monday night, April 15.

Scrums: 11–all. Penalties: Cronulla 12–3. Crowd: 15,108. Referee: Bill Harrigan. Halftime: Canterbury 12–4. Goalkickers: Halligan (Canterbury) 2/3, Rogers (Cronulla) 3/4. Reserves: Cronulla 12–8.

CANTERBURY: Silva; Halligan, Ryan, Timu, Halligan; Polla-Mounter, McRae; Newton, Hetherington, Haumono, Price, Gillies (c), Hughes. Interchange: Relf, Ward, Berrigan, Marteene.

CRONULLA: Peachey; Rogers, Ettingshausen (c), Bell, Barnett; Healey, Green; Lee, Treister, Strauss, McKenna, Long, Nikau. Interchange: Forrester, Pierce, Dykes, Richardson.

Sin bin: McRae (Canterbury).

STANDINGS: Brisbane 14, Penrith 10, Cronulla 8, Canterbury 8, Perth 8, Auckland 6, Hunter 4, Adelaide 4, Canberra 4, North Queensland 4.

TELSTRA CUP ROUND 8
APRIL 18, 19, 20, 21

Broncos lose unbeaten record

Inspired by 18-year-old halfback Craig Gower, Penrith scored a superb 27-26 win over Brisbane at Penrith Football Stadium, inflicting the first loss for the season upon the Broncos.

Selected to represent the Australian Super League side at hooker, Gower displayed his full bag of tricks at halfback, including the 77th minute field goal which brought victory for the home side.

Penrith went into the match without regular halfback Greg Alexander and experienced players Darren Brown and Steve Carter, but the 13 who ran on did the job admirably. They raced to a 14-0 lead (in 11 minutes) before the Broncos responded. The visitors hit the front after 50 minutes and looked set to run away with the match, but then centre Darren Smith scored his team's sixth try. A converted try to Penrith winger Andrew Hinson and Gower's late field goal finally turned the match around.

Adelaide scored their most significant victory when they overwhelmed Cronulla 29-18 at Shark Park. The Rams responded to some negative publicity following an incident in an Adelaide nightclub, by beginning the match at maximum intensity. They scored four first-half tries to lead 26-8 at the break. Cronulla fought back after halftime, trailing at one stage by just eight points, but a penalty goal to Luke Williamson and a Kurt Wrigley field goal put a seal on the match.

At Stockland Stadium, experienced pair Ricky Stuart and Laurie Daley helped Canberra climb from the bottom of the competition ladder with a comprehensive 40-16 win over a depleted North Queensland.

At Ericsson Stadium in Auckland, Canterbury fought back from a 12-2 deficit against the Auckland Warriors, scoring 36 of the next 38 points. Auckland crossed for two late consolation tries, but too late — the final score was a whopping 38-24 victory to Canterbury.

And at Breakers Stadium, the Hunter Mariners won their third consecutive match at home with a 36-16 win over Perth, after leading 36-0.

ROUND 8 — RESULTS

Hunter 36 (J.Carlaw 2, N.Goldthorpe 2, K.Beauchamp, R.Ross, R.Banister tries; R.Swain 2, Goldthorpe 2 goals) defeated **Perth** 16 (D.Higgins, M.Daylight, G.Fleming tries; J.O'Neill 2 goals) at Breakers Stadium, Friday night, April 18.

Scrums: Perth 7–6. Penalties: Perth 7–6. Crowd: 4139. Referee: Graham Annesley. Halftime: Hunter 8–0. Goalkickers: Swain (Hunter) 2/3, Goldthorpe (Hunter) 2/2, O'Neill (Perth) 2/3. Reserves: Perth 20–14.
HUNTER: Ross, Beauchamp, Carlaw, Zisti, Banister; Hill, Goldthorpe (c); Stone, McCormack, Brann, Doherty, Piccinelli, Swain. Interchange: Kimmorley, Poching, Maddison, Ebrill.
PERTH: O'Neill; Daylight, Fleming, Bell, Edgar; Wilson, Rodwell (c); Howe, Fuller, Kearns, Shiels, Lewis, Fritz. Interchange: Green, Higgins, Horan, Chapman.

Adelaide 29 (K.Campion, K.Wrigley, S.Topper, S.Stone tries; L.Williamson 6 goals; Wrigley field goal) defeated **Cronulla** 18 (R.Barnett, M.Healey, A.Ettingshausen tries; M.Rogers 3 goals) at Shark Park, Saturday night, April 19.

Scrums: Adelaide 6–2. Penalties: Cronulla 9–6. Crowd: 10,112. Referee: Tim Mander. Halftime: Adelaide 26–8. Goalkickers: Williamson (Adelaide) 6/6, Rogers (Cronulla) 3/4.
ADELAIDE: Maybon; Simonds, Quinn, Williamson, Tamani; Wrigley, Topper; Hick, Walters (c), Corvo, Pierce, Campion, Blair. Interchange: Mamando, Stone, Grimley, Cann.
CRONULLA: Peachey; Rogers, Ettingshausen (c), Bell, Barnett; Healey, Green; Greenhill, Treister, Lee, McKenna, Long, Nikau. Interchange: Strauss, Forrester, Sammut, Richardson.
Sin bin: Corvo (Adelaide), Long (Cronulla).

Canterbury 38 (H.El Masri 2, D.Halligan 2, J.Hetherington, R.Silva, M.Ryan tries; Halligan 5 goals) defeated **Auckland** 24 (S.Jones, S.Eru, I.Ropati, T.Ropati tries; M.Ellis 4 goals) at Ericsson Stadium, Sunday, April 20.

Scrums: 6 all. Penalties: Auckland 13–9. Crowd: 17,000. Referee: Steve Clark. Halftime: Canterbury 20–14. Goalkickers: Halligan (Canterbury) 5/8, Ellis (Auckland) 4/5. Reserves: 26–all.
CANTERBURY: Silva; El Masri, Ryan, Timu, Halligan; Polla-Mounter, McRae; Newton, Hetherington, Haumono, Price, Gillies (c), Hughes. Interchange: Relf, Ward.

AUCKLAND: Ellis; Hoppe, T.Ropati, A.Swann, I.Ropati; Ngamu, Jones; Vagana, Eru, Young, Betts, Kearney (c), Tuimavave. Interchange: Malam, Henare.

Canberra 40 (B.Mullins 2, R.Stuart, D.Furner, G.McNamara, R.Wiki, B.Kennedy tries; D.Furner 4, McNamara, L.Daley goals) defeated **North Queensland** 16 (L.Phillips, S.Walters, K.Warren tries; Phillips 2 goals) at Bruce Stadium, Sunday, April 20.

Scrums: North Queensland 8–7. Penalties: North Queensland 7–5. Crowd: 10,071. Referee: Brian Grant. Halftime: Canberra 22–10. Goalkickers: Furner (Canberra) 4/5, McNamara (Canberra) 1/1, Daley (Canberra) 1/1, Phillips (North Queensland) 2/3. Reserves: Canberra 23–10.
CANBERRA: Nagas; Boyle, Wiki, Mullins, McNamara; Daley, Stuart (c); Westley, Priddis, Davico, Kennedy, Furner, Clyde. Interchange: Pongia, Burnham, Woolford.
NORTH QUEENSLAND: Mahon; Phillips, Shipway, Warren, Loomans; Jones, Doyle; Murphy, Walters (c), Roberts, Smith, Scott, Cunningham. Interchange: Buttigieg, Cope.
Cited: Clyde (Canberra). **Charge:** Grade 1 dangerous throw. **Sentence:** One week. Priddis (Canberra). **Charge:** Grade 3 dangerous throw. **Sentence:** Exonerated.

Penrith 27 (G.Casey, J.Williams, R.Girdler, A.Hinson tries; Girdler 5 goals; C.Gower field goal) defeated **Brisbane** 26 (T.Carroll, D.Lockyer, M.Hancock, J.Plath, W.Sailor, D.Smith tries; Lockyer goal) at Penrith Football Stadium, Monday night, April 21.

Scrums: Brisbane 7–3. Penalties: Penrith 6–2. Crowd: 12,648. Referee: Bill Harrigan. Halftime: Penrith 20–12. Goalkickers: Girdler (Penrith) 5/5, Lockyer (Brisbane) 1/6. Reserves: Brisbane 26–6.
PENRITH: Jorgensen; Williams, Domic, Thompson, Hinson; Girdler (c), Gower; Johnson, Boyd, Macnamara, MacGillivray, M.Adamson, Casey. Interchange: P.Adamson, Drew, Farrar.
BRISBANE: Lockyer; Hancock, Smith, Carroll, Sailor; Walters, Langer (c); Lazarus, Driscoll, Gee, Thorn, Tallis, Ryan. Interchange: Plath, Webcke.
Sin bin: Lazarus (Brisbane).

STANDINGS: Brisbane 14, Penrith 12, Canterbury 10, Cronulla 8, Perth 8, Hunter 6, Canberra 6, Adelaide 6, Auckland 6, North Queensland 4.

TELSTRA CUP ROUND 9
APRIL 26, 27, 28

Brisbane bounce back

Brisbane recovered from their loss to Penrith (and the absence of players on representative duty in the lead-up to their clash with Canterbury) to score a convincing 34-16 win at ANZ Stadium.

With Canterbury starved of possession through a 9-3 penalty count, Brisbane were allowed to spend much of the match in attacking mode, and they scored six tries to the Bulldogs' three. Canterbury captain Simon Gillies staged a running battle with referee Graham Annesley over Annesley's interpretation of the offside rule.

Canterbury coach Chris Anderson described Annesley's control of the 10-metre rule as 'a bit excessive', and Gillies was concerned that referees had a preconceived view of Canterbury's tactics.

Canberra played their way into the top five for the first time in 1997 with a commanding 30-10 win over a depleted Perth Reds side at Bruce Stadium.

Captain Ricky Stuart limped from the field with a medial ligament tear, but a superb display by five-eighth Laurie Daley ensured the Raiders would take the two points.

Mat Rogers contributed 18 points to Cronulla's 26-0 defeat of the Hunter Mariners at Shark Park. The Sharks went into the match without Andrew Ettingshausen and had three players backing up from the previous night's Australia-New Zealand Test match.

A week after beating Cronulla at Shark Park, the Adelaide Rams scored their second successive away win against an established club with a 22-16 defeat of Penrith at Penrith Football Stadium. The Rams trailed by 14-2 at halftime but stormed home in the second half.

North Queensland led all the way to beat Auckland 30-22 just 48 hours after many of the Warriors' players turned out for in the Anzac Day Test match.

ROUND 9 — RESULTS

Cronulla 26 (M.Rogers 2, D.Peachey, C.McKenna tries; Rogers 5 goals) defeated **Hunter** 0 at Shark Park, Saturday night, April 26.

Scrums: Cronulla 7–4. Penalties: Hunter 10–8. Crowd: 12,284. Referee: Brian Grant. Halftime: Cronulla 10–0. Goalkickers: Rogers (Cronulla) 5/7, Goldthorpe (Hunter) 0/2. Reserves: Hunter 28–14.

CRONULLA: Peachey; Rogers, Richardson, Bell, Barnett; Healey (c), Green; Greenhill, Treister, Lee, Ryan, Long, Nikau. Interchange: McKenna, Strauss, Forrester, Sammut.

HUNTER: Ross; Beauchamp, Zisti, Carlaw, Thompson; Hill, Goldthorpe (c); Stone, McCormack, Brann, Swain, Doherty, Piccinelli. Interchange: Banister, Wise, Maddison, Poching.

Cited: Greenhill (Cronulla). **Charge:** Grade 3 careless tackle. **Sentence:** One week.

Adelaide 22 (R.Maybon, B.Mamando, S.Stone tries; K.Wrigley 5 goals) defeated **Penrith** 16 (B.Drew, A.Hinson tries; R.Girdler 4 goals) at Penrith Football Stadium, Sunday, April 27.

Scrums: 6–all. Penalties: 6–all. Crowd: 5815. Referee: Bill Harrigan. Halftime: Penrith 14–2. Goalkickers: Wrigley (Adelaide) 5/5, Girdler (Penrith) 4/4.

ADELAIDE: Maybon; Donnelly, Quinn, Grimley, Tamani; Wrigley, Topper; Hick, Walters (c), Corvo, Pierce, Campion, Blair. Interchange: Mamando, Schifilliti, Cann, Stone.

PENRITH: Jorgensen; Williamson, Girdler, Domic, Hinson; Carter (c), Gower; P.Adamson, Boyd, Macnamara, MacGillivray, M.Adamson, Brown. Interchange: Johnson, Farrar, Casey, Drew.

Cited: Boyd (Penrith). **Charge:** Grade 3 high tackle. **Sentence:** One week.

North Queensland 30 (R.Cressbrook, L.Phillips, P.Jones, S.Walters, L.Scott tries; Phillips 5 goals) defeated **Auckland** 22 (S.Endacott, S.Hoppe, T.Ropati tries; M.Ellis 5 goals) at Stockland Stadium, Sunday, April 27.

Scrums: North Queensland 6–1. Penalties: Auckland 12–5. Crowd: 12,464. Referee: Tim Mander. Halftime: North Queensland 14–4. Goalkickers: Phillips (North

Queensland) 5/6, Ellis (Auckland) 5/5. **Reserves:** North Queensland 26–0.
NORTH QUEENSLAND: Cressbrook; Warwick, Mahon, Shipway, Phillips; I.Dunemann, Doyle; Lomax, Walters, Roberts (c), Jones, Cunningham, Warren. Interchange: Scott, Murphy, Tabuai.
AUCKLAND: Ellis; Hoppe, T.Ropati, Swann, Staladi; Endacott, Jones; Malam, Eru, Horo, Betts, Kearney (c), Tuimavave. Interchange: Blake, Henare, Ngamu.

Brisbane 34 (T.Carroll 2, M.Hancock, A.Langer, D.Lockyer, W.Sailor tries; Lockyer 5 goals) defeated **Canterbury** 16 (P.Ryan 2, H.El Masri tries; D.Halligan 2 goals) at ANZ Stadium, Monday night, April 28.

Scrums: Brisbane 8–4. Penalties: Brisbane 9–3. Crowd: 17,921. Referee: Graham Annesley. Halftime: Brisbane 12–10. Goalkickers: Lockyer (Brisbane) 5/7, Halligan (Canterbury) 2/3. Reserves: Canterbury 20–18.
BRISBANE: Lockyer; Hancock, Smith, Carroll, Sailor; Walters, Langer (c); Lazarus, Driscoll, Webcke, Thorn, Tallis, Ryan. Interchange: Gee, Plath, Lee, B. Walker.
CANTERBURY: Silva; El Masri, Ryan, Timu, Halligan; Polla-Mounter, McRae; Newton, Hothorington, Relf, Price, Gillies (c), Hughes. Interchange: Ward, Haumono, Marteene, Berrigan.

Sin bin: Newton (Canterbury).

Canberra 30 (B.Mullins 2, R.Wiki, D.Boyle, R.Lightning tries; Lightning 4 goals; L.Daley 2 field goals) defeated **Perth** 10 (J.O'Neill, J.Millar tries; O'Neill goal) at Bruce Stadium, Monday night, April 28.

Scrums: Canberra 5–1. Penalties: Canberra 10–9. Crowd: 10,270. Referee: Stephen Clark. Halftime: Canberra 13–10. Goalkickers: Lightning (Canberra) 4/5, O'Neill (Perth) 1/2. Reserves: Canberra 20–18.
CANBERRA: Nagas; Lightning, Mullins, Wiki, Boyle; Daley, Stuart (c); Pongia, Priddis, Payten, Westley, Kennedy, Burnham. Interchange: Woolford, Atkins, Van Dalen.
PERTH: O'Neill; Fleming, Bell, Millar, Edgar; Horan, Rodwell (c); Kearns, Chapman, Green, Lewis, Shiels, Fritz. Interchange: Higgins, Trevitt, Mather, Brady–Smith.
Sent off: Trevitt (Perth), 65 min. **Charge:** Three Grade 3 high tackles. **Sentence:** Three weeks.

STANDINGS: Brisbane 16, Penrith 12, Cronulla 10, Canterbury 10, Canberra 8, Adelaide 8, Perth 8, Hunter 6, Auckland 6, North Queensland 6.

TELSTRA CUP ROUND 10
MAY 2, 4, 5, 12

Daley inspires Raiders

Canberra finally arrived as a force in Super League with a 22-8 win over Cronulla at Bruce Stadium.

Once again, five-eighth Laurie Daley was the inspiration for the Raiders. He set up an early try for centre Brett Mullins, scored a critical second-half try when he charged into open space from 10 metres out and should have scored another except for a dubious ruling by the video referee.

Canterbury's clash with the Hunter Mariners at Belmore Sports Ground developed into high farce with 84 points scored in the Bulldogs' 48-36 victory. Defence became a dirty word after halftime, when 54 points were racked up in just 40 minutes. The Mariners' tally of 36 was the highest score ever recorded by a losing team in either ARL or Super League competition.

Canterbury's Hazem El Masri topped the try tally with four.

First-placed Brisbane didn't have matters all their own way, despite a 34-18 scoreline over last-placed Auckland at Ericsson Stadium. Just days after dumping John Monie for national coach Frank Endacott, the Warriors rallied strongly and offered far stiffer opposition than in previous matches. Auckland led 12-10 at halftime, but the Broncos piled on four second-half tries.

An injury-stricken Penrith were no match for the Perth Reds, who ran up a 35-20 win at the WACA. The Panthers had 14 first-graders sidelined.

A try to fullback Reggie Cressbrook six minutes from fulltime enabled North Queensland to snatch a premiership point in a 14-all draw with Adelaide in wet conditions at Adelaide Oval.

ROUND 10 — RESULTS

Adelaide 14 (J.Tamani 2, L.Williamson tries; Williamson goal) drew with **North Queensland** 14 (I.Dunemann, M.Shipway, R.Cressbrook tries; L.Phillips goal) at Adelaide Oval, Friday night, May 2.

Scrums: Adelaide 11–5. Penalties: Adelaide 9–5. Crowd: 15,970. Referee: Graham Annesley. Halftime: Adelaide 8–6. Goalkickers: Williamson (Adelaide) 1/4, Phillips (North Queensland) 1/4.
ADELAIDE: Maybon; Donnelly, Grimley, Williamson, Tamani; Wrigley, Stone; Hick, Walters (c), Corvo, Campion, Pierce, Blair. Interchange: Mamando, Cann, Quinn, Stone.
NORTH QUEENSLAND: Cressbrook; Warwick, Mahon, Shipway, Phillips; I.Dunemann, Ferris; Roberts (c), Walters, Lomax, Cunningham, Jones, Warren. Interchange: Scott, Murphy, Tabuai.

Brisbane 34 (W.Sailor 2, K.Walters, D.Smith, D.Lockyer, B.Thorn tries; Lockyer 5 goals) defeated **Auckland** 18 (S.Hoppe 2, T.Ropati tries; M.Ellis 3 goals) at Ericsson Stadium, Sunday, May 4.

Scrums: Brisbane 6–3. Penalties: 6–all. Crowd: 16,471. Referee: Brian Grant. Halftime: Auckland 12–10. Goalkickers: Lockyer (Brisbane) 5/7, Ellis (Auckland) 3/3. Reserves: Auckland 26–24.
BRISBANE: Lockyer; Hancock, Smith, Carroll, Sailor; Walters, Langer (c); Lazarus, Driscoll, Webcke, Thorn, Tallis, Ryan. Interchange: Gee, Plath, Devere.
AUCKLAND: Ellis; Hoppe, T.Ropati, A.Swann, Staladi; Endacott, Jones; Malam, Eru, Horo, Henare, Kearney (c), L.Swann. Interchange: Vagana, Ngamu, Young.

Perth 35 (P.Bell, P.Shiels, T.Horan, G.Fleming, C.Ryan tries; D.Chapman 6, Ryan goals; Chapman field goal) defeated **Penrith** 20 (C.Gower, R.Girdler, J.Williams tries; Girdler 4 goals) at WACA, Sunday, May 4.

Scrums: Perth 8–5. Penalties: Penrith 11–6. Crowd: 7042. Referee: Bill Harrigan. Halftime: Perth 18–8. Goalkickers: Chapman (Perth) 6/8, Ryan (Perth) 1/1, Girdler (Penrith) 4/4. Reserves: Perth 34–12.
PERTH: Fleming; Ryan, Bell (c), Millar, Edgar; Wilson, Horan; Green, Chapman, Kearns, Shiels, Lewis, Fritz.

Interchange: Grieve, Higgins, Fuller, Rodwell.
PENRITH: Jorgensen; Williams, Thompson, Hinson, Beckett; Girdler, Carter (c); Macnamara, Gower, D.Alexander, Farrar, Hopkins, Gall. Interchange: Afoa, Puletua, Brown, Petersen.

Canberra 22 (B.Mullins 2, L.Daley, L.Priddis tries; R.Lightning 3 goals) defeated **Cronulla** 8 (P.Green try; M.Rogers 2 goals) at Bruce Stadium, Monday night, May 5.

Scrums: Cronulla 8–5. Penalties: Cronulla 5–4. Crowd: 13,875. Referee: Steve Clark. Halftime: Canberra 12–6. Goalkickers: Lightning (Canberra) 3/5, Rogers (Cronulla) 2/2. Reserves: Canberra 24–22.
CANBERRA: Nagas; Lightning, Mullins, Wiki, Boyle; Daley (c); McFadden; Davico, Priddis, Pongia, Kennedy, Burnham, Clyde. Interchange: Woolford, Payten, Shaw, Van Dalen.
CRONULLA: Peachey; Rogers, Ettingshausen (c), Bell, Barnett; Healey, Green; Lee, Treister, Lang, Long, Ryan, Nikau. Interchange: McKenna, Strauss, Richardson.

Canterbury 48 (H.El Masri 4, S.Gillies 2, R.Mears, M.Ryan tries; D.Halligan 8 goals) defeated **Hunter** 36 (W.Poching, D.Doherty, N.Zisti, R.Ross, B.Kimmorley, C.Wise, T.Iro tries; N.Goldthorpe 4 goals) at Belmore Sports Ground, Monday night, May 12.

Scrums: Canterbury 8–7. Penalties: Hunter 6–5. Crowd: 7126. Referee: Tim Mander. Halftime: Canterbury 18–12. Goalkickers: Halligan (Canterbury) 8/10, Goldthorpe (Hunter) 4/5, Poching (Hunter) 0/2, Zisti (Hunter) 0/1. Reserves: Canterbury 24–18.
CANTERBURY: Silva; El Masri, Ryan, Timu, Halligan, Polla-Mounter, McRae; Newton, Mears, Britt, Haumono, Gillies (c), Hughes. Interchange: Relf, Ward.
HUNTER: Ross; Beauchamp, Zisti, Carlaw, Wise; Hill, Goldthorpe (c); Stone, McCormack, Maddison, Doherty, Poching, Piccinelli. Interchange: Brann, Kimmorley, Iro.

STANDINGS: Brisbane 18, Penrith 12, Canterbury 12, Cronulla 10, Canberra 10, Perth 10, Adelaide 9, North Queensland 7, Hunter 6, Auckland 6.

TELSTRA CUP ROUND 11
MAY 16, 23, 24, 25, 26

Canberra move to third

Canberra joined Cronulla and Penrith in a share of third position on the Super League ladder with a 20-10 win over Auckland at Ericsson Stadium.

The Raiders went to halftime with an 8-6 lead before the second-half collapse by the Warriors that had become almost customary. Canberra scored three tries to two, but looked far more comfortable in the wet and slippery conditions. Centre Ruben Wiki sealed the result with a 40-metre try which featured a neat fend on former All Black Marc Ellis and a poor defensive effort from lock Denis Betts.

The Warriors lost their rudder when fullback and captain Matthew Ridge limped off with a hamstring injury early in the second half.

Cronulla made a welcome return to form with a 30-2 demolition of the Perth Reds at Shark Park.

The Sharks' defence led the way, denying the Reds a try, while their attack was in full voice in the second half, when they added five tries to their two in the first half.

The Brisbane Broncos were a weary bunch after the hectic Tri-series competition, and they played that way as they dropped a competition point to the lowly North Queensland Cowboys at ANZ Stadium. The Broncos led 20-8 with eight minutes remaining but ran out of steam, allowing the Cowboys two converted tries and a 20-all final score.

The Hunter Mariners continued their remarkable form on home soil with a comprehensive 30-6 defeat of Penrith at Breakers Stadium. Four days after conceding 48 points to Canterbury, the Mariners' defence had improved out of sight, and they conceded only one try to the Panthers.

Canterbury scored seven tries to four to thump the Adelaide Rams 42-22 at the Adelaide Oval, but the Bulldogs' defence again fell away late in the match; they conceded four tries in the final 10 minutes.

ROUND 11 — RESULTS

Hunter 30 (C.Wise 3, B.Godden, N.Zisti, N.Piccinelli tries; B.Kimmorley 2, Zisti goals) defeated **Penrith** 6 (R.Girdler try; Girdler goal) at Breakers Stadium, Friday night, May 16.
Scrums: Penrith 12–10. Penalties: 6–all. Crowd: 2198. Referee: Bill Harrigan. Halftime: Hunter 10–6. Goalkickers: Kimmorley (Hunter) 2/5, Zisti (Hunter) 1/1, Girdler (Penrith) 1/1. Reserves: Hunter 14–6.
HUNTER: Ross; Zisti, Wise, Godden, Thompson; Hill, Kimmorley; Stone (c), McCormack, Maddison, Doherty, Marquet, Piccinelli. Interchange: Poching, Brann, Dooley, T.Iro.
PENRITH: Jorgenson; Williams, Domic, Girdler, Hinson; Carter (c), Gower; D.Alexander, Farrar, MacNamara, MacGillivray, Gall, Brown. Interchange: P.Adamson, Puletua, Boyd.

Canterbury 42 (R.Silva, H.El Masri, M.Ryan, D.Halligan, S.Gillies, S.Price, R.Relf tries; Halligan 7 goals) defeated **Adelaide** 22 (R.Maybon, K.Walters, M.Corvo, L.Williamson tries; Williamson 3 goals) at Adelaide Oval, Friday night, May 23.
Scrums: Adelaide 8–6. Penalties: 6–all. Crowd: 15,022. Referee: Steve Clark. Halftime: Canterbury 24–0. Goalkickers: Halligan (Canterbury) 7/8, Williamson (Adelaide) 3/5.
CANTERBURY: Silva; El Masri, Ryan, Timu, Halligan; Polla-Mounter, McRae; Newton, Mears, Britt, Price, Gillies (c), Hughes. Interchange: Haumono, Ward, Relf, Pickering.
ADELAIDE: Maybon; Donnelly, Grimley, Williamson, Tamani, Wrigley, Topper, Hick, Walters (c), Conn, Campion, Pierce, Blair. Interchange: Mamando, Cann, Boughton, Schifilliti.
Sin bin: Pickering (Canterbury).

Cronulla 32 (C.McKenna 2, R.Richardson 2, A.Ettingshausen, G.Bell, M.Rogers tries; Rogers 2 goals) defeated **Perth** 2 (D.Chapman goal) at Shark Park, Saturday night, May 24.
Scrums: Cronulla 9–4. Penalties: Perth 11–7. Crowd: 9184. Referee: Brian Grant. Halftime: Cronulla 10–2. Goalkickers: Rogers (Cronulla) 2/8, Chapman (Perth) 1/2. Reserves: Perth 30–12.
CRONULLA: Peachey; Rogers, Ettingshausen (c), Bell, Richardson; Healey, Green; Lee, Treister, Stevens, Long, McKenna, Nikau. Interchange: Lang, Forrester, Sammut, Graham.
PERTH: Fleming; Ryan, Bell (c), Millar, Edgar; Wilson, Horan; Green, Chapman, Kearns, Lewis, Shiels, Fritz. Interchange: Grieve, Higgins, Fuller, Rodwell.

Brisbane 20 (D.Lockyer, S.Renouf, B.Thorn, J.Plath tries; D.Lockyer 2 goals) drew with **North Queensland** 20 (A.Dunemann, M.Shipway, I.Dunemann tries; L.Phillips 4 goals) at ANZ Stadium, Sunday, May 25.
Scrums: 6–all. Penalties: North Queensland 7–3. Crowd: 14,167. Referee: Tim Mander. Halftime: North Queensland 8–0. Goalkickers: Lockyer (Brisbane) 2/3, Phillips (North Queensland) 4/5. Reserves: North Queensland 36–10.
BRISBANE: Lockyer; Hancock, Renouf, Carroll, Sailor; Walters, Langer (c); Gee, Driscoll, Webcke, Tallis, Thorn, Ryan. Interchange: Lazarus, Smith, Plath, Mundine.
NORTH QUEENSLAND: Cressbrook; Phillips, Mahon, Shipway, Warwick; I.Dunemann, A.Dunemann; Roberts (c), Walters, Lomax, Cunningham, Jones, Warren. Interchange: Murphy, Scott, Vincent, Smith.
Cited: Ryan (Brisbane). **Charge:** Striking. **Sentence:** One week.

Canberra 20 (B.Kennedy, D.Boyle, R.Wiki tries; D.Furner 4 goals) defeated **Auckland** 10

(M.Ridge, M.Ellis tries; Ellis goal) at Ericsson Stadium, Monday night, May 26.

Scrums: Canberra 7–6. Penalties: 5–all. Crowd: 15,100. Referee: Graham Annesley. Halftime: Canberra 8–6. Goalkickers: Furner (Canberra) 4/4, Ellis (Auckland) 1/4. Reserves: Canberra 24–22.
CANBERRA: Nagas; Lightning, Mullins, Wiki, Boyle; Daley, Stuart (c); Westley, Priddis, Davico, Kennedy, Furner, Clyde. Interchange: Burnham, Hetherington, Woolford, Payten.

AUCKLAND: Ridge (c); Hoppe, T.Ropati, A.Swann, Ellis; Endacott, Jones; Young, Eru, Vagana, Henare, Kearney, Betts. Interchange: Malam, L.Swann, Ngamu, Staladi.

STANDINGS: Brisbane 19, Canterbury 14, Cronulla 12, Penrith 12, Canberra 12, Perth 10, Adelaide 9, Hunter 8, North Queensland 8, Auckland 6.

TELSTRA CUP ROUND 12
MAY 30, 31, JUNE 1, 2

Crowd riot at Belmore

More than 2,000 spectators became involved in an ugly riot at Belmore Sports Ground after Penrith upset Canterbury 28-20 in a Round 12 Monday night match. Police reinforcements were called after on-duty officers were menaced by the rioters. One policeman was put in a headlock, a touch judge was threatened and several spectators were arrested in a disturbing incident.

Referee Brian Grant came under heavy fire from Bulldogs' coach Chris Anderson, who described him as 'not up to scratch'. Anderson was dismayed at Grant's decision to disallow two Canterbury tries late in the match. 'I thought the refereeing for the whole game was fairly below standard,' he said.

Adding to the drama, the mother of Canterbury forward Solomon Haumono ran onto the field in the closing stages when her son was knocked out.

The credibility of the Hunter Mariners increased significantly after their shock 24-6 defeat of competition leaders Brisbane. The Mariners overwhelmed the visitors with four second-half tries after leading 6-0 at halftime. It was the Mariners' fifth straight win at home. Rookie Brett Kimmorley starred after again being preferred to Tri-series hero Noel Goldthorpe.

Cronulla coach John Lang declared that his team could win the inaugural Super League title after watching them tough out a 24-10 win over North Queensland in Townsville.

A dominant second-half performance helped the Canberra Raiders secure their sixth consecutive victory with a 34-18 win over the Adelaide Rams at the Adelaide Oval.

And at the WACA, Auckland Warriors coach Frank Endacott declared his team's season over after their 24-12 loss to the Perth Reds. Auckland went into the match without star players Stephen Kearney and Matthew Ridge.

ROUND 12 — RESULTS

Hunter 24 (N.Zisti 2, K.Beauchamp 2, R.Ross tries; B.Kimmorley, N.Goldthorpe goals) defeated **Brisbane** 6 (K.Walters try; D.Lockyer goal) at Topper Stadium, Friday night, May 16.

Scrums: 5–all. Penalties: Hunter 5–4. Crowd: 7124. Referee: Graham Annesley. Halftime: Hunter 6–0. Goalkickers: Kimmorley (Hunter) 1/4, Goldthorpe (Hunter) 1/3, Lockyer (Brisbane) 1/1. Reserves: Brisbane 18–16.
HUNTER: Ross; Beauchamp, Wise, Godden, Zisti; Hill, Kimmorley; Maddison, McCormack, Stone (c), Marquet, Doherty, Piccinelli. Interchange: Brann, T.Iro, Goldthorpe.
BRISBANE: Lockyer; Hancock, Renouf, Carroll, Sailor; Walters, Langer (c); Lazarus, Driscoll, Gee, Thorn,

Tallis, Webcke. Interchange: Mundine, Plath, Lee, Devere.

Cronulla 24 (A.Ettingshausen 2, D.Peachey, G.Bell tries; M.Rogers 4 goals) defeated **North Queensland** 10 (S.Mahon 2 tries; L.Phillips goal) at Stockland Stadium, Saturday night, May 31.

Scrums: Cronulla 13-9. Penalties: Cronulla 5-4. Crowd: 16,095. Referee: Tim Mander. Halftime: Cronulla 12-10. Goalkickers: Rogers (Cronulla) 4/5, Phillips (North Queensland) 1/3. Reserves: North Queensland 20-12.
CRONULLA: Peachey; Rogers, Ettingshausen (c), Richardson, Barnett; Healey, Green; Lee, Treister, Lang, McKenna, Long, Nikau. Interchange: Graham, Forrester, Bell.
NORTH QUEENSLAND: Cressbrook; Phillips, Shipway, Mahon, Warwick; I.Dunemann, A.Dunemann; Lomax, Death, Roberts (c), Jones, Cunningham, Warren. Interchange: Scott, Smith, Vincent, Murphy.

Canberra 34 (K.Nagas, R.Lightning, R.Wiki, L.Daley, A.McFadden, B.Kennedy tries; D.Furner 5 goals) defeated **Adelaide** 18 (M.Maguire, B.Mamando, S.Stone trios; L.Williamson 3 goals) at Adelaide Oval, Sunday, June 1.

Scrums: Canberra 5-4. Penalties: Canberra 11-5. Crowd: 13,894. Referee: Steve Clark. Halftime: Adelaide 18-14. Goalkickers: Furner (Canberra) 5/7, Williamson (Adelaide) 3/3.
CANBERRA: Nagas; Lightning, Mullins, Wiki, Boyle; Daley (c), McFadden, Davico, Priddis, Hetherington, Furner, Kennedy, Clyde. Interchange: Woolford, Westley, Burnham.
ADELAIDE: Maybon; Maguire, Williamson, Kiri, Grimley, Quinn, Schifilliti; Corvo, Walters (c), Cann, Campion, Boughton, Blair. Interchange: Mamando, Stone, Wrigley.

Perth 24 (S.Wilson, M.Daylight, D.Chapman, T.Horan tries; C.Ryan 2, Chapman 2 goals) defeated **Auckland** 12 (S.Eru, S.Hoppe tries; G.Ngamu 2 goals) at WACA, Sunday, June 1.

Scrums: Auckland 16-13. Penalties: Perth 4-3. Crowd: 10,203. Referee: Bill Harrigan. Halftime: Perth 12-0. Goalkickers: Chapman (Perth) 2/3, Ryan (Perth) 2/4, Ngamu (Auckland) 2/2. Reserves: Auckland 27-20.
PERTH: Fleming; Ryan, Bell (c), Horan, Daylight; Wilson, Rodwell; Green, Fuller, Kearns, Higgins, Shiels, Fritz. Interchange: Ridding, Grieve, Chapman, Matt Geyer.
AUCKLAND: Ngamu; Hoppe, T.Ropati, A.Swann, Ellis; Endacott, Jones; Tuimavave, Eru, Vagana, L.Swann, Henare, Betts. Interchange: Malam, Okesene, Noovao.

Penrith 28 (M.Adamson, R.Girdler, J.Gall, D.Farrar tries; R.Girdler 6 goals) defeated **Canterbury** 20 (H.El Masri, D.Halligan, D.McRae tries; Halligan 4 goals) at Belmore Sports Ground, Monday night, June 2.

Scrums: Penrith 8-6. Penalties: Canterbury 11-9. Crowd: 12,431. Referee: Brian Grant. Halftime: Penrith 18-10. Goalkickers: Girdler (Penrith) 6/7, Halligan (Canterbury) 4/5. Reserves: Canterbury 22-18.
PENRITH: Jorgensen; Williams, Domic, Girdler, Hinson; Carter, Gower; P.Adamson, Farrar, Macnamara, M.Adamson, Puletua, Gall. Interchange: Brown, Afoa, Thompson, Boyd.
CANTERBURY: Silva; El Masri, Ryan, Timu, Halligan; Polla-Mounter, McRae; Newton, Mears, Britt, Haumono, Price, Gillies (c). Interchange: Relf, Ward, Berrigan.
Sin bin: Gall (Penrith).

STANDINGS: Brisbane 19, Cronulla 14, Canberra 14, Canterbury 14, Penrith 14, Perth 12, Hunter 10, Adelaide 9, North Queensland 8, Auckland 6.

TELSTRA CUP ROUND 13
JUNE 27, 28, 29, 30

Awesome Sharks savage leaders

Cronulla emerged as genuine title contenders after a thumping 32-4 win over the Brisbane Broncos at Shark Park.

Cronulla's win was forged up front, where the Sharks' pack overpowered the Broncos' six in a dominating effort. In one of the most impressive displays of the season, Cronulla led 14-4 at halftime and went right on with the job in the second half.

The Broncos looked decidedly flat, and struggled to take the ball across the advantage line all night. Injuries to fullback Darren Lockyer and Gorden Tallis detracted from their cause, but the loss left coach Wayne Bennett with plenty to think about.

The giant-killing form of the Hunter Mariners continued at Topper Stadium, where they took another step towards a play-off berth in their first season with a 16-12 win over Canberra. The loss was Canberra's first since they fell to Auckland in Round 6. The Mariners survived a contentious video referee's call in the final two minutes, which disallowed a try to Raiders' replacement Simon Woolford.

Penrith coach Royce Simmons launched an astonishing verbal attack on referee Phil Houston after watching his team defeat Auckland 26-22 at Penrith Football Stadium. Simmons risked a fine from the Super League administration over his expletive-riddled outburst. Penrith led 26-12 before the Warriors crossed for two late tries.

Adelaide scored the biggest win of their debut season in the Super League competition with a 28-4 victory over the Perth Reds, but this was overshadowed by a referee's report linking Mark Geyer with a high tackle on Rams forward Cameron Blair. Geyer was in his first match back after a 10-week suspension.

At Stockland Stadium, a strong second-half surge by Canterbury gave them a 29-22 win over North Queensland.

ROUND 13 — RESULTS

Hunter 16 (W.Poching, B.Kimmorley, S.Hill tries; N.Piccinelli 2 goals) defeated **Canberra** 12 (N.Nadruku, B.Kennedy tries; D.Furner 2 goals) at Topper Stadium, Friday night, June 27.

Scrums: Canberra 13–6. Penalties: Canberra 8–5. Crowd: 7404. Referee: Brian Grant. Halftime: Hunter 12–6. Goalkickers: Piccinelli (Hunter) 2/4, Furner (Canberra) 2/2. Reserves: 18–all.
HUNTER: Ross; Carlaw, K.Iro, Godden, Beauchamp; Hill, Kimmorley; Stone, McCormack (c), Maddison, Marquet, Piccinelli, Poching. Interchange: Brann, Goldthorpe, Zisti, T.Iro.
CANBERRA: Nagas; Nadruku, Mullins, Wiki, Croker; Daley, Stuart (c); Davico, Priddis, Pongia, Kennedy, Furner, Clyde. Interchange: Westley, Boyle, Burnham, Woolford.

Canterbury 29 (M.Ryan, C.Polla-Mounter, S.Gillies, R.Relf tries; D.Halligan 6 goals; Polla-Mounter field goal) defeated **North Queensland** 22 (A.Warwick, I.Roberts, K.Warren, K.Tassell tries; L.Phillips 3 goals) at Stockland Stadium, Saturday night, June 28.

Scrums: North Queensland 7–6. Penalties: North Queensland 11–9. Crowd: 14,176. Referee: Steve Clark. Halftime: Canterbury 16–12. Goalkickers: Halligan (Canterbury) 6/6, Phillips (North Queensland) 3/6. Reserves: Canterbury 24–18.
CANTERBURY: Ryan; El Masri, Marteene, Timu, Halligan; Norton, Polla-Mounter; Britt, Mears, Price, Ward, Gillies, Hughes. Interchange: Relf, Newton, Haumono, Berrigan.
NORTH QUEENSLAND: Mahon; Phillips, Shipway, Bowman, Warwick; Doyle, A.Dunemann; Roberts, Walters, Locke, Cunningham, Lomax, Warren. Interchange: Murphy, Jones, Tassell, Scott.

Penrith 26 (S.Carter 2, C.Gower, J.Gall tries; R.Girdler 5 goals) defeated **Auckland** 22 (S.Eru 2, S.Jones, P.Staladi tries; G.Ngamu 3 goals) at Penrith Football Stadium, Sunday, June 29.

Scrums: Penrith 7–6. Penalties: Auckland 11–9. Crowd: 4446. Referee: Phil Houston. Halftime: Penrith 12–6. Goalkickers: Girdler (Canberra) 5/6, Ngamu (Auckland) 3/4. Reserves: Auckland 41–18.
PENRITH: Jorgensen; Williams, Domic, Girdler, Beckett; Carter, Gower; P.Adamson, Farrar, Macnamara, M.Adamson, Gall, Brown. Interchange: Afoa, MacGillivray, Thompson, Boyd.
AUCKLAND: Ellis; Hoppe, T.Ropati, A.Swann, Staladi; Ngamu, Jones; Malam, Eru, Vagana, Henare, Kearney (c), L.Swann. Interchange: Horo, Endacott.
Sin bin: Girdler (Penrith), Staladi (Auckland).

Adelaide 28 (K.Wrigley, K.Walters, B.Galea, R.Maybon tries; L.Williamson 4, K.Wrigley 2 goals) defeated **Perth** 4 (C.Ryan try) at WACA, Sunday, June 29.

Scrums: Adelaide 7–4. Penalties: Adelaide 11–4. Crowd: 7204. Referee: Tim Mander. Halftime: Adelaide 10–0. Goalkickers: Williamson (Adelaide) 4/5, Wrigley (Adelaide) 2/2, Ryan (Perth) 0/2.
ADELAIDE: Maybon; Simonds, Kiri, Quinn, Wrigley; Williamson, Schifilliti; Hick, Walters (c), Corvo, Galea, Boughton, Blair. Interchange: Mamando, Stone, Grimley, Paiyo.
PERTH: Fleming; Daylight, Bell, Brady–Smith, Ryan; Wilson, Rodwell (c); Green, Fuller, Kearns, Shiels, Mark Geyer, Fritz. Interchange: Higgins, Ridding, Evans, Chapman.
Cited: Geyer (Perth). **Charge:** Grade 3 reckless high tackle. **Sentence:** Three weeks. Boughton (Adelaide). **Charge:** Grade 2 reckless high tackle. **Sentence:** Exonerated.

Cronulla 32 (G.Bell 2, T.Nikau, A.Dykes, A.Ettingshausen tries; M.Rogers 6 goals) defeated **Brisbane** 4 (G.Tallis try) at Shark Park, Monday night, June 30.

Scrums: Brisbane 7–5. Penalties: 6–all. Crowd: 12,240. Referee: Bill Harrigan. Halftime: Cronulla 14–4. Goalkickers: Rogers (Cronulla) 6/7, Lockyer (Brisbane) 0/1. Reserves: Cronulla 26–4.
CRONULLA: Peachey; Rogers, Ettingshausen (c), Richardson, Barnett; Healey, Green; Lee, Treister, Stevens, Greenhill, McKenna, Nikau. Interchange: Lang, Davidson, Dykes, Bell.
BRISBANE: Lockyer; Carroll, Renouf, Mundine, Sailor; Walters, Langer (c); Lazarus, Driscoll, Webcke, Tallis, Thorn, Ryan. Interchange: Smith, Plath, Gee, Hancock.

STANDINGS: Brisbne 19, Cronulla 16, Canterbury 16, Penrith 16, Canberra 14, Hunter 12, Perth 12, Adelaide 11, North Queensland 8, Auckland 6.

TELSTRA CUP ROUND 14

JULY 4, 5, 6, 7

Raiders too quick

The surprise switch of Laurie Daley to fullback helped Canberra to an impressive 28-10 defeat of Canterbury at Bruce Stadium. This gave the Raiders a share of second place on the competition ladder.

Canberra coach Mal Meninga kept Daley's move in place of an injured Ken Nagas secret until the kick-off. The Raiders started superbly, running up 16 unanswered points in just 12 minutes of play. The Bulldogs responded with a try before halftime, but Canberra always had their opposition at arm's length.

With a chance to move into outright second position, Canterbury's form was dismal; they missed 23 tackles in the first half alone.

Auckland broke through for their first win in seven premiership matches with a shock 11-8 defeat of Cronulla at Ericsson Stadium. In a tough encounter, both sides scored one try, but the Warriors were favoured by two contentious decisions from referee Phil Houston.

Regrouping after their 32-4 loss to Cronulla in Round 13, Brisbane got well and truly back on track with a 50-14 annihilation of Perth at ANZ Stadium. The Broncos led 14-8 at halftime, but exploded into action in the second half to score seven tries to Perth's one. After a quiet game against the Sharks, halfback Allan Langer bounced back to his scheming best.

At Penrith, North Queensland youngster Ray Mercy scored a hat-trick of tries in the Cowboys' upset 33-26 win over the Panthers. Penrith coach Royce Simmons threatened changes to his team after the lacklustre effort.

The Hunter Mariners made it seven premiership victories at Topper Stadium with a 10-2 win over Adelaide in a match played on a heavy track in driving rain. This result, and the Cowboys defeat of Penrith, left the Warriors on their own at the foot of the ladder. Hunter, in contrast, were now just two points away from a five-way tie for second place.

ROUND 14 — RESULTS

North Queensland 33 (R.Mercy 3, L.Phillips 2, J.Loomans tries; Phillips 4 goals; A.Dunemann field goal) defeated **Penrith 26** (S.Carter, R.Girdler, S.Domic, D.Farrar tries; Girdler 4, C.Gower goals) at Penrith Football Stadium, Friday night, July 4.

Scrums: Penrith 10–8. Penalties: Penrith 5–3. Crowd: 5335. Referee: Brian Grant. Halftime: North Queensland 13–6. Goalkickers: Phillips (North Queensland) 4/7, Girdler (Penrith) 4/4, Gower (Penrith) 1/1. Reserves: North Queensland 26–20.

NORTH QUEENSLAND: Tassell; Phillips, Bowman, Mercy, Loomans; Doyle, A.Dunemann; Roberts (c), Walters, Lomax, Jones, Cunningham, Warren. Interchange: Murphy, Scott, Shipley, Locke.

PENRITH: Jorgensen; Williams, Domic, Girdler, Beckett; Carter (c), Gower; P.Adamson, Farrar, Macnamara, M.Adamson, Gall, Brown. Interchange: Boyd, MacGillivray, Afoa.

Hunter 10 (T.Iro, K.Beauchamp tries; N.Goldthorpe goal) defeated **Adelaide 2** (L.Williamson goal) at Topper Stadium, Saturday night, July 5.

Scrums: Hunter 9–7. Penalties: 9–all. Crowd: 2345. Referee: Steve Clark. Halftime: Hunter 4–0. Goalkickers: Goldthorpe (Hunter) 1/1, Piccinelli (Hunter) 0/1, Swain (Hunter) 0/1, Williamson (Adelaide) 1/1.

HUNTER: Thompson; Zisti, Carlaw, Godden, Beauchamp; Hill, Kimmorley; Stone, McCormack (c), Maddison, T.Iro, Marquet, Piccinelli. Interchange: Brann, Poohing, Goldthorpe, Swain.

ADELAIDE: Maybon; Simonds, Kiri, Quinn, Donnelly; Williamson, Schifiliti; Cann, Walters (c), Corvo, Galea, Boughton, Blair. Interchange: Hick, Campion, Stone, Wrigley.

Cited: Donnelly (Adelaide). **Charge:** Grade 2 striking.
Sentence: Two weeks.

Auckland 11 (M.Ellis try; M.Ridge 3 goals; S.Jones field goal) defeated **Cronulla** 8 (A.Dykes try; M.Rogers 2 goals) at Ericsson Stadium, Sunday, July 6.

Scrums: 6–all. Penalties: Auckland 9–6. Crowd: 12,568. Referee: Phil Houston. Halftime: Auckland 4–2. Goalkickers: Ridge (Auckland) 3/4, Rogers (Cronulla) 2/2. Reserves: Auckland 29–12.
AUCKLAND: Ridge (c); Hoppe, T.Ropati, A.Swann, Ellis; Ngamu, Jones; Vagana, Eru, Malam, Henare, Kearney, L.Swann. Interchange: Horo, Guttenbeil, Oudenryn,
CRONULLA: Peachey; Rogers, Ettingshausen (c), Richardson, Bell; Dykes, Green; Stevens, Sammut, Davidson, Greenhill, McKenna, Nikau. Interchange: Lang, Forrester, Howland.
Sin bin: Peachey (Cronulla).
Cited: Kearney (Auckland). **Charge:** Grade 1 careless high tackle. **Sentence:** 50 demerit points. **Cited:** McKenna (Cronulla). **Charge:** Grade 2 careless high tackle. **Sentence:** 75 demerit points.

Brisbane 50 (M.Devere 2, W.Sailor 2, S.Webcke 2, A.Langer, A.Mundine, D.Smith tries; D.Lockyer 7 goals) defeated **Perth** 14 (S.Wilson, P.Bell tries; C.Ryan 3 goals) at ANZ Stadium, Sunday, July 6.

Scrums: Brisbane 7–4. Penalties: Perth 4–2. Crowd: 11,806. Referee: Tim Mander. Halftime: Brisbane 14–8. Goalkickers: Lockyer (Brisbane) 7/10, Ryan (Perth) 3/3. Reserves: Brisbane 38–14.
BRISBANE: Lockyer; Devere, Renouf, Smith, Sailor;

Walters, Langer (c); Lazarus, Driscoll, Thorn, Ryan, Tallis, Mundine. Interchange: Webcke, Plath, Gee, Carroll.
PERTH: Matt Geyer; Brady–Smith, Ryan, Bell, Daylight; Wilson, Rodwell (c); Kearns, Fuller, Green, Evans, Higgins, Fritz. Interchange: Shiels, Ridding, Grieve, Devine.

Canberra 28 (D.Furner, L.Priddis, R.Wiki, R.Lightning, L.Davico tries; D.Furner 4 goals) defeated **Canterbury** 10 (B.Berrigan, D.Halligan tries; Halligan goal) at Bruce Stadium, Monday night, July 7.

Scrums: Canberra 11–7. Penalties: Canterbury 10–9. Crowd: 7791. Referee: Bill Harrigan. Halftime: Canberra 16–6. Goalkickers: Furner (Canberra) 4/5, Halligan (Canterbury) 1/2. Reserves: Canterbury 33–28.
CANBERRA: Daley; Nadruku, Boyle, Wiki, Lightning; Croker, Stuart (c); Pongia, Priddis, Hetherington, Kennedy, Furner, Clyde. Interchange: Westley, Davico, Burnham, Woolford.
CANTERBURY: Berrigan; El Masri, Marteene, Ryan, Halligan; Norton, Polla-Mounter; Britt, Hetherington, Price, Haumono, Ward, Gillies (c). Interchange: Newton, Relf, Pickering, Mears.
Cited: Polla-Mounter (Canterbury). **Charge:** Grade 2 careless high tackle. **Sentence:** Two weeks.

STANDINGS: Brisbane 21, Cronulla 16, Canterbury 16, Canberra 16, Penrith 16, Hunter 14, Perth 12, Adelaide 11, North Queensland 10, Auckland 8.

TELSTRA CUP ROUND 15
JULY 11, 12, 13, 14

Broncos stay well clear

Looking more like Super League's first champions every week, Brisbane outplayed the Canberra Raiders at Bruce Stadium to score a convincing 19-4 victory.

A disappointing crowd of only 13,067 watched the match between the breakaway competition's highest-profile teams. The same number left with the impression that it would take a team of outstanding ability to deny Brisbane the inaugural Super League title.

The Broncos led 9-0 at halftime after benefiting from a controversial decision by referee Bill Harrigan to penalise a number of Canberra defenders for 'running interference' for runaway Canberra fullback Ken Nagas. Raiders' captain Laurie Daley was sin-binned for his protest.

Continuing their irresistible form, the Broncos scored two second-half tries to lead 19-0 before a 77th minute try to Canberra hooker Simon Woolford.

Winger Mat Rogers piled on 22 points in Cronulla's 44-20 win over Penrith at Shark Park, which saw the Sharks retain second place on the table. Cronulla trailed 14-12 at halftime, but easily outplayed the sadly out-of-form Penrith in the second term. It was Penrith's fifth loss in seven competition matches.

Canterbury and Perth defied wet

conditions at Belmore to run in 11 tries in a high-scoring 38-26 win to the Bulldogs. For the eighth consecutive premiership match, the Bulldogs conceded more than 22 points.

Auckland scored only their second away win of the season to down the Adelaide Rams 18-8 at the Adelaide Oval. Missing Matthew Ridge, Gene Ngamu and Denis Betts, the Warriors led 12-2 at halftime and were rarely threatened after the break.

At Stockland Stadium, North Queensland led from start to finish to record their sixth win of the season with a 33-14 defeat of the Hunter Mariners.

ROUND 15 — RESULTS

Auckland 18 (L.Oudenryn 2, T.Ropati tries; M.Ellis 3 goals) defeated **Adelaide** 8 (W.Simonds try; L.Williamson 2 goals) at Adelaide Oval, Friday night, July 11.

Scrums: Adelaide 8–5. Penalties: Adelaide 6–4. Crowd: 13,278. Referee: Tim Mander. Halftime: Auckland 12–2. Goalkickers: Ellis (Auckland) 3/5, Williamson (Adelaide) 2/3.
AUCKLAND: Maybon; Simonds, Kiri, Quinn, Wrigley; Williamson, Schifilliti; Corvo, Walters (c), Cann, Boughton, Galea, Blair. Interchange: Whittaker, Henare, Horo.
ADELAIDE: Ellis; Hoppe, A.Swann, T.Ropati, Oudenryn; Endacott, Jones; Malam, Eru, Vagana, Kearney (c), Guttenbeil, L.Swann. Interchange: Hick, Mamando, Pierce, Stone.
Sin bin: Schifilliti (Adelaide).

Cronulla 44 (M.Rogers 2, G.Bell, D.Lee, R.Richardson, C.McKenna, P.Green tries; Rogers 7, Green goals) defeated **Penrith** 20 (R.Beckett, G.Thompson, D.Brown tries; R.Girdler 4 goals) at Shark Park, Saturday night, July 12.

Scrums: Cronulla 6–2. Penalties: Cronulla 5–3. Crowd: 11,914. Referee: Graham Annesley. Halftime: Penrith 14–12. Goalkickers: Rogers (Cronulla) 7/9, Green (Cronulla) 1/1, Girdler (Penrith) 4/4. Reserves: Cronulla 15–14.
CRONULLA: Peachey; Rogers, Ettingshausen (c), Richardson, Bell, Dykes, Green; Lee, Treister, Stevens, Davidson, McKenna, Nikau. Interchange: Lang, Greenhill, Howland.
PENRITH: Thompson, Jorgensen, Girdler, Domic, Beckett; Carter (c), Gower; Boyd, Farrar, M.Adamson, Gall, MacGillivray, Brown. Interchange: Puletua, P.Adamson, Williams, Macnamara.

Canterbury 38 (M.Ryan 2, H.El Masri, S.Marteene, R.Mears, S.Haumono tries; D.Halligan 7 goals) defeated **Perth** 26 (M.Rodwell, J.Millar, W.Evans, P.Shiels, T.Brady-Smith tries; Ryan 3 goals) at Belmore Sports Ground, Sunday, July 13.

Scrums: Canterbury 8–6. Penalties: 7–6. Crowd: 4290. Referee: Steve Clark. Halftime: Canterbury 18–10. Goalkickers: Halligan (Canterbury) 7/8, Ryan (Perth) 3/5. Reserves: Canterbury 22–6.
CANTERBURY: Silva; El Masri, Ryan, Marteene, Halligan; Hughes, Berrigan; Pickering, Mears, Price, Relf, Gillies (c), Norton. Interchange: Britt, Haumono, Mellor.

PERTH: Matt Geyer; Wilshere, Fleming, Ryan, Brady-Smith; Wilson, Rodwell (c); Green, Fuller, Kearns, Evans, Higgins, Millar. Interchange: Sapatu, Shiels, Horan.

North Queensland 33 (R.Mercy 2, A.Dunemann 2, J.Loomans, G.Murphy tries; L.Phillips 4 goals; Dunemann field goal) defeated **Hunter** 14 (D.Godden, J.Carlaw, N.Piccinelli tries; R.Swain goal) at Stockland Stadium, Sunday, July 13.

Scrums: Hunter 9–7. Penalties: Hunter 7–5. Crowd: 11,480. Referee: Brian Grant. Halftime: North Queensland 20–4. Goalkickers: Phillips (North Queensland) 4/7, Swain (Hunter) 1/2, Poching (North Queensland) 0/1, Goldthorpe (North Queensland) 0/1. Reserves: North Queensland 18–12.
NORTH QUEENSLAND: Cressbrook; Phillips, Mercy, Bowman, Loomans; Doyle, A.Dunemann; Roberts (c), Walters, Lomax, Cunningham, Murphy, Warren. Interchange: Locke, Death, Skardon, Buttigieg.
HUNTER: Thompson; Zisti, Carlaw, Godden, Beauchamp; Hill, Goldthorpe; Maddison, McCormack (c), Stone, Marquet, T.Iro, Piccinelli. Interchange: Doherty, Poching, Swain, Smith.
Cited: Poching (Hunter). **Charge:** High tackle. **Sentence:** One week.

Brisbane 19 (P.Ryan 2, W.Sailor tries; D.Lockyer 3 goals; A.Langer field goal) defeated **Canberra** 4 (S.Woolford try) at Bruce Stadium, Monday night, July 14.

Scrums: 8–all. Penalties: Canberra 12–1. Crowd: 13,067. Referee: Bill Harrigan. Halftime: Brisbane 9–0. Goalkickers: Lockyer (Brisbane) 3/4, Furner (Canberra) 0/1. Reserves: Canberra 20–8.
BRISBANE: Lockyer; Devere, Renouf, Mundine, Sailor; Walters, Langer (c); Lazarus, Gee, Thorn, Ryan, Tallis, Smith. Interchange: Webcke, Driscoll, Plath, Carroll.
CANBERRA: Nagas, Nadruku, Wiki, Croker, Boyle; Daley, Stuart (c); Pongia, Priddis, Hetherington, Kennedy, Furner, Clyde. Interchange: Westley, Woolford, Davico, Mullins.
Sin bin: Tallis (Brisbane), Daley (Canberra), Plath (Brisbane).
Cited: Plath (Brisbane). **Charge:** Spear tackle. **Sentence:** Two weeks.

STANDINGS: Brisbane 23, Cronulla 18, Canterbury 18, Canberra 16, Penrith 16, Hunter 14, North Queensland 12, Perth 12, Adelaide 11, Auckland 10.

TELSTRA CUP ROUND 15

TELSTRA CUP ROUND 16
AUGUST 8, 9, 10, 11

Canterbury remain on track

Canterbury remained on track for a place in the Super League top three with a 40-18 defeat of the Auckland Warriors at Belmore Sports Ground.

Winger Hazem El Masri scored three of his team's seven tries as the Bulldogs ran away with the match in the latter stages. A try to Auckland winger Sean Hoppe reduced Canterbury's lead to 28-18, 11 minutes from fulltime, and only a poor pass late in the game prevented the Warriors from trailing by just four points.

Brisbane's potent form continued, despite three weeks in England for the World Club Challenge, when they thumped Penrith 54-12 at ANZ Stadium. Stand-in skipper Kevin Walters maintained his perfect record as Broncos' captain with two tries. Canberra paid a high price for their 22-14 win over North Queensland in Townsville. The Raiders lost prop Luke Davico (dislocated wrist) and centre Ruben Wiki (broken arm) in a hard-fought encounter.

Cronulla continued their charge to the finals series with a workmanlike 28-6 win over Adelaide at the Adelaide Oval. The Sharks now equal second with Canterbury trailed 6-0 early, but a double to centre Russell Richardson helped his team assume control.

Fighting for their very future, the Perth Reds moved to within one win of fifth place with a 30-22 defeat of the Hunter Mariners at the WACA. Both sides scored five tries, but the Mariners could manage only one goal from seven attempts.

ROUND 16 — RESULTS

Cronulla 28 (R.Richardson 2, M.Rogers, G.Bell, A.Dykes, W.Forrester tries; Rogers 2 goals) defeated **Adelaide** 6 (K.Wrigley try; L.Williamson goal) at Adelaide Oval, Friday night, August 8.

Scrums: Cronulla 14–6. Penalties: Adelaide 6–2. Crowd: 7231. Referee: Tim Mander. Halftime: Cronulla 14–6. Goalkickers: Rogers (Cronulla) 2/6, Williamson (Adelaide) 1/1.

CRONULLA: Peachey; Rogers, Ettingshausen (c), Richardson, Bell; Healey, Green; Stevens, Dykes, Lee, Davidson, McKenna, Nikau. Interchange: Lang, Greenhill, Forrester, Howland.

ADELAIDE: Quinn; Donnelly, Kiri, Williamson, Simonds; Wrigley, Topper; Corvo, Walters (c), Campion, Boughton, Pierce, Blair. Interchange: Galea, Maguire, Campion, Tamani.

Canberra 22 (N.Nadruku, B.Kennedy, K.Nagas, B.Mullins tries; D.Furner 3 goals) defeated **North Queensland** 14 (P.Bowman, J.Lomax tries; L.Phillips 3 goals) at Stockland Stadium, Saturday night, August 9.

Scrums: North Queensland 13–7. Penalties: North Queensland 13–4. Crowd: 22,026. Referee: Steve Clark. Halftime: Canberra 10–8. Goalkickers: Furner (Canberra) 3/4, Phillips (North Queensland) 3/3. Reserves: North Queensland 32–14.

CANBERRA: Nagas; Nadruku, Mullins, Wiki, Lightning; Daley, Stuart (c); Davico, Priddis, Pongia, Furner, Kennedy, Clyde. Interchange: Croker, Burnham, Hetherington, Woolford.

NORTH QUEENSLAND: Mahon; Phillips, Mercy, Bowman, Loomans; Doyle, A.Dunemann; Locke, Walters (c), Buttigieg, Cunningham, Scott, Warren. Interchange: Murphy, Jones, Skardon, Lomax.

Perth 30 (M.Rodwell 2, D.Fritz, C.Ryan, J.Wilshere tries; S.Devine 3, D.Chapman 2 goals) defeated **Hunter** 22 (N.Zisti 2, J.Carlaw, P.Marquet, K.Iro tries; B.Kimmorley goal) at WACA, Sunday, August 10.

Scrums: Hunter 9–6. Penalties: Perth 9–4. Crowd: 5083. Referee: Brian Grant. Halftime: Perth 14–8. Goalkickers: Devine (Perth) 3/5, Chapman (Perth) 2/2, Kimmorley (Hunter) 1/4, Piccinelli (Hunter) 0/2, Swain (Hunter) 0/1. Reserves: Perth 38–20.

PERTH: Matt Geyer; Wilshere, Ryan, Fleming, Brady-Smith; Devine, Rodwell (c); Green, Fuller, Kearns, Evans, Higgins, Millar. Interchange: Mark Geyer, Fritz, Ridding, Chapman.

HUNTER: Ross; Beauchamp, K.Iro, Godden, Zisti; Hill, Kimmorley; Stone, McCormack (c), Maddison, Doherty, Marquet, Piccinelli. Interchange: Brann, T.Iro, Swain, Carlaw.

Brisbane 54 (K.Walters 2, S.Renouf 2, J.Plath, A.Mundine, M.Devere, D.Smith, A.Gee, W.Sailor tries; D.Lockyer 7 goals) defeated **Penrith** 12 (S.Carter, S.Domic tries; R.Girdler 2 goals) at ANZ Stadium, Sunday, August 10.

Scrums: Brisbane 6–3. Penalties: Brisbane 9–3. Crowd: 13,921. Referee: Bill Harrigan. Halftime: Brisbane 26–6. Goalkickers: Lockyer (Brisbane) 7/12, Girdler (Penrith) 2/2. Reserves: Penrith 32–23.
BRISBANE: Lockyer; Devere, Renouf, Smith, Sailor; Mundine, Walters (c); Gee, Driscoll, Webcke, Tallis, Thorn, Ryan. Interchange: Plath, Lee, Carroll, Walker.
PENRITH: Jorgensen; Williams, Girdler, Domic, Beckett; Carter (c), Gower; P.Adamson, Farrar, Macnamara, Gall, M.Adamson, Brown. Interchange: Puletua, Boyd, MacGillivray, Thompson.

Canterbury 40 (H.El Masri 3, R.Mears 2, M.Ryan, R.Silva tries; D.Halligan 6 goals) defeated **Auckland** 18 (A.Swann, L.Oudenryn, S.Hoppe tries; M.Ridge 3 goals) at Belmore Sports Ground, Monday night, August 11.

Scrums: Canterbury 10–6. Penalties: Canterbury 6–1. Crowd: 5126. Referee: Graham Annesley. Halftime: Canterbury 14–12. Goalkickers: Halligan (Canterbury) 6/8, Ridge (Auckland) 3/3. Reserves: Canterbury 58–4.
CANTERBURY: Silva; El Masri, Ryan, Timu, Halligan; Hughes, Polla-Mounter; Price, Mears, Britt, Relf, Gillies (c), Reardon. Interchange: Newton, Ward, Berrigan, Haumono.
AUCKLAND: Ridge (c); Hoppe, Endacott, A.Swann, Oudenryn; Ngamu, Jones, Vagana, Eru, Malam, L.Swann, Kearney, Betts. Interchange: Bailey, Horo, Guttenbeil.

STANDINGS: Brisbane 25, Cronulla 20, Canterbury 20, Canberra 18, Penrith 16, Hunter 14, Perth 14, North Queensland 12, Adelaide 11, Auckland 10.

TELSTRA CUP ROUND 17
AUGUST 15, 16, 17, 18

A perfect home record

Brisbane finished their regular season program with an undefeated home record, after accounting for the Hunter Mariners 34-16 at ANZ Stadium.

The major concern for the Broncos was the reporting of star centre Steve Renouf for dangerously lifting Hunter halfback Brett Kimmorley in a tackle.

Penrith staged a stunning form reversal when they swamped Canterbury 44-8. After three successive losses, the Panthers' return to form was as remarkable as the Bulldogs' slump. Centre Ryan Girdler contributed 24 points from three tries and six goals.

Cronulla continued their march towards a top three position by disposing of North Queensland 34-12. The Sharks scored four second-half tries after leading 12-2 at the break. The loss left the Cowboys in danger of claiming Super League's first wooden spoon.

Canberra produced one of their most impressive efforts of the season to thrash the Adelaide Rams 58-16 at Bruce Stadium. With lock Bradley Clyde in outstanding touch, the Raiders ran riot after a halftime lead of 18-10 — they scored a point a minute in the second half. Centre Brett Mullins collected a hat-trick of tries, while second-rower David Furner piled on 20 points from a try and eight goals.

Auckland leapfrogged Adelaide, vacating last place on the Super League table, with a 30-22 win over Perth at Ericsson Stadium. Matthew Ridge scored 18 points for the Warriors.

ROUND 17 — RESULTS

Penrith 44 (R.Girdler 3, P.Jorgensen 2, C.Gower, J.Gall, P.Adamson tries; Girdler 6 goals) defeated **Canterbury** 8 (H.El Masri try; D.Halligan 2 goals) at Penrith Football Stadium, Friday night, August 15.

Scrums: 7–all. Penalties: Penrith 6–4. Crowd: 8213. Referee: Bill Harrigan. Halftime: Penrith 14–2. Goalkickers: Girdler (Penrith) 6/8, Halligan (Canterbury) 2/2. Reserves: Canterbury 28–18.
PENRITH: Jorgensen; Williams, Domic, Girdler, Beckett; Carter (c), Gower; P.Adamson, Farrar, Macnamara,

Gall, Puletua, Brown. Interchange: MacGillivray, Boyd, Falcon, Thompson.
CANTERBURY: Silva; El Masri, Ryan, Timu, Halligan; Hughes, Polla-Mounter; Price, Mears, Britt, Gillies (c); Reardon, Norton. Interchange: Newton, Relf, Berrigan, Mellor.

Auckland 30 (M.Ridge 2, S.Kearney, D.Betts, S.Jones tries; Ridge 5 goals) defeated **Perth** 22 (S.Devine 2, C.Ryan, D.Higgins tries; Devine 3 goals) at Ericsson Stadium, Saturday night, August 16.

Scrums: 8–all. Penalties: Perth 12–7. Crowd: 13,142. Referee: Brian Grant. Halftime: Auckland 24–10. Goalkickers: Ridge (Auckland) 5/6, Devine (Perth) 3/4. Reserves: Perth 18–4.
AUCKLAND: Ridge (c); Hoppe, T.Ropati, A.Swann, Oudenryn; Ngamu, Jones; Vagana, Eru, Malam, L.Swann, Kearney, Betts. Interchange: Horo, Seu Seu, Bailey.
PERTH: Matt Geyer; Wilshere, Ryan, Fleming, Brady-Smith; Devine, Rodwell (c); Green, Fuller, Kearns, Higgins, Evans, Millar. Interchange: Mark Geyer, Fritz, Ridding.
Cited: Ridge (Auckland). **Charge:** Dropping knees, striking. **Sentence:** One week.

Cronulla 34 (M.Rogers, P.Green, A.Dykes, W.Forrester, D.Peachey, R.Richardson tries; Rogers 5 goals) defeated **North Queensland** 12 (L.Phillips, L.Scott tries; Phillips 2 goals) at Shark Park, Saturday night, August 16.

Scrums: Cronulla 13–8. Penalties: Cronulla 6–5. Crowd: 11,640. Referee: Tim Mander. Halftime: Cronulla 12–2. Goalkickers: Rogers (Cronulla) 5/7, Phillips (North Queensland) 2/3. Reserves: North Queensland 19–18.
CRONULLA: Peachey, Rogers, Ettingshausen (c), Richardson, Howland; Healey, Green; Stevens, Dykes, Lee, Davidson, McKenna, Nikau. Interchange: Greenhill, Forrester, Treister, Laumatia.
NORTH QUEENSLAND: Cressbrook; Phillips, Bowman, Mercy, Tassell; Jones, A.Dunemann; Roberts (c), Walters, Lomax, Scott, Cunningham, Warren. Interchange: Buttigieg, Locke, Doyle, Loomans.

Cited: Greenhill (Cronulla). **Charge:** Grade 3 dangerous throw. **Sentence:** Exonerated.

Canberra 58 (B.Mullins 3, B.Kennedy 2, K.Nagas, A.Fulivai, R.Stuart, S.Woolford, D.Furner tries; Furner 8, R.Lightning goals) defeated **Adelaide** 16 (R.Maybon, L.Williamson tries; Williamson 4 goals) at Bruce Stadium, Sunday, August 17.

Scrums: Adelaide 8–7. Penalties: Adelaide 9–8. Crowd: 7960. Referee: Steve Clark. Halftime: Canberra 18–10. Goalkickers: Furner (Canberra) 8/9, Lightning (Canberra) 1/1, Williamson (Adelaide) 4/4.
CANBERRA: Nagas; Lightning, Nadruku, Mullins, Fulivai; Daley, Stuart (c); Pongia, Priddis, Hetherington, Furner, Kennedy, Clyde. Interchange: Burnham, Woolford, Payten, Croker.
ADELAIDE: Maybon; Donnelly, Quinn, Kidwell, Tamani, Williamson, Stone; Corvo, Walters (c), Hick, Boughton, Pierce, Blair. Interchange: Schifilliti, Kiri, Galea.

Brisbane 34 (S.Renouf 2, G.Tallis, P.Ryan, D.Lockyer, W.Sailor tries; Lockyer 4, M.Devere goals) defeated **Hunter** 16 (N.Piccinelli, K.Beauchamp, M.Dorreen tries; K.Iro 2 goals) at ANZ Stadium, Monday night, August 18.

Scrums: Brisbane 11–4. Penalties: Hunter 8–4. Crowd: 13,830. Referee: Graham Annesley. Halftime: Brisbane 12–8. Goalkickers: Lockyer (Brisbane) 4/5, Devere (Brisbane) 1/1, K.Iro (Hunter) 2/2, Swain (Hunter) 0/1. Reserves: Brisbane 34–10.
BRISBANE: Lockyer; Carroll, Renouf, Smith, Sailor; Mundine, Walters (c); Gee, Plath, Webcke, Tallis, Thorn, Ryan. Interchange: Hancock, Devere, Lee, Walker.
HUNTER: Ross; Beauchamp, K.Iro, Carlaw, Thompson; Hill, Kimmorley; Stone, McCormack (c), Maddison, Doherty, Marquet, Piccinelli. Interchange: T.Iro, Brann, Swain, Dorreen.
Cited: Renouf (Brisbane). **Charge:** Grade 2 dangerous throw. **Sentence:** One week.

STANDINGS: Brisbane 27, Cronulla 22, Canberra 20, Canterbury 20, Penrith 18, Hunter 14, Perth 14, North Queensland 12, Auckland 12, Adelaide 11.

TELSTRA CUP ROUND 18
AUGUST 22, 23, 24, 25

Langer proves finals fitness

Brisbane warmed up for the final series when they defeated Canterbury 32-24 to round out Super League's first home-and-away season. The match was essentially a dead rubber — nothing could shake Brisbane's hold on first place on the ladder, and nothing could alter Canterbury's fourth position. Much to the relief of the Broncos, captain Allan Langer proved his fitness after a four-week lay-off with a groin injury.

Fullback Darren Lockyer starred for the Broncos with his dangerous running from broken play, but it was Solomon Haumono who produced the most memorable moment of the night with a thunderous tackle on Brisbane replacement Michael Hancock.

The Hunter Mariners' imposing record of seven consecutive premiership wins at Topper Stadium came to an end against a Cronulla, who scored a comfortable 28-16 victory. The win sealed second place on the ladder for the Sharks, giving them the home ground advantage for their first semi-final.

Adelaide steered clear of the wooden spoon with their best effort of their maiden season — a 36-16 win over semi-finalists Penrith at Adelaide Oval, while Canberra lost second-rower Ben Kennedy for the season with a broken arm during their 36-16 win over Perth at the WACA. The Raiders dominated, scoring seven tries to three.

North Queensland were left holding Super League's first wooden spoon after capitulating 50-22 to the Auckland Warriors at Ericsson Stadium. The Warriors saved their best till last, scoring nine tries in their biggest premiership win of the season.

ROUND 18 — RESULTS

Adelaide 36 (S.Kiri 2, J.Tamani, K.Wrigley, D.Boughton, C.Blair tries; Wrigley 6 goals) defeated **Penrith** 16 (J.Williams, G.Casey, C.Hicks tries; Casey 2 goals) at Adelaide Oval, Friday night, August 22.

Scrums: Penrith 9–8. Penalties: 4–all. Crowd: 11,211. Referee: Brian Grant. Halftime: Adelaide 22–4. Goalkickers: Wrigley (Adelaide) 6/7, Casey (Penrith) 2/3.
ADELAIDE: Maguire; Simonds, Kidwell, Kiri, Tamani; Wrigley, Schifilliti; Corvo, Walters (c), Hick, Cann, Galea, Boughton. Interchange: Blair, Peek, Quinn.
PENRITH: Jorgensen; Williams, Girdler, Beckett, Hicks; Carter (c), Gower; P.Adamson, Farrar, Macnamara, Puletua, Gall, Brown. Interchange: MacGillivray, Falcon, Casey, Boyd.

Canberra 36 (B.Kennedy 2, N.Nadruku 2, K.Nagas, L.Priddis, R.Lightning tries; D.Furner 4 goals) defeated **Perth** 16 (M.Rodwell, T.Brady-Smith, R.Kearns tries; D.Chapman 2 goals) at WACA, Saturday night, August 23.

Scrums: Canberra 12–9. Penalties: Perth 13–9. Crowd: 12,307. Referee: Steve Clark. Halftime: Canberra 26–6. Goalkickers: Furner (Canberra) 4/6, Lightning (Canberra) 0/1, Chapman (Perth) 2/4. Reserves: Perth 24–14.
CANBERRA: Nagas; Nadruku, Mullins, Fulivai, Lightning; Daley, Stuart (c); Pongia, Priddis, Hetherington, Kennedy, Furner, Clyde. Interchange: Crokor, Burnham, Payten, Woolford.
PERTH: Matt Geyer; Brady-Smith, Ryan, Fleming, Wilshere; Chapman, Rodwell (c); Kearns, Fuller, Green, Mark Geyer, Evans, Fritz. Interchange: Ridding, Millar, Taylor.

Auckland 50 (M.Ellis 3, S.Jones 2, A.Swann, D.Bailey, S.Hoppe, L.Oudenryn tries; G.Ngamu 7 goals) defeated **North Queensland** 22 (K.Warren, R.Mercy, L.Scott, J.Skardon tries; L.Phillips 3 goals) at Ericsson Stadium, Sunday, August 24.

Scrums: Auckland 7–5. Penalties: Auckland 7–6. Crowd: 12,000. Referee: Tim Mander. Halftime: Auckland 28–12. Goalkickers: Ngamu (Auckland) 7/9, Phillips (North Queensland) 3/4. Reserves: North Queensland 10–4.
AUCKLAND: Ellis; Hoppe, A.Swann, Bailey, Oudenryn; Ngamu, Jones; Vagana, Eru, Malam, L.Swann, Kearney (c), Betts. Interchange: Horo, Guttenbeil.
NORTH QUEENSLAND: Cressbrook; Phillips, Mercy, Bowman, Loomans; Doyle, A.Dunemann; Lomax, Death, Roberts (c), Cunningham, Jones, Warren. Interchange: Locke, Murphy, Scott, Skardon.

Cronulla 28 (D.Peachey 3, G.Bell, R.Barnett tries; M.Rogers 4 goals) defeated **Hunter** 16 (N.Zisti, S.Hill, T.Stone tries; W.Poching, R.Swain goals) at Topper Stadium, Sunday, August 24.

Scrums: Hunter 8–6. Penalties: 3–all. Crowd: 5122. Referee: Bill Harrigan. Halftime: Cronulla 24–6. Goalkickers: Rogers (Cronulla) 4/5, Poching (Hunter) 1/1, Swain (Hunter) 1/2. Reserves: Cronulla 10–6.
CRONULLA: Peachey; Rogers, Ettingshausen (c), Bell, Barnett; Dykes, Healey; Stevens, Treister, Lee, Ryan, Davidson, Nikau. Interchange: Forrester, Graham, Fisher.
HUNTER: Ross; Beauchamp, K.Iro, Carlaw, Zisti; Hill, Kimmorley; Stone, McCormack (c), Brann, Poching, Marquet, Smith. Interchange: Swain, Doherty, Dorreen.

Brisbane 32 (M.Devere, T.Carroll, S.Webcke, A.Mundine, D.Lockyer, P.Ryan tries; Lockyer 4 goals) defeated **Canterbury** 24 (R.Mears 2, R.Silva, M.Ryan tries; D.Halligan 4 goals) at Belmore Sports Ground, Monday night, August 25.

Scrums: Brisbane 5–4. Penalties: Canterbury 7–1. Crowd: 9781. Referee: Graham Annesley. Halftime: Brisbane 20–18. Goalkickers: Lockyer (Brisbane) 4/6, Halligan (Canterbury) 4/4. Reserves: Brisbane 34–30.
BRISBANE: Lockyer, Devere, Smith, Carroll, Sailor; Walters, Langer (c); Thorn, Driscoll, Gee, Webcke, Tallis, Mundine. Interchange: Ryan, Hancock, B. Walker, Lee.
CANTERBURY: Silva; El Masri, Ryan, Timu, Halligan; Hughes, Polla-Mounter; Price, Mears, Britt, Gillies (c), Haumono, Norton. Interchange: Newton, Relf, Berrigan, Reardon.

FINAL STANDINGS: Brisbane 29, Cronulla 24, Canberra 22, Canterbury 20, Penrith 18, Hunter 14, Auckland 14, Perth 14, Adelaide 13, North Queensland 12.

TELSTRA CUP ROUND 18

SUPER LEAGUE TELSTRA CUP 1997

FIRST GRADE

	P	W	L	D	F	A	Pts
Brisbane	18	14	3	1	481	283	29
Cronulla	18	12	6	-	403	230	24
Canberra	18	11	7	-	436	337	22
Canterbury	18	10	8	-	453	447	20
Penrith	18	9	9	-	431	462	18
Hunter	18	7	11	-	350	363	14
Auckland	18	7	11	-	332	406	14
Perth	18	7	11	-	321	456	14
Adelaide	18	6	11	1	303	402	13
North Qld	18	5	11	2	328	452	12

RESERVE GRADE

	P	W	L	D	F	A	Pts
Canterbury	16	12	3	1	419	278	29
Perth	16	10	6	-	389	287	24
North Qld	16	10	6	-	313	274	24
Auckland	16	8	6	2	303	335	22
Cronulla	16	8	8	-	276	284	20
Brisbane	16	7	9	-	333	313	18
Canberra	16	6	8	2	283	399	18
Hunter	16	5	10	1	282	315	15
Penrith	16	3	13	-	294	407	10

TOP POINTSCORERS
(After 18 premiership rounds)

Player	Tries	Goals	FG	Points
Ryan Girdler *(Penrith)*	11	71	-	186
Daryl Halligan *(Canterbury)*	6	76	-	176
Mat Rogers *(Cronulla)*	11	61	-	166
Darren Lockyer *(Brisbane)*	7	60	-	148
Luke Phillips *(North Qld)*	8	45	-	122
David Furner *(Canberra)*	5	45	-	110
Kurt Wrigley *(Adelaide)*	5	30	1	81
Nick Zisti *(Hunter)*	9	20	-	76
Marc Ellis *(Auckland)*	5	25	1	71
Luke Williamson *(Adelaide)*	3	29	-	70
Matt Ryan *(Canterbury)*	17	-	-	68
Hazem El Masri *(Canterbury)*	16	-	-	64
Ben Kennedy *(Canberra)*	15	-	-	60

RUGBY LEAGUE 1998

Player	Tries	Goals	FG	Points
Wendell Sailor *(Brisbane)*	14	-	-	56
Julian O'Neill *(Perth)*	6	14	1	53
Matthew Ridge *(Auckland)*	3	18	-	48
Geoff Bell *(Cronulla)*	11	-	-	44
Sean Hoppe *(Auckland)*	11	-	-	44
Chris Ryan *(Perth)*	5	12	-	44
Brett Mullins *(Canberra)*	10	-	-	40
Royston Lightning *(Canberra)*	5	9	-	38
Steve Renouf *(Brisbane)*	9	-	-	36
Damien Chapman *(Perth)*	1	15	1	35

TOP TRYSCORERS
(After 18 premiership rounds)

Player	Tries	Player	Tries
Matt Ryan *(Canterbury)*	17	John Carlaw *(Hunter)*	8
Hazem El Masri *(Canterbury)*	16	David Peachey *(Cronulla)*	8
Ben Kennedy *(Canberra)*	15	Luke Phillips *(North Qld)*	8
Wendell Sailor *(Brisbane)*	14	Darren Smith *(Brisbane)*	8
Geoff Bell *(Cronulla)*	11	Keith Beauchamp *(Hunter)*	7
Ryan Girdler *(Penrith)*	11	Steve Carter *(Penrith)*	7
Sean Hoppe *(Auckland)*	11	Craig Gower *(Penrith)*	7
Mat Rogers *(Cronulla)*	11	Stacey Jones *(Auckland)*	7
Brett Mullins *(Canberra)*	10	Noa Nadruku *(Canberra)*	7
Steve Renouf *(Brisbane)*	9	Kevin Walters *(Brisbane)*	7
Nick Zisti *(Hunter)*	9	Jason Williams *(Penrith)*	7

TOP GOALKICKERS
(After 18 premiership rounds)

Player	Goals	Attempts
Daryl Halligan *(Canterbury)*	76	97
Ryan Girdler *(Penrith)*	71	78
Mat Rogers *(Cronulla)*	61	88
Darren Lockyer *(Brisbane)*	60	97
David Furner *(Canberra)*	45	66
Luke Phillips *(North Qld)*	45	72
Kurt Wrigley *(Adelaide)*	30	36
Luke Williamson *(Adelaide)*	29	37
Marc Ellis *(Auckland)*	25	37
Nick Zisti *(Hunter)*	20	33
Matthew Ridge *(Auckland)*	18	22
Damien Chapman *(Perth)*	15	19
Julian O'Neill *(Perth)*	14	29
Gene Ngamu *(Auckland)*	12	17
Chris Ryan *(Perth)*	12	20

SUPER LEAGUE FINALS SERIES

Broncos, Sharks set for decider

Cronulla launched Super League's first finals series in sizzling style with a 22-18 win over Canberra at Shark Park. The Sharks took control early through a try to captain Andrew Ettingshausen, and never looked like relinquishing their grip on the semi-final.

Ettingshausen and winger Mat Rogers combined superbly on the right for Cronulla, Rogers finishing with two tries and Ettingshausen one. Cronulla raced to a 12-0 lead after 15 minutes and were 16-6 ahead at halftime. Canberra rallied to trail 16-12 in the 65th minute, before Rogers ran 60 metres from dummy-half to seal the win. Veteran forwards Les Davidson and Danny Lee led the way up front for Cronulla, while Canberra five-eighth Laurie Daley was the pick for his side.

Canterbury became the first team eliminated from the finals series after a one-point loss to Penrith in the minor preliminary semi-final at Belmore Sports Ground.

The Bulldogs went down 15-14 after trailing 15-8 at halftime. The difference was a field goal kicked by Penrith centre Ryan Girdler on the stroke of halftime. Penrith posted all their points in the first half, but on a wet night which made ball-handling difficult, their seven-point lead proved sufficient.

Canterbury started the match aggressively but, as usual in their 1997 season, they were unable to sustain their defensive effort. A 70-metre try by winger Robbie Beckett and a storming try by schoolboy second-rower Tony Puletua just before halftime highlighted Canterbury's defensive deficiencies.

A week later, Brisbane blasted into the grand final with a thumping 34-2 victory over Cronulla at Townsville's Stockland Stadium. The Broncos blew Cronulla away with a first-half assault that realised five tries and gave them an unassailable 30-2 lead.

The star of the match was 20-year-old Brisbane fullback Darren Lockyer, whose kick returns overshadowed those of Cronulla's David Peachey, the player who had earlier been regarded as the premier runner from broken play in the Super League competition.

Centre Steve Renouf returned from a one-match suspension to score two early tries for the Broncos. Cronulla's preparation was disrupted by the withdrawal of captain Andrew Ettingshausen, who was suffering a virus.

Canberra readied themselves for a rematch with Cronulla in the preliminary final after eliminating Penrith 32-12 at Bruce Stadium.

The Raiders overcame the loss of goalkicking second-rower David Furner in the opening minutes to score a satisfying win. Five-eighth Laurie Daley took over the goalkicking duties with excellent results — he landed six goals from eight attempts. Despite suffering injury problems of their own, Penrith competed well and it was not until Canberra hooker Luke Priddis scored late in the match that the Raiders opened up a sizeable margin. Furner was later ruled out for six weeks with a serious knee injury.

Brisbane's grand final opponents were decided when Cronulla scored a scrambling 10-4 win over Canberra in the preliminary final at Shark Park.

Cronulla led 10-0 at halftime and did enough in the second term to deny the Raiders, despite conceding an early try to second-rower Jason Croker. Just as it looked as if the Raiders were fighting their way back, they lost their way with some poor options and a lack of ball control. Cronulla scored their only try in the 18th minute, through winger Mat Rogers, who also landed a conversion and two penalty goals — all his side's points. The video referee made a vital decision midway through the second half when he disallowed a try to Canberra winger Albert Fulivai.

Major preliminary semi-final

Cronulla 22 (M.Rogers 2, A.Ettingshausen, R.Richardson tries; Rogers 3 goals) defeated **Canberra** 18 (J.Croker, L.Priddis, A.Fulivai tries; D.Furner 3 goals) at Shark Park, Saturday night, August 30.
Scrums: 7-all. Penalties: Canberra 6-3. Crowd: 17,137. Referee: Bill Harrigan. Halftime: Cronulla 16-6. Goalkickers: Rogers (Cronulla) 3/5, Furner (Canberra) 3/3. Reserves: North Queensland def. Perth 12-8.
CRONULLA: Peachey; Rogers, Ettingshausen (c), Richardson, Barnett; Healey, Green; Lee, Treister, Stevens, McKenna, Davidson, Nikau. Interchange: Lang, Greenhill, Bell, Dykes.
CANBERRA: Nagas; Nadruku, Mullins, Croker, Lightning; Daley, Stuart (c); Pongia, Priddis, Hetherington, Furner, Croker, Clyde. Interchange: Atkins, Woolford, Burnham.

Minor preliminary semi-final

Penrith 15 (R.Beckett, T.Puletua tries; R.Girdler 3 goals; Girdler field goal) defeated **Canterbury** 14 (J.Hetherington, R.Silva tries; D.Halligan 3 goals) at Belmore Sports Ground, Monday night, September 1.
Scrums: Canterbury 12-8. Penalties: 6-all. Crowd: 10,492. Referee: Graham Annesley. Halftime: Penrith 15-8. Goalkickers: Girdler (Penrith) 3/3, Halligan (Canterbury) 3/4. Reserves: Auckland def. Cronulla 21-14.
PENRITH: Jorgensen; Beckett, Girdler, Thompson, Williams; Carter (c), Gower; P.Adamson, Farrar, Macnamara, M.Adamson, Gall, Brown. Interchange: Puletua, MacGillivray, Boyd, Casey.
CANTERBURY: Silva; El Masri, Ryan, Timu, Halligan; Polla-Mounter, Berrigan; Price, Hetherington, Britt, Haumono, Gillies (c), Norton. Interchange: Reit, Reardon, Mears, Newton.

Major semi-final

Brisbane 34 (S.Renouf 2, K.Walters, W.Sailor, M.Devere, B.Thorn tries; D.Lockyer 5 goals) defeated **Cronulla** 2 (M.Rogers goal) at Stockland Stadium, Saturday night, September 6.
Scrums: Cronulla 5-4. Penalties: Cronulla 9-4. Crowd: 26,256. Referee: Bill Harrigan. Halftime: Brisbane 30-2. Goalkickers: Lockyer (Brisbane) 5/7, Rogers (Cronulla) 1/1. Reserves: Canterbury def. North Queensland 27-14.
BRISBANE: Lockyer; Devere, Renouf, Mundine, Sailor; Walters, Langer (c); Webcke, Gee, Thorn, Tallis, Ryan, Smith. Interchange: Driscoll, Hancock, Plath, Carroll.
CRONULLA: Peachey; Rogers, Bell, Richardson, Laumatia; Healey (c), Green; Lee, Treister, Stevens, Davidson, McKenna, Nikau. Interchange: Dykes, Ryan, Greenhill, Long.

Minor semi-final

Canberra 32 (K.Nagas, A.Fulivai, L.Priddis, S.Woolford, L.Daley tries; Daley 6 goals) defeated **Penrith** 12 (S.Carter, R.Beckett tries; R.Girdler 2 goals) at Bruce Stadium, Monday night, September 8.
Scrums: Penrith 9-8. Penalties: Canberra 8-4. Crowd: 10,153. Referee: Graham Annesley. Halftime: Canberra 16-6. Goalkickers: Daley (Canberra) 6/8, Girdler (Penrith) 2/2. Reserves: Auckland def. Perth 18-14.
CANBERRA: Nagas; Nadruku, Mullins, Croker, Fulivai; Daley, Stuart (c); Pongia, Priddis, Hetherington, Clyde, Furner, Burnham. Interchange: Boyle, Woolford, Davico, Atkins.
PENRITH: Jorgensen; Beckett, Girdler, Thompson, Williams; Carter (c), Gower; P.Adamson, Farrar, Macnamara, M.Adamson, Gall, Brown. Interchange: Puletua, Boyd, Falcon, MacGillivray.

Preliminary final

Cronulla 10 (M.Rogers try; Rogers 3 goals) defeated **Canberra** 4 (J.Croker try) at Shark Park, Saturday night, September 13.
Scrums: Canberra 9-8. Penalties: 6-all. Crowd: 17,638. Referee: Bill Harrigan. Halftime: Cronulla 8-0. Goalkickers: Rogers (Cronulla) 3/4, Daley (Canberra) 0/1. Reserves: Auckland def. North Queensland 30-14.
CRONULLA: Peachey; Rogers, Ettingshausen (c), Richardson, Bell; Healey, Green; Lee, Treister, Stevens, Greenhill, McKenna, Nikau. Interchange: Dykes, Ryan, Davidson.
CANBERRA: Nagas; Nadruku, Mullins, Boyle, Fulivai; Daley, Stuart (c); Davico, Priddis, Hetherington, Croker, Burnham, Clyde. Interchange: Payten, McFadden, Woolford.

SUPER LEAGUE FINALS

SUPER LEAGUE GRAND FINAL
SEPTEMBER 20

Brisbane take inaugural title

GRAND FINAL
Brisbane 26, Cronulla 8

Brisbane proved themselves the champion team in Super League with an emphatic 26-8 grand final win over Cronulla before a record crowd for a league match in Brisbane of 58,912.

The Broncos overwhelmed their opponents, scoring four tries to one, including three in the final 25 minutes. Centre Steve Renouf enjoyed a memorable night with a hat-trick of tries.

The Broncos dominated the opening period, but a series of missed opportunities saw them score only one first-half try. Their 10-2 halftime lead was cut to just two points when winger Wendell Sailor threw an ill-directed pass close to his own line for Cronulla centre Russell Richardson to score four minutes after the resumption.

Brisbane recovered quickly, though, and Renouf's second try in the 55th minute reinstated the eight-point margin. The try followed a crunching tackle by second-rower Peter Ryan on Cronulla fullback David Peachey which dislodged the ball in front of the Cronulla posts.

Renouf completed his hat-trick nine minutes later and the premiership was safe in the Broncos' keeping. Long-serving winger Michael Hancock was rewarded with Brisbane's final try two minutes from fulltime.

Cronulla had only themselves to blame for a below-par performance in which they committed too many fundamental errors and failed to kick intelligently in open play. The Sharks' over-aggressive approach was out of character, and did not help the team settle into their stride. Danny Lee and Les Davidson were placed on report for incidents involving Brisbane's John Plath.

Renouf was a popular choice as man of the match, although front-rower Shane Webcke played a mighty hand in building momentum for the Broncos, and with pack-mates Peter Ryan, Andrew Gee, Gorden Tallis and Darren Smith, helped subdue the power of the Cronulla pack. At the back, fullback Darren Lockyer handled Cronulla's bombing raids with great composure.

The Broncos' win was achieved without strike forward Glenn Lazarus, with Allan Langer struggling from a groin injury and with second-rower Tallis needing pain-killing injections to mask a rib cartilage injury.

Brisbane 26 (S.Renouf 3, M.Hancock tries; D.Lockyer 5 goals) defeated **Cronulla** 8 (R.Richardson try; M.Rogers 2 goals) at ANZ Stadium, Saturday night, September 20.

Scrums: Cronulla 9-2. Penalties: 5-all. Crowd: 58,912 (ground record). Referee: Bill Harrigan. Halftime: Brisbane 10-2. Goalkickers: Lockyer (Brisbane) 5/6, Rogers (Cronulla) 2/2. Reserves: Canterbury def. Auckland 40-12. Under-19s: Penrith def. Auckland 22-18.

BRISBANE: Lockyer; Devere, Renouf, Mundine, Sailor; Walters, Langer (c); Thorn, Gee, Webcke, Tallis, Ryan, Smith. Interchange: Carroll, Plath, Hancock, Walker.

CRONULLA: Peachey; Rogers, Ettingshausen (c), Richardson, Bell; Healey, Green; Lee, Treister, Stevens, Greenhill, McKenna, Nikau. Interchange: Dykes, Ryan, Davidson, Long.

Cited: Lee (Cronulla). **Charge:** Head-butting. **Sentence:** 95 demerit points. **Cited:** Davidson (Cronulla). **Charge:** Punching. **Sentence:** 95 demerit points.

SUPER LEAGUE WORLD NINES
JANUARY 31, FEBRUARY 1, 2

Aussies crash out of Nines

For the second successive year, the Australian Super League side was bundled out of the World Nines by New Zealand in a semi-final. In a repeat of their loss in Fiji 12 months earlier, the Australians fell 12-10 to the Kiwis, who went on to win their second title.

Australia's 20-8 pool victory over the Western Samoans was laced with controversy when Western Samoan player Joe Galauvao was wrongfully awarded a try. The ball had been clearly grounded by Australian winger Michael Hancock, but in an embarrassment for the Super League hierarchy, video ref Brian Grant awarded the points to Western Samoa.

RESULTS
DAY ONE
Pool A
Australia defeated USA 24-0, Cook Islands defeated Papua New Guinea 26-0, Western Samoa defeated Fiji 12-6, Australia defeated Cook Islands 18-4, Western Samoa defeated USA 30-10, Fiji defeated PNG 22-10.

Pool B
New Zealand defeated France 12-10, Great Britain defeated Tonga 20-0, South Africa defeated Japan 42-6, New Zealand defeated Tonga 14-4, France defeated Japan 28-0, Great Britain defeated South Africa 28-10.

DAY TWO
Pool A
Australia defeated Western Samoa 20-8, Fiji defeated Cook Islands 12-8, Papua New Guinea defeated USA 38-8, Australia defeated Fiji 26-10, Western Samoa defeated Papua New Guinea 16-4, Cook Islands defeated USA 24-6, Western Samoa defeated Cook Islands 18-10, Fiji defeated USA 19-8, Australia defeated Papua New Guinea 34-4.

Pool B
New Zealand defeated Japan 50-4, South Africa drew with Tonga 10-all, Great Britain defeated France 20-0, New Zealand defeated South Africa 34-8, Great Britain defeated Japan 46-0, France defeated Tonga 8-6, Great Britain defeated New Zealand 12-10, South Africa defeated France 18-4, Tonga defeated Japan 44-0.

FINALS DAY
BOWL SEMI-FINALS
Papua New Guinea defeated Japan 20-0, Tonga defeated USA 26-4.

BOWL FINAL
Tonga defeated Papua New Guinea 16-8.

PLATE SEMI-FINALS
Fiji defeated France 24-8, South Africa defeated Cook Islands 8-4.

PLATE FINAL
Fiji defeated South Africa 22-6.

TROPHY SEMI-FINALS
New Zealand defeated Australia 12-10, Western Samoa defeated Great Britain 10-0.

TROPHY FINAL
New Zealand 16 (T.Iro, Q.Pongia, R.Wiki tries; M.Ellis 2 goals) defeated Western Samoa 0, Sunday February 2.

NEW ZEALAND: Quentin Pongia, Richard Barnett, Marc Ellis, Ruben Wiki, John Timu, Robbie Paul, Stacey Jones, Shane Endacott, Jason Williams, Stephen Kearney (c), Tony Iro, Tony Tatupu, Joe Vagana, Tyran Smith. Coach: Graeme Norton.

WESTERN SAMOA: John Schuster, Jerry Seu Seu, Willie Swann, Tony Tuimavave, Bryan Laumatia, Nigel Vagana, Anthony Swann, Joe Galauvao, Matt Sauvao, Fela Sina, Philip Leuluai, Vila Matautia, Apollo Perelini. Coach: Mark Graham.

AUSTRALIAN TEAM: Andrew Ettingshausen, Allan Langer, Wendell Sailor, Steve Renouf, Gorden Tallis, Jason Croker, Brett Hetherington, David Furner, Paul Green, Steve Walters, Michael Hancock, Glenn Lazarus, Kevin Walters, Ryan Girdler. Coach: Tim Sheens.

Crowds: Friday 10,530. Saturday 12,360. Sunday 13,423. Total 36,313.

All matches played at Stockland Stadium, Townsville from January 31 to February 2.

NINES WINNERS
1996 New Zealand
1997 New Zealand

SUPER LEAGUE TRI-SERIES
PRELIMINARY ROUNDS

Blues win amazing finale

Game 1 — NSW 38, Qld 10
Sydney Football Stadium, April 11

Underdogs New South Wales drew first blood in Super League's Tri-Series competition with a 38-10 demolition of Queensland at the Sydney Football Stadium. Inspired by a vintage display from 32-year-old halfback Greg Alexander, the Blues led 22-4 at halftime and continued to dominate after the break.

New South Wales entered the match with 10 interstate newcomers, however it was the Queensland side who were made to look like novices. Alexander scored one try and set up two others in the first half, while centre Andrew Ettingshausen, who finished with a hat-trick of tries, and five-eighth Laurie Daley were also key figures in the win.

The Maroons were rocked by the loss of centre Steve Renouf, whose jaw was broken in a head-clash with New South Wales replacement forward Solomon Haumono in the 28th minute. Haumono was placed on report by referee Bill Harrigan for using a swinging arm in the tackle, but he was later cleared of all responsibility for Renouf's injury.

The Blues' victory was soured by news that Alexander would be missing for a long period after suffering a broken bone in his foot, while Queensland captain Allan Langer described the loss as one of the worst of his representative career.

New South Wales 38 (A.Ettingshausen 3, K.Nagas 2, D.Peachey, G.Alexander tries; R.Girdler 5 goals) defeated **Queensland** 10 (W.Sailor, P.Ryan tries; M.Rogers goal) at Sydney Football Stadium, Friday night, April 11.

Scrums: NSW 12-5. Penalties: 2-all. Crowd: 26,731. Referee: Bill Harrigan. Halftime: NSW 22-4. Goalkickers: Girdler (NSW) 5/7, Rogers (Queensland) 1/2.

NEW SOUTH WALES: David Peachey; Ken Nagas, Ryan Girdler, Andrew Ettingshausen, Matt Ryan; Laurie Daley (c), Greg Alexander; Rodney Howe, Craig Gower, Glenn Lazarus, Sean Ryan, Simon Gillies, David Furner. Interchange: Solomon Haumono, Matt Adamson, Robbie Ross, Noel Goldthorpe.

QUEENSLAND: Julian O'Neill; Wendell Sailor, Steve Renouf, Geoff Bell, Mat Rogers; Kevin Walters, Allan Langer (c); Brad Thorn, Steve Walters, Andrew Gee, Owen Cunningham, Gorden Tallis, Darren Smith. Interchange: Peter Ryan, Chris McKenna, Paul Green, Shane Webcke.

Game 2 — Qld 26, NZ 12
Ericsson Stadium, May 9

Irrepressible Queensland halfback Allan Langer took his team a step closer to a place in the Tri-Series final with an inspired performance in his team's 26-12 win over New Zealand at Ericsson Stadium.

Queensland held a 10-6 lead at halftime and maintained their advantage through the early stages of a tense second half. After a long break from centre Darren Smith, Langer withstood a high tackle from New Zealand centre Ruben Wiki and somehow managed to slip a pass to five-eighth Kevin Walters, who scored for Queensland. Mat Rogers' conversion gave the Maroons a 16-6 lead, but New Zealand hit back quickly through centre John Timu, putting them back in the match at 16-12.

However, Langer struck again six minutes from fulltime when from close range, he slipped between New Zealand defenders Tawera Nikau and Quentin

176 RUGBY LEAGUE 1998

Pongia to score a crucial try. Rogers converted for 22-12 and then scored himself right on fulltime for the 26-12 result.

The 14-point margin gave Queensland the same for and against difference as the Kiwis, leaving New Zealand with the task of beating New South Wales at Bruce Stadium in order to qualify for the Tri-Series final.

Queensland 26 (S.Webcke, T.Carroll, K.Walters, A.Langer, M.Rogers tries; Rogers 3 goals) defeated **New Zealand** 12 (S.Jones, J.Timu tries; G.Ngamu 2 goals) at Ericsson Stadium, Friday night, May 9.

Scrums: New Zealand 8-5. Penalties: 4-all. Crowd: 18,000. Referee: Graham Annesley. Halftime: 6-all. Goalkickers: Rogers (Queensland) 3/5, Ngamu (New Zealand) 2/2.

QUEENSLAND: Darren Lockyer; Wendell Sailor, Tonie Carroll, Darren Smith, Mat Rogers; Kevin Walters, Allan Langer (c); Brad Thorn, Steve Walters, Craig Greenhill, Gorden Tallis, Owen Cunningham, Peter Ryan. Interchange: Shane Webcke, Michael Hancock, Kevin Campion, Paul Green.

NEW ZEALAND: Anthony Swann; Sean Hoppe, Tea Ropati, Ruben Wiki, Richie Barnett; Gene Ngamu, Stacey Jones; Quentin Pongia, Syd Eru, Joe Vagana, Tony Iro, Steve Kearney (c), Tawera Nikau. Interchange: John Timu, Brady Malam, Tyran Smith, Marc Ellis.

Game 3 — NSW 20, NZ 15
Bruce Stadium, May 14

An incorrect no-try ruling cost New Zealand the chance of playing in the final of the Tri-Series competition after a tough contest against New South Wales at Canberra's Bruce Stadium. With his team trailing 20-15 right on fulltime, Kiwi five-eighth Gene Ngamu launched a last-ditch bomb 20 metres out from the New South Wales line. Winger Sean Hoppe leapt above the New South Wales defence to claim the ball and touch down for what appeared a fair try.

But referee Steve Clark had received an offside call from touch judge Jim Neal and instead of awarding a New Zealand try, he ruled a penalty to New South Wales. Replays of the incident showed Hoppe was well on-side when the ball was kicked. A try to New Zealand at that point would have cut the Blues' lead to 20-19, with a conversion attempt from the sideline to follow.

The decision provoked an almighty outburst from New Zealand officials and the Kiwi media, who compared the incident to cricket's underarm controversy.

The incident overshadowed a hard-fought game of football, in which New South Wales scored four tries to two. New South Wales winger Ken Nagas crossed for two long-range tries, while second-rower Simon Gillies also collected a double. On a night of doubles, New Zealand centre Ruben Wiki scored both his team's tries.

New South Wales 20 (S.Gillies 2, K.Nagas 2 tries; R.Girdler 2 goals) defeated **New Zealand** 15 (R.Wiki 2 tries; G.Ngamu 3 goals; Ngamu field goal) at Bruce Stadium, Wednesday night, May 14.

Scrums: NSW 11-6. Penalties: 10-all. Crowd: 13,836. Referee: Steve Clark. Halftime: 10-all. Goalkickers: Girdler (NSW) 2/4, Daley (NSW) 0/1, Ngamu (New Zealand) 3/4.

NEW SOUTH WALES: David Peachey; Ken Nagas, Andrew Ettingshausen, Ryan Girdler, Brett Mullins; Laurie Daley (c), Noel Goldthorpe; Glenn Lazarus, Luke Priddis, Ian Roberts, Simon Gillies, David Furner, Bradley Clyde. Interchange: Solomon Haumono, Matt Ryan, Scott Wilson, Danny Lee.

NEW ZEALAND: Anthony Swann; Sean Hoppe, Tea Ropati, Ruben Wiki, Richie Barnett; Gene Ngamu, Stacey Jones; Quentin Pongia, Syd Eru, Joe Vagana, Steve Kearney (c), Tyran Smith, Tawera Nikau. Interchange: John Timu, Brady Malam, Tony Iro, Marc Ellis.

FINAL — NSW 23, Qld 22
ANZ Stadium, May 19

A result in the Tri-Series final took 103 minutes and 47 seconds to decide and finally came about through a field goal to New South Wales halfback Noel Goldthorpe. In a thrilling and tension-packed match before a crowd of 35,507 at Brisbane's ANZ Stadium, Goldthorpe's field goal broke a 22-all deadlock between New South Wales and

Queensland, and gave the Blues victory in the inaugural Tri-Series competition.

The teams were forced to play an extra 20 minutes after the scores were locked 22-all at the end of regular time. But with no further score in the overtime period, under Super League rules, a period of sudden-death was installed.

New South Wales survived an attempt at penalty goal by Queensland fullback Darren Lockyer after two minutes of sudden-death, before Goldthorpe launched his attempt at field goal less than two minutes later. After missing with two earlier attempts, Goldthorpe made no mistake from 24 metres out.

During the two periods of overtime, three tries were disallowed and six attempts at field goal missed as the large crowd lapped up the excitement.

Both sides scored four tries in the 80 minutes of regular play which was again marked by controversial decisions by match officials.

Late in the first half, referee Bill Harrigan disallowed what might have been a fair try to New South Wales winger Brett Mullins after centre Andrew Ettingshausen flicked the ball back from the Queensland dead-ball line. Harrigan declined to call on the video referee, despite the closeness of the call. Then, five minutes after halftime, Mullins was awarded a try even though a video replay revealed that winger Ken Nagas had placed a foot on the touchline during a play leading up to the try.

Mullins had earlier scored the Blues' first try when he outleapt Lockyer from a Laurie Daley bomb.

Queensland centre Steve Renouf laid on his team's first try with a neat pass to centre partner Tonie Carroll, who sprinted 70 metres to score. Renouf scored himself just before halftime when he effortlessly beat the tackles of Matt Ryan and David Peachey, establishing a 10-6 halftime lead for the Maroons.

New South Wales assumed a 12-10 lead when David Furner converted Mullins' second try, but Queensland quickly regained the ascendancy when Renouf crossed for his second try, created by Allan Langer and Kevin Walters.

The lead changed again when Mullins completed his hat-trick after accepting a difficult pass from Ryan and the Blues went to a 22-16 lead. Then Mullins reciprocated for Ryan to score in the 62nd minute. Queensland levelled five minutes later when winger Michael Hancock scored from a Langer crossfield kick, leaving Lockyer with a simple conversion.

Queensland missed with two field goal attempts which could have broken the deadlock before the match went into extra-time.

The 104-minute epic was the longest match of top-level football ever played.

New South Wales 23 (B.Mullins 3, M.Ryan tries; D.Furner 3 goals; N.Goldthorpe field goal) defeated **Queensland** 22 (S.Renouf 2, M.Hancock, T.Carroll tries; M.Rogers 2, D.Lockyer goals) after 20 minutes extra-time and four minutes of sudden-death, at ANZ Stadium, Monday night, May 19.

Scrums: Queensland 14-5. Penalties: 5-all. Crowd: 35,570. Referee: Bill Harrigan. Halftime: Queensland 10-6. Goalkickers: Furner (NSW) 3/4, Rogers (Queensland) 2/3, Lockyer (Queensland) 1/2.

NEW SOUTH WALES: David Peachey; Ken Nagas, Andrew Ettingshausen, Matt Ryan, Brett Mullins; Laurie Daley (c), Noel Goldthorpe; Glenn Lazarus, Craig Gower, Ian Roberts, David Furner, Simon Gillies, Bradley Clyde. Interchange: Robbie Kearns, Solomon Haumono, Robbie Ross, Luke Priddis.

QUEENSLAND: Darren Lockyer; Wendell Sailor, Tonie Carroll, Steve Renouf, Mat Rogers; Kevin Walters, Allan Langer (c); Brad Thorn, Steve Walters, Owen Cunningham, Gorden Tallis, Peter Ryan, Darren Smith. Interchange: Kevin Campion, Paul Green, Michael Hancock, Shane Webcke.

SUPER LEAGUE WORLD CLUB CHALLENGE

A costly competition

Before a ball was kicked in Super League's World Club Challenge, administrators were planning ways to modify future versions of what was quickly recognised to be a costly and ill-conceived competition.

The WCC sprang forth from the Super League 'vision' of taking the game to the world. And in its infancy Super League hailed the WCC as a triumph, the first truly international contest of Rugby League clubs. However, the first series of matches, in early June, showed up the competition for what it was — a folly of monumental proportions. Australian sides won nine of the 10 matches played, most by wide margins. Only Wigan restored a semblance of British pride, with a 22-18 defeat of Canterbury.

But not even the former world champions of club football were exempt from the lopsided scores of their countrymen. A week later they were trounced 34-0 by Brisbane, and then 56-22 by Canberra after the Raiders led 42-6 at halftime.

The results followed a predictable pattern. By the end of the second three-week period, Euroleague clubs had won a dismal eight games out of 60, a success rate of little more than 13 per cent.

The competition reached farcical proportions in the final pool match at Penrith Football Stadium, where the Panthers required a win by 47 points or more against St Helens to qualify for the quarter-finals, despite an undefeated record in their previous five games. Their 32-26 victory meant Penrith had won all six matches, yet failed to qualify for the quarter-finals. In contrast, under the cockeyed WCC qualification process, St Helens, who failed to win one of their six pool matches, won through to the quarter-finals via a play-off with Paris-St Germain.

The programming of matches was another blight on the competition. Super League's premiership, gathering momentum after 12 rounds, was placed on hold while the first three rounds of the WCC was played. Half the Super League clubs jetted off to England for three weeks, before returning to play Rounds 13 to 15 of their premiership. The second three-week period of the WCC, in which the remaining Australian clubs spent time abroad, forced yet another break in the premiership.

Super League went into damage control, attempting to defend what to most was indefensible. They claimed the competition was necessary to expose the gulf in standards between the Australian and the British games. Many million of dollars says it was a costly way to expose what most already suspected. However, for individual clubs such as the Auckland Warriors, the Hunter Mariners and the Brisbane Broncos, who picked up $1 million for finally winning the disjointed contest in mid-October, the competition had its benefits.

Playing against weaker opposition helped the Warriors climb from a sizeable hole they had dug for themselves and their new-found confidence had a flow-on effect when they returned to premiership football. The Mariners, in their first season, breezed through their pool matches and then upset Wigan at Central Park and Cronulla at Shark Park to earn a place in the final against the Broncos.

Centre Steve Renouf ran in five tries as Brisbane monstered St Helens out of the competition with a 66-12 quarter-final win and then they knocked over an improved Auckland with a 22-16 win in one of the few quality contests of the whole sorry competition.

The final itself, played before sparsely filled stands at Auckland's Ericsson Stadium, was as much a no-contest as so many of the games that preceded it. A month after taking out the inaugural Super League premiership, the Broncos shook off their lethargy to run up a 26-4 halftime lead against the Mariners before ultimately winning 36-12.

Super League's support base was significantly eroded by the failure of the WCC. Poor crowds and the dislocation caused to the Super League premiership also led to substantially lower crowds over the last six rounds of the competition.

ROUND 1
Pool A

Brisbane 42 (Kevin Walters 2, Wendell Sailor, Darren Lockyer, Steve Renouf, Anthony Mundine, Tonie Carroll tries; Lockyer 7 goals) defeated **London** 22 (Scott Roskell 2, Andrew Duncan, Robbie Beazley tries; Greg Barwick 3 goals) at ANZ Stadium, Friday night, June 6.
Scrums: Brisbane 13-8. Penalties: Brisbane 9-2. Crowd: 18,193. Referee: Bill Harrigan. Halftime: London 18-12.

Auckland 42 (Anthony Swann 2, Sean Hoppe 2, Stephen Kearney, Stacey Jones, Tea Ropati tries; Matthew Ridge 7 goals) defeated **St Helens** 14 (Anthony Sullivan, Alan Hunte tries; Bobbie Goulding 2, Paul Anderson goals) at Knowsley Road, Friday night, June 6.
Scrums: Auckland 9-8. Penalties: St Helens 12-4. Crowd: 8911. Referee: Stuart Cummings. Halftime: Auckland 20-8.

Canberra 70 (Ken Nagas 6, Jason Croker 2, Brett Hetherington, David Boyle, Ben Kennedy, David Westley, Simon Woolford tries; David Furner 7, Royston Lightning, Luke Davico goals) defeated **Halifax** 6 (Carl Gillespie try; Martin Pearson goal) at Bruce Stadium, Sunday, June 8.
Scrums: Halifax 9-8. Penalties: Canberra 8-3. Crowd: 7780. Referee: Brian Grant. Halftime: Canberra 38-6.

Cronulla 40 (Russell Richardson 4, David Peachey, Wade Forrester, Mat Rogers, Richard Barnett tries; Rogers 4 goals) defeated **Warrington** 12 (Nigel Vagana, Kelly Shelford tries; Lee Briers 2 goals) at Wilderspool Stadium, Sunday, June 8.
Scrums: 5-all. Penalties: 5-all. Crowd: 3378. Referee: Russell Smith. Halftime: Cronulla 26-0.

Wigan 22 (Jason Robinson 2, Simon Haughton, Andy Johnson tries; Andy Farrell 2, Henry Paul goals) defeated **Canterbury** 18 (Jason Hetherington, John Timu, Matthew Ryan tries; Daryl Halligan 3 goals) at Belmore Sports Ground, Monday night, June 19.
Scrums: Canterbury 9-6. Penalties: Canterbury 7-2. Crowd: 10,680. Referee: Graham Annesley. Halftime: Wigan 10-0.

Penrith 20 (Peter Jorgensen, Ryan Girdler, Darren Brown, Sid Domic tries; Girdler 2 goals) defeated **Bradford** 16 (Jon Scales, Danny Peacock, Stuart Spruce tries; Steve McNamara 2 goals) at Odsal Stadium, Monday night, June 19.
Scrums: 6-all. Penalties: Bradford 11-4. Crowd: 14,378. Referee: David Campbell. Halftime: Bradford 16-6.

Pool B

North Queensland 42 (Glen Murphy 2, Reggie Cressbrook, Peter Jones, Luke Phillips, Mark Shipway, Bert Tabuai, Adam Warwick tries; Phillips 5 goals) defeated **Leeds** 20 (Paul Sterling 2, Damien Gibson, Wayne Collins tries; Iestyn Harris 2 goals) at Stockland Stadium, Saturday night, June 7.
Scrums: Leeds 9-7. Penalties: North Queensland 9-7. Crowd: 14,561. Referee: Stephen Clark. Halftime: North Queensland 26-10.

Adelaide 50 (Solomon Kiri 2, Rod Maybon 2, Kerrod Walters, Steve Stone, Cameron Blair, Bruce Mamando tries; Luke Williamson 6, Kurt Wrigley 3 goals) defeated **Salford** 8 (Gary Broadbent try; Steve Blakeley 2 goals) at Adelaide Oval, Sunday, June 8.
Scrums: Salford 3-2. Penalties: 7-all. Crowd: 11,346. Referee: Tim Mander. Halftime: Adelaide 16-6.

Perth 24 (Peter Shiels, Jon Grieve, Scott Wilson, Matthew Rodwell tries; Chris Ryan 4 goals) defeated **Castleford** 16 (Jason Critchley, Ian Tonks, David Chapman tries; Tonks, Danny Orr goals) at Wheldon Road, Sunday, June 8.
Scrums: Castleford 12-10. Penalties: Perth 5-3. Crowd: 3590. Referee: Robert Connolly. Halftime: Perth 18-4.

Hunter 28 (Keith Beauchamp, Robbie Ross, Brad Godden, Anthony Brann, Scott Hill tries; Neil Piccinelli 4 goals) defeated **Paris-St Germain** 12 (Deon Bird, Fabien Devecchi tries; Matt O'Connor 2 goals) at Charlety Stadium, Sunday, June 8.
Scrums: 6-all. Penalties: Paris 5-4. Crowd: 3500. Referee: Steve Presley. Halftime: Hunter 16-6.

ROUND 2
Pool A

Auckland 20 (Matthew Ridge, Stacey Jones, Paul Staladi tries; Ridge 4 goals) defeated **Bradford** 16 (Mike Forshaw, Graeme Bradley tries; Steve McNamara 3, Paul Loughlin goals) at Odsal Stadium, Saturday, June 14.
Penalties: Auckland 15-14. Crowd: 13,133. Referee: Russell Smith. Halftime: Auckland 8-2.

Canterbury 58 (Matthew Ryan 2, Hazem El Masri 2, John Timu, Daryl Halligan, Duncan McRae, Craig Polla-Mounter, Steven Price, Barry Ward tries; Halligan 9 goals) defeated **Halifax** 6 (Michael Jackson try; Martin Pearson goal) at Belmore Sports Ground, Sunday, June 15.
Scrums: Halifax 8-4. Penalties: Canterbury 8-7. Crowd: 5034. Referee: Brian Grant. Halftime: Canterbury 26-2.

Canberra 66 (Laurie Daley 3, Brett Mullins 2, Ken Nagas 2, Ruben Wiki 2, Royston Lightning, Luke Davico tries; David Furner 11 goals) defeated **London** 20 (Martin Offiah, Scott Roskell, Josh White, Terry Matterson tries; Matterson 2 goals) at Bruce Stadium, Sunday, June 15.
Scrums: Canberra 13-7. Penalties: Canberra 6-3. Crowd: 6471. Referee: Tim Mander. Halftime: Canberra 24-8.

Penrith 52 (Ryan Girdler 3, Robbie Beckett 2, Darron Drown, Jody Gall, Andrew Hinson, Danny Farrar tries; Girdler 7, Brad Drew goals) defeated **Warrington** 22 (Shaun Geritas, Mark Foster, Toa Kohe-Love, Willie Swann tries; Lee Briers 2, Chris Rudd goals) at Wilderspool Stadium, Sunday, June 15.
Penalties: Warrington 10-5. Crowd: 3850. Referee: Robert Connolly. Halftime: Penrith 28-10.

Brisbane 34 (Darren Lockyer 2, Kevin Walters, Tonie Carroll, Allan Langer, Gorden Tallis tries; Lockyer 5 goals) defeated **Wigan** 0 at ANZ Stadium, Monday night, June 16.
Scrums: 8-all. Penalties: 4-all. Crowd: 14,833. Referee: Bill Harrigan. Halftime: Brisbane 10-0.

Cronulla 48 (Tawera Nikau 2, Russell Richardson, Richard Barnett, Mat Rogers, Jason Stevens, Wade Forrester, Paul Green tries; Rogers 8 goals) defeated **St Helens** 8 (Alan Hunte try; Sean Long 2 goals) at Knowsley Road, Monday night, June 16.

Scrums: St Helens 8-6. Penalties: St Helens 14-3. Crowd: 8039. Referee: David Campbell. Halftime: Cronulla 30-2.

Pool B

Adelaide 34 (Chris Quinn 2, Steve Stone 2, Luke Williamson, Rod Maybon tries; Williamson 5 goals) defeated **Leeds** 8 (Ryan Sheridan, Leroy Rivett tries) at Adelaide Oval, Friday night, June 13.
Scrums: Adelaide 7-5. Penalties: Adelaide 11-5. Crowd: 14,630. Referee: Stephen Clark. Halftime: Adelaide 8-4.

Hunter 42 (Robbie Ross 2, John Carlaw 2, Noel Goldthorpe, Tony Iro, Scott Hill, Troy Stone tries; Noel Goldthorpe 5 goals) defeated **Castleford** 14 (Andrew Shick, Chris Smith, Mike Ford tries; Ian Tonks goal) at Wheldon Road, Friday night, June 13.
Penalties: 8-all. Crowd: 3087. Referee: Stuart Cummings. Halftime: Hunter 16-6.

North Queensland 54 (Reggie Cressbrook 2, Steve Walters 2, Shane Vincent 2, Glen Murphy, Luke Phillips, Andrew Dunemann, Mark Shipway tries; Phillips 7 goals) defeated **Oldham** 16 (David Jones, John Clarke, Alfei Leuila tries; Luke Goodwin 2 goals) at Stockland Stadium, Saturday night, June 14.
Scrums: North Queensland 12-9. Penalties: Oldham 9-8. Crowd: 12,631. Referee: Graham Annesley. Halftime: North Queensland 20-4.

Sheffield 26 (Nick Pinkney 2, Willie Morganson, Lynton Scott tries; Mark Aston 5 goals) defeated **Perth** 22 (Paul Bell, Matthew Rodwell, Chris Ryan, Scott Wilson tries; Ryan 3 goals) at Don Valley Stadium, Sunday, June 15.
Penalties: Sheffield 12-7. Crowd: 3500. Referee: John Connolly. Halftime: Perth 22-8.

ROUND 3
Pool A

Cronulla 30 (Mat Rogers 3, Tiaan Strauss tries; Rogers 7 goals) defeated **Bradford** 10 (Paul Loughlin, Sonny Nickle tries; Loughlin goal) at Odsal Stadium, Friday night, June 20.
Scrums: Cronulla 6-4. Penalties: Bradford 11-8. Crowd: 10,756. Referee: Stuart Cummings. Halftime: Cronulla 16-4.

Brisbane 76 (Wendell Sailor 3, Darren Smith 3, Anthony Mundine 2, Steve Renouf, Allan Langer, Glenn Lazarus, John Plath, Shane Webcke, Gorden Tallis, Tonie Carroll tries; Darren Lockyer 8 goals) defeated **Halifax** 0 at ANZ Stadium, Sunday, June 22.
Scrums: Brisbane 8-2. Penalties: Brisbane 4-2. Crowd: 11,358. Referee: Tim Mander. Halftime: Brisbane 42-0.

Canberra 56 (Noa Nadruku 2, Luke Priddis 2, Ruben Wiki 2, Bradley Clyde 2, Brett Mullins,

SUPER LEAGUE WORLD CLUB CHALLENGE

David Westley tries; David Furner 8 goals) defeated **Wigan** 22 (Kris Radlinski 2, Martin Hall, Gary Connolly tries; Andy Farrell 3 goals) at Bruce Stadium, Sunday, June 22.
Scrums: Canberra 9-6. Penalties: Wigan 8-7. Crowd: 9098. Referee: Stephen Clark. Halftime: Canberra 42-6.

Penrith 50 (Ryan Girdler 2, Darren Brown 2, Danny Farrar 2, Jody Gall, Sid Domic, Robbie Beckett tries; Girdler 7 goals) defeated **St Helens** 30 (Anthony Sullivan 2, Keiron Cunningham 2, Steve Prescott tries; Sean Long 5 goals) at Knowsley Road, Sunday, June 22.
Scrums: Penrith 8-6. Penalties: St Helens 11-4. Crowd: 6671. Referee: John Connolly. Halftime: Penrith 36-10.

Canterbury 34 (Jason Hetherington 2, Hazem El Masri, Barry Ward, Travis Norton tries; Daryl Halligan 7 goals) defeated **London** 18 (Martin Offiah, Scott Roskell, Shaun Edwards, David Krause tries; Terry Matterson goal) at Belmore Sports Ground, Monday night, June 23.
Scrums: 6-all. Penalties: Auckland 5-3. Crowd: 6272. Referee: Bill Harrigan. Halftime: Canterbury 20-4.

Auckland 56 (Tea Ropati 4, Anthony Swann 2, Gene Ngamu, Stephen Kearney, Joe Vagana, Matthew Ridge tries; Ridge 8 goals) defeated **Warrington** 28 (Lee Briers, Richard Henare, Kelly Shelford, Willie Swann, Mark Forster tries; Briers 4 goals) at Wilderspool Stadium, Monday night, June 23.
Scrums: Auckland 8-6. Penalties: Auckland 5-3. Crowd: 4428. Referee: Steve Presley. Halftime: Auckland 20-12.

Pool B

Adelaide 42 (Luke Williamson, Steve Stone, Wayne Simonds, Rod Maybon, Brett Galea, Kurt Wrigley, Andrew Hick tries; Williamson 6, Wrigley goals) defeated **Oldham** 14 (Paul Topping, Joe Faimalo, Francis Maloney tries; Maloney goal) at Adelaide Oval, Friday night, June 20.
Scrums: Adelaide 9-5. Penalties: Adelaide 5-2. Crowd: 13,852. Referee: Graham Annesley. Halftime: Adelaide 18-6.

Hunter 40 (Robbie Ross 3, Darrien Doherty, Keith Beauchamp, Willie Poching, John Carlaw, Brett Kimmorley tries; Noel Goldthorpe 2, Neil Piccinelli 2 goals) defeated **Sheffield** 4 (Mark Aston 2 goals) at Don Valley Stadium, Friday night, June 20.
Scrums: 6-all. Penalties: Sheffield 7-5. Crowd: 2350. Referee: Russell Smith. Halftime: Hunter 20-2.

Paris-St Germain 24 (Jason Eade 2, Phil Bergman, David Lomax, Deon Bird tries; Matt O'Connor 2 goals) defeated **Perth** 0 at Charlety Stadium, Friday night, June 20.

Scrums: Paris 8-3. Penalties: Paris 6-3. Crowd: 3500. Referee: David Campbell. Halftime: Paris 10-0.

North Queensland 44 (Adam Warwick 2, Reggie Cressbrook, Paul Bowman, Owen Cunningham, Bert Tabuai, Mark Shipway, Ian Dunemann tries; Luke Phillips 6 goals) defeated **Salford** 8 (Nathan McAvoy try; Steve Blakeley 2 goals) at Stockland Stadium, Saturday night, June 21.
Scrums: 10-all. Penalties: North Queensland 9-4. Crowd: 15,560. Referee: Brian Grant. Halftime: 8-all.

ROUND 4
Pool A

Penrith 48 (Matt Adamson 3, Bobby Thompson, Sid Domic, Jason Williams, Ryan Girdler, Danny Farrar tries; Girdler 8 goals) defeated **Warrington** 12 (Jon Roper 2, Mark Forster tries) at Penrith Football Stadium, Friday night, July 18.
Scrums: Penrith 12-9. Penalties: Penrith 10-8. Crowd: 5642. Referee: Brian Grant. Halftime: Penrith 24-8.

Auckland 64 (Tea Ropati 3, Sean Hoppe 2, Lee Oudenryn, Marc Ellis, Denis Betts, Gene Ngamu, Stephen Kearney, Syd Eru tries; Ngamu 12 goals) defeated **Bradford** 14 (Graeme Bradley, James Lowes, Brian McDermott tries; Paul Loughlin goal) at Ericsson Stadium, Sunday, July 20.
Scrums: Auckland 6-5. Penalties: Auckland 8-6. Crowd: 13,500. Referee: Bill Harrigan. Halftime: Auckland 24-8.

Canterbury 40 (Hazem El Masri 3, Steve Reardon, Travis Norton, Daryl Halligan, Robert Mears tries; Halligan 6 goals) defeated **Halifax** 22 (Simon Baldwin, David Bouveng, Daio Powell, Paul Highton tries; John Schuster 3 goals) at Thrum Hall, Sunday, July 20.
Scrums: 7-all. Penalties: Halifax 7-5. Crowd: 3500. Referee: Steve Presley. Halftime: Canterbury 22-6.

Brisbane 30 (Kevin Waters, Anthony Mundine, Steve Renouf, Darren Lockyer, Wendell Sailor tries; Darren Lockyer 5 goals) defeated **Wigan** 4 (Andy Farrell 2 goals) at Central Park, Sunday, July 20.
Scrums: Wigan 7-4. Penalties: Wigan 8-4. Crowd: 13,476. Referee: Stuart Cummings. Halftime: Brisbane 6-4.

Cronulla 28 (Andrew Ettingshausen 2, Geoff Bell, Paul Donaghy, Adam Dykes tries; Paul Green 4 goals) defeated **St Helens** 12 (Keiron Cunningham, Paul Newlove tries; Bobbie Goulding 2 goals) at Shark Park, Monday night, July 21.
Scrums: Cronulla 8-6. Penalties: St Helens 6-5. Crowd: 7721. Referee: Graham Annesley.

Halftime: Cronulla 14-4.
London 38 (Terry Matterson 2, Greg Barwick, Peter Gill, Tulsen Tollett, Scott Roskell tries; Barwick 7 goals) defeated **Canberra** 18 (David Boyle 2, Luke Priddis, Jason Burnham tries; David Furner goal) at The Stoop, Monday night, July 21.
Scrums: London 5-2. Penalties: London 11-5. Crowd: 7819. Referee: John Connolly. Halftime: 14-all.

Pool B

Oldham 20 (Paul Davidson 2, Brett Goldsink tries; Luke Goodwin 4 goals) defeated **North Queensland** 16 (Ray Mercy, Luke Phillips, Paul Bowman tries; Phillips 2 goals) at Boundary Park, Friday night, July 18.
Scrums: 8-all. Penalties: Oldham 7-5. Crowd: 2961. Referee: Robert Connolly. Halftime: Oldham 10-8.

Leeds 22 (Damien Gibson, Phil Hassan, Paul Sterling tries; Iestyn Harris 5 goals) defeated **Adelaide** 14 (Solomon Kiri, Dean Schifilliti tries; Luke Williamson 3 goals) at Headingley, Friday night, July 18.
Scrums: Leeds 12-10. Penalties: Leeds 13-10. Crowd: 11,269. Referee: Russell Smith. Halftime: Leeds 8-0.

Hunter 26 (Keith Beauchamp 2, John Carlaw 2, Tony Iro, Kevin Iro tries; Noel Goldthorpe goal) defeated **Castleford** 8 (Jason Critchley, Chris Smith tries) at Topper Stadium, Sunday, July 20.
Scrums: Hunter 14-7. Penalties: Hunter 3-2. Crowd: 3379. Referee: Tim Mander. Halftime: Hunter 18-4.

Perth 48 (Wayne Evans 2, Shaun Devine, Chris Ryan, Darren Higgins, Fred Sapatu, Matthew Rodwell, Matt Geyer, John Wilshere tries; Devine 6 goals) defeated **Sheffield** 12 (Lynton Scott, Whetu Taewa tries; Mark Aston 2 goals) at WACA, Sunday, July 20.
Scrums: Sheffield 10-6. Penalties: Perth 8-6. Crowd: 7429. Referee: Stephen Clark. Halftime: Perth 24-6.

ROUND 5

Pool A

Auckland 70 (Gene Ngamu 3, Sean Hoppe 2, Lee Oudenryn 2, Syd Eru 2, Denis Betts, Marc Ellis, Stacey Jones tries; Matthew Ridge 11 goals) defeated **St Helens** 6 (Alan Hunte try; Bobbie Goulding goal) at Ericsson Stadium, Friday night, July 25.
Scrums: Auckland 8-3. Penalties: 8-all. Crowd: 18,500. Referee: Stephen Clark. Halftime: Auckland 36-0.

Cronulla 44 (Paul Green 2, Russell Richardson 2, Andrew Ettingshausen 2, Chris McKenna, Ben Sammut tries; Green 6 goals) defeated **Warrington** 0 at Shark Park, Saturday night, July 26.
Scrums: Cronulla 9-4. Penalties: Cronulla 10-5. Crowd: 6112. Referee: Tim Mander. Halftime: Cronulla 16-0.

Canberra 42 (Ben Kennedy 3, David Furner 2, Jason Croker, Ken Nagas, Bradley Clyde tries; Furner 4, Laurie Daley goals) defeated **Halifax** 12 (Karl Harrison, David Bouveng tries; Martin Pearson 2 goals) at Thrum Hall, Saturday, July 26.
Scrums: Halifax 9-6. Penalties: Halifax 12-6. Crowd: 3620. Referee: Robert Connolly. Halftime: Canberra 20-6.

Brisbane 34 (Wendell Sailor 2, Darren Smith 2, Anthony Mundine 2, Kevin Walters tries; Darren Lockyer 3 goals) defeated **London** 16 (Peter Gill, Scott Roskell, Nick Mardon tries; Greg Barwick 2 goals) at The Stoop, Sunday July 27.
Scrums: London 6-2. Penalties: Brisbane 6-4. Crowd: 9846. Referee: Stuart Cummings. Halftime: Brisbane 16-6.

Penrith 54 (Ryan Girdler 2, Peter Jorgensen, Craig Gower, Andrew Hinson, Bobby Thompson, Matt Adamson, Darren Brown, Danny Farrar tries; Girdler 9 goals) defeated **Bradford** 14 (Danny Peacock, Matt Calland, Mike Forshaw tries; Andy Hodgson goal) at Penrith Football Stadium, Monday night, July 28.
Scrums: Bradford 4-3. Penalties: Penrith 14-4. Crowd: 5336. Referee: Bill Harrigan. Halftime: Penrith 22-6.

Wigan 31 (Kris Radlinski, Andy Farrell, Jason Robinson, Neil Cowie, Gary Connolly tries; Andy Farrell 5 goals; Farrell field goal) defeated **Canterbury** 24 (Daryl Halligan 2, Simon Gillies, Robert Mears tries; Halligan 4 goals) at Central Park, Monday night, July 28.
Scrums: 7-all. Penalties: Wigan 13-8. Crowd: 10,280. Referee: Russell Smith. Halftime: Canterbury 18-12.

Pool B

Adelaide 18 (Wayne Simonds, Steve Stone, Danny Grimley tries; Luke Williamson 3 goals) defeated **Oldham** 2 (Luke Goodwin goal) at Boundary Park, Friday night, July 25.
Scrums: Adelaide 13-7. Penalties: Oldham 9-7. Crowd: 3513. Referee: John Connolly. Halftime: Adelaide 6-2.

North Queensland 24 (Luke Phillips, Ray Mercy, Owen Cunningham, John Skandon tries; Phillips 4 goals) defeated **Salford** 14 (Darren Rogers, Peter Edwards tries; Steve Blakeley 3 goals) at The Willows, Saturday, July 26.
Scrums: North Queensland 8-4. Penalties: North Queensland 8-7. Crowd: 6448. Referee: Steve

SUPER LEAGUE WORLD CLUB CHALLENGE

Presley. Halftime: North Queensland 12-8.

Hunter 32 (Scott Hill 2, Gavin Thompson 2, Kevin Iro, Willie Poching tries; Richard Swain 3, Tim Maddison goals) defeated **Paris-St Germain** 0 at Topper Stadium, Sunday July 27.

Scrums: Hunter 7-5. Penalties: 5-all. Crowd: 2110. Referee: Graham Annesley. Halftime: Hunter 4-0.

Perth 24 (Mark Geyer, Shaun Devine, Matt Geyer tries; Devine 6 goals) defeated **Castleford** 14 (Jason Roach, Jason Flowers, Jason Critchley tries; Graham Steadman goal) at WACA, Sunday, July 27.

Scrums: Castleford 13-8. Penalties: Perth 6-3. Crowd: 6114. Referee: Brian Grant. Halftime: Perth 20-0.

ROUND 6

Pool A

Canterbury 44 (Mitch Newton 2, Shane Marteene, Simon Gillies, Robert Mears, Hazem El Masri, John Timu, Rod Silva tries; Daryl Halligan 6 goals) defeated **London** 22 (Wes Cotton 2, Shaun Edwards, Kim Howard tries; Greg Barwick 3 goals) at The Stoop, Friday night, August 1.

Scrums: Canterbury 6-4. Penalties: Canterbury 8-4. Crowd: 6923. Referee: John Connolly. Halftime: Canterbury 24-6.

Cronulla 40 (Russell Richardson, Mat Rogers, Chris McKenna, Adam Dykes, Tawera Nikau, Andrew Ettingshausen, Brett Howland tries; Rogers 6 goals) defeated **Bradford** 12 (Graeme Bradley 2 tries; Steve McNamara 2 goals) at Shark Park, Saturday night, August 2.

Scrums: Bradford 9-8. Penalties: Cronulla 10-5. Crowd: 8272. Referee: Brian Grant. Halftime: Cronulla 24-0.

Canberra 50 (Ken Nagas 2, Royston Lightning 2, Noa Nadruku, Albert Fulivai, Ruben Wiki, Ben Kennedy, Jason Burnham tries; Lightning 5, David Furner 2 goals) defeated **Wigan** 10 (Simon Haughton try; Andy Farrell 3 goals) at Central Park, Saturday, August 2.

Scrums: Canberra 7-5. Penalties: Canberra 9-3. Crowd: 12,504. Referee: Steve Presley. Halftime: Canberra 20-10.

Auckland 16 (Stephen Kearney, Stacey Jones, Syd Eru tries; Matthew Ridge 2 goals) defeated **Warrington** 4 (Ian Knott try) at Lancaster Park, Christchurch, Sunday, August 3.

Scrums: 11-all. Penalties: Auckland 9-2. Crowd: 8500. Referee: Graham Annesley. Halftime: Auckland 12-0.

Penrith 32 (Ryan Girdler 2, Tony Puletua, Steve Carter, Sid Domic, Craig Gower tries; Girdler 4 goals) defeated **St Helens** 26 (Anthony Sullivan, Andy Haigh, Danny Arnold, Keiron Cunningham, Sean Long tries; Bobbie Goulding 3 goals) at Penrith Football Stadium, Monday night, August 4.

Scrums: St Helens 10-6. Penalties: Penrith 2-1. Crowd: 5053. Referee: Bill Harrigan. Halftime: Penrith 20-10.

Brisbane 54 (Steve Renouf 4, Wendell Sailor 3, Shane Webcke, John Plath, Gorden Tallis tries; Darren Lockyer 7 goals) defeated **Halifax** 10 (Fereti Tuialgi, Kevin O'Loughlin tries; Martin Pearson goal) at Thrum Hall, Monday night, August 4.

Scrums: Brisbane 11-2. Penalties: Halifax 8-2. Crowd: 3255. Referee: Robert Connolly. Halftime: Brisbane 20-0.

Pool B

Perth 30 (Matt Fuller 2, Greg Fleming, Chris Ryan, Matt Geyer tries; Shaun Devine 4, Damian Chapman goals) defeated **Paris-St Germain** 12 (Phil Bergman, Jason Martin tries; Matt O'Connor 2 goals) at WACA, Friday night, August 1.

Scrums: Perth 12-8. Penalties: Paris 8-6. Crowd: 5960. Referee: Tim Mander. Halftime: Perth 18-8.

Hunter 58 (Brad Godden 2, Nick Zisti 2, Anthony Brann 2, Neil Piccinelli, Noel Goldthorpe, Willie Poching, Robbie Ross, Brett Kimmorley tries; Richard Swain 7 goals) defeated **Sheffield** 12 (Darren Turner, Jean-Marc Garcia tries; Mark Aston 2 goals) at Topper Stadium, Sunday August 3.

Scrums: Hunter 5-4. Penalties: Hunter 11-7. Crowd: 1965. Referee: Stephen Clark. Halftime: Hunter 24-8.

North Queensland 48 (Andrew Dunemann 2, Luke Phillips 2, Ray Mercy, Reggie Cressbrook, Glen Murphy, Mark Shipway tries; Phillips 8 goals) defeated **Leeds** 14 (Adrian Morley, Gary Mercer (penalty) tries; Graham Holroyd 3 goals) at Headingley, Sunday, August 3.

Scrums: North Queensland 8-5. Penalties: North Queensland 6-5. Crowd: 12,224. Referee: Russell Smith. Halftime: North Queensland 18-8.

Salford 14 (Darren Rogers try; Steve Blakeley 4 goals; Mark Lee 2 field goals) defeated **Adelaide** 12 (Chris Quinn, Danny Grimley tries; Kurt Wrigley 2 goals) at The Willows, Sunday, August 3.

Scrums: Adelaide 6-5. Penalties: Adelaide 9-4. Crowd: 6995. Referee: Stuart Cummings. Halftime: Adelaide 12-8.

WORLD CLUB CHALLENGE — FINAL STANDINGS

Australasia Pool A

	P	W	L	D	F	A	Pts	+/-
BRISBANE	6	6	-	-	270	52	12	218
AUCKLAND	6	6	-	-	268	82	12	186
CRONULLA	6	6	-	-	230	54	12	176
PENRITH	6	6	-	-	256	120	12	136
CANBERRA	6	5	1	-	302	108	10	194
CANTERBURY	6	4	2	-	218	121	8	97

Europe Pool B

	P	W	L	D	F	A	Pts	+/-
WIGAN	6	2	4	-	89	212	4	-123
LONDON	6	1	5	-	136	238	2	-102
BRADFORD	6	-	6	-	82	228	-	-146
ST HELENS	6	-	6	-	96	270	-	-174
WARRINGTON	6	-	6	-	78	256	-	-178
HALIFAX	6	-	6	-	56	340	-	-284

Australasia Pool B

	P	W	L	D	F	A	Pts	+/-
HUNTER	6	6	-	-	226	50	12	176
NORTH QLD	6	5	1	-	228	92	10	136
ADELAIDE	6	4	2	-	170	66	8	104
PERTH	6	4	2	-	148	104	8	44

Europe Pool B

	P	W	L	D	F	A	Pts	+/-
PARIS	4	1	3	-	48	90	6	-42
LEEDS	4	1	3	-	64	138	6	-74
OLDHAM	4	1	3	-	52	130	6	-78
SALFORD	4	1	3	-	42	130	6	-88
SHEFFIELD	4	1	3	-	54	168	6	-114
CASTLEFORD	4	-	4	-	52	116	4	-64

The Australasian qualifiers were the top three Pool A teams, plus the top team in Pool B.

The European qualifiers were the top three Pool A teams, plus the fourth Pool A team, St Helens, who won a play-off against the top Pool B team, Paris-St Germain.

Play-off

St Helens 42 (Joey Hayes 2, Chris Morley, Alan Hunte, Sean Long, Anthony Sullivan, Koiron Cunningham, Andy Haigh tries; Long 5 goals) defeated **Paris-St Germain** 4 (Shaun Mahoney try) at Knowsley Road, Wednesday, August 13. Crowd: 3641.

Quarter-Finals

Auckland 62 (Sean Hoppe 2, Matthew Ridge 2, Stacey Jones, Syd Eru, Logan Swann, Brady Malam, Anthony Swann, Gene Ngamu, Marc Ellis tries; Ridge 9 goals) defeated **Bradford** 14 (Abi Ekoku, Graeme Bradley tries; Steve McNamara 3 goals) at Ericsson Stadium, Friday night, October 3.
Scrums: Auckland 7-5. Penalties: Bradford 10-9. Crowd: 12,063. Referee: Bill Harrigan. Halftime: Auckland 20-14.

Brisbane 66 (Steve Renouf 5, Gorden Tallis 2, Shane Webcke 2, Anthony Mundine 2, Andrew Gee tries; Ben Walker 5, Michael Devere 4 goals) defeated **St Helens** 12 (Alan Hunte,

Simon Booth tries; Sean Long 2 goals) at ANZ Stadium, Saturday night, October 4.
Scrums: Brisbane 14-3. Penalties: Brisbane 6-2. Crowd: 6438. Referee: Stephen Clark. Halftime: Brisbane 32-0.

Hunter 22 (Nick Zisti 2, John Carlaw, Scott Hill, Richard Swain tries; Kevin Iro goal) defeated **Wigan** 18 (Danny Ellison 2, Kris Radlinski tries; Andy Farrell 3 goals) at Central Park, Saturday, October 4.
Crowd: 9563. Referee: Russell Smith. Halftime: Wigan 10-4.

Cronulla 40 (Sean Ryan 3, Russell Richardson 2, David Peachey 2, Mat Rogers tries; Rogers 4 goals) defeated **London** 16 (Tony Martin 2, Butch Fatnowna tries; Martin, Terry Matterson goals) at The Stoop, Monday night, October 6. Crowd: 6239. Halftime: Cronulla 16-10.

Semi-Finals

Brisbane 22 (Ben Walker 2, Kevin Walters, Gorden Tallis tries; Walker 3 goals) defeated **Auckland** 16 (Lee Oudenryn 2, Shane Endacott tries; Matthew Ridge 2 goals) at ANZ Stadium, Friday night, October 10.
Scrums: Auckland 8-6. Penalties: 6-all. Crowd: 9686. Referee: Graham Annesley. Halftime: 10-all.

Hunter 22 (Brett Kimmorley 2, Nick Zisti, Darrien Doherty tries; Kevin Iro 2, Richard Swain goals) defeated **Cronulla** 18 (Mat Rogers, Andrew Ettingshausen, Russell Richardson tries; Rogers 3 goals) at Shark Park, Saturday night, October 11.
Scrums: 9-all. Penalties: Cronulla 4-2. Crowd: 5214. Referee: Bill Harrigan. Halftime: 12-all.

Final

Brisbane 36 (D.Smith 3, K.Walters, J.Plath, W.Sailor, S.Renouf tries; M.Devere 3, B.Walker goals) defeated **Hunter** 12 (N.Zisti 2, J.Carlaw tries; Swain goals) at Ericsson Stadium, Friday night, October 17.
Scrums: Brisbane 9-4. Penalties: Hunter 5-3. Crowd: 10,000. Referee: Graham Annesley. Halftime: Brisbane 26-4. Goalkickers: Devere (Brisbane) 3/5, Walker (Brisbane) 1/2, K.Iro (Hunter) 0/2, Swain (Hunter) 0/2.

BRISBANE: Darren Lockyer; Michael Devere, Steve Renouf, Darren Smith, Wendell Sailor; Kevin Walters, Allan Langer (c); Andrew Gee, John Plath, Shane Webcke, Gorden Tallis, Brad Thorn, Peter Ryan. Interchange: Michael Hancock, Philip Lee, Tonie Carroll, Ben Walker.

HUNTER: Robbie Ross; Nick Zisti, Brad Godden, Kevin Iro, John Carlaw; Scott Hill, Brett Kimmorley; Anthony Brann, Robbie McCormack (c), Troy Stone, Darrien Doherty, Paul Marquet, Tyran Smith. Interchange: Tim Maddison, Richard Swain, Keith Beauchamp, Tony Iro.

AUSTRALIA-NEW ZEALAND SUPER LEAGUE TESTS

Anzac battles split

Anzac Day Test
Australia 34, New Zealand 22
Sydney Football Stadium, April 25

Return Test match
New Zealand 30, Australia 12
North Harbour Stadium, Sept 26

Australia's Super League side made light work of their first foray into the international arena with a thumping 34-22 defeat of a more experienced New Zealand outfit in the Anzac Day Test at the Sydney Football Stadium. Eleven members of the Australian squad of 17 made their debut at international level.

Captained by Laurie Daley, Australia went to the break leading 20-0.

New Zealand did make a bold fightback after halftime, thanks mainly to halfback Stacey Jones.

The staging of the match on Anzac Day and the use of Anzac imagery to promote the match drew heavy criticism in some quarters. A moderate crowd of 23,829 attended.

New Zealand reversed their Anzac Day loss to the Australians with a crushing 30-12 win at Auckland's North Harbour Stadium in a Test played six days after the Super League grand final.

The New Zealanders outmuscled and out-manouevered the inexperienced Australian line-up for virtually the entire match. In fact, fullback Darren Lockyer was the only Australian player to survive the match with his reputation intact. Australian forward Craig Greenhill was placed on report by English referee Russell Smith after an ugly first-half punch-up with second-rower Stephen Kearney, while several Australian players finished the worst for wear after copping a battering from their Trans-Tasman rivals.

Australia 34 (W.Sailor 2, D.Furner 2, D.Smith, C.Gower tries; R.Girdler 5 goals) defeated **New Zealand** 22 (S.Jones, D.Halligan, S.Hoppe, R.Paul tries; Halligan 3 goals) at Sydney Football Stadium, Friday night, April 25.
Scrums: Australia 6-5. Penalties: New Zealand 8-7. Crowd: 23,829. Referee: Stuart Cummins (England). Halftime: Australia 20-0. Goalkickers: Girdler (Australia) 5/7, Halligan (New Zealand) 3/4.
AUSTRALIA: David Peachey; Ken Nagas, Andrew Ettingshausen, Ryan Girdler, Wendell Sailor; Laurie Daley (c), Allan Langer; Glenn Lazarus, Craig Gower, Rodney Howe, Brad Thorn, David Furner, Darren Smith. Interchange: Paul Green, Julian O'Neill, Solomon Haumono, Matt Adamson.
NEW ZEALAND: Richard Barnett; Sean Hoppe, Ruben Wiki, John Timu, Daryl Halligan; Gene Ngamu, Stacey Jones; Grant Young, Syd Eru, Quentin Pongia, Tony Iro, Steve Kearney (c), Tawera Nikau. Interchange: Joe Vagana, Tyran Smith, Tea Ropati, Robbie Paul.

New Zealand 30 (S.Jones 2, S.Eru 2, M.Ridge, T.Iro tries; Ridge 3 goals) defeated **Australia** 12 (D.Lockyer 2 tries; R.Girdler 2 goals) at North Harbour, Friday night, September 26.
Scrums: Australia 4-3. Penalties: New Zealand 10-8. Crowd: 17,500. Referee: Russell Smith (England). Halftime: New Zealand 10-8. Goalkickers: Ridge (New Zealand) 3/6, Girdler (Australia) 2/2.
NEW ZEALAND: Matthew Ridge (c); Sean Hoppe, Richie Blackmore, Kevin Iro, Richard Barnett; Gene Ngamu, Stacey Jones; John Lomax, Syd Eru, Quentin Pongia, Tony Iro, Steve Kearney, Logan Swann. Interchange: Joe Vagana, Tyran Smith, Robbie Paul, John Timu.
AUSTRALIA: Darren Lockyer; Ken Nagas, Ryan Girdler, Steve Renouf, Wendell Sailor; Laurie Daley (c), Paul Green; Jason Stevens, Craig Gower, Brad Thorn, Matt Adamson, Bradley Clyde, Darren Smith. Interchange: Shane Webcke, Craig Greenhill, Brett Mullins, Luke Priddis.

AUSTRALIA-GREAT BRITAIN SUPER LEAGUE SERIES

Aussies prevail in three

Australian squad: Matt Adamson (Penrith), Bradley Clyde (Canberra), Laurie Daley (Canberra - c), Andrew Ettingshausen (Cronulla), Ryan Girdler (Penrith), Craig Gower (Penrith), Craig Greenhill (Cronulla), Robbie Kearns (Perth), Brett Kimmorley (Hunter), Danny Lee (Cronulla), Darren Lockyer (Brisbane), Brett Mullins (Canberra), Ken Nagas (Canberra), David Peachey (Cronulla), Luke Priddis (Canberra), Russell Richardson (Cronulla), Wendell Sailor (Brisbane), Darren Smith (Brisbane), Jason Stevens (Cronulla), Gorden Tallis (Brisbane), Brad Thorn (Brisbane), Steve Walters (North Queensland). Allan Langer (Brisbane), Steve Renouf (Brisbane) and Shane Webcke (Brisbane) were selected but withdrew through injury. Lee, Peachey and Priddis were their replacements.

FIRST TEST
Australia 38, Great Britain 14
Wembley Stadium, November 1

Australian captain Laurie Daley scored a hat-trick of tries before halftime to pave the way for his team's commanding 38-14 win over Great Britain in the first Test at Wembley Stadium. The Australians put aside the hoodoo that had afflicted previous touring teams to run in seven tries to their opponents' two.

Daley was in mesmerising touch, with tries in the 12th, 34th and 37th minutes as well as a hand in a number of others scored by the Australians, who looked primed from the outset to turn in a strong display.

Great Britain did well to reclaim the lead from the Australians at one point of the first half, but Daley's two tries in the lead-up to halftime ensured it was the visitors who were ahead at the break. Great Britain were unable to match the firepower of the Australian forwards, who created a strong platform from which Daley and his backs could dominate. Centre Ryan Girdler landed five goals and played an impressive support role to man-of-the-match Daley.

Australia 38 (L.Daley 3, B.Mullins 2, C.Gower, D.Smith tries; R.Girdler 5 goals) defeated **Great Britain** 14 (J.Robinson, J.Lowes tries; A.Farrell 3 goals) at Wembley Stadium, London, Saturday, November 1. Scrums: Great Britain 7-5. Penalties: Great Britain 8-5. Crowd: 41,135. Referee: Phil Houston (New Zealand). Halftime: Australia 22-14. Goalkickers: Girdler (Australia) 5/8, Farrell (Great Britain) 3/4.

AUSTRALIA: Lockyer; Mullins, Ettingshausen, Girdler, Sailor; Daley (c), Gower; Thorn, Walters, Stevens, Tallis, Adamson, Smith. Replacements: Kearns, Greenhill, Nagas, Kimmorley. Coach: John Lang.

GREAT BRITAIN: Jason Robinson; Alan Hunte, Kris Radlinski, Paul Newlove, Anthony Sullivan; Andy Farrell (c), Bobbie Goulding; Brian McDermott, James Lowes, Paul Broadbent, Mick Cassidy, Chris Joynt, Paul Sculthorpe. Replacements: Steve McNamara, Paul Atcheson, Adrian Morley, Dean Sampson. Coach: Andy Goodway.

SECOND TEST
Great Britain 20, Australia 12
Old Trafford, November 8

Australia were made to pay for a poorly disciplined performance in the second Test when they were beaten by a more enthusiastic and aggressive British side 20-12 at Old Trafford. Australian second-rower Gorden Tallis

AUSTRIALIA V GREAT BRITAIN   187

was the worst offender. He was penalised three times for high tackles before being placed on report and later sin-binned for back-chatting.

Great Britain were eager to atone for their disappointing effort in the first Test and began the match full of fire. The forward pack, roundly criticised after Wembley, laid a firm platform for the backs and quality tries followed to Andy Farrell in the first half and Jason Robinson in the second.

Australian captain Laurie Daley worked hard to settle his players but, with a young and inexperienced outfit, his messages often went unheeded.

Australia looked to be getting on top when halfback Craig Gower sent Steve Walters into a yawning gap and then Gower scored himself to reduce Great Britain's lead to four points inside the final 20 minutes. However, the tourists self-destructed when Tallis conceded a vital penalty and was then sin-binned and Darren Smith failed to hold a pass from replacement back Russell Richardson which, if held, would have meant a certain four points.

Great Britain 20 (A.Farrell, J.Robinson tries; Farrell 6 goals) defeated **Australia** 12 (S. Walters, C.Gower tries; D.Lockyer 2 goals) at Old Trafford, Manchester, Saturday, November 8.
Scrums: Australia 12-8. Penalties: Great Britain 13-10. Crowd: 40,324. Referee: Phil Houston (New Zealand). Halftime: Great Britain 10-6. Goalkickers: Farrell (Great Britain) 6/7, Lockyer (Australia) 2/3.
GREAT BRITAIN: Paul Atcheson; Jason Robinson, Kris Radlinski, Paul Newlove, Alan Hunte; Andy Farrell (c), Bobbie Goulding; Brian McDermott, James Lowes, Paul Broadbent, Adrian Morley, Chris Joynt, Paul Sculthorpe. Replacements: Simon Haughton, Mike Forshaw. Coach: Andy Goodway.
AUSTRALIA: Lockyer; Nagas, Ettingshausen, Mullins, Sailor; Daley (c), Gower; Thorn, Walters, Stevens, Tallis, Adamson, Smith. Replacements: Kearns, Greenhill, Richardson. Coach: John Lang.
Sin bin: Tallis (Australia).

THIRD TEST
Australia 37, Great Britain 20
Elland Road, November 16

Australia bounced back from their shock defeat at Old Trafford to wrap up Super League's three-Test series with a crushing 37-20 victory in the final Test, at Elland Road.

The Australians dominated from the outset, with the first try coming to Ken Nagas from a precision Laurie Daley kick after just 40 seconds play. Darren Lockyer created the extra-man for Wendell Sailor to score soon after and then a long Ryan Girdler break led to Sailor's second try in quick succession. Daley scored Australia's fourth try when British fullback Paul Atcheson lost possession in a tackle and Brad Thorn picked up a fifth before halftime.

When lock Darren Smith crossed soon after the resumption, the tourists looked primed for a record-breaking score. But with the series safely in their keeping, the Australians relaxed.

Australia 37 (W.Sailor 2, K.Nagas, L.Daley, B.Thorn, D.Smith, R.Kearns tries; R.Girdler 4 goals; D.Lockyer field goal) defeated **Great Britain** 20 (S.Haughton 2, J.Robinson tries; A.Farrell 4 goals) at Elland Road, Leeds, Sunday, November 16.
Scrums: 9-all. Penalties: Great Britain 13-6. Crowd: 39,337. Referee: Phil Houston (New Zealand). Halftime: Austria 25-2. Goalkickers: Girdler (Australia) 4/7, Farrell (Great Britain) 4/4.
AUSTRALIA: Lockyer; Nagas, Ettingshausen, Girdler, Sailor; Daley (c), Gower; Thorn, Walters, Stevens, Tallis, Clyde, Smith. Replacements: Kearns, Adamson, Kimmorley, Richardson. Coach: John Lang.
GREAT BRITAIN: Paul Atcheson; Jason Robinson, Kris Radlinski, Paul Newlove, Alan Hunte; Andy Farrell (c), Bobbie Goulding; Brian McDermott, James Lowes, Paul Broadbent, Adrian Morley, Chris Joynt, Paul Sculthorpe. Replacements: Simon Haughton, Mike Forshaw, Sean Long, Steve McNamara. Coach: Andy Goodway.
Sin bin: Smith (Australia).

Super League Clubs

ADELAIDE

Adelaide had a lot of reasons not to do well in 1997, but it would take only the most strident critic to suggest their year was not one of outstanding achievement. Thrown together in haste, Adelaide were the last club to join Super League for its inaugural season and with a limited pool of players from which to choose, they always appeared destined to struggle in their first year.

Establishing a club in parochial AFL territory only made the challenge greater.

By season's end the Rams had won six and drawn one of their 18 premiership matches to avoid the wooden spoon — a feat few believed they could achieve.

Even more impressive was the support the club was able to attract to its games at the Adelaide Oval. Despite having no 'home-grown' talent, the Rams drew average crowds of more than 15,500. The highlight was a bumper crowd of 27,435 which turned out to watch the club's first home game, against the Hunter Mariners. Spurred on by the massive support, the Rams repaid their new fans with a 10-8 victory. Ironically, though, it was one of only two premiership wins on home soil in 1997.

Their second came in their final match of the year with a 36-16 defeat of semi-final bound Penrith, a win that saw them leapfrog the North Queensland Cowboys and avoid the ignominy of finishing in last place on the ladder.

The Rams' four away victories came at the expense of semi-finalists Cronulla and Penrith, along with Auckland and Perth. Wins against Cronulla (29-18) and Penrith (22-16) were achieved in successive weeks early in the year and helped to establish the credibility of the newcomers.

Coach Rod Reddy, who had served a long apprenticeship in England and with St George in Sydney, did a good job to mould his players into a cohesive outfit, particularly with limited resources.

The Rams did not field a reserve-grade side, a situation which prevented players from obtaining match fitness if they were left out of the top-grade squad, or if they were making returns from injury.

Injuries cut deep into Reddy's squad,

PLAYERS RECORDS 1997

Player	App	Int	T	G	FG	Pts
Cameron Blair	15	1	3	-	-	12
David Boughton	13	1	1	-	-	4
Kevin Campion	11	3	1	-	-	4
Alan Cann	4	7	-	-	-	0
Mark Corvo	16	-	1	-	-	4
Jason Donnelly	6	-	-	-	-	0
Brett Galea	6	5	2	-	-	8
Danny Grimley	4	2	-	-	-	0
Andrew Hick	10	6	-	-	-	0
David Kidwell	2	-	-	-	-	0
Solomon Kiri	0	1	2	-	-	8
Michael Maguire	3	2	1	-	-	4
Bruce Mamando	-	15	4	-	-	16
Rod Maybon	13	-	5	-	-	20
Marty McKenzie	3	2	1	-	-	4
Elias Paiyo	2	6	-	-	-	0
Adam Peek	-	1	-	-	-	0
Andrew Pierce	12	2	1	-	-	4
Chris Quinn	13	4	1	-	-	4
Dean Schifilliti	10	4	-	-	-	0
Wayne Simonds	13	1	4	-	-	16
Steve Stone	7	7	3	-	-	12
Joe Tamani	13	1	4	-	-	16
Stuart Topper	6	-	1	-	-	4
Kerrod Walters	17	-	3	-	-	12
Luke Williamson	12	-	3	29	-	70
Kurt Wrigley	14	1	5	30	1	81
27 players	18		46	59	1	303

CAPTAINCY: Walters 17, Schifilliti 1

with fullback Rod Maybon (eight weeks) and winger Joe Tamani (six weeks) out for long periods. In addition, prop Bruce Mamando broke his leg in England during the World Club Challenge and team-mates Kevin Campion, Marty McKenzie, Jason Donnelly and Brett Galea were all sidelined for varying lengths of time.

Adelaide's best player in 1997 was front-rower Mark Corvo, who linked with the club after playing all his previous football in Canberra. He won a place in the top grade after the first couple of matches in 1997 and didn't look back. The club's best emerging talent was centre or five-eighth Luke Williamson. A Queenslander by birth, Williamson played 12 top-grade matches and impressed with his attacking talents as well as some accurate goalkicking. He represented Super League's Australian Under-19 side during the year.

The most disappointing aspects of the season for the fledgling Rams were a 58-16 pummelling at the hands of Canberra in Round 17 and a disappointing English leg of the club's World Club Challenge campaign. Undefeated in three matches against British clubs at the Adelaide Oval, the Rams slumped to defeats against Leeds and Salford to bow out of the tournament.

The Rams will be looking to new recruit, halfback Noel Goldthorpe, to provide on-field direction and leadership in 1998, while former Cronulla and Perth winger Matt Daylight and Auckland lower grader Meti Noovao should add some much-needed zip to the backline. The club released a number of players at the end of the 1997 season including Cameron Blair, Jason Donnelly, Solomon Kiri, Michael Maguire, Elias Paiyo, Kurt Wrigley and Stuart Topper.

MATCH RECORDS 1997

Played	Ground	Result	Score
North Qld	Stockland	Lost	16-24
Brisbane	ANZ	Lost	12-28
Hunter	Adelaide	Won	10-8
Auckland	Ericsson	Won	16-12
Perth	Adelaide	Lost	16-18
Canterbury	Belmore	Lost	22-34
Brisbane	Adelaide	Lost	10-20
Cronulla	Shark Park	Won	29-18
Penrith	Penrith	Won	22-16
North Qld	Adelaide	Drew	14-all
Canterbury	Adelaide	Lost	22-42
Canberra	Adelaide	Lost	18-34
Perth	WACA	Won	28-4
Hunter	Topper	Lost	2-10
Auckland	Adelaide	Lost	8-18
Cronulla	Adelaide	Lost	6-28
Canberra	Bruce	Lost	16-58
Penrith	Adelaide	Won	36-16

Played 18: won 6, lost 11, drew 1, for 303, against 402

REPRESENTATIVE PLAYERS
QUEENSLAND: Kevin Campion
WORLD CLUB CHALLENGE
Salford (Adelaide) won 50-8; Leeds (Adelaide) won 34-8, Oldham (Adelaide) won 42-14, Leeds (Headingley) lost 14-22, Oldham (Boundary Park) won 18-2, Salford (The Willows) lost 12-14. Played 6, won 4, lost 2, for 170, against 68.
First Grade 1997: Coach: Rod Reddy. Finished 9th.
Reserve Grade 1997: Did not field a side.

AUCKLAND

Success came late for the Auckland Warriors, who experienced a season of mixed fortunes both on and off the playing arena. The departure of chief executive Ian Robson and coach John Monie followed a period of instability and acrimony which saw the Warriors plunge to the premiership cellar.

The club were beaten in seven successive competition matches and only a late-season recovery helped them avoid finishing in last place. It took a crushing 50-22 defeat of North Queensland in the last match to stave off the wooden spoon.

The turning point for the Warriors came in the World Club Challenge competition, a competition pilloried by most, but viewed as a godsend by Auckland coach Frank Endacott.

It was during Auckland's three-week stint in England that the Warriors got together, out of the glare of the pervasive Auckland media spotlight, to work through their on-field deficiencies. The weaker standard of the British sides helped the Warriors regain their confidence and composure and the results were carried back to the Southern Hemisphere.

Endacott nominated the Warriors' 20-16 defeat of British champions Bradford as his club's most important win of the season. With a large and parochial Odsal Stadium crowd cheering on the locals, Auckland overcame the loss of hooker Syd Eru early in the game to score an outstanding win.

Returning to Australia, the Warriors breezed through their final three WCC matches and won four of their last five premiership games. The Warriors reached the semi-finals of the WCC before being eliminated by Brisbane in a high-quality match at ANZ Stadium.

Auckland officials are hoping the positive end-of-season results will provide the springboard to a far more successful 1998 season. Coach Endacott's faith in 'home-grown' talent will be tested in '98, with only one foreign player on the club's books– Australian winger Lee Oudenryn.

Former Canberra prop Quentin Pongia will add some necessary starch and experience to the Warriors' front row and he returns to his native New Zealand after five seasons in Australia's capital.

The Warriors will be hoping for a larger contribution from influential fullback Matthew Ridge, who missed half the 1997 season through injury. His leadership and experience are viewed as crucial components to a successful Auckland side. Second-rower Stephen Kearney performed admirably in Ridge's absence and he continued to display outstanding form, despite his club's roller-coaster season.

Missing in 1998 will be international forward Denis Betts, who announced his return to the north of England, despite still having two years of a five-year contract with the Warriors to run. Prop Mark Horo announced his retirement at the end of the season and props Grant Young and Hitro Okesene were released from the club.

Despite the up-and-down results of the season, the Warriors managed to attract average crowds of over 16,000 to Ericsson Stadium in 1997.

PLAYERS RECORDS 1997

Player	App	Int	T	G	FG	Pts
David Bailey	1	2	1	-	-	4
Denis Betts	14	-	3	-	-	12
Phil Blake	1	1	-	-	-	0
Steve Buckingham	-	2	-	-	-	0
Marc Ellis	16	-	5	25	1	71
Shane Endacott	6	3	1	-	-	4
Syd Eru	18	-	5	-	-	20
Awen Guttenbeil	1	3	-	-	-	0
Bryan Henare	5	6	1	-	-	4
Sean Hoppe	18	-	11	-	-	44
Mark Horo	8	7	-	-	-	0
Stacey Jones	18	-	7	-	1	29
Stephen Kearney	17	-	2	-	-	8
Brady Malam	9	6	-	-	-	0
Gene Ngamu	14	3	-	12	-	24
Meti Noovao	-	1	-	-	-	0
Hitro Okesene	-	1	-	-	-	0
Lee Oudenryn	4	1	4	-	-	16
Matthew Ridge	9	-	3	18	-	48
Iva Ropati	2	3	3	-	-	12
Tea Ropati	16	-	5	-	-	20
Jerry Seu Seu	-	1	-	-	-	0
Paul Staladi	3	1	1	-	-	4
Anthony Swann	18	-	2	-	-	8
Logan Swann	12	1	-	-	-	0
Tony Tuimavave	6	1	1	-	-	4
Joe Vagana	11	6	-	-	-	0
Aaron Whittaker	-	2	-	-	-	0
Grant Young	7	2	-	-	-	0
29 players	18		55	55	2	332

CAPTAINCY: Ridge 9, Kearney 8, Betts 1

SUPER LEAGUE CLUBS

REPRESENTATIVE PLAYERS

NEW ZEALAND (Tri-Series): Marc Ellis, Syd Eru, Sean Hoppe, Stacey Jones, Stephen Kearney, Brady Malam, Gene Ngamu, Tea Ropati, Anthony Swann, Joe Vagana.

NEW ZEALAND (Test): Syd Eru, Sean Hoppe, Stacey Jones, Stephen Kearney, Gene Ngamu, Matthew Ridge, Tea Ropati, Logan Swann, Joe Vagana, Grant Young.

WORLD CLUB CHALLENGE

St Helens (Knowsley Road) won 42-14, Bradford (Odsal) won 20-16, Warrington (Wilderspool) won 56-28, Bradford (Ericsson) won 64-14, St Helens (Ericsson) won 70-6, Warrington (Christchurch) won 16-4, Bradford (Ericsson, quarter-final) won 62-14, Brisbane (ANZ, semi-final) lost 16-22. Played 8, won 7, lost 1, for 346, against 118.

First Grade 1997: Coach: Frank Endacott (replaced John Monie). Finished 7th.

Reserve Grade 1997: Coach: John Ackland (replaced Frank Endacott). Finished 2nd.

MATCH RECORDS 1997

Played	Ground	Result	Score
Brisbane	ANZ	Lost	2-14
Hunter	Ericsson	Won	18-14
Cronulla	Shark Park	Lost	8-34
Adelaide	Ericsson	Lost	12-16
Penrith	Ericsson	Won	16-14
Canberra	Bruce	Won	31-24
Hunter	Breakers	Lost	10-18
Canterbury	Ericsson	Lost	24-38
North Qld	Stockland	Lost	22-30
Brisbane	Ericsson	Lost	18-34
Canberra	Ericsson	Lost	10-20
Perth	WACA	Lost	12-24
Penrith	Penrith	Lost	22-26
Cronulla	Ericsson	Won	11-8
Adelaide	Adelaide	Won	18-8
Canterbury	Belmore	Lost	18-40
Perth	Ericsson	Won	30-22
North Qld	Ericsson	Won	50-22

Played 18: won 7, lost 11, for 332, against 406l

BRISBANE

The Brisbane Broncos put three years of disappointments behind them in 1997 to win everything on offer to them. Super League premiers and World Club Challenge champs was the imposing bounty hauled in by Wayne Bennett's team during one of the club's most successful seasons.

In 29 matches in both competitions, the Broncos lost only three times. They went through the World Club Challenge competition undefeated and won their last seven premiership matches, culminating in an emphatic 26-8 grand final victory over Cronulla at ANZ Stadium. For the first time in the club's history, they went through the season undefeated on home soil, winning 14 and drawing one of 15 matches at ANZ Stadium.

It was a powerful turnaround by the Broncos, who had been bundled out of the ARL final series for three successive seasons following their premiership victories of 1992 and 1993.

In a Super League competition in which only Cronulla and Canberra could have been labelled as genuine threats to their supremacy, the Broncos showed determination from the outset to claim the major prizes on offer. They won their first seven games, before a mini-slump during the representative season saw them win only two of their next six matches. During the period, they suffered their first defeat (27-26) in a highly entertaining game against Penrith, drew 20-all with North Queensland at ANZ Stadium after leading 20-8 with three minutes to play, were stunned 24-6 by the Hunter Mariners at Breakers Stadium and were thumped 32-4 by Cronulla at Shark Park.

The 28-point loss to Cronulla was a humbling experience and it served as a reality check for the club in the lead-up to the big end-of-season games. From that point, the Broncos advanced to win 13 games straight on the way to collecting the two pieces of silverware. When they next met Cronulla, in the major semi-final at Stockland Stadium in , the Broncos produced their most brilliant effort of the season. In an unparalleled 40-minute period, the Broncos destroyed Cronulla's hopes to lead 30-2, before finally winning the match 34-2.

The grand final was a closer contest, but in the end Brisbane, playing in front of 58,912 people at ANZ Stadium, had far too much class and claimed the title with a 26-8 win.

Their run home was not without its difficulties, with prop Glenn Lazarus missing after breaking his leg during the British section of their World Club Challenge campaign, and inspirational captain Allan Langer struggling through with a restrictive groin injury.

The loss of Lazarus brought out the best in young prop Shane Webcke, who graduated to Australian Super League honours late in the year, and also produced improved efforts from forwards such as Brad Thorn, Peter Ryan and Gorden Tallis.

They will have to get on with business without Lazarus on a permanent basis in 1998 when the experienced international heads to Melbourne to head up the game's newest team. Also missing will be utility player Anthony Mundine, who had difficulty settling in with the Broncos and returns to St George in 1998.

The Broncos have opted not to add to their playing roster, instead they will be relying on the wealth of talent already on hand. The brightest star in 1997 was undoubtedly 20-year-old fullback Darren Lockyer, who developed into a player of world class.

MATCH RECORDS 1997

Played	Ground	Result	Score
Auckland	ANZ	Won	14-2
Adelaide	ANZ	Won	28-12
Perth	WACA	Won	26-16
Canberra	ANZ	Won	24-8
Cronulla	ANZ	Won	14-12
North Qld	Stockland	Won	42-16
Adelaide	Adelaide	Won	20-10
Penrith	Penrith	Lost	26-27
Canterbury	ANZ	Won	34-16
Auckland	Ericsson	Won	34-18
North Qld	ANZ	Drew	20-all
Hunter	Topper	Lost	6-24
Cronulla	Shark Park	Lost	4-32
Perth	ANZ	Won	50-14
Canberra	Bruce	Won	19-4
Penrith	ANZ	Won	54-12
Hunter	ANZ	Won	34-16
Canterbury	Belmore	Won	32-24
CRONULLA	STOCKLAND	WON	34-2
CRONULLA	ANZ	WON	26-8

Played 20: won 16, lost 3, drawn 1, for 541, against 293

His maturity and composure under pressure brought comparisons with Wally Lewis and Allan Langer at the same age and he is expected to fill Langer's mantle as the club's most dominant player in the coming years.

Other youngsters to show vast improvement in 1997 included winger Michael Devere, who kept Michael Hancock out of first grade for much of the season, centre Tonie Carroll, who represented Queensland in the Tri-Series, and young halfback Ben Walker, who earned his chance when Langer

PLAYERS RECORDS 1997

Player	App	Int	T	G	FG	Pts
Tonie Carroll	13	6	6	-	-	24
Michael Devere	10	5	7	2	-	32
John Driscoll	15	3	-	-	-	0
Andrew Gee	15	5	1	-	-	4
Michael Hancock	9	5	5	-	-	20
Allan Langer	18	-	5	-	1	21
Glenn Lazarus	14	1	-	-	-	0
Philip Lee	-	7	1	-	-	4
Darren Lockyer	20	-	7	70	-	168
Anthony Mundine	9	2	3	-	-	12
John Plath	2	17	3	-	-	12
Steve Renouf	15	-	14	-	-	56
Peter Ryan	14	5	6	-	-	24

Player	App	Int	T	G	FG	Pts
Wendell Sailor	20	-	15	-	-	60
Dennis Scott	-	4	-	-	-	0
Darren Smith	17	2	8	-	-	32
Gorden Tallis	18	1	3	-	-	12
Brad Thorn	19	1	4	-	-	16
Ben Walker	-	6	-	-	-	0
Shane Walker	-	2	-	-	-	0
Kevin Walters	20	-	0	-	-	0
Shane Webcke	12	6	3	-	-	12
22 players	20	-	99	72	1	541

CAPTAINCY: Langer 18, Walters 2

SUPER LEAGUE CLUBS

was battling his groin injury late in the year.

Despite their record year, the Broncos' home crowds for the regular season slipped 16 percent on 1996 figures, to average just under 20,000 for the year. A number of home crowds during the World Club Challenge fell below 10,000.

REPRESENTATIVE PLAYERS
NSW: Glenn Lazarus.
QUEENSLAND: Tonie Carroll, Andrew Gee, Michael Hancock, Allan Langer, Darren Lockyer, Steve Renouf, Peter Ryan, Wendell Sailor, Darren Smith, Gorden Tallis, Brad Thorn, Kevin Walters, Shane Webcke.
AUSTRALIA: Allan Langer, Glenn Lazarus, Darren Lockyer, Steve Renouf, Wendell Sailor, Darren Smith, Gorden Tallis, Brad Thorn, Shane Webcke.

WORLD CLUB CHALLENGE
London (ANZ) won 42-22, Wigan (ANZ) won 34-0, Halifax (ANZ) won 76-0, Wigan (Central Park) won 30-4, London (The Stoop) won 34-16, Halifax (Thrum Hall) won 54-10, St Helens (ANZ, quarter-final) won 66-12, Auckland (ANZ, semi-final) won 22-16, Hunter Mariners (Ericsson, final) won 36-12. Played 9, won 9, for 394, against 92.

First Grade 1997: Coach Wayne Bennett. Finished 1st.
Reserve Grade 1997: Coach Ivan Henjak. Finished 6th.

CANBERRA

Life was difficult for the Canberra Raiders in the winter of 1997, when off-field disruptions, a horror injury crisis and a team under pressure made every game a battle of survival in the Super League competition.

New coach Mal Meninga felt the blowtorch of media scrutiny from the outset of his coaching career. A new order in the nation's capital, combined with a series of early injuries left the Raiders languishing at the tail of the Super League field after the first six weeks of the competition. Consecutive losses to Cronulla, Penrith, Canterbury and Brisbane saw knives sharpened for Meninga, who had stepped into the top-grade arena with no previous coaching experience.

The recovery began at Penrith in Round 7 when the Raiders ground out a 30-20 win over the Panthers. Over the next 11 rounds of the competition, Canberra was beaten only twice and their effort in qualifying for the finals in third place was a credit to the team's determination.

The Raiders began the year without representative players Brett Mullins and Jason Croker and had key players Ricky Stuart and Bradley Clyde returning from long-term injuries. This undoubtedly contributed to the dismal start. And although these players returned to play important roles in the Raiders' resurgence, the Green Machine could not shake their injury curse.

In a short space of time they lost Noa Nadruku, Graham Appo, Damon Booby and Queensland Rugby Union recruit Barry Lea with long-term injuries

MATCH RECORDS 1997

Played	Ground	Result	Score
Cronulla	Stadium	Lost	4-26
Penrith	Bruce	Lost	20-33
Canterbury	Belmore	Lost	26-38
Brisbane	ANZ	Lost	8-24
Hunter	Bruce	Won	18-12
Auckland	Bruce	Lost	24-31
Penrith	Penrith	Won	30-20
North Qld	Bruce	Won	40-16
Perth	Bruce	Won	30-10
Cronulla	Bruce	Won	22-8
Auckland	Ericsson	Won	20-10
Adelaide	Adelaide	Won	34-18
Hunter	Topper	Lost	12-16
Canterbury	Bruce	Won	28-10
Brisbane	Bruce	Lost	4-19
North Qld	Stockland	Won	22-14
Adelaide	Bruce	Won	58-16
Perth	WACA	Won	36-16
CRONULLA	SHARK PARK	LOST	18-22
PENRITH	BRUCE	WON	32-12
CRONULLA	SHARK PARK	LOST	4-10

Played 21: won 12, lost 9, for 490, against 381

and had Kiwi prop Quentin Pongia outed through suspension. By the time Canberra played in the preliminary final against Cronulla at Shark Park, injuries had cost them the services of David Furner, David Westley, Ruben Wiki, Quentin Pongia and Ben Kennedy. The Raiders' season ended that night, despite a brave showing, with a 10-4 loss to the Sharks.

The club's off-field dramas centred around a long-running dispute between club chief executive Kevin Neil and captain Ricky Stuart. Tensions which had bubbled beneath the surface for much of the year came to a head at the end of the season when Stuart was stripped of the club's captaincy in favour of five-eighth Laurie Daley. For a time it seemed Stuart would leave the club, but a series of meetings appeared to settle the issue.

Another drama which enveloped the club brought further negative publicity at the end of the year.

Winger Noa Nadruku's acquittal on two assault charges because a magistrate ruled he was 'too drunk' to form an intent sparked national outrage and led to Raiders' management cancelling Nadruku's contract. The Fijian winger had been a star performer for the Raiders since 1993 and scored over 70 top-grade tries for the club.

On the positive side was the continued resounding form of champion five-eighth Laurie Daley, who again confirmed his status as one of the superstars of Rugby League. He took out Super League's official player-of-the-year award and regularly inspired the Raiders to victory.

Teenage hooker Luke Priddis emerged from obscurity to win a place in the NSW Tri-Series team after only a few top-grade matches and late in the year he was further rewarded with selection in Super League's Australian team.

The Raiders ran up almost 200 points in three World Club Challenge matches at Bruce Stadium, including a 70-6 annihilation of Halifax, before losing their way with a 38-18 loss to the London Broncos in London. Coach Mal Meninga described the team's display that day as the worst in his 12 years with the club.

At season's end, the Raiders farewelled prop Quentin Pongia after five years with the club. He returns to his native New Zealand to link with the Auckland Warriors. Canberra's side of a swap deal landed them promising junior New Zealand representative Lesley Vainikolo.

PLAYERS RECORDS 1997

Player	App	Int	T	G	FG	Pts	Player	App	Int	T	G	FG	Pts
David Atkins	-	3	-	-	-	0	Brett Mullins	14	1	10	-	-	40
Damon Booby	2	-	2	-	-	8	Noa Nadruku	14	-	7	-	-	28
David Boyle	10	1	2	-	-	8	Ken Nagas	18	-	5	-	-	20
Jason Burnham	7	12	-	-	-	0	Craig O'Neall	4	1	1	3	-	10
Bradley Clyde	19	-	1	-	-	4	Todd Payten	1	10	1	-	-	4
Jason Croker	6	4	2	-	-	8	Quentin Pongia	13	1	-	-	-	0
Laurie Daley	21	-	5	7	2	36	Luke Priddis	18	2	7	-	-	28
Luke Davico	12	5	1	-	-	4	Ben Rauter	-	1	-	-	-	0
Albert Fulivai	5	-	3	-	-	12	Darren Shaw	-	2	-	-	-	0
David Furner	18	-	5	48	-	116	Ricky Stuart	16	-	2	-	-	8
Matt Gaffa	1	1	-	-	-	0	Tim Van Dalen	-	2	-	-	-	0
Brett Hetherington	16	1	1	-	-	4	David Westley	5	0	1	-	-	4
Ben Kennedy	15	3	15	-	-	60	Ruben Wiki	16	-	5	-	-	20
Barry Lea	-	1	-	-	-	0	Simon Woolford	4	16	4	-	-	16
Royston Lightning	10	-	5	9	-	38	31 players	21		88	68	2	490
Andrew McFadden	2	1	1	-	-	4							
Geoff McNamara	6	-	2	1	-	10	CAPTAINCY. Stuart 16, Daley 5						

SUPER LEAGUE CLUBS

REPRESENTATIVE PLAYERS
NSW: Bradley Clyde, Laurie Daley, David Furner, Brett Mullins, Ken Nagas, Luke Priddis
NEW ZEALAND (Tri-Series): Quentin Pongia, Ruben Wiki
AUSTRALIA: Bradley Clyde, Laurie Daley, David Furner, Brett Mullins, Ken Nagas, Luke Priddis
NEW ZEALAND (Test): Quentin Pongia, Ruben Wiki

WORLD CLUB CHALLENGE
Halifax (Bruce) won 70-6, London (Bruce) 66-20, Wigan (Bruce) 56-22, London (The Stoop) lost 18-38, Halifax (Thrum Hall) won 42-12, Wigan (Central Park) won 50-10. Played 6, won 5, lost 1, for 302, against 108.

First Grade 1997: Coach Mal Meninga. Finished 3rd. **Reserve Grade 1997:** Coach Gary Greinke. Finished 7th.

CANTERBURY

Canterbury will enter a new era in 1998 following the departure of coach Chris Anderson, the man who has prepared the club from the start of the decade. Those who watched the Bulldogs in 1997 will suggest the time was right for change after the club's proud defensive record took a battering during the season.

The Bulldogs may have qualified for the finals, but they were a long way short of the standard set by premiers Brisbane and grand finalists Cronulla.

A club which established a reputation in the 1980s for its fearsome defensive style was a pale shadow of its former self. From conceding an average of 15 points per game in their 1995 premiership year, the Bulldogs allowed over 24 per game in 1997. Instead of intimidating their rivals as they did in the '80s, the Bulldogs presented their opponents with simple tryscoring opportunities.

In two matches against the Broncos, Canterbury conceded 66 points. They allowed Penrith to score 44 a fortnight before the finals, conceded 36 points to the Hunter Mariners (but still won) and 34 points to Perth.

Super League's accelerated play-the-ball undoubtedly affected Canterbury and their defensive patterns more than any other team. Captain Simon Gillies was regularly at loggerheads with referees over the interpretation of the play-the-balls and the team finished on the wrong end of the penalty count more often than not.

It was a frustrating year for the club and for Anderson in particular. After a long association with the Bulldogs which stretched back to 1970, Anderson reluctantly severed his ties with the club in September, to take up residence at Melbourne Storm. Reports of political in-fighting involving Anderson and the influential Hughes family is said to have hastened Anderson's decision.

On the positive side, Canterbury provided Super League's two leading tryscorers in centre Matt Ryan (17) and exciting Lebanese winger Hazem El Masri (16). Ryan left a nightmare run of injuries behind him to play every match

MATCH RECORDS 1997

Played	Ground	Result	Score
Hunter	Breakers	Won	20-16
Cronulla	Belmore	Lost	12-13
Canberra	Belmore	Won	38-26
Perth	Perth	Lost	6-34
North Qld	Belmore	Lost	14-16
Adelaide	Belmore	Won	34-22
Cronulla	Shark Park	Won	16-6
Auckland	Ericsson	Won	38-24
Brisbane	ANZ	Lost	16-34
Hunter	Belmore	Won	48-36
Adelaide	Adelaide	Won	42-22
Penrith	Belmore	Lost	20-28
North Qld	Stockland	Won	29-22
Canberra	Bruce	Lost	10-28
Perth	Belmore	Won	38-26
Auckland	Belmore	Won	40-18
Penrith	Penrith	Lost	8-44
Brisbane	Belmore	Lost	24-32
PENRITH	BELMORE	LOST	14-15

Played 19: won 10, lost 9, for 467, against 462

RUGBY LEAGUE 1998

PLAYERS RECORDS 1997

Player	App	Int	T	G	FG	Pts
Barry Berrigan	3	12	1	-	-	4
Darren Britt	14	1	-	-	-	0
Hazem El Masri	19	-	16	-	-	64
Simon Gillies	19	-	6	-	-	24
Tony Grimaldi	-	1	-	-	-	0
Daryl Halligan	19	-	6	79	-	182
Solomon Haumono	12	5	4	-	-	16
Jason Hetherington	11	-	3	-	-	12
Glen Hughes	11	1	-	-	-	0
Shane Marteene	7	3	3	-	-	12
Duncan McRae	7	-	1	-	-	4
Robert Mears	8	2	6	-	-	24
Paul Mellor	-	2	-	-	-	0
Mitch Newton	12	6	-	-	-	0
Travis Norton	12	1	1	-	-	4
James Pickering	1	2	-	-	-	0
Craig Polla-Mounter	17	-	1	-	1	5
Steve Price	13	2	2	-	-	8
Steve Reardon	7	2	-	-	-	0
Robert Relf	4	15	3	-	-	12
Matthew Ryan	19	-	17	-	-	68
Kevin Schraader	-	2	-	-	-	0
Rod Silva	13	1	7	-	-	28
Michael Smith	-	5	-	-	-	0
John Timu	17	-	-	-	-	0
Barry Ward	2	8	-	-	-	0
26 players	19		77	79	1	467

CAPTAINCY: Gillies 19

for the Bulldogs and was rewarded with selection in the New South Wales Tri-Series team. El Masri became a highly popular figure on the Bulldogs' flank and showed signs of a representative future given a continuation of his 1997 form.

Although at times inconsistent, forward Solomon Haumono earned selection for NSW in the Tri-Series and for the Australian Super League side early in the year. He provided a number of magic moments for the Belmore faithful with a storming try against Cronulla in Round 2 and a thunderous tackle on Brisbane winger Michael Hancock in the final home-and-away match in August. Robert Mears was a strong performer at hooker in the absence of the injured Jason Hetherington, while Steven Price graduated successfully from lock to the front row and was voted the players' player for 1997.

Incoming coach Steve Folkes, a member of the Bulldogs' intimidating forward packs of the 1980s, has vowed to turnabout the worrying defensive lapses of 1997.

REPRESENTATIVE PLAYERS
NSW: Simon Gillies, Solomon Haumono, Matt Ryan
NEW ZEALAND (Tri-Series): John Timu
AUSTRALIA: Solomon Haumono
NEW ZEALAND (Test): Daryl Halligan, John Timu

WORLD CLUB CHALLENGE
Wigan (Belmore) lost 18-22, Halifax (Belmore) won 58-6, London (Belmore) won 34-18, Halifax (Thrum Hall) won 40-22, Wigan (Central Park) lost 24-31, London (The Stoop) won 44-22. Played 6, won 4, lost 2, for 218, against 121.

First Grade 1997: Coach Chris Anderson. Finished 5th.
Reserve Grade 1997: Coach Steve Folkes. Finished 1st.

CRONULLA

Cronulla enjoyed their best season in almost 20 years in 1997, yet there was a feeling within the club that the Sharks had missed one of their best opportunities to win a first-grade title. They had returned from the British leg of their World Club Challenge campaign to whip short-priced premiership favourites Brisbane 32-4 in a Round 13 clash at Shark Park. It was at that point Cronulla looked capable of finally breaking their 30-year-old premiership duck.

They went on to win four of their next five premiership games, qualifying for the finals in second position. Continuing their run, the Sharks outlasted Canberra to win their opening semi-final 22-18 at Shark Park, and set up a major semi-final duel with Brisbane in Townsville. But as Cronulla were to dis-

SUPER LEAGUE CLUBS

cover again in the grand final, Brisbane had another level to which no side in the Super League competition could reach.

The Sharks, missing experienced captain Andrew Ettingshausen, were blown away by a stunning first-half assault by the Broncos at Stockland Stadium, before eventually losing 34-2. After a second finals win over Canberra at Shark Park, the Sharks again confronted Brisbane, this time in the grand final at ANZ Stadium.

Early in the second half a try to 20-year-old Cronulla centre Russell Richardson reduced Brisbane's lead to 10-8, opening the door for the Sharks to take the upper hand. But once again, the Broncos accelerated away, scoring three further tries to take the title 26-8.

It was a different story — but the same result — in the World Club Challenge competition. The Sharks cruised through the preliminary rounds undefeated, but after the disappointment of losing the domestic grand final, had real trouble motivating themselves for the WCC final series.

Cronulla flew halfway across the globe to meet London in the quarter-final, sweeping them aside 40-16, and a week later returned home to play the Hunter Mariners in a semi-final. The Sharks were headed for another final showdown when they led 18-12 late in the game, but the Mariners scored two late tries to win 22-18.

In many respects, the Sharks did well to achieve what they did. Forwards Les Davidson, Craig Greenhill, Jason Stevens, Nathan Long, Sean Ryan, Martin Lang and Paul Fisher all spent extended periods on the sidelines through injury, while backs Richie Barnett, Paul Donaghy, Adam Dykes and Brett Howland were also missing for varying lengths of time.

Winger Mat Rogers was a brilliant performer for the club throughout the season, topping both the tryscoring and pointscoring charts and forming a deadly combination with captain Andrew Ettingshausen. Centre Russell Richardson developed into one of the game's most promising players and won selection in Australia's Super League squad for the Great Britain Test series.

He was one of seven Cronulla players to represent the Australian Super League side during the season. Fullback David Peachey, halfback Paul Green, centre Andrew Ettingshausen and props Craig Greenhill, Danny Lee and Jason Stevens also achieved the honour.

Lock Tawera Nikau was one of the

PLAYERS RECORDS 1997

Player	App	Int	T	G	FG	Pts
Richard Barnett	14	-	3	-	-	12
Geoff Bell	18	3	11	-	-	44
Les Davidson	12	2	1	-	-	4
Adam Dykes	5	11	4	-	-	16
Paul Donaghy	-	1	-	-	-	0
A. Ettingshausen	20	-	7	-	-	28
Paul Fisher	-	2	-	-	-	0
Wade Forrester	-	9	2	-	-	8
Nick Graham	-	4	1	-	-	4
Paul Green	21	-	3	1	-	14
Craig Greenhill	5	6	-	-	-	0
Mitch Healey	20	-	1	1	1	7
Brett Howland	2	3	2	-	-	8
Martin Lang	2	6	-	-	-	0
Bryan Laumatia	1	1	-	-	-	0
Danny Lee	19	-	2	-	-	8
Nathan Long	11	2	-	-	-	0
Chris McKenna	14	6	6	-	-	24
Tawera Nikau	22	-	1	-	-	4
David Peachey	22	-	8	-	-	32
Stuart Pierce	1	3	-	-	-	0
Russell Richardson	12	5	8	-	-	32
Mat Rogers	21	-	14	70	-	196
Sean Ryan	9	3	-	-	-	0
Ben Sammut	1	6	-	-	-	0
Jason Stevens	12	3	-	-	-	0
Paul Stevens	-	1	-	-	-	0
Tiaan Strauss	3	6	-	-	-	0
Dean Treister	19	1	1	-	-	4
28 players	22		75	72	1	445

CAPTAINCY: Ettingshausen 20, Healey 2

Sharks' most consistent performers, however he was unable to negotiate a new deal for 1998 and departed the club, bound for Melbourne. Test winger Richie Barnett left for Sydney City, while South African prop Tiaan Strauss was allowed to return to Rugby Union.

The Sharks announced no new signings for 1998.

REPRESENTATIVE PLAYERS

NSW: Andrew Ettingshausen, Danny Lee, David Peachey, Sean Ryan
QUEENSLAND: Geoff Bell, Paul Green, Craig Greenhill, Chris McKenna, Mat Rogers
NEW ZEALAND (Tri-Series): Richie Barnett, Tawera Nikau.
AUSTRALIA: Andrew Ettingshausen, Paul Green, Craig Greenhill, Danny Lee, David Peachey, Russell Richardson, Jason Stevens
NEW ZEALAND (Test): Richie Barnett, Tawera Nikau.

WORLD CLUB CHALLENGE

Warrington (Wilderspool) won 40-12, St Helens (Knowsley Road) won 48-8, Bradford (Odsal) won 30-10, St Helens (Shark Park) won 28-12, Warrington (Shark Park) won 44-0, Bradford (Shark Park) won 40-12, London (The Stoop, quarter-final) won 40-16, Hunter (Shark Park, semi-final) lost 18-22. Played 8, won 7, lost 1, for 288, against 92.

MATCH RECORDS 1997

Played	Ground	Result	Score
Canberra	Stadium	Won	26-4
Canterbury	Belmore	Won	13-12
Auckland	Shark Park	Won	34-8
Penrith	Penrith	Lost	10-38
Brisbane	ANZ	Lost	12-14
Perth	WACA	Won	20-6
Canterbury	Shark Park	Lost	6-16
Adelaide	Shark Park	Lost	18-29
Hunter	Shark Park	Won	26-0
Canberra	Bruce	Lost	8-22
Perth	Shark Park	Won	32-2
North Qld	Stockland	Won	24-10
Brisbane	Shark Park	Won	32-4
Auckland	Ericsson	Lost	8-11
Penrith	Shark Park	Won	44-20
Adelaide	Adelaide	Won	28-6
North Qld	Shark Park	Won	34-12
Hunter	Topper	Won	28-16
CANBERRA	SHARK PARK	WON	22-18
BRISBANE	STOCKLAND	LOST	2-34
CANBERRA	SHARK PARK	WON	10-4
BRISBANE	ANZ	LOST	8-26

Played 22: won 14, lost 8, for 445, against 312

First Grade 1997: Coach John Lang. Finished 2nd.
Reserve Grade 1997: Coach Dave Stores (replaced Stuart Raper). Finished 5th.

HUNTER

The Hunter Mariners battled overwhelming odds in 1997 as the despised second team in the ARL-stronghold of Newcastle. But despite a minimal following at Topper Stadium, the Mariners performed credibly to reach the final of the maligned World Club Challenge and finish sixth in the Super League premiership.

The Mariners finished ahead of Auckland, Perth, Adelaide and North Queensland in the premiership and won seven of nine matches on home soil. No team in their first season of an ARL or Super League competition has boasted a more impressive home-ground record. However, not even wins against Brisbane (24-6) and Canberra (16-12) could lift home crowd averages past a dismal 5,549 for the season.

The Mariners' inability to win away from Newcastle was the rock on which they perished in the Super League premiership. A 0-9 away record cost the Mariners any chance of reaching the finals in their first season. They lost only narrowly to Auckland (14-18), Adelaide (8-10) and Canberra (12-18) in their early away games, but away performances deteriorated from that point. Their clash with Canterbury at Belmore was one of the most bizarre games of the season. Despite scoring 36 points, the Mariners lost 48-36. Their losing total was the highest ever in a Super League or ARL premiership match.

Goalkicking was another major stumbling block for the new outfit. No

SUPER LEAGUE CLUBS

MATCH RECORDS 1997

Played	Ground	Result	Score
Canterbury	Breakers	Lost	16-20
Auckland	Ericsson	Lost	14-18
Adelaide	Adelaide	Lost	8-10
North Qld	Breakers	Won	38-10
Canberra	Bruce	Lost	12-18
Penrith	Penrith	Lost	24-36
Auckland	Breakers	Won	18-10
Perth	Breakers	Won	36-16
Cronulla	Shark Park	Lost	0-26
Canterbury	Belmore	Lost	36-48
Penrith	Breakers	Won	30-6
Brisbane	Topper	Won	24-6
Canberra	Topper	Won	16-12
Adelaide	Topper	Won	10-2
North Qld	Stockland	Lost	14-33
Perth	WACA	Lost	22-30
Brisbane	ANZ	Lost	16-34
Cronulla	Topper	Lost	16-28

Played 18: won 7, lost 11, for 350, against 363

fewer than nine players were given the kicking role during the season, with only moderate results. Former St George winger Nick Zisti finished as the club's top scorer with 76 points from nine tries and 20 goals.

After failing to qualify for the finals, the Mariners devoted their energies towards the World Club Challenge competition. They had breezed through the preliminary rounds undefeated with home and away victories over Paris-St Germain, Castleford and Sheffield and were drawn to play Wigan in a quarter-final at Central Park.

The Mariners triumphed against the former world champions 22-18. Returning to Australia a week later, the Mariners scored their first away win on Australian soil, when they downed Cronulla by the same score. The win cast Graham Murray's outfit into the final against the Brisbane Broncos at Auckland's Ericsson Stadium. They met their match on this occasion, however, with the Broncos scoring a commanding 36-12 win.

Prop Tim Maddison was voted the club's players' player and also the player of the year. Once a part-time first-grader with Newcastle and Sydney City, Maddison was a regular in Murray's line-up and was a contender for selection in the Australian Super League side in November.

Halfback Brett Kimmorley enjoyed a remarkable rise to prominence in 1997. Elevated to first grade after Murray controversially dropped NSW Tri-Series hero Noel Goldthorpe, Kimmorley repaid his coach's faith with a series of outstanding displays late in the season. One of the brightest newcomers in the game, Kimmorley capped his first year in the top grade with selection in the Australian Super League side.

PLAYERS RECORDS 1997

Player	App	Int	T	G	FG	Pts
Robbie Banister	1	1	1	-	-	4
Keith Beauchamp	17	-	7	-	-	28
Anthony Brann	4	12	-	-	-	0
Andrew Carige	-	1	-	-	-	0
John Carlaw	12	1	8	-	-	32
Stuart Collins	-	1	-	-	-	0
Darrien Doherty	7	4	1	-	-	4
Justin Dooley	1	3	-	-	-	0
Mike Dorreen	-	4	1	-	-	4
Steve Ebrill	-	1	-	-	-	0
Brad Godden	9	2	2	-	-	8
Noel Goldthorpe	11	3	3	8	-	28
Scott Hill	18	-	2	-	-	8
Kevin Iro	4	-	1	2	-	8
Tony Iro	8	6	3	-	-	12
Brett Kimmorley	7	3	2	4	-	16
Tim Maddison	14	2	1	-	-	4
Paul Marquet	15	-	3	-	-	12
Rob McCormack	15	-	-	-	-	0
Troy Miles	-	3	1	-	-	4
Neil Piccinelli	17	-	6	2	-	28
Willie Poching	3	10	3	1	-	14
Robbie Ross	16	-	5	-	-	20
Tyran Smith	1	1	-	-	-	0
Troy Stone	17	1	1	-	-	4
Richard Swain	6	17	-	4	-	8
Gavin Thompson	12	-	3	-	-	12
Craig Wise	3	2	4	-	-	16
Nick Zisti	16	1	9	20	-	76
28 players	18		67	41	-	350

CAPTAINCY: Goldthorpe 7, McCormack 6, T.Iro 3, Stone 2

Prop Troy Stone and five-eighth Scott Hill also enjoyed outstanding seasons for the Mariners and both played in all 18 premiership matches.

REPRESENTATIVE PLAYERS
NSW: Noel Goldthorpe, Robbie Ross
AUSTRALIA: Brett Kimmorley
NEW ZEALAND (Tri-Series): Tony Iro
NEW ZEALAND (Test): Kevin Iro, Tony Iro, Tyran Smith

WORLD CLUB CHALLENGE
Paris-St Germain (Charlety Stadium) won 28-12, Castleford (Wheldon Road) won 42-14, Sheffield (Don Valley Stadium) won 40-4, Castleford (Topper Stadium) won 30-6, Paris-St Germain (Topper Stadium) won 32-0, Sheffield (Topper Stadium) won 58-12, Wigan (Central Park, quarter-final) won 22-18, Cronulla (Shark Park, semi-final) won 22-18, Brisbane (Ericsson Stadium, final) lost 12-36. Played 9, won 8, lost 1, for 282, against 122.

First Grade 1997: Coach Graham Murray. Finished 6th. **Reserve Grade 1997:** Coach Mark Winkler. Finished 8th.

NORTH QUEENSLAND

The North Queensland Cowboys failed to live up to the intense weight of public expectation in 1997, despite the biggest off-season recruitment drive in the club's short history. The arrival of three-times premiership-winning coach Tim Sheens, internationals Ian Roberts, Steve Walters, John Lomax and Tyran Smith and other top-liners such as Owen Cunningham, Scott Mahon and Jason Ferris produced hopes of a semi-final finish for the club in '97, but the Cowboys' season was all over by the end of August. To add insult to injury, the team was saddled with Super League's first wooden spoon.

Earlier, Sheens' men had been bundled out of the World Club Challenge competition with an embarrassing 20-16 loss to lowly Oldham in England, just weeks after they had thrashed the same team 54-16 at Stockland Stadium.

After 15 rounds of the premiership, the Cowboys were only four points adrift of fifth place, but a 22-14 loss at home to Canberra ended the club's hopes of reaching the finals. A week later they went down 34-12 to Cronulla at Shark Park, leaving them with a Round-18 clash with Auckland in which to avoid the wooden spoon. Instead of rising to the challenge, the Cowboys capitulated completely, losing 50-22 in their poorest effort of the year.

The Cowboys finished Super League's first season with five wins and two draws, their best results in their three seasons in major competition, but still fell way short of the hopes of their army of supporters. At times, the Cowboys showed far more impressive capabilities, particularly in a Round-11 clash with Brisbane at ANZ Stadium. Trailing 20-8 late in the match, the Cowboys scored two converted tries in the dying minutes to finish with a 20-all draw. They were the only team to take a point from the Broncos at ANZ Stadium in 1997.

In Round 5, the Cowboys scored

MATCH RECORDS 1997

Played	Ground	Result	Score
Adelaide	Stockland	Won	24-16
Perth	Stockland	Lost	20-22
Penrith	Stockland	Lost	12-19
Hunter	Breakers	Lost	10-38
Canterbury	Belmore	Won	16-14
Brisbane	Stockland	Lost	16-42
Perth	WACA	Lost	4-6
Canberra	Bruce	Lost	16-40
Auckland	Stockland	Won	30-22
Adelaide	Adelaide	Drew	14-all
Brisbane	ANZ	Drew	20-all
Cronulla	Stockland	Lost	10-24
Canterbury	Stockland	Lost	22-29
Penrith	Penrith	Won	33-26
Hunter	Stockland	Won	33-14
Canberra	Stockland	Lost	14-22
Cronulla	Shark Park	Lost	12-34
Auckland	Ericsson	Lost	22-50

Played 18: won 5, lost 11, drew 2, for 328, against 452

SUPER LEAGUE CLUBS **201**

PLAYERS RECORDS 1997

Player	App	Int	T	G	FG	Pts
Jim Ahmat	2	1	1	-	-	4
Paul Bowman	10	-	2	-	-	8
John Buttigieg	2	3	-	-	-	0
Dion Cope	5	2	-	-	-	0
Reggie Cressbrook	7	3	3	-	-	12
Owen Cunningham	18	-	-	-	-	0
Jason Death	3	5	2	-	-	8
John Doyle	11	1	-	4	-	8
Andrew Dunemann	11	3	3	-	2	14
Ian Dunemann	5	1	2	-	-	8
Jason Ferris	7	-	1	-	-	4
Paul Galea	1	-	-	-	-	0
Peter Jones	12	4	1	-	-	4
Aaron Ketchell	-	3	-	-	-	0
Martin Locke	6	6	-	-	-	0
John Lomax	14	1	1	-	-	4
Justin Loomans	6	1	2	-	-	8
Scott Mahon	14	-	3	-	-	12
Ray Mercy	6	-	6	-	-	24
Marshall Miller	1	-	-	-	-	0
Glen Murphy	2	9	1	-	-	4
Luke Phillips	17	-	8	45	-	122
Ian Roberts	17	-	2	-	-	8
Jason Ryan	1	-	-	-	-	0
Luke Scott	3	10	3	-	-	12
Mark Shipway	12	-	3	-	-	12
John Skardon	-	4	1	-	-	4
Tyran Smith	5	4	1	-	-	4
Bert Tabuai	2	4	-	-	-	0
Kris Tassell	2	1	1	-	-	4
Shane Vincent	-	2	-	-	-	0
Steve Walters	15	-	4	-	-	16
Kyle Warren	12	2	5	-	-	20
Adam Warwick	5	2	1	-	-	4
34 players	18		57	49	2	328

CAPTAINCY: Roberts 10, Walters 8

their first ever win at Belmore Sports Ground, when they downed Canterbury 16-14, despite the dismissal of hooker Steve Walters 14 minutes from the end. The Cowboys scored sizeable wins over Leeds, Oldham and Salford in their three World Club Challenge matches at Stockland Stadium, but lost the first match on their English leg, costing them any chance of qualifying for the finals of the competition.

A highlight of the season was a record 30,122 crowd for the Round-6 clash with Brisbane at Stockland Stadium. The Cowboys finished the year with average home crowds of over 17,000, second only to the Broncos in both ARL and Super League competitions.

The Cowboys' reserve-grade side became the first North Queensland team to qualify for a final series and failed by just one win to reach the grand final.

Veteran forward Owen Cunningham was named the club's player of the year in his first season with the Cowboys. The former Manly workhorse powered his way through a huge defensive workload in every match of the premiership and he represented Queensland in the Tri-Series competition.

Hooker Steve Walters was selected in Super League's Australian squad for the November Test series against Great Britain.

REPRESENTATIVE PLAYERS
NSW: Ian Roberts
QUEENSLAND: Owen Cunningham, Steve Walters
AUSTRALIA: Steve Walters
NEW ZEALAND (Tri-Series): Tyran Smith
NEW ZEALAND (Test): John Lomax, Tyran Smith
WORLD CLUB CHALLENGE
Leeds (Stockland Stadium) won 42-20, Oldham (Stockland Stadium) won 54-16, Salford (Stockland Stadium) won 44-8, Oldham (Boundary Park) lost 16-20, Salford (The Willows) won 24-14, Leeds (Headingley) won 48-14. Played 6, won 5, lost 1, for 228, against 92.
First Grade 1997: Coach Tim Sheens. Finished 10th.
Reserve Grade 1997: Coach Murray Hurst. Finished 3rd.

PENRITH

Penrith were one of Super League's biggest surprise packets in 1997. Written off by many critics in the pre-season, the Panthers got off to a flyer, winning six of their first eight matches to set a course for the final series. A mid-season injury crisis and a slump in form resulted in them winning only three of their next 10 games, but their efforts were enough to snare fifth place in Super League's five-team final series.

Along the way Penrith beat every team in the competition with the exception of the newcomers, the Adelaide Rams, who scored upset wins at Penrith (22-16) and in Adelaide (36-16), the latter in the final match of the regular season.

The Panthers beat Canterbury three times during the year, including a gripping 15-14 victory in the first preliminary semi-final. They toughed out a 28-20 win at Belmore, before humiliating the Bulldogs 44-8 at Penrith late in the season. The Panthers made it all the way to the minor semi-final, before bowing out with a 32-12 loss to Canberra at Bruce Stadium.

A high injury toll cost the Panthers the services of Greg Alexander, Steve Carter, Jody Gall, Sid Domic, Andrew Hinson, Morvin Edwards, Steve Waddell, Barry Walker and Paul Johnson for varying periods of the season. The most costly loss was veteran halfback Alexander, who was in rare form until his injury in the first Tri-Series match.

MATCH RECORDS 1997

Played	Ground	Result	Score
Perth	Penrith	Won	30-20
Canberra	Bruce	Won	33-20
North Qld	Stockland	Won	19-12
Cronulla	Penrith	Won	38-10
Auckland	Ericsson	Lost	14-16
Hunter	Penrith	Won	36-24
Canberra	Penrith	Lost	20-30
Brisbane	Penrith	Won	27-26
Adelaide	Penrith	Lost	16-22
Perth	WACA	Lost	20-35
Hunter	Breakers	Lost	6-30
Canterbury	Belmore	Won	28-20
Auckland	Penrith	Won	26-22
North Qld	Penrith	Lost	26-33
Cronulla	Shark Park	Lost	20-44
Brisbane	ANZ	Lost	12-54
Canterbury	Penrith	Won	44-8
Adelaide	Adelaide	Lost	16-36
CANTERBURY	BELMORE	WON	15-14
CANBERRA	BRUCE	LOST	12-32

Played 20: won 10, lost 10, for 458, against 508

PLAYERS RECORDS 1997

Player	App	Int	T	G	FG	Pts
Matt Adamson	16	-	2	-	-	8
Phil Adamson	9	8	2	-	-	8
Fa'ausu Afoa	-	1	-	-	-	0
David Alexander	2	-	-	-	-	0
Greg Alexander	6	-	2	1	2	10
Robbie Beckett	9	1	3	-	-	12
Brett Boyd	3	13	-	-	-	0
Darren Brown	17	2	3	-	-	12
Steve Carter	14	-	8	-	-	32
Garen Casey	2	4	2	2	-	12
Sid Domic	16	-	4	-	-	16
Brad Drew	-	5	2	-	-	8
Morvin Edwards	1	-	-	-	-	0
Gordon Falcon	1	7	-	-	-	0
Danny Farrar	11	2	3	-	-	8
Jody Gall	14	-	3	-	-	12
Ryan Girdler	19	-	11	76	1	197
Craig Gower	20	-	7	1	1	31
Chris Hicks	1	2	1	-	-	4
Andrew Hinson	11	-	6	-	-	24
Lee Hopkins	1	-	-	-	-	0
Paul Johnson	7	2	-	-	-	0
Peter Jorgensen	20	-	5	-	-	20
D. MacGillivray	6	8	-	-	-	0
Carl Macnamara	19	1	-	-	-	0
Fred Petersen	-	3	-	-	-	0
Tony Puletua	3	6	1	-	-	4
Bob Thompson	12	5	1	-	-	4
Steve Waddell	1	2	-	-	-	0
Jason Williams	19	1	7	-	-	28
30 players		20	72	83	4	458

CAPTAINCY: Carter 12, Alexander 6, Brown 1, Girdler 1

Alexander was forced to undergo operations on both feet and made only six appearances for the club in 1997. His form for NSW suggested he was well on the way to representing the Australian Super League side in the Anzac Day Test against New Zealand.

Gower filled in capably for Alexander at halfback, but coach Royce Simmons views the youngster as a more valuable commodity at dummy-half and he is likely to be the club's long-term choice at hooker. At just 18 years of age, Gower displayed remarkable maturity in his first full season at the top level. He represented New South Wales and Australia and never looked out of his depth.

Ryan Girdler and Matt Adamson also experienced their finest seasons in Rugby League, with both representing SL's Australian team during the year. Girdler topped the competition's pointscoring tables, with 197 points from 11 tries, 76 goals and one field goal.

The Panthers were left scratching their heads after completing the preliminary rounds of the World Club Challenge competition with an undefeated record. Six wins from six games was not enough to guarantee them a place in the quarter-finals against English sides that had failed to win one of their preliminary matches. Under the WCC's wacky qualifying rules, the Panthers were knocked out on points differences.

REPRESENTATIVE PLAYERS
NSW: Matt Adamson, Greg Alexander, Ryan Girdler, Craig Gower
AUSTRALIA: Matt Adamson, Ryan Girdler, Craig Gower

WORLD CLUB CHALLENGE
Bradford (Odsal Stadium) won 20-16, Warrington (Wilderspool) won 52-22, St Helens (Knowsley Road) won 50-30, Warrington (Penrith) won 48-12, Bradford (Penrith) won 54-14, St Helens (Penrith) won 32-26. Played 6, won 6, for 256, against 120.

First Grade 1997: Coach Royce Simmons. Finished 4th.
Reserve Grade 1997: Coach Len Stacker. Finished 9th.

PERTH

Rugby League in Western Australia, established for 50 years, was dealt a body blow by News Limited's decision late in 1997 to close the door on the Perth Reds.

Super League's vision of taking the game to the world was blind to the ambitions of those in the west, who had worked hard in trying circumstances for so long. A debt spiralling upwards of $10 million was the reason given by News' number-crunchers for the abolition of the club.

Ironically, it was the massively inflated player payments brought about by News' raids on the ARL in 1995 which produced much of the debt.

The Reds ended three years in national competition with a disappointing season in which a cloud of uncertainty hung over the club.

Speculation that the Reds were to be either closed or relocated presented a massive distraction to coach Dean Lance and his players, the majority of whom had undertaken a major lifestyle change to shift to Perth in the first place.

The season started well enough, with a 50 per cent record after 12 rounds of the premiership, but the turning point came in a confidence-sapping three weeks in England during the World Club Challenge competition. The Reds were beaten by both Sheffield and Paris-St Germain and could not recover their form after their return to Australia. They slumped to win only one of their remaining six premiership games.

The early departure of troubled fullback Julian O'Neill and the continued disciplinary breaches of captain Mark Geyer added to the instability within the club. O'Neill began strongly, with selection in the Queensland and Australian Super League outfits, and a personal haul of 26 points (four tries and five goals) in a Round-4 match against Canterbury, but his repeated off-field transgressions led to the Reds tearing up his contract in May. Geyer was suspended twice during the season, for a total of 10 weeks, denying the team his considerable playing talents.

The Reds were also hard-hit by the season-ending knee injury to prop Rodney Howe, who rose to selection in SL's Australian team for the Anzac Day Test against New Zealand. His efforts in the front row, along with Robbie Kearns, who also represented the SL Australian side late in the year, gave the Reds' pack a powerful authority.

The Reds introduced a number of new players to first grade during the season, including Jared Millar, Matt Geyer, Tristan Brady-Smith and John Wilshere. Millar became the Reds' first 'home-grown' player to appear in the top grade.

REPRESENTATIVE PLAYERS
NSW: Rodney Howe, Robbie Kearns, Scott Wilson
QUEENSLAND: Julian O'Neill

MATCH RECORDS 1997

Played	Ground	Result	Score
Penrith	Penrith	Lost	20-30
North Qld	Stockland	Won	22-20
Brisbane	WACA	Lost	16-26
Canterbury	Perth	Won	34-6
Adelaide	Adelaide	Won	18-16
Cronulla	WACA	Lost	6-20
North Qld	WACA	Won	6-4
Hunter	Breakers	Lost	16-36
Canberra	Bruce	Lost	10-30
Penrith	WACA	Won	35-20
Cronulla	Shark Park	Lost	2-32
Auckland	WACA	Won	24-12
Adelaide	WACA	Lost	4-28
Brisbane	ANZ	Lost	14-50
Canterbury	Belmore	Lost	26-38
Hunter	WACA	Won	30-22
Auckland	Ericsson	Lost	22-30
Canberra	WACA	Lost	16-36

Played 18: won 7, lost 11, for 321, against 456

AUSTRALIA: Rodney Howe, Robbie Kearns, Julian O'Neill

WORLD CLUB CHALLENGE
Castleford (Wheldon Road) won 24-16, Sheffield (Don Valley Stadium) lost 22-26, Paris St Germain (Charlety Stadium) lost 0-24, Sheffield (WACA) won 48-12, Castleford (WACA) won 24-14, Paris St Germain (WACA) won 30-12. Played 6, won 4, lost 2, for 148, against 104.

First Grade 1997: Coach Dean Lance. Finished 8th.

Reserve Grade 1997: Coach Peter Parr. Finished 4th.

PLAYERS RECORDS 1996

Player	App	Int	T	G	FG	Pts
Paul Bell	14	-	4	-	-	16
Tristan Brady-Smith	6	1	2	-	-	8
Damien Chapman	4	7	1	15	1	35
Matt Daylight	11	-	3	-	-	12
Chris Dever	3	2	-	-	-	0
Shaun Devine	2	1	2	6	-	20
Jeff Doyle	-	2	1	-	-	4
Eamonn Edgar	5	-	1	-	-	4
Wayne Evans	5	1	1	-	-	4
Greg Fleming	15	-	6	-	-	24
Dale Fritz	15	2	2	-	-	8
Matthew Fuller	15	2	-	-	1	1
Mark Geyer	6	2	1	-	-	4
Matthew Geyer	5	1	-	-	-	0
Brett Green	10	8	-	-	-	0
Jon Grieve	2	8	1	-	-	4
Darren Higgins	6	11	2	-	-	8
Tim Horan	4	5	2	-	-	8
Rodney Howe	8	-	-	-	-	0
Robbie Kearns	18	-	2	-	-	8
Cameron Lewis	4	-	-	-	-	0
Barrie-Jon Mather	1	1	-	-	-	0
Jared Millar	6	1	2	-	-	8
Julian O'Neill	7	1	6	14	1	53
Corin Ridding	-	6	-	-	-	0
Matthew Rodwell	16	2	4	-	-	16
Chris Ryan	15	-	5	12	-	44
Fred Sapatu	-	1	-	-	-	0
Peter Shiels	13	2	3	-	-	12
Ricky Taylor	-	2	-	-	-	0
Peter Trevitt	-	1	-	-	-	0
John Wilshere	4	-	1	-	-	4
Scott Wilson	14	-	4	-	-	16
33 players	18		56	47	3	321

CAPTAINCY: Rodwell 11, Geyer 4, Bell 3

SUPER LEAGUE CLUBS

AUSTRALIAN SCOREBOARD

NEW SOUTH WALES

MMI Country Divisional Championships
Preliminary rounds — Illawarra defeated Northern Division 30–10, Newcastle defeated Monaro Division 36–8, Northern Rivers defeated Western Divison 20–14, North Coast defeated Southern Division 40–8.
Semi-finals: Newcastle defeated Illawarra 34–18, North Coast defeated Northern Rivers 26–10.
Final: Newcastle 28 (S.Storrie 2, B.Cullen 2, A.Hall tries; B.Christiansen 4 goals) defeated North Coast 18 (M.Bye 2, D.Briggs tries; B.Davis 3 goals) at International Stadium, Coffs Harbour, April 12. Referee: Ray Inskip.
NEWCASTLE: Brett Christiansen (Cessnock); Brett Cullen (Western Suburbs), Michael Reid (South Newcastle), Steve Storrie (Western Suburbs), Adam Hall (Lakes United); Paul Skovgaard (Western Suburbs), Darren Forward (South Newcastle); Kiel Emerton (Lakes United), Tony Hutton (Western Suburbs), Paul Davies (South Newcastle), Todd Anderson (Western Suburbs), Steve Henderson (Waratah Mayfield), Peter Riding (Cessnock). Reserves: Brendon Dooley (Kurri Kurri), Todd Buckingham (South Newcastle), Heath Aland (Cessnock), Ken Kerr (Kurri Kurri), Craig Hibberd (Lakes United).
NORTH COAST: Brad Sims (Sawtell); David Briggs (Woolgoolga), Matt Donovan (Orara), Shane Bru (Forster Dragons), Andrew Gray (Coffs Harbour); Brett Davis (Nambucca), Matt Bye (Orara); Blair Sankey (Woolgoolga), Scott Sullivan (Wingham Hotel), Wayne Taekata (Coffs Harbour), Darren Leaney (Bellingen), Brett Winkler (Coffs Harbour), Greg Watts (Wauchope). Reserves: Allan Lewis (Wauchope), Peter Denham (Bellingen), Paul Hilton (Nambucca), Andrew Korn (Coffs Harbour).
Under-19s Final: North Coast def Northern Division 32–10.

COUNTRY DIVISIONAL CHAMPIONS 1960–97

1960	Riverina	1971	Illawarra
1961	Western Div	1972	Illawarra
1962	Western Div	1973	Newcastle
1963	Newcastle	1974	Illawarra
1964	Newcastle	1975	Riverina
1965	Newcastle	1976	Illawarra
1966	Newcastle	1977	Monaro
1967	Northern Div	1978	Illawarra
1968	Newcastle	1979	Newcastle
1969	Newcastle	1980	Southern Div
1970	Northern Div	1981	Newcastle
1982	Riverina	1990	Northern Rivers
1983	Southern Div	1991	Newcastle
1984	Newcastle	1992	Newcastle
1985	Riverina	1993	Central Coast
1986	Western Div	1994	Newcastle
1987	Northern Rivers	1995	Newcastle
1988	Riverina	1996	Newcastle
1989	Northern Div	1997	Newcastle

MMI Country Player of the Year: Darren Leaney (Bellingen)
MMI Country Origin Player of the Year: Paul McGregor (Illawarra)

NSW COUNTRY PLAYERS OF THE YEAR 1965–97

1965	Laurie Moraschi (Griffith)
1966	Terry Pannowitz (Maitland)
1967	Allan Thomson (Lakes United, Newcastle)
1968	Allan Thomson (Lakes United, Newcastle)
1969	John Cootes (Western Suburbs, Newcastle)
1970	Les Hutchings (Condobolin)
1971	Dick Jeffrey (Glen Innes)
1972	Brian Burke (Maitland)
1973	John Donnelly (Gunnedah)
1974	Michael Cronin (Gerringong)
1975	Steve Hewson (Queanbeyan United)
1976	Peter Kennedy (Forbes)
1977	Barry Pearson (Western Suburbs, Illawarra)
1978	Ray Brown (Griffith Waratahs)
1979	Pat Smith (Maitland)
1980	Perry Haddock (Erina)
1981	Terry Regan (Cessnock)
1982	Willie Tarry (Cessnock)
1983	Paul Field (Cootamundra)
1984	Ross Gibson (Wyong)
1985	Peter Hawthorne (Griffith)
1986	Neil Moy (Parkes)
1987	Steve Walters (Lakes United, Newcastle)
1988	Chris Cumming (Aberdeen)
1989	Mark Ryan (Moree)
1990	Paul Danes (Wagga Magpies)
1991	Richard Jones (South Newcastle)
1992	Trevor Crow (South Newcastle)
1993	Warren Douch (Erina)
1994	Brian Quinton (Kurri)
1995	Jamy Forbes (Cessnock)
1996	Brett Gallard (Orange CYMS)
1997	Darren Leaney (Bellingen)

CLAYTON CUP WINNERS 1937–97

1937	West Tamworth		
1938	Nimmitabel	1941-45	No awards
1939	Wagga Magpies	1946	Port Kembla
1940	Henty	1947	Bombala

1948	Cootamundra		United
1949	Tumut	1975	Albury Blues
1950	Bathurst Railway	1976	Bombala
1951	North Tamworth	1977	Belconnen United
1952	Gundagai	1978	Sawtell
1953	Young	1979	Scone
1954	Orange CYMS	1980	Narwan
1955	Young	1981	Bellingen
1956	Maitland	1982	Warilla
1957	Temora	1983	Tweed Heads Seagulls
1958	Coonamble		
1959	Dubbo Macquarie	1984	Bourke
1960	Goulburn Workers	1985	Tumbarumba
1961	Ballina	1986	Tumbarumba
1962	Warialda	1987	Lismore Marist Brothers
1963	Tweed Heads Seagulls		
		1988	Bega
1964	Oberon	1989	Tweed Heads Seagulls
1965	Tullibigeal		
1966	Picton Magpies	1990	Singleton
1967	Casino	1991	Mittagong
1968	Darlington Point	1992	Wstrn Suburbs, Newcastle
1969	Tarcutta		
1970	Delegate	1993	Rankins Springs
1971	Cobar	1994	Forster-Tuncurry
1972	Cobar	1995	Forster-Tuncurry
1973	Gunnedah	1996	Werris Creek
1974	Queanbeyan	1997	Eden

NSW COUNTRY GRAND FINALS

Newcastle: Western Suburbs def Lakes United 26–16

Illawarra: Collegians def Dapto 32–16

Canberra District: West Belconnen def Goulburn 26–8

Central Coast: Wyong def Gosford 32–6

Group 1: Lismore Marist Brothers def Ballina 20–10

Group 2: Orara Valley def Coffs Harbour 40–32

Group 3: Wingham District def Forster-Tuncurry 26–16

Group 4: Werris Creek def Wee Waa 22–21

Group 6: Camden def Picton 27–21

Group 7: Warilla def Albion Park-Oak Flats 18–16

Group 9: Tumbarumba def Harden-Murrumburrah 28–22

Group 10: Bathurst Penguins def City of Orange Hawks 12–9

Group 11: Cobar def Parkes 42–10

Group 12: Wilcannia def Menindee 56–48

Group 14: Gilgandra def Walgett 33–20

Group 16: Eden def Moruya 23–8

Group 17: Rankins Springs def Whitton 50–10

Gold Coast-Group 18: Runaway Bay def Cudgen 18–17

Group 19: Armidale def Guyra 34–24

Group 20: Leeton def Griffith Waratahs 25–18

Group 21: Denman def Muswellbrook 34–16

Mid-west: Gulgong def Wallerawang 52–0

METROPOLITAN CUP GRAND FINAL

Newtown 18 (J.Lintmeijer, D.Howlett, P.Baumgart tries; C.Shaw 3 goals) defeated **Guildford** 8 (A.Xuereb try; Xuereb 2 goals) at Parramatta Stadium, August 9. Referee: Neil Almond.

NEWTOWN: Craig Shaw; Duane Roberts, David Howlett, Jason Evans, John Lintmeijer; Matt O'Keefe, Brad Westaway; Peter Baumgart, Trent Brown, Dayle Bonner, Brett Taper, Tony Catton (c), Paul Danes. Reserves: Gavin Orr, Mark Lavender, Shaun O'Bryan, Brad Williams, Michael Speechley, Greg Jordan, Tony Gerasimou, Tim Araullo, Luke Ellis. **Coach:** Col Murphy.

GUILDFORD: Scott Casey; Richard Kairouz, Marcel Nassar, Darren Thorson, Chris Tolar; Aaron Milan, Kim Bray, Troy Cassell, Michael Brown (c), Kandy Tamer, Bernard Boys, Mark Barnes, Anthony Xuereb. Reserves: Scott Prebble, Darren Matthews, Eden Hughes, Tony Sakr, Veramu Dikidikilati, Chris Bulgin, Jason Hedges, Ben Tickle, Paul Fuller. **Coach:** Steve Ghosn.

Reserve Grade Grand Final: Wentworthville defeated Kellyville 14–12.

Bill Buckley Medal winner: Justin Holbrook (Moorebank)

COUNTRY FIRSTS V SYDNEY METRO

Country Firsts 16 (B.Cullen 2, D.Saddler tries; B.Christiansen 2 goals) defeated **Sydney Metros** 0 at Marathon Stadium, April 25. Referee: Ray Inskip.

COUNTRY FIRSTS: Brett Christiansen (Cessnock); Brett Cullen (Newcastle Wests), Craig McKeough (Runaway Bay), Dean Saddler (Blayney), Adam Hall (Lakes United); Steve Storrie (Newcastle Wests), Graham Russell (Casino – c); Blair Sankey (Woolgoolga), Tony Hutton (Newcastle Wests), Jason Darcy (Orange Hawks), Darren Leaney (Bellingen), Jason Priest (Mudgee), Greg Watts (Wauchope). Reserves: Ken Kerr (Kurri Kurri), Brett Davis (Nambucca Heads), Martin Sedgwick (Collegians), Steve Henderson (Waratah-Mayfield). **Coach:** John Harvey.

SYDNEY METRO: Brett Wheelhouse (Ryde); Craig Shaw (Newtown), Jason Evans (Newtown), Anthony Xuereb (Guildford), Ashley Rhodes (Bondi Roosters); Aaron Milan (Guildford), Paul Danes (Newtown); Stephen Boss (Kellyville), Scott Fleming (Newtown), Brett Langford (Moorebank), Dave Moffatt (St Marys), Bernard Boys (Guildford), Jason Benge

AUSTRALIAN SCOREBOARD

(St Marys). Reserves: Shayne Boyd (Wentworthville), Brad Williams (Newtown), Jason Small (St Marys), Paul Fuller (Guildford). **Coach**: Col Murphy.

BRASCH-BELLEW SHIELD

Sydney Metros 26 (J.Evans 2, J.Benge, J.Small, B.Wheelhouse tries; A.Xuereb 3 goals) defeated **Brisbane Capitals** 12 (D.Williams, T.Kalauta tries; A.Singleton 2 goals) at Leichhardt Oval, April 9. Referee: Mick Lewis.
SYDNEY METROS: Brett Wheelhouse (Ryde-Eastwood); John Lintmeijer (Newtown), Jason Evans (Newtown), Anthony Xuereb (Guildford), Ashley Rhodes (Bondi Roosters); Aaron Milan (Guildford), Paul Danes (Newtown); Stephen Boss (Kellyville), Scott Fleming (Newtown), Brett Langford (Moorebank), Dave Moffatt (St Marys), Bernard Boys (Guildford), Jason Benge (St Marys). Reserves: Shayne Boyd (Wentworthville), Brad Williams Newtown), Jason Small (St Marys), Paul Fuller (Guildford). **Coach**: Col Murphy.
BRISBANE CAPITALS: Adam Mogg (Redcliffe); Tokofe Kalauta (Souths), George Wilson (Redcliffe), Travis Baker (Easts), Matt Fisher (Brothers); Anthony Singleton (Redcliffe), Kevin Carmichael (Norths); Graham Cotter (Easts), Dale Williams (Easts), Scott Collis (Logan City), James Hinchey (Redcliffe), Mark Sessarago (Easts), Tony Gould (Redcliffe). Reserves: Jeff Hassan (Wynnum), Chris Essex (Redcliffe), Shane O'Flanaghan (Wests), Leon Yeatman (Easts), Jason Twist (Wests). **Coach**: Mark Murray.

INTERSTATE CHALLENGE

Queensland Residents 14 (G.Wilson 2, J.Hinchey tries; A.Singleton goal) defeated **NSW Residents** 4 (J.Evans try) at Sydney Football Stadium, June 25. Referee: Rod Lawrence.
QUEENSLAND RESIDENTS: Scott Schultz (Toowoomba); Jeff Slater (Toowoomba), George Wilson (Redcliffe), David Maiden (Cairns), Matt Fisher (Brothers); Anthony Singleton (Redcliffe), Kevin Carmichael (Norths); Michael Searle (Gold Coast-Burleigh), Dale Williams (Easts), Graham Cotter (Easts), James Hinchey (Redcliffe), Danny Burgess (Gold Coast-Burleigh), Tony Gould (Redcliffe – c). Reserves: Graham White (Central), Cameron Hurren (Redcliffe), Tony Evans (Toowoomba), Chris Beattie (Ipswich). **Coach**: Gary Lawrence.
NSW RESIDENTS: Brett Christiansen (Cessnock); Brett Cullen (Wests Newcastle), Craig McKeough (Runaway Bay), Dean Saddler (Blayney), Jason Evans (Newtown); Steve Storrie (Wests Newcastle), Jason Small (St Marys), Brad Williams (Newtown), Scott Fleming (Newtown), Jason Darcy (Orange Hawks), Darren Leaney (Bellingen), Dave Moffatt (St Marys), Greg Watts (Wauchope). Reserves: Brett Wheelhouse (Ryde-Eastwood), Aaron Milan (Guildford), Paul Danes (Newtown), Blair Sankey (Woolgoolga). **Coach**: John Harvey.

QUEENSLAND

CHANNEL NINE CUP GRAND FINAL

Redcliffe 18 (J.Hinchey 2, A.Singleton tries; Singleton 3 goals) defeated **Easts** 16 (L.Yeatman, D.Williams, R.Braun tries; S.Sipple 2 goals) at Suncorp Stadium, September 6. Referee: Stuart Berndt.
REDCLIFFE: Adam Mogg; Cameron Hurren, Bevan Canning, George Wilson, Aaron Douglas; Anthony Singleton, Peter Robinson (c); Grant Cleal, Richard Ackerman, Troy Lindsay, Ian Graham, James Hinchey, Tony Gould. Replacements: Russell Lahiff, Wayne Miller, Chris Essex, Selwyn Toby. **Coach**: John Boxsell.
EASTS: Leon Yeatman; Rob Braun, Chris Beattie, Travis Baker, Peter Turner; Scott Sipple, Brett McPherson; Graham Cotter, Dale Williams, Scott Neilson, Doug Evans, Mark Sessarago (c), Jeff Wakefield. Replacements: Phil Lockwood, Steve Mills, Jamie Day, Aaron Smith. **Coach**: Gavin Payne.

BRISBANE

Fourex Premier League Grand Final: **Redcliffe** 35 (A.Douglas 3, A.Mogg, C.Hurren, B.Canning tries; A.Singleton 5 goals; I.Graham field goal) defeated **Easts** 6 (S.Sipple try; Sipple goal) at Suncorp Stadium, September 21. Referee: Stuart Berndt.
REDCLIFFE: Adam Mogg; Selwyn Toby, Cameron Hurren, Bevan Canning, Aaron Douglas; Anthony Singleton, Peter Robinson (c); Grant Cleal, Richard Ackerman, Troy Lindsay, Ian Graham, James Hinchey, Tony Gould. Replacements: Russell Lahiff, Chris Essex, Wayne Miller, George Wilson. **Coach**: John Boxsell.
EASTS: Leon Yeatman; Rob Braun, Chris Beattie, Travis Baker, Peter Turner; Scott Sipple, Brett McPherson; Graham Cotter, Dale Williams, Scott Neilson, Doug Evans, Mark Sessarago (c), Jeff Wakefield. Replacements: Phil Lockwood, Steve Mills, Jamie Day, Aaron Smith. **Coach**: Gavin Payne.
A Grade: Redcliffe defeated Easts 30–26.
Colts: Redcliffe defeated Easts 46–4.

CITY V COUNTRY

City 20 (M.Sessarago, K.Carmichael, M.Fisher, G.Wilson tries; A.Singleton 2 goals) defeated **Country** 16 (S.Bell, S.Busby, S.Schultz tries; D.Richens, G.White goals) at Langlands Park, June 7. Referee: Stuart Berndt.

CITY: Bevan Canning (Redcliffe); Takofe Kalauta (Souths), Cameron Hurren (Redcliffe), George Wilson (Redcliffe), Matt Fisher (Brothers); Anthony Singleton (Redcliffe), Kevin Carmichael (Norths); Tony Gould (Redcliffe), James Hinchey (Redcliffe), Mark Sessarago (Easts), Grant Cleal (Redcliffe), Dale Williams (Easts), Graham Cotter (Easts). Reserves: Scott Ward (Logan City), Chris Essex (Redcliffe), Neil Stanley (Norths), Ian Graham (Redcliffe).

COUNTRY: Scott Schultz (Toowoomba); Damien Richters (Wide Bay), Steve Bell (Central Qld), David Maiden (Cairns), Heath Egglestone (Central Qld); Graham White (Central Qld), Robbie Schmidt (Cairns); Michael Searle (Gold Coast), Eddie Fallins (Gold Coast), Steve Worsley (Mackay), Tony Evans (Toowoomba), Danny Burgess (Gold Coast), David Anderson (Toowoomba). Reserves: Chris Beattie (Ipswich), Sime Busby (Central Qld), Shannon Van Balen (Cairns), Jeff Slater (Toowoomba).

QUEENSLAND COUNTRY GRAND FINALS

Thursday Island: Federal Sharks def Torres Eels 36–28
Cairns: Southern Suburbs def Brothers 20–12
Mt Isa: Town def Brothers 38–24
Townsville: Centrals def Brothers 31–20
Mid-west: Hughenden Raiders def Richmond 24–22
Mackay: Brothers def Magpies 20–18
Central Highlands: Gemfields def Middlemount 24–10
Rockhampton: Yeppoon def Norths 30–28
Extended League: Rockhampton Brothers def Wallabies 26–24
Gladstone: Tannum def Wallabies 32–28
Central West: Longreach def Barcaldine 24–16
47th Battalion Shield: Sunshine Coast def Bundaberg 30–10
Group 1: Bundaberg Brothers def Bundaberg Wests 22–14
Maryborough-Hervey Bay: Wallaroos def Rovers 21–12
Bundaberg: Wests def Brothers 10–8
Northern Districts: Isis def Avondale 32–16
South Burnett: Cherbourg def Blackbutt-Yarraman 44–2
Central Burnett: Eidsvold def Monto 30–18
Sunshine Coast-Gympie: Noosa def Maroochydore/Coolum 16–10
Toowoomba: Wattles def Newtown 42–8
Roma: Wallumbilla def St George 40–36
Western League: Cunnamulla def Quilpie 34–24
Ipswich: Booval Swifts def Fassifern 38–6
Border: Texas def Tenterfield 28–22

WESTERN AUSTRALIA

Perth: Fremantle def South Perth 12–10
Goldfields: Kalgoorlie Broncos def. Kambalda Roosters 22–14
Pilbara: Wickham def. South Hedland Cougars 34–32
Newman: Dragons def United 18–16

NORTHERN TERRITORY

Darwin: Litchfield def University 28–14
Alice Springs: Central-Memorial def United 43–34

VICTORIA

Melbourne: Altona def St Kilda 28–12
Gippsland: Sale def Traralgon 29–24
Goulburn-Murray: Southern Riverina Jets def Corowa 28–6

SOUTH AUSTRALIA

Adelaide: South Adelaide def Kilburn 18–16

TASMANIA

Northern Suburbs def Launceston 18–16

JUNIOR REPRESENTATIVE

President's Cup

The President's Cup was the trophy on offer for the second grade competition in 1997. For grand final details see Lower Grades (Page 108).

President's Cup Champions 1910–97

Year	Team	Year	Team
1910	Easts	1934	Southern Dis
1911	Easts	1935	St George
1912	Balmain	1936	Souths
1913	Easts	1937	Northern Sub
1914	Balmain	1938	Easts
1915	Easts	1939	Balmain
1918	Norths	1940	Balmain
1919	Newtown	1941	St George
1920	Easts	1942	Souths
1921	Newtown	1943	Souths
1922	Easts	1944	Newtown
1923	Easts	1945	Wests
1924	Easts	1946	Manly
1925	Wests	1947	Wests
1926	Balmain	1948	Easts
1927	Easts	1949	Easts
1928	Newtown	1950	Newtown
1929	Balmain	1951	Souths
1930	Balmain	1952	Balmain
1931	Canterbury	1953	Souths
1932	Balmain	1954	Balmain
1933	Norths	1955	Easts

AUSTRALIAN SCOREBOARD

1956	Newtown	1977	Souths
1957	St George	1978	Easts
1958	Wests	1979	Parramatta
1959	Balmain	1980	Souths
1960	Souths	1981	St George
1961	Souths	1982	Souths
1962	Souths	1983	Souths
1963	Souths	1984	Illawarra
1964	Souths	1985	Penrith
1965	Souths	1986	Penrith
1966	Balmain	1987	Easts
1967	Balmain	1988	Parramatta*
1968	Souths	1989	Souths*
1969	Souths	1990	Canberra*
1970	Manly	1991	Canterbury*
1971	Souths	1992	Wests*
1972	Souths	1993	Easts*
1973	Balmain	1994	Cronulla*
1974	Souths	1995	Canberra
1975	Parramatta	1996	South Qld
1976	Canterbury	1997	Parramatta*

* Run in conjunction with senior competitions

H. "Jersey" Flegg Memorial Trophy

The H. "Jersey" Flegg Memorial Trophy was the prize on offer for the Under-20s competition in 1997. For grand final details see 'Lower Grades'.

H. "Jersey" Flegg Memorial Trophy Champions 1961–97

1961	Manly	1980	Balmain
1962	Souths	1981	Wests
1963	Canterbury	1982	Balmain
1964	Souths	1983	Canterbury
1965	Wests	1984	St George
1966	Souths	1985	St George
1967	Souths	1986	Parramatta
1968	Souths	1987	Manly
1969	Souths	1988	Manly
1970	Parramatta	1989	Canberra
1971	Canterbury	1990	Parramatta
1972	Canterbury	1991	Newcastle
1973	Balmain	1992	Newcastle
1974	Manly	1993	Canberra
1975	St George	1994	Balmain
1976	Canterbury	1995	Sydney City
1977	Penrith	1996	St George
1978	Souths	1997	Balmain*
1979	Canterbury		

* Run in conjunction with senior competitions

SG Ball Cup Final

Sydney City 11 (D.Mancuso, D.Widders tries; D.Lambert goal; G.Wardle field goal) defeated **Newcastle** 10 (C.Tallon, S.Rudder tries; K.Rudder goal) at North Sydney Oval, June 21.
SYDNEY CITY: Gavin Lamb; Brock Thompson, Anthony Minichiello, Ronald Prince, Dainan Mancuso; Andrew Large, Gavin Wardle; Brendan Currie, Nick Windeatt, Nelson Lomi, David Lambert, Andrew Roberts, Dean Widders (c). Reserves: Sean Daras Wells, Lee Trasler, Marcelo Loustau, Nathan DeBartolo, Solomone Vukici, Andrew Lomu, Mark Riddell, Paul Farah. **Coach**: Brian Gray.
NEWCASTLE: Willy Baker; Damian Griffiths, Chad Dillenger, Clint Tallon, Trent Estatheo; Graham Blackhall, Sean Rudder; Mark White, Ben Donaldson, Aaron Dyett, Craig Greenaway, Paul Delaney, Kurt Rudder. Reserves: Corey Hammond, Nathan Miller, Todd Polglase, Steve Simpson, Russell Richards, Scott Lyne, Ben Callen. **Coach**: Steve Burraton.

SG Ball Cup Champions 1965–97

1965	Souths	1982	Balmain
1966	Parramatta	1983	Parramatta
1967	Parramatta	1984	St George
1968	Parramatta	1985	Parramatta
1969	Souths	1986	Souths
1970	St George	1987	Parramatta
1971	Wests	1988	Parramatta
1972	Canterbury	1989	Illawarra
1973	Parramatta	1990	Newcastle
1974	Souths	1991	Parramatta
1975	Souths	1992	St George
1976	Souths	1993	Parramatta
1977	Penrith	1994	Souths
1978	Canterbury	1995	Canberra
1979	Souths	1996	Illawarra
1980	Souths	1997	Sydney City
1981	Penrith		

Harold Matthews Shield Final

Parramatta 28 (E.Quiokacikaci, P.Maguire, L.Burt, M.Robertson, B.Sargeant tries; Burt 3 goals; S.Hogan 2 field goals) defeated **Norths** 10 (S.McLean, M.O'Meley tries; McLean goal) at North Sydney Oval, June 21.
PARRAMATTA: Brett Stafford; Eturte Quiokacikaci, Peter Maguire, Luke Burt, Mark Robertson; Scott Ella, Matthew McPherson (c); Michael Egan-Hirst, Daniel Irvine, Brett Sargent, George Alam, Jason Powell, Joel Webb. Reserves: Scott Hogan, Damian Broad, Mitchell Cook, Marcus Orley, Danny Swindells, Luke Taggart, Adam Donaldson, Luke Ross, Michael Meigan, Steve Dean. **Coach**: Gary Freeman.
NORTHS: Nick Calandra; Haysam Elysee, Scott McLean, Ryan Gregory, Brent Keegan; Steven Hales, Jamie Seeton (c); Michael Maryska, Jye Simon, Mark O'Meley, Scott Simpson, Aaron Hardman, Adam Close. Reserves: Craig Cawey, Dame Swaney, Ben Dreyer, Matt Sulkowicz, Davis Duffy, Steve Butler, Mark Salvaterra, Luke Bickhoff, Clint L'Estrange, Stuart Jones, Moses Alone. **Coach**: Wayne Lambkin.

Harold Matthews Shield Champions 1970–97

Year	Team	Year	Team
1970	Parramatta	1984	Canberra
1971	Parramatta	1985	Penrith
1972	Parramatta	1986	Parramatta
1973	Cronulla	1987	Illawarra
1974	Souths	1988	Parramatta
1975	Parramatta	1989	Penrith
1976	Parramatta	1990	Parramatta
1977	Cronulla	1991	Gold Coast
1978	Canberra	1992	Newcastle
1979	Penrith	1993	Canberra
1980	Group 12	1994	Parramatta
1981	Parramatta	1995	Canberra
1982	Parramatta	1996	Illawarra
1983	Group 6	1997	Parramatta

Junior City–Country Matches
NSW Under-18s

Sydney 34 (D.Heckenberg 2, L.Hookey 2, P.Rossi, B.Currie, E.Wignall tries; R.Prince 3 goals) defeated **Country** 8 (G.Brodbeck try; G.Taggart 2 goals) at Marathon Stadium, April 25. Referee: A.Riolo.
SYDNEY: Luke Patten (Illawarra); Paul Rossi (Illawarra), Ronald Prince (Sydney City), Erin Wignall (Norths), Lee Hookey (Souths); Adam Gooden (Sydney City – c), Sean Rudder (Newcastle); Brendan Currie (Sydney City), Ben Donaldson (Newcastle), Aaron Dyett (Newcastle), Robert Stolk (Parramatta), Greg Ebrill (Manly), Dean Widders (Sydney City). Reserves: Joel Penny (Norths), Todd Eadie (Manly), Daniel Heckenberg (Wests), Tevita Amone (Wests). **Coach**: Steve Hood.
COUNTRY: Gavin Taggart (Uralla); Dylan Coleman (Lismore Marist), Lee Grant (Yanco Wamoon), Grant Brodbeck (Armidale YCW), Shannon Trindall (Armidale YCW); Nathan Cross (Byron Bay), Michael Sullivan (Wingham); Grant Schubert (Macleay Valley Mustangs), Grant Coleman (Macleay Valley Mustangs – c), Heath Summerville (Macksville), Philip Charles (Bay & Basin), Phil Bailey (Inverell), Ben Cameron (Sawtell). Reserves: Nathan Towney (Wellington), Michael Ronan (Nambucca Heads), Damien Bower (Lismore Marist), Shaun Coe (Lismore Marist). **Coach**: Craig Higgins.

Queensland Under-17s

Country 38 (L.Wallis 2, D.Flint, B.Ross, T.Williams, M.Johnson, P.Mladenovic tries; D.Lambert 4, N.Doyle goals) defeated **City** 12 (M.Wheeler, D.Raveendrakumar tries; B.Ebert, T.Green goals) at Bishop Park, May 17. Referee: Gavin Williams.
COUNTRY: Peter Mladenovic (Toowoomba Valleys); Leon Wallis (Innisfail Brothers), Dudley McGuire (Caloundra), Chris Flannery (Kawana), Damien Flint (Redbank Plains); Bevan Costello (Murgon), Denny Lambert (Ipswich Brothers); Nathan Doyle (Gladstone Valleys), Zac Nogar (Townsville Centrals – c), Benjamin Ross (Nambour), James Brown (Southport), Tony Jensen (Newtown, Toowoomba), Ben Cook (Caloundra). Reserves: Stephen Robinson (Toowoomba Valleys), Ty Williams (Innisfail), Max Johnson (Mareeba), Nick Bowman (Dalby). **Coach**: Ray Tolley.
CITY: Tony Green (Souths); Benjamin Centirh (Redcliffe), Michael Crocker (Redcliffe), Raymond Vis (Redcliffe), Matthew Wheeler (Souths – c); Brad Watts (Redcliffe), Sam Obst (Redcliffe); Anthony McCormack (Souths), Nathan Venn (Aspley), Michael Anderson (Wynnum/Cannon Hill), Ron Poll (Redcliffe), Ben Ebert (Redcliffe), Cameron Mann (Wynnum/Cannon Hill). Reserves: David Oliphant (Redcliffe), Lucas Beatson (Carina), Jacob Christie (Souths), Dushan Raveendrakumar (Logan Brothers). **Coach**: Alan Cann.

Queensland Under-19s

City 40 (N.Wobber 2, B.Bryzak, M.Dux, A.Stacey, M.Roberts, S.Sanderson, A.Dudson tries; Webber 4 goals) defeated **Country** 16 (M.Mitchell, T.Gollan, T.Benson tries; L.Brown 2 goals) at Bishop Park, May 17. Referee: Michael Smith.
CITY: Ben Bryzak (Logan City); Matthew Dux (Redcliffe), Adam Stacey (Redcliffe), Nathan Webber (Norths), Skye Davidson (Brothers); John Paul Cherry (Redcliffe – c), Michael Roberts (Redcliffe); Simon Vanzanten (Logan City), Jamie Tomlinson (Redcliffe), Luke Bishop (Redcliffe), Shane Sanderson (Redcliffe), Steven Carr (Souths), Ashley Dudson (Redcliffe). Reserves: Selwyn Toby (Redcliffe), Brett Simmonds (Logan City), Darren Payne (Wests), Damien Currie (Brothers). **Coach**: James Box.
COUNTRY: Craig Wehrman (Goodna); Leroy Brown (Cairns), Jim Castles (Burleigh), Robert David (Cairns), Darrell Solomon (Tannum Sands); Michael Mitchell (Charters Towers), Steve Singleton (Cairns Souths); Ben Walsh (Dysart), George Gattis (Townsville Centrals), Boyd Lorimer (Innisfail Brothers), Peter McGhie (Townsville Centrals), Joe Davoui (Charters Towers), Tony Gollan (Toowoomba Valleys – c). Reserves: Colin Frohloff (Kingaroy), Geoff Black (Roma), Terry Benson (Dysart), Casey Harvey (Toowoomba All Whites). **Coach**: Max Shoesmith.

Junior Interstate Matches
Under-17s

NSW 38 (L.Patten, M.Pink, J.Penny, T Estathoo, J.Gamgee, S Geddes, M.Riddell tries; Pink 4, A.Maroun goals) defeated **Queensland** 14 (L.Wallis 2, C.Flannery tries; D.Lambert goal) at Sydney Football Stadium, June 25. Referee: Moghseen Jadwat.

AUSTRALIAN SCOREBOARD

NSW: Luke Patten (Illawarra); Matthew Pink (Norths), Joel Penny (Norths), Anthony Minichiello (Sydney City), Trent Estatheo (Newcastle); Damien Bower (Lismore Marist), Josh Gamgee (Balmain); Tevita Amone (Wests), Grant Coleman (Macleay Valley Mustangs), Chad Robinson (Parramatta), Scott Geddes (Parramatta), Phil Bailey (Inverell), Kurt Rudder (Newcastle). Reserves: Mark Riddell (Sydney City), Jason Cayless (Parramatta), Anthony Maroun (Parramatta), Kurt Hancock (Norths). **Coach**: David Brooks.

QUEENSLAND: Chris Flannery (Kawana); Leon Wallis (Innisfail Brothers), Casey McGuire (Caloundra), Mark Eacott (South Queensland), Peter Mladenovic (Toowoomba Valleys); Stephen Robinson (Toowoomba Wattles); Denny Lambert (Ipswich Brothers); Nathan Doyle (Gladstone Valleys), Nathan Venn (Aspley – c), Benjamin Ross (Nambour), James Brown (Southport), Tony Jensen (Newtown, Toowoomba), Ben Cook (Caloundra). Reserves: Matthew Wheeler (Souths), Bevan Costello (Murgon), Max Johnson (Mareeba), Nick Bowman (Dalby). **Coach**: Neil Wharton.

Under-19s

NSW 44 (K.Herring 3, R.Prince 2, D.Cook, M.Simon, T.Wozniak, G.Wood tries; C.Cater 3, L.Krilich goals) defeated **Queensland** 10 (S.Toby, J.Tomlinson tries; N.Webber goal) at Suncorp Stadium, May 28. Referee: Darren McKenzie.

NSW: Clint Cater (Parramatta); John Kaho (Balmain), Ronald Prince (Sydney City), David Cook (Norths), Wes Tillot (Norths); Mark Simon (Illawarra), Keiron Herring (Parramatta); Justin Doyle (Souths), Matthew Relf (Sydney City), Aaron Grainger (Newcastle), Leigh Krilich (Manly), Troy Wozniak (Balmain – c), Kurt Bryant (Norths). Reserves: Garth Wood (Souths), Tim Stocker (Manly), John Faulks (Norths), Luke Faul (Manly). **Coach**: Wayne Portlock.

QUEENSLAND: Selwyn Toby (Redcliffe); Leroy Brown (Cairns), Adam Stacey (Redcliffe), Skye Davidson (Brothers), Nathan Webber (Norths); John Paul Cherry (Redcliffe – c), Michael Mitchell (Charters Towers); Ben Walsh (Dysart), Jamie Tomlinson (Redcliffe), Boyd Lorimer (Innisfail Bros), Shane Sanderson (Redcliffe), Luke Bishop (Redcliffe), Ashley Dudson (Redcliffe). Reserves: Geoff Black (Roma), Tony Gollan (Toowoomba Valleys), Ben Bryzak (Logan City), Brett Simmonds (Logan City). **Coach**: Paul Canning.

SCHOOLBOYS

NATIONAL CHAMPIONSHIPS

Australian Under-15 Championship Final: Queensland beat NSW Combined High Schools 21–0 at Cairns.

Australian Under-15 merit squad: Justin Hodges (Trinity Bay, Qld), Paul Franze (Broadmeadow, NSW), Bart Foster (Trinity, Lismore, NSW), Brad Graham (Trinity Bay, Qld), Gray Viane (Westfields Sports High, NSW), Brent Tate (Clontarf, Qld), Steven Witt (Harristown, Qld), Michael Luck (Lockyer, Qld), Daniel Irvine (Parramatta Marist, NSW), Roy Friend (Westfields, NSW), Corey Parker (Beaudesert, Qld), Michael Meigan (Westfields, NSW), Michael Howell (St Gregory's, Campbelltown, NSW), Danny Swindells (St Patricks, Campbelltown, NSW), Matthew Hilder (Woolooware, NSW), Danny Sullivan (Westfields, NSW), Andrew Dallalana (Endeavour High, NSW).

Australian Open Age Championship Final: NSW Combined Catholic Colleges defeated NSW Combined High Schools 22–12 at Pioneer Oval, Parkes.

Australian Schoolboys: Luke Patten (Keira); Blake Revell (St Gregory's, Campbelltown), Craig Frawley (Southern Cross, Qld), Casey McGuire (Caloundra, Qld), Lenny Beckett (Westfields Sports); Mark McLinden (Hawker, ACT), Joel Penny (Kincumber); Troy Thompson (Dickson, ACT), Paul Dalsanto Dapto), Daniel Heckenberg (St Gregory's, Campbelltown), Bradley Meyers (Villanova, Qld), Dane Carlaw (Padua, Qld), Michael Hodgson (St Francis Xavier, Qld). Reserves: Barry Davis (Patrician Brothers, Fairfield), Chad Robinson (Parramatta Marist), Robert Stolk (Westfields Sports), Luke Bailey (Warilla). Lincoln Withers (Erindale, ACT) was selected but withdrew through injury. **Coach**: Brian Hetherington (St Joseph's Regional High). Manager: Michael Fischer (Holsworthy).

BARLA Great Britain Young Lions touring squad: James Aramayo (West Hull), Paul Ashton (Saddleworth Rangers), Christopher Beever (Elland), David Best (Saddleworth Rangers), Ryan Birkby (Dalton), Rodney Bowker (Leigh East), Nicholas Cammann (Pilkington Recs), Christopher Cooke (Blackbrook), Simon Cowap (Woolston Rovers), William Cowell (Kells), Andrew Fisher (Blackbrook), Neil Gregg (Wath Brow Hornets), Chris Halliwell (Leigh East), Ryan Halloran (Thornhill), Marc Jackson (Wath Brow Hornets), Stephen Kirkbride (Kells), Ian Lewis (Leigh East), Garry Purdham (Egremont Rangers), Andrew Rigby (Ulverston), Karl Schwab (Kells), Philip Sherwin (Wath Brow Hornets), Andrew Spink (Thornhill), Philip Thacker (West Hull), Paul Toole (Blackbrook), Graham Wilson (Egremont Rangers), John Young (Egremont Rangers). **Coach**: Phil Kitchin.

First "Test"
Australian Schoolboys 50 (L.Beckett 5, C.Frawley 2, M.McLinden, L.Bailey, J.Penny tries; Penny 3, C.McGuire 2 goals) defeated **BARLA** 0 at West Port Park, Port Macquarie, Saturday, August 9.

Second "Test"
Australian Schoolboys 54 (L.Patten 3, B. Revell 2, J.Penny, D.Heckenberg, M.Hodgson, L.Bailey, B.Meyers tries; Penny 7 goals) defeated **BARLA** 2 (M.Jackson goal) at Kougari Oval, Wynnum, Saturday, August 16.

AUSSIE HOME LOANS CUP FINAL
Erindale College 26 (D.Whitehead, A.Mullins, L.Withers, D.Jeffery, R.Villasanti tries; M.Adams 3 goals) defeated **Parramatta Marist High** 12 (A.Rizk, M.Haig tries; Haig, J.Power goals) at Sydney Football Stadium, September 13. Scrums: Erindale 3–2. Penalties: 5–all. Referee: Sean Hampstead. Player of the match: Matt Adams (Erindale). Peter Sterling Medal winner: Greg Keary (Parramatta Marist).
ERINDALE COLLEGE: David Mulhall (c); Damon Jeffery, Aaron Mullins, Clinton Scott-Knight, Brent Kite; Matt Adams, Lincoln Withers; Adam Taylor, Todd Clark, Ben Pijpers, Terry Martin, Richard Villasanti, Daryl O'Connor. Reserves: Peter Rose, Scott Clendenning-Fenton, Daniel Whitehead, Adrian Veamatahan, Bryce Lloyd, Rohan Ditton, Joe Winkerei. **Coach**: Peter Sollis.
PARRAMATTA MARIST HIGH: Luke Schembri; Daniel Irvine, Andrew DeCelis, Jason Power, Brett Stafford; Tony Robinson, Matthew Haig; Jason Cayless, Greg Keary (c), Chad Robinson, Anthony Rizk, Brett Sargeant, Sean Goncalves. Reserves: Charles Robertson, Damien Gallagher, Scott Townsend, Paul Pafumi, Joseph Saliby, John Nehme, Brett Keegan, Scott Hogan, Michael Egan-Hirst, Ben Hutchinson, Phillip Takchi. **Coach**: David Dwyer.

Aussie Home Loans Cup Champions 1975–97
1975	Fairfield Patrician Brothers
1976	Blacktown High
1977	Ashcroft High
1978	Fairfield Patrician Brothers
1979	St Gregory's, Campbelltown
1980	St Gregory's, Campbelltown
1981	Holy Cross, Ryde
1982	Fairfield Patrician Brothers
1983	Fairfield Patrician Brothers
1984	St Gregory's, Campbelltown
1985	Ashcroft High
1986	St Gregory's, Campbelltown
1987	Fairfield Patrician Brothers
1988	Parramatta Marist
1989	St Gregory's, Campbelltown
1990	St Gregory's, Campbelltown
1991	St Gregory's, Campbelltown
1992	Fairfield Patrician Brothers
1993	St Gregory's, Campbelltown
1994	John Paul II, Marayong
1995	Parramatta Marist
1996	John Paul II, Marayong
1997	Erindale College, ACT

* Amco Shield 1975–79, Commonwealth Bank Cup 1980–April, 1997

Amco Player of the Series
1976	Steve White (Blacktown High)
1977	Alan Emery (Ashcroft High)
1978	Peter Sterling (Fairfield Patrician Bros)
1979	Ivan Henjak (St Gregory's, Campbelltown)

Commonwealth Bank Player of the Series
1980	Ben Elias (Holy Cross, Ryde)
1981	Ben Elias (Holy Cross, Ryde)
1982	Paul Langmack (Fairfield Patrician Bros)
1983	Greg Alexander (Fairfield Patrician Bros)
1984	Paul Osborne (Lewisham Christian Bros)
1985	David Rowles (Ashcroft High)
1986	Damian Kenniff (St Gregory's, Campbelltown)
1987	David Danes (Fairfield Patrician Bros)
1988	David Bayssari (Parramatta Marist)
1989	Jason Taylor (St Gregory's, Campbelltown)
1990	Troy Dicinoski (St John's, Woodlawn)
1991	Damian Chapman (St Gregory's, Campbelltown)
1992	Andrew Dunemann (Harristown)
1993	Kris Flint (St Gregory's, Campbelltown)
1994	Michael Withers (John Paul II, Marayong)
1995	Nathan Cayless (Parramatta Marist)

Peter Sterling Medal
1996	Chris Smith (John Paul II, Marayong)
1997	Greg Keary (Parramatta Marist)

WESTMONT SHIELD
Final: Terrigal 12 (Ben Uhler, Gavin French tries; Mitchell J Hall goal) defeated Ross Hill 7 (Bradley Charter try; Nick Doig goal) at WIN Stadium, Saturday, September 20. (Mod-league pointscoring rules applied)

Westmont Shield Champions 1975–97
1975	Mount Warrigal	1987	Shalvey
1976	Lethbridge Park	1988	Woy Woy
1977	La Perouse	1989	Tweed Heads
1978	Lethbridge Park		South
1979	Port Macquarie	1990	Eden
1980	La Perouse	1991	Blairmount
1981	Wauchope	1992	Toormina
1982	Warners Bay	1993	Toormina
1983	Ashcroft	1994	Farnborough Rd
1984	Hayes Park	1995	Ramsgate
1985	Young	1996	St Andrews
1986	Scone	1997	Terrigal

AUSTRALIAN SCOREBOARD

BUCKLEY SHIELD

Final: Westfields Sports High 24 (Dayne Neirinck 2, David Djukic, Joven Clarke tries; Kurt Minard 4 goals) defeated Scone High 10 (Nathan Robinson 2 tries; Todd Lowrie goal) at WIN Stadium, Saturday, September 20.

Buckley Shield Champions 1974–97

1974	Coffs Harbour	1986	Newtown
1975	Wyong	1987	Ashcroft
1976	Maitland	1988	Yanco
1977	James Cook	1989	Nowra
1978	Narromine	1990	Nowra
1979	Bomaderry	1991	Woolooware
1980	James Cook	1992	Blacktown
1981	Kempsey	1993	Blacktown
1982	Ashcroft	1994	Westfields Sports
1983	Forbes	1995	Mt Austin
1984	James Cook	1996	Westfields Sports
1985	Belmore	1997	Westfields Sports

UNIVERSITY SHIELD

Final: Camden High 34 (A.Wheeler 2, A.Brazenall, K.Fisher, M.Lowe tries; Lowe 7 goals) defeated Toormina High 28 (B.Cameron 3, N.Johnston, J.Farmer tries; B.Hope 4 goals) at WIN Stadium, Saturday September 20.

CAMDEN: Liam Franklin; Aaron Clifton, Mark Lowe, Kevin Fisher, Mark Garrick; Lincoln Young, Joshua Patterson; Adam Wheeler (c), Adam O'Brien, Aaron Patterson, Nathan Shears, Simon Hand, Adam Brazenall. Reserves: Steven Casserly, Aaron Lewis, Kristian Marrow, Shaun Humphries, David Lowe, Nathan Couley, Adrian Toovey, Travis McNamara. **Coach**: Brett Smith.

TOORMINA: Craig O'Loughlin; Brent Strugnell, Damien Irvine, Jase Farmer, Steve Palmer; Brendan Hope, Mark Curtis; Rob Merchant, Nathan Johnson, Heath Langdon, Brad McKay, Adam Watson, Ben Cameron (c). Reserves: Brenton Morris, Jo Lupton, Kurt McInerny, Jo Bishenden, Isaac Baxter, Kyle Wolfe, Luke Brooks. **Coach**: Chris Gardiner.

University Shield Champions 1922–97

1922	Goulburn	1961	Tamworth
1923	Goulburn	1962	Newcastle
1924	Goulburn	1963	Newcastle
1925	Sydney Tech		Tech
1926	Tamworth	1964	Tamworth
1927	Tamworth	1965	Tamworth
1928	Tamworth	1966	Griffith
1929	Tamworth	1967	Orange
1930	Randwick	1968	Orange &
1931	Tamworth		Tamworth
1932	Newcastle		(shared)
1933	Cessnock	1969	Tamworth
1934	Combined	1970	Yanco
	Techs	1971	Tamworth
1935	Newcastle	1972	Yanco
1936	Newcastle	1973	Moree
1937	Cessnock	1974	Gosford
1938	Cessnock	1975	Tamworth
1939	Newcastle	1976	Ashcroft
1940	Newcastle	1977	Ashcroft
1941	Newcastle	1978	Tamworth
1942	Newcastle	1979	Blacktown
1943	Newcastle	1980	Chatham
1944	Sydney Tech	1981	Chatham
1945	Sydney Tech	1982	James Cook
1946	Newcastle	1983	James Cook
1947	Maitland	1984	Ashcroft
1948	Taree	1985	Ashcroft
1949	Gosford	1986	Toormina
1950	Gosford	1987	Yanco
1951	Gosford	1988	Melville
1952	Gosford	1989	James Cook
1953	Muswellbrook	1990	Yanco
1954	Newcastle	1991	Dubbo South
1955	Gosford	1992	Yanco
1956	Newcastle	1993	Kingsgrove
1957	Tamworth	1994	Kingsgrove
1958	Newcastle	1995	Sarah Redfern
1959	Newcastle	1996	Yanco
1960	Newcastle	1997	Camden

ARL Premiership Records

Most First Grade Premierships
South Sydney	20
St George	15
Sydney Tigers	11
Sydney City	11
Canterbury	7
Manly-Warringah	6

Most First Grade Grand Final Victories
St George	14
South Sydney	9
Canterbury	6
Manly-Warringah	6
Balmain	4
Western Suburbs	4

Most Reserve Grade Premierships
South Sydney	20
Balmain	16
North Sydney	8
Sydney City	8
St George	6
Newtown	6

Most Third Grade Premierships
(Competition variously known as Third Grade, President's Cup and Under-20s)
Balmain	14
St George	14
Sydney City	12
South Sydney	10
Western Suburbs	9

Most Club Championships
St George	18
Sydney City	10
Parramatta	9
South Sydney	9

Most Points in a season by a club
779	Canberra	1994
727	Manly	1995
715	Parramatta	1983
715	Manly	1983
673	Parramatta	1982

Most wins in a premiership season by a club
23	Parramatta	1982
23	Manly	1983
22	Easts	1975
22	Manly	1995

Undefeated in a season
Balmain	1915
North Sydney	1921
South Sydney	1925
Easts	1936
Easts	1937
St George	1959

Won all three grades in a season
Balmain	1915
Balmain	1916
South Sydney	1925
St George	1963

Most points by an individual in one match
Points	Player	Club	Opponent	Venue	Date	How Scored
45	Dave Brown	Easts	Canterbury	Sports Ground	May 18, 1935	5T,15G
38	Dave Brown	Easts	Canterbury	Pratten Park	August 10, 1935	6T,10G
38	Mal Meninga	Canberra	Easts	Bruce Stadium	April 16, 1990	5T,9G
36	Les Griffin	St George	Canterbury	Earl Park	May 11, 1935	2T,15G
36	Jack Lindwall	St George	Manly	Hurstville Oval	May 3, 1947	6T,9G
32	Frank Burge	Glebe	University	Agricultural Ground	June 19, 1920	8T,4G
32	Dave Brown	Easts	Balmain	3CG	August 31, 1935	6T,7G
30	Ron Howles	Manly	Canterbury	Brookvale Oval	July 24, 1954	4T,9G
30	Matthew Ridge	Manly	Wests	Brookvale Oval	August 25, 1996	2T,11G

Most points by an individual in one season
Points	Player	Club	Year	Trs	Gls	FG
282	Mick Cronin	Parramatta	1978	16	117	-
270	Mick Cronin	Parramatta	1982	11	123	-
270	Daryl Halligan	Canterbury	1994	12	110	2
265	Eric Simms	Souths	1969	1	112	19
257	Matthew Ridge	Manly	1995	11	106	1
256	Mike Eden	Easts	1983	12	103	2
253	Mick Cronin	Parramatta	1979	15	104	-

Most points in first grade career

Points	Player	Years	Trs	Gls	FG
1,971	Mick Cronin	1977-86	74	865	2
1,917	Graham Eadie	1971-83	71	847	3
1,841	Eric Simms	1965-75	23	803	86
1,554	Graeme Langlands	1963-76	86	648	-
1,519	Keith Barnes	1955-68	11	742	1
1,442	Terry Lamb	1980-96	164	386	44
1,388	Steve Gearin	1976-86	78	566	-
1,374	Steve Rogers	1973-85	90	543	10
1,365	Jason Taylor	1990-97	30	608	29
1,296	John Dorahy	1974-89	55	553	11

Most points for one club (in all grades)
Graham Eadie, 2070 points for Manly Warringah, 1971-83.

Top pointscorers by position

Position	Player	Club	Points	Year
Fullback	Eric Simms	Souths	265	1969
Winger	Daryl Halligan	Canterbury	270	1994
Centre	Mick Cronin	Parramatta	282	1978
Five-eighth	Mike Eden	Easts	256	1983
Halfback	Jason Taylor	Norths	242	1997
Prop	Harry Bath	St George	205	1959
Hooker	Mal Cochrane	Manly	172	1986
Second Rower	Harry Bath	St George	225	1958
Lock	Wayne Bartrim	St George	176	1996

Most tries by an individual in one match

Tries	Player	Club	Opponent	Venue	Date
8	Frank Burge	Glebe	University	Agricultural Ground	June 19, 1920
7	Rod O'Loan	Easts	University	Sports Ground	May 11, 1935
6	Frank Burge	Glebe	Norths	Wentworth Park	July 1, 1916
6	Alan Ridley	Wests	Newtown	Pratten Park	July 11, 1936
6	Dave Brown	Easts	Canterbury	Pratten Park	August 10, 1935
6	Dave Brown	Easts	Balmain	SCG	August 31, 1935
6	Jack Lindwall	St George	Manly	Hurstville Oval	May 3, 1947
6	Jack Troy	Newtown	Easts	Sports Ground	July 8, 1950

Most tries by an individual in one season

Tries	Player	Club	Year
38	Dave Brown	Easts	1935
34	Ray Preston	Newtown	1954
29	Les Brennan	Souths	1954
28	Bob Lulham	Balmain	1947
28	Johnny Graves	Souths	1951
27	Rod O'Loan	Easts	1935
27	Norm Jacobson	Newtown	1948
27	Phil Blake	Manly	1983

Most tries in first grade career

Tries	Player	Years
212	Ken Irvine	1958-73
164	Terry Lamb	1980-96
152	Harold Horder	1912-24
147	Bob Fulton	1966-79
146	Frank Burge	1911-27
144	Benny Wearing	1921-33
143	Johnny King	1960-71
138	Phil Blake	1982-96
137	Eddie Lumsden	1955-66
136	Andrew Ettingshausen	1983-96

Most tries in first grade for one club

Tries	Player	Club	Years
171	Ken Irvine	Norths	1958-70
144	Benny Wearing	Souths	1921-33
143	Johnny King	St George	1960-71
137	Frank Burge	Glebe	1911-26
136	Eddie Lumsden	St George	1957-66
136	Andrew Ettingshausen	Cronulla	1983-96

Top tryscorers by position

Position	Player	Club	Tries	Year
Fullback	Brett Mullins	Canberra	22	1994
Winger	Ray Preston	Newtown	34	1954
Centre	Dave Brown	Easts	38	1935
Five-eighth	Arthur McCabe	Souths	18	1910
Halfback	Phil Blake	Manly	27	1983
Prop	Frank Burge	Glebe	24	1918
Hooker	Steve Martin	Penrith	13	1979
Second Rower	Steve Menzies	Manly	22	1995
Lock	Chick Cahill	Newtown	13	1945

Most goals by an individual in one match

Goals	Player	Club	Opponent	Venue	Date
15	Dave Brown	Easts	Canterbury	Sports Ground	May 18, 1935
15	Les Griffin	St George	Canterbury	Earl Park	May 11, 1935
14	Graham Eadie	Manly	Penrith	Penrith Park	July 29, 1973
12	Les Mead	Wests	Canterbury	Pratten Park	August 31, 1935
12	Graham Eadie	Manly	Souths	Brookvale Oval	August 24, 1975

Most goals by an individual in one season

Goals	Player	Club	Year
123	Mick Cronin	Parramatta	1982
117	Mick Cronin	Parramatta	1978
112	Eric Simms	Souths	1969
110	Daryl Halligan	Canterbury	1994
108	Harry Bath	St George	1958
108	Jason Taylor	Norths	1996

Most goals in first grade career

Goals	Player	Years
865	Mick Cronin	1977-86
847	Graham Eadie	1971-83
803	Eric Simms	1965-75
742	Keith Barnes	1955-68
648	Graeme Langlands	1963-76
608	Jason Taylor	1990-97
605	Ron Willey	1948-64
566	Steve Gearin	1976-86
564	Ken Wilson	1971-83
553	John Dorahy	1974-89

Most field goals in one match

FG	Player	Club	Opponent	Venue	Date
5	Eric Simms	Souths	Penrith	Penrith Park	July 27, 1969

Most field goals in one season

FG	Player	Club	Year
29	Barry Glasgow	Wests	1969
29	Eric Simms	Souths	1969

Most field goals in first grade career

FG	Player	Club	Years
86	Eric Simms	Souths	1965-75

Most appearances in first grade

App	Player	Years
349	Terry Lamb	1980-96
303	Geoff Gerard	1974-89
300	Paul Langmack	1983-97
287	Cliff Lyons	1985-97
287	Des Hasler	1982-97
284	Bob O'Reilly	1967-82
274	Mario Fenech	1981-95
272	Steve Mortimer	1977-88
272	Ian Schubert	1975-89
269	Phil Blake	1982-96

Most appearances in all grades

App	Player	Years
357	Terry Lamb	1980-96
348	Geoff Gerard	1974-89
334	Max Krilich	1970-83

Most consecutive first grade appearances

App	Player	Years
143	Roy Fisher	1954-62
	(all for Parramatta)	

Most consecutive appearances in all grades

App	Player	Years
187	Michael Bolt	1983-90
	(all for Illawarra)	

ARL PREMIERSHIP RECORDS

Highest winning margins

Points	Score	Venue	Date
85	St George 91, Canterbury 6	Earl Park	May 11, 1935
80	Easts 87, Canterbury 7	Sports Ground	May 18, 1935
68	Canberra 68, Parramatta 0	Bruce Stadium	August 22, 1993
67	Souths 67, Wests 0	Agricultural Ground	July 23, 1910
63	Souths 63, University 0	Sports Ground	April 17, 1937
63	Manly 70, Penrith 7	Penrith Park	July 29, 1973
62	Balmain 64, Wests 2	Pratten Park	July 29, 1944
62	Canberra 66, Easts 4	Bruce Stadium	April 15, 1990
62	Sydney Bulldogs 66, North Qld 4	Belmore	August 27, 1995
62	Sydney City 62, Souths 0	Football Stadium	April 25, 1996

Lowest scoring matches

Score	Teams	Venue	Date
0-all	Newtown v Canterbury	Henson Park	March 28, 1982
1-0	Newtown v St George	SCG	May 12, 1973

Highest drawn score

Score	Teams	Venue	Date
34-all	Parramatta v Norths	Parramatta Oval	June 25, 1949
34-all	Illawarra v Manly	WIN Stadium	May 4, 1997

Highest score by losing side

Score	Teams	Venue	Date
34	Cronulla v Brisbane (38)	ANZ Stadium	July 18, 1993

Most consecutive victories

Wins	Club	Year
19	Easts	1975
15	Manly	1995
14	Souths	1932
12	Souths	1925
12	St George	1958
12	Parramatta	1964
12	Parramatta	1977
12	Manly	1987
12	Souths	1989

Most consecutive losses

Losses	Club	Dates
42	University	April 28, 1934 to August 29, 1936

Failed to win a match

Annandale	1918
Annandale	1920
University	1921
University	1935
University	1937
Souths	1946
Easts	1966

Best start to a season

Wins	Club	Year
15	Manly	1995
12	Souths	1925
11	Wests	1934
11	Balmain	1966
10	St George	1959
10	Sydney City	1996

Highest crowds at premiership matches

78,056	St George v Souths	SCG	September 18, 1965 (grand final)
69,860	St George v Wests	SCG	August 24, 1963 (grand final)
65,959	St George v Parramatta	SCG	September 24, 1977 (grand final)
63,282	St George v Wests	SCG	September 13, 1958 (grand final)
63,047	Easts v St George	SCG	September 20, 1975 (grand final)

Highest crowds at regular season matches (non-finals)

58,593	Brisbane v St George	ANZ Stadium	August 27, 1993
57,212	Brisbane v Gold Coast	ANZ Stadium	June 18, 1993
55,934	St George v Balmain	SCG	June 19, 1966
54,751	Brisbane v Canterbury	ANZ Stadium	July 25, 1993
54,645	Brisbane v Auckland	ANZ Stadium	August 27, 1995
53,146	St George v Souths	SCG	August 2, 1969
51,517	Brisbane v Parramatta	ANZ Stadium	March 28, 1993
50,153	St George v Souths	SCG	July 22, 1967
50,130	Easts v Manly	SCG	May 4, 1974

FIRST GRADE PREMIERS AND RUNNERS-UP

Year	Premiers	Runners Up	Year	Premiers	Runners Up
1908	South Sydney	Eastern Subs	1953	South Sydney	St George
1909	South Sydney	Balmain	1954	South Sydney	Newtown
1910	Newtown	South Sydney	1955	South Sydney	Newtown
1911	Eastern Subs	Glebe	1956	St George	Balmain
1912	Eastern Subs	Glebe	1957	St George	Manly-W'gah
1913	Eastern Subs	Newtown	1958	St George	Western Subs
1914	South Sydney	Newtown	1959	St George	Manly-W'gah
1915	Balmain	Glebe	1960	St George	Eastern Subs
1916	Balmain	South Sydney	1961	St George	Western Subs
1917	Balmain	South Sydney	1962	St George	Western Subs
1918	South Sydney	Western Subs	1963	St George	Western Subs
1919	Balmain	Eastern Subs	1964	St George	Balmain
1920	Balmain	South Sydney	1965	St George	South Sydney
1921	North Sydney	Eastern Subs	1966	St George	Balmain
1922	North Sydney	Glebe	1967	South Sydney	Canterbury
1923	Eastern Subs	South Sydney	1968	South Sydney	Manly-W'gah
1924	Balmain	South Sydney	1969	Balmain	South Sydney
1925	South Sydney	Western Subs	1970	South Sydney	Manly-W'gah
1926	South Sydney	University	1971	South Sydney	St George
1927	South Sydney	St George	1972	Manly-W'gah	Eastern Subs
1928	South Sydney	Eastern Subs	1973	Manly-W'gah	Cron-Sutherland
1929	South Sydney	Newtown	1974	Eastern Subs	Canterbury
1930	Western Subs	St George	1975	Eastern Subs	St George
1931	South Sydney	Eastern Subs	1976	Manly-W'gah	Parramatta
1932	South Sydney	Western Subs	1977	St George	Parramatta
1933	Newtown	St George	1978	Manly-W'gah	Cron-Sutherland
1934	Western Subs	Eastern Subs	1979	St George	Canterbury
1935	Eastern Subs	South Sydney	1980	Canterbury	Eastern Subs
1936	Eastern Subs	Balmain	1981	Parramatta	Newtown
1937	Eastern Subs	South Sydney	1982	Parramatta	Manly-W'gah
	St George (tie)		1983	Parramatta	Manly-W'gah
1938	Canterbury	Eastern Subs	1984	Canterbury	Parramatta
1939	Balmain	South Sydney	1985	Canterbury	St George
1940	Eastern Subs	Canterbury	1986	Parramatta	Canterbury
1941	St George	Eastern Subs	1987	Manly-W'gah	Canberra
1942	Canterbury	St George	1988	Canterbury	Balmain
1943	Newtown	North Sydney	1989	Canberra	Balmain
1944	Balmain	Newtown	1990	Canberra	Penrith
1945	Eastern Subs	Balmain	1991	Penrith	Canberra
1946	Balmain	St George	1992	Brisbane	St George
1947	Balmain	Canterbury	1993	Brisbane	St George
1948	Western Subs	Balmain	1994	Canberra	Canterbury
1949	St George	South Sydney	1995	Sydney Bulldogs	Manly-W'gah
1950	South Sydney	Western Subs	1996	Manly-W'gah	St George
1951	South Sydney	Manly-W'gah	1997	Newcastle	Manly-W'gah
1952	Western Subs	South Sydney			

ARL PREMIERSHIP RECORDS

GRAND FINALS (MANDATORY)

Year	Premiers		Runners Up		Crowd
1954	South Sydney	23	Newtown	15	45,759
1955	South Sydney	12	Newtown	11	42,466
1956	St George	18	Balmain	12	61,987
1957	St George	31	Manly-Warringah	9	54,399
1958	St George	20	Western Suburbs	9	63,282
1959	St George	20	Manly-Warringah	0	49,457
1960	St George	31	Eastern Suburbs	6	53,156
1961	St George	22	Western Suburbs	0	61,196
1962	St George	9	Western Suburbs	6	44,184
1963	St George	8	Western Suburbs	3	69,860
1964	St George	11	Balmain	6	61,369
1965	St George	12	South Sydney	8	78,056
1966	St George	23	Balmain	4	61,129
1967	South Sydney	12	Canterbury-Banks	10	56,368
1968	South Sydney	13	Manly-Warringah	9	54,255
1969	Balmain	11	South Sydney	2	61,129
1970	South Sydney	23	Manly-Warringah	12	53,241
1971	South Sydney	16	St George	10	62,828
1972	Manly-Warringah	19	Eastern Suburbs	14	54,357
1973	Manly-Warringah	10	Cronulla-Suth	7	52,044
1974	Eastern Suburbs	19	Canterbury-Banks	4	57,214
1975	Eastern Suburbs	38	St George	0	63,047
1976	Manly-Warringah	13	Parramatta	10	57,343
1977	St George	9	Parramatta	9	65,959
1977+	St George	22	Parramatta	0	48,828
1978	Manly-Warringah	11	Cronulla-Suth	11	51,510
1978+	Manly-Warringah	16	Cronulla-Suth	0	33,552
1979	St George	17	Canterbury-Banks	13	50,991
1980	Canterbury-Banks	18	Eastern Suburbs	4	52,881
1981	Parramatta	20	Newtown	11	57,333
1982	Parramatta	21	Manly-Warringah	8	52,186
1983	Parramatta	18	Manly-Warringah	6	40,285
1984	Canterbury-Banks	6	Parramatta	4	47,076
1985	Canterbury-Banks	7	St George	6	44,569
1986	Parramatta	4	Canterbury-Banks	2	45,843
1987	Manly-Warringah	18	Canberra	8	50,201
1988	Canterbury-Banks	24	Balmain	12	40,000
1989	Canberra	19	Balmain	14	40,500
1990	Canberra	18	Penrith	14	41,535
1991	Penrith	19	Canberra	12	41,815
1992	Brisbane	28	St George	8	41,560
1993	Brisbane	14	St George	6	42,329
1994	Canberra	36	Canterbury	12	42,234
1995	Sydney Bulldogs	17	Manly	4	41,127
1996	Manly-Warringah	20	St George	8	40,985
1997	Newcastle	22	Manly-Warringah	16	42,482

+ indicates grand final replay
Note: Drawn grand finals — 1977, 9-all (after extra-time), St George v Parramatta (St George won replay 22-0); 1978, 11-all (no extra-time), Manly v Cronulla (Manly won replay 16-0). The 1989 grand final between Canberra and Balmain finished 14-all at fulltime. Canberra won 19-14 after 20 minutes of extra-time.

FIRST GRADE MINOR PREMIERS AND WOODEN SPOONERS

Year	Minor Premiers	Wooden Spooners	Year	Minor Premiers	Wooden Spooners
1908	South Sydney*	Cumberland	1953	South Sydney*	Western Subs
1909	South Sydney*	Western Subs	1954	Newtown	Parramatta
1910	Newtown*	Western Subs	1955	Newtown	Western Subs
1911	Glebe	Balmain	1956	St George*	Parramatta
1912	Eastern Subs*	Western Subs	1957	St George*	Parramatta
1913	Eastern Subs*	Western Subs	1958	St George*	Parramatta
1914	South Sydney*	Annandale	1959	St George*	Parramatta
1915	Balmain*	North Sydney	1960	St George*	Parramatta
1916	Balmain*	Western Subs	1961	Western Subs	Parramatta
1917	Balmain*	North Sydney	1962	St George*	South Sydney
1918	South Sydney*	Annandale	1963	St George*	Eastern Subs
1919	Balmain*	North Sydney	1964	St George*	Canterbury
1920	Balmain*	Annandale	1965	St George*	Eastern Subs
1921	North Sydney*	University	1966	St George*	Eastern Subs
1922	North Sydney*	St George	1967	St George	Cronulla
1923	Eastern Subs*	University	1968	South Sydney*	Newtown
1924	Balmain*	Newtown	1969	South Sydney	Cronulla
1925	South Sydney*	Newtown	1970	South Sydney*	Parramatta
1926	South Sydney*	St George	1971	Manly-Warringah	Western Subs
1927	South Sydney*	University	1972	Manly-Warringah*	Parramatta
1928	St George	Newtown	1973	Manly-Warringah*	Penrith
1929	South Sydney*	University	1974	Eastern Subs*	Balmain
1930	Western Subs*	University	1975	Eastern Subs*	South Sydney
1931	Eastern Subs	University	1976	Manly-Warringah*	Newtown
1932	South Sydney*	North Sydney	1977	Parramatta	Newtown
1933	Newtown*	Western Subs	1978	Western Subs	Newtown
1934	Eastern Subs	University	1979	St George*	North Sydney
1935	Eastern Subs*	University	1980	Eastern Subs	Penrith
1936	Eastern Subs*	University	1981	Eastern Subs	Balmain
1937	Eastern Subs*	University	1982	Parramatta*	Canberra
1938	Canterbury*	St George	1983	Manly-Warringah	Western Subs
1939	Balmain*	Newtown	1984	Canterbury*	Western Subs
1940	Eastern Subs*	Western Subs	1985	St George	Illawarra
1941	Eastern Subs	North Sydney	1986	Parramatta*	Illawarra
1942	Canterbury*	Western Subs	1987	Manly-Warringah*	Western Subs
1943	Newtown*	Canterbury	1988	Cronulla	Western Subs
1944	Newtown	Canterbury	1989	South Sydney	Illawarra
1945	Eastern Subs*	South Sydney	1990	Canberra*	South Sydney
1946	St George	South Sydney	1991	Penrith*	Gold Coast
1947	Canterbury	Parramatta	1992	Brisbane*	Gold Coast
1948	Western Subs*	North Sydney	1993	Canterbury	Gold Coast
1949	South Sydney	Eastern Subs	1994	Canterbury	Balmain
1950	South Sydney*	North Sydney	1995	Manly-Warringah	North Qld
1951	South Sydney*	North Sydney	1996	Manly-Warringah*	South Qld
1952	Western Subs*	Parramatta	1997	Manly-Warringah	South Qld

Denotes premiers
From 1997 the minor premiers were awarded the J.J.Giltinan Shield.

ARL PREMIERSHIP RECORDS

RESERVE GRADE

Year	Team
1908	East Subs
1909	East Subs
1910	East Subs
1911	East Subs
1912	Glebe
1913	Sth Sydney
1914	Sth Sydney
1915	Balmain
1916	Balmain
1917	Sth Sydney
1918	Glebe
1919	Glebe
1920	Glebe
1921	Glebe
1922	Newtown
1923	Sth Sydney
1924	Sth Sydney
1925	Sth Sydney
1926	Sth Sydney
1927	Sth Sydney
1928	Balmain
1929	Sth Sydney
1930	Balmain
1931	Sth Sydney
1932	Sth Sydney
1933	Balmain
1934	Sth Sydney
1935	East Subs
1936	West Subs
1937	East Subs
1938	St George
1939	Canterbury
1940	Nth Sydney
1941	Balmain
1942	Nth Sydney
1943	Sth Sydney
1944	Balmain
1945	Sth Sydney
1946	Balmain
1947	Newtown
1948	Newtown
1949	East Subs
1950	Balmain
1951	Newtown
1952	Sth Sydney
1953	Sth Sydney
1954	Manly-W'gah
1955	Nth Sydney
1956	Sth Sydney
1957	Balmain
1958	Balmain
1959	Nth Sydney
1960	Manly-W'gah
1961	West Subs
1962	St George
1963	St George
1964	St George
1965	Balmain
1966	Sth Sydney
1967	Balmain
1968	Sth Sydney
1969	Manly-W'gah
1970	Newtown
1971	Canterbury
1972	Canterbury
1973	Manly-W'gah
1974	Newtown
1975	Parramatta
1976	St George
1977	Parramatta
1978	Balmain
1979	Parramatta
1980	Canterbury
1981	West Subs
1982	Balmain
1983	Sth Sydney
1984	Balmain
1985	St George
1986	East Subs
1987	Penrith
1988	Manly-W'gah
1989	Nth Sydney
1990	Brisbane
1991	Nth Sydney
1992	Nth Sydney
1993	Nth Sydney
1994	Cronulla
1995	Newcastle
1996	Cronulla

Second Grade

Year	Team
1997	Parramatta

THIRD GRADE

Year	Team
1908	Sydney
1909	Sth Syd Fed
1910	Sydney
1911	Leichhardt
1912	Sth Sydney
1913	Sth Syd Fed
1914	East Subs
1915	Balmain
1916	Balmain
1917	East Subs
1918	Sth Sydney
1919	Balmain
1920	Newtown
1921	Mascot
1922	Mascot
1923	Kensington
1924	East Subs
1925	Sth Sydney
1926	Balmain
1927	Glebe
1928	Sth Sydney
1929	East Subs
1930	East Subs
1931	East Subs
1932	East Subs
1933	Sth Sydney
1934	Balmain
1935	Newtown
1936	West Subs
1937	Nth Sydney
1938	West Subs
1939	West Subs
1940	St George
1941	East Subs
1942	St George
1943	Newtown
1944	West Subs
1945	Nth Sydney
1946	Nth Sydney
1947	East Subs
1948	Balmain
1949	St George
1950	Balmain
1951	St George
1952	Manly-W'gah
1953	St George
1954	Balmain
1955	Balmain
1956	Balmain
1957	St George
1958	West Subs
1959	Nth Sydney
1960	Balmain
1961	West Subs
1962	Sth Sydney
1963	St George
1964	Parramatta
1965	St George
1966	St George
1967	West Subs
1968	Balmain
1969	Sth Sydney
1970	East Subs
1971	Canterbury
1972	St George

Under-23s

Year	Team
1973	Balmain
1974	St George
1975	Cronulla
1976	East Subs
1977	West Subs
1978	Penrith
1979	Parramatta
1980	Parramatta
1981	Sth Sydney

Third Grade

Year	Team
1982	Parramatta
1983	St George
1984	Parramatta

Under-23s

Year	Team
1985	St George
1986	Sth Sydney
1987	St George

President's Cup (U-21)

1988	Parramatta	1943		Balmain	1971		St George
1989	Sth Sydney	1944		Balmain	1972		Manly-W'gah
1990	Canberra	1945		Eastern Subs	1973		Newtown
1991	Canterbury	1946		St George	1974		Eastern Subs
1992	West Subs	1947		Balmain	1975		Eastern Subs
1993	East Subs	1948		Western Subs	1976		Parramatta
1994	Cronulla	1949		St George	1977		Parramatta
1995	Canberra	1950		Balmain	1978		Parramatta
1996	South Qld	1951		St George	1979		Parramatta
Under-20s		1952		Sth Sydney	1980		Parramatta
1997	Balmain	1953		Sth Sydney	1981		Parramatta
		1954		Sth Sydney	1982		Parramatta
		1955		St George	1983		Manly-W'gah
CLUB CHAMPIONSHIP		1956		St George	1984		St George
		1957		St George	1985		St George
1930	Eastern Subs	1958		St George	1986		Parramatta
1931	Eastern Subs	1959		St George	1987		Manly-W'gah
1932	Sth Sydney	1960		Western Subs	1988		Manly-W'gah
1933	Sth Sydney	1961		Western Subs	1989		Sth Sydney
1934	Eastern Subs	1962		St George	1990		Canberra
1935	Eastern Subs	1963		St George	1991		Western Subs
1936	Eastern Subs	1964		St George	1992		Brisbane
1937	Eastern Subs	1965		St George			Newcastle (tie)
1938	Canterbury	1966		St George	1993		Canterbury
1939	Canterbury	1967		Sth Sydney	1994		Canterbury
1940	St George	1968		Sth Sydney	1995		Cronulla
1941	Balmain	1969		Sth Sydney	1996		Brisbane
1942	St George	1970		Eastern Subs	1997		Parramatta

GRAND FINAL RECORDS

Most tries: 4, Johnny Graves (Souths), 1951
Most goals: 8, Harry Bath (St George), 1957
Most points: 16, Harry Bath (St George), 1957 (8 goals)
Most successful player: Norm Provan (St George), 10 wins
Most successful captain: Ken Kearney (St George), 5 wins, 1956-60
Most successful coach: Ken Kearney (St George), 5 wins, 1957-61; Jack Gibson, 5 wins (Easts 1974-75, Parramatta 1981-83).
Grand finals for three different clubs: Phil Sigsworth - Newtown, 1981; Manly, 1983; Canterbury, 1986
Most tries (team): 8, Newtown 1943; Souths, 1951; Easts, 1975
Most goals (team): 9, Souths (1951)
Most points (team): 42, Souths (1951)
Biggest winning margin: 38-0, Easts v St George, 1975
Lowest scoring: Parramatta 4, Canterbury 2, 1986
Tryless grand finals: 1986, Parramatta 4, Canterbury 2
Highest scoring: Souths 42, Manly 14, 1951
Most grand final wins (team): St George, 14
Most consecutive wins (team): St George, 11, 1956-66
Most appearances (player): Norm Provan (St George), 10, Brian Clay (Newtown, St George), 10.
Most appearances (referee): Darcy Lawler, 7 (1956-61, 1963)
Most points in all grand finals: Eric Simms (Souths), 41 (16 goals, 5 field goals).
Fathers and sons in grand finals: Fathers and sons in grand finals: Jack Spencer (Balmain, 1946-47) and John Spencer (Balmain, 1969); Bob McCarthy (Souths, 1967, 1970-71) and Darren McCarthy (Canterbury, 1988); Doug Daley (Manly, 1957) and Phil Daley (Manly, 1987); Robin Gourley (St George 1965-66) and Scott Gourley (St George 1992-93 and 1996); Bill Mullins (Easts 1972, 1974-75 and Brett Mullins (Canberra, 1994); Garry Hughes (Canterbury, 1979-80) and Steven Hughes (Canterbury, 1994); Garry Hughes (Canterbury, 1979-80) and Glen Hughes (Bulldogs, 1995); Clive Gartner (Canterbury, 1967) and Daniel Gartner (Manly, 1995-97); Gil MacDougall (Wests, 1962-63) and Adam MacDougall (Newcastle, 1997).
Sent off: Bryan Orrock (Souths) and Hec Farrell (Wests), 1952; Harry Bath (St George) and Rex Mossop (Manly), 1958, Dilan Wright (Easts) and Kevin Ryan (St George), 1960; Billy Wilson (St George), 1962; Phil Sigsworth (Canterbury), 1986.
Won Clive Churchill Medal twice: Bradley Clyde (Canberra), 1989, 1991

ARL PREMIERSHIP RECORDS

Club-by-Club Records

AUCKLAND

Year entered premiership: 1995 (Auckland competed in the 1997 Super League competition)
First match: March 10, 1995, lost 22-25 v Brisbane, Ericsson Stadium
Colours: Blue, white, red and green
Emblem: Warrior
Home ground: Ericsson Stadium
Attendance record: 30,112, Auckland v Manly, April 7, 1995

TITLES: Nil

Most tries in a match

Player	Tries	Opponent	Venue	Date
Phil Blake	4	Wests	Ericsson Stadium	March 26, 1995
Tea Ropati	3	Gold Coast	Ericsson Stadium	July 9, 1995
Gene Ngamu	3	North Queensland	Ericsson Stadium	August 3, 1996

(Marc Ellis scored three tries in a Super League match against North Queensland at Ericsson Stadium on August 24, 1997)

Most tries in a season

Player	Tries	Year
Sean Hoppe	19	1995
Phil Blake	14	1995
Tea Ropati	12	1995
John Kirwan	10	1996
Greg Alexander	8	1995

(Sean Hoppe scored 11 tries in the 1997 Super League competition)

Most tries for club

Player	Tries
Sean Hoppe	26
Phil Blake	17
Tea Ropati	17
John Kirwan	13
Greg Alexander	11
Richie Blackmore	11
Stacey Jones	11

(Hoppe's total does not include 11 Super League tries, Ropati 5 and Jones 7)

Most goals in a match

Player	Goals	Opponent	Venue	Date
Gene Ngamu	8	North Queensland	Ericsson Stadium	August 3, 1996
Gene Ngamu	7	Wests	Ericsson Stadium	March 26, 1995
Frano Botica	6	Sydney Tigers	Ericsson Stadium	June 4, 1995
Frano Botica	6	Gold Coast	Ericsson Stadium	July 9, 1995

(Gene Ngamu kicked seven goals in a Super League match against North Queensland at Ericsson Stadium on August 24, 1997)

Most points in a match

Player	Points	Opponent	Venue	Date
Gene Ngamu	28 (3T, 8G)	North Queensland	Ericsson Stadium	August 3, 1996
Gene Ngamu	18 (1T, 7G)	Wests	Ericsson Stadium	March 26, 1995
Phil Blake	16 (4T)	Wests	Ericsson Stadium	March 26, 1995
Frano Botica	16 (1T, 6G)	Gold Coast	Ericsson Stadium	July 9, 1995

(Matthew Ridge scored 18 points (2T, 5G) in a Super League match against Perth at Ericsson Stadium August 16, 1997)

Most points in a season

Player	Points		Year
Gene Ngamu	120	(5T, 50G)	1996
Gene Ngamu	84	(3T, 36G)	1995
Sean Hoppe	76	(19T)	1995
Phil Blake	56	(14T)	1995
Tea Ropati	48	(12T)	1995

(Marc Ellis scored 71 points (5T, 25G, 1FG) and Matthew Ridge scored 48 points (3T, 18G) in the 1997 Super League competition)

Most points for club

Player	Points	
Gene Ngamu	204	(8T, 86G)
Sean Hoppe	104	(26T)
Phil Blake	68	(17T)
Tea Ropati	68	(17T)
Stacey Jones	64	(11T, 9G, 2FG)

(Ngamu's total does not include 24 Super League points, Hoppe 44, Ropati 20 and Jones 29)

Biggest wins
52-6 v North Qld, Ericsson, August 3, 1996
40-4 v Parramatta, Parramatta, April 23, 1995
46-12 v Wests, Ericsson, March 26, 1995
44-16 v Gold Coast, Ericsson, July 9, 1995
38-12 v Illawarra, Ericsson, April 16, 1995
(Auckland beat North Queensland 50-22 in a Super League match at Ericsson Stadium on August 24, 1997)

Worst defeats
48-6 v Newcastle, Marathon, May 7, 1995
48-10 v Norths, North Sydney Oval, April 1, 1995
44-6 v Brisbane, ANZ Stadium, August 27, 1995
47-14 v St George, Ericsson, August 6, 1995
38-6 v Brisbane, Ericsson, August 30, 1996

Most first grade games

Sean Hoppe	42	Tea Ropati	41	John Kirwan	35
Stephen Kearney	41	Greg Alexander	37	Andy Platt	35
Gene Ngamu	41	Stacey Jones	35		

(Hoppe's total does not include 18 Super League games, Kearney 17, Ngamu 14, Ropati 15 and Jones 18)

CLUB INTERNATIONALS (New Zealand, 17) Richie Blackmore, Logan Edwards, Marc Ellis, Syd Eru, Sean Hoppe, Stacey Jones, Stephen Kearney, Gene Ngamu, Hitro Okesene, Matthew Ridge, Tea Ropati, Anthony Swann, Logan Swann, Tony Tatupu, Tony Tuimavave, Joe Vagana, Grant Young.

Test captains: Stephen Kearney (1997), Matthew Ridge (1997)
Rothmans Medal winners: Nil

BALMAIN

Year entered premiership: 1908 (Known as Sydney Tigers 1995-96)
First match: April 20, 1908, won 20-0 v Wests, Birchgrove Oval
Colours: Black and gold
Emblem: Tiger
Home ground: Leichhardt Oval
Attendance record: 22,750, Balmain v Penrith, August 27, 1989. 23,000 Cronulla v Souths (KB Cup final), August 12, 1981.

TITLES
First grade: 1915, 1916, 1917, 1919, 1920, 1924, 1939, 1944, 1946, 1947, 1969
Runners-up: 1909, 1936, 1945, 1948, 1956, 1964, 1966, 1988, 1989
Reserve grade: 1915, 1916, 1928, 1930, 1933, 1941, 1944, 1946, 1950, 1957, 1958, 1965, 1967, 1978, 1982, 1984
Third grade (Under-20s): 1915, 1916, 1919, 1926, 1934, 1948, 1950, 1954, 1955, 1956, 1960, 1968, 1973, 1997
Club Championship: 1941, 1943, 1944, 1947, 1950
Pre-season Cup: 1967, 1976
Amco Cup: 1976
National Panasonic Cup: 1985, 1987
Sevens: 1989

Most tries in a match

Player	Tries	Opponent	Venue	Date
Sid Goodwin	5	University	Leichhardt Oval	April 4, 1935
Arthur Patton	5	Easts	SCG	August 12, 1944
Bob Lulham	5	Parramatta	Leichhardt Oval	August 2, 1947
Dave Topliss	5	Newtown	Henson Park	August 7, 1977

Most tries in a season

Bobby Lulham	20	1947
Larry Corowa	24	1978
Arthur Patton	19	1944
Sid Goodwin	18	1939
Paul Cross	18	1971

Most tries for club

Arthur Patton	95
Sid Goodwin	86
Tim Brasher	82
Jack Robinson	78
Bob Mara	70

CLUB-BY-CLUB RECORDS

Most goals in a match

Player	Goals	Opponent	Venue	Date
Frank Driese	11	Wests	Pratten Park	July 29, 1944
Keith Barnes	11	Norths	Sports Ground	July 24, 1960

Most points in a match

Player	Points	Opponent	Venue	Date
Frank Driese	22 (11G)	Wests	Pratten Park	July 29, 1944
Keith Barnes	22 (11G)	Norths	Sports Ground	July 24, 1960
Ross Conlon	22 (1T, 9G)	Wests	Leichhardt Oval	April 4, 1985

Most points in a season

Len Killeen	207	(9T, 84G, 6FG)	1969
Ross Conlon	196	(4T, 90G)	1985
Ross Conlon	196	(4T, 90G)	1986
Ross Conlon	196	(5T, 88G)	1987
Greg Cox	187	(3T, 89G)	1977

Most points for club

Keith Barnes	1,519	(11T, 742G, 1FG)
Ross Conlon	756	(15T, 348G)
Joe Jorgenson	734	(22T, 334G)
Len Killeen	664	(36T, 270G, 8FG)
Wayne Miranda	541	(12T, 252G)
Tim Brasher	538	(82T, 105G)

Biggest wins

64-2 v Wests, Pratten Park, July 29, 1944
57-0 v University, Birchgrove Oval, April 23, 1921
59-8 v Easts, Leichhardt Oval, August 23, 1952
60-13 v University, Birchgrove, May 22, 1920
49-2 v University, Birchgrove, August 21, 1920

Worst defeats

62-5 v Wests, Lidcombe Oval, March 31, 1974
50-0 v Brisbane, ANZ Stadium, August 13, 1993
56-10 v Manly, Parramatta, August 6, 1995
42-0 v Manly, Leichhardt Oval, May 28, 1994
41-0 v St George, SCG, August 7, 1965

Most first grade games

Garry Jack	244	Wayne Pearce	192	Reg Latta	176	Trevor Ryan	159
Ben Elias	234	Tim Brasher	185	Garry Leo	173	Bob Boland	157
Paul Sironen	225	Charles Fraser	185	John Davidson	172	Jack Robinson	156
Keith Barnes	194	Steve Roach	185	John Spencer, jnr	161	Peter Provan	155

CLUB INTERNATIONALS (39) Keith Barnes, Arthur Beetson, George Bishop, Tim Brasher, Larry Corowa, Jim Craig, Robert Craig, Fred de Belin, Pat Devery, Alf Dobbs, Ben Elias, Charles Fraser, Sid Goodwin, Robert Graves, Frank Griffiths, Arthur Halloway, Garry Jack, Joe Jorgenson, Bill Kelly, Reg Latta, Bob Lulham, Bruce McGuire, Allan McMahon, Charles McMurtrie, Barry McTaggart, Bill Marsh, Rod Morris, Dave Parkinson, Wayne Pearce, Peter Provan, Steve Roach, Jack Robinson, Bill Schultz, Paul Sironen, Geoff Starling, Dennis Tutty, Tom Tyrrell, Horrie Watt, Fred Woolley

Test captains: Robert Graves (1909), Arthur "Pony" Halloway (1919), Charles Fraser (1921), Joe Jorgenson (1946), Keith Barnes (1959-62)
World Cup captains: Keith Barnes (1960)
Rothmans Medal winners: Wayne Pearce (1985)
Major sponsor 1997: Meriton
First grade 1997: Coach Wayne Pearce. Finished 8th
Second grade 1997: Coach Dan Stains. Finished 2nd
Under-20s 1997: Coach Peter Camroux. Finished 1st

1997 Representative players: City - Tim Brasher, Darren Senter. Country - William Kennedy, Glenn Morrison. NSW - Tim Brasher. Australia - Tim Brasher.

BRISBANE

Year entered premiership: 1988 (Brisbane competed in the 1997 Super League competition)
First match: March 6, 1988, won 44-10 v Manly, Lang Park
Colours: Maroon, white and yellow
Emblem: Bronco
Home ground: ANZ Stadium
Attendance record: 58,593, Brisbane v St George, August 27, 1993 (58,912 attended the 1997 Super League grand final between Brisbane and Cronulla, September 20, 1997).

TITLES:
First grade: 1992, 1993
(Brisbane won the 1997 Super League competition)
Reserve grade: 1990
Club Championship: 1992, 1996
Panasonic Cup: 1989
Lotto Challenge: 1991
Tooheys Challenge: 1995
(Brisbane also won the 1997 Super League World Club Challenge)

Most tries in a match

Player	Tries	Opponent	Venue	Date
Steve Renouf	4	Norths	Lang Park	August 9, 1991
Steve Renouf	4	Canterbury	ANZ Stadium	July 25, 1993
Steve Renouf	4	Balmain	Melbourne	April 23, 1994
Steve Renouf	4	Auckland	ANZ Stadium	August 27, 1995

Most tries in a season

Player	Tries	Year
Steve Renouf	23	1994
Steve Renouf	19	1996
Willie Carne	17	1993
Steve Renouf	16	1993
Wally Lewis	15	1988
Willie Carne	15	1990
Steve Renouf	15	1991
Michael Hancock	15	1995
Steve Renouf	15	1995

(Wendell Sailor scored 15 tries in the 1997 Super League competition)

Most tries for club

Player	Tries
Steve Renouf	102
Michael Hancock	96
Allan Langer	79
Willie Carne	72
Chris Johns	50

(Renouf's total does not include 14 Super League tries, Hancock 5, Langer 5)

Most goals in a match

Player	Goals	Opponent	Venue	Crowd
Terry Matterson	8	Manly	Lang Park	March 6, 1988
Julian O'Neill	8	Parramatta	Parramatta Stadium	June 25, 1995

Most points in a match

Player	Points	Opponent	Venue	Crowd
Terry Matterson	24 (2T, 8G)	Manly	Lang Park	March 6, 1988
Julian O'Neill	20 (1T, 8G)	Parramatta	Parramatta	June 25, 1995

Most points in a season

Player	Points		Year
Julian O'Neill	193	(8T, 79G, 3FG)	1995
Terry Matterson	156	(2T, 74G)	1992
Terry Matterson	150	(8T, 59G)	1988
Willie Carne	146	(7T, 59G)	1990
Terry Matterson	144	(7T, 58G)	1993

(Darren Lockyer scored 168 points (7T, 70G) in the 1997 Super League competition)

Most points for club

Player	Points	
Terry Matterson	744	(29T, 314G)
Julian O'Neill	480	(33T, 169G, 10FG)
Willie Carne	414	(72T, 63G)
Steve Renouf	408	(102T)
Michael Hancock	388	(96T)

(Renouf's total does not include 56 Super League points, Hancock 20)

CLUB-BY-CLUB RECORDS

Biggest wins
50-0 v Balmain, ANZ Stadium, August 13, 1993
56-6 v Souths, ANZ Stadium, August 13, 1995
54-4 v Illawarra, ANZ Stadium, April 6, 1996
60-14 v Parramatta, Parramatta, June 25, 1995
54-8 v Souths, ANZ Stadium, July 2, 1993

Worst defeats
38-8 v Cronulla, Caltex Field, April 23, 1988
32-4 v Canberra, SFS, September 16, 1990
26-0 v Manly, Brookvale Oval, July 14, 1991
26-0 v Canberra, Bruce Stadium, April 28, 1995
38-14 v Cronulla, Parramatta, August 29, 1989
(Brisbane was beaten 32-4 by Cronulla in a Super League match at Shark Park, June 30, 1997)

Most first grade games

Allan Langer	186	Chris Johns	170	Andrew Gee	145	Mark Hohn	117
Michael Hancock	184	Terry Matterson	152	Willie Carne	135	Julian O'Neill	105
Kerrod Walters	181	Kevin Walters	151	Steve Renouf	132	Glenn Lazarus	103

(Langer's total does not include 18 Super League games, Hancock 14, Kevin Walters 20, Gee 20, Renouf 15 and Lazarus 15)

CLUB INTERNATIONALS (19) Sam Backo, Willie Carne, Greg Conescu, Tony Currie, Andrew Gee, Michael Hancock, Paul Hauff, Mark Hohn, Peter Jackson, Chris Johns, Allan Langer, Glenn Lazarus, Wally Lewis, Gene Miles, Steve Renouf, Wendell Sailor, Dale Shearer, Kerrod Walters, Kevin Walters *(Allan Langer, Glenn Lazarus, Darren Lockyer, Steve Renouf, Wendell Sailor, Darren Smith, Brad Thorn and Shane Webcke represented the Australian Super League side)*

Test captains: Wally Lewis (1988-89)
World Cup captains: Wally Lewis (1988-89)
Rothmans Medal winners: Allan Langer (1992)
Clive Churchill Medal winners: Allan Langer (1992)
Year entered premiership: 1988
Colours: Maroon, white and yellow
Emblem: Bronco
Home ground: ANZ Stadium

CANBERRA

Year entered premiership: 1982 (Canberra competed in the 1997 Super League competition)
First match: February 27, 1982, lost 7-37 v Souths, Redfern Oval
Colours: Lime green, white, blue and gold arm bands
Emblem: Raider
Home ground: Bruce Stadium
Attendance record: 25,253, Canberra v Wests, August 21, 1994

TITLES
First grade: 1989, 1990, 1994
Runners-up: 1987, 1991
Reserve grade: Nil
President's Cup: 1990, 1995
Club Championship: 1990
Channel TEN Challenge: 1990
Tooheys Challenge: 1993

Most tries in a match

Player	Tries	Opponent	Venue	Date
Mal Meninga	5	Easts	Bruce Stadium	April 16, 1990
John Ferguson	4	Gold Coast	Seiffert Oval	April 17, 1988
Phil Carey	4	Illawarra	Seiffert Oval	April 25, 1989
Gary Coyne	4	Manly	Football Stadium	September 7, 1991
Jason Croker	4	Cronulla	Caltex Field	August 14, 1993
Ruben Wiki	4	Newcastle	Bruce Stadium	March 27, 1994
Brett Mullins	4	Souths	Football Stadium	July 24, 1994
Brett Mullins	4	Newcastle	Marathon Stadium	July 29, 1994
Ken Nagas	4	South Queensland	Bruce Stadium	August 27, 1995
Ruben Wiki	4	North Queensland	Bruce Stadium	April 14, 1996
Noa Nadruku	4	South Queensland	Suncorp Stadium	September 1, 1996

Most tries in a season
Noa Nadruku	22	1993
Jason Croker	22	1994
Brett Mullins	22	1994
Noa Nadruku	21	1996
John Ferguson	20	1988

Most tries for club
Mal Meninga	74
Laurie Daley	70
Gary Belcher	69
Brett Mullins	67
Jason Croker	66
Noa Nadruku	66
Chris O'Sullivan	62

(Daley's total does not include five Super League tries, Mullins 10, Croker 2 and Nadruku 7)

Most goals in a match
Player	Goals	Opponent	Venue	Crowd
David Furner	10	Parramatta	Bruce Stadium	August 22, 1993
Gary Belcher	9	Cronulla	Seiffert Oval	April 3, 1988
Mal Meninga	9	Easts	Bruce Stadium	April 15, 1990

Most points in a match
Player	Points	Opponent	Venue	Date
Mal Meninga	38 (5T, 9G)	Easts	Bruce Stadium	April 16, 1990
Mal Meninga	26 (3T, 7G)	Wests	Seiffert Oval	April 19, 1987
Laurie Daley	22 (2T, 7G)	Canterbury	Seiffert Oval	April 16, 1989
David Furner	22 (3T, 5G)	Parramatta	Bruce Stadium	June 7, 1992
Gary Belcher	20 (2T, 6G)	Brisbane	Lang Park	May 22, 1988
David Furner	20 (10G)	Parramatta	Bruce Stadium	August 22, 1993

(Furner scored 20 points (1T, 8G) in a Super League match against Adelaide at Bruce Stadium, August 17, 1997)

Most points in a season
Gary Belcher	218	(10T, 89G)	1988
Mal Meninga	212	(17T, 72G)	1990
David Furner	198	(10T, 79G)	1995
David Furner	196	(6T, 86G)	1994
Ron Giteau	193	(5T, 86G, 1FG)	1983

Most points for club
Mal Meninga	864	(74T, 283G, 2FG)
David Furner	802	(30T, 341G)
Gary Belcher	572	(69T, 148G)
Ron Giteau	527	(14T, 234G, 3FG)
Laurie Daley	358	(70T, 37G, 4FG)

(Furner's total does not include 116 Super League points, Daley 36)

Biggest wins
68-0 v Parramatta, Bruce, August 22, 1993
66-4 v Easts, Bruce Stadium, April 15, 1990
66-10 v North Qld, Bruce Stadium, April 14, 1996
58-4 v South Qld, Bruce, August 27, 1995
56-6 v Gold Coast, Bruce, August 13, 1995

Worst defeats
54-3 v Parramatta, Belmore, April 11, 1982
45-0 v Illawarra, Wollongong, April 25, 1982
50-6 v St George, Seiffert Oval, August 25, 1982
61-20 v Manly, Brookvale Oval, July 11, 1982
55-15 v Easts, SSG, May 23, 1982
50-10 v Parramatta, Parramatta, June 23, 1996

Most first grade games
Steve Walters	228	Mal Meninga	166	Gary Belcher	148	Bradley Clyde	137
Chris O'Sullivan	204	Dean Lance	160	Craig Bellamy	148	Ashley Gilbert	135
Ricky Stuart	171	Gary Coyne	158	Laurie Daley	167	Jason Croker	121

(Stuart's total does not include 16 Super League games, Daley 21, Clyde 19 and Croker 9)

CLUB INTERNATIONALS (12) Sam Backo, Gary Belcher, Bradley Clyde, Gary Coyne, Laurie Daley, David Furner, Peter Jackson, Glenn Lazarus, Mal Meninga, Brett Mullins, Ricky Stuart, Steve Walters
(Bradley Clyde, Laurie Daley, David Furner, Brett Mullins, Ken Nagas and Luke Priddis represented the Australian Super League team)

Test captains: Mal Meninga (1990-94), Laurie Daley (1993)
(Laurie Daley captained the 1997 Australian Super League team)
World Cup captains: Mal Meninga (1990-92)
Rothmans Medal winners: Ricky Stuart (1993)
(Laurie Daley won the 1997 Super League best and fairest award)
Clive Churchill Medal winners: Bradley Clyde (1989, 1991), Ricky Stuart (1990), David Furner (1994)

CLUB-BY-CLUB RECORDS

CANTERBURY-BANKSTOWN

Year entered premiership: 1935 (Canterbury competed in the 1997 Super League competition. Known as Sydney Bulldogs 1995-96)
First match: April 25, 1935, lost 5-20 v Norths, North Sydney Oval
Colours: Blue and white
Emblem: Bulldog
Home ground: Belmore Sports Ground
Attendance record: 27,804, Canterbury v Parramatta, April 12, 1993

TITLES
First grade: 1938, 1942, 1980, 1984, 1985, 1988, 1995
Runners-up: 1940, 1947, 1967, 1974, 1979, 1986, 1994
Reserve grade: 1939, 1971, 1972, 1980
(Canterbury won the 1997 Super League reserve grade competition)
Third grade (President's Cup): 1971, 1991
Club Championship: 1938, 1939, 1993, 1994
Craven Mild Cup: 1962, 1970

Most tries in a match

Player	Tries	Opponent	Venue	Date
Edgar Newham	5	Balmain	Sydney Cricket Ground	August 15, 1942
Tony Nash	4	Souths	Sydney Cricket Ground	May 23, 1942
Eddie Burns	4	Newtown	Belmore Sports Ground	July 11, 1942
Bernie Lowther	4	Penrith	Penrith Park	June 30, 1974
Peter Mortimer	4	Wests	Lidcombe Oval	August 19, 1984
Andrew Farrar	4	Wests	Lidcombe Oval	June 2, 1985
Terry Lamb	4	Wests	Belmore Sports Ground	March 21, 1987
Ewan McGrady	4	Souths	Belmore Sports Ground	August 11, 1991

(Hazem El Masri scored four tries in a Super League match against Hunter at Belmore Sports Ground, May 12, 1997)

Most tries in a season

Player	Tries	Year
Chris Anderson	19	1983
Terry Lamb	17	1984
Terry Lamb	16	1987
Chris Anderson	16	1974
Morrie Murphy	14	1947
Barry Stenhouse	14	1953
Steve Gearin	14	1980
Greg Brentnall	14	1982
Ewan McGrady	14	1991

(Matthew Ryan scored 17 Super League tries in 1997, Hazem El Masri 16)

Most tries for club

Player	Tries
Terry Lamb	123
Chris Anderson	93
Steve Mortimer	79
Peter Mortimer	78
Steve Gearin	63
Eddie Burns	60

Most goals in a match

Player	Goals	Opponent	Venue	Date
George Taylforth	9	Newtown	Sports Ground	May 14, 1967
George Taylforth	9	Cronulla	Endeavour Field	May 11, 1969
Henry Tatana	9	Balmain	Belmore Sports Ground	July 15, 1973
Terry Lamb	9	Wests	Sydney Cricket Ground	June 23, 1986

Most points in a match

Player	Points	Opponent	Venue	Date
Terry Lamb	26 (4T, 5G)	Wests	Belmore Sports Ground	March 21, 1987
Steve Gearin	25 (3T, 8G)	Balmain	Leichhardt Oval	April 20, 1981
George Taylforth	24 (2T, 9G)	Cronulla	Endeavour Field	May 11, 1969
Steve Gearin	22 (2T, 8G)	Souths	Belmore Sports Ground	August 16, 1981
Terry Lamb	22 (1T, 9G)	Wests	SCG	June 23, 1986
Daryl Halligan	22 (2T, 7G)	Newcastle	Belmore Sports Ground	April 9, 1994
Daryl Halligan	22 (2T, 7G)	Souths	Parramatta Stadium	July 29, 1995

Most points in a season

Daryl Halligan	270	(12T, 110G, 2FG)	1994
Steve Gearin	244	(12T, 104G)	1979
Daryl Halligan	222	(12T, 87G)	1995
Steve Gearin	220	(14T, 89G)	1980
Terry Lamb	210	(12T, 76G, 10FG)	1986
George Taylforth	204	(2T, 99G)	1967

Most points for club

Terry Lamb	1,276	(123T, 375G, 37FG)
Steve Gearin	1,006	(63T, 405G)
Daryl Halligan	638	(31T, 256G, 2FG)
Les Johns	545	(14T, 233G, 19FG)
George Taylforth	410	(8T, 192G, 1FG)

(Halligan's total does not include 182 Super League points)

Biggest wins
66-4 v North Qld, Belmore, August 27, 1995
52-0 v Wests, Lidcombe Oval, June 2, 1985
54-4 v Wests, SCG, June 23, 1986
50-6 v Norths, North Sydney Oval, May 18, 1975
42-0 v Western Reds, Parramatta, April 9, 1995

Worst defeats
91-6 v St George, Earl Park, May 11, 1935*
87-7 v Easts, SSG, May 18, 1935
65-10 v Easts, Pratten Park, August 10, 1935
65-11 v Wests, Pratten Park, August 31, 1935
63-12 v St George, Kogarah Oval, June 15, 1959
* premiership record

Most first grade games

Steve Mortimer	267	Chris Anderson	232	Peter Mortimer	190	Bill Noonan	161
Terry Lamb	261	Fred Anderson	215	Andrew Farrar	186	Roy Kirkaldy	160
Steve Folkes	243	Ray Gartner	200	Paul Langmack	174	Henry Porter	156
Eddie Burns	232	Chris Mortimer	191	Mark Hughes	164		

CLUB INTERNATIONALS (28) Chris Anderson, Ron Bailey, Greg Brentnall, Ross Conlon, Ron Costello, Tony Currie, Brett Dallas, Paul Dunn, Jim Dymock, Andrew Farrar, Steve Folkes, David Gillespie, Kevin Goldspink, Johnny Greaves, Bruce Hopkins, Les Johns, Terry Lamb, Paul Langmack, Bruce McGuire, Chris Mortimer, Steve Mortimer, Dean Pay, George Peponis, Tim Pickup, John Rhodes, Jason Smith, Peter Tunks, Ron Willey *(Solomon Haumono represented the Australian Super League side in 1997)*

Test captains: Ron Bailey (1946), George Peponis (1979-80)
World Cup captains: nil
Rothmans Medal winners: Greg Brentnall (1982), Terry Lamb (1984), Ewan McGrady (1991)
Clive Churchill Medal winners: Paul Dunn (1988), Jim Dymock (1995)

CRONULLA-SUTHERLAND

Year entered premiership: 1967 (Cronulla competed in the 1997 Super League competition)
First match: April 2, 1967, won 11-5 v Easts, Sydney Sports Ground
Colours: Blue, black and white
Emblem: Shark
Home ground: Shark Park (formerly known as Endeavour Field and Caltex Field)
Attendance record: 20,168, Cronulla v Manly, April 9, 1994

TITLES
First grade: Nil
Runners-up: 1973, 1978
(Cronulla were runners-up to Brisbane in the 1997 Super League competition)
Reserve grade: 1994, 1996
Third grade (President's Cup) 1975, 1994
Club Championship: 1995
Amco Cup: 1979

Most tries in a match

Player	Tries	Opponent	Venue	Date
Andrew Ettingshausen	5	Illawarra	Caltex Field	August 27, 1989
Andrew Ettingshausen	5	Souths	Caltex Field	August 27, 1994
John Monie	4	Newtown	Endeavour Field	August 10, 1968
Ray Corcoran	4	Souths	Endeavour Field	May 18, 1975
Martin Raftery	4	Souths	Endeavour Field	May 16, 1976
Rick Bourke	4	Newtown	Endeavour Field	July 17, 1977
Mat Rogers	4	Newcastle	Marathon Stadium	August 25, 1995

CLUB-BY-CLUB RECORDS

Most tries in a season
Andrew Ettingshausen	18	1994
Ray Corcoran	17	1971
Chris Gardner	17	1983
Andrew Ettingshausen	17	1988

Most tries for club
Andrew Ettingshausen	136
Steve Rogers	82
Ray Corcoran	63
Jonathan Docking	57
Mick Mullane	53

(Ettingshausen's total does not include 7 Super League tries)

Most goals in a match
Player	Goals	Opponent	Venue	Crowd
Steve Rogers	10	Wests	Pratten Park	August 6, 1977
George Taylforth	9	Norths	Endeavour Field	March 28, 1971
Barry Andrews	9	Newtown	Endeavour Field	July 17, 1977
Steve Rogers	9	Balmain	Endeavour Field	July 12, 1980

Most points in a match
Player	Points	Opponent	Venue	Date
Steve Rogers	26 (2T, 10G)	Wests	Pratten Park	August 6, 1977
Steve Rogers	24 (2T, 9G)	Balmain	Endeavour Field	July 12, 1980
Andrew Ettingshausen	20 (5T)	Illawarra	Caltex Field	August 27, 1989
Greg Carberry	20 (3T, 4G)	Easts	Caltex Field	July 28, 1991
Andrew Ettingshausen	20 (5T)	Souths	Caltex Field	August 27, 1994
Mat Rogers	20 (1T, 8G)	Parramatta	Parramatta Stadium	August 13, 1995
Mat Rogers	20 (4T, 2G)	Newcastle	Marathon Stadium	August 25, 1995
Mat Rogers	20 (2T, 6G)	Sydney Tigers	Parramatta Stadium	April 21, 1996

(Mat Rogers scored 22 points (2T, 7G) in a Super League match against Penrith at Shark Park, July 12, 1997)

Most points in a season
George Taylforth	202	(4T, 95G)	1970
Steve Rogers	194	(14T, 76G)	1981
Dean Carney	194	(11T, 75G)	1985
Mat Rogers	192	(14T, 68G)	1995
Steve Rogers	187	(9T, 79G, 2FG)	1982

(Mat Rogers scored 196 points (14T, 70G) in the 1997 Super League competition)

Most points for club
Steve Rogers	1,253	(82T, 501G, 5FG)
Barry Andrews	657	(17T, 303G)
Andrew Ettingshausen	544	(136T)
Allan Wilson	520	(37T, 185G, 2FG)
Terry Hughes	388	(8T, 171G, 11FG)

(Ettingshausen's total does not include 28 Super League points)

Biggest wins
46-0 v Gold Coast, Caltex Field, June 5, 1994
44-0 v Newtown, Endeavour Field, July 23, 1978
42-0 v Souths, Caltex Field, August 27, 1994
44-4 v Balmain, Caltex Field, March 24, 1991
43-4 v Penrith, Penrith Park, July 9, 1978
44-5 v Canberra, Seiffert Oval, May 2, 1982
42-3 v Norths, Endeavour Field, March 28, 1971

Worst defeats
56-12 v Canberra, Bruce Stadium, July 16, 1994
46-6 v Canberra, Bruce Stadium, April 11, 1993
43-4 v Souths, Redfern Oval, April 11, 1969
40-2 v Brisbane, Lang Park, May 31, 1991
44-6 v Illawarra, Wollongong, August 4, 1991

Most first grade games
A Ettingshausen	253	David Hatch	185	Mark McGaw	159	Dan Stains	135
Dane Sorensen	216	Gavin Miller	180	Michael Porter	154	John Maguire	134
Greg Pierce	206	Danny Lee	174	Rick Bourke	153	Mitch Healey	133
Steve Rogers	198	Jonathan Docking	162	Craig Dimond	143	Chris Gardner	130

(Ettingshausen's total does not include 19 Super League games, Lee 19 and Healey 20)

CLUB INTERNATIONALS (11) Andrew Ettingshausen, Steve Kneen, Mark McGaw, Ken Maddison, Gavin Miller, Greg Pierce, Aaron Raper, Steve Rogers, Dan Stains, Ron Turner, David Waite *(Andrew Ettingshausen, Paul Green, Craig Greenhill, Danny Lee, Russell Richardson, David Peachey and Jason Stevens represented the Australian Super League side in 1997)*

Test captains: Greg Pierce (1978), Steve Rogers (1981)
World Cup captains: Nil
Rothmans Medal winners: Terry Hughes (1968), Ken Maddison (1973), Steve Rogers (1975), Barry Russell (1988), Gavin Miller (1989), Paul Green (1995)

GOLD COAST

Year entered premiership: 1988
First match: March 5, 1988, lost 10-21 v Canterbury, Seagulls Stadium
Colours: Jade, black, purple and gold
Emblem: Charger (formerly Giant, Seagull)
Home ground: Carrara Stadium
Attendance record: 22,688, Gold Coast v Brisbane, March 18, 1994

TITLES: Nil

Most tries in a match

Player	Tries	Opponent	Venue	Date
Shane Russell	4	Wests	Campbelltown Sports Ground	March 8, 1997
Danny Peacock	3	Penrith	Penrith Football Stadium	May 28, 1995

Most tries in a season

Player	Tries	Year
Danny Peacock	14	1995
Wes Patten	12	1997
Wayne Bartrim	10	1994
Scott Mieni	8	1988
Lee Oudenryn	8	1990

Most tries for club

Player	Tries
Danny Peacock	28
Jamie Goddard	20
Wayne Bartrim	18
Jeremy Schloss	14
Ben Gonzales	12
Wes Patten	12
Brett French	11

Most goals in a match

Player	Goals	Opponent	Venue	Date
Brendan Hurst	8	Sth Queensland	Suncorp Stadium	July 21, 1996
Mike Eden	6	Easts	Seagulls Stadium	April 29, 1989
Mike Eden	6	Manly	Seagulls Stadium	July 2, 1989
Wayne Bartrim	6	Easts	Sydney Football Stadium	August 27, 1994

Most points in a match

Player	Points	Opponent	Venue	Date
Wayne Bartrim	20 (2T, 6G)	Balmain	Seagulls	July 31, 1994
Brendan Hurst	20 (1T, 8G)	Sth Queensland	Suncorp Stadium	July 21, 1996
Mike Eden	17 (1T, 6G, 1FG)	Manly	Seagulls	July 2, 1989
Mike Eden	16 (1T, 6G)	Easts	Seagulls	April 29, 1989
Craig Weston	16 (2T, 4G)	Souths	Stadium	June 21, 1992
Wayne Bartrim	16 (1T, 6G)	Easts	Stadium	August 27, 1994
Shane Russell	16 (4T)	Wests	Campbelltown	March 8, 1997

Most points in a season

Player	Points		Year
Wayne Bartrim	124	(10T, 42G)	1994
Brendan Hurst	107	(3T, 47G, 1FG)	1996
Brendan Hurst	90	(2T, 41G)	1995
Brendan Hurst	88	(3T, 37G, 2FG)	1997
Mike Eden	79	(1T, 36G, 3FG)	1988

Most points for club

Player	Points	
Brendan Hurst	285	(8T, 125G, 3FG)
Wayne Bartrim	224	(18T, 76G)
Mike Eden	142	(4T, 61G, 4FG)
Danny Peacock	112	(28T)
Peter Benson	104	(8T, 36G)

Biggest wins

52-4 v South Qld, Suncorp Stadium, July 21, 1996
38-12 v Souths, SFS, August 5, 1990
32-6 v Balmain, Seagulls Stadium, July 31, 1994
28-4 v Souths, Carrara Stadium, June 7, 1997
29-6 v Manly, Seagulls Stadium, July 2, 1989

Worst defeats

56-6 v Canberra, Bruce, August 13, 1995
46-0 v Manly, Brookvale Oval, August 15, 1993
46-0 v Cronulla, Caltex Field, June 5, 1994
50-6 v Canberra, Bruce Stadium, April 17, 1988
46-2 v Balmain, Seagulls Stadium, June 23, 1990
48-4 v Canberra, Bruce Stadium, May 22, 1993
50-0 v Newcastle, Marathon Stadium, August 22, 1993

CLUB-BY-CLUB RECORDS

Most first grade games

Brett Horsnell	82	Robert Simpkins	72	Danny Peacock	67	Billy Johnstone	61
Clinton Mohr	82	Peter Gill	68	Tony Durheim	65	Ben Gonzales	58
Wayne Bartrim	77	Chris Close	67	Jamie Goddard	63	Geoff Bagnall	56
Brendan Hurst	74						

CLUB INTERNATIONALS: (2) Wally Lewis, Dale Shearer
Test captains: Nil
World Cup captains: Nil
Rothmans Medal winners: Nil
Major sponsor 1997: Chandlers
First grade 1997: Coach Phil Economidis. Finished 6th
Second grade 1997: Coach Fred Teasdell. Finished 8th
Under-20s 1997: Coach Graham Eadie. Finished 11th

1997 Representative players: Queensland - Jamie Goddard, Jeremy Schloss. Rest of the World: Marcus Bai, Tom O'Reilly, Chris Nahi.

ILLAWARRA

Year entered premiership: 1982
First match: February 28, 1982, lost 7-17 v Penrith, Wollongong Showground
Colours: Scarlet and white
Emblem: Steeler
Home ground: WIN Stadium (formerly known as Wollongong Showground and Steelers Stadium)
Attendance record: 17,527, Illawarra v St George, May 21, 1993

TITLES:
Tooheys Challenge: 1992

Most tries in a match

Player	Tries	Opponent	Venue	Date
Alan McIndoe	5	Gold Coast	Wollongong	May 4, 1991
Brett Rodwell	4	Auckland	Steelers Stadium	March 18, 1995

Most tries in a season

Player	Tries	Year
Alan McIndoe	19	1991
Shane McKellar	18	1983
Wayne Clifford	14	1997
Rod Wishart	14	1996
John Sparks	13	1982
Shane McKellar	13	1982

Most tries for club

Player	Tries
Alan McIndoe	65
Rod Wishart	65
Brett Rodwell	60
Paul McGregor	38
John Cross	32

Most goals in a match

Player	Goals	Opponent	Venue	Date
Rod Wishart	10	Parramatta	Steelers Stadium	July 16, 1995
Rod Wishart	9	Wests	Steelers Stadium	August 27, 1995
Rod Wishart	8	Canterbury	Wollongong	March 31, 1991
Rod Wishart	8	Souths	Steelers Stadium	April 14, 1996

Most points in a match

Player	Points	Opponent	Venue	Date
Rod Wishart	22 (1T, 9G)	Wests	Steelers Stadium	August 27, 1995
Rod Wishart	22 (3T, 5G)	Newcastle	Marathon Stadium	August 4, 1996
Rod Wishart	22 (2T, 7G)	Penrith	Steelers Stadium	August 25, 1996
Rod Wishart	22 (2T, 7G)	Souths	WIN	March 9, 1997

Most points in a season

Player	Points		Year
Rod Wishart	176	(11T, 66G)	1995
John Dorahy	175	(5T, 76G, 3FG)	1983
Dean Carney	162	(8T, 64G, 2FG)	1987
Rod Wishart	160	(14T, 52G)	1996
John Dorahy	159	(6T, 70G, 1FG)	1982

Most points for club

Player	Points	
Rod Wishart	986	(65T, 363G)
John Dorahy	463	(14T, 204G, 5FG)
Alan McIndoe	260	(65T)
Brett Rodwell	256	(60T, 8G)
Dean Carney	198	(12T, 74G, 2FG)

Biggest wins
45-0 v Canberra, Wollongong, April 25, 1982
46-4 v Gold Coast, Wollongong, May 4, 1991
56-14 v Souths, Steelers, April 14, 1996
44-4 v Canterbury, Wollongong, March 31, 1991
52-12 v Parramatta, Steelers, July 16, 1995
46-6 v Wests, Steelers, August 27, 1995
42-2 v Penrith, Steelers, August 25, 1996
50-10 v Souths, WIN Stadium, March 9, 1997

Worst defeats
51-0 v Newtown, Henson Park, May 2, 1982
55-5 v Parramatta, Belmore, May 30, 1982
54-4 v Brisbane, ANZ Stadium, April 6, 1996
47-2 v Easts, SSG, March 11, 1983
48-6 v Easts, Henson Park, April 16, 1989

Most first grade games

Michael Bolt	167	Brian Hetherington	144	Alan McIndoe	125	Ian Russell	110
Brett Rodwell	156	Rod Wishart	142	John Simon	120	David Walsh	106
Neil Piccinelli	145	John Cross	137	Paul McGregor	111	Greg Mackey	103

CLUB INTERNATIONALS (4) Bob Lindner, Paul McGregor, Alan McIndoe, Rod Wishart

Test captains: Nil
World Cup captains: Nil
Rothmans Medal winners: Nil
Major sponsor 1997: BHP
First grade 1997: Coach Andrew Farrar. Finished 7th
Second grade 1997: Coach Ian Millward. Finished 5th
Under-20s 1997: Coach Phil Ostwald. Finished 7th

1997 Representative players: Country - Paul McGregor. NSW - Rod Wishart, Paul McGregor, Trent Barrett. Queensland - Craig Smith. Australia - Paul McGregor. Rest of the World - Craig Smith.

MANLY-WARRINGAH

Year entered premiership: 1947
First match: April 12, 1947, lost 13-15 v Wests, Brookvale Oval
Colours: Maroon and white
Emblem: Sea Eagle
Home ground: Brookvale Oval
Attendance record: 27,655, Manly v Parramatta, August 31, 1986

TITLES
First grade: 1972, 1973, 1976, 1978, 1987, 1996
Runners-up: 1951, 1957, 1959, 1968, 1970, 1982, 1983, 1995, 1997
Reserve grade: 1954, 1960, 1969, 1973, 1988
Third grade (President's Cup): 1952
Club Championship: 1972, 1983, 1987, 1988
Pre-season Cup: 1980
KB Cup: 1982, 1983
Sevens: 1990, 1994, 1995

Most tries in a match

Player	Tries	Opponent	Venue	Date
Les Hanigan	5	Cronulla	Brookvale Oval	May 14, 1967

Most tries in a season

Phil Blake	27	1983
Kevin Junee	23	1974
Steve Menzies	22	1995
Terry Hill	22	1997
Bob Fulton	21	1976
John Hopoate	21	1995
John Ribot	20	1982
Steve Menzies	20	1996

Most tries for club

Bob Fulton	129
Tom Mooney	83
Cliff Lyons	77
Des Hasler	72
Graham Eadie	71
Steve Menzies	71
Phil Blake	66
Alan Thompson	62
Gordon Willoughby	60
Craig Hancock	59
Michael O'Connor	54
Nick Yakich	52

CLUB BY CLUB RECORDS

Most goals in a match

Player	Goals	Opponent	Venue	Date
Graham Eadie	14	Penrith	Penrith Park	July 29, 1973
Graham Eadie	12	Souths	Brookvale Oval	August 24, 1975
Mike Eden	11	Canberra	Brookvale Oval	July 11, 1982
Matthew Ridge	11	Wests	Brookvale Oval	March 26, 1994
Matthew Ridge	11	Wests	Brookvale Oval	August 25, 1996

Most points in a match

Player	Points		Opponent	Venue	Date
Ron Rowles	30	(4T, 9G)	Canterbury	Brookvale Oval	July 24, 1954
Matthew Ridge	30	(2T, 11G)	Wests	Brookvale Oval	August 25, 1996
Graham Eadie	28	(14G)	Penrith	Penrith Park	July 29, 1973
Matthew Ridge	28	(3T, 8G)	Western Reds	Brookvale Oval	June 25, 1995
Ron Rowles	27	(3T, 9G)	Easts	Brookvale Oval	April 17, 1954
Graham Eadie	27	(1T, 12G)	Souths	Brookvale Oval	August 24, 1975

Most points in a season

Player	Points		Year
Matthew Ridge	257	(11T, 106G, 1FG)	1995
Graham Eadie	242	(14T, 100G)	1975
Matthew Ridge	234	(5T, 106G, 2FG)	1994
Graham Eadie	233	(9T, 103G)	1976
Graham Eadie	226	(7T, 99G)	1983
Ron Rowles	221	(13T, 91G)	1954
Ron Rowles	220	(12T, 92G)	1951
Graham Eadie	216	(10T, 93G)	1974

Most points for club

Graham Eadie	1,917	(71T, 847G, 3FG)
Bob Batty	1,154	(40T, 502G, 15FG)
Matthew Ridge	1,093	(32T, 477G, 11FG)
Ron Willey	958	(20T, 449G)
Ron Rowles	842	(46T, 352G)
Michael O'Connor	578	(54T, 180G, 2FG)
Bob Fulton	510	(129T, 10G, 56FG)

Biggest wins
70-7 v Penrith, Penrith Park, July 29, 1973
61-0 v St George, Brookvale Oval, July 3, 1994
66-8 v Wests, Brookvale Oval, March 26, 1994
54-0 v Souths, Brookvale Oval, August 24, 1975
53-0 v Easts, SSG, July 17, 1966

Worst defeats
61-11 v St George, Hurstville Oval, May 3, 1947
50-6 v Newtown, SCG, June 13, 1955
39-0 v St George, Brookvale Oval, May 5, 1963
40-2 v Easts, SSG, August 21, 1982
41-5 v Newtown, Erskineville Oval, May 7, 1949

Most number of games for the club (first grade)

Player	Games	Player	Games	Player	Games	Player	Games
Cliff Lyons	264	Fred Jones	243	Bob Fulton	213	Bob Batty	205
Alan Thompson	263	Graham Eadie	237	Terry Randall	208	Paul Vautin	204
Des Hasler	255	Max Krilich	215				

CLUB INTERNATIONALS (59) Johnny Bliss, Martin Bella, Kerry Boustead, Les Boyd, Bill Bradstreet, Ray Branighan, Dave Brown, Ray Brown, Roy Bull, Peter Burke, Mark Carroll, Noel Cleal, Chris Close, Phil Daley, Bill Delamere, Graham Eadie, Bob Fulton, Daniel Gartner, Russel Gartner, Geoff Gerard, Johnny Gibbs, David Gillespie, Bill Hamilton, Les Hanigan, Des Hasler, Terry Hill, John Hopoate, Fred Jones, Nik Kosef, Max Krilich, Jack Lumsden, Cliff Lyons, John McDonald, Paul McCabe, Steve Martin, Steve Menzies, Danny Moore, John Morgan, Rex Mossop, Wally O'Connell, Michael O'Connor, John O'Neill, Terry Randall, John Ribot, Ray Ritchie, Ian Roberts, Kevin Schubert, Dale Shearer, Jack Sinclair, Frank Stanton, Alan Thompson, Ian Thomson, Geoff Toovey, Paul Vautin, Mick Veivers, Bruce Walker, Dennis Ward, Gordon Willoughby, Nick Yakich

Test captains: Max Krilich (1982-83), Geoff Toovey (1996)
World Cup captains: Nil
Rothmans Medal winners: Graham Eadie (1974), Mal Cochrane (1986)
Clive Churchill Medal winners: Cliff Lyons (1987), Geoff Toovey (1996)
Major sponsor 1997: Pepsi-Cola Bottlers
First grade 1997: Coach Bob Fulton. Finished 2nd
Second grade 1997: Coach Frank Ponissi. Finished 6th
Under-20s 1997: Coach: Charlie Haggett. Finished 5th

1997 Representative players: City - Mark Carroll, Craig Field, Daniel Gartner, Craig Hancock, Terry Hill, John Hopoate, Steve Menzies, Geoff Toovey. Country - David Gillespie, Nik Kosef. NSW - Mark Carroll, Terry Hill, Nik Kosef, Steve Menzies, Geoff Toovey. Queensland - Danny Moore, Neil Tierney. Australia - Mark Carroll, Terry Hill, Nik Kosef, Steve Menzies, Geoff Toovey. Rest of the World - Craig Innes.

NEWCASTLE

Year entered premiership: 1988 (A team from the Newcastle and Hunter district played in the NSWRL premiership in 1908-09, figuring in the 1909 semi-finals. The side wore colours of red and white. They withdrew to form their own club competition in 1910).
First match: March 5, 1988, lost 4-28 v Parramatta, Newcastle International Sports Centre
Colours: Red and blue
Emblem: Knight
Home ground: Marathon Stadium (formerly known as Newcastle International Sports Centre)
Attendance record: 32,642, Newcastle v Manly, July 21, 1995

TITLES:
First grade: 1997
Reserve grade: 1995
Club Championship: 1992
Sevens: 1991, 1996

Most tries in a match

Player	Tries	Opponent	Venue	Date
Ashley Gordon	3	St George	Newcastle	May 6, 1990
Ashley Gordon	3	Easts	Newcastle	June 24, 1990
Mark Sargent	3	Canberra	Marathon Stadium	August 30, 1992
Adam Muir	3	Parramatta	Marathon Stadium	May 15, 1994
Nathan Barnes	3	Auckland	Marathon Stadium	May 7, 1995
Jamie Ainscough	3	Sydney Bulldogs	Marathon Stadium	June 25, 1995
Jamie Ainscough	3	St George	Kogarah Oval	April 8, 1996
Jamie Ainscough	3	Illawarra	Marathon Stadium	August 4, 1996
Adam Muir	3	Sth Queensland	Marathon Stadium	March 23, 1997
Darren Albert	3	Wests	Marathon Stadium	July 25, 1997
Owen Craigie	3	Wests	Marathon Stadium	July 25, 1997

Most tries in a season

Player	Tries	Year
Darren Albert	18	1997
Jamie Ainscough	17	1995
Ashley Gordon	15	1990
Jamie Ainscough	14	1993
Robbie O'Davis	13	1997
Nathan Barnes	12	1995
Owen Craigie	12	1997

Most tries for club

Player	Tries
Jamie Ainscough	47
Robbie O'Davis	45
Ashley Gordon	38
Adam Muir	29
Darren Albert	21

Most goals in a match

Player	Goals	Opponent	Venue	Date
Andrew Johns	9	Western Reds	Marathon Stadium	March 19, 1995
Andrew Johns	8	Auckland	Marathon Stadium	May 7, 1995
Ashley Gordon	7	Wests	Newcastle	April 1, 1990
John Schuster	7	Gold Coast	Marathon Stadium	April 19, 1992
Andrew Johns	7	Souths	Football Stadium	March 13, 1994
Andrew Johns	7	Sydney Tigers	Parramatta Stadium	April 2, 1995
Andrew Johns	7	Sydney Bulldogs	Marathon Stadium	June 25, 1995
Andrew Johns	7	Gold Coast	Marathon Stadium	May 12, 1996

Most points in a match

Player	Points	Opponent	Venue	Date
Andrew Johns	23 (2T, 7G, 1FG)	Souths	Sydney Football Stadium	March 13, 1994*
Ashley Gordon	20 (3T, 4G)	Easts	Newcastle	June 24, 1990

* Record achieved on first grade debut

Most points in a season

Player	Points		Year
Andrew Johns	194	(6T, 85G)	1995
Andrew Johns	162	(7T, 65G, 4FG)	1994
John Schuster	152	(4T, 68G)	1992
Andrew Johns	142	(3T, 64G, 2FG)	1996
Ashley Gordon	130	(15T, 35G)	1990

Most points for club

Player	Points	
Andrew Johns	592	(18T, 257G, 6FG)
Ashley Gordon	266	(38T, 56G, 2FG)
John Schuster	266	(16T, 101G)
Robbie O'Davis	261	(45T, 40G, 1FG)
Jamie Ainscough	198	(47T, 4G, 2FG)

CLUB-BY-CLUB RECORDS

Biggest wins
50-6 v Gold Coast, Marathon, August 22, 1993
44-0 v South Qld, Marathon, March 23, 1997
48-6 v Auckland, Marathon Stadium, May 7, 1995
42-0 v Sydney Bulldogs, Marathon, June 25, 1995
42-0 v Gold Coast, Marathon, May 12, 1996

Worst defeats
52-16 v Canberra, Marathon, July 29, 1994
39-4 v Canberra, Bruce, June 30, 1995
40-6 v Norths, North Sydney Oval, April 17, 1988
44-12 v Manly, Brookvale, March 27, 1988
30-0 v Parramatta, Parramatta, June 30, 1991
30-0 v Canterbury, Belmore, June 13, 1993
34-4 v Norths, North Sydney, August 15, 1993

Most first grade games

Marc Glanville	188	Paul Harragon	149	David Boyd	110	Matthew Johns	105
Tony Butterfield	158	Mark Sargent	126	Paul Marquet	110	Adam Muir	99
Rob McCormack	154	Michael Hagan	111	Robbie O'Davis	125	Brad Godden	89

CLUB INTERNATIONALS (8) Jamie Ainscough, Brad Godden, Paul Harragon, Andrew Johns, Matthew Johns, Adam Muir, Robbie O'Davis, Mark Sargent

Test captains: Paul Harragon (1995)
World Cup captains: Paul Harragon (1995)
Rothmans Medal winners: Mark Sargent (1989)
Clive Churchill Medal winners: Robbie O'Davis (1997)
Major sponsor 1997: Stockland
First grade 1997: Coach Malcolm Reilly. Finished 1st
Second grade 1997: Coach Steve Linnane. Finished 11th
Under-20s 1997: Coach Peter Robertson. Finished 12th

1997 Representative players: Country - Darren Albert, Matthew Gidley, Marc Glanville, Paul Harragon, Wayne Richards. NSW - Paul Harragon, Andrew Johns, Adam Muir. Queensland - Robbie O'Davis. Australia - Paul Harragon, Andrew Johns, Robbie O'Davis. Rest of the World - Lee Jackson.

NORTH QUEENSLAND

Year entered premiership: 1995 (North Queensland competed in the 1997 Super League competition)
First match: March 11, 1995, lost 16-32 v Canterbury, Stockland Stadium
Colours: Navy blue, grey, white and gold
Emblem: Cow Horns
Nickname: Cowboys
Home ground: Stockland Stadium
Attendance record: 27,096, North Queensland v Souths, July 20, 1996 *(30,122 attended the 1997 Super League match between North Queensland and Brisbane, April 5, 1997)*

TITLES: Nil

Most tries in a match

Player	Tries	Opponent	Venue	Date
Justin Loomans	2	Manly	Stockland Stadium	April 22, 1995
David Bouveng	2	Illawarra	Steelers Stadium	April 30, 1995
Justin Loomans	2	Sydney City	Stockland Stadium	May 20, 1995
Justin Loomans	2	Souths	Sydney Football Stadium	July 15, 1995
Kris Tassell	2	Sydney Tigers	Stockland Stadium	April 6, 1946
Kris Tassell	2	Illawarra	Stockland Stadium	May 11, 1996
Justin Loomans	2	Newcastle	Stockland Stadium	June 15, 1996
Marshall Miller	2	Wests	Campbelltown Sports Ground	July 14, 1996
Marshall Miller	2	Sth Queensland	Stockland Stadium	August 9, 1996
Damian Gibson	2	St George	Kogarah Oval	August 25, 1996

(Ray Mercy scored three tries in a Super League match against Penrith at Penrith Football Stadium, July 4, 1997; Steve Walters, 2, against Adelaide, Stockland Stadium, March 1, 1997; Jason Death, 2, against Brisbane, Stockland Stadium, April 5, 1997; Scott Mahon, 2, against Cronulla, Stockland Stadium, May 31, 1997; Luke Phillips, 2, against Penrith, Penrith Football Stadium, July 4, 1997; Mercy, 2, against Hunter, Stockland Stadium, July 13, 1997; Andrew Dunemann, 2, against Hunter, Stockland Stadium, July 13, 1997)

Most tries in a season
David Bouveng	9	1995
Justin Loomans	9	1995
Jutsin Loomans	8	1996
Kris Tassell	8	1996

(Luke Phillips scored eight tries in the 1997 Super League competition)

Most tries for club
Justin Loomans	17
David Bouveng	10
Kris Tassell	8
Damian Gibson	7

(Loomans' total does not include two Super League tries, Tassell 1)

Most goals in a match
Player	Goals	Opponent	Venue	Date
Shane Howarth	6	Gold Coast	Carrara Stadium	July 26, 1996
Jonathan Davies	5	Wests	Stockland Stadium	July 8, 1995

(Luke Phillips kicked five goals in a Super League match against Auckland, Stockland Stadium, April 27, 1997)

Most points in a match
Player	Points	Opponent	Venue	Date
Shane Howarth	16 (1T, 6G)	Gold Coast	Carrara Stadium	July 26, 1996
Jonathan Davies	11 (5G, 1FG)	Wests	Stockland Stadium	July 8, 1995

(Luke Phillips scored 16 points (2T, 4G) in a Super League match against Penrith, Penrith Football Stadium, July 4, 1997; Phillips 14 points (1T, 5G) against Auckland, Stockland Stadium, April 27, 1997; Phillips 12 points (1T, 4G) against Adelaide, Stockland Stadium, March 1, 1997)

Most points in a season
Shane Howarth	49	(1T, 21G, 3FG)	1996
Jonathan Davies	43	(1T, 19G, 1FG)	1995
David Bouveng	36	(9T)	
Justin Loomans	36	(9T)	

(Luke Phillips scored 122 points (8T, 45G) in the 1997 Super League competition)

Most points for club
Justin Loomans	68	(17T)
Shane Howarth	49	(1T, 21G, 3FG)
Jonathan Davies	43	(1T, 19G, 1FG)
Reggie Cressbrook	42	(2T, 17G)
David Bouveng	40	(10T)

(Loomans' total does not include 8 Super League points, Cressbrook 12)

Biggest wins
31-12 v Wests, Stockland Stadium, July 8, 1995
26-16 v Newcastle, Stockland, June 15, 1996
17-2 v Sydney Tigers, Stockland, April 6, 1996
24-14 v Gold Coast, Carrara, July 26, 1996
16-10 v Cronulla, Stockland, June 22, 1996
(North Queensland beat Hunter 33-14 in a Super League match at Stockland Stadium, July 13, 1997; Adelaide 24-16, Stockland Stadium, March 1, 1997; Auckland 30-22, Stockland Stadium, April 27, 1997)

Worst defeats
66-4 v Sydney Bulldogs, Belmore, August 27, 1995
66-10 v Canberra, Bruce Stadium, April 14, 1996
60-6 v Norths, North Sydney Oval, April 16, 1995
52-6 v Auckland, Ericsson, August 3, 1996
58-14 v Brisbane, ANZ Stadium, April 21, 1996

Most first grade games
Adrian Vowles	41	Damien Gibson	31	George Bartlett	27	Paul Galea	24
Justin Loomans	37	Peter Jones	31	Ian Dunemann	26	Reggie Cressbrook	23
Wayne Sing	36						

(Loomans' total does not include seven Super League games, Jones 16, Dunemann 6 and Cressbrook 11)

CLUB INTERNATIONALS: Nil

Test captains: Nil
World Cup captains: Nil
Rothmans Medal winners: Nil

NORTH SYDNEY

Year entered premiership: 1908
First match: April 20, 1908, lost 7-11 v Souths, Birchgrove Oval
Colours: Red, black and white
Emblem: Bear
Home ground: North Sydney Oval
Attendance record: 23,089, Norths v Manly, May 13, 1994

TITLES
First grade: 1921, 1922
Runners-up: 1943
Reserve grade: 1940, 1942, 1955, 1959, 1989, 1991, 1992, 1993
Third grade (President's Cup): 1937, 1945, 1946, 1959
Club Championship: Nil
Pre-season: Nil

Most tries in a game
Player	Tries	Opponent	Venue	Date
Cec Blinkhorn	5	Annandale	North Sydney Oval	August 28, 1920
Johnny Bliss	5	Easts	North Sydney Oval	July 8, 1944

Most tries in a season
Player	Tries	Year
Cec Blinkhorn	20	1922
Peter O'Brien	20	1952
Ken Irvine	19	1959
John McClean	18	1952
Horrie Toole	18	1953

Most tries for club
Player	Tries
Ken Irvine	171*
Cec Blinkhorn	79
Peter O'Brien	67
Horrie Toole	67
Greg Florimo	64
Herman Peters	62

* premiership record

Most goals in a match
Player	Goals	Opponent	Venue	Date
Allen Arkey	10	Wests	North Sydney Oval	July 11, 1953
Allen Arkey	10	Easts	North Sydney Oval	June 26, 1954
Fred Griffiths	10	Newtown	Henson Park	May 4, 1963
Noel Cavanagh	10	Penrith	North Sydney Oval	June 29, 1969
Peter Inskip	10	Penrith	Penrith Park	April 9, 1972

Most points in a match
Player	Points	Opponent	Venue	Date
Harold Horder	26 (4T, 7G)	St George	North Sydney Oval	August 19, 1922
Jason Taylor	26 (3T, 7G)	Souths	North Sydney Oval	August 25, 1996
Jason Taylor	26 (2T, 9G)	St George	North Sydney Oval	April 27, 1997
R.Crossley	22 (2T, 8G)	Parramatta	Parramatta Oval	June 25, 1949
Owen O'Donnell	21 (3T, 6G)	Parramatta	North Sydney Oval	August 16, 1970

Most points in a season
Player	Points		Year
Jason Taylor	242	(10T, 98G, 6FG)	1997
Jason Taylor	238	(5T, 108G, 2FG)	1996
Jason Taylor	217	(6T, 93G, 7FG)	1994
Daryl Halligan	196	(13T, 72G)	1991
Jason Taylor	182	(3T, 84G, 2FG)	1995

Most points for club
Player	Points	
Jason Taylor	879	(24T, 383G, 17FG)
Allen Arkey	689	(1T, 343G)
Ken Irvine	633	(171T, 59G, 1FG)
Fred Griffiths	590	(8T, 283G)
Daryl Halligan	544	(23T, 225G, 2FG)

Biggest wins
60-6 v North Qld, North Sydney, April 16, 1995
55-3 v Penrith, North Sydney Oval, July 16, 1978
45-0 v Cumberland, Wentworth, July 25, 1908
50-6 v North Qld, Stockland, April 27, 1996
45-2 v Canterbury, Belmore, April 17, 1954

Worst defeats
59-3 v Glebe, Wentworth Park, July 17, 1915
53-0 v Souths, SSG, August 12, 1939
56-4 v Manly, Nortth Sydney Oval, July 22, 1984
51-0 v Wests, St Luke's, Burwood, June 14, 1919
53-4 v Souths, Agricultural Ground, July 20, 1910

Most first grade games
Greg Florimo	261	Don McKinnon	183	George Ambrum	157	Mark Soden	137
Norm Strong	210	Ken Irvine	176	David Hall	153	John McArthur	133
Gary Larson	190	Billy Moore	168	John Adam	152	Adrian Toole	129
Ross Warner	186	David Fairleigh	158	Mark Graham	146		

CLUB INTERNATIONALS (38) George Ambrum, Martin Bella, Tom Berecry, Cec Blinkhorn, Albert Broomham, Michael Buettner, Brian Carlson, Tedda Courtney, Arch Crippin, Brett Dallas, Sid Deane, Jim Devereux, Peter Diversi, David Fairleigh, Greg Florimo, Nevyl Hand, Harold Horder, Ken Irvine, Clarrie Ives, Peter Jackson, Les Kiss, Gary Larson, Dinny Lutge, Ken McCaffery, Don McKinnon, Keith Middleton, Billy Moore, Andy Morton, Fred Nolan, Herman Peters, Tim Pickup, Con Sullivan, Bob Sullivan, Duncan Thompson, Roy Thompson, Laurie Ward, Lloyd Weier, Billy Wilson

Test captains: Dinny Lutge (1908), Sid Deane (1914), Brian Carlson (1959-61), Billy Wilson (1963)
World Cup captains: nil
Rothmans Medal winners: David Fairleigh (1994), Jason Taylor (1996)
Major sponsor 1997: Citibank
First grade 1997: Coach Peter Louis. Finished 3rd
Second grade 1997: Coach Les Kiss. Finished 9th
Under-20s 1997: Coach Paul Conlon. Finished 6th

1997 Representative players: City - Michael Buettner, Josh Stuart. Country - Matt Seers. NSW - David Fairleigh, Matt Seers, Michael Buettner. Queensland - Brett Dallas, Ben Ikin, Gary Larson, Billy Moore. Rest of the World - Willie McLean.

PARRAMATTA

Year entered premiership: 1947
First match: April 12, 1947, lost 12-34 v Newtown, Parramatta Oval
Colours: Blue and gold
Emblem: Eel
Home ground: Parramatta Stadium
Attendance record: 27,243, Parramatta v Souths, August 17, 1986. (29,913 attended Nissan Sevens, February 11, 1991)

TITLES
First grade: 1981, 1982, 1983, 1986
Runners-up: 1976, 1977, 1984
Reserve (Second) grade: 1975, 1977, 1979, 1997
Third grade (President's Cup) 1964, 1979, 1980, 1982, 1984, 1988
Club Championship: 1976, 1977, 1978, 1979, 1980, 1981, 1982, 1986, 1997
Pre-season Cup: 1975
Tooth Cup: 1980
National Panasonic Cup: 1986
Sevens: 1997

Most tries in a match

Player	Tries	Opponent	Venue	Date
Mitchell Wallace	4	Balmain	Parramatta Oval	April 23, 1949
Dick Thornett	4	Canterbury	Cumberland Oval	July 21, 1968
Owen Stephens	4	Souths	Redfern Oval	May 24, 1975
Ray Price	4	Souths	Redfern Oval	August 13, 1978
Eric Grothe	4	Canberra	Belmore Sports Ground	April 11, 1982
Eric Grothe	4	Wests	Belmore Sports Ground	July 1, 1984
Paul Taylor	4	Canberra	Parramatta Stadium	April 24, 1988

Most tries in a season

Steve Ella	23	1982
Brett Kenny	21	1983
Neil Hunt	20	1983
Mitchell Wallace	18	1949
Mitchell Wallace	18	1951

Most tries for club

Brett Kenny	110
Steve Ella	92
Eric Grothe	78
Ray Price	70
Mick Cronin	75

Most goals in a match

Player	Goals	Opponent	Venue	Date
Mick Cronin	11	Illawarra	Belmore Sports Ground	May 30, 1982
Brian Jones	10	Canterbury	Cumberland Oval	August 20, 1955
Mick Cronin	10	Newtown	Henson Park	August 20, 1978

Most points in a match

Player	Points	Opponent	Venue	Date
Mick Cronin	27 (3T, 9G)	Norths	North Sydney Oval	May 13, 1979
Mick Cronin	27 (3T, 9G)	Canberra	Belmore Sports Ground	April 11, 1982
Mick Cronin	26 (2T, 10G)	Newtown	Henson Park	August 20, 1978
Mick Cronin	25 (1T, 11G)	Illawarra	Belmore Sports Ground	May 30, 1982
Mick Cronin	24 (2T, 9G)	Norths	Cumberland Oval	March 26, 1978
Scott Mahon	22 (1T, 9G)	Easts	Henson Park	July 1, 1990

CLUB-BY-CLUB RECORDS

Most points in a season
Mick Cronin	282	(16T, 117G)	1978*
Mick Cronin	279	(11T, 123g)	1982
Mick Cronin	253	(15T, 104G)	1979
Mick Cronin	226	(4T, 105G)	1983
Mick Cronin	225	(7T, 101G, 2FG)	1977
Mick Cronin	204	(6T, 90G)	1985

* premiership record

Most points for club
Mick Cronin	1,971	(74T, 865G, 2FG)*
Steve Ella	544	(92T, 104G, 6FG)
Arch Brown	460	(24T, 194G)
Brett Kenny	410	(110T)
Keith Campbell	381	(13T, 171G)

* premiership record

Biggest wins
54-3 v Canberra, Belmore, April 11, 1982
55-5 v Illawarra, Belmore, May 30, 1982
54-4 v Newtown, Henson Park, June 5, 1983
62-18 v Newtown, Henson Park, August 20, 1978
52-10 v South Qld, Parramatta, June 8, 1997

Worst defeats
68-0 v Canberra, Bruce Stadium, August 22, 1993
61-4 v St George, Cumberland Oval, June 7, 1959
52-0 v St George, Sydney Cricket Ground, April 2, 1960
64-12 v Manly, Parramatta Stadium, March 20, 1988
56-6 v St George, Kogarah Oval, May 21, 1995

Most first grade games
Brett Kenny	265	Mick Cronin	216	Bill Rayner	203	Dick Thornett	168
Ray Price	258	Bob O'Reilly	216	Ron Lynch	202	John McMartin	167
Peter Sterling	227	Mark Laurie	205				

CLUB INTERNATIONALS (34) Ron Boden, Keith Campbell, Mick Crocker, Mick Cronin, Garry Dowling, Jim Dymock, Steve Ella, Denis Fitzgerald, Geoff Gerard, Neville Glover, Eric Grothe, Brian Hambly, Ray Higgs, Ron Hilditch, Ian Johnston, Brett Kenny, John Kolc, Bob Lindner, Ron Lynch, John Muggleton, Graham Olling, Bob O'Reilly, Dean Pay, John Peard, Jim Porter, Ray Price, John Quayle, Bill Rayner, John Simon, Jason Smith, Peter Sterling, Ken Thornett, Dick Thornett, Peter Wynn.

Test captains: Nil
World Cup captains: Nil
Rothmans Medal winners: Ray Higgs (1976), Mick Cronin (1977, 1978), Ray Price (1979), Peter Sterling (1987, 1990)
Clive Churchill Medal winners: Peter Sterling (1986)
Major sponsor 1997: Asics
First grade 1997: Coach Brian Smith. Finished 5th
Second grade 1997: Coach Peter Sharp. Finished 1st
Under-20s 1997: Coach John Kolc. Finished 4th

1997 Representative players: City - Jim Dymock. Country - John Simon. NSW - Jim Dymock, Dean Pay, John Simon. Queensland - Jason Smith, Stuart Kelly. Australia - John Simon, Dean Pay. Rest of the World - Jarrod McCracken.

PENRITH

Year entered premiership: 1967 (Penrith competed in the 1997 Super League competition)
First match: April 2, 1967, lost 12-15 v Canterbury, Belmore Sports Ground
Colours: Black with white, red, green and yellow stripes
Emblem: Panther
Home ground: Penrith Football Stadium
Attendance record: 21,956, Penrith v Manly, August 14, 1988

TITLES
First grade: 1991
Runners-up: 1990
Reserve grade: 1987
Third grade (President's Cup): 1978
(Penrith won the Super League Under-19 competition in 1997)
Pre-season series: 1968

Most tries in a match
Player	Tries	Opponent	Venue	Date
Peter Langmack	5	St George	Penrith Park	July 7, 1974
Glenn West	4	Balmain	Penrith Park	May 5, 1974
Gary Freeman	4	Wests	Campbelltown	May 8, 1994

Most tries in a season
Player	Tries	Year
Graham Mackay	16	1991
Greg Alexander	15	1989
Graham Mackay	15	1994
Glenn West	14	1974
Greg Alexander	14	1985
Alan McIndoe	14	1990

Most tries for club
Player	Tries
Greg Alexander	93
Brad Izzard	73
Graham Mackay	43
Steve Carter	42
Kevin Dann	40

(Alexander's total does not include two Super League tries, Carter 8)

Most goals in a match
Player	Goals	Opponent	Venue	Date
Greg Alexander	10	Souths	Penrith Park	June 17, 1990
Shane Marshall	9	Canberra	Penrith Park	August 15, 1982
Greg Alexander	9	Cronulla	Penrith Park	August 24, 1986
Ryan Girdler	9	Western Reds	Penrith Football Stadium	May 12, 1996

Most points in a match
Player	Points	Opponent	Venue	Date
Shane Marshall	24 (2T, 9G)	Canberra	Penrith Park	August 15, 1982
Greg Alexander	24 (1T, 10G)	Souths	Penrith Park	June 17, 1990
Ryan Girdler	24 (2T, 8G)	Gold Coast	Penrith Football Stadium	May 28, 1995

(Girdler scored 24 points (3T, 6G) in a Super League match against Canterbury, Penrith Football Stadium, August 15, 1997)

Most points in a season
Player	Points		Year
Greg Alexander	196	(14T, 69G, 2FG)	1985
Greg Alexander	183	(11T, 69G, 1FG)	1986
Greg Alexander	170	(13T, 59G)	1990
Ryan Girdler	162	(8T, 65G)	1996
Bob Landers	158	(6T, 70G)	1969

(Girdler scored 197 points (11T, 76G, 1FG) in the 1997 Super League competition)

Most points for club
Player	Points	
Greg Alexander	1,053	(93T, 335G, 11FG)
Bob Landers	428	(18T, 187G)
Mark Levy	428	(20T, 178G)
Ryan Girdler	374	(29T, 129G)
Kevin Dann	318	(40T, 98G, 1FG)

(Alexander's total does not include 18 Super League points, Girdler 197)

Biggest wins
43-2 v Souths, Penrith Park, July 3, 1977
44-6 v Souths, Penrith Park, June 17, 1990
37-0 v Wests, Orana Park, August 20, 1989
50-14 v Cronulla, Penrith Park, August 24, 1986
47-12 v Gold Coast, Penrith Park, May 15, 1988
(Penrith beat Canterbury 44-8 in a Super League match at Penrith Football Stadium, Aug 15, 1997)

Worst defeats
70-7 v Manly, Penrith Park, July 29, 1973
59-5 v Souths, Redfern Oval, May 11, 1980
55-3 v Norths, North Sydney Oval, July 16, 1978
46-5 v Balmain, Penrith Park, July 20, 1980
42-2 v Illawarra, Steelers, August 25, 1996
(Penrith were beaten 54-12 by Brisbane in a Super League match at ANZ Stadium, August 10, 1997)

Most first grade games
Royce Simmons	233						
Brad Izzard	206	Tim Sheens	166	Grahame Moran	121	Lew Zivanovic	115
Greg Alexander	196	Steve Carter	152	Brad Fittler	119	Kevin Dann	115
John Cartwright	184	Warren Fenton	129	Barry Walker	117	Col Van der Voort	115

(Alexander's total does not include six Super League games and Carter 14)

CLUB INTERNATIONALS (7) Greg Alexander, John Cartwright, Brad Fittler, Mark Geyer, Graham Mackay, Royce Simmons, Matt Sing *(Matt Adamson, Ryan Girdler and Craig Gower represented the Australian Super League side in 1997)*

Test captains: Brad Fittler (1995)
World Cup captains: Brad Fittler (1995)
Rothmans Medal winners: Nil

CLUB-BY-CLUB RECORDS

ST GEORGE

Year entered premiership: 1921
First match: April 23, 1921, lost 3-4 v Glebe, Sydney Sports Ground
Colours: Red and white
Emblem: Dragon
Home ground: Kogarah Jubilee Oval
Attendance record: 23,582, St George v South Sydney, May 4, 1975

TITLES
First grade: 1941, 1949, 1956, 1957, 1958, 1959, 1960, 1961, 1962, 1963, 1964, 1965, 1966, 1977, 1979
Runners-up: 1927, 1930, 1933, 1937, 1942, 1946, 1953, 1971, 1975, 1985, 1992, 1993, 1996
Reserve grade: 1938, 1962, 1963, 1964, 1976, 1985
Third grade (President's Cup): 1940, 1942, 1949, 1951, 1953, 1957, 1963, 1965, 1966, 1972, 1974, 1983, 1985, 1987
Club Championship: 1940, 1942, 1946, 1949, 1951, 1955, 1956, 1957, 1958, 1959, 1962, 1963, 1964, 1965, 1966, 1971, 1984, 1985
Pre-season Cup: 1963, 1964, 1965, 1971
Panasonic Cup: 1988

Player	Tries	Opponent	Venue	Date
Jack Lindwall	6	Manly	Hurstville Oval	May 3, 1947
Merv Lees	5	Norths	Sydney Cricket Ground	July 24, 1954

Most tries in a season

Tommy Ryan	26	1957	
Ron Roberts	25	1949	
Reg Gasnier	25	1960	
Reg Gasnier	24	1963	
Stan Gorton	22	1968	

Most tries for club

Johnny King	143
Eddie Lumsden	136
Reg Gasnier	127
Jack Lindwall	110
Ricky Walford	104
Steve Morris	102

Most goals in a match

Player	Goals	Opponent	Venue	Date
Les Griffin	15	Canterbury	Earl Park	May 11, 1935*
Harry Bath	11	Parramatta	Cumberland Oval	June 7, 1959
Brian Graham	11	Parramatta	SCG	April 2, 1960
Ray Lindwall	10	Norths	Hurstville Oval	July 25, 1942
Noel Pidding	10	Canterbury	Kogarah Oval	April 14, 1951
Doug Fleming	10	Parramatta	Kogarah Oval	May 4, 1957
Brian Graham	10	Newtown	Kogarah Oval	July 30, 1961

*equals premiership record

Most points in a match

Player	Points	Opponent	Venue	Date
Les Griffin	36 (2T, 15G)	Canterbury	Earl Park	May 11, 1935
Jack Lindwall	36 (6T, 9G)	Manly	Hurstville Oval	May 3, 1947
Graeme Langlands	27 (3T, 9G)	Parramatta	SCG	Sept 5, 1964
Ricky Walford	26 (4T, 5G)	Canterbury	Kogarah Oval	August 5, 1989
Harry Bath	25 (1T, 11G)	Parramatta	Cumberland Oval	June 7, 1959
Brian Graham	25 (1T, 11G)	Parramatta	SCG	April 2, 1960
Graeme Langlands	25 (3T, 8G)	Norths	Sports Ground	July 28, 1963

Most points in a season

Harry Bath	225	(3T, 108G)	1958
George Grant	211	(1T, 104G)	1979
Harry Bath	205	(5T, 95G)	1959
Noel Pidding	200	(14T, 79G)	1951
Graeme Langlands	196	(14T, 77G)	1971

Most points for club

Graeme Langlands	1,554	(86T, 648G)
Ricky Walford	874	(104T, 229G)
Brian Graham	634	(20T, 287G)
Noel Pidding	626	(34T, 262G)
Doug Fleming	604	(15T, 281G)

Biggest wins
91-6 v Canterbury, Earl Park, May 11, 1935*
65-5 v University, SCG, May 22, 1937
61-4 v Parramatta, Cumberland, June 7, 1959
65-9 v Newtown, SSG, July 30, 1961
52-0 v Parramatta, SCG, April 2, 1960
* premiership record

Worst defeats
61-0 v Manly, Brookvale Oval, July 3, 1994
55-7 v Newtown, SCG, August 26, 1944
52-7 v Newtown, SCG, June 3, 1944
44-2 v Easts, SCG, March 20, 1987
42-0 v Norths, North Sydney Oval, May 5, 1996

Most first grade games

Norm Provan	256	Michael Beattie	210	Graeme Wynn	195	Mark Coyne	184
Billy Smith	234	Ricky Walford	207	Barry Beath	198	Brian Clay	183
Craig Young	234	Rod Reddy	204	Johnny King	191	Johnny Raper	180
Graeme Langlands	227						

CLUB INTERNATIONALS (49) Wayne Bartrim, Barry Beath, Tony Branson, Bob Bugden, George Carstairs, Brian Clay, Mark Coyne, Percy Fairall, Wally Fullerton Smith, Fred Gardner, Reg Gasnier, Ted Goodwin, Scott Gourley, Johnny Hawke, Phil Hawthorne, Jack Holland, Pat Jarvis, Albert "Ricketty" Johnston, Brian Johnston, Arthur Justice, Ken Kearney, Johnny King, Ross Kite, Graeme Langlands, Eddie Lumsden, Matt McCoy, Doug McRitchie, Brad Mackay, Noel Mulligan, Kevin O'Brien, Michael O'Connor, Bryan Orrock, Noel Pidding, Norm Provan, Graham Quinn, Johnny Raper, Elton Rasmussen, Rod Reddy, John Riley, Ron Roberts, Steve Rogers, Kevin Ryan, Tommy Ryan, Billy Smith, Ian Walsh, Billy Wilson, John Wittenberg, Graeme Wynn, Craig Young

Test captains: Ken Kearney (1956), Reg Gasnier (1962-67), Ian Walsh (1963-66), Johnny Raper (1967), Phil Hawthorne (1970), Graeme Langlands (1970-74)
World Cup captains: Johnny Raper (1968), Billy Smith (1970). Graeme Langlands (1972-77)
Rothmans Medal winners: Nil
Clive Churchill Medal winners: Brad Mackay (1993)
Major sponsor 1997: Newmans Motor Group
First grade 1997: Coach David Waite. Finished 10th
Second grade 1997: Coach Shane Millard. Finished 3rd
Under-20s 1997: Coach Peter O'Sullivan. Finished 8th

1997 Representative players: City - Colin Ward. NSW - Jamie Ainscough. Queensland - Wayne Bartrim, Mark Coyne, Tony Hearn. Australia - Mark Coyne. Rest of the World - Darren Rameka, Andrew Tangata-Toa.

SOUTH SYDNEY

Year entered premiership: 1908
First match: April 20, 1908, won 11-7 v Norths, Birchgrove Oval
Colours: Red and green
Emblem: Rabbit
Home ground: Sydney Football Stadium
Attendance record: 26,433 v Eastern Suburbs, April 9, 1993 (officially Easts' home game, but still Souths' biggest crowd for a club match at Sydney Football Stadium)

TITLES
First grade: 1908, 1909, 1914, 1918, 1925, 1926, 1927, 1928, 1929, 1931, 1932, 1950, 1951, 1953, 1954, 1955, 1967, 1968, 1970, 1971
Runners-up: 1910, 1916, 1917, 1920, 1923, 1924, 1935, 1937, 1930, 1949, 1952, 1965, 1969
Reserve grade: 1913, 1914, 1917, 1923, 1924, 1925, 1926, 1927, 1929, 1931, 1932, 1934, 1943, 1945, 1952, 1953, 1956, 1966, 1968, 1983
Third grade (President's Cup): 1912, 1918, 1925, 1928, 1933, 1962, 1969, 1981, 1986, 1989
Club Championship: 1932, 1933, 1952, 1953, 1954, 1967, 1968, 1969, 1989
Pre-season Cup: 1966, 1969, 1972, 1978
Tooth Cup: 1981
Tooheys Challenge: 1994
Sevens: 1988

CLUB-BY-CLUB RECORDS

Most tries in a match

Player	Tries	Opponent	Venue	Date
Harold Horder	5	Norths	Showground	June 4, 1917
Harold Horder	5	Norths	Showground	July 14, 1917
Alan Quinlivan	5	University	Earl Park	July 11, 1936
Don Manson	5	University	Sports Ground	April 17, 1937
John Graves	5	Easts	Redfern Oval	July 16, 1949
Ian Moir	5	Parramatta	Redfern Oval	June 6, 1957
Eric Sladden	5	Parramatta	Cumberland Oval	August 10, 1957

Most tries in a season

Les Brennan	29	1954
Johnny Graves	28	1951
Ian Moir	23	1953
Harold Horder	21	1918
Ian Moir	21	1954

Most tries for club

Benny Wearing	144
Ian Moir	105
Harold Horder	102
Bob McCarthy	100
Johnny Graves	79
Mike Cleary	76

Most goals in a match

Player	Goals	Opponent	Venue	Date
Eric Simms	11	Cronulla	Redfern Oval	April 11, 1969
Eric Simms	11	Penrith	Penrith Park	July 27, 1969*
Arthur Oxford	10	University	Marrickville Oval	September 1, 1920
E.Butler	10	Parramatta	Sports Ground	April 19, 1947
Johnny Graves	10	Easts	Sports ground	June 7, 1952
Johnny Graves	10	Newtown	Redfern Oval	August 9, 1952
Steve Walsh	10	Penrith	Redfern Oval	May 11, 1980

* Includes five field goals

Most points in a match

Player	Points	Opponent	Venue	Date
Johnny Graves	29 (3T, 10G)	Easts	Sports Ground	June 7, 1952
Johnny Graves	27 (5T, 6G)	Easts	Redfern Oval	July 16, 1949
Johnny Graves	23 (3T, 7G)	Parramatta	Redfern Oval	June 26, 1948
Johnny Graves	23 (1T, 10G)	Newtown	Redfern Oval	August 9, 1952
Eric Simms	22 (11G)	Cronulla	Redfern Oval	April 11, 1969
Eric Simms	22 (6G, 5FG)	Penrith	Penrith Park	July 27, 1969
Mark Ross	22 (2T, 8G)	St George	Redfern Oval	June 27, 1981
Tony Melrose	22 (1T, 9G)	Cronulla	Redfern Oval	April 24, 1983

Most points in a season

Eric Simms	265	(1T, 112G, 19FG)	1969
Eric Simms	241	(3T, 96G, 20FG)	1970
Eric Simms	233	(3T, 100G, 12FG)	1967
Eric Simms	212	(77G, 29FG)	1968
Tony Melrose	188	(8T, 80G, 4FG)	1982

Most points for club

Eric Simms	1,841	(23T, 803G, 86FG)
Bernie Purcell	1,126	(36T, 509G)
Benny Wearing	836	(144T, 202G)
Johnny Graves	553	(79T, 158G)
Neil Baker	501	(15T, 205G, 31FG)

Biggest wins

67-0 v Wests, Sydney, July 23, 1910
63-0 v University, SSG, April 17, 1937
59-5 v Penrith, Redfern Oval, May 11, 1980
53-0 v Norths, SSG, August 12, 1939
50-0 v Easts, SSG, June 7, 1952

Worst defeats

62-0 v Sydney City, SFS, April 25, 1996
54-0 v Manly, Brookvale Oval, August 24, 1975
56-6 v Brisbane, ANZ Stadium, August 13, 1995
48-0 v Canberra, SFS, August 26, 1990
46-0 v Manly, Brookvale Oval, May 15, 1983
54-8 v Brisbane, ANZ Stadium, July 2, 1993

Most first grade games

Bob McCarthy	211	Jack Rayner	195	Michael Andrews	182	Les Cowie	176
Craig Coleman	208	John Sattler	195	Howard Hallett Snr	181	Bernie Purcell	173
Eric Simms	206	Alf Blair	186	Mario Fenech	181	Denis Donoghue	166
Benny Wearing	196						

CLUB INTERNATIONALS (60) Tommy Anderson, Jim Armstrong, Alf "Smacker" Blair, Cec Blinkhorn, Ray Branighan, Arthur Butler, Billy Cann, Mark Carroll, Clive Churchill, Michael Cleary, Ron Coote, Les Cowie, Frank Curran, Steve Darmody, Les Davidson, Jim Davis, Denis Donoghue, Terry Fahey, Harry Finch, Herb Gilbert, Bob Grant, Johnny Graves, Howard Hallett, Ernie Hammerton, Greg Hawick, Arthur Hennessy, Bob Honan, Harold Horder, Brian James, Harry Kadwell, Clem Kennedy, John Kerwick, Jack Levison, Eric Lewis, Jim Lisle, Paddy Maher, Bob McCarthy, Ted McGrath, Ian Moir, Ray Norman, Alf O'Connor, Frank O'Connor, John O'Neill, Arthur Oxford, George Piggins, Denis Pittard, Bernie Purcell, Jack Rayner, Eddie Root, Johnny Rosewell, Paul Sait, John Sattler, Eric Simms, Bill Spence, Gary Stevens, George Treweek, Elwyn Walters, Benny Wearing, Jack Why, Percy Williams

Test captains: Arthur Hennessy (1908), Clive Churchill (1950-55), John Sattler (1969-70), Bob McCarthy (1973)
World Cup captains: Clive Churchill (1954), Ron Coote (1970)
Rothmans Medal winners: Denis Pittard (1969, 1971)
Major sponsor 1997: Canon
First grade 1997: Coach Ken Shine. Finished 11th
Second grade 1997: Coach Craig Coleman. Finished 10th
Under-20s 1997: Coach Darryl Neville. Finished 3rd

1997 Representative players: Queensland - Julian O'Neill. Rest of the World - Phil Howlett.

SYDNEY CITY

Year entered premiership: 1908 (Known as Eastern Suburbs 1908-94)
First match: April 20, 1908, won 32-16 v Newtown, Wentworth Park
Colours: Red, white and blue
Emblem: Rooster (formerly Tricolours)
Home ground: Sydney Football Stadium
Attendance record: 37,981, Sydney City v Manly, July 22, 1996

TITLES
First grade: 1911, 1912, 1913, 1923, 1935, 1936, 1937, 1940, 1945, 1974, 1975
Runners-up: 1908, 1919, 1921, 1928, 1931, 1934, 1938, 1941, 1960, 1972, 1980
Reserve grade: 1908, 1909, 1910, 1911, 1935, 1937, 1949, 1986
Third grade (President's Cup): 1914, 1917, 1924, 1929, 1930, 1931, 1932, 1941, 1947, 1970, 1976, 1993
Club Championship: 1930, 1931, 1934, 1935, 1936, 1937, 1945, 1970, 1974, 1975
Pre-season Cup: 1974, 1977, 1979, 1981
Amco Cup: 1975, 1978
Sevens: 1993

Most tries in a match

Player	Tries	Opponent	Venue	Date
Rod O'Loan	7	University	Sports Ground	May 11, 1935
Dave Brown	6	Canterbury	Pratten Park	August 10, 1935
Dave Brown	6	Balmain	Sydney Cricket Ground	August 31, 1935
Gordon Wright	5	Balmain	Agricultural Ground	July 24, 1920
Dave Brown	5	Canterbury	Sydney Sports Ground	May 18, 1935
Brian Allsop	5	Parramatta	Sydney Sports Ground	June 18, 1955

Most tries in a season

Player	Tries	Year
Dave Brown	38	1935*
Rod O'Loan	27	1935
Fred Tottey	25	1936
Bill Mullins	23	1974
Rod O'Loan	20	1936

* premiership record

Most tries for club

Player	Tries
Bill Mullins	104
Dave Brown	93
Mark Harris	86
Fred Tottey	77
Rod O'Loan	76
Kevin Junee	69

CLUB-BY-CLUB RECORDS

Most goals in a match

Player	Goals	Opponent	Venue	Date
Dave Brown	15	Canterbury	Sydney Sports Ground	May 18, 1935*
Mike Eden	11	St George	Kogarah Oval	July 24, 1983
Wally Messenger	10	Wests	Sydney Sports Ground	July 8, 1916
Dave Brown	10	Canterbury	Pratten Park	August 10, 1935
Allan McKean	10	Parramatta	Sydney Sports Ground	April 16, 1972

* equals premiership record

Most points in a match

Player	Points	Opponent	Venue	Date
Dave Brown	45 (5T, 15G)	Canterbury	Sports Ground	May 18, 1935*
Dave Brown	38 (6T, 10G)	Canterbury	Pratten Park	August 10, 1935
Dave Brown	32 (6T, 7G)	Balmain	Sydney Cricket Ground	August 31, 1935
Dave Brown	26 (4T, 7G)	Norths	Sydney Cricket Ground	August 17, 1935
Rex Norman	25 (3T, 8G)	University	Sydney Cricket Ground	June 18, 1921
Mike Eden	25 (1T, 11G)	St George	Kogarah Oval	July 24, 1983

* premiership record

Most points in a season

Player	Points		Year
Mike Eden	256	(12T, 103G, 2FG)	1983
Dave Brown	244	(38T, 65G)	1935
Allan McKean	220	(7T, 99G, 1FG)	1972
John Brass	213	(8T, 94G, 1FG)	1974
Ivan Cleary	194	(8T, 81G)	1997

Most points for club

Player	Points	
Allan McKean	903	(18T, 422G, 3FG)
John Brass	715	(33T, 295G, 17FG)
Dave Brown	667	(93T, 194G)
Bob Landers	629	(41T, 253G)
Wally Messenger	624	(50T, 237G)

Biggest wins
87-7 v Canterbury, SSG, May 18, 1935
62-0 v Souths, SFS, April 25, 1996
61-5 v University, SSG, May 11, 1935
65-10 v Canterbury, Pratten, August 10, 1935
53-0 v Wests, SSG, July 8, 1916

Worst defeats
66-4 v Canberra, Bruce, April 16, 1990
53-0 v Manly, SSG, July 17, 1966
59-8 v Balmain, Leichhardt, August 23, 1952
50-0 v Souths, SSG, June 7, 1952
46-0 v St George, Kogarah, June 20, 1993

Most first grade games

Player	Games	Player	Games	Player	Games	Player	Games
Kevin Hastings	217	Bill Mullins	190	Kevin Junee	163	Charlie Lees	153
Barry Reilly	198	Ray Stehr	184	Brendan Hall	156	Harry Pierce	152
Mark Harris	195	Sid (Sandy) Pearce	176	Sid (Joe) Pearce	153	Ken Ashcroft	152

CLUB INTERNATIONALS (62) Ferris Ashton, Royce Ayliffe, Jack Beaton, Arthur Beetson, Kerry Boustead, John Brass, Dave Brown, Vic Bulgin, Joe Busch, Hugh Byrne, Harry Caples, Lionel Cooper, Ron Coote, Les Cubitt, Col Donohoe, John Ferguson, Brad Fittler, Dan Frawley, Mick Frawley, Bob Fulton, Arthur Halloway, Nelson Hardy, Mark Harris, Lou Jones, Kevin Junee, John Lang, Ian Mackay, Paul McCabe, Allan McKean, Ross McKinnon, Jeff Masterman, John Mayes, Herbert (Dally) Messenger, Wally Messenger, Jim Morgan, Ernie Norman, Ray Norman, Rex Norman, Andy Norval, Wally O'Connell, Larry O'Malley, Arthur Oxford, Sid (Sandy) Pearce, Sid (Joe) Pearce, John Peard, Harry Pierce, Jim Porter, Albert Rosenfeld, Ron Saddler, Craig Salvatori, Ian Schubert, Bill Shankland, Matt Sing, Ray Stehr, Viv Thicknesse, Bob Tidyman, David Trewhella, Andrew Walker, Elwyn Walters, Jack Watkins, George Watt, Bob Williams

Test captains: Herbert (Dally) Messenger (1908-10), Larry O'Malley (1909), Dave Brown (1935-36), Wally O'Connell (1948), Arthur Beetson (1973-74), Bob Fulton (1978), Brad Fittler (1996-97)
World Cup captains: Arthur Beetson (1975-77), John Brass (1975)
Rothmans Medal winners: Kevin Junee (1970), Kevin Hastings (1981), Mike Eden (1983)
Provan-Summons Medal winners: Brad Fittler (1997)
Major sponsor 1997: Samsung
First grade 1997: Coach Phil Gould. Finished 4th
Second grade 1997: Coach Joe Thomas. Finished 7th
Under-20s 1997: Coach Arthur Kitinas. Finished 2nd

1997 Representative players: City - Brad Fittler, Luke Ricketson, Shane Rigon. Country - Scott Gourley. Queensland - Adrian Lam, Matt Sing. Australia - Brad Fittler, Matt Sing. Rest of the World - Terry Hermansson, Adrian Lam, Jason Lowrie.

WESTERN SUBURBS

Year entered premiership: 1908
First match: April 20, 1908, lost 0-24 v Balmain, Birchgrove Oval
Colours: Black and white
Emblem: Magpie
Home ground: Campbelltown Sports Ground
Attendance record: 17,286, Wests v St George, August 2, 1991

TITLES
First grade: 1930, 1934, 1948, 1952
Runners-up: 1918, 1925, 1932, 1950, 1958, 1961, 1962, 1963
Reserve grade: 1936, 1961, 1981
Third grade (President's Cup): 1936, 1938, 1939, 1944, 1958, 1961, 1967, 1977, 1992
Club Championship: 1948, 1960, 1961, 1991
Amco Cup: 1977

Most tries in a match

Player	Tries	Opponent	Venue	Date
Alan Ridley	6	Newtown	Pratten Park	July 11, 1936
Dick Vest	4	University	Pratten Park	August 7, 1920
Dick Fifield	4	Norths	Pratten Park	August 28, 1926
Tony Redmond	4	Glebe	Pratten Park	July 16, 1927
Alan Brady	4	Glebe	Wentworth Park	August 17, 1929
Ray Morris	4	Easts	Sydney Sports Ground	May 10, 1930
Alan Ridley	4	Norths	Sydney Cricket Ground	April 27, 1935
Neville Charlton	4	Balmain	Leichhardt Oval	August 21, 1954
Keith Cullen	4	Souths	Sydney Cricket Ground	April 4, 1953
Peter Dimond	4	Souths	Pratten Park	August 11, 1962
Jim Leis	4	Penrith	Lidcombe Oval	April 5, 1980
Steve Broughton	4	Canberra	Lidcombe Oval	June 13, 1982

Most tries in a season

Alan Ridley	18	1932
Paul Smith	18	1994
Steve Broughton	17	1982
John Ribot	16	1980
Mark Bell	16	1992

Most tries for club

Peter Dimond	84
Keith Holman	70
Alan Ridley	64
Alan Brady	56
W.Collins	52
Russell Mullins	51

Most goals in a match

Player	Goals	Opponent	Venue	Date
Les Mead	12	Canterbury	Pratten Park	August 31, 1935
Darcy Russell	11	Souths	Pratten Park	April 6, 1957
Darcy Russell	11	Norths	Sydney Cricket Ground	May 3, 1958
Darcy Russell	11	Canterbury	Pratten Park	May 2, 1959
Peter Flanders	11	Canterbury	Lidcombe Oval	March 28, 1971
Tony Ford	11	Parramatta	Lidcombe Oval	June 11, 1972

Most points in a match

Player	Points	Opponent	Venue	Date
Les Mead	27 (1T, 12G)	Canterbury	Pratten Park	August 31, 1935
Peter Flanders	25 (1T, 11G)	Canterbury	Lidcombe Oval	March 28, 1971
Tony Ford	23 (1T, 10G)	Balmain	Lidcombe Oval	March 31, 1974
Darcy Russell	23 (1T, 10G)	Souths	Pratten Park	June 21, 1958
Darcy Russell	22 (11G)	Souths	Pratten Park	April 6, 1957
Darcy Russell	22 (11G)	Norths	Sydney Cricket Ground	May 3, 1958
Darcy Russell	22 (11G)	Canterbury	Pratten Park	May 2, 1959
Tony Ford	22 (11G)	Parramatta	Lidcombe Oval	June 11, 1972

CLUB-BY-CLUB RECORDS

Most points in a season

Peter Rowles	229	(8T, 101G, 3FG)	1978
Darcy Russell	206	(6T, 94G)	1959
Darcy Russell	204	(4T, 96G)	1958
Darcy Russell	185	(3T, 88G)	1960
John Dorahy	183	(11T, 75G)	1975

Most points for club

Bill Keato	776	(6T, 379G)
Darcy Russell	764	(16T, 358G)
Tony Ford	667	(11T, 317G)
Andrew Leeds	547	(25T, 221G, 5FG)
John Dorahy	545	(29T, 228G, 2FG)
Jason Taylor	486	(6T, 225G, 12FG)
George Bain	482	(12T, 223G)

Biggest wins
62-5 v Balmain, Lidcombe, March 31, 1974
65-11 v Canterbury, Pratten, August 31, 1935
51-0 v Norths, St Luke's, Burwood, June 14, 1919
52-3 v Annandale, Pratten, July 31, 1920
52-4 v Norths, SCG, May 3, 1958

Worst defeats
67-0 v South Sydney, Agricultural, July 23, 1910
64-2 v Balmain, Pratten Park, July 29, 1944
66-8 v Manly, Brookvale Oval, March 26, 1994
53-0 v Easts, SSG, July 8, 1916
52-0 v Canterbury, Lidcombe Oval, June 2, 1985

Most first grade games

Tom Raudonikis	201	Wayne Smith	161	John Donnelly	148	Rangi Joass	139
Keith Holman	199	Trevor Cogger	160	Nev Charlton	143	Bob Lindfield	138
Tedda Courtney	161	Peter Dimond	155	Frank McMillan	141		

CLUB INTERNATIONALS (40) Jim Abercrombie, Les Boyd, Bill Brogan, Tedda Courtney, Bill Carson, Arthur Clues, Arthur Collinson, Peter Dimond, John Donnelly, John Dorahy, John Elford, Viv Farnsworth, Cec Fifield, Herb Gilbert, David Gillespie, Kevin Hansen, Darcy Henry, Vic Hey, Keith Holman, Ian Johnston, Noel Kelly, Steve Knight, Jim Leis, Bob Lindner, Frank McMillan, Col Maxwell, Les Mead, Ian Moir, Kel O'Shea, Don Parish, Cliff Pearce, Clarrie Prentice, Tom Raudonikis, John Ribot, Alan Ridley, Jim Serdaris, Kevin Smyth, Frank Stanmore, Arthur Summons, Dick Vest, Harry Wells

Test captains: Herb Gilbert (1920), Frank McMillan (1933), Col Maxwell (1948), Arthur Summons (1962-63), Tom Raudonikis (1973)
World Cup captains: Nil
Rothmans Medal winners: Tom Raudonikis (1972)
Major sponsor 1997: LG Electronics
First grade 1997: Coach Tom Raudonikis. Finished 9th
Second grade 1997: Coach Jason Alchin. Finished 12th
Under-20s 1997: Coach Michael Liubinskas. Finished 9th

1997 Representative players: Country - Bill Dunn, Ciriaco Mescia, Brandon Pearson, Darren Willis. NSW - Ken McGuinness.

Extinct Clubs
ANNANDALE

Year entered premiership: 1910
First match: April 30, 1910, lost 6-31 v Newtown, Wentworth Park
Last match: September 1, 1920, lost 0-15 v Easts, SCG No. 2
Colours: Maroon and Gold
Nickname: The Dales
Home ground: Wentworth Park

TITLES
First grade: Nil
Runners-up: Nil
Reserve grade: Nil
Third grade: Nil

Most tries in a match

Player	Tries	Opponent	Venue	Date
Ray Norman	3	Norths	North Sydney Oval	August 2, 1913
J.Bain	3	Easts	Agricultural Ground	June 16, 1917

Most tries in a season

Roy Norman	8	1910
Roy Norman	8	1911
J.Larkin	8	1915
J.Bain	6	1917
G.Jolly	6	1918

Most tries for club

Player	Tries
J.Bain	16
Roy Norman	15
Ray Norman	12
G.Jolly	11
W.Geoghegan	9
Rex Norman	9
Bob Stuart	9

Most goals in a match

Player	Goals	Opponent	Venue	Date
W.Doyle	6	Norths	North Sydney Oval	May 29, 1915

Most points in a match

Player	Points	Opponent	Venue	Date
Lyall Wall	12 (2T, 3G)	Wests	Wentworth Park	August 9, 1913
W.Doyle	12 (6G)	Norths	North Sydney Oval	May 29, 1915
F.Greshier	11 (1T, 4G)	Norths	Wentworth Park	July 29, 1911

Most points in a season

Player	Points		Year
W.Doyle	46	(2T, 20G)	1916
Lyall Wall	42	(2T, 18G)	1913
Charlie Hedley	32	(16G)	1910
Roy Norman	28	(8T, 2G)	1910
Roy Norman	24	(6T, 3G)	1911

Worst defeats
52-3 v Wests, Pratten Park, July 31, 1920
43-0 v Balmain, Birchgrove Oval, June 3, 1918
43-0 v Glebe, Birchgrove Oval, May 1, 1920
44-3 v Norths, North Sydney, August 28, 1920
42-3 v Wests, St Luke's, Burwood, June 15, 1918

Most points for club

Player	Points	
Ray Norman	84	(12T, 24G)
W.Doyle	83	(3T, 37G)
Roy Norman	55	(15T, 5G)
J.Bain	50	(16T, 1G)
Lyall Wall	42	(2T, 18G)

Most first grade games

W Haddock	80
J.Bain	61
Rex Norman	56
P.Coll	54
W.Palmer	54
G.Eves	51

Biggest wins
25-3 v Wests, Wentworth Park, August 27, 1910
30-8 v Norths, North Sydney, May 29, 1915
31-11 v Norths, Wentworth, July 20, 1911
18-0 v Wests, Wentworth, August 9, 1913
21-10 v Norths, North Sydney, July 2, 1910

CLUB INTERNATIONALS (1) Bob Stuart.

Test captains: Nil

CUMBERLAND

Year entered premiership: 1908
First match: May 9, 1908, lost 2-23 v Souths, Agricultural Ground
Last match: July 25, 1908, lost 0-45 v Norths, Wentworth Park
Colours: Blue and Gold
Home ground: none

TITLES
First grade: Nil
Runners-up: Nil
Reserve grade: Nil
Third grade: Nil

Most tries in a match
Player	Tries	Opponent	Venue	Date
E.Bellamy	1	Glebe	Wentworth Park	May 30, 1908
E.Bellamy	1	Easts	Agricultural Ground	June 27, 1908
J.Cribb	1	Wests	Birchgrove Oval	July 4, 1908
H.Bloomfield	1	Wests	Birchgrove Oval	July 4, 1908

Most tries in a season
E.Bellamy   2   1908

Most tries for club
E.Bellamy   2

Most goals in a match
Player	Goals	Opponent	Venue	Date
H.Bloomfield	4	Wests	Birchgrove Oval	July 4, 1908
E.Bellamy	3	Newtown	Birchgrove Oval	May 23, 1908

Most points in a match
Player	Points	Opponent	Venue	Date
H.Bloomfield	11 (1T, 4G)	Wests	Birchgrove Oval	July 4, 1908
E.Bellamy	8 (1T, 2G)	Glebe	Wentworth Park	May 30, 1908

Most points in a season
H.Bloomfield   19   (1T, 8G)   1908
E.Bellamy   16   (2T, 5G)   1908

Most points for club
H.Bloomfield   19   (1T, 8G)
E.Bellamy   16   (2T, 5G)

Biggest win
14-6 v Wests, Birchgrove Oval, July 4, 1908

Worst defeats
45-0 v Norths, Wentworth Park, July 25, 1908
37-0 v Newcastle, Agricultural, May 16, 1908
23-2 v Souths, Agricultural Ground, May 9, 1908
26-5 v Easts, Agricultural Ground, June 27, 1908
22-7 v Glebe, Wentworth Park, May 30, 1908

Most first grade games
H.Bloomfield	8	S.Jarvis	8	F.O'Grady	8
A.Halling	8	T.Lalor	8	R.Casey	7

CLUB INTERNATIONALS: Nil

Test captains: Nil

GLEBE

Year entered premiership: 1908
First match: April 20, 1908, won 8-5 v Newcastle, Wentworth Park
Last match: August 31, 1929, drew 24-all v Norths, North Sydney Oval
Colours: Maroon and white
Nickname: Dirty Reds
Home ground: Wentworth Park

TITLES
First grade: Nil
Runners-up: 1911, 1912, 1915, 1922
Reserve grade: 1912, 1918, 1919, 1920, 1921
Third grade: 1927

Most tries in a match
Player	Tries	Opponent	Venue	Date
Frank Burge	8	University	Agricultural Ground	June 19, 1920
Frank Burge	6	Norths	Wentworth Park	July 1, 1916
Roy Algie	4	Newtown	Wentworth Park	July 27, 1912
Tom Leggo	4	Norths	Wentworth Park	July 17, 1915
Frank Burge	4	Wests	Wentworth Park	July 22, 1916
Frank Burge	4	Newtown	Wentworth Park	June 4, 1917
Bill Benson	4	Annandale	Wentworth Park	June 23, 1917
Frank Burge	4	Norths	Wentworth Park	June 15, 1918
Frank Burge	4	Annandale	Wentworth Park	June 22, 1918
Frank Burge	4	Annandale	Birchgrove Oval	July 24, 1920
Charlie Ogle	4	Newtown	Sydney Cricket Ground	June 17, 1920
Frank Burge	4	Annandale	Birchgrove Oval	July 24, 1920

Most tries in a season
Frank Burge	24	1918
Frank Burge	22	1916
Frank Burge	20	1915
Jack Toohey	18	1922
Frank Burge	16	1920

Most tries for club
Frank Burge	137
Tom Leggo	41
Charlie Ogle	40
Bert Gray	31
Jack Toohey	31

Most goals in a match
Player	Goals	Opponent	Venue	Date
Frank Burge	8	Annandale	Birchgrove Oval	May 1, 1920
Jack Hickey	8	Balmain	Birchgrove Oval	April 23, 1927
Frank Burge	7	Annandale	Birchgrove Oval	July 24, 1920
Frank Burge	7	University	Birchgrove	May 21, 1921
Tony Redmond	7	St George	Sydney Sports Ground	May 27, 1922

Most points in a match
Player	Points	Opponent	Venue	Date
Frank Burge	32 (8T, 4G)	University	Agricultural Ground	June 19, 1920
Frank Burge	26 (4T, 7G)	Annandale	Birchgrove Oval	July 24, 1920
Frank Burge	20 (2T, 7G)	University	Birchgrove Oval	May 21, 1921

Most points in a season
Frank Burge	110	(16T, 31G)	1920
J. "Tony" Redmond	84	(42G)	1922
Frank Burge	74	(24T, 1G)	1918
Alex Bolewski	73	(3T, 32G)	1916
Frank Burge	66	(22T)	1916

Most points for club
Frank Burge	509	(137T, 49G)
Alex Bolewski	213	(7T, 96G)
Albert "Son" Burge	206	(10T, 88G)
Jack Toohey	177	(31T, 42G)
Tom Leggo	159	(41T, 18G)

Biggest wins
59-3 v Norths, Wentworth Park, July 17, 1915
43-0 v Annandale, Birchgrove, May 1, 1920
41-0 v University, Agricultural, June 19, 1920
41-0 v St George, SSG, May 27, 1922
41-2 v Balmain, Wentworth, August 19, 1911

Worst defeats
36-0 v Easts, Agricultural, September 10, 1910
38-5 v Easts, Wentworth, April 24, 1909
35-3 v Norths, SCG, September 6, 1922
40-9 v Balmain, Birchgrove Oval, July 21, 1917
38-11 v St George, Earl Park, July 30, 1927
31-4 v Souths, SSG, July 13, 1929

Most first grade games
Frank Burge	138	Bert Gray	99	Tom Leggo	87	Tom McGrath	80
Sid Pert	115	Bill "Binghi" Benson	94	Ned Goddard	82	M. Scannell	75
Ted Swinson	107						

CLUB INTERNATIONALS (11) Alex Burdon, Frank Burge, Peter Burge, Albert Conlon, Bert Gray, Arthur "Pony" Halloway, Charlie Hedley, Jack Hickey, Tom McCabe, Chris McKivat, Peter Moir

Test captains: Alex Burdon (1908-09), Chris McKivat (1911-12)

CLUB-BY-CLUB RECORDS — EXTINCT CLUBS

NEWCASTLE

Year entered premiership: 1908
First game: April 20, 1908, lost 5-8 v Glebe, Wentworth Park
Last game: August 14, 1909, lost 0-20 v Souths, Agricultural Ground
Colours: Red and White
Home ground: Newcastle Showground

TITLES
First grade: Nil
Runners-up: Nil
Reserve grade: Nil
Third grade: Nil

Most tries in a match
Player	Tries	Opponent	Venue	Date
Bill "Jerry" Bailey	3	Glebe	Wentworth Park	June 19, 1909
Bill "Jerry" Bailey	3	Wests	Newcastle	June 26, 1909

Most tries in a season
Player	Tries	Year
Bill "Jerry" Bailey	9	1908
Bill "Jerry" Bailey	9	1909

Most tries for club
Player	Tries
Bill "Jerry" Bailey	18
A.Coleman	10
E.McGuinness	7
G.Cox	5
S.Carpenter	4
C.Croft	4
R.Lawson	4

Most goals in a match
Player	Goals	Opponent	Venue	Date
Stan Carpenter	5	Easts	Newcastle	May 29, 1909
Stan Carpenter	4	Newtown	Agricultural Ground	June 13, 1908
Stan Carpenter	4	Easts	Agricultural Ground	July 25, 1908
Stan Carpenter	4	Glebe	Wentworth Park	June 19, 1909
Stan Carpenter	4	Wests	Agricultural Ground	July 17, 1909

Most points in a match
Player	Points	Opponent	Venue	Date
Bill "Jerry" Bailey	13 (3T, 2G)	Wests	Newcastle	June 26, 1909
Stan Carpenter	10 (2T, 2G)	Cumberland	Wentworth Park	May 16, 1908
Stan Carpenter	10 (5G)	Easts	Newcastle	May 29, 1909

Most points in a season
Player	Points	Year
Stan Carpenter	38 (2T, 16G)	1908
Bill "Jerry" Bailey	33 (9T, 3G)	1909
Bill "Jerry" Bailey	29 (9T, 1G)	1908

Most points for club
Player	Points
Stan Carpenter	80 (4T, 34G)
Bill "Jerry" Bailey	62 (18T, 4G)
A.Coleman	30 (10T)
E.McGuinness	27 (7T, 3G)
L.Carpenter	22 (2T, 8G)

Biggest wins
37-0 v Cumberland, Wentworth, May 16, 1908
34-0 v Wests, Newcastle, June 26, 1909
28-5 v Balmain, Birchgrove, July 4, 1908
28-5 v Wests, Agricultural, July 17, 1909
24-2 v Wests, Agricultural, May 23, 1908

Worst defeats
20-0 v Souths, Agricultural, August 14, 1909
30-11 v Souths, Agricultural, June 27, 1908
28-9 v Souths, Agricultural, May 1, 1909
34-17 v Easts, Agricultural, July 25, 1908
21-9 v Norths, Birchgrove Oval, May 30, 1908

Most first grade games
Player	Games	Player	Games	Player	Games	Player	Games
E.McGuinness	20	G.Cox	17	L.Carpenter	16	E.Patfield	14
Stan Carpenter	19	Bill "Jerr" Bailey	16	A.Coleman	16		

CLUB INTERNATIONALS (2) Bill "Jerry" Bailey, Pat Walsh.
Test captains: Nil

NEWTOWN

Year entered premiership: 1908
First game: April 20, 1908, lost 16-32 v Easts, Wentworth Park
Last game: August 27, 1983, won 9-6 v Canberra, Orana Park
Colours: Sky blue
Emblems: Blue Bag, Jet
Home grounds: Metters Ground (Erskineville), Erskineville Oval, Marrickville Oval, Henson Park, Orana Park
Attendance record: 21,588 v St George, Henson Park, June 9, 1957

TITLES
First grade: 1910, 1933, 1943
Runners-up: 1913, 1914, 1929, 1944, 1954, 1955, 1981
Reserve grade: 1922, 1947, 1948, 1951, 1970, 1974
Third grade: 1920, 1935, 1943
Club Championship: 1973
Pre-season competition: 1973

Most tries in a match

Player	Tries	Opponent	Venue	Date
Jack Troy	6	Easts	Sydney Sports Ground	July 8, 1950
Norm Jacobson	5	Parramatta	Erskineville Oval	April 17, 1948
Viv Farnsworth	4	Annandale	Wentworth Park	April 30, 1910
W. Cockburn	4	Annandale	Erskineville Oval	June 1, 1918
Lou Boyd	4	University	Henson Park	May 12, 1937
Len Smith	4	St George	Sydney Cricket Ground	August 26, 1944
Norm Jacobson	4	Parramatta	Erskineville Oval	June 28, 1947
Ray Preston	4	Manly	Erskineville Oval	July 18, 1953
Bob Whitton	4	Canterbury	Belmore Sports Ground	June 14, 1954
Kevin Considine	4	St George	Sydney Cricket Ground	September 11, 1954
Dick Poole	4	Easts	Sydney Cricket Ground	August 13, 1955
Ray Preston	4	Easts	Henson Park	April 7, 1956
Ray Preston	4	Manly	Sydney Cricket Ground	April 28, 1956
Bruce Pickett	4	Balmain	Henson Park	July 22, 1973
John Ferguson	4	Penrith	Penrith Park	August 29, 1982

Most tries in a season

Ray Preston	34	1954
Norm Jacobson	27	1948
Sid Goodwin	22	1944
Kevin Considine	21	1954
Ray Preston	18	1953
John Bradstock	18	1972

Most tries for club

Player	Tries
Ray Preston	109
Brian Moore	90
Kevin Considine	84
Norm Jacobson	69
Dick Poole	51

Most goals in a match

Player	Goals	Opponent	Venue	Date
Tom Kirk	11	St George	Sydney Cricket Ground	June 3, 1944
Tom Kirk	11	St George	Sydney Cricket Ground	August 26, 1944
Tom Kirk	10	Canterbury	Henson Park	June 2, 1945
Gordon Clifford	10	Manly	Sydney Cricket Ground	June 13, 1955
John Bonham	10	Parramatta	Henson Park	July 12, 1970
Ken Wilson	10	Illawarra	Henson Park	May 2, 1982

Most points in a match

Player	Points	Opponent	Venue	Date
Tom Kirk	25 (1T, 11G)	St George	Sydney Cricket ground	August 26, 1944
Ken Wilson	24 (1T, 10G, 1FG)	Illawarra	Henson Park	May 2, 1982
John Bonham	23 (1T, 10G)	Parramatta	Henson Park	July 12, 1970
Tom Kirk	22 (11G)	St George	Sydney Cricket Ground	June 3, 1944
Tom Kirk	21 (1T, 9G)	Easts	Sydney Cricket Ground	May 20, 1944

CLUB-BY-CLUB RECORDS — EXTINCT CLUBS

Most points in a season
Ken Wilson	197	(5T, 90G, 2FG)	1980
Tom Kirk	185	(3T, 88G)	1944
Bob Lanigan	185	(3T, 88G)	1966
Gordon Clifford	184	(92G)	1955
Gordon Clifford	163	(1T, 80G)	1954

Most points for club
Ken Wilson	1,001	(25T, 447G, 28FG)
Gordon Clifford	919	(7T, 449G)
Tom Kirk	680	(14T, 319G)
Tom Ellis	559	(3T, 275G)
Bob Lanigan	455	(11T, 204G, 7FG)
Kevin Considine	436	(84T, 92G)
John Bonham	436	(14T, 195G, 2FG)

Biggest wins
51-0 v Illawarra, Henson Park, May 2, 1982
55-7 v St George, SCG, August 26, 1944
48-3 v University, Henson Park, May 12, 1937
52-7 v St George, SCG, June 3, 1944
50-6 v Manly, SCG, June 13, 1955

Worst defeats
65-9 v St George, Kogarah Oval, July 30, 1961
57-6 v Manly, Henson Park, May 16, 1976
54-4 v Parramatta, Belmore, June 5, 1983
50-2 v Manly, Brookvale Oval, August 14, 1977
54-10 v St George, Kogarah Oval, July 24, 1960
44-0 v Cronulla, Endeavour Field, July 23, 1978
62-18 v Parramatta, Henson, August 20, 1978

Most first grade games
Frank Farrell	204	Bob Keyes	163	Kevin Considine	133	Felix Ryan	125
Brian Moore	173	Ken Wilson	150	Tom Ellis	128	Les Bull	124
Bob Whitton	171	Tommy Nevin	142	Graham Wilson	128		

CLUB INTERNATIONALS (34) Jack Barnett, Tony Brown, Frank Cheadle, Gordon Clifford, Tedda Courtney, Bill Farnsworth, Viv Farnsworth, Frank Farrell, Arthur Folwell, Keith Froome, Col Geelan, Henry Holloway, Jack Holmes, Frank Johnson, Albert "Ricketty" Johnston, Paddy McCue, Brian Moore, Noel Mulligan, Joe Murray, Herb Narvo, William "Webby" Neill, Bill Noble, Dick Poole, Paul Quinn, Tom Raudonikis, Charlie "Boxer" Russell, Felix Ryan, Phil Sigsworth, Len Smith, Gary Sullivan, Dick Townsend, Jack Troy, Lionel Williamson, Graham Wilson.

Test captains: Albert "Ricketty" Johnston (1919-20), Len Smith (1948), Keith Froome (1949).
World Cup captains: Dick Poole (1954)
Rothmans Medal winners: Geoff Bugden (1980)

SOUTH QUEENSLAND

Year entered premiership: 1995
First game: March 11, 1995, lost 6-24 v Canberra, Suncorp Stadium
Last game: August 31, 1997, won 39-18 v Wests, Suncorp Stadium
Colours: Aztec gold, blue and red
Emblem: Steam Train
Nickname: Crushers
Home ground: Suncorp Stadium
Attendance record: 34,263, South Queensland v Brisbane, April 12, 1996

TITLES:
President's Cup: 1996

Most tries in a match
Player	Tries	Opponent	Venue	Date
Dale Shearer	3	Parramatta	Suncorp Stadium	April 30, 1995
Darren Plowman	2	Newcastle	Suncorp Stadium	May 21, 1995
David Krause	2	Penrith	Suncorp Stadium	June 25, 1995
David Krause	2	Western Reds	WACA	July 28, 1995
Fili Seru	2	North Queensland	Suncorp Stadium	August 6, 1995
Troy Pezet	2	Parramatta	Suncorp Stadium	March 29, 1996
Nigel Gaffey	2	Sydney City	Suncorp Stadium	May 25, 1996
Jason Hudson	2	Norths	Suncorp Stadium	May 10, 1997
Clinton Schifcofske	2	Sydney City	Suncorp Stadium	May 23, 1997

Most tries in a season

David Krause	9	1995
Jason Hudson	9	1997
Clinton Schifcofske	6	1997
Darren Plowman	5	1995
Travis Norton	5	1995
Craig Weston	5	1996
Michael Eagar	5	1997
Matt Toshack	5	1997

Most tries for club

Jason Hudson	11
David Krause	10
Travis Norton	7
Clinton Schifcofske	7
Troy Pezet	6
Darren Plowman	6
Craig Weston	6

Most goals in a match

Player	Goals	Opponent	Venue	Date
Clinton Schifcofske	7	Wests	Suncorp Stadium	August 31, 1997
Tony Kemp	6	Penrith	Suncorp Stadium	June 25, 1995
Graham Mackay	6	Parramatta	Suncorp Stadium	March 29, 1996

Most points in a match

Player	Points	Opponent	Venue	Date
Clinton Schifcofske	18 (1T, 7G)	Wests	Suncorp Stadium	August 31, 1997
Tony Kemp	16 (1T, 6G)	Penrith	Suncorp Stadium	June 25, 1995
Clinton Schifcofske	16 (2T, 4G)	Sydney City	Suncorp Stadium	May 23, 1997
Dale Shearer	12 (3T)	Parramatta	Suncorp Stadium	April 30, 1995
Graham Mackay	12 (6G)	Parramatta	Suncorp Stadium	March 29, 1995
Troy Pezet	12 (1T, 4G)	Manly	Suncorp Stadium	March 29, 1997

Most points in a season

Clinton Schifcofske	94	(6T, 35G)	1997
Jason Hudson	42	(9T, 3G)	1997
Tony Kemp	38	(2T, 15G)	1995
Travis Norton	38	(5T, 9G)	1995
David Krause	36	(9T)	1995
St John Ellis	30	(1T, 13G)	1995
Graham Mackay	26	(2T, 9G)	1996

Most points for club

Clinton Schifcofske	108	(7T, 40G)
Travis Norton	56	(7T, 14G)
Jason Hudson	50	(11T, 3G)
David Krause	40	(10T)
Tony Kemp	38	(2T, 15G)

Biggest wins

39-18 v Wests, Suncorp, August 31, 1997
28-8 v Penrith, Suncorp, June 25, 1995
33-14 v Parramatta, Suncorp, April 30, 1995
23-6 v Parramatta, Suncorp, March 16, 1997
22-6 v North Qld, Suncorp, August 6, 1995

Worst defeats

58-4 v Canberra, Bruce, August 27, 1995
52-4 v Gold Coast, Suncorp, July 21, 1996
44-0 v Newcastle, Marathon, March 23, 1997
52-10 v Parramatta, Parramatta, June 8, 1997
46-12 v Manly, Brookvale Oval, July 6, 1997
42-8 v Norths, North Sydney, August 24, 1997

Most first grade games

Craig Teevan	58	Brett Horsnell	38	Travis Norton	33
Trevor Gillmeister	41	Mark Protheroe	34	Clinton O'Brien	30
Jason Hudson	39	Grant Young	33	Chris McKenna	29

CLUB INTERNATIONALS (1) Trevor Gillmeister

Test captains: Nil
World Cup captains: Nil
Rothmans Medal winners: Nil
Major sponsor 1997: AV Jennings
First grade 1997: Coach Steve Bleakley. Finished 12th
Second grade 1997: Coach Graham Herlihy. Finished 4th
Under-20s 1997: Coach Gary O'Brien. Finished 10th

1997 Representative players: Queensland - Clinton O'Brien.

UNIVERSITY

Year entered premiership: 1920
First game: May 8, 1920, lost 12-36 v Norths, North Sydney Oval
Last game: June 19, 1937, lost 0-17 v Canterbury, Belmore Sports Ground
Colours: Blue and Gold
Nickname: The Students
Home ground: None

TITLES
First grade: Nil
Runners-up: 1926
Reserve grade: Nil
Third grade: Nil

Most tries in a match
Player	Tries	Opponent	Venue	Date
Jack Gray-Spence	3	St George	Sydney Sports Ground	July 15, 1933
J.McNeill	3	Easts	Agricultural Ground	September 6, 1930

Most tries in a season
Player	Tries	Year
Jack Gray-Spence	11	1933
Gordon Favelle	10	1933
Rod O'Loan	10	1930
Eddie Ryan	9	1926
R.O'Brien	8	1926
Harley Hanrahan	8	1929
J.McNeill	8	1930

Most tries for club
Player	Tries
E. "Sammy" Ogg	24
Eddie Ryan	20
Gordon Favelle	16
Jim Flattery	15
Jack Gray-Spence	15
Frank O'Rourke	15

Most goals in a match
Player	Goals	Opponent	Venue	Date
Jimmy Craig	6	Balmain	Birchgrove Oval	July 29, 1922
J.McIntyre	6	Newtown	Wentworth Park	July 7, 1928
J.McIntyre	6	Newtown	Marrickville Oval	August 18, 1928
W.Flanagan	6	Easts	Wentworth Park	July 6, 1929

Most points in a match
Player	Points	Opponent	Venue	Date
Jimmy Craig	15 (1T, 6G)	Balmain	Birchgrove Oval	July 29, 1922
W.Flanagan	15 (1T, 6G)	Easts	Wentworth Park	July 6, 1929

Most points in a season
Player	Points		Year
J.McIntyre	86	(2T, 40G)	1928
J.McIntyre	60	(30G)	1927
Frank O'Rourke	48	(6T, 15G)	1925
Hec Courtenay	42	(21G)	1922
Eddie Ryan	39	(9T, 6G)	1926

Most points for club
Player	Points	
T.McInerney	178	(8T, 77G)
Jim McIntyre	176	(4T, 82G)
E. "Sammy" Ogg	104	(24T, 16G)
W.Flanagan	100	(12T, 32G)
Eddie Ryan	96	(20T, 18G)

Biggest wins
42-8 v St George, SSG, July 15, 1933
29-3 v Glebe, SCG, September 4, 1926
35-16 v Easts, Wentworth Park, July 6, 1929
21-2 v Norths, North Sydney Oval, May 20, 1933
19-3 v Easts, Wentworth Park, May 15, 1926
24-8 v St George, Earl Park, July 10, 1926

Worst defeats
63-0 v Souths, SSG, April 17, 1937
65-5 v St George, SCG May 22, 1937
57-0 v Balmain, Birchgrove Oval, April 23, 1921
61-5 v Easts, SSG, May 11, 1935
60-13 v Balmain, Birchgrove Oval, May 22, 1920
49-2 v Balmain, Birchgrove Oval, August 21, 1920
52-5 v Easts, SSG, May 8, 1937

Most first grade games
Player	Games	Player	Games	Player	Games
E. "Sammy" Ogg	116	Frank Benning	66	Ted Barry	53
Harry Finn	70	Eddie Ryan	66	Paddy McCormack	50
		M Cunningham	53		
		T.McInerney	53		

CLUB INTERNATIONALS (1) Ray Morris.
Test captains: Nil

WESTERN REDS

Year entered premiership: 1995 (Known as the Perth Reds in the 1997 Super League competition)
First game: March 12, 1995, won 28-16 v St George, WACA Ground
Last game: August 23, 1997, lost 16-36 v Canberra, WACA Ground (Super League competition)
Colours: Black, red, yellow and white
Emblem: Red kangaroo
Home ground: The WACA Ground
Attendance record: 24,392, Western Reds v St George, March 12, 1995 (debut premiership match)

TITLES: Nil

Most tries in a match

Player	Tries	Opponent	Venue	Date
Matthew Rodwell	3	Auckland	WACA Ground	July 20, 1996
Matt Fuller	2	Sydney Tigers	WACA Ground	April 14, 1995
Greg Fleming	2	Canberra	Bruce Stadium	April 23, 1995
Chris Ryan	2	Parramatta	WACA Ground	July 21, 1995
Greg Fleming	2	Newcastle	WACA Ground	August 18, 1995
Darren Higgins	2	Cronulla	WACA Ground	April 7, 1996
Greg Fleming	2	Gold Coast	WACA Ground	July 5, 1996
Barrie-Jon Mather	2	Illawarra	WACA Ground	July 8, 1996
Matt Fuller	2	Nth Queensland	WACA Ground	August 17, 1996
Paul Evans	2	Newcastle	Marathon Stadium	August 24, 1996
Matt Fuller	2	St George	WACA Ground	August 30, 1996

(Julian O'Neill scored four tries in a Super League match against Canterbury, Perth Oval, March 23, 1997; Greg Fleming, 2, against Penrith, Penrith Football Stadium, March 2, 1997; Fleming, 2, against North Queensland, Stockland Stadium, March 7, 1997; Matthew Rodwell, 2, against Hunter, WACA Ground, August 10, 1997; Shaun Devine, 2, against Auckland, Ericsson Stadium, August 16, 1997)

Most tries in a season

Matt Fuller	10	1995
Chris Ryan	9	1995
Matthew Rodwell	9	1996
Greg Fleming	7	1995
Chris Ryan	7	1996

Most tries for club

Chris Ryan	16
Matt Fuller	14
Greg Fleming	10
Matthew Rodwell	10
Julian O'Neill	6

(Ryan's total does not include five Super League tries, Fleming 6, Rodwell 4 and O'Neill 6)

Most goals in a match

Player	Goals	Opponent	Venue	Date
Julian O'Neill	6	Auckland	WACA Ground	July 20, 1996
Chris Ryan	5	Newcastle	WACA Ground	August 18, 1995
Julian O'Neill	5	North Queensland	WACA Ground	August 17, 1996

(Damien Chapman kicked six goals in a Super League match against Penrith, WACA Ground, May 4, 1997; Julian O'Neill, 5, against Canterbury, Perth Oval, March 23, 1997)

Most points in a match

Player	Points	Opponent	Venue	Date
Julian O'Neill	16 (1T, 6G)	Auckland	WACA Ground	July 20, 1996
Chris Ryan	12 (1t, 4G)	Gold Coast	Seagulls Stadium	July 1, 1995
Chris Ryan	12 (1T, 4G)	Illawarra	WACA Ground	July 8, 1995
Chris Ryan	12 (2T, 2G)	Parramatta	WACA Ground	July 21, 1995
Matthew Rodwell	12 (3T)	Auckland	WACA Ground	July 20, 1996

(Julian O'Neill scored 26 points (4T, 5G) in a Super League match against Canterbury, Perth Oval, March 23, 1997; Shaun Devine 14 points (2T, 3G) against Auckland, Ericsson Stadium, August 16, 1997; Damien Chapman 12 points (6G), against Penrith, WACA Ground, May 4, 1997)

Most points in a season

Chris Ryan	136	(9T, 50G)	1995
Julian O'Neill	125	(6T, 49G, 3FG)	1996
Matt Fuller	40	(10T)	1995
Matthew Rodwell	36	(9T)	1996
Chris Ryan	30	(7T, 1G)	1996

(Julian O'Neill scored 53 points (6T, 14G, 1FG) in the 1997 Super League competition, Chris Ryan 44 (5T, 12G) and Damien Chapman 35 (1T, 15G, 1FG))

Most points for club

Chris Ryan	166	(16T, 51G)
Julian O'Neill	125	(6T, 49G, 3FG)
Matt Fuller	56	(14T)
Greg Fleming	40	(10T)
Matthew Rodwell	40	(10T)

(Ryan's total does not include 44 Super League points, O'Neill 53, Fuller 1, Fleming 24 and Rodwell 16)

Biggest wins

30-4 v North Qld, WACA, August 17, 1996
32-12 v Auckland, WACA Ground, July 20, 1996
28-10 v Illawarra, WACA Ground, July 8, 1995
22-6 v Sydney Tigers, WACA, April 14, 1995
22-8 v Newcastle, WACA, August 18, 1995
(Perth beat Canterbury 34-6 in a Super League match at Perth Oval, March 23, 1997; and Penrith 35-20 at the WACA Ground, May 4, 1997)

Worst defeats

42-0 v Sydney Bulldogs, Parramatta, April 9, 1995
54-14 v Newcastle, Marathon, March 19, 1995
52-12 v Norths, WACA Ground, June 5, 1995
46-12 v Penrith, Penrith, May 12, 1996
28-2 v Cronulla, WACA Ground, March 31, 1995
32-6 v Wests, Campbelltown, May 12, 1995
(Perth were beaten 50-14 by Brisbane in a Super League match at ANZ Stadium, July 6, 1997, and 32-2 by Cronulla at Shark Park, May 24, 1997)

Most first grade games

Matt Fuller	42	Dale Fritz	41	Jeff Doyle	35	Rodney Howe	32
Chris Ryan	42	Matt Rodwell	40	David Boyd	35	Brett Goldspink	26
Jason Eade	24	Greg Fleming	40	Peter Shiels	33	Mark Geyer	25

(Fuller's total does not include 17 Super League games, Ryan 15, Fritz 17, Rodwell 17, Fleming 15, Doyle 2, Shiels 15, Howe 8 and Geyer 8)

CLUB INTERNATIONALS: Nil *(Rodney Howe and Julian O'Neill represented the Australian Super League side in 1997)*

Test captains: Nil
World Cup captains: Nil
Rothmans Medal winners: Nil

City v Country
1927–1997

Most tries in one match

Alan Ridley	4	City I	1935
Fred Felsch	4	City I	1938
Ian Moir	4	City II	1952
Ian Moir	4	City I	1957
Brian Carlson	4	City I	1958
Mark Harris	4	City I	1972
Graham Eadie	4	City I	1980
Graham Lyons	4	City I	1990
Jason Edwards	4	Country I	1990

Most goals in one match

Noel Pidding 12 City I 1950

Most points in one match

Noel Pidding 27 (1T, 12G) City I 1950

Most points

Mick Cronin 115 (5T, 50G) — 11 matches for Country and City (1972-82).

Biggest win (City): 66-7, 1927

Biggest win (Country Origin): 22-2, 1994

RESULTS

Year	Team	Score	Team	Score	Year	Team	Score	Team	Score
1927	Metropolis I	66	Country I	7	1947	City I	33	Country I	10
	Metropolis II	19	Country II	10		City II	25	Country II	22
1928	Country I	35	City I	34	1948	City I	28	Country I	13
	City II	28	Country II	0		City II	19	Country II	3
	Country	23	City	14		City I	6	Country I	5
1929	City I	16	Country I	5	1949	City I	23	Country I	2
	City II	34	Country II	13		City II	9	Country II	2
	City	13	Country	9	1950	City I	51	Country I	13
1930	Country I	35	City I	26		City II	32	Country II	19
	City II	27	Country II	17	1951	City I	24	Country I	6
1931	City I	17	Country I	15		City II	25	Country I	20
	City II	45	Country II	12	1952	City I	23	Country I	21
1932	City I	27	Country I	15		City II	48	Country II	9
	City II	21	Country II	0	1953	Country I	28	City I	27
	Country	39	City	23		City II	31	Country II	13
	City	25	Country	19	1954	City I	50	Country I	9
1933	City I	47	Country I	6		Country II	16	City II	15
	City II	26	Country II	9	1955	City I	31	Country I	18
	City I	17	Country I	17		City II	34	Country II	7
1934	City I	28	Country I	14	1956	City I	32	Country I	17
	Country II	13	City II	11		City II	29	Country II	13
	City I	32	Country I	29		City	34	Country	22
1935	City I	20	Country I	5	1957	City I	53	Country I	2
	Country II	12	City II	3		City II	15	Country II	12
1936	City I	41	Country I	8	1958	City I	55	Country I	14
	City II	37	Country II	3		City II	39	Country II	6
1937	Country I	20	City I	12	1959	City I	37	Country I	7
	City II	30	Country II	4		City II	28	Country II	24
	Country I	15	City I	5		City	19	Country	18
1938	City I	42	Country I	12	1960	City I	20	Country I	2
	City II	31	Country II	15		City II	26	Country II	12
1939	City I	38	Country I	17		Metropolitan	27	Country	18
	City II	21	Country II	8	1961	Country I	19	City I	5
1940	City	28	Country	10		City II	5	Country II	5
1941	City I	44	Country I	21	1962	Country I	18	City I	8
	City II	40	Country II	21		City II	17	Country II	8
1942	Country I	14	City I	11	1963	City I	35	Country I	11
1943	City I	37	Country I	25		City II	20	Country I	8
1944	City I	17	Country I	10		City	15	Country	10
1945	City	41	Country	12	1964	City I	27	Country I	4
1946	City I	31	Country I	10		City II	29	Country II	2
	City II	35	Country II	7	1965	City I	32	Country I	2

Year	Match	Score	Match	Score	Year	Match	Score	Match	Score
	City II	23	Country II	5	1981	City II	17	Country II	16
1966	City I	18	Country I	14		City I	38	Country I	7
	Country II	16	City II	6		City II	12	Country II	3
1967	City I	18	Country I	17	1982	City I	47	Country I	3
	Country II	19	City II	18		City II	29	Country II	10
	Country	16	City	12	1983	City I	30	Country I	14
1968	City I	34	Country I	14		City II	24	Country II	12
	City II	12	Country II	11	1984	City I	38	Country I	12
1969	City I	27	Country I	20		Country II	28	City II	22
	Country II	24	City II	18	1985	City I	18	Country I	12
1970	City I	22	Country I	18		City II	24	Country II	6
	City II	24	Country II	13	1986	City I	34	Country I	18
	City	26	Country	20		City II	36	Country II	8
1971	City I	17	Country I	0	1987	City Origin	30	Ctry Origin	22
	City II	19	Country II	5		City I	52	Country I	12
1972	City I	35	Country I	8		City II	42	Country II	12
	City II	34	Country II	5	1988	City Origin	20	Ctry Origin	18
1973	City I	33	Country I	17		City I	54	Country I	16
	City II	34	Country II	3	1989	City Origin	16	Ctry Origin	8
1974	City I	23	Country I	0		City I	18	Country I	10
	City II	41	Country II	5	1990	City Origin	28	Ctry Origin	26
1975	Country I	19	City I	9		City I	38	Country I	26
	City II	28	Country II	8	1991	City Origin	22	Ctry Origin	12
1976	City I	47	Country I	0		City I	36	Country I	20
	City II	37	Country II	5	1992	Ctry Origin	17	City Origin	10
1977	City I	36	Country I	0		Country I	20	City I	18
	City II	25	Country II	2	1993	City Origin	7	Ctry Origin	0
1978	City I	30	Country I	13		City I	40	Country I	4
	City II	35	Country II	14	1994	Ctry Origin	22	City Origin	2
1979	City I	29	Country I	0	1995	City Origin	16	Ctry Origin	8
	City II	36	Country II	16	1996	Ctry Origin	18	City Origin	16
1980	City I	55	Country I	2	1997	Ctry Origin	17	City Origin	4

New South Wales v Queensland 1908–1997

NSW RECORDS 1908–97

Most appearances
Graeme Langlands	33
Wally Prigg	32
Ray Stehr	30
Joe Pearce	29
Clive Churchill	27
Harry Wells	27
Michael Cronin	25
Andrew Ettingshausen	25
Keith Holman	24
Ken Irvine	24
Johnny Raper	24
Jim Gibbs	23

Most tries: Ken Irvine, 30
Most tries in one match: Sid Goodwin, 6, Sydney 1939
Most goals: Les Johns, 77
Most goals in one match: Greg Hawick, 15, Sydney 1957
Most points: Michael Cronin, 173 (7T, 76G)
Most points in one match: "Dally" Messenger, 32 (4T, 10G) 1911
Biggest win: 69-5, Sydney Cricket Ground, June 4, 1957.
Worst defeat: 36-6, Lang Park, May 23, 1989.

NSW STATE OF ORIGIN RECORDS 1980–97

Most appearances
Andrew Ettingshausen	25
Ben Elias	19
Michael O'Connor	19
Rod Wishart	19
Brad Fittler	18
Paul Harragon	18
Garry Jack	17
Steve Roach	17
Brad Mackay	17
Laurie Daley	17
Brett Kenny	16
Glenn Lazarus	16
Tim Brasher	16

Most tries: Michael O'Connor, 11
Most tries in one match: Chris Anderson, 3, Lang Park, July 28, 1983
Most goals: Michael O'Connor, 42
Most goals in one match: Ross Conlon, 5, Lang Park, July 17, 1984. Michael O'Connor, 5, Lang Park, May 28, 1985
Most points: Michael O'Connor, 129 (11T, 42G, 1FG)
Most points in one match: Michael O'Connor, 18 (2T, 5G), Lang Park, May 28, 1985
Biggest win: 18-2, Lang Park, May 28, 1985.
Worst defeat: 36-6, Lang Park, May 23, 1989.

QUEENSLAND RECORDS 1908–97

Most appearances
Mal Meninga	38
Les Heidke	35
Wally Lewis	35
Mick Madsen	34
Herb Steinohrt	33
Brian Davies	31
Eddie "Babe" Collins	28
Allan Langer	27
Bob Banks	26
Tom Gorman	26
Fred Laws	26
Dale Shearer	26

Most tries: Eddie "Babe" Collins, 20
Most tries in one match: Alan Smith, 4, Sydney, 1979
Most goals: Mal Meninga, 78
Most goals in one match: Dan O'Connor, 12, Brisbane, 1940
Most points: Mal Meninga, 188 (9T, 78G)
Most points in one match: Dan O'Connor, 24 (12G), 1940
Biggest win: 38-0, Brisbane, July 3, 1926.
Worst defeat: 69-5, Sydney Cricket Ground, June 5, 1957.

QUEENSLAND STATE OF ORIGIN RECORDS 1980–97

Most appearances
Mal Meninga	32
Wally Lewis	31
Allan Langer	27
Dale Shearer	26
Bob Lindner	25
Paul Vautin	22
Trevor Gillmeister	22
Martin Bella	21
Gary Larson	21
Greg Conescu	20
Gene Miles	20
Mark Coyne	19
Colin Scott	18

Most tries: Dale Shearer, 12
Most tries in one match: Kerry Boustead, 3, Lang Park, May 29, 1984
Most goals: Mal Meninga, 69
Most goals in one match: Mal Meninga, 7, Lang Park, July 8, 1980
Most points: Mal Meninga, 161 (5T, 69G)
Most points in one match: Mal Meninga, 16 (2T, 4G), Lang Park, May 23, 1989. Dale Shearer, 16 (2T, 4G), Lang Park, June 28, 1989
Biggest win: 36-6, Lang Park, May 23, 1989.
Worst defeat: 18-2, Lang Park, May 28, 1985.

TRADITIONAL INTERSTATE MATCHES 1908–81

Year	Result				Venue
1908	NSW	43	Qld	0	Syd
1908	NSW	37	Qld	8	Syd
1908	NSW	12	Qld	3	Syd
1910	NSW	40	Qld	21	Bris
1910	NSW	32	Qld	18	Bris
1910	NSW	19	Qld	3	Bris
1911	NSW	65	Qld	9	Syd
1911	NSW	49	Qld	0	Syd
1911	NSW	32	Qld	8	Syd
1912	NSW	65	Qld	9	Syd
1912	NSW	32	Qld	4	Syd
1913	NSW	27	Qld	12	Bris
1913	NSW	21	Qld	17	Bris
1915	NSW	53	Qld	9	Syd
1915	NSW	39	Qld	6	Syd
1919	NSW	33	Qld	18	Syd
1919	NSW	12	Qld	7	Syd
1919	NSW	24	Qld	10	Bris
1919	NSW	13	Qld	10	Bris
1920	NSW	40	Qld	18	Syd
1921	NSW	37	Qld	11	Syd
1921	NSW	34	Qld	20	Bris
1922	Qld	25	NSW	9	Syd
1923	Qld	18	NSW	13	Syd
1923	Qld	25	NSW	10	Bris
1924	Qld	22	NSW	20	Syd
1924	Qld	20	NSW	7	Syd
1924	Qld	36	NSW	6	Bris
1925	Qld	23	NSW	15	Syd
1925	Qld	27	NSW	13	Syd
1925	NSW	27	Qld	16	Syd
1925	Qld	26	NSW	8	Bris
1925	Qld	23	NSW	18	Bris
1926	NSW	30	Qld	17	Syd
1926	NSW	5	Qld	3	Syd
1926	Qld	26	NSW	11	Newc
1926	Qld	38	NSW	0	Bris
1926	Qld	37	NSW	19	Bris
1927	NSW	14	Qld	10	Syd
1927	NSW	13	Qld	11	Syd
1927	Qld	11	NSW	7	Bris
1927	NSW	15	Qld	11	Bris
1928	Qld	25	NSW	9	Syd
1928	NSW	16	Qld	7	Syd
1928	Qld	28	NSW	17	Bris
1928	Qld	21	NSW	10	Bris
1929	NSW	21	Qld	8	Syd
1929	NSW	17	Qld	8	Syd
1929	NSW	12	Qld	10	Syd
1929	NSW	16	Qld	14	Bris
1929	NSW	11	Qld	8	Bris
1930	NSW	16	Qld	11	Syd
1930	Qld	25	NSW	11	Syd
1930	NSW	15	Qld	12	Bris
1931	NSW	39	Qld	17	Syd
1931	Qld	23	NSW	20	Syd
1931	NSW	28	Qld	6	Syd
1931	Qld	15	NSW	8	Bris
1931	Qld	4	NSW	3	Bris
1932	Qld	23	NSW	15	Syd
1932	NSW	9	Qld	9	Syd
1932	Qld	19	NSW	9	Bris
1933	NSW	24	Qld	0	Syd
1933	NSW	15	Qld	13	Syd
1933	NSW	17	Qld	14	Syd
1933	Qld	10	NSW	8	Bris
1934	NSW	13	Qld	0	Syd
1934	NSW	42	Qld	9	Syd
1934	Qld	14	NSW	10	Syd
1934	Qld	25	NSW	25	Bris
1934	Qld	22	NSW	20	Bris
1935	NSW	33	Qld	16	Syd
1935	NSW	18	Qld	14	Syd
1935	NSW	51	Qld	8	Syd
1935	Qld	22	NSW	20	Bris
1935	NSW	23	Qld	9	Bris
1936	NSW	30	Qld	13	Syd
1936	NSW	24	Qld	13	Syd

Year	Result				Venue	Year	Result				Venue
1936	NSW	16	Qld	14	Bris	1956	Qld	28	NSW	20	Syd
1937	NSW	21	Qld	9	Syd	1956	NSW	26	Qld	18	Bris
1937	NSW	31	Qld	3	Syd	1956	NSW	23	Qld	19	Bris
1937	NSW	16	Qld	11	Bris	1957	NSW	49	Qld	11	Bris
1938	NSW	20	Qld	19	Syd	1957	NSW	29	Qld	12	Bris
1938	NSW	44	Qld	7	Syd	1957	NSW	69	Qld	5	Syd
1938	Qld	36	NSW	22	Bris	1957	NSW	45	Qld	12	Syd
1939	NSW	50	Qld	15	Syd	1958	NSW	25	Qld	14	Syd
1939	NSW	54	Qld	13	Syd	1958	NSW	29	Qld	20	Bris
1939	Qld	29	NSW	13	Bris	1958	NSW	23	Qld	15	Bris
1939	Qld	23	NSW	13	Bris	1959	Qld	17	NSW	15	Bris
1940	NSW	52	Qld	11	Syd	1959	NSW	24	Qld	14	Bris
1940	Qld	19	NSW	16	Syd	1959	Qld	23	NSW	11	Syd
1940	Qld	45	NSW	8	Bris	1959	Qld	18	NSW	14	Syd
1940	Qld	23	NSW	15	Bris	1960	NSW	22	Qld	21	Syd
1941	NSW	18	Qld	14	Syd	1960	Qld	17	NSW	12	Syd
1941	NSW	44	Qld	10	Syd	1960	Qld	13	NSW	0	Bris
1941	NSW	23	Qld	16	Bris	1960	NSW	33	Qld	14	Bris
1941	Qld	27	NSW	21	Bris	1961	Qld	15	NSW	2	Syd
1942-44	No matches because of World War II					1961	Qld	20	NSW	17	Bris
1945	NSW	37	Qld	12	Syd	1961	NSW	21	Qld	20	Syd
1945	NSW	30	Qld	19	Bris	1961	NSW	18	Qld	2	Syd
1946	NSW	46	Qld	10	Syd	1962	Qld	20	NSW	17	Bris
1946	NSW	24	Qld	6	Syd	1962	NSW	28	Qld	8	Syd
1946	NSW	30	Qld	14	Bris	1962	NSW	19	Qld	14	Syd
1947	NSW	29	Qld	15	Syd	1962	NSW	25	Qld	12	Bris
1947	Qld	18	NSW	9	Syd	1963	NSW	20	Qld	10	Bris
1947	NSW	22	Qld	10	Bris	1963	NSW	53	Qld	7	Bris
1947	NSW	13	Qld	13	Bris	1963	NSW	31	Qld	5	Syd
1948	NSW	23	Qld	9	Syd	1963	NSW	13	Qld	5	Syd
1948	NSW	17	Qld	15	Syd	1964	NSW	28	Qld	12	Syd
1948	Qld	9	NSW	8	Bris	1964	NSW	41	Qld	3	Syd
1948	NSW	17	Qld	13	Bris	1964	NSW	31	Qld	5	Bris
1949	NSW	19	Qld	3	Syd	1964	NSW	22	Qld	11	Bris
1949	NSW	33	Qld	3	Syd	1965	NSW	31	Qld	7	Syd
1949	NSW	44	Qld	20	Bris	1965	NSW	22	Qld	4	Syd
1949	NSW	33	Qld	13	Bris	1965	NSW	30	Qld	9	Bris
1950	NSW	45	Qld	12	Syd	1965	NSW	22	Qld	15	Bris
1950	NSW	9	Qld	0	Syd	1966	NSW	16	Qld	6	Syd
1950	NSW	25	Qld	5	Bris	1966	NSW	28	Qld	10	Syd
1951	Qld	29	NSW	18	Syd	1966	NSW	28	Qld	20	Bris
1951	NSW	31	Qld	8	Syd	1966	NSW	27	Qld	3	Bris
1951	Qld	39	NSW	23	Bris	1967	NSW	14	Qld	8	Syd
1952	NSW	18	Qld	17	Syd	1967	NSW	28	Qld	9	Syd
1952	NSW	27	Qld	10	Syd	1967	Qld	16	NSW	16	Bris
1952	NSW	38	Qld	17	Bris	1968	Qld	13	NSW	11	Bris
1953	NSW	26	Qld	15	Syd	1968	NSW	30	Qld	7	Syd
1953	NSW	27	Qld	16	Syd	1968	Qld	15	NSW	8	Bris
1953	Qld	32	NSW	23	Bris	1968	NSW	29	Qld	11	Bris
1953	Qld	22	NSW	13	Bris	1969	NSW	28	Qld	0	Bris
1954	NSW	26	Qld	23	Syd	1969	NSW	32	Qld	13	Bris
1954	NSW	18	Qld	13	Syd	1969	NSW	33	Qld	17	Syd
1954	NSW	46	Qld	7	Bris	1969	NSW	22	Qld	2	Newc
1954	NSW	26	Qld	21	Bris	1970	Qld	16	NSW	16	Bris
1955	NSW	17	Qld	15	Syd	1970	NSW	00	Qld	0	Bris
1955	Qld	30	NSW	28	Syd	1970	NSW	34	Qld	8	Syd
1955	NSW	25	Qld	18	Bris	1970	NSW	12	Qld	3	Newc
1955	Qld	34	NSW	12	Bris	1971	NSW	30	Qld	2	Bris
1956	NSW	28	Qld	26	Syd	1971	NSW	17	Qld	15	Syd

NSW v QUEENSLAND 1908–1997

Year	Result				Venue	Year	Result				Venue
1972	NSW	29	Qld	5	Bris	1976	NSW	15	Qld	13	Bris
1972	NSW	27	Qld	6	Bris	1977	NSW	19	Qld	3	Bris
1973	NSW	26	Qld	0	Syd	1977	NSW	14	Qld	13	Bris
1973	NSW	16	Qld	0	Bris	1978	NSW	25	Qld	19	Bris
1973	NSW	10	Qld	0	Bris	1978	NSW	12	Qld	11	Bris
1974	NSW	13	Qld	13	Bris	1978	NSW	28	Qld	12	Syd
1974	Qld	4	NSW	4	Bris	1979	NSW	30	Qld	5	Bris
1974	NSW	22	Qld	13	Syd	1979	NSW	31	Qld	7	Bris
1975	Qld	14	NSW	8	Bris	1979	NSW	35	Qld	20	Syd
1975	NSW	27	Qld	18	Bris	1980	NSW	35	Qld	3	Bris
1975	NSW	9	Qld	8	Syd	1980	NSW	17	Qld	7	Syd
1976	NSW	33	Qld	9	Syd	1981	NSW	10	Qld	2	Bris
1976	NSW	10	Qld	5	Bris	1981	NSW	22	Qld	9	Syd

Played 221, NSW 160, Qld 54, drawn 7

STATE OF ORIGIN MATCHES 1980–97

Year	Result				Venue	Year	Result				Venue
1980	Qld	20	NSW	10	Lang	1989	Qld	36	NSW	16	Lang
1981	Qld	22	NSW	15	Lang	1990	NSW	8	Qld	0	SFS
1982	Qld	20	NSW	16	Lang	1990	NSW	12	Qld	6	Melb
1982	Qld	11	NSW	7	Lang	1990	Qld	14	NSW	10	Lang
1982	Qld	10	NSW	5	SCG	1991	Qld	6	NSW	4	Lang
1983	Qld	24	NSW	12	Lang	1991	NSW	14	Qld	12	SFS
1983	NSW	10	Qld	6	SCG	1991	Qld	14	NSW	12	Lang
1983	Qld	43	NSW	22	Lang	1992	NSW	14	Qld	6	SFS
1984	Qld	29	NSW	12	Lang	1992	Qld	5	NSW	4	Lang
1984	Qld	14	NSW	2	SCG	1992	NSW	16	Qld	4	SFS
1984	NSW	22	Qld	12	Lang	1993	NSW	14	Qld	10	Lang
1985	NSW	18	Qld	2	Lang	1993	NSW	16	Qld	12	SFS
1985	NSW	21	Qld	14	SCG	1993	Qld	24	NSW	12	Lang
1985	Qld	20	NSW	6	Lang	1994	Qld	16	NSW	12	SFS
1986	NSW	22	Qld	16	Lang	1994	NSW	14	Qld	0	MCG
1986	NSW	24	Qld	20	SCG	1994	NSW	27	Qld	12	Suncorp
1986	NSW	18	Qld	16	Lang	1995	Qld	2	NSW	0	SFS
1987	NSW	20	Qld	16	Lang	1995	Qld	20	NSW	12	MCG
1987	Qld	12	NSW	6	SCG	1995	Qld	24	NSW	16	Suncorp
1987	Qld	10	NSW	8	Lang	1996	NSW	14	Qld	6	Suncorp
1987	NSW	30	Qld	18	California	1996	NSW	18	Qld	6	SFS
1988	Qld	26	NSW	18	SFS	1996	NSW	15	Qld	14	Suncorp
1988	Qld	16	NSW	6	Lang	1997	NSW	8	Qld	6	Suncorp
1988	Qld	38	NSW	22	SFS	1997	NSW	15	Qld	14	MCG
1989	Qld	36	NSW	6	Lang	1997	Qld	18	NSW	12	SFS
1989	Qld	16	NSW	12	SFS						

Played 51, NSW 24, Qld 27

STATE OF ORIGIN MATCH-BY-MATCH RECORDS

1980

Match 1, Lang Park, July 8, 1980

QUEENSLAND: Colin Scott; Kerry Boustead, Mal Meninga, Chris Close, Brad Backer; Alan Smith, Greg Oliphant; Wally Lewis, Rod Reddy, Rohan Hancock, Arthur Beetson (c); Johnny Lang, Rod Morris. Replacements: Norm Carr, Bruce Astill. Coach: John McDonald.
NEW SOUTH WALES: Graham Eadie; Chris Anderson, Steve Rogers, Mick Cronin, Greg Brentnall; Alan Thompson, Tom Raudonikis (c); Jim Leis, Graeme Wynn, Bob Cooper, Craig Young, Steve Edge, Gary Hambly. Replacements: Steve Martin, Robert Stone. Coach: Ted Glossop.
Queensland 20 (Boustead, Close tries; Meninga 7 goals) defeated **New South Wales** 10 (Raudonikis, Brentnall tries; Cronin 2 goals).
Crowd: 33,210. **Referee**: Billy Thompson (Great Britain). **Man of the match**: Chris Close (Queensland).

1981

Match 2, Lang Park, July 28, 1981

QUEENSLAND: Colin Scott; Brad Backer, Mal Meninga, Chris Close, Mitch Brennan; Wally Lewis (c), Ross Henrick; Chris Phelan, Paul McCabe, Rohan Hancock, Rod Morris, Greg Conescu, Paul Khan. Replacements: Norm Carr, Mark Murray. Coach: Arthur Beetson.
NEW SOUTH WALES: Phil Sigsworth; Terry Fahey, Mick Cronin, Steve Rogers (c), Eric Grothe; Terry Lamb, Peter Sterling; Ray Price, Les Boyd, Peter Tunks, Ron Hilditch, Barry Jensen, Steve Bowden. Replacements: Garry Dowling, Graham O'Grady. Coach: Ted Glossop.
Queensland 22 (Backer, Close, Lewis, Meninga (pen) tries; Meninga 5 goals) defeated **New South Wales** 15 (Grothe 2, Cronin tries; Cronin 3 goals).
Crowd: 25,613. **Referee**: Kevin Steele (New Zealand). **Man of the match**: Chris Close (Queensland).

1982

Match 3, Lang Park, June 1, 1982

NEW SOUTH WALES: Greg Brentnall; Chris Anderson, Ziggy Niszczot, Mick Cronin, Steve Rogers; Alan Thompson, Steve Mortimer; Ray Price, John Muggleton, Tony Rampling, Craig Young, Max Krilich (c), John Coveney. Replacements: Brad Izzard, Royce Ayliffe. Coach: Frank Stanton.
QUEENSLAND: Colin Scott; John Ribot, Mitch Brennan, Mal Meninga, Kerry Boustead; Wally Lewis (c), Mark Murray; Paul Vautin, Paul McCabe, Bruce Walker, Paul Khan, John Dowling, Rohan Hancock. Replacements: Bob Kellaway, Gene Miles. Coach: Arthur Beetson.
New South Wales 20 (Niszczot 2, Mortimer, Izzard tries; Cronin 4 goals) defeated **Queensland** 16 (Ribot, Brennan tries; Meninga 5 goals).
Crowd: 27,326. **Referee**: Kevin Roberts (NSW). **Man of the match**: Mal Meninga (Queensland).

Match 4, Lang Park, June 8, 1982

QUEENSLAND: Colin Scott; John Ribot, Graham Quinn, Gene Miles, Brad Backer; Wally Lewis (c), Mark Murray; Norm Carr, Paul McCabe, Rod Morris, Paul Khan, John Dowling, Rohan Hancock. Replacements: Paul Vautin, Greg Holben. Coach: Arthur Beetson.
NEW SOUTH WALES: Greg Brentnall; Tony Melrose, Brad Izzard, Steve Rogers, Ziggy Niszczot; Alan Thompson, Steve Mortimer; Ray Price, John Muggleton, Tony Rampling, Craig Young, Max Krilich (c), John Coveney. Replacements: Brett Kenny, Royce Ayliffe. Coach: Frank Stanton.
Queensland 11 (Ribot, Miles, Vautin tries; Scott goal) defeated **New South Wales** 7 (Izzard try; Melrose 2 goals).
Crowd: 19,435. **Referee**: Barry Gomersall (Queensland). **Man of the match**: Rod Morris (Queensland).

Match 5, Sydney Cricket Ground, June 22, 1982

QUEENSLAND: Mitch Brennan; John Ribot, Gene Miles, Mal Meninga, Kerry Boustead; Wally Lewis (c), Mark Murray; Norm Carr, Paul McCabe, Rohan Hancock, Paul Khan, John Dowling, Rod Morris. Replacements: Paul Vautin, Tony Currie. Coach: Arthur Beetson.
NEW SOUTH WALES: Phil Sigsworth; Terry Fahey, Mick Cronin, Brad Izzard, Phillip Duke; Brett Kenny, Steve Mortimer; Ray Price, Les Boyd, Paul Merlo, Don McKinnon, Max Krilich (c), Royce Ayliffe. Replacements: Alan Thompson, Craig Young. Coach: Frank Stanton.
Queensland 10 (Hancock, Lewis tries; Meninga 2 goals) defeated **New South Wales** 5 (Duke try; Cronin goal).
Crowd: 20,242. **Referee**: Don Wilson (New Zealand). **Man of the match**: Wally Lewis (Queensland).

1983

Match 6, Lang Park, June 7, 1983

QUEENSLAND: Colin Scott; John Ribot, Mal Meninga, Gene Miles, Steve Stacey; Wally Lewis

STATE OF ORIGIN MATCH-BY-MATCH

(c), Mark Murray; Wally Fullerton-Smith, Paul Vautin, Bryan Niebling, Darryl Brohman, Greg Conescu, Brad Tessmann. Replacements: Brett French, Dave Brown. Coach: Arthur Beetson.
NEW SOUTH WALES: Greg Brentnall; Chris Anderson, Brett Kenny, Phil Sigsworth, Eric Grothe; Alan Thompson, Peter Sterling; Ray Price, Wayne Pearce, Les Boyd, Geoff Bugden, Max Krilich (c), Geoff Gerard. Replacements: Steve Ella, Ray Brown. Coach: Ted Glossop.
Queensland 24 (Lewis 2, Murray tries; Meninga 6 goals) defeated **New South Wales** 12 (Grothe, Ella tries; Sigsworth 2 goals).
Crowd: 29,412. **Referee**: Barry Gomersall (Queensland). **Man of the match**: Wally Lewis (Queensland).

Match 7, Sydney Cricket Ground, June 21, 1983.

NEW SOUTH WALES: Marty Gurr; Neil Hunt, Mick Cronin, Steve Ella, Eric Grothe; Brett Kenny, Peter Sterling; Ray Price (c), Paul Field, Gavin Miller, Lindsay Johnston, Ray Brown, Geoff Gerard. Replacements: Steve Mortimer, Stan Jurd. Coach: Ted Glossop.
QUEENSLAND: Colin Scott; Terry Butler, Mal Meninga, Gene Miles, Chris Close; Wally Lewis (c), Mark Murray; Paul Vautin, Wally Fullerton-Smith, Bryan Niebling, Dave Brown, Greg Conescu, Brad Tessmann. Replacements: Brett French, Ross Henrick. Coach: Arthur Beetson.
New South Wales 10 (Hunt, Ella tries; Cronin goal) defeated **Queensland** 6 (Meninga try; Meninga goal).
Crowd: 21,620. **Referee**: John Gocher (NSW). **Man of the match**: Peter Sterling (NSW).

Match 8, Lang Park, June 28, 1983

QUEENSLAND: Colin Scott; Mitch Brennan, Mal Meninga, Gene Miles, Steve Stacey; Wally Lewis (c), Mark Murray; Paul Vautin, Wally Fullerton-Smith, Bryan Niebling, Dave Brown, Greg Conescu, Brad Tessmann. Replacements: Bruce Astill, Gavin Jones. Coach: Arthur Beetson.
NEW SOUTH WALES: Marty Gurr; Chris Anderson, Mick Cronin, Steve Ella, Neil Hunt; Brett Kenny, Steve Mortimer; Gavin Miller, Paul Field, Stan Jurd, Lindsay Johnston, Max Krilich (c), Geoff Bugden. Replacements: Kevin Hastings, Ray Brown. Coach: Ted Glossop.
Queensland 43 (Brennan 2, Miles, Stacey, Brown, Conescu, Niebling tries; Meninga 6, Scott goals; Lewis field goal) defeated **New South Wales** 22 (Anderson 3, Mortimer tries; Cronin 3 goals).
Crowd: 26,084. **Referee**: Robin Whitfield (England). **Man of the match**: Wally Lewis (Queensland).

1984

Match 9, Lang Park, May 29, 1984

QUEENSLAND: Colin Scott; Kerry Boustead, Gene Miles, Mal Meninga, Chris Close; Wally Lewis (c), Mark Murray; Paul Vautin, Wally Fullerton-Smith, Bryan Niebling, Dave Brown, Greg Conescu, Greg Dowling. Replacements: Brett French, Bob Lindner. Coach: Arthur Beetson.
NEW SOUTH WALES: Garry Jack; Ross Conlon, Brett Kenny, Steve Ella, Eric Grothe; Alan Thompson, Peter Sterling; Ray Price (c), Wayne Pearce, Noel Cleal, Steve Roach, Rex Wright, Craig Young. Replacements: Pat Jarvis, Brian Hetherington. Coach: Frank Stanton.
Queensland 29 (Boustead 3, Vautin, Lewis, Miles tries; Meninga 2 goals; Lewis field goal) defeated **New South Wales** 12 (Cleal try; Conlon 4 goals).
Crowd: 33,662. **Referee**: Kevin Roberts (New South Wales). **Man of the match**: Wally Lewis (Queensland).

Match 10, Sydney Cricket Ground, June 19, 1984

QUEENSLAND: Colin Scott; Kerry Boustead, Gene Miles, Chris Close, Mal Meninga; Wally Lewis (c), Mark Murray; Paul Vautin, Wally Fullerton-Smith, Bryan Niebling, Dave Brown, Greg Conescu, Greg Dowling. Replacements: Tony Currie, Bob Lindner. Coach: Arthur Beetson.
NEW SOUTH WALES: Garry Jack; Eric Grothe, Brett Kenny, Andrew Farrar, Ross Conlon; Terry Lamb, Steve Mortimer; Ray Price (c), Wayne Pearce, Noel Cleal, Peter Tunks, Royce Simmons, Steve Roach. Replacements: Steve Ella, Pat Jarvis. Coach: Frank Stanton.
Queensland 14 (Dowling, Miles tries; Meninga 3 goals) defeated **New South Wales** 2 (Conlon goal).
Crowd: 29,088. **Referee**: Barry Gomersall (Queensland). **Man of the match**: Wally Lewis (Queensland).

Match 11, Lang Park, July 17, 1984

NEW SOUTH WALES: Garry Jack; Steve Morris, Chris Mortimer, Brian Johnston, Ross Conlon; Brett Kenny, Steve Mortimer (c); Peter Wynn, Noel Cleal, Chris Walsh, Pat Jarvis, Royce Simmons, Steve Roach. Replacements: Mick Potter, Peter Tunks. Coach: Frank Stanton.
QUEENSLAND: Colin Scott; John Ribot, Mal Meninga, Brett French, Kerry Boustead; Wally Lewis (c), Ross Henrick; Bob Lindner, Wally Fullerton-Smith, Chris Phelan, Dave Brown, Greg Conescu, Greg Dowling. Replacements: Tony Currie, Bob Kellaway. Coach: Arthur Beetson.
New South Wales 22 (Johnston 2, Cleal tries;

Conlon 5 goals) defeated **Queensland** 12 (Lindner, Boustead tries; Meninga 2 goals).
Crowd: 16,559. **Referee:** Kevin Roberts (NSW).
Man of the match: Steve Mortimer (NSW).

1985

Match 12, Lang Park, May 28, 1985

NEW SOUTH WALES: Garry Jack; Eric Grothe, Michael O'Connor, Chris Mortimer, John Ferguson; Brett Kenny, Steve Mortimer (c); Wayne Pearce, Peter Wynn, Noel Cleal, Steve Roach, Ben Elias, Pat Jarvis. Replacements: Steve Ella, Peter Tunks. Coach: Terry Fearnley.
QUEENSLAND: Colin Scott; John Ribot, Mal Meninga, Chris Close, Dale Shearer; Wally Lewis (c), Mark Murray; Bob Lindner, Paul McCabe, Paul Vautin, Dave Brown, Greg Conescu, Greg Dowling. Replacements: Brett French, Ian French. Coach: Des Morris.
New South Wales 18 (O'Connor 2 tries; O'Connor 5 goals) defeated **Queensland** 2 (Meninga goal).
Crowd: 33,011. **Referee:** Kevin Roberts (NSW).
Man of the match: Peter Wynn (NSW).

Match 13, Sydney Cricket Ground, June 11, 1985

NEW SOUTH WALES: Garry Jack; Eric Grothe, Michael O'Connor, Chris Mortimer, John Ferguson; Brett Kenny, Steve Mortimer (c); Wayne Pearce, Peter Wynn, Noel Cleal, Steve Roach, Ben Elias, Pat Jarvis. Replacements: Steve Ella, Peter Tunks. Coach: Terry Fearnley.
QUEENSLAND: Colin Scott; John Ribot, Mal Meninga, Chris Close, Dale Shearer; Wally Lewis (c), Mark Murray; Bob Lindner, Wally Fullerton-Smith, Paul Vautin, Dave Brown, Greg Conescu, Greg Dowling. Replacements: Tony Currie, Ian French. Coach: Des Morris.
New South Wales 21 (C.Mortimer, Elias, Kenny tries; O'Connor 4 goals; O'Connor field goal) defeated **Queensland** 14 (Lindner, French tries; Meninga 3 goals).
Crowd: 39,068. **Referee:** Barry Gomersall (Queensland). **Man of the match:** Wally Lewis (Queensland).

Match 14, Lang Park, July 23, 1985

QUEENSLAND: Colin Scott; John Ribot, Mal Meninga, Chris Close, Dale Shearer; Wally Lewis (c), Mark Murray; Paul Vautin, Wally Fullerton-Smith, Ian French, Dave Brown, Greg Conescu, Greg Dowling. Replacements: Tony Currie, Cavill Heugh. Coach: Des Morris.
NEW SOUTH WALES: Garry Jack; John Ferguson, Chris Mortimer, Michael O'Connor, Eric Grothe; Brett Kenny, Des Hasler; Wayne Pearce (c), David Brooks, Peter Wynn, Steve Roach, Ben Elias, Pat Jarvis. Replacements:

Steve Ella, Tony Rampling. Coach: Terry Fearnley.
Queensland 20 (Shearer 2, Ribot, French tries; Meninga 2 goals) defeated **New South Wales** 6 (Ella try; O'Connor goal).
Crowd: 18,825. **Referee:** Barry Gomersall (Queensland). **Man of the match:** Wally Fullerton-Smith (Queensland).

1986

Match 15, Lang Park, May 27, 1986

NEW SOUTH WALES: Garry Jack; Steve Morris, Michael O'Connor, Chris Mortimer, Andrew Farrar; Brett Kenny, Peter Sterling; Wayne Pearce (c), Noel Cleal, Steve Folkes, Peter Tunks, Royce Simmons, Steve Roach. Replacements: Terry Lamb, David Gillespie. Coach: Ron Willey.
QUEENSLAND: Colin Scott; Dale Shearer, Mal Meninga, Gene Miles, Chris Close; Wally Lewis (c), Mark Murray; Bob Lindner, Gavin Jones, Bryan Niebling, Dave Brown, Greg Conescu, Greg Dowling. Replacements: Peter Jackson, Ian French. Coach: Wayne Bennett.
New South Wales 22 (Jack, Mortimer, Farrar, Simmons tries; O'Connor 3 goals) defeated **Queensland** 16 (Miles, Dowling tries; Meninga 4 goals).
Crowd: 33,066. **Referee:** Kevin Roberts (NSW).
Man of the match: Royce Simmons (NSW).

Match 16, Sydney Cricket Ground, June 10, 1986

NEW SOUTH WALES: Garry Jack; Brian Hetherington, Chris Mortimer, Michael O'Connor, Andrew Farrar; Brett Kenny, Peter Sterling; Wayne Pearce (c), Noel Cleal, Steve Folkes, Steve Roach, Royce Simmons, Peter Tunks. Replacements: Terry Lamb, David Gillespie. Coach: Ron Willey.
QUEENSLAND: Gary Belcher; Dale Shearer, Gene Miles, Mal Meninga, Les Kiss; Wally Lewis (c), Mark Murray; Ian French, Gavin Jones, Bob Lindner, Darryl Brohman, Greg Conescu, Cavill Heugh. Replacements: Peter Jackson, Brad Tessmann. Coach: Wayne Bennett.
New South Wales 24 (O'Connor, Farrar, Kenny, Pearce, Cleal tries; O'Connor 2 goals) defeated **Queensland** 20 (Shearer, Kiss, French, Lindner tries; Meninga 2 goals).
Crowd: 40,707. **Referee:** Barry Gomersall (Queensland). **Man of the match:** Peter Sterling (NSW).

Match 17, Lang Park, July 1, 1986

NEW SOUTH WALES: Garry Jack; Brian Johnston, Michael O'Connor, Chris Mortimer, Eric Grothe; Brett Kenny, Peter Sterling; Wayne Pearce (c), Noel Cleal, Steve Folkes, Peter

STATE OF ORIGIN MATCH-BY-MATCH

Tunks, Royce Simmons, Steve Roach. Replacements: Terry Lamb, David Gillespie. Coach: Ron Willey.
QUEENSLAND: Gary Belcher; Dale Shearer, Mal Meninga, Gene Miles, Les Kiss; Wally Lewis (c), Mark Murray; Bob Lindner, Gavin Jones, Bryan Niebling, Cavill Heugh, Greg Conescu, Brad Tessmann. Replacements: Grant Rix, Ian French. Coach: Wayne Bennett.
New South Wales 18 (Pearce, O'Connor, Tunks tries; O'Connor 3 goals) defeated **Queensland** 16 (Belcher, Kiss, Conescu, Shearer tries).
Crowd: 21,097. **Referee**: Kevin Roberts (NSW).
Man of the match: Brett Kenny (NSW).

1987

Match 18, Lang Park, June 2, 1987

NEW SOUTH WALES: Garry Jack; Andrew Ettingshausen, Mark McGaw, Brian Johnston, Michael O'Connor; Brett Kenny, Peter Sterling; Wayne Pearce (c), Noel Cleal, Steve Folkes, Les Davidson, Royce Simmons, Pat Jarvis. Replacements: David Boyle, Des Hasler. Coach: Ron Willey.
QUEENSLAND: Gary Belcher; Dale Shearer, Gene Miles, Peter Jackson, Tony Currie; Wally Lewis (c), Allan Langer; Ian French, Paul Vautin, Trevor Gillmeister, Martin Bella, Greg Conescu, Greg Dowling. Replacements: Colin Scott, Gary Smith. Coach: Wayne Bennett.
New South Wales 20 (O'Connor 2, McGaw, Davidson tries; O'Connor 2 goals) defeated **Queensland** 16 (Shearer, Currie, Dowling tries; Jackson, Belcher goals).
Crowd: 33,411. **Referee**: Michael Stone (NSW).
Man of the match: Les Davidson (NSW).

Match 19, Sydney Cricket Ground, June 10, 1987

QUEENSLAND: Gary Belcher; Colin Scott, Peter Jackson, Gene Miles, Dale Shearer; Wally Lewis (c), Allan Langer; Bob Lindner, Paul Vautin, Trevor Gillmeister, Martin Bella, Greg Conescu, Greg Dowling. Replacements: Tony Currie, Ian French. Coach: Wayne Bennett.
NEW SOUTH WALES: Garry Jack; Mark McGaw, Michael O'Connor, Brian Johnston, Andrew Farrar; Brett Kenny, Peter Sterling; Wayne Pearce (c), Les Davidson, Steve Folkes, Pat Jarvis, Royce Simmons, David Boyle. Replacements: Des Hasler, Paul Langmack. Coach: Ron Willey.
Queensland 12 (Shearer, Dowling, Scott tries) defeated **New South Wales** 6 (Farrar try; O'Connor goal).
Crowd: 42,048. **Referee**: Barry Gomersall (Queensland). **Man of the match**: Peter Sterling (NSW).

Match 20, Lang Park, July 15, 1987

QUEENSLAND: Gary Belcher; Colin Scott, Peter Jackson, Gene Miles, Dale Shearer; Wally Lewis (c), Allan Langer; Bob Lindner, Paul Vautin, Trevor Gillmeister, Bryan Niebling, Greg Conescu, Greg Dowling. Replacements: Tony Currie, Ian French. Coach: Wayne Bennett.
NEW SOUTH WALES: Garry Jack; Brian Johnston, Andrew Ettingshausen, Brett Kenny, Michael O'Connor; Cliff Lyons, Peter Sterling; Wayne Pearce (c), Les Davidson, David Boyle, Phil Daley, Royce Simmons, Peter Tunks. Replacements: Mark McGaw, Steve Folkes. Coach: Ron Willey.
Queensland 10 (Shearer, Lindner tries; Shearer goal) defeated **New South Wales** 8 (Boyle try; O'Connor 2 goals).
Crowd: 32,602. **Referee**: Barry Gomersall (QLD). **Man of the match**: Allan Langer (Queensland).

Match 21, Veterans Stadium, Long Beach, California, August 6, 1987

NEW SOUTH WALES: Jonathan Docking; Brian Johnston, Mark McGaw, Michael O'Connor, Andrew Ettingshausen; Cliff Lyons, Peter Sterling (c); Paul Langmack, Noel Cleal, Les Davidson, Peter Tunks, Royce Simmons, Phil Daley. Replacements: Des Hasler, David Boyle. Coach: Ron Willey.
QUEENSLAND: Gary Belcher; Dale Shearer, Peter Jackson, Gene Miles, Tony Currie; Wally Lewis (c), Allan Langer; Bob Lindner, Paul Vautin, Trevor Gillmeister, Bryan Niebling, Greg Conescu, Greg Dowling. Replacements: Colin Scott, Ian French. Coach: Wayne Bennett.
New South Wales 30 (Ettingshausen, McGaw, Docking, O'Connor, Lyons tries; O'Connor 5 goals) defeated **Queensland** 18 (Currie, Miles, Shearer tries; Shearer 3 goals).
Crowd: 12,349. **Referee**: Michael Stone (NSW).
Man of the match: Peter Sterling (NSW).

1988

Match 22, Sydney Football Stadium, May 17, 1988

QUEENSLAND: Gary Belcher; Alan McIndoe, Tony Currie, Gene Miles, Joe Kilroy; Peter Jackson, Allan Langer; Paul Vautin (c), Bob Lindner, Wally Fullerton-Smith, Sam Backo, Greg Conescu, Martin Bella. Replacements: Brett French, Scott Tronc. Coach: Wayne Bennett.
NEW SOUTH WALES: Jonathan Docking; Brian Johnston, Mark McGaw, Michael O'Connor, Andrew Ettingshausen; Cliff Lyons, Peter Sterling; Wayne Pearce (c), Noel Cleal, Steve Folkes, Steve Roach, Royce Simmons, Les Davidson. Replacements: Terry Lamb, David Trewhella. Coach: John Peard.

Queensland 26 (Langer 2, Jackson, McIndoe, Belcher tries; Belcher 3 goals) defeated **New South Wales** 18 (O'Connor, Ettingshausen, McGaw tries; O'Connor 3 goals).
Crowd: 26,441. **Referee**: Barry Gomersall (QLD).
Man of the match: Allan Langer (QLD).

Match 23, Lang Park, May 31, 1988

QUEENSLAND: Gary Belcher; Alan McIndoe, Peter Jackson, Gene Miles, Tony Currie; Wally Lewis (c), Allan Langer; Paul Vautin, Bob Lindner, Wally Fullerton-Smith, Sam Backo, Greg Conescu, Martin Bella. Replacements: Brett French, Trevor Gillmeister. Coach: Wayne Bennett.
NEW SOUTH WALES: Garry Jack; Jonh Ferguson, Mark McGaw, Michael O'Connor, Andrew Ettingshausen; Terry Lamb, Peter Sterling; Paul Langmack, Steve Folkes, Wayne Pearce (c), Steve Roach, Ben Elias, Phil Daley. Replacements: Paul Dunn, Des Hasler. Coach: John Peard.
Queensland 16 (Backo, Langer tries; Belcher 4 goals) defeated **New South Wales** 6 (O'Connor try; O'Connor goal).
Crowd: 31,817. **Referee**: Michael Stone (NSW).
Man of the match: Sam Backo (Queensland).

Match 24, Sydney Football Stadium, June 21, 1988

QUEENSLAND: Gary Belcher; Alan McIndoe, Tony Currie, Peter Jackson, Joe Kilroy; Wally Lewis (c), Allan Langer; Paul Vautin, Bob Lindner, Wally Fullerton-Smith, Sam Backo, Greg Conescu, Martin Bella. Replacements: Brett French, Trevor Gillmeister. Coach: Wayne Bennett.
NEW SOUTH WALES: Garry Jack; John Ferguson, Mark McGaw, Michael O'Connor, Andrew Ettingshausen; Cliff Lyons, Des Hasler; Paul Langmack, Wayne Pearce (c), Steve Folkes, Steve Roach, Ben Elias, Steve Hanson. Replacements: Noel Cleal, Greg Florimo. Coach: John Peard.
Queensland 38 (Backo 2, Kilroy, Langer, Lewis tries; Belcher 5 goals) defeated **New South Wales** 22 (Ferguson, O'Connor, Pearce, Hanson tries; O'Connor 3 goals).
Crowd: 16,910. **Referee**: Greg McCallum (New South Wales). **Man of the match**: Sam Backo (Queensland).

1989

Match 25, Lang Park, May 23, 1989

QUEENSLAND: Gary Belcher; Michael Hancock, Tony Currie, Mal Meninga, Alan McIndoe; Wally Lewis (c), Allan Langer; Martin Bella, Kerrod Walters, Dan Stains, Paul Vautin, Gene Miles, Bob Lindner. Replacements: Trevor Gillmeister, Dale Shearer, Gary Coyne, Michael Hagan. Coach Arthur Beetson.
NEW SOUTH WALES: Garry Jack; Chris Johns, Andrew Farrar, Laurie Daley, John Ferguson; Terry Lamb, Des Hasler; John Cartwright, Mario Fenech, Paul Dunn, Paul Sironen, Gavin Miller (c), Bradley Clyde. Replacements: Glenn Lazarus, Greg Alexander, Andrew Ettingshausen, Chris Mortimer. Coach: Jack Gibson.
Queensland 36 (Hancock 2, Meninga 2, McIndoe, Langer, Lindner tries; Meninga 4 goals) defeated **New South Wales** 6 (Ettingshausen try; Daley goal).
Crowd: 33,088. **Referee**: Michael Stone (NSW).
Man of the match: Martin Bella (Queensland).

Match 26, Sydney Football Stadium, June 14, 1989

QUEENSLAND: Gary Belcher; Michael Hancock, Tony Currie, Mal Meninga, Alan McIndoe; Wally Lewis (c), Allan Langer; Martin Bella, Kerrod Walters, Sam Backo, Paul Vautin, Gene Miles, Bob Lindner. Replacements: Michael Hagan, Dale Shearer, Trevor Gillmeister, Gary Coyne. Coach: Arthur Beetson.
NEW SOUTH WALES: Garry Jack; Chris Johns, Andrew Ettingshausen, Laurie Daley, John Ferguson; Chris Mortimer, Greg Alexander; Peter Kelly, Mario Fenech, Paul Dunn, Bruce McGuire, Gavin Miller (c), Bradley Clyde. Replacements: Des Hasler, John Cartwright, Brad Mackay, Alan Wilson. Coach: Jack Gibson.
Queensland 16 (Hancock, Walters, Lewis tries; Meninga, Belcher goals) defeated **New South Wales** 12 (Daley, Johns tries; Alexander 2 goals).
Crowd: 40,000. **Referee**: David Manson (Queensland). **Man of the match**: Wally Lewis (Queensland).

Match 27, Lang Park, June 28, 1989

QUEENSLAND: Gary Belcher; Michael Hancock, Dale Shearer, Tony Currie, Alan McIndoe; Wally Lewis (c), Michael Hagan; Martin Bella, Kerrod Walters, Sam Backo, Gene Miles, Dan Stains, Paul Vautin. Replacements: Peter Jackson, Gary Coyne, Trevor Gillmeister, Kevin Walters. Coach: Arthur Beetson.
NEW SOUTH WALES: Garry Jack; Michael O'Connor, Brian Johnston, Chris Johns, John Ferguson; Des Hasler, Greg Alexander; Bruce McGuire, David Trewhella, Peter Kelly, Gavin Miller (c), Mark Geyer, Brad Mackay. Replacements: Terry Matterson, John Cartwright, Phil Blake, Alan Wilson. Coach: Jack Gibson.
Queensland 36 (Shearer 2, McIndoe, Hancock, Kerrod Walters, Belcher, Currie tries; Shearer 4 goals) defeated **New South Wales** 16 (Hasler, Trewhella, McGuire tries; O'Connor 2 goals).
Crowd: 33,268. **Referee**: Greg McCallum

STATE OF ORIGIN MATCH-BY-MATCH

(NSW). **Man of the match**: Kerrod Walters (Queensland).

1990

Match 28, Sydney Football Stadium, May 9, 1990

NEW SOUTH WALES: Andrew Ettingshausen; Rod Wishart, Michael O'Connor, Mark McGaw, Ricky Walford; Laurie Daley, Ricky Stuart; Ian Roberts, Ben Elias (c), Steve Roach, Bruce McGuire, David Gillespie, Bradley Clyde. Replacements: Paul Sironen, Glenn Lazarus, Graham Lyons, Geoff Toovey. Coach: Jack Gibson.
QUEENSLAND: Gary Belcher; Alan McIndoe, Dale Shearer, Mal Meninga, Les Kiss; Michael Hagan, Allan Langer; Dan Stains, Steve Walters, Martin Bella, Wally Fullerton-Smith, Paul Vautin (c), Bob Lindner. Replacements: Trevor Gillmeister, Gary Coyne, Kevin Walters, Mark Coyne. Coach: Arthur Beetson.
New South Wales 8 (McGaw try; O'Connor 2 goals) defeated **Queensland** 0.
Crowd: 41,235. **Referee**: David Manson (Queensland). **Man of the match**: Ben Elias (New South Wales).

Match 29, Olympic Park, Melbourne, May 30, 1990

NEW SOUTH WALES: Andrew Ettingshausen; Rod Wishart, Brad Mackay, Mark McGaw, Graham Lyons, Des Hasler, Ricky Stuart; Ian Roberts, Ben Elias (c), Steve Roach, Bruce McGuire, David Gillespie, Bradley Clyde. Replacements: Andrew Farrar, Glenn Lazarus, Paul Sironen, Brad Fittler. Coach: Jack Gibson.
QUEENSLAND: Gary Belcher; Alan McIndoe, Dale Shearer, Mal Meninga, Les Kiss; Wally Lewis (c), Allan Langer; Sam Backo, Kerrod Walters, Martin Bella, Gary Coyne, Dan Stains, Bob Lindner. Replacements: Trevor Gillmeister, Andrew Gee, Mark Coyne, Kevin Walters (not used). Coach: Arthur Beetson.
New South Wales 12 (Stuart, Mackay tries; Wishart 2 goals) defeated **Queensland** 6 (Kiss try; Meninga goal).
Crowd: 25,800. **Referee**: Greg McCallum (NSW). **Man of the match**: Ricky Stuart (NSW).

Match 30, Lang Park, Brisbane, June 13, 1990

QUEENSLAND: Gary Belcher; Alan McIndoe, Dale Shearer, Peter Jackson, Willie Carne; Wally Lewis (c), Allan Langer; Sam Backo, Kerrod Walters, Martin Bella, Gary Coyne, Trevor Gillmeister, Bob Lindner. Replacements: Andrew Gee, Kevin Walters, Steve Jackson, Michael Hagan. Coach: Arthur Beetson.
NEW SOUTH WALES: Andrew Ettingshausen; Graham Lyons, Michael O'Connor, Mark McGaw, Rod Wishart; Brad Mackay, Ricky Stuart; Ian Roberts, Ben Elias (c), Glenn Lazarus, Bruce McGuire, David Gillespie, Bradley Clyde. Replacements: Mark Sargent, Paul Sironen, Greg Alexander, Andrew Farrar. Coach: Jack Gibson.
Queensland 14 (Belcher, Steve Jackson tries; Belcher 2, Lewis goals) defeated **New South Wales** 10 (Lazarus, McGaw tries; Wishart goal).
Crowd: 31,416. **Referee**: David Manson (Queensland). **Man of the match**: Bob Lindner (Queensland). **Man of the series**: Ben Elias (New South Wales).

1991

Match 31, Lang Park, Brisbane, May 8, 1991

QUEENSLAND: Paul Hauff; Michael Hancock, Peter Jackson, Mal Meninga, Willie Carne; Wally Lewis (c), Allan Langer; Steve Jackson, Steve Walters, Martin Bella, Mike McLean, Andrew Gee, Gary Larson. Interchange: Kevin Walters, Steve Renouf, Gary Coyne, Gavin Allen. Coach: Graham Lowe.
NEW SOUTH WALES: Greg Alexander; Chris Johns, Andrew Ettingshausen, Laurie Daley, Michael O'Connor; Cliff Lyons, Ricky Stuart; Ian Roberts, Ben Elias (c), Steve Roach, Paul Sironen, Mark Geyer, Des Hasler. Interchange: Glenn Lazarus, David Gillespie, Mark McGaw, Brad Fittler. Coach: Tim Sheens.
Queensland 6 (Meninga try; Meninga goal) defeated **New South Wales** 4 (Daley try).
Crowd: 32,400. **Referee**: Bill Harrigan (NSW). **Man of the match**: Wally Lewis (Queensland).

Match 32, Sydney Football Stadium, May 29, 1991

NEW SOUTH WALES: Andrew Ettingshausen; Chris Johns, Laurie Daley, Michael O'Connor, Rod Wishart, Cliff Lyons, Ricky Stuart; David Gillespie, Ben Elias (c), Steve Roach, Mark Geyer, Ian Roberts, Bradley Clyde. Interchange: Des Hasler, Mark McGaw, Brad Mackay, John Cartwright. Coach: Tim Sheens.
QUEENSLAND: Paul Hauff; Michael Hancock, Peter Jackson, Mal Meninga, Willie Carne; Wally Lewis (c), Allan Langer; Steve Jackson, Steve Walters, Martin Bella, Mike McLean, Andrew Gee, Gary Larson. Interchange: Kevin Walters, Dale Shearer, Gary Coyne, Gavin Allen. Coach: Graham Lowe.
New South Wales 14 (Johns, McGaw tries; O'Connor 3 goals) defeated **Queensland** 12 (Carne, Shearer tries; Meninga 2 goals).
Crowd: 41,520. **Referee**: David Manson (Queensland). **Man of the match**: Steve Walters (Queensland).

Match 33, Lang Park, Brisbane, June 12, 1991

QUEENSLAND: Paul Hauff; Michael Hancock, Peter Jackson, Mal Meninga, Willie Carne; Wally Lewis (c), Allan Langer; Steve Jackson, Steve Walters, Martin Bella, Mike McLean, Andrew Gee, Gary Larson. Interchange: Dale Shearer, Gary Coyne, Bob Lindner, Kevin Walters (not used). Coach: Graham Lowe.
NEW SOUTH WALES: Greg Alexander; Chris Johns, Mark McGaw, Michael O'Connor, Rod Wishart; Brad Fittler, Ricky Stuart; David Gillespie, Ben Elias (c), Steve Roach, Bradley Clyde, John Cartwright, Brad Mackay. Interchange: Des Hasler, Brad Izzard, Craig Salvatori, David Fairleigh. Coach: Tim Sheens.
Queensland 14 (Hauff, Hancock, Shearer tries; Meninga goal) defeated **New South Wales** 12 (Johns, O'Connor, Hasler tries).
Crowd: 33,226. **Referee**: Bill Harrigan (NSW). **Man of the match**: Martin Bella (Queensland).

1992

Match 34, Sydney Football Stadium, May 6, 1992

NEW SOUTH WALES: Andrew Ettingshausen; Graham Mackay, Brad Fittler, Paul McGregor, Rod Wishart; Laurie Daley (c), John Simon; Glenn Lazarus, Ben Elias, Paul Harragon, Paul Sironen, John Cartwright, Bradley Clyde. Interchange: Robbie McCormack, Craig Salvatori, Brad Mackay, David Gillespie. Coach: Phil Gould.
QUEENSLAND: Dale Shearer; Michael Hancock, Mal Meninga (c), Peter Jackson, Willie Carne; Kevin Walters, Allan Langer; Martin Bella, Steve Walters, Steve Jackson, Bob Lindner, Trevor Gillmeister, Gary Larson. Interchange: Mark Coyne, Gary Coyne, Steve Renouf, Gavin Allen. Coach: Graham Lowe.
New South Wales 14 (Clyde, Salvatori tries; Wishart 3 goals) defeated **Queensland** 6 (Langer try; Meninga goal).
Crowd: 40,039. **Referee**: David Manson. **Man of the match**: Ben Elias (NSW).

Match 35, Lang Park, May 20, 1992

QUEENSLAND: Dale Shearer; Michael Hancock, Mal Meninga (c), Mark Coyne, Adrian Brunker; Peter Jackson, Allan Langer; Martin Bella, Steve Walters, Gavin Allen, Bob Lindner, Gary Larson, Billy Moore. Interchange: Kevin Walters, Trevor Gillmeister, Darren Smith, Mike McLean. Coach: Graham Lowe.
NEW SOUTH WALES: Andrew Ettingshausen; Graham Mackay, Brad Fittler, Paul McGregor, Rod Wishart; Laurie Daley (c), Ricky Stuart; Glenn Lazarus, Ben Elias, Paul Harragon, Paul Sironen, John Cartwright, Bradley Clyde. Interchange: Craig Salvatori, Brad Mackay, David Gillespie, Steve Carter. Coach: Phil Gould.
Queensland 5 (Moore try; Langer field goal) defeated **New South Wales** 4 (Wishart 2 goals).
Crowd: 31,500. **Referee**: Bill Harrigan. **Man of the match**: Bob Lindner (Queensland).

Match 36, Sydney Football Stadium, June 3, 1992

NEW SOUTH WALES: Andrew Ettingshausen; Rod Wishart, Paul McGregor, Brad Fittler, Chris Johns; Laurie Daley (c), Ricky Stuart; Glenn Lazarus, Benny Elias, Paul Harragon, Paul Sironen, John Cartwright, Bradley Clyde. Interchange: Craig Salvatori, David Gillespie, Tim Brasher, Brad Mackay. Coach: Phil Gould.
QUEENSLAND: Dale Shearer; Michael Hancock, Mark Coyne, Mal Meninga (c), Adrian Brunker; Peter Jackson, Allan Langer; Martin Bella, Steve Walters, Gavin Allen, Gary Larson, Mike McLean, Billy Moore. Interchange: Kevin Walters, Darren Smith, Steve Jackson, Gary Coyne. Coach: Graham Lowe.
New South Wales 16 (Stuart, Ettingshausen, Cartwright tries; Brasher 2 goals) defeated **Queensland** 4 (Meninga 2 goals).
Crowd: 41,878. **Referee**: Eddie Ward. **Man of the match**: Ricky Stuart (NSW).

1993

Match 37, Lang Park, May 3, 1993

NEW SOUTH WALES: Tim Brasher; Andrew Ettingshausen, Paul McGregor, Brad Fittler, Rod Wishart; Laurie Daley (c), Ricky Stuart; Glenn Lazarus, Ben Elias, Ian Roberts, Paul Sironen, Paul Harragon, Brad Mackay. Reserves: David Fairleigh, Craig Salvatori. Brett Mullins and Jason Taylor were not used. Coach: Phil Gould.
QUEENSLAND: Gary Belcher; Willie Carne, Mal Meninga (c), Steve Renouf, Michael Hancock; Kevin Walters, Allan Langer; Steve Jackson, Steve Walters, Martin Bella, Bob Lindner, Gary Larson, Billy Moore. Reserves: Mark Coyne, Dale Shearer, Mark Hohn, Andrew Gee. Coach: Wally Lewis.
New South Wales 14 (Wishart, Stuart tries; Wishart 3 goals) defeated **Queensland** 10 (Lindner, Carne tries; Meninga goal).
Crowd: 33,000. **Referee**: Greg McCallum. **Man of the match**: Ricky Stuart (NSW).

Match 38, Sydney Football Stadium, May 17, 1993

NEW SOUTH WALES: Tim Brasher; Andrew Ettingshausen, Paul McGregor, Brad Fittler, Rod Wishart; Laurie Daley (c), Ricky Stuart; Glenn Lazarus, Robbie McCormack, Ian Roberts, Paul

STATE OF ORIGIN MATCH-BY-MATCH

Sironen, Paul Harragon, Brad Mackay. Reserves: David Fairleigh, David Gillespie, Jason Taylor, Jason Croker. Coach: Phil Gould.
QUEENSLAND: Dale Shearer; Willie Carne, Mal Meninga (c), Mark Coyne, Adrian Brunker; Kevin Walters, Allan Langer; Mark Hohn, Steve Walters, Martin Bella, Trevor Gillmeister, Gary Larson, Bob Lindner. Reserves: Julian O'Neill, Steve Jackson, Billy Moore, Darren Smith. Coach: Wally Lewis.
New South Wales 16 (Daley, Mackay, Wishart tries; Wishart 2 goals) defeated **Queensland** 12 (Meninga, Kevin Walters tries; Brunker, Shearer goals).
Crowd: 41,895. Referee: Eddie Ward. **Man of the match**: Tim Brasher (NSW).

Match 39, Lang Park, May 31, 1993

QUEENSLAND: Dale Shearer; Brett Dallas, Mal Meninga (c), Mark Coyne, Willie Carne; Julian O'Neill, Allan Langer; Martin Bella, Steve Walters, Mark Hohn, Gary Larson, Trevor Gillmeister, Bob Lindner. Interchange: Kevin Walters, Darren Smith, Steve Jackson, Billy Moore. Coach: Wally Lewis.
NEW SOUTH WALES: Tim Brasher; Rod Wishart, Brad Fittler, Andrew Ettingshausen, Graham Mackay; Laurie Daley (c), Ricky Stuart; Glenn Lazarus, Ben Elias, David Fairleigh, Paul Sironen, Paul Harragon, Brad Mackay. Interchange: David Gillespie, Terry Hill, Scott Gourley, Jason Taylor. Coach: Phil Gould.
Queensland 24 (Carne 2, S.Walters, Lindner tries; Meninga 2, O'Neill 2 goals) defeated **New South Wales** 12 (Ettingshausen, Harragon tries; Wishart 2 goals).
Crowd: 31,500. Referee: Greg McCallum. **Man of the match**: Dale Shearer (Queensland). **Sin bin**: Bella, S.Walters (Queensland), Harragon, Elias (New South Wales).

1994

Match 40, Sydney Football Stadium, May 23, 1994

QUEENSLAND: Julian O'Neill; Michael Hancock, Mal Meninga (c), Steve Renouf, Willie Carne; Kevin Walters, Allan Langer; Andrew Gee, Steve Walters, Martin Bella, Trevor Gillmeister, Gary Larson, Billy Moore. Interchange: Mark Coyne, Darren Smith, Mark Hohn, Darren Fritz. Coach: Wally Lewis.
NEW SOUTH WALES: Tim Brasher; Graham Mackay, Brad Fittler, Paul McGregor, Rod Wishart; Laurie Daley (c), Ricky Stuart; Glenn Lazarus, Ben Elias, Ian Roberts, Paul Sironen, Paul Harragon, Brad Mackay. Interchange: Andrew Ettingshausen, Chris Johns, David Gillespie, David Barnhill. Coach: Phil Gould.
Queensland 16 (O'Neill, Carne, Coyne tries; Meninga 2 goals) defeated **New South Wales** 12 (B.Mackay, Harragon tries; Wishart, G.Mackay goals).
Crowd: 41,859. Referee: Bill Harrigan. **Man of the match**: Willie Carne (Queensland).

Match 41, Melbourne Cricket Ground, June 8, 1994

NEW SOUTH WALES: Tim Brasher; Andrew Ettingshausen, Brad Fittler, Paul McGregor, Brett Mullins; Laurie Daley (c), Ricky Stuart; Glenn Lazarus, Ben Elias, Paul Harragon, Paul Sironen, Dean Pay, Bradley Clyde. Interchange: Brad Mackay, David Barnhill, Ken Nagas. Chris Johns wasn't used. Coach: Phil Gould.
QUEENSLAND: Julian O'Neill; Michael Hancock, Mal Meninga (c), Mark Coyne, Willie Carne; Kevin Walters, Allan Langer; Andrew Gee, Kerrod Walters, Darren Fritz, Trevor Gillmeister, Gary Larson, Billy Moore. Interchange: Darren Smith, Mark Hohn, Gorden Tallis, Adrian Vowles. Coach: Wally Lewis.
New South Wales 14 (Lazarus, McGregor tries; Brasher 3 goals) defeated **Queensland** 0.
Crowd: 87,161 (Australian record). Referee: Graham Annesley. **Man of the match**: Paul Harragon (NSW).

Match 42, Suncorp Stadium, June 20, 1994

NEW SOUTH WALES: Tim Brasher; Andrew Ettingshausen, Brad Fittler, Paul McGregor, Brett Mullins; Laurie Daley (c), Ricky Stuart; Ian Roberts, Ben Elias, Paul Harragon, Paul Sironen, Dean Pay, Bradley Clyde. Interchange: Ken Nagas, Chris Johns, Brad Mackay, David Barnhill. Coach: Phil Gould.
QUEENSLAND: Julian O'Neill; Michael Hancock, Mal Meninga (c), Steve Renouf, Willie Carne; Kevin Walters, Allan Langer; Mark Hohn, Steve Walters, Darren Fritz, Billy Moore, Gary Larson, Jason Smith. Interchange: Mark Coyne, Darren Smith, Andrew Gee, Gorden Tallis. Coach: Wally Lewis.
New South Wales 27 (Clyde, Daley, Mullins, Fittler tries; Brasher 4 goals; Elias 2, Fittler field goals) defeated **Queensland** 12 (Gee, Renouf tries; O'Neill 2 goals).
Crowd: 40,665. Referee: Bill Harrigan. **Man of the match**: Ben Elias (New South Wales).

1995

Match 43, Sydney Football Stadium, May 15, 1995

QUEENSLAND: Robbie O'Davis; Brett Dallas, Mark Coyne, Danny Moore, Matt Sing; Dale Shearer, Adrian Lam; Tony Hearn, Wayne Bartrim, Gavin Allen, Gary Larson, Trevor Gillmeister (c), Billy Moore. Interchange: Terry

Cook, Ben Ikin, Mark Hohn, Craig Teevan. Coach: Paul Vautin.
NEW SOUTH WALES: Tim Brasher; Rod Wishart, Terry Hill, Paul McGregor, Craig Hancock; Matthew Johns, Andrew Johns; Paul Harragon, Jim Serdaris, Mark Carroll, Brad Mackay, Steven Menzies, Brad Fittler (c). Interchange: Greg Florimo, David Fairleigh, Matthew Seers, Adam Muir. Coach: Phil Gould. **Queensland** 2 (Bartrim goal) defeated **New South Wales** 0.
Crowd: 39,841. **Referee**: Eddie Ward. **Man of the match**: Gary Larson (Queensland).

Match 44, Melbourne Cricket Ground, May 31, 1995

QUEENSLAND: Robbie O'Davis; Brett Dallas, Mark Coyne, Danny Moore, Matt Sing; Jason Smith, Adrian Lam; Gavin Allen, Wayne Bartrim, Tony Hearn, Trevor Gillmeister (c), Gary Larson, Billy Moore. Interchange: Ben Ikin, Terry Cook, Mark Hohn, Craig Teevan. Coach: Paul Vautin.
NEW SOUTH WALES: Tim Brasher; Rod Wishart, Terry Hill, Paul McGregor, John Hopoate; Brad Fittler (c), Andrew Johns; Dean Pay, Jim Serdaris, Paul Harragon, Greg Florimo, David Barnhill, Brad Mackay. Interchange: Brett Rodwell, Adam Muir, Steven Menzies, David Fairleigh. Coach: Phil Gould.
Queensland 20 (Coyne, Lam, Dallas tries; Bartrim 4 goals) defeated **New South Wales** 12 (Rodwell, Serdaris tries; Wishart 2 goals).
Crowd: 52,994. **Referee**: Eddie Ward. **Man of the match**: Jason Smith (Queensland).

Match 45, Suncorp Stadium, June 12, 1995

QUEENSLAND: Robbie O'Davis; Brett Dallas, Mark Coyne, Danny Moore, Matt Sing; Jason Smith, Adrian Lam; Gavin Allen, Wayne Bartrim, Tony Hearn, Trevor Gillmeister (c), Gary Larson, Billy Moore. Interchange: Ben Ikin, Terry Cook, Mark Hohn, Craig Teevan. Coach: Paul Vautin.
NEW SOUTH WALES: Tim Brasher; Rod Wishart, Terry Hill, Paul McGregor, David Hall; Matthew Johns, Geoff Toovey; Paul Harragon, Jim Serdaris, Mark Carroll, Steven Menzies, Adam Muir, Brad Fittler (c). Interchange: Matt Seers, Greg Florimo, David Fairleigh, David Barnhill. Coach: Phil Gould.
Queensland 24 (Moore, Smith, Dallas, Ikin tries; Bartrim 4 goals) defeated **New South Wales** 16 (Wishart, Muir, Brasher tries; Wishart 2 goals).
Crowd: 40,189. **Referee**: David Manson. **Man of the match**: Adrian Lam (Queensland).

1996

Match 46, Suncorp Stadium, May 20, 1996

NEW SOUTH WALES: Tim Brasher; Rod Wishart, Andrew Ettingshausen, Laurie Daley, Brett Mullins; Brad Fittler (c), Geoff Toovey; Glenn Lazarus, Andrew Johns, Paul Harragon, David Furner, Dean Pay, Adam Muir. Interchange: Jim Dymock, Jamie Ainscough, Jason Croker, Steve Menzies. Coach: Phil Gould.
QUEENSLAND: Robbie O'Davis; Brett Dallas, Steve Renouf, Matt Sing, Wendell Sailor; Jason Smith, Allan Langer; Tony Hearn, Wayne Bartrim, Gary Larson, Trevor Gillmeister (c), Brad Thorn, Billy Moore. Interchange: Adrian Lam, Michael Hancock, Alan Cann, Craig Greenhill. Coach: Paul Vautin.
New South Wales 14 (Ettingshausen, Menzies tries; Johns 3 goals) defeated **Queensland** 6 (Langer try; Bartrim goal).
Crowd: 39,348. **Referee**: David Manson. **Man of the match**: Geoff Toovey (NSW).

Match 47, Sydney Football Stadium, June 3, 1996

NEW SOUTH WALES: Tim Brasher; Rod Wishart, Andrew Ettingshausen, Laurie Daley, Brett Mullins; Brad Fittler (c), Geoff Toovey; Glenn Lazarus, Andrew Johns, Paul Harragon, David Furner, Dean Pay, Adam Muir. Interchange: Jim Dymock, Jamie Ainscough, Jason Croker, Steve Menzies. Coach: Phil Gould.
QUEENSLAND: Wendell Sailor; Brett Dallas, Steve Renouf, Mark Coyne, Matt Sing; Julian O'Neill, Allan Langer (c); Tony Hearn, Steve Walters, Andrew Gee, Gary Larson, Brad Thorn, Billy Moore. Interchange: Adrian Lam, Kevin Walters, Jason Smith, Craig Greenhill. Coach: Paul Vautin.
New South Wales 18 (Mullins 2, Wishart tries; Johns 3 goals) defeated **Queensland** 6 (Renouf try; O'Neill goal).
Crowd: 41,955. **Referee**: David Manson. **Man of the match**: Andrew Johns (NSW). **Sent off**: Greenhill (Queensland), 62 min. **Charge**: High tackle. **Sentence**: Four matches.

Match 48, Suncorp Stadium, June 17, 1996

NEW SOUTH WALES: Tim Brasher; Rod Wishart, Andrew Ettingshausen, Laurie Daley, Brett Mullins; Brad Fittler (c), Geoff Toovey; Glenn Lazarus, Andrew Johns, Paul Harragon, David Furner, Dean Pay, Adam Muir. Interchange: Jim Dymock, Jamie Ainscough, Jason Croker, Steve Menzies. Coach: Phil Gould.
QUEENSLAND: Wendell Sailor; Brett Dallas, Steve Renouf, Mark Coyne, Willie Carne; Dale Shearer, Allan Langer (c); Tony Hearn, Steve Walters, Andrew Gee, Gary Larson, Brad Thorn, Billy Moore. Interchange: Adrian Lam, Matt Sing, Jason Smith, Owen Cunningham. Coach: Paul Vautin.
New South Wales 15 (Ettingshausen, Mullins tries; Wishart 2, Johns goals; Fittler field goal)

defeated **Queensland** 14 (Dallas, Coyne tries; Carne 3 goals).
Crowd: 38,217. **Referee**: David Manson. **Man of the match**: Steve Menzies (NSW).

1997

Match 49, Suncorp Stadium, May 28, 1997

NEW SOUTH WALES: Tim Brasher; Rod Wishart, Terry Hill, Paul McGregor, Jamie Ainscough; Jim Dymock, Geoff Toovey (c); Paul Harragon, Andrew Johns, Mark Carroll, Steve Menzies, Adam Muir, Nik Kosef. Interchange: David Fairleigh, Dean Pay, John Simon, Ken McGuinness. Coach: Tom Raudonikis.
QUEENSLAND: Robbie O'Davis; Brett Dallas, Matt Sing, Mark Coyne, Danny Moore; Ben Ikin, Adrian Lam (c); Neil Tierney, Jamie Goddard, Craig Smith, Gary Larson, Billy Moore, Wayne Bartrim. Interchange: Jason Smith, Jeremy Schloss, Tony Hearn, Stuart Kelly. Coach: Paul Vautin.
New South Wales 8 (McGregor try; Johns, Wishart goals) defeated **Queensland** 6 (Lam try; Bartrim goal).
Crowd: 28,222. **Referee**: Kelvin Jeffes. **Man of the match**: Geoff Toovey (NSW).

Match 50, Melbourne Cricket Ground, June 11, 1997

NEW SOUTH WALES: Tim Brasher; Ken McGuinness, Paul McGregor, Terry Hill, Jamie Ainscough; Jim Dymock, John Simon; Paul Harragon, Geoff Toovey (c), Mark Carroll, Steve Menzies, Adam Muir, Nik Kosef. Interchange: David Fairleigh, Dean Pay, Matt Seers. Aaron Raper did not play. Coach: Tom Raudonikis.
QUEENSLAND: Robbie O'Davis; Brett Dallas, Stuart Kelly, Mark Coyne, Matt Sing; Ben Ikin, Adrian Lam (c); Neil Tierney, Wayne Bartrim, Craig Smith, Gary Larson, Jason Smith, Billy Moore. Interchange: Jamie Goddard, Jeremy Schloss, Clinton O'Brien, Julian O'Neill. Coach: Paul Vautin.
New South Wales 15 (McGuinness, Kosef, Dymock tries; Simon goal; Simon field goal) defeated **Queensland** 14 (Sing, O'Davis, Dallas tries; O'Neill goal).
Crowd: 25,105. **Referee**: David Manson. **Man of the match**: Paul McGregor (NSW).

Match 51, Sydney Football Stadium, June 25, 1997

QUEENSLAND: Robbie O'Davis; Brett Dallas, Mark Coyne, Julian O'Neill, Matt Sing; Ben Ikin, Adrian Lam (c); Clinton O'Brien, Jamie Goddard, Neil Tierney, Gary Larson, Jason Smith, Billy Moore. Interchange: Stuart Kelly, Jeremy Schloss, Craig Smith, Wayne Bartrim. Coach: Paul Vautin.
NEW SOUTH WALES: Tim Brasher; Ken McGuinness, Jamie Ainscough, Terry Hill, Matt Seers; Trent Barrett, Geoff Toovey (c); Mark Carroll, Andrew Johns, Paul Harragon, Adam Muir, Steve Menzies, Nik Kosef. Interchange: John Simon, Michael Buettner, Dean Pay, David Fairleigh. Coach: Tom Raudonikis.
Queensland 18 (Ikin, O'Neill, Coyne tries; O'Neill 3 goals) defeated **New South Wales** 12 (Ainscough, Johns tries; Simon, Johns goals).
Crowd: 33,241. **Referee**: Eddie Ward. **Man of the match**: Gary Larson (Queensland).

STATE OF ORIGIN PLAYERS' RECORDS 1980–97

NEW SOUTH WALES

AINSCOUGH Jamie (Newcastle, St George): Matches 3 (+3R). 1996 (0+3R), 1997 (3). One try – four points.
ALEXANDER Greg (Penrith): Matches 4 (+1R). 1989 (2), 1990 (0+1R), 1991 (2). Two goals – four points.
ANDERSON Chris (Canterbury): Matches 4. 1980 (1), 1982 (1), 1983 (2). Three tries – 12 points.
AYLIFFE Royce (Easts): Matches 1 (+2R). 1982 (1+2R). Points – nil.
BARNHILL David (St George): Matches 1 (+4R). 1994 (0+3R), 1995 (2). Points – nil.
BARRETT Trent (Illawarra): Matches 1. 1997 (1). Points – nil.
BLAKE Phil (Souths): Matches 0 (+1R). 1989 (0+1R). Points – nil.
BOWDEN Steve (Newtown): Matches 1. 1981 (1). Points – nil.
BOYD Les (Manly): Matches 3. 1981 (1), 1982 (1), 1983 (1). Points – nil.
BOYLE David (Souths): Matches 2 (+2R). 1987 (2+2R). One try – four points
BRASHER Tim (Balmain): Matches 15 (+1R). 1992 (0+1R), 1993 (3), 1994 (3), 1995 (3), 1996 (3), 1997 (3). One try, nine goals – 22 points.
BRENTNALL Greg (Canterbury): Matches 4. 1980 (1), 1982 (2), 1983 (1). One try – 3 points.
BROOKS David (Balmain): Matches 1. 1985 (1). Points – nil.
BROWN Ray (Manly): Matches 1 (+2R). 1983 (1+2R). Points – nil.
BUETTNER Michael (Norths): Matches 0 (+1R). 1997 (0+1R). Points – nil.
BUGDEN Geoff (Newtown): Matches 2. 1983 (2). Points – nil.
CARROLL Mark (Manly): Matches 5. 1995 (2), 1997 (3). Points – nil.
CARTER Steve (Penrith): Matches 0 (+1R). 1992 (0+1R). Points – nil.
CARTWRIGHT John (Penrith): Matches 5 (+3R). 1989 (1+2R), 1991 (1+1R), 1992 (3). One try – 4 points.
CLEAL Noel (Manly): Matches 11 (+1R). 1984 (3). 1985 (2), 1986 (3), 1987 (2). 1988 (1+1). Three tries – 12 points.
CLYDE Bradley (Canberra): Matches 11. 1989 (2), 1990 (3), 1991 (2), 1992 (3), 1994 (2). Two tries – 8 points.
CONLON Ross (Canterbury): Matches 3. 1984 (3). 10 goals – 20 points.
COOPER Bob (Wests): Matches 1. 1980 (1). Points – nil.
COVENEY John (Canterbury): Matches 2. 1982 (2). Points – nil.
CROKER Jason (Canberra): Matches 0 (+4R). 1993 (0+1R), 1996 (0+3R). Points – nil.
CRONIN Mick (Parramatta): Matches 6. 1980 (1), 1981 (1), 1982 (2), 1983 (2). One try, 14 goals – 31 points.
DALEY Laurie (Canberra): Matches 17. 1989 (2), 1990 (1), 1991 (2), 1992 (3), 1993 (3), 1994 (3), 1996 (3). Four tries, one goal – 18 points.
DALEY Phil (Manly): Matches 3. 1987 (2), 1988 (1). Points – nil.
DAVIDSON Les (Souths): Matches 5. 1987 (4). 1988 (1). One try – 4 points
DOCKING Jonathan (Cronulla): Matches 2. 1987 (1), 1988 (1). One try – 4 points.
DOWLING Garry (Parramatta): Matches 0 (+1R). 1981 (0+1R). Points – nil.
DUKE Phil (Moree Boomerangs): Matches 1. 1982 (1). One try – 3 points.
DUNN Paul (Canterbury): Matches 2 (+1R). 1988 (0+1R).

1989 (2). Points – nil.
DYMOCK Jim (Parramatta): Matches 2 (+3R). 1996 (0+3R), 1997 (2). One try – four points.
EADIE Graham (Manly): Matches 1. 1980 (1). Points – nil.
EDGE Steve (Parramatta): Matches 1. 1980 (1). Points – nil.
ELIAS Ben (Balmain): Matches 19. 1985 (3), 1988 (2), 1990 (3), 1991 (3), 1992 (3), 1993 (2), 1994 (3). One try, 2 field goals – 6 points.
ELLA Steve (Parramatta): Matches 3 (+5R). 1983 (2+1R), 1984 (1+1R), 1985 (0+3R). Three tries – 12 points.
ETTINGSHAUSEN Andrew (Cronulla): Matches 23 (+2R). 1987 (3), 1988 (3), 1989 (1+1R), 1990 (3), 1991 (2), 1992 (3), 1993 (3), 1994 (2+1R), 1996 (3). Seven tries – 28 points.
FAHEY Terry (Easts): Matches 2. 1981 (1), 1982 (1). Points – nil.
FAIRLEIGH David (Norths): Matches 1 (+9R). 1991 (0+1R), 1993 (1+2R), 1995 (0+3R), 1997 (0+3R). Points – nil.
FARRAR Andrew (Canterbury): Matches 5 (+2R). 1984 (1), 1986 (2), 1987 (1), 1989 (1), 1990 (0+2R). Three tries – 12 points.
FENECH Mario (Souths): Matches 2. 1989 (2). Points – nil.
FERGUSON John (Easts, Canberra): Matches 8. 1985 (3), 1988 (2), 1989 (3). One try – 4 points.
FIELD Paul (Cootamundra): Matches 2. 1983 (2). Points – nil.
FITTLER Brad (Penrith, Sydney City): Matches 16 (+2R). 1990 (0+1R), 1991 (1+1R), 1992 (3), 1993 (3), 1994 (3), 1995 (3), 1996 (3). One try, 2 field goals, 6 points.
FLORIMO Greg (Norths): Matches 1 (+3R). 1988 (0+1R), 1995 (1+2R). Points – nil.
FOLKES Steve (Canterbury): Matches 8 (+1R). 1986 (3). 1987 (2+1R). 1988 (3). Points – nil.
FURNER David (Canberra): Matches 3. 1996 (3). Points – nil.
GERARD Geoff (Manly): Matches 2. 1983 (2). Points – nil.
GEYER Mark (Penrith): Matches 3. 1989 (1), 1991 (2). Points – nil.
GILLESPIE David (Canterbury, Wests, Manly): Matches 5 (+10R). 1986 (0+3R), 1990 (3), 1991 (2+1R), 1992 (0+3R), 1993 (0+2R), 1994 (0+1R). Points – nil.
GOURLEY Scott (St George): Matches 0 (+1R). 1993 (0+1R). Points – nil.
GROTHE Eric (Parramatta): Matches 9. 1981 (1), 1983 (2), 1984 (2), 1985 (3), 1986 (1). Three tries – 10 points.
GURR Marty (Easts): Matches 2. 1983 (2). Points – nil.
HALL David (Norths): Matches 1. 1995 (1). Points – nil.
HAMBLY Gary (Souths): Matches 1. 1980 (1). Points – nil.
HANCOCK Craig (Manly): Matches 1. 1995 (1). Points – nil.
HANSON Steve (Norths): Matches 1. 1988 (1). One try – 4 points.
HARRAGON Paul (Newcastle): Matches 18. 1992 (3), 1993 (3), 1994 (3), 1995 (3), 1996 (3), 1997 (3). Two tries – 8 points.
HASLER Des (Manly): Matches 6 (+7R). 1985 (1), 1987 (0+3R), 1988 (1+1R), 1989 (2+1R), 1990 (1), 1991 (1+2R). Two tries – 8 points.
HASTINGS Kevin (Easts): Matches 0 (+1R). 1983 (0+1R). Points – nil.
HETHERINGTON Brian (Illawarra): Matches 1 (+1R). 1984 (0+1R), 1986 (1). Points – nil.

STATE OF ORIGIN MATCH-BY-MATCH

HILDITCH Ron (Parramatta): Matches 1. 1981 (1). Points – nil.
HILL Terry (Wests, Manly): Matches 6 (+1R). 1993 (0+1R), 1995 (3), 1997 (3). Points – nil.
HOPOATE John (Manly): Matches 1. 1995 (1). Points – nil.
HUNT Neil (Parramatta): Matches 2. 1983 (2). One try – 4 points.
IZZARD Brad (Penrith): Matches 2 (+2R). 1982 (2+1R), 1991 (0+1R). Two tries – 6 points.
JACK Garry (Balmain): Matches 17. 1984 (3), 1985 (3), 1986 (3), 1987 (3), 1988 (2), 1989 (3). One try – 4 points.
JARVIS Pat (St George, Canterbury): Matches 6 (+2R). 1984 (1+2R), 1985 (3), 1987 (2). Points – nil.
JENSEN Barry (Newtown): Matches 1. 1981 (1).
JOHNS Andrew (Newcastle): Matches 7. 1995 (2), 1996 (3), 1997 (2). One try, nine goals – 22 points.
JOHNS Chris (Broncos): Matches 7 (+2R). 1989 (3), 1991 (3), 1992 (1), 1994 (0+2R). Three tries – 12 points.
JOHNS Matthew (Newcastle): Matches 2. 1995 (2). Points – nil.
JOHNSTON Brian (St George): Matches 8. 1984 (1), 1986 (1), 1987 (4), 1988 (1), 1989 (1). Two tries – 8 points.
JOHNSTON Lindsay (Norths): Matches 2. 1983 (2). Points – nil.
JURD Stan (Parramatta): Matches 2 (+1R). 1983 (2+1R). Points – nil.
KENNY Brett (Parramatta): Matches 15 (+1R). 1982 (1+1R), 1983 (2), 1984 (3), 1985 (3), 1986 (3), 1987 (3). Two tries – 8 points.
KELLY Peter (Penrith): Matches 2. 1989 (2). Points – nil.
KOSEF Nik (Manly): Matches 3. 1997 (3). One try – four points.
KRILICH Max (Manly): Matches 5. 1982 (3), 1983 (2). Points – nil.
LAMB Terry (Wests, Canterbury): Matches 4 (+4R). 1981 (1), 1984 (1), 1986 (0+3R), 1988 (1+1R), 1989 (1). Points – nil.
LANGMACK Paul (Canterbury): Matches 3 (+1R). 1987 (1+1R), 1988 (2). -Points – nil.
LAZARUS Glenn (Canberra, Broncos): Matches 12 (+4R). 1989 (0+1R), 1990 (1+2R), 1991 (0+1R), 1992 (3), 1993 (3), 1994 (2), 1996 (3). Two tries – 8 points.
LEIS Jim (Wests): Matches 1. 1980 (1). Points – nil.
LYONS Cliff (Manly): Matches 6. 1987 (2), 1988 (2), 1991 (2). One try – 4 points.
LYONS Graham (Souths): Matches 2 (+1R). 1990 (2+1R). Points – nil.
MACKAY Brad (St George, Western Reds): Matches 10 (+7R). 1989 (1+1R), 1990 (2), 1991 (1+1R), 1992 (0+3R), 1993 (3), 1994 (1+2R), 1995 (2). Three tries – 12 points.
MACKAY Graham (Penrith): Matches 4. 1992 (2), 1993 (1), 1994 (1). One goal – 2 points.
MARTIN Steve (Manly): Matches 0 (+1R). 1980 (0+1R). Points – nil.
MATTERSON Terry (Broncos): Matches 0 (+1R). 1989 (0+1R). Points – nil.
McCORMACK Robbie (Newcastle). Matches 1 (+1R). 1990 (0+1R). 1993 (1). Points – nil.
McGAW Mark (Cronulla): Matches 10 (+2R). 1987 (3+1R), 1988 (3), 1990 (3), 1991 (1+2R). Six tries – 24 points.
McGREGOR Paul (Illawarra): Matches 13. 1992 (3), 1993 (2), 1994 (3), 1995 (3), 1997 (2). Two tries – 8 points.
McGUINNESS Ken (Wests): Matches 2 (+1R). 1997 (2+1R). One try – four points.
McGUIRE Bruce (Balmain): Matches 5. 1989 (2). 1990 (3). One try – 4 points.
McKINNON Don (Norths): Matches 1. 1982 (1). Points – nil.
MELROSE Tony (Souths): Matches 1. 1982 (1). Two goals – 4 points.
MENZIES Steven (Manly): Matches 5 (+4R). 1995 (2+1R), 1996 (0+3R), 1997 (3). One try – 4 points.
MERLO Paul (Wests): Matches 1. 1982 (1). Points – nil.
MILLER Gavin (Cronulla): Matches 5. 1983 (2), 1989 (3). Points – nil.
MORRIS Steve (St George): Matches 2. 1984 (1), 1986 (1). Points – nil.
MORTIMER Chris (Canterbury, Penrith): Matches 8 (+1R). 1984 (1), 1985 (3), 1986 (3), 1989 (1+1R). Two tries – 8 points.
MORTIMER Steve (Canterbury): Matches 8 (+1R). 1982 (3), 1983 (1+1R), 1984 (2), 1985 (2). Two tries – 7 points.
MUGGLETON John (Parramatta): Matches 2. 1982 (2). Points – nil.
MUIR Adam (Newcastle): Matches 7 (+2R). 1995 (1+2R), 1996 (3), 1997 (3). One try – 4 points.
MULLINS Brett (Canberra): Matches 5. 1994 (2), 1996 (3). Four tries – 16 points.
NAGAS Ken (Canberra): Matches 0 (+2R). 1994 (0+2R). Points – nil.
NISZCZOT Ziggy (Souths): Matches 2. 1982 (2). Two tries – 6 points.
O'CONNOR Michael (St George, Manly): Matches 19. 1985 (3), 1986 (3), 1987 (4), 1988 (3), 1989 (1), 1990 (2), 1991 (3). Eleven tries, 42 goals, 1 field goal – 129 points.
O'GRADY Graham (Newtown): Matches 0 (+1R). 1981 (0+1R). Points – nil.
PAY Dean (Canterbury, Parramatta): Matches 6 (+3R). 1994 (2), 1995 (1), 1996 (3), 1997 (0+3R). Points – nil.
PEARCE Wayne (Balmain): Matches 15. 1983 (1), 1984 (2), 1985 (3), 1986 (3), 1987 (3), 1988 (3). Three tries – 12 points.
POTTER Mick (Canterbury): Matches 0 (+1R). 1984 (0+1R). Points – nil.
PRICE Ray (Parramatta): Matches 8. 1981 (1), 1982 (3), 1983 (2), 1984 (2). Points – nil.
RAMPLING Tony (Souths): Matches 2 (+1R). 1982 (2), 1985 (0+1R). Points – nil.
RAUDONIKIS Tom (Newtown): Matches 1. 1980 (1). One try – 3 points.
ROACH Steve (Balmain): Matches 17. 1984 (3), 1985 (3), 1986 (3), 1988 (3), 1990 (2), 1991 (3). Points – nil.
ROBERTS Ian (Manly): Matches 9. 1990 (3), 1991 (2), 1993 (2), 1994 (2). Points – nil.
RODWELL Brett (Illawarra): Matches 0 (+1R). 1995 (0+1R). One try – 4 points.
ROGERS Steve (Cronulla): Matches 4. 1980 (1), 1981 (1), 1982 (2). Points – nil.
SALVATORI Craig (Easts): Matches 0 (+5R). 1991 (0+1R), 1992 (0+3R), 1993 (0+1R). One try – 4 points.
SARGENT Mark (Newcastle): Matches 0 (+1R). 1990 (0+1R). Points – nil.
SEERS Matthew (Norths): Matches 1 (+3R). 1995 (0+2R), 1997 (1+1R). Points – nil.
SERDARIS Jim (Wests): Matches 3. 1995 (3). One try – 4 points.
SIGSWORTH Phil (Newtown, Manly): Matches 3. 1981 (1), 1982 (1), 1983 (1). Two goals – 4 points.
SIMMONS Royce (Penrith): Matches 10. 1984 (2), 1986 (3), 1987 (4), 1988 (1). One try – 4 points.
SIMON John (Illawarra, Parramatta): Matches 2 (+2R). 1992 (1), 1997 (2+1R). Two goals, one field goal – 5 points.
SIRONEN Paul (Balmain): Matches 11 (+3R). 1989 (1), 1990 (0+3R), 1991 (1), 1992 (3), 1993 (3), 1994 (3).

Points – nil.
STERLING Peter (Parramatta): Matches 13. 1981 (1), 1983 (2), 1984 (1), 1986 (3), 1987 (4), 1988 (2). Points – nil.
STONE Robert (St George): Matches 1. 1980 (1). Points – nil.
STUART Ricky (Canberra): Matches 14. 1990 (3), 1991 (3), 1992 (2), 1993 (3), 1994 (3). Three tries – 12 points.
TAYLOR Jason (Wests): Matches 0 (+2R). 1993 (0+2R). Points – nil.
THOMPSON Alan (Manly): Matches 5 (+1R). 1980 (1), 1982 (2+1R), 1983 (1), 1984 (1). Points – nil.
TOOVEY Geoff (Manly): Matches 7 (+1R). 1990 (0+1R), 1995 (1), 1996 (3), 1997 (3). Points – nil.
TREWHELLA David (Easts): Matches 1 (+1R). 1989 (1+1R). One try – 4 points.
TUNKS Peter (Souths, Canterbury): Matches 7 (+3R). 1981 (1), 1984 (1+1R), 1985 (0+2R), 1986 (3), 1987 (2). One try – 4 points.
WALFORD Ricky (St George): Matches 1. 1990 (1). Points – nil.
WALSH Chris (St George): Matches 1. 1984 (1). Points – nil.
WILSON Alan (Cronulla): Matches 0 (+2R). 1989 (0+2R). Points – nil.
WISHART Rod (Illawarra): Matches 19. 1990 (3), 1991 (2), 1992 (3), 1993 (3), 1994 (1), 1995 (3), 1996 (3), 1997 (1). Four tries, 23 goals – 62 points.
WRIGHT Rex (North Newcastle): Matches 1. 1984 (1). Points – nil.
WYNN Graeme (St George): Matches 1. 1980 (1). Points – nil.
WYNN Peter (Parramatta): Matches 4. 1984 (1), 1985 (3). Points – nil.
YOUNG Craig (St George): Matches 4 (+1R). 1980 (1), 1982 (2+1R), 1984 (1). Points – nil.

QUEENSLAND

ALLEN Gavin (Broncos): Matches 5 (+3R). 1991 (0+2R), 1992 (2+1R), 1995 (3). Points – nil.
ASTILL Bruce (Souths Brisbane): Matches 0 (+2R). 1980 (0+1R), 1983 (0+1R). Points – nil.
BACKER Brad (Easts Brisbane): Matches 3. 1980 (1), 1981 (1), 1982 (1). One try – 3 points.
BACKO Sam (Canberra, Broncos): Matches 7. 1988 (3), 1989 (2), 1990 (2). Three tries – 12 points.
BARTRIM Wayne (St George): Matches 6 (+1R). 1995 (3), 1996 (1), 1997 (2+1R). Eleven goals, 22 points.
BEETSON Arthur (Parramatta): Matches 1. 1980 (1). Points – nil.
BELCHER Gary (Canberra): Matches 16. 1986 (2), 1987 (4), 1988 (3), 1989 (3), 1990 (3), 1993 (1). Four tries, 16 goals – 48 points.
DELLA Martin (Norths, Manly, Canterbury): Matches 21. 1987 (2), 1988 (3), 1989 (3), 1990 (0), 1991 (3), 1992 (3), 1993 (3), 1994 (1). Points – nil.
BOUSTEAD Kerry (Easts, Manly): Matches 6. 1980 (1), 1982 (2), 1984 (3). Five tries – 19 points.
BRENNAN Mitch (Souths, Redcliffe): Matches 4. 1981 (1), 1982 (2), 1983 (1). Three tries – 11 points.
BROHMAN Darryl (Penrith): Matches 2. 1983 (1), 1986 (1). Points – nil.
BROWN Dave (Manly, Easts): Matches 9 (+1R). 1983 (2+1R), 1984 (3), 1985 (1). One try – 4 points
BRUNKER Adrian (Newcastle): Matches 3. 1992 (2), 1993 (1). One goal, 2 points.
BUTLER Terry (Wynnum): Matches 1. 1983 (1). Points – nil.
CANN Alan (Broncos): Matches 0 (+1R). 1996 (0+1R). Points – nil.
CARNE Willie (Broncos): Matches 12. 1990 (1), 1991

(3), 1992 (1), 1993 (3), 1994 (3), 1996 (1). Five tries, three goals – 26 points.
CARR Norm (Wests Brisbane): Matches 2. 1980 (0+1R), 1981 (0+1R), 1982 (2). Points – nil.
CLOSE Chris (Redcliffe, Manly): Matches 9. 1980 (1), 1981 (1), 1983 (1), 1984 (2), 1985 (3), 1986 (1). Two tries – 6 points.
CONESCU Greg (Norths Brisbane, Gladstone Brothers, Redcliffe): Matches 20. 1981 (1), 1983 (3), 1984 (3), 1985 (3), 1986 (3), 1987 (4), 1988 (3). Two tries – 8 points.
COOK Terry (Crushers): Matches 0 (+3R). 1995 (0+3R). Points – nil.
COYNE Gary (Canberra): Matches 2 (+9R). 1989 (0+3R), 1990 (2+1R), 1991 (0+3R), 1992 (0+2R). Points – nil.
COYNE Mark (St George): Matches 13 (+6R). 1990 (0+2R), 1992 (2+1R), 1993 (2+1R), 1994 (1+2R), 1995 (3), 1996 (2), 1997 (3). Four tries – 16 points.
CUNNINGHAM Owen (Manly): Matches 0 (+1R). 1996 (0+1R). Points – nil.
CURRIE Tony (Wests Brisbane, Redcliffe, Broncos): Matches 8 (+7R). 1982 (0+1R), 1984 (0+2R), 1985 (0+2R), 1987 (2+2R), 1988 (3), 1989 (3). Three tries – 12 points.
DALLAS Brett (Canterbury, Norths): Matches 10. 1993 (1), 1995 (3), 1996 (3). Four tries – 16 points.
DOWLING Greg (Wynnum, Brisbane Norths): Matches 11. 1984 (3), 1985 (3), 1986 (1), 1987 (4). Four tries – 16 points.
DOWLING John (St George): Matches 3. 1982 (3). Points – nil.
FRENCH Brett (Wynnum, Norths): Matches 1 (+7R). 1983 (0+2R), 1984 (1+1R), 1985 (0+1R), 1988 (0+3R). One try – 4 points.
FRENCH Ian (Wynnum, Norths): Matches 3 (+7R). 1985 (1+2R), 1986 (1+2R), 1987 (1+3R). Three tries – 12 points.
FRITZ Darren (Illawarra): Matches 2 (+1R). 1994 (2+1R). Points – nil.
FULLERTON SMITH Wally (Redcliffe, St George): Matches 12. 1983 (3), 1984 (3), 1985 (2), 1988 (3), 1990 (1). Points – nil.
GEE Andrew (Broncos): Matches 7 (+4R). 1990 (0+2R), 1991 (3), 1993 (0+1R), 1994 (2+1R), 1996 (2). One try – 4 points.
GILLMEISTER Trevor (Easts, Broncos, Penrith, Crushers): Matches 14 (+8R). 1987 (4), 1988 (0+2R), 1989 (0+3R), 1990 (1+2R), 1992 (1+1R), 1993 (3), 1994 (2), 1995 (3), 1996 (1). Points – nil.
GODDARD Jamie (Gold Coast): Matches 2 (+1R). 1997 (2+1R). Points – nil.
GREENHILL Craig (Cronulla): Matches 0 (+2R). 1996 (0+2R). Points – nil.
HAGAN Michael (Newcastle): Matches 2 (+3R). 1989 (1+2R), 1990 (1+1R). Points – nil
HANCOCK Michael (Broncos): Matches 13 (+1R). 1989 (3), 1991 (3), 1992 (3), 1993 (1), 1994 (3), 1996 (0+1R). Five tries – 20 points.
HANCOCK Rohan (Toowoomba Wattles): Matches 5. 1980 (1), 1981 (1), 1982 (3). One try – 3 points.
HAUFF Paul (Broncos): Matches 3. 1991 (3). One try – 4 points.
HEARN Tony (Norths, Crushers, St George): Matches 6 (+1R). 1995 (3), 1996 (3), 1997 (0+1R). Points – nil.
HENRICK Ross (Norths Brisbane, Valleys): Matches 2 (+1R). 1981 (1), 1983 (0+1R), 1984 (1). Points – nil.
HEUGH Gavill (Easts Brisbane): Matches 2 (+1R). 1985 (0+1R), 1986 (2). Points – nil.
HOHN Mark (Broncos, Crushers): Matches 3 (+6R). 1993 (2+1R), 1994 (1+2R), 1995 (0+3R). Points – nil.
HOLBEN Greg (Easts Brisbane): Matches 0 (+1R). 1982 (0+1R). Points – nil.
IKIN Ben (Gold Coast, Norths): Matches 3 (+3R). 1995

STATE OF ORIGIN PLAYERS' RECORDS 1980–97

(0+3R), 1997 (3). Two tries – 8 points.
JACKSON Peter (Souths Brisbane, Canberra, Broncos, Norths): Matches 14 (+3R). 1986 (0+2R), 1987 (4), 1988 (3), 1989 (0+1R), 1990 (1), 1991 (3), 1992 (3). Two tries, one goal – 10 points.
JACKSON Steve (Wests, Gold Coast): Matches 5 (+4R). 1990 (0+1R), 1991 (3), 1992 (1+1R), 1993 (1+2R). One try – 4 points.
JONES Gavin (Easts Brisbane, Norths): Matches 3 (+1R). 1983 (0+1R), 1986 (3). Points – nil.
KELLAWAY Bob (Brothers, Souths Brisbane): Matches 0 (+2R). 1982 (0+1R), 1984 (0+1R). Points – nil.
KELLY Stuart (Parramatta): Matches 1 (+2R). 1997 (1+2R). Points – nil.
KHAN Paul (Cronulla, Easts Brisbane): Matches 4. 1981 (1), 1982 (3). Points – nil.
KILROY Joe (Broncos): Matches 2. 1988 (2). One try – 4 points.
KISS Les (Norths): Matches 4. 1986 (2), 1990 (2). Three tries – 12 points.
LAM Adrian (Sydney City): Matches 6 (+3R). 1995 (3), 1996 (0+3R), 1997 (3). Two tries – 8 points.
LANG Johnny (Easts): Matches 1. 1980 (1). Points – nil.
LANGER Allan (Ipswich, Broncos): Matches 27. 1987 (4), 1988 (3), 1989 (2), 1990 (3), 1991 (3), 1992 (3), 1993 (3), 1994 (3), 1996 (3). Seven tries, 1 field goal – 29 points.
LARSON Gary (Norths): Matches 21. 1991 (3) 1992 (3), 1993 (3), 1994 (3), 1995 (3), 1996 (3), 1997 (3). Points – nil.
LEWIS Wally (Valleys, Wynnum, Broncos, Gold Coast): Matches 31. 1980 (1), 1981 (1), 1982 (3), 1983 (3), 1984 (3), 1985 (3), 1986 (3), 1987 (4), 1988 (2), 1989 (3), 1990 (2), 1991 (3). Seven tries, 1 goal, 2 field goals – 30 points.
LINDNER Bob (Souths Brisbane, Wynnum, Broncos, Gold Coast, Wests, Illawarra): Matches 22 (+3R). 1984 (1+2R), 1985 (2), 1986 (3), 1987 (3), 1988 (3), 1989 (2), 1990 (3), 1991 (0+1R), 1992 (2), 1993 (3). Seven tries – 28 points.
McCABE Paul (Easts, Manly): Matches 5. 1981 (1), 1982 (3), 1985 (1). Points – nil.
McINDOE Alan (Illawarra, Penrith): Matches 9. 1988 (3), 1989 (3), 1990 (3). Three tries – 12 points.
McLEAN Mike (Newcastle, Gold Coast): Matches 4 (+1R). 1991 (3), 1992 (1+1R). Points – nil.
MENINGA Mal (Souths Brisbane, Canberra): Matches 32. 1980 (1), 1981 (1), 1982 (2), 1983 (3), 1984 (3), 1985 (3), 1986 (3), 1988 (2), 1990 (2), 1991 (3), 1992 (3), 1993 (3), 1994 (3). Six tries, 69 goals – 161 points.
MILES Gene (Wynnum, Broncos): Matches 19 (+1R). 1982 (2+1R), 1983 (3), 1984 (2), 1986 (3), 1987 (4), 1988 (2), 1989 (3). Six tries – 25 points.
MOORE Billy (Norths): Matches 15 (+2R). 1992 (2), 1993 (1+2R), 1994 (3), 1995 (3), 1996 (3), 1997 (3). One try – 4 points.
MOORE Danny (Manly): Matches 4. 1995 (3), 1997 (1). One try – 4 points.
MORRIS Rod (Balmain, Wynnum): Matches 4. 1980 (1), 1981 (1), 1982 (2). Points – nil.
MURRAY Mark (Norths Brisbane, Valleys, Redcliffe): Matches 14 (+1R). 1981 (0+1R), 1982 (3), 1983 (3), 1984 (2), 1985 (3), 1986 (3). One try – 4 points.
NIEBLING Bryan (Valleys, Redcliffe): Matches 9. 1983 (3), 1984 (2), 1986 (3), 1987 (2). One try – 4 points.
O'BRIEN Clinton (Crushers): Matches 1 (+1R). 1997 (1+1R). Points – nil.
O'DAVIS Robbie (Newcastle): Matches 7. 1995 (3), 1996 (1), 1997 (3). One try – four points.
OLIPHANT Greg (Balmain): Matches 1. 1980 (1). Points – nil.

O'NEILL Julian (Broncos, Western Reds, Souths): Matches 6 (+2R). 1993 (1+1R), 1994 (3), 1996 (1), 1997 (1+1R). Two tries, nine goals, 26 points.
PHELAN Chris (Souths Brisbane, Parramatta): Matches 2. 1981 (1), 1984 (1). Points – nil.
QUINN Graham (St George): Matches 1. 1982 (1). Points – nil.
REDDY Rod (St George): Matches 1. 1980 (1). Points – nil.
RENOUF Steve (Broncos): Matches 6 (+2R). 1991 (0+1R), 1992 (0+1R), 1993 (1), 1994 (2), 1996 (3). Two tries – 8 points.
RIBOT John (Manly, Redcliffe): Matches 8. 1982 (3), 1983 (1), 1984 (1), 1985 (3). Three tries – 10 points.
RIX Grant (Valleys): Matches 0 (+1R). 1986 (0+1R). Points – nil.
SAILOR Wendell (Broncos): Matches 3. 1996 (3). Points – nil.
SCHLOSS Jeremy (Gold Coast): Matches 0 (+3R). 1997 (0+3R). Points – nil.
SCOTT Colin (Easts Brisbane, Wynnum): Matches 16 (+2R). 1980 (1). 1981 (1), 1982 (2), 1983 (3), 1984 (3), 1985 (3), 1986 (1), 1987 (2+2R). One try, 2 goals – 8 points.
SHEARER Dale (Manly, Broncos, Gold Coast, Crushers): Matches 21 (+5R). 1985 (3), 1986 (3), 1987 (4), 1989 (1+2R), 1990 (3), 1991 (0+2R), 1992 (3), 1993 (2+1R), 1995 (1), 1996 (1). Twelve tries, nine goals – 66 points.
SING Matt (Penrith, Sydney City): Matches 8. 1995 (3), 1996 (2), 1997 (3). One try – four points.
SMITH Alan (Norths): Matches 1. 1980 (1). Points – nil.
SMITH Craig (Illawarra): Matches 2 (+1R). 1997 (2+1R). Points – nil.
SMITH Gary (Brothers): Matches 0 (+1R). 1987 (0+1R). Points – nil.
SMITH Darren (Canterbury): Matches 0 (+7R). 1992 (0+2R), 1993 (0+2R), 1994 (0+3R). Points – nil.
SMITH Jason (Canterbury, Parramatta): Matches 6 (+3R). 1994 (1), 1995 (2), 1996 (1+2R), 1997 (2+1R). One try – 4 points.
STACEY Steve (Easts Brisbane): Matches 2. 1983 (2). One try – 4 points.
STAINS Dan (Cronulla): Matches 4. 1989 (2), 1990 (2). Points – nil.
TALLIS Gorden (St George): Matches 0 (+2R). 1994 (0+2R). Points – nil.
TEEVAN Craig (Crushers): Matches 0 (+3R). 1995 (0+3R). Points – nil.
TESSMANN Brad (Souths Brisbane, Easts): Matches 4 (+1R). 1983 (3), 1986 (1+1R). Points – nil.
THORN Brad (Broncos): Matches 3. 1996 (3). Points – nil.
TIERNEY Neil (Manly): Matches 3. 1997 (3). Points – nil.
TRONC Scott (Wests): Matches 0 (+1R). 1988 (0+1R). Points – nil.
VAUTIN Paul (Manly, Easts): Matches 20 (+2R). 1982 (1+2R), 1983 (3), 1984 (2), 1985 (3), 1987 (4), 1988 (3), 1989 (3), 1990 (1). Two tries – 7 points.
VOWLES Adrian (Gold Coast): Matches 0 (+1R). 1994 (0+1R). Points – nil.
WALKER Bruce (Manly): Matches 1. 1982 (1). Points – nil.
WALTERS Kerrod (Broncos): Matches 6. 1989 (3), 1990 (2), 1994 (1). Two tries – 8 points.
WALTERS Kevin (Canberra, Broncos): Matches 6 (+9R). 1989 (0+1R), 1990 (0+2R), 1991 (0+2R), 1992 (1+2R), 1993 (2+1R), 1994 (3), 1996 (0+1R). One try – 4 points.
WALTERS Steve (Canberra): Matches 14. 1990 (1), 1991 (3), 1992 (3), 1993 (3), 1994 (2), 1996 (2). One try – 4 points.

AUSTRALIAN TEST RESULTS 1908-97

AUSTRALIA'S TEST RECORD

Australia v.	P	W	L	D
Great Britain	111	54	53	4
New Zealand	76	54	21	1
France	46	32	12	2
Papua New Guinea	7	7	-	-
South Africa	3	3	-	-
England	2	1	1	-
Fiji	2	2	-	-
Rest of the World	1	1	-	-
TOTALS	248	154	87	7

AUSTRALIA v GREAT BRITAIN

1908	Australia	22	England	22	London	2,000
1909	England	15	Australia	5	Newcastle	22,000
1909	England	6	Australia	5	Birmingham	9,000
1910	England	27	Australia	20	Sydney	42,000
1910	England	22	Australia	17	Brisbane	18,000
1911	Australasia	19	England	10	Newcastle	6,500
1911	Australasia	11	England	11	Edinburgh	6,000
1911	Australasia	33	England	8	Birmingham	4,000
1914	England	23	Australia	5	Sydney	40,000
1914	Australia	12	England	7	Sydney	55,000
1914	England	14	Australia	6	Sydney	34,420
1920	Australia	8	England	4	Brisbane	20,000
1920	Australia	21	England	8	Sydney	40,000
1920	England	23	Australia	13	Sydney	32,000
1921	England	6	Australia	5	Leeds	32,000
1921	Australia	16	England	2	Hull	21,504
1922	England	6	Australia	0	Salford	21,000
1924	England	22	Australia	3	Sydney	50,000
1924	England	5	Australia	3	Sydney	33,842
1924	Australia	21	England	11	Brisbane	36,000
1928	England	15	Australia	12	Brisbane	39,200
1928	England	8	Australia	0	Sydney	44,548
1928	Australia	21	England	14	Sydney	37,380
1929	Australia	31	England	8	Hull	20,000
1929	England	9	Australia	3	Leeds	31,402
1930	Australia	0	England	0	Swinton	34,709
1930	England	3	Australia	0	Rochdale	16,743
1932	England	8	Australia	6	Sydney	70,204
1932	Australia	15	England	6	Brisbane	26,574
1932	England	18	Australia	13	Sydney	50,053
1933	England	4	Australia	0	Manchester	34,000
1933	England	7	Australia	5	Leeds	29,618
1933	England	19	Australia	16	Swinton	10,990
1936	Australia	24	England	8	Sydney	63,920
1936	England	12	Australia	7	Brisbane	29,486
1936	England	12	Australia	7	Sydney	53,546
1937	England	5	Australia	4	Leeds	31,949
1937	England	13	Australia	3	Swinton	31,724
1937	Australia	13	England	3	Huddersfield	9,093
1946	Australia	8	England	8	Sydney	64,527
1946	England	14	Australia	5	Brisbane	40,500
1946	England	20	Australia	7	Sydney	35,294
1948	GB	23	Australia	21	Leeds	36,529
1948	GB	16	Australia	7	Swinton	36,354
1949	GB	23	Australia	9	Bradford	42,000
1950	GB	6	Australia	4	Sydney	47,215
1950	Australia	15	GB	3	Brisbane	35,000
1950	Australia	5	GB	2	Sydney	47,178
1952	GB	19	Australia	6	Leeds	34,505
1952	GB	21	Australia	5	Swinton	32,421
1952	Australia	27	GB	7	Bradford	30,509
1954	Australia	37	GB	12	Sydney	65,884
1954	GB	38	Australia	21	Brisbane	46,355

AUSTRALIAN TEST RESULTS 1908-97

Year	Team1	Score1	Team2	Score2	Venue	Attendance
1954	Australia	20	GB	16	Sydney	67,577
1956	GB	21	Australia	10	Wigan	22,473
1956	Australia	22	GB	9	Bradford	23,634
1956	GB	19	Australia	0	Swinton	17,542
1958	Australia	25	GB	8	Sydney	68,777
1958	GB	25	Australia	18	Brisbane	32,965
1958	GB	40	Australia	17	Sydney	68,720
1959	Australia	22	GB	14	Swinton	35,224
1959	GB	11	Australia	10	Leeds	30,184
1959	GB	18	Australia	12	Wigan	26,089
1962	GB	31	Australia	12	Sydney	70,174
1962	GB	17	Australia	10	Brisbane	34,766
1962	Australia	18	GB	17	Sydney	42,104
1963	Australia	28	GB	2	London	13,946
1963	Australia	50	GB	12	Swinton	30,833
1963	GB	16	Australia	5	Leeds	20,497
1966	GB	17	Australia	13	Sydney	57,962
1966	Australia	6	GB	4	Brisbane	45,057
1966	Australia	19	GB	14	Sydney	63,503
1967	GB	16	Australia	11	Leeds	22,293
1967	Australia	17	GB	11	London	17,445
1967	Australia	11	GB	3	Swinton	13,615
1970	Australia	37	GB	15	Brisbane	42,807
1970	GB	28	Australia	7	Sydney	60,962
1970	GB	21	Australia	17	Sydney	61,258
1973	GB	21	Australia	12	London	9,874
1973	Australia	14	GB	6	Leeds	16,674
1973	Australia	15	GB	5	Warrington	10,019
1974	Australia	12	GB	6	Brisbane	30,280
1974	GB	16	Australia	11	Sydney	48,006
1974	Australia	22	GB	18	Sydney	55,505
1978	Australia	15	GB	9	Wigan	17,664
1978	GB	18	Australia	14	Bradford	26,447
1978	Australia	23	GB	6	Leeds	29,627
1979	Australia	35	GB	0	Brisbane	23,051
1979	Australia	24	GB	16	Sydney	26,387
1979	Australia	28	GB	2	Sydney	16,844
1982	Australia	40	GB	4	Hull	26,771
1982	Australia	27	GB	6	Wigan	23,216
1982	Australia	32	GB	8	Leeds	17,318
1984	Australia	25	GB	8	Sydney	30,190
1984	Australia	18	GB	6	Brisbane	26,534
1984	Australia	20	GB	7	Sydney	18,756
1986	Australia	38	GB	16	Manchester	50,583
1986	Australia	34	GB	4	Leeds	30,908
1986	Australia	24	GB	15	Wigan	20,169
1988	Australia	17	GB	6	Sydney	24,202
1988	Australia	34	GB	14	Brisbane	27,130
1988	GB	26	Australia	12	Sydney	15,944
1990	GB	19	Australia	12	London	54,569
1990	Australia	14	GB	10	Manchester	46,615
1990	Australia	14	GB	0	Leeds	32,500
1992	Australia	22	GB	6	Sydney	40,141
1992	GB	33	Australia	10	Melbourne	31,005
1992	Australia	16	GB	10	Brisbane	32,300
1994	GB	8	Australia	4	London	57,034
1994	Australia	38	GB	8	Manchester	43,930
1994	Australia	23	GB	4	Leeds	39,468

* Although representative of the whole of Great Britain, British teams played as "England" until 1948.

AUSTRALIA v FRANCE

Year	Team1	Score1	Team2	Score2	Venue	Attendance
1938	Australia	35	France	6	Paris	11,500
1938	Australia	16	France	11	Marseilles	24,000
1949	Australia	29	France	10	Marseilles	15,796
1949	Australia	10	France	0	Bordeaux	17,365
1951	France	26	Australia	15	Sydney	60,160

1951	Australia	23	France	11	Brisbane	35,000
1951	France	35	Australia	14	Sydney	67,009
1952	Australia	16	France	12	Paris	18,327
1952	France	5	Australia	0	Bordeaux	23,419
1953	France	13	Australia	5	Lyons	17,454
1955	Australia	20	France	8	Sydney	67,748
1955	France	29	Australia	28	Brisbane	45,745
1955	France	8	Australia	5	Sydney	62,458
1956	Australia	15	France	8	Paris	10,789
1956	Australia	10	France	6	Bordeaux	11,379
1957	Australia	25	France	21	Lyons	5,743
1959	Australia	20	France	19	Paris	9,864
1959	Australia	17	France	2	Bordeaux	8,848
1960	Australia	16	France	8	Roanne	3,437
1960	Australia	8	France	8	Sydney	49,868
1960	Australia	56	France	6	Brisbane	32,644
1960	France	7	Australia	5	Sydney	29,127
1963	France	8	Australia	5	Bordeaux	4,261
1963	Australia	21	France	9	Toulouse	6,932
1964	Australia	16	France	8	Paris	5,979
1964	Australia	20	France	6	Sydney	20,270
1964	Australia	27	France	2	Brisbane	20,076
1964	Australia	35	France	9	Sydney	16,731
1967	Australia	7	France	7	Marcoilles	5,193
1967	France	10	Australia	3	Carcassonne	4,193
1967	France	16	Australia	13	Toulouse	5,000
1973	Australia	21	France	11	Perpignan	7,630
1973	Australia	14	France	3	Toulouse	5,000
1978	France	13	Australia	10	Carcassonne	7,000
1978	France	11	Australia	10	Toulouse	7,060
1981	Australia	43	France	3	Sydney	16,277
1981	Australia	17	France	2	Brisbane	14,000
1982	Australia	15	France	4	Avignon	8,000
1982	Australia	23	France	9	Narbonne	7,000
1986	Australia	44	France	2	Perpignan	6,000
1986	Australia	52	France	0	Carcassonne	5,000
1990	Australia	34	France	2	Parkes	12,348
1990	Australia	60	France	4	Avignon	3,000
1990	Australia	34	France	10	Perpignan	2,000
1994	Australia	58	France	0	Parramatta	27,318
1994	Australia	74	France	0	Bezier	6,000

AUSTRALIA v NEW ZEALAND

1908	NZ	11	Australia	10	Sydney	20,000
1908	NZ	24	Australia	12	Brisbane	6,000
1908	Australia	14	NZ	9	Sydney	13,000
1909	NZ	19	Australia	11	Sydney	6,000
1909	Australia	10	NZ	5	Brisbane	6,000
1909	Australia	25	NZ	5	Sydney	6,000
1919	Australia	44	NZ	21	Wellington	8,000
1919	NZ	26	Australia	10	Christchurch	7,200
1919	Australia	34	NZ	23	Auckland	24,300
1919	Australia	32	NZ	2	Auckland	15,000
1935	NZ	22	Australia	14	Auckland	20,000
1935	Australia	29	NZ	8	Auckland	8,000
1935	Australia	31	NZ	8	Auckland	20,000
1937	Australia	12	NZ	8	Auckland	12,000
1937	NZ	16	Australia	15	Auckland	25,000
1948	NZ	21	Australia	19	Sydney	55,866
1948	Australia	10	NZ	4	Brisbane	23,013
1949	NZ	26	Australia	21	Wellington	7,737
1949	Australia	13	NZ	10	Auckland	12,361
1952	Australia	25	NZ	13	Sydney	56,326
1952	NZ	49	Australia	25	Brisbane	29,245
1952	NZ	19	Australia	9	Sydney	44,916
1953	NZ	25	Australia	5	Christchurch	5,509

AUSTRALIAN TEST RESULTS 1908–97

1953	NZ	12	Australia	11	Wellington	5,394
1953	Australia	18	NZ	16	Auckland	13,350
1956	Australia	12	NZ	9	Sydney	46,766
1956	Australia	8	NZ	2	Brisbane	28,361
1956	Australia	31	NZ	14	Sydney	46,735
1959	Australia	9	NZ	8	Sydney	38,613
1959	Australia	38	NZ	10	Brisbane	30,994
1959	NZ	28	Australia	12	Sydney	31,629
1961	NZ	12	Australia	10	Auckland	11,485
1961	Australia	10	NZ	8	Auckland	12,424
1963	Australia	7	NZ	3	Sydney	48,330
1963	NZ	16	Australia	13	Brisbane	30,748
1963	Australia	14	NZ	0	Sydney	45,567
1965	Australia	13	NZ	8	Auckland	13,295
1965	NZ	7	Australia	5	Auckland	11,383
1967	Australia	22	NZ	13	Sydney	33,416
1967	Australia	35	NZ	22	Brisbane	30,122
1967	Australia	13	NZ	9	Sydney	27,530
1969	Australia	20	NZ	10	Auckland	13,459
1969	NZ	18	Australia	14	Auckland	9,848
1971	NZ	24	Australia	3	Auckland	13,917
1972	Australia	36	NZ	11	Sydney	29,714
1972	Australia	31	NZ	7	Brisbane	24,000
1978	Australia	24	NZ	2	Sydney	16,577
1978	Australia	38	NZ	7	Brisbane	14,000
1978	Australia	33	NZ	16	Sydney	6,541
1980	Australia	27	NZ	6	Auckland	12,321
1980	Australia	15	NZ	6	Auckland	9,706
1982	Australia	11	NZ	8	Brisbane	14,000
1982	Australia	20	NZ	2	Sydney	16,775
1983	Australia	16	NZ	4	Auckland	15,000
1983	NZ	19	Australia	12	Brisbane	20,000
1985	Australia	26	NZ	20	Brisbane	22,000
1985	Australia	10	NZ	6	Auckland	19,132
1985	NZ	18	Australia	0	Auckland	15,327
1986	Australia	22	NZ	8	Auckland	14,566
1986	Australia	29	NZ	12	Sydney	34,302
1986	Australia	32	NZ	12	Brisbane	26,000
1987	NZ	13	Australia	6	Brisbane	16,500
1989	Australia	26	NZ	6	Christchurch	17,000
1989	Australia	8	NZ	0	Rotorua	26,000
1989	Australia	22	NZ	14	Auckland	15,000
1990	Australia	24	NZ	6	Wellington	25,000
1991	NZ	24	Australia	8	Melbourne	26,900
1991	Australia	44	NZ	0	Sydney	34,911
1991	Australia	40	NZ	12	Brisbane	30,000
1993	Australia	14	NZ	14	Auckland	22,994
1993	Australia	16	NZ	8	Palmerston North	19,000
1993	Australia	16	NZ	4	Brisbane	31,000
1995	Australia	26	NZ	10	Brisbane	25,304
1995	Australia	20	NZ	10	Sydney	27,568
1995	Australia	46	NZ	10	Brisbane	20,803
1995	Australia	30	NZ	20	Huddersfield	16,608

AUSTRALIA v SOUTH AFRICA

1963	Australia	34	SA	6	Brisbane	10,210
1963	Australia	54	SA	21	Sydney	16,995
1995	Australia	86	SA	6	Gateshead	9191

AUSTRALIA v PAPUA NEW GUINEA

1982	Australia	38	PNG	2	Port Moresby	15,000
1986	Australia	62	PNG	12	Port Moresby	17,000
1988	Australia	70	PNG	8	Wagga	11,685
1991	Australia	58	PNG	2	Goroka	13,000
1991	Australia	40	PNG	6	Port Moresby	14,500
1992	Australia	36	PNG	14	Townsville	12,470
1996	Australia	52	PNG	6	Port Moresby	15,000

AUSTRALIA V ENGLAND

| 1995 | England | 20 | Australia | 16 | London | 41,271 |
| 1995 | Australia | 16 | England | 8 | London | 66,540 |

AUSTRALIA V FIJI

| 1995 | Australia | 66 | Fiji | 0 | Huddersfield | 7,127 |
| 1996 | Australia | 84 | Fiji | 14 | Newcastle | 19,244 |

AUSTRALIA V REST OF THE WORLD

| 1997 | Australia | 28 | Rest | 8 | Brisbane | 14,927 |

* 1995 World Cup matches were classified as Tests

NOTABLE TEST ACHIEVEMENTS

Biggest win: 86-6 v. South Africa, Gateshead, October 10, 1995
Biggest loss: 49-25 v. New Zealand, Brisbane, June 28, 1952
Most points in a Test: 32 (2 tries, 12 goals), by Andrew Johns v. Fiji, Marathon Stadium, Newcastle, July 12, 1996

Most Points

Player	T	G	FG	Pts
Mal Meninga	21	96	-	272
Michael Cronin	5	93	-	201
Michael O'Connor	17	61	-	190
Graeme Langlands	17	69	-	189
Rod Wishart	13	43	-	138
Noel Pidding	6	53	-	124
Ken Irvine	33	11	-	121
Andrew Johns	5	50	-	120
Keith Barnes	-	54	-	108
Dave Brown	7	26	-	73
Les Johns	2	30	-	66

Note: Up to and including the second Test against France in 1982, tries were worth three points. In all Tests since that match, tries have been worth four points.

Most Goals

Mal Meninga	96
Michael Cronin	93
Graeme Langlands	69
Michael O'Connor	61
Keith Barnes	54
Noel Pidding	53
Andrew Johns	50
Rod Wishart	43
Les Johns	30
Dave Brown	26
Gordon Clifford	24

Most Tries

Ken Irvine	33
Reg Gasnier	26
Mal Meninga	21
Graeme Langlands	17
Michael O'Connor	17
Kerry Boustead	15
Keith Holman	14
Andrew Ettingshausen	14
Rod Wishart	13
Bob Fulton	12
Steve Menzies	12

Most Appearances

Mal Meninga	45
Reg Gasnier	36
Clive Churchill	34
Graeme Langlands	34
Wally Lewis	33
Johnny Raper	33
Keith Holman	32
Ken Irvine	31
Brian Davies	27
Kerry Boustead	25
Ken Kearney	25
Noel Kelly	25
Ian Walsh	25
Andrew Ettingshausen	25
Brad Fittler	23
Bob Lindner	23
Roy Bull	22
Michael Cronin	22
Duncan Hall	22
Barry Muir	22
Ray Price	22
Steve Rogers	21
Paul Sironen	21
Harry Wells	21
Bob Fulton	20
Garry Jack	20
Tom Raudonikis	20
Dale Shearer	20
Craig Young	20

Most Appearances as Captain

Clive Churchill	24
Wally Lewis	23
Mal Meninga	23
Keith Barnes	12
Ian Walsh	10
Max Krilich	10
Brad Fittler	9
Ken Kearney	9
Reg Gasnier	8
Tom Gorman	7
Wally Prigg	7
Graeme Langlands	7
Bob Fulton	7
Dave Brown	6
Arthur Summons	5
George Peponis	5
John Raper	4

AUSTRALIAN TEST RESULTS 1908–97

AUSTRALIAN INTERNATIONALS 1908–1997

Below is the complete list of Australian internationals and their records from 1908 to 1997. Teams in brackets are the clubs the player represented when he wore the Australian jumper.
Key: GB = Great Britain, NZ = New Zealand, F = France, PNG = Papua New Guinea, E = England, FJ = Fiji, SA = South Africa, ROW = Rest of the World, f = Test played in France, w = Test played during World Cup.

ABERCROMBIE Jim (Sydney Wests): Tests 2. GB (2) 1908. 1908-09 Kangaroo tour. Points – nil.
ADAMS Don "Bandy" (Maitland): Tests 5. NZ (3) 1956, GB (1) 1956, F (1) 1956. 1956-57 Kangaroo tour. Five tries – 15 points.
AINSCOUGH Jamie (Newcastle Knights): Tests 1. NZ (1) 1995. One try – 4 points.
ALEXANDER Greg (Penrith): Tests 6. NZ (2) 1989, GB (2) 1990, F (2) 1990 (f). 1986 Kangaroo tour, 1989 NZ tour, 1990 Kangaroo tour. Four tries, 10 goals – 36 points.
AMBRUM George (North Sydney): Tests 2. NZ (2) 1972. Two tries – 6 points.
ANDERSON Chris (Canterbury-Bankstown): Tests 8. GB (3) 1978, F (2) 1978, GB (1) 1979, NZ (2) 1980. 1975 World Series, 1978 Kangaroo tour, 1980 NZ tour, 1982 Kangaroo tour. Points – nil.
ANDERSON Tommy (South Sydney): Tests 1. NZ (1) 1908. 1908-09 Kangaroo tour. One try – 3 points.
ANDERSON Vic (South Brisbane): Tests 1. NZ (1) 1909. Points – nil.
ANDREWS Ned (Mackay): Tests 1. GB (1) 1950. Points – nil.
ANLEZARK Arthur (Lismore): Tests 1. GB (1) 1909. 1908-09 Kangaroo tour. Points – nil.
ARMBRUSTER Vic (Toowoomba, Brisbane Grammars, Brisbane Valleys): Tests 8. GB (2) 1924, GB (3) 1928, GB (3) 1929. 1929-30 Kangaroo tour. Two tries – 6 points.
ARMSTRONG Jim (South Sydney): Tests 1. GB (1) 1946. Points – nil.
ASHTON Ferris (Sydney Easts): Tests 8. NZ (2) 1952, GB (2) 1952, F (3) 1952, NZ (1) 1953. 1952-53 Kangaroo tour, 1953 NZ tour. Two tries – 6 points.
AYLIFFE Royce (Sydney Easts): Tests 1. F (1) 1981. Points – nil.
AYNSLEY Cecil (Brisbane Wests): Tests 4, GB (3) 1924, GB (1) 1928. Three tries, three goals – 15 points.
BACKO Sam (Canberra, Broncos): Tests 6. GB (3) 1988, NZ (3) 1989. 1988 v Rest of the World, 1989 NZ tour. Three tries – 12 points.
BAILEY Bill (Newcastle): 1908-09 Kangaroo tour.
BAILEY Ron (Canterbury-Bankstown): Tests 2. GB (2) 1946. One try – 3 points.
BAIRD Eddie (Brisbane): Tests 1. NZ (1) 1908. Points – nil.
BANKS Gary (Newcastle): Tests 1. GB (1) 1966. One try – 3 points.
BANKS Bob (Toowoomba, Cunnamulla): Tests 13. NZ (3) 1953, GB (2) 1954, GB (3) 1956, F (3) 1956, F (1) 1960, GB (1) 1962. 1953 NZ tour, 1954 World Cup, 1956-57 Kangaroo tour. Two tries, one goal – 8 points.
BARNES Keith (Balmain): Tests 14. NZ (2) 1959, GB (3) 1959, F (3) 1959, F (3) 1960, GB (1) 1962, GB (2) 1966. 1957 World Cup, 1959-60 Kangaroo tour, 1960 World Cup. 54 goals – 108 points.
BARNETT Jack (Newtown): Tests 2. GB (2) 1910. Two tries – 6 points.
BARTRIM Wayne (St George): Tests 6. NZ (2) 1995, E (1) 1995, SA (1) 1995, FJ (1) 1995, PNG (1) 1996. 1995 World Cup. Three tries – 12 points.
BEATH Barry (Eugowra, St George): 1965, 1971 NZ tours.
BEATON Jack (Sydney Easts): Tests 10. GB (3) 1936, NZ (2) 1937, GB (3) 1937, F (2) 1938. 1937-38 Kangaroo tour. One try, 14 goals – 31 points.
BEATTIE Dud (Ipswich): Tests 12. NZ (3) 1959, GB (2) 1959, F (2) 1959, F (1) 1960, NZ (1) 1961, GB (3) 1962. 1959-60 Kangaroo tour, 1960 World Cup, 1961 NZ tour. One try – 3 points.
BEAVEN Ray (Tumut): 1961 NZ tour.
BEETSON Arthur (Balmain, Sydney Easts): Tests 14. GB (1) 1966, GB (3) 1970, NZ (2) 1972, GB (3) 1973, F (2) 1973, GB (3) 1974. 1968 World Cup, 1972 World Cup, 1973 Kangaroo tour, 1975, 1977 World Series. Points – nil.
BELCHER Gary (Canberra): Tests 15. GB (3) 1988, NZ (3) 1989, F (1) 1990, NZ (1) 1990, GB (3) 1990, F (2) 1990 (f), PNG (2) 1991. 1986 Kangaroo tour, 1989 NZ tour, 1990 Kangaroo tour, 1991 PNG tour. Three tries, six goals – 24 points.
BELLA Martin (North Sydney, Manly-Warringah): Tests 9. GB (1) 1988, F (1) 1990, NZ (1) 1990, GB (1) 1990, NZ (3) 1991, PNG (2) 1991. 1986 Kangaroo tour, 1989 NZ tour, 1990 Kangaroo tour, 1991 PNG tour. Points – nil.
BENNETT Jim (Toowoomba): Tests 3. GB (3) 1924. Points – nil.
BENNETT Wayne (Toowoomba): 1971 NZ tour.
BENTON Henry (Townsville): 1948-49 Kangaroo tour.
BERECRY Tom (North Sydney): Tests 1. GB (1) 1911. 1911-12 Kangaroo tour. Two tries – 6 points.
BICHEL Henry (Ipswich): 1935 NZ tour.
BISHOP George (Balmain): Tests 2. GB (2) 1929. 1929-30 Kangaroo tour. One try – 3 points.
BLAIR Alf "Smacker" (South Sydney): Tests 1. GB (1) 1924. Points – nil.
BLINKHORN Cecil (North Sydney, South Sydney): Tests 4. GB (3) 1921, GB (1) 1924. 1921-22 Kangaroo tour. Three tries – 9 points.
BLISS Johnny (Manly-Warringah): Tests 1. F (1) 1951. Points – nil.
BODEN Ron (Toowoomba, Parramatta): Tests 2. F (2) 1960. 1959-60 Kangaroo tour, 1960 World Cup. Points – nil.
BOLEWSKI Henry (Bundaberg): Tests 1. GB (1) 1914. One goal – 2 points.
BOLEWSKI Mick (Bundaberg): Tests 4. GB (3) 1908, NZ (1) 1909. 1908-09 Kangaroo tour. Two tries – 6 points.
BOUSTEAD Kerry (Innisfail, Sydney Easts, Manly-Warringah): Tests 25. NZ (3) 1978, GB (3) 1978, F (2) 1978, GB (2) 1979, NZ (1) 1980, F (1) 1981, GB (3) 1982, F (2) 1982, NZ (2) 1982, PNG (1) 1982, GB (3) 1983, GB (3) 1984. 1978 Kangaroo tour, 1980 NZ tour, 1982 Kangaroo tour. 15 tries – 46 points.
BOYD Les (Sydney Wests, Manly-Warringah): Tests 17. GB (2) 1978, F (1) 1978, GB (3) 1979, NZ (2) 1980, F (2) 1981, F (2) 1982, GB (3) 1982, F (2) 1982. 1978 Kangaroo tour, 1980 NZ tour, 1982 Kangaroo tour. Four tries – 12 points.

BRACKENREG Herb (South Brisbane, North Brisbane): Tests 3. NZ (2) 1909, GB (1) 1910. Seven goals – 14 points
BRADSTREET Bill (Manly-Warringah): Tests 1. GB (1) 1966. Points – nil.
BRANIGHAN Ray (South Sydney, Manly-Warringah): Tests 8. NZ (1) 1971, GB (3) 1973, F (2) 1973, GB (2) 1974. 1970 World Cup, 1971 NZ tour, 1972 World Cup, 1973 Kangaroo tour, 1975 World Series. Two tries, two goals – 10 points.
BRANSON Tony (Nowra, St George): Tests 6. GB (2) 1967, F (3) 1967, NZ (1) 1971. 1967-68 Kangaroo tour, 1968 World Cup, 1971 NZ tour. One try – 3 points.
BRASHER Tim (Balmain): Tests 14. F (1) 1994, GB (1) 1994, F (1) 1994 (f), NZ (3) 1995, E (2) 1995, SA (1) 1995, FJ (1) 1995, NZ (1) 1995 (w), FJ (1) 1996, PNG (1) 1996, ROW (1) 1997. 1992 World Cup, 1994 Kangaroo tour, 1995 World Cup. Nine tries – 36 points.
BRASS John (Sydney Easts): Tests 3. GB (3) 1970. 1975 World Series. Points – nil.
BRENTNALL Greg (Canterbury-Bankstown): Tests 13. NZ (2) 1980, F (2) 1981, NZ (2) 1982, GB (3) 1982, F (2) 1982, PNG (1) 1982, NZ (1) 1983. 1980 NZ tour, 1982 Kangaroo tour. Four tries – 12 points.
BROADFOOT Neville (Grammar Brisbane): Tests 1. GB (1) 1920. 1921-22 Kangaroo tour. Points – nil.
BROGAN Bill (Sydney Wests): Tests 3. GB (3) 1929. 1929-30 Kangaroo tour. Points – nil.
BROOMHAM Albert (North Sydney): Tests 5. NZ (3) 1909, GB (1) 1910, GB (1) 1911. 1911-12 Kangaroo tour. One try – 3 points.
BROSNAN Eddie (Brisbane Brothers): Tests 1. NZ (1) 1948. 1948-49 Kangaroo tour. Points – nil.
BROWN Tony (Newtown): Tests 7. GB (2) 1958, NZ (3) 1959, F (1) 1969, F (1) 1960. 1959-60 Kangaroo tour, 1960 World Cup. Points – nil.
BROWN Dave (Sydney Easts): Tests 9. GB (3) 1933, NZ (3) 1935, GB (3) 1936. 1933-34 Kangaroo tour, 1935 NZ tour. Seven tries, 26 goals – 73 points.
BROWN Dave (Manly-Warringah): Tests 5. NZ (2) 1983, GB (3) 1984. Points – nil.
BROWN Edwin (Toowoomba): 1921-22 Kangaroo tour.
BROWN Johnny (North Brisbane): 1970 World Cup.
BROWN Ray (Manly-Warringah): Tests 5. PNG (1) 1982, GB (?) 1982, F (1) 1982, NZ (1) 1983. 1982 Kangaroo tour. Points – nil.
BUCKLEY Edward (Brisbane Valleys): Tests 1. GB (1) 1910. Points – nil.
BUETTNER Michael (North Sydney): Tests 1. PNG (1) 1996. Two tries – 8 points.
BUGDEN Bob (St George): Tests 2. F (2) 1960. 1959-60 Kangaroo tour. Four tries – 12 points.
BULGIN Vic (Sydney Easts, Bourke): 1948-49 Kangaroo tour, 1949 NZ tour.
BULL Roy (Manly-Warringah): Tests 22. NZ (1) 1949, GB (1) 1952, F (1) 1952, NZ (1) 1953, GB (2) 1954, F (3) 1955, NZ (3) 1956, GB (3) 1956, F (3) 1956. 1949, 1953 New Zealand tours, 1954 World Cup, 1956-57 Kangaroo tour. One try – 3 points.
BUMAN Allan (Newcastle): Tests 2. NZ (2) 1967. 1965 NZ tour. Points – nil.
BURDON Alex (Glebe): Tests 2. GB (2) 1908. 1908-09 Kangaroo tour. Points – nil.
BURGE Frank (Glebe): Tests 13. GB (3) 1914, NZ (4) 1919, GB (3) 1920, GB (3) 1921. 1910 NZ tour, 1921-22 Kangaroo tour. Seven tries, seven goals – 35 points.
BURGE Peter (Glebe): 1911-12 Kangaroo tour.
BURKE Peter (Manly-Warringah): 1959-60 Kangaroo tour.
BUSCH Joe "Chimpy" (Sydney Easts): Tests 6. GB (2) 1928, GB (4) 1929. 1929-30 Kangaroo tour. Points – nil.
BUTLER Arthur (South Sydney): Tests 3. GB (2) 1908, NZ (1) 1909. 1908-09 Kangaroo tour. One try – 3 points.
BYRNE Hugh (Sydney Easts): Tests 1. GB (1) 1928. Points – nil.
CAMPBELL Keith (Parramatta): Tests 1. NZ (1) 1971. 1971 NZ tour. One try – 3 points.
CANN Bill (South Sydney): Tests 8. NZ (1) 1908, NZ (2) 1909, GB (3) 1911, GB (2) 1914. 1908-09 Kangaroo tour, 1911-12 Kangaroo tour. One try, one goal – 5 points.
CAPLES Harry (Sydney Easts): Tests 2. GB (1) 1921. 1921-22 Kangaroo tour. Points – nil.
CARLSON Brian (Wollongong, Newcastle, North Sydney, Blackall): Tests 17. GB (2) 1952, F (1) 1953, GB (2) 1953, GB (3) 1954, GB (3) 1958, NZ (1) 1959, GB (2) 1959, F (2) 1959, NZ (1) 1961. 1952-53 Kangaroo tour, 1953 NZ tour, 1957 World Cup, 1959-60 Kangaroo tour, 1960 World Cup, 1961 NZ tour. Ten tries, five goals – 40 points.
CARNE Willie (Brisbane Broncos): Tests 9. NZ (2) 1991, PNG (2) 1991, GB (1) 1992, PNG (1) 1992, NZ (3) 1993. 1991 PNG tour, 1992 World Cup, 1993 NZ tour. Ten tries – 40 points.
CARROLL Mark (South Sydney, Manly-Warringah): Tests 12. F (1) 1990, NZ (3) 1995, E (2) 1995, SA (1) 1995, FJ (1) 1995, NZ (1) 1995 (w), FJ (1) 1996, PNG (1) 1996, ROW (1) 1997. 1990 Kangaroo tour, 1995 World Cup. Points – nil.
CARSON Bill (Sydney Wests): Tests 2. GB (2) 1962. Points – nil.
CARSTAIRS George (St George): Tests 2. GB (1) 1921. 1921-22 Kangaroo tour. Points – nil.
CARTWRIGHT John (Penrith): Tests 6. GB (1) 1990, NZ (3) 1991, GB (1) 1992, PNG (1) 1992. 1990 Kangaroo tour, 1992 World Cup. Points – nil.
CAVANAGH Noel (Brisbane Brothers): 1965 NZ tour.
CHAPMAN Darrell (Kempsey): 1959-60 Kangaroo tour.
CHEADLE Frank (Newtown): Tests 5. NZ (3) 1908, NZ (2) 1909. 1908-09 Kangaroo tour. Points – nil.
CHRISTIE Bill (Coorparoo): Tests 1. GB (1) 1932. Points – nil.
CHURCHILL Clive (South Sydney): Tests 34. NZ (1) 1948, GB (3) 1948, F (2) 1949, NZ (2) 1949, GB (3) 1950, F (3) 1951, NZ (3) 1952, GB (3) 1952, F (3) 1952, NZ (3) 1953, GB (3) 1954, F (3) 1955, GB (1) 1956, F (1) 1956. 1948-49 Kangaroo tour, 1949 NZ tour, 1952-53 Kangaroo tour, 1953 NZ tour, 1954 World Cup, 1956-57 Kangaroo tour. Ten goals – 20 points.
CLAY Brian (St George): Tests 5. GB (3) 1959, F (2) 1959. 1957 World Cup, 1959-60 Kangaroo tour. Points – nil.
CLEAL Noel (Manly-Warringah): Tests 8. NZ (2) 1985, NZ (3) 1986, PNG (1) 1986, GB (2) 1986. 1985 NZ tour, 1986 Kangaroo tour. Three tries – 12 points.
CLEARY John (Ipswich): 1963-64 Kangaroo tour.
CLEARY Michael (South Sydney): Tests 8. GB (1) 1962, NZ (1) 1963, F (1) 1963, F (3) 1964, NZ (2) 1965. 1963-64 Kangaroo tour, 1965, 1969 NZ tours. Five tries – 15 points.
CLIFFORD Gordon (Newtown): Tests 8. NZ (1) 1956, GB (2) 1956, F (2) 1956, GB (3) 1958. 1956-57 Kangaroo tour. 24 goals – 48 points.
CLOSE Chris (Redcliffe, Manly-Warringah): Tests 3. NZ (3) 1985. 1980, 1985 NZ tours. One try – 4 points.
CLUES Arthur (Sydney Wests): Tests 3. GB (3) 1946. Points – nil.
CLYDE Bradley (Canberra): Tests 18. NZ (3) 1989, NZ (3) 1991, PNG (2) 1991, GB (3) 1992, NZ (3) 1993, GB

(3) 1994, F (1) 1994 (f). 1989 NZ tour, 1991 PNG tour, 1992 World Cup, 1993 NZ tour, 1994 Kangaroo tour. Six tries – 24 points.
COLLINS Edward (North Brisbane): 1935 NZ tour, 1937-38 Kangaroo tour.
COLLINSON Arthur (Sydney Wests): Tests 3. GB (2) 1952, F (1) 1952. 1952-53 Kangaroo tour. Points – nil.
CONESCU Greg (North Brisbane, Redcliffe, Gladstone, Broncos): Tests 9. GB (3) 1984, NZ (2) 1985, GB (3) 1988, PNG (1) 1988. 1982 Kangaroo tour, 1985 NZ tour, 1988 v Rest of the World. Two tries – 8 points.
CONLON Albert (Glebe): Tests 3. GB (1) 1909, NZ (2) 1909. 1908-09 Kangaroo tour. One try – 3 points.
CONLON Ross (Canterbury-Bankstown): Tests 1. GB (1) 1984. Four goals – 8 points.
CONNELL Cyril (Rockhampton): Tests 2. NZ (2) 1956. 1956-57 Kangaroo tour. Points – nil.
CONNELL Geoff (Brisbane Easts): Tests 1. NZ (1) 1967. Points – nil.
COOPER Lionel (Sydney Easts): Tests 3. GB (3) 1946. Two tries – 6 points.
COOTE Ron (South Sydney, Sydney Easts): Tests 13. GB (2) 1967, F (3) 1967, NZ (2) 1969, GB (3) 1970, GB (3) 1974. 1967-68 Kangaroo tour, 1968 World Cup, 1969 NZ tour, 1970 World Cup, 1975 World Series. Seven tries – 21 points.
COOTES John (Newcastle): Tests 4. NZ (2) 1969, GB (2) 1970. 1969 NZ tour, 1970 World Cup. One try – 3 points.
COROWA Larry (Balmain): Tests 2. GB (2) 1979. 1978 Kangaroo tour. One try – 3 points.
COSTELLO Ron (Illawarra Collegians, Canterbury-Bankstown): Tests 3. NZ (1) 1969, GB (1) 1970, NZ (1) 1971. 1969 NZ tour, 1970 World Cup, 1971 NZ tour. Points – nil.
COURTNEY Tedda (Newtown, North Sydney, Sydney Wests): Tests 11. GB (3) 1908, NZ (2) 1909, GB (1) 1910, GB (2) 1911, GB (3) 1914. 1908-09 Kangaroo tour, 1911-12 Kangaroo tour. One try – 3 points.
COWIE Les (South Sydney): Tests 6. NZ (2) 1949, GB (3) 1950, NZ (1) 1953. 1948-49 Kangaroo tour, 1953 NZ tour. One try – 3 points.
COYNE Gary (Canberra): Tests 2. PNG (2) 1991. 1991 PNG tour. Points – nil.
COYNE Mark (St George): Tests 9. NZ (2) 1995, E (2) 1995, FJ (1) 1995, NZ (1) 1995 (w), FJ (1) 1996, PNG (1) 1996. 1995 World Cup, ROW (1) 1997. Two tries – 8 points.
CRAIG Jimmy (Balmain, Ipswich): Tests 7. GB (1) 1921, GB (3) 1924, GB (3) 1928. 1921-22 Kangaroo tour. Six goals – 12 points.
CRAIG Robert (Balmain): Tests 7. GB (2) 1910, GB (3) 1911, GB (2) 1914. 1911-12 Kangaroo tour. One try – 3 points.
CREAR Steve (Brisbane Wests): 1977 World Series.
CREMA Angelo (Tully): Tests 1. GB (1) 1966. Points – nil.
CRIPPIN Arch (North Sydney): Tests 3. GB (3) 1936. One try – 3 points.
CROCKER Harold "Mick" (South Brisbane, Parramatta): Tests 15. GB (2) 1950, F (3) 1951, NZ (1) 1952, GB (1) 1952, F (1) 1953, NZ (3) 1953, GB (2) 1954, F (2) 1955. 1952-53 Kangaroo tour, 1953 NZ tour. Three tries – 9 points.
CRONIN Michael (Gerringong, Parramatta): Tests 22. F (2) 1973, GB (3) 1974, NZ (3) 1978, GB (3) 1978, F (2) 1978, GB (3) 1979, NZ (2) 1980, F (2) 1981, NZ (2) 1982. 1973 Kangaroo tour, 1975 World Series, 1977 World Series, 1978 Kangaroo tour, 1980 NZ tour. Five tries, 93 goals – 201 points.
CROWE Ron (West Wyalong): Tests 5. NZ (2) 1961, F (2) 1964, GB (1) 1966. 1961 NZ tour. Points – nil.
CUBITT Les (Sydney Easts): Tests 4. NZ (4) 1919. 1919 NZ tour, 1921-22 Kangaroo tour. Five tries – 15 points.
CURRAN Frank (South Sydney): Tests 10. NZ (3) 1935, GB (3) 1936, GB (2) 1937, F (2) 1938. 1933-34 Kangaroo tour, 1935 NZ tour, 1937-38 Kangaroo tour. One try – 3 points.
CURRIE Tony (Canterbury-Bankstown, Broncos): Tests 7. GB (3) 1988, PNG (1) 1988, NZ (3) 1989. 1989 NZ tour. Two tries – 8 points.
DALEY Laurie (Canberra): Tests 19. F (1) 1990, NZ (1) 1990, GB (2) 1990, F (1) 1990 (f), NZ (2) 1991, GB (3) 1992, PNG (1) 1992, NZ (3) 1993, F (1) 1994, GB (3) 1994, F (1) 1994 (f). 1990 Kangaroo tour, 1993 NZ tour, 1994 Kangaroo tour. 11 tries, 2 field goals – 46 points.
DALEY Phil (Manly-Warringah): Tests 3. GB (2) 1988, PNG (1) 1988. 1986 Kangaroo tour. Points – nil.
DALLAS Brett (Sydney Bulldogs, North Sydney): Tests 6. NZ (1) 1995, SA (1) 1995, FJ (1) 1995, NZ (1) 1995 (w), E (1) 1995, FJ (1) 1996. 1995 World Cup. Nine tries – 36 points.
DARMODY Steve (South Sydney): 1911-12 Kangaroo tour.
DAVIDSON Les (South Sydney): Tests 4. GB (1) 1986, F(2) 1986, NZ (1) 1987. 1986 Kangaroo tour. Points – nil.
DAVIES Brian (Brisbane Brothers): Tests 27. F (3) 1951, NZ (2) 1952, GB (3) 1952, F (3) 1952, NZ (3) 1953, GB (1) 1954, F (1) 1955, NZ (3) 1956, GB (2) 1956, F (1) 1956, GB (3) 1958. 1952-53 Kangaroo tour, 1953 NZ tour, 1954 World Cup, 1956-57 Kangaroo tour, 1957 World Cup. Five tries, six goals – 27 points.
DAVIS James (South Sydney): Tests 3. NZ (2) 1908, NZ (1) 1909. 1908-09 Kangaroo tour. One try, one goal – 5 points.
DAWSON Les (Newcastle): Tests 5. NZ (1) 1937, GB (2) 1937, F (2) 1938. 1937-38 Kangaroo tour. Three tries – 9 points.
DAY Ken (Brisbane Wests): Tests 9. NZ (3) 1963, SA (2) 1963, GB (1) 1963, F (1) 1963, F (2) 1964. 1961 NZ tour, 1963-64 Kangaroo tour. Three tries – 9 points.
DEANE Sid (North Sydney): Tests 5. GB (2) 1908, GB (3) 1914. 1908-09 Kangaroo tour. One try – 3 points.
DE BELIN Fred (Balmain): Tests 8. NZ (2) 1948, GB (1) 1949, F (2) 1949, NZ (1) 1949, GB (2) 1950. 1948-49 Kangaroo tour, 1949 NZ tour. Two tries – 6 points.
DELAMERE Bill (Manly-Warringah): 1959-60 Kangaroo tour.
DEMPSEY Dan (Ipswich): Tests 7. GB (1) 1928, GB (1) 1929, GB (2) 1932, GB (1) 1933. 1929-30, 1933-34 Kangaroo tours. Points – nil.
DENMAN Jeff (Brisbane Easts): 1969 NZ tour.
DENNY Henry (Brisbane Wests): 1933-34 Kangaroo tour.
DEVEREUX Jim (North Sydney): Tests 5. NZ (3) 1908, GB (2) 1908. 1908-09 Kangaroo tour. Three tries, one goal – 11 points.
DEVERY Pat (Balmain): Tests 3. GB (3) 1946. Points – nil.
DICKENS Harry (Brisbane Valleys): Tests 1. NZ (1) 1909. Points – nil.
DIMOND Peter (Sydney Wests): Tests 10. GB (2) 1958, GB (1) 1962, GB (3) 1963, F (3) 1963, GB (1) 1966. 1963-64 Kangaroo tour. Three tries – 9 points.
DIMOND Bobby (Dapto): 1948-49 Kangaroo tour.
DIVERSI Peter (North Sydney): Tests 2. GB (1) 1954, F (1) 1955. 1954 World Cup. One try – 3 points.
DOBBS Alf "Bullock" (Balmain): 1908-09 Kangaroo tour.
DONNELLY John (Sydney Wests): Tests 1. NZ (1) 1978. 1975 World Series. Points – nil.

DONOGHUE Denis (South Sydney): Tests 2. F (2) 1951. Points – nil.
DONOHOE Col (Sydney Easts): Tests 2. NZ (1) 1952, GB (1) 1952. 1952-53 Kangaroo tour. Points – nil.
DOONAR Frank (Ipswich): 1933-34 Kangaroo tour.
DORAHY John (Sydney Wests): Tests 2. NZ (2) 1978. One try – 3 points.
DORE Mike (Brisbane): Tests 3. NZ (2) 1908, NZ (1) 1909. Points – nil.
DOWLING Garry (Parramatta): Tests 2. NZ (2) 1980. 1980 NZ tour. Points – nil.
DOWLING Greg (Wynnum-Manly, North Brisbane): Tests 12. GB (3) 1984, NZ (3) 1985, GB (3) 1986, F (2) 1986, NZ (1) 1987. 1985 NZ tour, 1986 Kangaroo tour. Points – nil.
DOYLE Ian "Ripper" (Toowoomba): Tests 7. NZ (3) 1956, GB (2) 1956, F (2) 1956. 1956-57 Kangaroo tour. Points – nil.
DOYLE Joe (Toowoomba): Tests 1. GB (1) 1933. 1933-34 Kangaroo tour. Points – nil.
DRAKE Frank (South Brisbane): Tests 2. NZ (1) 1961, GB (1) 1962. 1961 NZ tour. One try – 3 points.
DREW Bernie (Bundaberg, Ipswich): Tests 3. F (2) 1951, NZ (1) 1953. 1953 NZ tour. Points – nil
DUFFIN George (Toombul). Tests 1. NZ (1) 1909 Points – nil.
DUNCAN Rees (Kurri Kurri): Tests 2. NZ (2) 1952. 1952-53 Kangaroo tour. Points – nil.
DUNN Paul (Canterbury-Bankstown): Tests 6. PNG (1) 1986, GB (2) 1986, F (2) 1986, PNG (1) 1988. 1986 Kangaroo tour, 1988 World Cup. Points – nil.
DYMOCK Jim (Sydney Bulldogs, Parramatta): Tests 6. E (2) 1995, SA (1) 1995, FJ (1) 1995, NZ (1) 1995 (w), FJ (1) 1996. 1995 World Cup. One try – 4 points.
EADIE Graham (Manly-Warringah): Tests 12. GB (2) 1973, GB (1) 1974, NZ (1) 1978, GB (3) 1978, F (2) 1978, GB (3) 1979. 1973 Kangaroo, 1975, 1977 World Series, 1978 Kangaroo. Two tries, five goals – 16 points.
EATHER Trevor (Boggabri): Tests 1. GB (1) 1946. Points – nil.
EDWARDS Arthur (Brisbane Valleys): Tests 1. GB (1) 1928. Points – nil.
ELFORD John (Sydney Wests): Tests 2. NZ (2) 1972. 1972 World Cup. Two tries – 6 points.
ELIAS Ben (Balmain): Tests 5. NZ (1) 1985, GB (2) 1990, F (2) 1990 (f). 1985 NZ tour, 1986 Kangaroo tour, 1988 World Cup, 1990 Kangaroo tour. One try – 4 points.
ELLA Steve (Parramatta): Tests 4. NZ (1) 1983, NZ (3) 1985. 1982 Kangaroo tour, 1985 NZ tour. One try, 4 points.
ETTINGSHAUSEN Andrew (Cronulla-Sutherland): Tests 25. GB (3) 1988, F (1) 1990, NZ (1) 1990, QD (3) 1990, F (2) 1990 (f), NZ (3) 1991, PNG (2) 1991, GB (3) 1992, NZ (2) 1993, F (1) 1994, GB (3) 1994, F (1) 1994 (f). 1988 v Rest of the World, 1990 Kangaroo tour, 1991 PNG tour, 1993 NZ tour, 1994 Kangaroo tour. 14 tries – 56 points.
FAHEY Terry (Wellington, South Sydney, Sydney Easts): Tests 3. NZ (1) 1978, GB (1) 1979, F (1) 1981. 1975, 1977 World Series. Three tries – 9 points.
FAIRALL Percy (St George): Tests 5. NZ (3) 1935, GB (2) 1936. 1935 NZ tour, 1937-38 Kangaroo tour. Two tries – 6 points.
FAIRLEIGH David (North Sydney): Tests 5. F (1) 1994, GB (1) 1994, F (1) 1994 (f), FJ (1) 1996, PNG (1) 1996. 1994 Kangaroo tour. Two tries – 8 points.
FARNSWORTH Viv (Newtown, Sydney Wests): Tests 6. GB (3) 1911, GB (2) 1920. 1911-12 Kangaroo tour. Four tries – 12 points.
FARNSWORTH Bill (Newtown): Tests 4. GB (2) 1910, GB (2) 1911. 1911-12 Kangaroo tour. Points – nil.
FARRAR Andrew (Canterbury-Bankstown): 1988 World Cup.
FARRELL Frank "Bumper" (Newtown): Tests 4. GB (3) 1946, NZ (1) 1948. Points – nil.
FERGUSON John (Sydney Easts): Tests 3. NZ (3) 1985. 1985 NZ tour. Points – nil.
FEWIN Harry (Brisbane Carltons): Tests 1. GB (1) 1920. Points – nil.
FIFIELD Cec (Sydney Wests): Tests 4. GB (4) 1929. 1929-30 Kangaroo tour. Points – nil.
FIHELLY Jack (Brisbane): 1908-09 Kangaroo tour.
FINCH Harry (South Sydney): 1929-30 Kangaroo tour.
FITTLER Brad (Penrith, Sydney City): Tests 22. PNG (2) 1991, GB (2) 1992, PNG (1) 1992, NZ (3) 1993, F (1) 1994, GB (3) 1994, F (1) 1994 (f), NZ (3) 1995, E (2) 1995, FJ (1) 1995, NZ (1) 1995 (w), FJ (1) 1996, ROW (1) 1997. 1990 Kangaroo tour, 1991 PNG tour, 1992 World Cup, 1993 NZ tour, 1994 Kangaroo tour, 1995 World Cup. Seven tries, one field goal – 29 points.
FITZGERALD Denis (Parramatta): 1975, 1977 World Series.
FITZSIMMONS Brian (Townsville): Tests 3. NZ (1) 1967, GB (1) 1970, NZ (1) 1971. 1968 World Cup, 1969, 1971 NZ tours. Points – nil.
FLANNERY Denis (Ipswich): Tests 13. GB (1) 1950, F (2) 1951, NZ (2) 1952, GB (1) 1952, F (2) 1955, GB (2) 1956, F (1) 1956. 1952-53, 1956-57 Kangaroo tours. 1954 World Cup. Four tries – 12 points.
FLORIMO Greg (North Sydney): Tests 4. GB (2) 1994, NZ (2) 1995. 1994 Kangaroo tour. One field goal – 1 point.
FOLKES Steven (Canterbury-Bankstown): Tests 5. NZ (3) 1986. F (1) 1986, GB (1) 1988. 1986 Kangaroo tour. Two tries – 8 points.
FOLWELL Arthur (Newtown): Tests 2. GB (2) 1933. 1933-34 Kangaroo tour. Points – nil.
FRANCIS Arthur (New Zealand): Tests 2. GB (1) 1911. 1911-12 Kangaroo Tour. One try, two goals, 7 points.
FRASER Charles "Chook" (Balmain): Tests 11. GB (1) 1911, GB (2) 1914, NZ (2) 1919, GB (3) 1920, GB (1) 1921. 1911-12 Kangaroo tour, 1919 NZ tour, 1921-22 Kangaroo tour. Two tries, one goal – 8 points.
FRAUENFELDER Eric (Ipswich): Tests 3. GB (3) 1924. Points – nil.
FRAWLEY Dan (Sydney Easts): Tests 7. GB (2) 1909, NZ (1) 1909, GB (2) 1911, GB (2) 1914. 1908-09, 1911-12 Kangaroo tours. Four tries, two goals – 16 points.
FRAWLEY Mick (Sydney Easts): Tests 1. NZ (1) 1909. Points – nil.
FREESTONE Eric (Tumut): Tests 1. GB (1) 1928. One goal – 2 points.
FROOME Keith (Newtown): Tests 8. NZ (2) 1948, GB (2) 1948, F (2) 1949, NZ (2) 1949. 1948-49 Kangaroo tour, 1949 NZ tour. Two tries, 12 goals – 30 points.
FULLERTON-SMITH Wally (Redcliffe, St George): Tests 8. NZ (2) 1983, GB (2) 1984, GB (3) 1988, PNG (1) 1988. 1985 NZ tour, 1988 v Rest of the World. One try – 4 points.
FULTON Bob (Manly-Warringah, Sydney Easts): Tests 20. GB (1) 1970, NZ (1) 1971, NZ (2) 1972, GB (3) 1973, F (2) 1973, GB (3) 1974, NZ (3) 1978, GB (3) 1978, F (2) 1978. 1968, 1970 World Cups, 1971 NZ tour, 1972 World Cup, 1973 Kangaroo tour, 1975 World Series, 1978 Kangaroo tour. 12 tries, four field goals – 40 points.
FURNER David (Canberra): Tests 1. GB (1) 1994. 1994 Kangaroo tour. Points – nil.
FURNER Don (Toowoomba): Tests 1. GB (1) 1956. 1956-57 Kangaroo tour. Points – nil.
GALLAGHER Noel (Bundaberg): Tests 2. GB (1) 1967,

F (1) 1967. 1967-68 Kangaroo tour. Points – nil.
GALLAGHER Peter (Brisbane Brothers): Tests 17. NZ (3) 1963, SA (2) 1963, GB (1) 1963, F (2) 1963, NZ (3) 1967, GB (3) 1967, F (3) 1967. 1963-64, 1967-68 Kangaroo tours. One try – 3 points.
GARDNER Fred (St George): Tests 1. GB (1) 1933. 1933-34 Kangaroo tour. Points – nil.
GARTNER Daniel (Manly-Warringah): Tests 1. PNG (1) 1996. Points – nil.
GARTNER Russel (Manly-Warringah): 1977 World Series.
GASNIER Reg (St George): Tests 36. NZ (3) 1959, GB (3) 1959, F (3) 1959, F (3) 1960, NZ (2) 1961, GB (2) 1962, NZ (3) 1963, SA (2) 1963, GB (3) 1963, F (3) 1963, F (3) 1964, NZ (2) 1965, NZ (3) 1967, GB (1) 1967. 1959-60 Kangaroo tour, 1960 World Cup, 1961 NZ tour, 1963-64 Kangaroo tour, 1965 NZ tour, 1967-68 Kangaroo tour. 26 tries – 78 points.
GEE Andrew (Brisbane Broncos): 1991 PNG tour.
GEE Hector (Ipswich): Tests 3. GB (3) 1932. Two tries – 6 points.
GEELAN Col (Newtown): Tests 8. F (1) 1951, NZ (3) 1952, GB (2) 1952, F (2) 1952. 1952-53 Kangaroo tour. Four tries – 12 points.
GEHRKE Bob (Redcliffe): 1961 NZ tour.
GEIGER Nick (North Brisbane): 1977 World Series.
GERARD Geoff (Parramatta, Manly-Warringah): Tests 6. GB (3) 1978, F (2) 1978, NZ (1) 1983. 1978 Kangaroo tour. One try – 3 points.
GEYER Mark (Penrith): Tests 3. F (1) 1990 (f), NZ (2) 1991. 1990 Kangaroo tour. One try – 4 points.
GIBBS Alf (Newcastle): Tests 5. GB (3) 1948, F (2) 1949. 1948-49 Kangaroo tour. One try – 3 points.
GIBBS Jimmy (Newcastle): Tests 7. GB (2) 1933, NZ (1) 1935, NZ (2) 1937, GB (2) 1937. 1933-34 Kangaroo tour, 1935 NZ tour, 1937-38 Kangaroo tour. Points – nil.
GIBBS John (Manly-Warringah): 1978 Kangaroo tour.
GIL Alan (Cairns): Tests 2. GB (2) 1962. 1961 NZ tour. Points – nil.
GILBERT Fred (Toowoomba): Tests 4. GB (1) 1936, GB (1) 1937, F (2) 1938. 1933-34 Kangaroo tour, 1935 NZ tour, 1937-38 Kangaroo tour. Two tries – 6 points.
GILBERT Herb (South Sydney, Sydney Wests): Tests 7. GB (3) 1911, NZ (2) 1919, GB (2) 1920. 1911-12 Kangaroo tour, 1919 NZ tour. Two tries, one goal – 8 points.
GILL Charlie (Newcastle): Tests 7. NZ (3) 1952, GB (1) 1952, NZ (3) 1953. 1952-53 Kangaroo tour, 1953 NZ tour. Points – nil.
GILLESPIE David (Canterbury-Bankstown, Sydney Wests, Manly): Tests 17. F (1) 1990, GB (1) 1990, F (2) 1990 (f), NZ (2) 1991, GB (3) 1992, PNG (1) 1992, NZ (2) 1993, NZ (3) 1995, E (1) 1995. 1988 World Cup, 1990 Kangaroo tour, 1992 World Cup, 1993 NZ tour, 1995 World Cup. Three tries – 12 points.
GILLETT George (New Zealand): 1911-12 Kangaroo tour.
GILLMEISTER Trevor (South Queensland): Tests 3. NZ (3) 1995. Points – nil.
GLASHEEN E. Melville (Townsville): 1933-34 Kangaroo tour.
GLEESON John (Toowoomba, Wynnum-Manly, Brisbane Brothers): Tests 10. F (2) 1964, GB (2) 1966, NZ (1) 1967, GB (3) 1967. 1963-64 Kangaroo tour, 1965 NZ tour, 1967-68 Kangaroo tour. Two tries – 6 points.
GLOVER Neville (Parramatta): Tests 2. NZ (2) 1978. Two tries – 6 points.
GODDEN Brad (Newcastle Knights): 1992 World Cup.
GOLDSPINK Kevin (Canterbury-Bankstown): 1967-68 Kangaroo tour.

GOODWIN Ted (St George): Tests 4. NZ (1) 1972, GB (1) 1973, F (2) 1973. 1973 Kangaroo tour. Two tries – 6 points.
GOODWIN Sid (Balmain): Tests 3. NZ (3) 1935. 1935 NZ tour. Two tries – 6 points.
GORMAN Tom (Toowoomba, Brisbane Brothers): Tests 10. GB (3) 1924, GB (3) 1928, GB (4) 1929. 1929-30 Kangaroo tour. Points – nil.
GOURLEY Scott (St George): Tests 1. PNG (1) 1991. 1991 PNG tour. Points – nil.
GRANT John (South Brisbane): 1972 World Cup.
GRANT Bob (South Sydney): Tests 2. GB (1) 1970, NZ (1) 1971. 1971 NZ tour, 1972 World Cup. Points – nil.
GRAVES Johnny (South Sydney): Tests 7. NZ (2) 1948, GB (2) 1948, NZ (1) 1949, GB (1) 1950, F (1) 1951. 1948-49 Kangaroo tour, 1949 NZ tour. Five tries, 14 goals – 43 points.
GRAVES Bob (Balmain): Tests 6. NZ (3) 1908, GB (1) 1909, NZ (2) 1909. 1908-09 Kangaroo tour. One try – 3 points.
GRAY Bert (Glebe): Tests 4. GB (3) 1920, GB (1) 1921. 1921-22 Kangaroo tour. One try – 3 points.
GREAVES Johnny (Canterbury-Bankstown): Tests 8. GB (2) 1966, NZ (1) 1967, GB (2) 1967, F (3) 1967. 1967-68 Kangaroo tour, 1968 World Cup. Three tries – 9 points.
GRICE John (South Brisbane): Tests 2. GB (2) 1946. Points – nil.
GRIFFITHS Frank (Balmain): 1937-38 Kangaroo tour.
GRIFFITHS Ron (Ipswich): 1949 NZ tour.
GROTHE Eric (Parramatta): Tests 8. GB (2) 1982, F (2) 1982, NZ (2) 1983, GB (2) 1984. 1982 Kangaroo tour. Ten tries – 34 points.
HAGAN Bob (Toowoomba): Tests 2. GB (1) 1962, NZ (1) 1963. Two goals – 4 points.
HALL Duncan (Brisbane Valleys, Toowoomba, Brisbane Wests): Tests 22. NZ (1) 1948, GB (2) 1948, F (2) 1949, GB (2) 1950, F (3) 1951, GB (3) 1952, F (3) 1952, GB (3) 1954, F (3) 1955. 1948-49, 1952-53 Kangaroo tours, 1954 World Cup. Nine tries – 27 points.
HALLETT Howard (South Sydney): Tests 6. GB (3) 1911, GB (3) 1914. 1911-12 Kangaroo tour. One try – 3 points.
HALLOWAY Arthur "Pony" (Glebe, Sydney Easts, Balmain): Tests 10. NZ (1) 1908, GB (1) 1908, NZ (2) 1909, GB (3) 1914, NZ (3) 1919. 1908-09, 1911-12 Kangaroo tours, 1919 NZ tour. Points – nil.
HAMBLY Brian (Wagga, Parramatta): Tests 18. GB (3) 1959, F (3) 1959, F (2) 1960, NZ (2) 1963, GB (2) 1963, F (3) 1963, F (1) 1964, NZ (2) 1965. 1959-60 Kangaroo tour, 1960 World Cup, 1963-64 Kangaroo tour, 1965 NZ tour. Two tries, two goals – 10 points.
HAMILTON Bill (Manly-Warringah): 1973 Kangaroo tour.
HAMMERTON Ernie (South Sydney): Tests 1. F (1) 1951. 1956-57 Kangaroo tour. Points – nil.
HANCOCK Michael (Brisbane Broncos): Tests 13. NZ (3) 1989, NZ (1) 1990, GB (1) 1990, GB (3) 1992, PNG (1) 1992, NZ (3) 1993, F (1) 1994. 1989 NZ tour, 1990 Kangaroo tour, 1992 World Cup, 1993 NZ tour, 1994 Kangaroo tour. Five tries – 20 points.
HANCOCK Rohan (Toowoomba): Tests 3. NZ (2) 1982, PNG (1) 1982. 1980 NZ tour, 1982 Kangaroo tour. Points – nil.
HAND Nevyl (North Sydney): Tests 2. NZ (1) 1948, GB (1) 1948. 1948-49 Kangaroo tour. Points – nil.
HANIGAN Les (Manly-Warringah): Tests 2. NZ (2) 1967. 1967-68 Kangaroo tour. Three tries – 9 points.
HANSEN Kevin (Sydney Wests): Tests 1. NZ (1) 1952. 1949 NZ tour. Points – nil.
HARDCASTLE Bill (Ipswich): Tests 2. NZ (2) 1908.

1908-09 Kangaroo tour. One try – 3 points.
HARDY Nelson (Sydney Easts): Tests 3. GB (3) 1928. Points – nil.
HARRAGON Paul (Newcastle Knights): Tests 16. GB (3) 1992, NZ (3) 1993, F (1) 1994, GB (1) 1994, F (1) 1994 (f), NZ (2) 1995, E (1) 1995, SA (1) 1995, FJ (1) 1996, PNG (1) 1996, ROW (1) 1997. 1992 World Cup, 1993 NZ tour, 1994 Kangaroo tour, 1995 World Cup. Three tries – 12 points.
HARRIS Mark (Sydney Easts): Tests 1. NZ (1) 1972. 1970, 1972 World Cups, 1975, 1977 World Series. Points – nil.
HARRISON Earl (Gilgandra): Tests 9. NZ (3) 1963, SA (2) 1963, GB (3) 1963, F (1) 1963. 1963-64 Kangaroo tours. Three tries – 9 points.
HASLER Des (Manly-Warringah): Tests 12. NZ (1) 1985, PNG (1) 1986, PNG (1) 1988, NZ (2) 1989, NZ (1) 1990, GB (2) 1990, F (2) 1990 (f), NZ (2) 1991. 1985 NZ tour, 1986 Kangaroo tour, 1988 v Rest of the World, 1989 NZ tour, 1990 Kangaroo tour. Two tries – 8 points.
HAUFF Paul (Brisbane Broncos) Tests 1. NZ (1) 1991. Points – nil.
HAWICK Greg (South Sydney, Wagga): Tests 6. GB (1) 1952, F (1) 1953, NZ (2) 1953, GB (2) 1958. 1952-53 Kangaroo tour, 1953 NZ tour, 1954, 1957 World Cups. One try – 3 points.
HAWKE Johnny (Canberra, St George): Tests 6. GB (2) 1948, F (2) 1949, NZ (1) 1949, F (1) 1951. 1948-49 Kangaroo tour, 1949 NZ tour. Points – nil.
HAWTHORNE Phil (St George): Tests 3. GB (3) 1970. Three goals – 6 points.
HAZELTON Charlie (Port Kembla): Tests 1. NZ (1) 1937. 1937-38 Kangaroo tour. Two tries – 6 points.
HAZZARD Noel (Bundaberg, Roma): Tests 13. F (3) 1951, NZ (3) 1952, GB (3) 1952, F (3) 1952, GB (1) 1954. 1952-53 Kangaroo tours. Two tries – 6 points.
HEDLEY Charlie (Glebe): Tests 3. NZ (2) 1908, GB (1) 1909. 1908-09 Kangaroo tour. Points – nil.
HEIDKE Les (Ipswich): Tests 9. GB (2) 1932, GB (3) 1936, GB (2) 1937, F (2) 1938. 1933-34, 1937-38 Kangaroo tours. Points – nil.
HEIDKE Bill (Bundaberg): Tests 4. GB (2) 1908, NZ (1) 1909, GB (1) 1910. 1908-09 Kangaroo tour. Points – nil.
HENDERSON Arthur (Booval Swifts): 1929-30 Kangaroo tour.
HENNESSY Arthur (South Sydney): Tests 2. NZ (2) 1908. 1908-09 Kangaroo tour. Points – nil.
HENRY Darcy (Forbes, Sydney Wests): Tests 2, F (1) 1955, NZ (1) 1956. One try – 3 points.
HEY Vic (Sydney Wests, Toowoomba): Tests 6. GB (3) 1933, GB (3) 1936. 1933-34 Kangaroo tour. Two tries – 6 points.
HICKEY Jack (Glebe): Tests 2. GB (2) 1910. One try, one goal – 5 points.
HIGGS Ray (Nambour, Parramatta): Tests 1. GB (1) 1974. 1975, 1977 World Series. Points – nil.
HILDITCH Ron (Parramatta): Tests 3. F (1) 1978, F (2) 1981. 1978 Kangaroo tour. Points – nil.
HILL Terry (Manly-Warringah): Tests 8. NZ (1) 1995, E (2) 1995, FJ (1) 1995, NZ (1) 1995 (w), FJ (1) 1996, PNG (1) 1996, ROW (1) 1997. 1994 Kangaroo tour, 1995 World Cup. Six tries – 24 points.
HINES Ray (Maitland): Tests 8. NZ (3) 1935. 1935 NZ tour. Three tries – 9 points.
HOHN Mark (Brisbane Broncos): Tests 1. F (1) 1994. Points – nil.
HOLLAND Jack (Newtown): Tests 7. NZ (1) 1948, GB (1) 1948, NZ (2) 1949, GB (3) 1950. 1948-49 Kangaroo tour, 1949 NZ tour. One goal – 2 points.
HOLLOWAY Henry (Newtown): Tests 3. F (3) 1955. One try – 3 points.
HOLMAN Keith (Sydney Wests): Tests 32. GB (3) 1950, F (3) 1951, NZ (2) 1952, GB (2) 1952, F (3) 1952, NZ (1) 1953, GB (3) 1954, F (3) 1955, NZ (3) 1956, GB (3) 1956, F (3) 1956, GB (3) 1958. 1952-53 Kangaroo tour, 1953 NZ tour, 1954 World Cup, 1956-57 Kangaroo tour, 1957 World Cup. 14 tries, six goals – 54 points.
HOLMES Jack (Newtown): 1929-30 Kangaroo tour.
HONAN Bob (South Sydney): Tests 2. NZ (2) 1969. 1969 NZ tour. Points – nil.
HOPKINS Bruce (Canterbury-Bankstown): 1948-49 Kangaroo tour.
HOPOATE John (Manly-Warringah): Tests 2. E (1) 1995, SA (1) 1995. 1995 World Cup. Three tries – 12 points.
HORDER Harold (South Sydney, North Sydney): Tests 13. GB (1) 1914, NZ (4) 1919, GB (3) 1920, GB (3) 1921, GB (2) 1924. 1919 NZ tour, 1921-22 Kangaroo tour. 11 tries, 10 goals – 53 points.
HORNERY Alan (South Brisbane): 1953 NZ tour.
HORRIGAN Jack (Brisbane Valleys): Tests 1. GB (1) 1948. 1948-49 Kangaroo tour. One try – 3 points.
HUNT Johnny (Ipswich): Tests 2. GB (2) 1924. Points – nil.
HUTCHINSON Jack (Newcastle): Tests 1. GB (1) 1946. Points – nil.
IRVINE Ken (North Sydney): Tests 31. F (1) 1959, F (3) 1960, NZ (2) 1961, GB (3) 1962, NZ (3) 1963, SA (2) 1963, GB (3) 1963, F (2) 1963, F (3) 1964, NZ (2) 1965, GB (3) 1966, NZ (3) 1967, F (1) 1967. 1959-60 Kangaroo tour, 1960 World Cup, 1961 NZ tour, 1963-64 Kangaroo tour, 1965 NZ tour, 1967-68 Kangaroo tour. 33 tries, 11 goals – 121 points.
IVES Clarrie (North Sydney): Tests 1. GB (1) 1924. 1921-22 Kangaroo tour. Points – nil.
JACK Garry (Balmain): Tests 20. GB (3) 1984, NZ (3) 1985, NZ (3) 1986, PNG (1) 1986, GB (3) 1986, F (2) 1986, NZ (1) 1987, GB (3) 1988, PNG (1) 1988. 1985 NZ tour, 1986 Kangaroo tour, 1988 v Rest of the World, 1988 World Cup. 11 tries – 44 points.
JACKSON Peter (Canberra, Broncos, North Sydney): Tests 9. GB (3) 1988, PNG (1) 1988, NZ (2) 1991, PNG (1) 1991, GB (2) 1992. 1989 NZ tour, 1991 PNG tour. Four tries – 16 points.
JAMES Brian (South Sydney): 1968 World Cup.
JARVIS Pat (St George): Tests 1. NZ (1) 1983. Points – nil.
JOHNS Andrew (Newcastle Knights): Tests 7. SA (1) 1995, FJ (1) 1995, NZ (1) 1995 (w), E (1) 1995, FJ (1) 1996, PNG (1) 1996, ROW (1) 1997. 1995 World Cup. Five tries, 50 goals – 120 points.
JOHNS Chris (Brisbane Broncos) Tests 9. F (1) 1990 (f), NZ (3) 1991, PNG (2) 1991, GB (2) 1992, PNG (1) 1992. 1990 Kangaroo tour, 1991 PNG tour, 1992 World Cup. One try – 4 points.
JOHNS Les (Canterbury-Bankstown): Tests 14. SA (2) 1963, F (1) 1964, NZ (2) 1965, GB (1) 1966, GB (3) 1967, F (3) 1967, NZ (2) 1969. 1963-64 Kangaroo tour, 1965 NZ tour, 1967-68 Kangaroo tour, 1969 NZ tour. Two tries, 30 goals – 66 points.
JOHNS Matthew (Newcastle Knights): Tests 6. NZ (2) 1995, E (1) 1995, SA (1) 1995, NZ (1) 1995 (w), FJ (1) 1996. 1995 World Cup. One try – 4 points.
JOHNSON Frank (Newtown) 1948-49 Kangaroo tour.
JOHNSTON Brian (St George): Tests 1. NZ (1) 1987. Points – nil.
JOHNSTON Albert "Ricketty" (Newtown, St George): Tests 8. NZ (4) 1919, GB (3) 1920, GB (1) 1921. 1919 NZ tour, 1921-22 Kangaroo tour. Two tries – 6 points.
JOHNSTON Ian (Sydney Wests, Parramatta): Tests 1. NZ (1) 1949. 1949 NZ tour, 1956-57 Kangaroo tour. Three goals – 6 points.

AUSTRALIAN INTERNATIONALS 1908–1997

JONES Fred (Manly-Warringah): 1968, 1972 World Cups.
JONES Lou (Sydney Easts): Tests 1. NZ (1) 1908. 1908-09 Kangaroo tour. One try – 3 points.
JORGENSON Joe (Balmain): Tests 3. GB (3) 1946. Four goals – 8 points.
JUNEE Kevin (Sydney Easts): 1967-68 Kangaroo tour.
JUSTICE Arthur "Snowy" (St George): Tests 5. GB (3) 1928, GB (2) 1930. 1929-30 Kangaroo tour. Points – nil.
KADWELL Harry (South Sydney): 1929-30 Kangaroo tour.
KAY Reg (South Brisbane): Tests 3. GB (3) 1946. Points – nil.
KEARNEY Ken (St George): Tests 25. GB (1) 1952, F (3) 1952, NZ (3) 1953, GB (3) 1954, F (3) 1955, NZ (3) 1956, GB (3) 1956, F (3) 1956, GB (3) 1958. 1952-53 Kangaroo tour, 1953 NZ tour, 1954 World Cup, 1956-57 Kangaroo tour, 1957 World Cup. One try – 3 points.
KELLY Noel (Ipswich, Ayr, Sydney Wests): Tests 25. NZ (3) 1959, F (1) 1960, NZ (1) 1963, SA (2) 1963, GB (3) 1963, F (1) 1963, F (2) 1964, GB (2) 1966, NZ (3) 1967, GB (3) 1967, F (2) 1967. 1959-60 Kangaroo tour, 1960 World Cup, 1963-64, 1967-68 Kangaroo tours. Two tries – 6 points.
KELLY Bill (Balmain): Tests 1. GB (1) 1914. One try – 3 points.
KENNEDY Clem (South Sydney): Tests 1. GB (1) 1946. One try – 3 points.
KENNY Brett (Parramatta): Tests 17. PNG (1) 1982, GB (3) 1982, F (2) 1982, GB (2) 1984, NZ (3) 1986, GB (3) 1986, F (2) 1986, NZ (1) 1987. 1982, 1986 Kangaroo tours. 10 tries – 36 points.
KERWICK John (South Sydney): 1919 NZ tour.
KING Johnny (St George): Tests 13. GB (3) 1966, NZ (1) 1967, GB (3) 1967, F (3) 1967, GB (3) 1970. 1967-68 Kangaroo tour, 1968 World Cup. Six tries – 18 points.
KINGSTON Jack (Young): Tests 3. GB (1) 1928, GB (2) 1930. 1929-30 Kangaroo tour. Points – nil.
KISS Les (North Sydney): Tests 4. NZ (2) 1986, PNG (1) 1986, GB (1) 1986. 1986 Kangaroo tour. Two tries – 8 points.
KITE Ross (St George, Wagga): Tests 5. F (3) 1955, GB (2) 1958. Three tries – 9 points.
KNEEN Steve (Cronulla-Sutherland): 1978 Kangaroo tour.
KNIGHT Stephen (Sydney Wests): 1972 World Cup.
KOLC John (Parramatta): 1977 World Series.
KOSEF Nik (Manly-Warringah): Tests 5. SA (1) 1995, FJ (1) 1995, NZ (1) 1995 (w), PNG (1) 1996, ROW (1) 1997. 1995 World Cup. One try – 4 points.
KRILICH Max (Manly-Warringah): Tests 13. NZ (1) 1978, GB (2) 1978, NZ (2) 1982, GB (3) 1982, F (2) 1982, PNG (1) 1982, NZ (2) 1983. 1978, 1982 Kangaroo tours. One try – 3 points.
LAING Bert (New Zealand): 1921-22 Kangaroo tour.
LAIRD Graham (Toowoomba): Tests 2. F (2) 1955. Two tries – 6 points.
LAIRD Ray (Mackay): Tests 1. GB (1) 1970. Points – nil.
LAMB Terry (Canterbury-Bankstown): Tests 7. NZ (2) 1986, GB (3) 1986, F (2) 1986. 1986 Kangaroo tour, 1988 World Cup. Points – nil.
LANG John (Brisbane Easts, Sydney Easts): Tests 3. F (1) 1973, GB (1) 1974, GB (1) 1978. 1973 Kangaroo tour, 1975 World Series, 1980 NZ tour. One try – 3 points.
LANGER Allan (Brisbane Broncos): Tests 19. PNG (1) 1988, F (1) 1990, NZ (1) 1990, GB (1) 1990, NZ (3) 1991, GB (3) 1992, PNG (1) 1992, NZ (3) 1993, F (1) 1994, GB (3) 1994, F (1) 1994 (f). 1988 v Rest of the World, 1988 World Cup, 1990 Kangaroo tour, 1992 World Cup, 1993 NZ tour, 1994 Kangaroo tour. Three

tries – 12 points.
LANGLANDS Graeme (St George): Tests 34. NZ (3) 1963, SA (2) 1963, GB (3) 1963, F (2) 1963, F (2) 1964, NZ (2) 1965, GB (2) 1966, NZ (3) 1967, GB (3) 1967, F (3) 1967, NZ (2) 1969, GB (1) 1970, NZ (1) 1971, NZ (2) 1972, GB (1) 1973, GB (2) 1974. 1963-64 Kangaroo tour, 1965 NZ tour, 1967-68 Kangaroo tour, 1968 World Cup, 1969, 1971 NZ tour, 1972 World Cup, 1974 Kangaroo tour, 1975 World Series. 17 tries, 69 goals – 189 points.
LANGMACK Paul (Canterbury-Bankstown): 1986 Kangaroo tour.
LARSON Gary (North Sydney): Tests 9. NZ (3) 1995, FJ (1) 1995, NZ (1) 1995 (w), E (1) 1995, FJ (1) 1996, PNG (1) 1996, ROW (1) 1997. 1995 World Cup. One try – 4 points.
LATTA Reg (Balmain): Tests 4. GB (1) 1922, GB (3) 1924. 1919 NZ tour, 1921-22 Kangaroo tour. Points – nil.
LAWS Fred (Toowoomba): Tests 6. GB (1) 1928, GB (1) 1930, GB (3) 1932, GB (1) 1933. 1929-30, 1933-34 Kangaroo tours. Points – nil.
LAZARUS Glenn (Canberra, Broncos): Tests 18. NZ (1) 1990, GB (3) 1990, F (2) 1990 (f), PNG (2) 1991, GB (3) 1992, PNG (1) 1992, NZ (3) 1993, GB (2) 1994, F (1) 1994 (f). 1990 Kangaroo tour, 1991 PNG tour, 1992 World Cup, 1993 NZ tour, 1994 Kangaroo tour. One try – 4 points.
LEIS Jim (Sydney Wests): 1980 NZ tour.
LEVISON Jack (South Sydney): Tests 1. NZ (1) 1909. Points – nil.
LEWIS Eric (South Sydney): Tests 9. NZ (2) 1935, NZ (2) 1937, GB (3) 1937, F (2) 1938. 1935 NZ tour, 1937-38 Kangaroo tour. Points – nil.
LEWIS Wally (Brisbane Valleys, Wynnum-Manly, Broncos, Gold Coast): Tests 33. F (2) 1981, NZ (2) 1982, GB (2) 1982, F (1) 1982, NZ (2) 1983, GB (3) 1984, NZ (3) 1985, NZ (3) 1986, PNG (1) 1986, GB (3) 1986, F (2) 1986, NZ (1) 1987, GB (3) 1988, PNG (1) 1988, NZ (3) 1989, NZ (1) 1991. 1982 Kangaroo tour, 1985 NZ tour, 1986 Kangaroo tour, 1988 v Rest of the World, 1988 World Cup, 1989 NZ tour. 11 tries, two field goals – 45 points.
LINDNER Bob (Wynnum-Manly, Parramatta, Sydney Wests, Illawarra): Tests 23. PNG (1) 1986, GB (3) 1986, F (2) 1986, NZ (1) 1987, GB (3) 1988, NZ (1) 1990, GB (3) 1990, F (1) 1990 (f), NZ (1) 1991, GB (3) 1992, PNG (1) 1992, NZ (3) 1993. 1986 Kangaroo tour, 1990 Kangaroo tour, 1992 World Cup, 1993 NZ tour. Six tries – 24 points.
LISLE Jimmy (South Sydney): Tests 6. GB (1) 1962, F (3) 1964, NZ (2) 1965. 1963-64 Kangaroo tour, 1965 NZ tour. Points – nil.
LITTLE Jack (Brisbane Valleys): Tests 1. GB (1) 1932. 1933-34 Kangaroo tour. Points – nil.
LULHAM Bobby (Balmain): Tests 3. GB (1) 1949, F (2) 1949. 1948-49 Kangaroo tour. One try – 3 points.
LUMSDEN Eddie (St George): Tests 15. NZ (2) 1959, GB (3) 1959, F (1) 1959, F (1) 1960, NZ (2) 1961, GB (2) 1962, NZ (1) 1963, SA (1) 1963. 1959-60 Kangaroo tour, 1961 NZ tour. Four tries – 12 points.
LUMSDEN Jack (Manly-Warringah): Tests 1. NZ (1) 1952. Points – nil.
LUTGE Dinny (North Sydney): Tests 3. NZ (3) 1908. 1908-09 Kangaroo tour. Two tries – 6 points.
LYE Graeme (Wollongong Wests): 1969 NZ tour.
LYNCH Ron (Parramatta): Tests 12. NZ (2) 1961, GB (1) 1962, GB (2) 1966, NZ (2) 1967, GB (2) 1967, F (2) 1967, GB (1) 1970. 1961 NZ tour, 1967-68 Kangaroo tour. One try – 3 points.
LYONS Cliff (Manly-Warringah): Tests 6. GB (2) 1990, F

(2) 1990 (f), PNG (2) 1991. 1990 Kangaroo tour, 1991 PNG tour. Two tries – 8 points.
MACKAY Brad (St George): Tests 12. F (1) 1990, NZ (1) 1990, GB (2) 1990, F (2) 1990 (f), GB (2) 1992, PNG (1) 1992, NZ (2) 1993, F (1) 1994. 1990 Kangaroo tour, 1993 NZ tour. Six tries – 24 points.
MACKAY Graham (Penrith): Tests 1. PNG (1) 1992. 1992 World Cup. Two tries – 8 points.
MACKAY Ian (Sydney Easts): 1975 World Series.
MacLENNAN Gordon (Cooma): 1937-38 Kangaroo tour.
McCABE Paul (Sydney Easts, Manly-Warringah): Tests 6. F (2) 1981, GB (1) 1982, F (2) 1982, NZ (1) 1983. 1982 Kangaroo tour. Two tries – 6 points.
McCABE Tom (Glebe): Tests 2. NZ (1) 1908, GB (1) 1909. 1908-09 Kangaroo tour. Points – nil.
McCAFFERY Ken (Toowoomba, North Sydney): Tests 5. NZ (3) 1953, GB (1) 1954, F (1) 1955. 1952-53 Kangaroo tour, 1953 NZ tour, 1954, 1957 World Cups. Four tries – 12 points.
McCARTHY Bob (South Sydney): Tests 10. NZ (2) 1969, GB (1) 1970, NZ (1) 1971, NZ (2) 1972, GB (2) 1973, GB (2) 1974. 1969 NZ tour, 1970 World Cup, 1971 NZ tour, 1972 World Cup, 1973 Kangaroo tour. Six tries – 18 points.
McCOY Matt (St George): Tests 2. NZ (2) 1949. 1949 NZ tour. Two tries, one goal – 8 points.
McCROHON Ken (Brisbane Wests): Tests 1. NZ (1) 1956. Points – nil.
McCUE Paddy (Newtown): Tests 4. GB (3) 1911, GB (1) 1914. 1911-12 Kangaroo tour. Two tries – 6 points.
McDONALD John (Toowoomba, Manly-Warringah): Tests 13. GB (1) 1966, NZ (2) 1967, GB (3) 1967, F (2) 1967, NZ (1) 1969, GB (3) 1970. 1967-68 Kangaroo tour, 1969 NZ tour. Five tries, nine goals – 33 points.
McDONALD Trevor (Toowoomba): Tests 1. NZ (1) 1959. Points – nil.
McGAW Mark (Cronulla-Sutherland): Tests 3. F (1) 1990, NZ (1) 1990, GB (1) 1990. 1988 v Rest of the World, 1988 World Cup, 1990 Kangaroo tour, 1991 PNG tour. Four tries – 16 points.
McGOVERN Des (Toowoomba): Tests 7. NZ (1) 1952, NZ (1) 1953, NZ (2) 1956, GB (2) 1956, F (1) 1956. 1952-53 Kangaroo tour, 1953 NZ tour, 1956-57 Kangaroo tour. One try – 3 points.
McGRATH Ted (South Sydney): 1921-22 Kangaroo tour.
McGREGOR Dugald (Bundaberg): Tests 2. NZ (1) 1909, GB (1) 1910. Points – nil.
McGREGOR Paul (Illawarra): Tests 4. F (1) 1994, SA (1) 1995, FJ (1) 1995, ROW (1) 1997. 1994 Kangaroo tour, 1995 World Cup. Three tries – 12 points.
McGUIRE Bruce (Balmain, Canterbury): Tests 2. NZ (2) 1989. 1989 NZ tour, 1991 PNG tour. Points – nil.
McINDOE Alan (Illawarra): 1988 v Rest of the World.
McKEAN Allan (Sydney Easts): Tests 1. GB (1) 1970. Seven goals – 14 points.
McKINNON Don (North Sydney): 1982 Kangaroo tour.
McKINNON Ross (Sydney Easts): Tests 8. NZ (2) 1935, NZ (2) 1937, GB (2) 1937, F (2) 1938. 1935 NZ tour, 1937-38 Kangaroo tour. Three tries – 9 points.
McKIVAT Chris (Glebe): Tests 5. GB (2) 1910, GB (3) 1911. 1911-12 Kangaroo tour. Four tries – 12 points.
McLEAN Doug (Brisbane): Tests 1. NZ (1) 1908. Points – nil.
McLEAN Doug (Ipswich): Tests 2. GB (1) 1937. 1937-38 Kangaroo tour. Three tries – 9 points.
McMAHON Allan (Balmain): 1975, 1977 World Series, 1978 Kangaroo tour.
McMAHON Pat (Toowoomba): Tests 9. NZ (2) 1948, GB (3) 1948, F (2) 1949, NZ (2) 1949. 1948-49 Kangaroo tour, 1949 NZ tour. Five tries – 15 points.

McMILLAN Frank (Sydney Wests): Tests 9. GB (4) 1929, GB (3) 1932, GB (2) 1933. 1929-30, 1933-34 Kangaroo tours. Points – nil.
McMURTRIE Charlie (Balmain): 1911-12 Kangaroo tour.
McRITCHIE Doug (St George): Tests 6. GB (2) 1948, F (2) 1949, GB (2) 1950. 1948-49 Kangaroo tour. Points – nil.
McTAGGART Barry (Balmain): 1970 World Cup.
MADDISON Ken (Cronulla-Sutherland): Tests 4. GB (3) 1973, F (1) 1973. 1973 Kangaroo tour. Three tries – 9 points.
MADSEN Peter "Mick" (Toowoomba): Tests 9. GB (2) 1929, GB (3) 1932, GB (3) 1933, GB (1) 1936. 1929-30, 1933-34 Kangaroo tour. Points – nil.
MAHER Pat (South Sydney): Tests 1. GB (1) 1928. 1929-30 Kangaroo tour. Points – nil.
MAHON Bill (Toowoomba): Tests 1. NZ (1) 1935. 1935 NZ tour. Points – nil.
MANTEIT Dennis (Brisbane Brothers): Tests 3. GB (2) 1967, F (1) 1967. 1967-68 Kangaroo tour, 1968 World Cup, 1969 NZ tour. Points – nil.
MARSH Bill (Cootamundra, Balmain): Tests 5. GB (1) 1956, F (1) 1957, GB (3) 1958. 1956-57 Kangaroo tour, 1957 World Cup. One try – 3 points.
MARTIN Steve (Manly-Warringah): Tests 1. F (1) 1978. 1978 Kangaroo tour. 1980 NZ tour. Points – nil.
MASTERMAN Jeff (Sydney Easts): Tests 2. F (2) 1981. One try – 3 points.
MAXWELL Col (Sydney Wests): Tests 1. GB (1) 1948. 1948-49 Kangaroo tour. Points – nil.
MAYES Johnny (Sydney Easts): 1975 World Series.
MEAD Les (Sydney Wests): Tests 1. GB (1) 1933. 1933-34 Kangaroo tour. Points – nil.
MENINGA Mal (South Brisbane, Canberra): Tests 45. NZ (1) 1982, PNG (1) 1982, GB (3) 1982, F (2) 1982, NZ (2) 1983, GB (2) 1984, NZ (3) 1985, PNG (1) 1986, GB (3) 1986, PNG (1) 1988, NZ (3) 1989, F (1) 1990, NZ (1) 1990, GB (3) 1990, F (2) 1990 (f), GB (3) 1991, PNG (2) 1991, GB (3) 1992, PNG (1) 1992, NZ (2) 1993, F (1) 1994, GB (3) 1994, F (1) 1994 (f). 1982 Kangaroo tour, 1985 NZ tour, 1986 Kangaroo tour, 1988 v Rest of the World, 1989 NZ tour, 1990 Kangaroo tour, 1991 PNG tour, 1992 World Cup, 1993 NZ tour, 1994 Kangaroo tour. 21 tries, 96 goals – 272 points.
MENZIES Steve (Manly-Warringah): Tests 9. NZ (3) 1995, E (2) 1995, FJ (1) 1995, NZ (1) 1995 (w), FJ (1) 1996, ROW (1997). 1994 Kangaroo tour, 1995 World Cup. Twelve tries – 48 points.
MESSENGER Herbert "Dally" (Sydney Easts): Tests 7. NZ (3) 1908, GB (2) 1908, GB (2) 1910. 1908 Kangaroo tour. Four tries, 16 goals – 44 points.
MESSENGER Wally (Sydney Easts): Tests 2. GB (2) 1914. One try, three goals – 9 points.
MIDDLETON Keith (North Sydney): Tests 3. GB (3) 1950. Points – nil.
MILES Gene (Wynnum-Manly, Broncos): Tests 14. NZ (1), 1983, GB (3) 1984, NZ (3) 1986, PNG (1) 1986, GB (3) 1986, F (2) 1986, NZ (1) 1987. 1982, 1986 Kangaroo tours, 1988 v Rest of the World. 8 tries – 32 points.
MILLER Gavin (Cronulla-Sutherland): Tests 1. PNG (1) 1988. 1988 v Rest of the World, 1988 World Cup. One try – 4 points.
MOIR Ian (South Sydney, Sydney Wests): Tests 8. NZ (1) 1956, GB (1) 1956, F (1) 1957, GB (2) 1958, NZ (3) 1958. 1954 World Cup, 1956-57 Kangaroo tour, 1957 World Cup. Six tries – 18 points.
MOIR Peter (Glebe): 1908-09 Kangaroo tour.
MOORE Brian (Newtown): 1967-68 Kangaroo tour.
MOORE Billy (North Sydney): Tests 3. SA (1) 1995, FJ (1) 1996, ROW (1997). 1995 World Cup. Points – nil.
MOORE Danny (Manly-Warringah): Tests 4. NZ (3)

AUSTRALIAN INTERNATIONALS 1908–1997 293

1995, SA (1) 1995. 1995 World Cup. Three tries – 12 points.
MORGAN Jim (Sydney Easts): Tests 2. GB (2) 1970. Two tries – 6 points.
MORGAN John (Manly-Warringah): Tests 2. NZ (2) 1965. 1965 NZ tour. Points – nil.
MORGAN Lionel (Wynnum-Manly): Tests 2. F (2) 1960. 1960 World Cup. Two tries – 6 points.
MORRIS Ray (University): 1933-34 Kangaroo tour.
MORRIS Rod (Brisbane Easts, Balmain, Wynnum-Manly): Tests 15. NZ (2) 1978, GB (1) 1978, F (1) 1978, GB (3) 1979, NZ (2) 1980, F (2) 1981, NZ (2) 1982, GB (1) 1982, F (1) 1982. 1977 World Series, 1978 Kangaroo tour, 1980 NZ tour, 1982 Kangaroo tour. One try – 3 points.
MORRIS Steve (Dapto): Tests 1. NZ (1) 1978. Points – nil.
MORTIMER Chris (Canterbury-Bankstown): Tests 1. PNG (1) 1986. 1986 Kangaroo tour. One try – 4 points.
MORTIMER Steve (Canterbury-Bankstown): Tests 8. F (2) 1981, NZ (2) 1982, PNG (1) 1982, NZ (1) 1983, GB (2) 1984. 1982 Kangaroo tour. Two tries – 6 points.
MORTON Andy (North Sydney): Tests 1. GB (1) 1909. 1908-09 Kangaroo tour. Points – nil.
MOSSOP Rex (Manly-Warringah): Tests 9. GB (3) 1958, GB (3) 1959, F (1) 1959, F (2) 1960. 1959-60 Kangaroo tour, 1960 World Cup. One try – 3 points.
MUGGLETON John (Parramatta): Tests 3. NZ (2) 1982, PNG (1) 1982. 1982 Kangaroo tour. One try – 3 points.
MUIR Adam (Newcastle Knights): Tests 3. NZ (1) 1995, SA (1) 1995, FJ (1) 1996. 1995 World Cup. One try – 4 points.
MUIR Barry (Brisbane Wests): Tests 22. NZ (3) 1959, GB (3) 1959, F (3) 1959, F (1) 1960, NZ (2) 1961, GB (1) 1962, NZ (2) 1963, SA (1) 1963, GB (3) 1963, F (3) 1963. 1959-60 Kangaroo tour, 1960 World Cup, 1961 NZ tour, 1963-64 Kangaroo tour. Two tries – 6 points.
MULLIGAN Noel (Newtown, Bowral, St George): Tests 10. GB (2) 1946, GB (3) 1948, F (2) 1949, NZ (2) 1949, F (1) 1951. 1948-49 Kangaroo tour, 1949 NZ tour. Two tries – 6 points.
MULLINS Brett (Canberra): Tests 5. F (1) 1994, GB (3) 1994, F (1) 1994 (f). Five tries – 20 points.
MURPHY Jim (South Brisbane): Tests 1. NZ (1) 1972. 1971 NZ tour. Points – nil.
MURRAY Joe (Newtown): 1911-12 Kangaroo tour.
MURRAY Mark (Brisbane Valleys, Redcliffe): Tests 6. PNG (1) 1982, NZ (1) 1983, GB (2) 1984, NZ (2) 1985. 1982 Kangaroo tour, 1985 NZ tour. One try – 4 points.
NARVO Herb (Newtown): Tests 4. GB (2) 1937, F (2) 1938. 1937-38 Kangaroo tour. Two tries – 6 points.
NEILL William "Webby" (Newtown): 1911-12 Kangaroo tour.
NEUMANN Fred (Brisbane Valleys): Tests 1. GB (1) 1932. 1933-34 Kangaroo tour. Points – nil.
NEWHAM Edgar (Cowra): Tests 2. GB (2) 1946. Points – nil.
NICHOLSON Robert (South Brisbane): Tests 2. NZ (1) 1909, GB (1) 1910. One try – 3 points.
NIEBLING Bryan (Redcliffe): Tests 13. GB (3) 1984, NZ (3) 1986, PNG (1) 1986, GB (3) 1986, F (2) 1986, NZ (1) 1987. 1986 Kangaroo tour. One try – 4 points.
NOBLE Bill (Newtown): Tests 6. NZ (3) 1909, GB (1) 1910, GB (2) 1911. 1908-09, 1911-12 Kangaroo tours. Points – nil.
NOLAN Fred (North Sydney): Tests 2. NZ (2) 1937. 1937-38 Kangaroo tour. One try – 3 points.
NORMAN Ernie (Sydney Easts): Tests 12. GB (2) 1932, NZ (1) 1935, GB (3) 1936, NZ (2) 1937, GB (2) 1937. 1935 NZ tour, 1937-38 Kangaroo tour. One try – 3 points.

NORMAN Ray (South Sydney, Sydney Easts): Tests 2. GB (1) 1914, NZ (1) 1919. 1919 NZ tour. One try – 3 points.
NORMAN Rex (Sydney Easts): 1921-22 Kangaroo tour.
NORVAL Andy (Sydney Easts): Tests 3. F (1) 1937, F (2) 1938. 1937-38 Kangaroo tour. Three tries – 9 points.
O'BRIEN Kevin (St George): 1956-57 Kangaroo tour.
O'CONNELL Wally (Sydney Easts, Wollongong, Manly-Warringah): Tests 10. NZ (2) 1948, GB (3) 1948, F (2) 1949, NZ (2) 1949, F (1) 1951. 1948-49 Kangaroo tour, 1949 NZ tour. Two tries – 6 points.
O'CONNOR Alf (South Sydney): Tests 3. GB (3) 1924. Points – nil.
O'CONNOR Frank (South Sydney): Tests 4. GB (2) 1932, GB (2) 1933. 1933-34 Kangaroo tour. One try – 3 points.
O'CONNOR Michael (St George, Manly-Warringah): Tests 17. NZ (3) 1986, PNG (1) 1986, GB (3) 1986, F (2) 1986, NZ (1) 1987, GB (3) 1988, PNG (1) 1988, NZ (2) 1989, F (1) 1990. 1985 NZ tour, 1986 Kangaroo tour, 1988 World Cup, 1989 NZ tour. 17 tries, 61 goals – 190 points.
O'DAVIS Robbie (Newcastle Knights): Tests 6. NZ (2) 1995, SA (1) 1995, FJ (1) 1995, NZ (1) 1995 (w), ROW (1) 1997. 1995 World Cup. Six tries – 24 points.
O'DONNELL Claude (Brisbane Carltons): Tests 4. NZ (4) 1919. 1919 NZ tour. Points – nil.
OLIPHANT Greg (Redcliffe): Tests 2. NZ (2) 1978. 1978 Kangaroo tour. Points – nil.
OLLING Graham (Parramatta): Tests 4. NZ (2) 1978, GB (2) 1978. 1977 World Series, 1978 Kangaroo tour. Points – nil.
O'MALLEY Larry "Jersey" (Sydney Easts): Tests 5. GB (3) 1908, NZ (2) 1909. 1908-09 Kangaroo tour. Points – nil.
O'NEILL John (South Sydney, Manly-Warringah): Tests 2. F (1) 1973, GB (1) 1974. 1970, 1972 World Cups, 1973 Kangaroo tour, 1975 World Series. Points – nil.
O'REILLY Bob (Parramatta): Tests 9. NZ (1) 1971, NZ (2) 1972, GB (3) 1973, F (1) 1973, GB (2) 1974. 1970 World Cup, 1971 NZ tour, 1972 World Cup, 1973 Kangaroo tour. Points – nil.
ORR Warren (Brisbane Wests): Tests 2. GB (2) 1974. 1973 Kangaroo tour. One try – 3 points.
ORROCK Bryan (St George): Tests 2. GB (1) 1956, F (1) 1956. 1956-57 Kangaroo tour. Points – nil.
O'SHEA Kel (Ayr Colts, Sydney Wests): Tests 15. GB (3) 1954, NZ (3) 1956, GB (3) 1956, F (3) 1956, GB (3) 1958. 1954 World Cup, 1956-57 Kangaroo tour, 1957 World Cup. Two tries – 6 points.
OWEN Bill (Newcastle): Tests 1. GB (1) 1962. 1961 NZ tour. Points – nil.
OXFORD Arthur (South Sydney, Sydney Easts): Tests 5. NZ (3) 1919, GB (2) 1924. 1919 NZ tour. One try, seven goals – 17 points.
PANNOWITZ Terry (Maitland): 1965 NZ tour.
PARCELL Gary (Ipswich): Tests 6. GB (2) 1959, F (2) 1959, F (1) 1960, GB (1) 1962. 1959-60 Kangaroo tour, 1960 World Cup. Points – nil.
PARISH Don (Dubbo, Sydney Wests): Tests 3. NZ (2) 1961, GB (1) 1962. 1959-60 Kangaroo tour, 1961 NZ tour. One try, seven goals – 17 points.
PARKINSON Dave (Balmain): Tests 3. GB (3) 1946. Points – nil.
PATEN Bill (Ipswich): Tests 2. NZ (1) 1919, GB (1) 1924. 1919 NZ tour. One try – 3 points.
PATERSON Jim (Townsville): Tests 8. NZ (3) 1959, F (2) 1959, F (1) 1960, NZ (2) 1961. 1959-60 Kangaroo tour, 1961 NZ tour. Points – nil.
PAUL Albert (Newcastle): Tests 4. NZ (3) 1952, GB (1) 1952. 1952-53 Kangaroo tour, 1953 NZ tour. One try –

3 points.
PAY Dean (Canterbury-Bankstown, Parramatta): Tests 9. GB (3) 1994, F (1) 1994 (f), E (2) 1995, FJ (1) 1995, NZ (1) 1995 (w), ROW (1) 1997. 1994 Kangaroo tour, 1995 World Cup. One try – 4 points.
PAYNE Tom (Toowoomba): Tests 1. F (1) 1957. 1956-57 Kangaroo tour. One try – 3 points.
PEARCE Cliff (Tamworth, Sydney Wests): Tests 7. GB (1) 1928, GB (3) 1932, GB (3) 1933. 1933-34 Kangaroo tour. One try – 3 points.
PEARCE Sid "Sandy" (Sydney Easts): Tests 14. NZ (2) 1908, GB (3) 1908, NZ (1) 1909, GB (3) 1914, GB (3) 1920, GB (2) 1921. 1908-09, 1921-22 Kangaroo tours. Points – nil.
PEARCE Sid "Joe" (Sydney Easts): Tests 13. GB (3) 1932, GB (2) 1933, NZ (3) 1935, GB (3) 1936, NZ (2) 1937. 1933-34 Kangaroo tour, 1935 NZ tour, 1937-38 Kangaroo tour. One try, one goal – 5 points.
PEARCE Wayne (Balmain): Tests 18. GB (3) 1982, F (2) 1982, GB (3) 1984, NZ (3) 1985, NZ (2) 1986, NZ (1) 1987, GB (2) 1988, PNG (1) 1988. 1982 Kangaroo tour, 1985 NZ tour, 1988 v Rest of the World, 1988 World Cup. Six tries – 21 points.
PEARD John (Sydney Easts, Parramatta): 1975, 1977 World Series.
PEGG Len (South Brisbane): Tests 2. NZ (2) 1948. 1948-49 Kangaroo tour. One try – 3 points.
PEPONIS George (Canterbury-Bankstown): Tests 8. NZ (1) 1978, GB (1) 1978, F (1) 1978, GB (3) 1979, NZ (2) 1980. 1978 Kangaroo tour, 1980 NZ tour. Two tries – 6 points.
PETERS Herman (North Sydney): 1921-22 Kangaroo tour.
PICKUP Tim (North Sydney, Canterbury-Bankstown): Tests 7. NZ (2) 1972, GB (2) 1973, F (2) 1973, GB (1) 1974. 1973 Kangaroo tour, 1975 World Series. Points – nil.
PIDDING Noel (St George, Maitland): Tests 16. NZ (1) 1948, GB (1) 1950, F (2) 1951, NZ (2) 1952, GB (2) 1952, F (2) 1952, NZ (3) 1953, GB (3) 1954. 1952-53 Kangaroo tour, 1953 NZ tour, 1954 World Cup. Six tries, 53 goals - 124 points.
PIERCE Greg (Cronulla-Sutherland): Tests 3. F (1) 1973, NZ (2) 1978. 1973 Kangaroo tour, 1975, 1977 World Series, 1978 Kangaroo tour. One try – 3 points.
PIERCE Harry (Sydney Easts): Tests 5. GB (3) 1937, F (2) 1938. 1937-38 Kangaroo tour. One try – 3 points.
PIGGINS George (South Sydney): 1975 World Series.
PITTARD Denis (South Sydney): Tests 2. NZ (2) 1969. 1969 NZ tour, 1970 World Cup. One try – 3 points.
PLATZ Greg (Toowoomba): Tests 1. NZ (1) 1978. Points – nil.
PLATZ Lew (Wynnum-Manly): 1975 World Series.
POOLE Dick (Newtown): Tests 10. F (1) 1955, NZ (3) 1956, GB (3) 1956, F (3) 1956. 1956-57 Kangaroo tour, 1957 World Cup. Four tries – 12 points.
POPE Norm (Brisbane Valleys): Tests 1. NZ (1) 1956. Five goals – 10 points.
PORTER Jim (Parramatta): 1975 World Series.
POTTER Norm (Brisbane Wests, Ipswich): Tests 7. NZ (1) 1919, GB (3) 1920, GB (3) 1924. 1919 NZ tour, 1921-22 Kangaroo tour. One try – 3 points.
PRENTICE Clarrie (Sydney Wests): Tests 5. NZ (2) 1919, GB (3) 1921. 1919 NZ tour, 1921-22 Kangaroo tour. Points – nil.
PRICE Ray (Parramatta): Tests 22. NZ (3) 1978, GB (3) 1978, F (2) 1978, GB (3) 1979, NZ (2) 1980, F (2) 1981, NZ (1) 1982, GB (2) 1982, PNG (1) 1982, NZ (1) 1983, GB (2) 1984. 1978 Kangaroo tour, 1980 NZ tour, 1982 Kangaroo tour. 10 tries – 31 points.

PRIGG Wally (Newcastle): Tests 19. GB (2) 1929, GB (1) 1932, GB (3) 1933, NZ (3) 1935, GB (3) 1936, NZ (2) 1937, GB (3) 1937, F (2) 1938. 1929-30, 1933-34 Kangaroo tours, 1935 NZ tour, 1937-38 Kangaroo tour. Four tries – 12 points.
PROVAN Norm (St George): Tests 14. GB (3) 1954, F (3) 1956, GB (1) 1958, NZ (3) 1959, F (2) 1960. 1954 World Cup, 1956-57 Kangaroo tour, 1957 World Cup. Seven tries – 21 points.
PROVAN Peter (Balmain): Tests 1. NZ (1) 1963. Points nil.
PURCELL Bernie (South Sydney): Tests 1. GB (1) 1950. 1956-57 Kangaroo tour. Points – nil.
QUAYLE John (Parramatta): 1975 World Series.
QUINN Graham (St George): Tests 1. NZ (1) 1980. 1980 NZ tour. Points – nil.
QUINN Paul (Gerringong, Newtown): Tests 7. SA (1) 1963, GB (2) 1963, F (1) 1963, F (1) 1964, NZ (2) 1965. 1963-64 Kangaroo tour, 1965 NZ tour. Points – nil.
RANDALL Terry (Manly-Warringah): 1973 Kangaroo tour. 1975, 1977 World Series.
RAPER Aaron (Cronulla-Sutherland): Tests 1. SA (1) 1995. 1995 World Cup. One try – 4 points.
RAPER John (St George): Tests 33. NZ (3) 1959, GB (1) 1959, F (2) 1959, F (3) 1960, GB (2) 1962, NZ (3) 1963, SA (2) 1963, GB (3) 1963, F (2) 1963, F (3) 1964, GB (1) 1966, NZ (3) 1967, GB (2) 1967, F (3) 1967. 1959-60 Kangaroo tour, 1960 World Cup, 1963-64, 1967-68 Kangaroo tours, 1968 World Cup. Nine tries – 27 points.
RASMUSSEN Elton (Toowoomba, St George): Tests 15. GB (1) 1959, F (1) 1960, F (3) 1960, NZ (2) 1961, GB (2) 1962, GB (3) 1967, F (3) 1967. 1959-60 Kangaroo tour, 1960 World Cup, 1961 NZ tour, 1967-68 Kangaroo tour, 1968 World Cup. Points – nil.
RAUDONIKIS Tom (Sydney Wests, Newtown): Tests 20. NZ (2) 1972, GB (3) 1973, F (1) 1973, GB (3) 1974, NZ (1) 1978, GB (3) 1978, F (2) 1978, GB (3) 1979, NZ (2) 1980. 1971 NZ tour, 1972 World Cup, 1973 Kangaroo tour, 1975, 1977 World Series, 1978 Kangaroo tour, 1980 NZ tour. Two tries – 6 points.
RAYNER Jack (South Sydney): Tests 5. NZ (1) 1948, GB (2) 1948, NZ (2) 1949. 1948-49 Kangaroo tour, 1949 NZ tour. One try – 3 points.
RAYNER Billy (Parramatta): Tests 2. F (2) 1960. 1960 World Cup. Points – nil.
REARDON Jack (North Brisbane): Tests 4. GB (3) 1937, F (1) 1938. 1937-38 Kangaroo tour. Two tries – 6 points.
REDDY Rod (St George): Tests 16. NZ (3) 1978, GB (3) 1978, F (1) 1978, GB (3) 1979, NZ (2) 1980, PNG (1) 1982, GB (3) 1982, F (1) 1982. 1977 World Series, 1978 Kangaroo tour, 1980 NZ tour, 1982 Kangaroo tour. Seven tries – 21 points.
RENOUF Steve (Brisbane Broncos): Tests 6. NZ (1) 1993, F (1) 1994, GB (3) 1994, F (1) 1994 (f). 1992 World Cup, 1993 NZ tour, 1994 Kangaroo tour. Seven tries – 28 points.
RHODES Johnny (Canterbury-Bankstown, Wynnum-Manly): 1968 World Cup, 1975 World Series.
RIBOT John (Sydney Wests, Manly-Warringah, Redcliffe): Tests 9. F (2) 1981, NZ (2) 1982, GB (1) 1982, PNG (1) 1982, NZ (3) 1985. 1982 Kangaroo tour, 1985 NZ tour. Nine tries, two goals – 34 points.
RICHARDS Bill (Brisbane Wests): Tests 4. GB (3) 1920, GB (1) 1922. 1921-22 Kangaroo tour. Points – nil.
RICHARDSON Geoff (Brisbane Wests): Tests 2. GB (2) 1974. Points – nil.
RIDLEY Alan (Queanbeyan, Sydney Wests): Tests 5. GB (2) 1933, GB (3) 1936. 1929-30, 1933-34 Kangaroo tours. One try – 3 points.

AUSTRALIAN INTERNATIONALS 1908–1997

RILEY John (St George): Tests 1. GB (1) 1959. 1959-60 Kangaroo tour. Points – nil.
RITCHIE Ray (Manly-Warringah): 1957 World Cup.
ROACH Steve (Balmain): Tests 19. NZ (3) 1985, NZ (3) 1986, PNG (1) 1986, GB (1) 1986, NZ (3) 1989, F (1) 1990, NZ (1) 1990, GB (3) 1990, F (2) 1990 (f), NZ (1) 1991. 1985 NZ tour, 1986 Kangaroo tour, 1988 v Rest of the World, 1988 World Cup, 1989 NZ tour, 1990 Kangaroo tour, 1991 PNG tour. Three tries – 12 points.
ROBERTS Ian (Manly-Warringah): Tests 13. NZ (1) 1990, NZ (3) 1991, PNG (2) 1991, NZ (2) 1993, F (1) 1994, GB (3) 1994, F (1) 1994 (f). 1991 PNG tour, 1993 NZ tour, 1994 Kangaroo tour. Three tries – 12 points.
ROBERTS Ron (St George): Tests 2. NZ (1) 1949, GB (1) 1950. 1949 NZ tour. One try – 3 points.
ROBINSON Jack (Balmain): Tests 5. NZ (4) 1919, GB (1) 1920. 1919 NZ tour. Three tries – 9 points.
ROBISON Harry (Toowoomba): 1937-38 Kangaroo tour.
ROBSON Ian (Brisbane Wests): 1969 NZ tour.
ROGERS Steve (Cronulla-Sutherland, St George): Tests 21. NZ (3) 1978, GB (3) 1978, F (1) 1978, GB (3) 1979, F (2) 1981, NZ (2) 1982, GB (3) 1982, F (2) 1982, PNG (1) 1982, NZ (1) 1983. 1973 Kangaroo tour, 1975 World Series, 1978, 1982 Kangaroo tours. Ten tries, 2 goals – 35 points.
ROONEY Jack (Toowoomba): Tests 2. NZ (2) 1952. 1952-53 Kangaroo tour. Points – nil.
ROOT Eddie (South Sydney): 1929-30 Kangaroo tour.
ROSENFELD Albert (Sydney Easts): Tests 4. NZ (3) 1908, GB (1) 1909. 1908-09 Kangaroo tour. One try – 3 points.
ROSEWELL John (South Sydney): Tests 1. NZ (1) 1908. 1908-09 Kangaroo tour. Points – nil.
RUSHWORTH Barry (Lithgow): Tests 1. F (1) 1964. 1963-64 Kangaroo tour. One try – 3 points.
RUSSELL Charlie "Boxer" (Newtown): Tests 3. GB (1) 1910, GB (2) 1911. 1911-12 Kangaroo tour. One try – 3 points.
RYAN Felix (Newtown): Tests 4. NZ (2) 1919, GB (2) 1921. 1919 NZ tour, 1921-22 Kangaroo tour. One try – 3 points.
RYAN Kevin (St George): Tests 2. F (2) 1964. 1963-64 Kangaroo tour. Points – nil.
RYAN Tommy (St George): Tests 4. GB (1) 1952, F (3) 1952. 1952-53 Kangaroo tour. Four tries – 12 points.
SADDLER Ron (Sydney Easts): 1967-68 Kangaroo tour.
SAILOR Wendell (Brisbane Broncos): Tests 1. GB (1) 1994. 1994 Kangaroo tour. Points – nil.
SAIT Paul (South Sydney): Tests 7. NZ (1) 1971, GB (3) 1973, F (1) 1973, GB (2) 1974. 1970 World Cup, 1971 NZ tour, 1972 World Cup, 1973 Kangaroo tour. Points – nil.
SALVATORI Craig (Sydney Easts): Tests 2. NZ (2) 1991. 1991 PNG tour. Points – nil.
SARGENT Mark (Newcastle Knights): Tests 4. GB (1) 1990, F (2) 1990 (f), PNG (1) 1992. 1990 Kangaroo tour, 1992 World Cup. One try – 4 points.
SATTLER John (South Sydney): Tests 4. NZ (2) 1969, GB (1) 1970, NZ (1) 1971. 1967-68 Kangaroo tour, 1969, 1971 NZ tours. Points – nil.
SAVORY, Charlie (New Zealand): 1911-12 Kangaroo Tour.
SCHOFIELD Don (Muswellbrook): 1957 World Cup.
SCHUBERT Ian (Sydney Easts): 1975 World Series, 1978, 1982 Kangaroo tours.
SCHUBERT Kevin (Wollongong, Manly-Warringah): Tests 19. NZ (2) 1948, GB (3) 1948, F (2) 1949, NZ (2) 1949, GB (3) 1950, F (2) 1951, NZ (3) 1952, GB (2) 1952. 1948-49 Kangaroo tour, 1949 NZ tour, 1952-53 Kangaroo tour. Points – nil.
SCHULTZ Bill (Balmain): Tests 7. NZ (2) 1919, GB (3) 1920, GB (2) 1921. 1919 NZ tour, 1921-22 Kangaroo tour. Points – nil.
SCOTT Colin (Wynnum-Manly): Tests 1. NZ (1) 1983. Points – nil.
SELLARS Les (Ipswich): 1929-30 Kangaroo tour.
SERDARIS Jim (Sydney Wests): Tests 1. NZ (1) 1995. 1994 Kangaroo tour. Points – nil.
SHANKLAND Bill (Sydney Easts): Tests 4. GB (4) 1929. 1929-30 Kangaroo tour. Three tries – 9 points.
SHEARER Dale (Manly-Warringah, Broncos, Gold Coast): Tests 20. NZ (1) 1986, GB (2) 1986, F (2) 1986, NZ (1) 1987, NZ (3) 1989, F (1) 1990, NZ (1) 1990, GB (3) 1990, F (2) 1990 (f), NZ (1) 1991, NZ (3) 1993. 1986 Kangaroo tour, 1988 World Cup, 1989 NZ tour, 1990 Kangaroo tour, 1993 NZ tour. 12 tries, 6 goals – 60 points.
SHIELDS Mick (Quirindi): 1935 NZ tour.
SIGSWORTH Phil (Newtown): Tests 1. F (1) 1981. Points – nil.
SIMMONS Royce (Penrith): Tests 10. NZ (3) 1986, PNG (1) 1986, GB (3) 1986, F (2) 1986, NZ (1) 1987. 1986 Kangaroo tour. Points – nil.
SIMMS Eric (South Sydney): 1968, 1970 World Cups.
SIMON John (Parramatta): Tests 1. ROW (1) 1997. One goal – 2 points.
SINCLAIR Jack (Manly-Warringah): Tests 1. NZ (1) 1961. 1961 NZ tour. Points – nil.
SING Matt (Penrith, Sydney City): Tests 3. NZ (1) 1995, PNG (1) 1996, ROW (1) 1997. One try – four points.
SIRONEN Paul (Balmain): Tests 21. PNG (1) 1986, F (1) 1986, NZ (2) 1989, F (1) 1990, NZ (1) 1990, GB (3) 1990, F (2) 1990 (f), GB (3) 1992, PNG (1) 1992, NZ (3) 1993, F (1) 1994, GB (2) 1994. 1986 Kangaroo tour, 1988 World Cup, 1989 NZ tour, 1990 Kangaroo tour, 1992 World Cup, 1993 NZ tour, 1994 Kangaroo tour. Three tries – 12 points.
SMITH George (Lithgow): Tests 1. GB (1) 1962. Points – nil.
SMITH Jason (Canterbury-Bankstown, Parramatta): Tests 9. NZ (3) 1995, E (2) 1995, SA (1) 1995, FJ (1) 1995, NZ (1) 1995 (w), PNG (1) 1996. 1994 Kangaroo tour, 1995 World Cup. One try – 4 points.
SMITH Len (Newtown): Tests 2. NZ (2) 1948. Points – nil.
SMITH Billy (St George): Tests 18. F (3) 1964, NZ (2) 1965, GB (3) 1966, NZ (3) 1967, GB (2) 1967, F (3) 1967, GB (2) 1970. 1965 NZ tour, 1967-68 Kangaroo tour, 1968, 1970 World Cups. Points – nil.
SMITH Bill "Circy" (Ipswich): Tests 1. GB (1) 1933. 1933-34 Kangaroo tour. Points – nil.
SMYTH Kevin (Sydney Wests): Tests 2. F (2) 1963. 1963-64 Kangaroo tour. Points – nil.
SPENCE Bill (South Sydney): Tests 1. GB (1) 1910. Points – nil.
SPENCER Bill (Bundaberg): Tests 4. GB (4) 1929. 1929-30 Kangaroo tour. One try – 3 points.
STAINS Dan (Cronulla-Sutherland): 1989 NZ tour.
STANMORE Frank (Sydney Wests): Tests 10. GB (3) 1950, F (2) 1951, GB (2) 1952, F (3) 1952. 1949 NZ tour, 1952-53 Kangaroo tour. Points – nil.
STANTON Frank (Manly-Warringah): 1963-64 Kangaroo tour.
STARLING Geoff (Balmain): Tests 7. NZ (2) 1972, GB (3) 1973, F (2) 1973. 1971 NZ tour, 1972 World Cup, 1973 Kangaroo tour. Five tries – 15 points.
STEHR Ray (Sydney Easts): Tests 11. GB (2) 1933, NZ (3) 1935, GB (3) 1936, NZ (2) 1937, GB (1) 1937. 1933-34 Kangaroo tour, 1935 NZ tour, 1937-38 Kangaroo tour. Two tries – 6 points.
STEINOHRT Herb (Toowoomba): Test 9. GB (3) 1928, GB (3) 1929, GB (1) 1932. 1929-30 Kangaroo tour. Points – nil.

STERLING Peter (Parramatta): Tests 18. GB (3) 1982, F (2) 1982, NZ (1) 1983, NZ (3) 1986, GB (3) 1986, F (2) 1986, NZ (1) 1987, GB (3) 1988. 1982, 1986 Kangaroo tours. Four tries, one field goal – 16 points.
STEVENS Gary (South Sydney): Tests 5. GB (2) 1973, F (1) 1973, GB (2) 1974. 1972 World Cup, 1973 Kangaroo tour, 1975 World Series. Points – nil.
STEWART Wayne (Brisbane Wests): Tests 1. NZ (1) 1972. Five goals – 10 points.
STRUDWICK Ross (Brisbane Valleys): 1975 World Series.
STUART Bob (Annandale): 1911-12 Kangaroo tour.
STUART Ricky (Canberra): Tests 9. GB (3) 1990, F (2) 1990 (f), GB (3) 1994, F (1) 1994 (f). 1990 Kangaroo tour, 1992 World Cup, 1994 Kangaroo tour. One try, one field goal – 5 points.
SULLIVAN Con (North Sydney): Tests 5. GB (1) 1910, GB (1) 1911, GB (3) 1914. 1911-12 Kangaroo tour. Points – nil.
SULLIVAN Gary (Newtown): Tests 2. NZ (2) 1972. 1970, 1972 World Cups. Two tries – 6 points.
SULLIVAN Bob (North Sydney): Tests 1. GB (1) 1954. Points – nil.
SUMMONS Arthur (Sydney Wests): Tests 9. NZ (2) 1961, GB (3) 1962, NZ (1) 1963, SA (1) 1963, F (2) 1963. 1961 NZ tour, 1963-64 Kangaroo tour. Four tries – 12 points.
SWEENEY Tom (Brisbane Wests): Tests 2. NZ (2) 1919. 1919 NZ tour. Points – nil.
TESSMANN Brad (South Brisbane): Tests 1. NZ (1) 1983. Points – nil.
THICKNESSE Viv (Sydney Easts): Tests 7. GB (2) 1933, NZ (3) 1935, GB (2) 1936. 1933-34 Kangaroo tour, 1935 NZ tour. Points – nil.
THOMAS Mark (Brisbane Brothers): 1977 World Series.
THOMPSON Alan (South Brisbane): Tests 3. GB (2) 1950, F (1) 1951. 1949 NZ tour. Points – nil.
THOMPSON Alan (Manly-Warringah): Tests 7. GB (2) 1978, GB (3) 1979, NZ (2) 1980. 1978 Kangaroo tour, 1980 NZ tour. Two tries – 6 points.
THOMPSON Duncan (North Sydney, Toowoomba): Tests 9. NZ (2) 1919, GB (2) 1920, GB (3) 1921, GB (2) 1924. 1919 NZ tour, 1921-22 Kangaroo tour. One try, four goals – 11 points.
THOMPSON Roy (North Sydney): 1937-38 Kangaroo tour.
THOMPSON Bill (Toowoomba): Tests 1. GB (1) 1948. 1948-49 Kangaroo tour, 1949 NZ tour. Points – nil.
THOMSON Allan (Newcastle): Tests 3. NZ (2) 1967, F (1) 1968. 1967-68 Kangaroo tour. Points – nil.
THOMSON Ian (Manly-Warringah): Tests 3. NZ (1) 1978, GB (1) 1978, F (1) 1978. 1978 Kangaroo tour. Points – nil.
THORNETT Ken (Parramatta): Tests 12. NZ (3) 1963, SA (1) 1963, GB (3) 1963, F (3) 1963, F (2) 1964. 1963-64 Kangaroo tour. Six tries – 18 points.
THORNETT Dick (Parramatta): Tests 11. SA (2) 1963, GB (3) 1963, F (1) 1963, F (1) 1964, GB (2) 1966. 1963-64 Kangaroo tour, 1968 World Cup. One try – 3 points.
THOROGOOD Charlie (Coorparoo): Tests 2. NZ (2) 1919. 1919 NZ tour. Points – nil.
TIDYMAN Bob (Sydney Easts): Tests 2. GB (2) 1914. Points – nil.
TOOVEY Geoff (Manly-Warringah): Tests 12. PNG (2) 1991, NZ (3) 1995, E (2) 1995, FJ (1) 1995, NZ (1) 1995 (w), FJ (1) 1996, PNG (1) 1996, ROW (1) 1997. 1991 PNG tour, 1995 World Cup. Points – nil.
TOWNSEND Dick (Newtown): Tests 3. NZ (2) 1919, GB (1) 1921. 1919 NZ tour, 1921-22 Kangaroo tour. Points – nil.
TREWEEK George (South Sydney): Tests 7. GB (3) 1928, GB (4) 1929. 1929-30 Kangaroo tour. One try – 3 points.
TREWHELLA David (Sydney Easts): 1989 NZ tour.
TROY Jack (Newtown): Tests 2. GB (2) 1950. Points – nil.
TUBMAN Bob (Ipswich): Tests 2. NZ (1) 1908, GB (1) 1910. Points – nil.
TUNKS Peter (Canterbury-Bankstown): Tests 6. NZ (2) 1985, NZ (3) 1986, NZ (1) 1987. 1985 NZ tour. Points – nil.
TURNER Ron (Cronulla-Sutherland): Tests 1. GB (1) 1974. 1970 World Cup. Points – nil.
TUTTY Dennis (Balmain): Tests 1. NZ (1) 1967. Points – nil.
TYQUIN Tom (South Brisbane): Tests 6. NZ (3) 1956, GB (2) 1956, F (1) 1956. 1956-57 Kangaroo tour, 1957 World Cup. Points – nil.
TYQUIN Bill (South Brisbane): Tests 6. NZ (2) 1948, GB (2) 1949, F (2) 1949. 1948-49 Kangaroo tour. Three tries – 9 points.
TYRRELL Tom (Balmain): Tests 2. NZ (1) 1952, GB (1) 1952. 1952-53 Kangaroo tour. Points – nil.
UPTON Jack (Toowoomba): 1929-30 Kangaroo tour.
VAUTIN Paul (Manly-Warringah): Tests 13. NZ (1) 1982, NZ (2) 1983, GB (1) 1984, NZ (2) 1985, GB (3) 1988, PNG (1) 1988, NZ (3) 1989. 1985, 1989 NZ tours. Points – nil.
VEIVERS Greg (South Brisbane): 1975, 1977 World Series.
VEIVERS Mick (South Brisbane, Manly-Warringah): Tests 6. GB (2) 1962, NZ (2) 1965, GB (2) 1966. 1965 NZ tour. Points – nil.
VEST Dick (Sydney Wests): Tests 7. NZ (1) 1919, GB (3) 1920, GB (3) 1921. 1919 NZ tour, 1921-22 Kangaroo tour. Four tries – 12 points.
WAITE David (Wollongong Wests, Cronulla-Sutherland): Tests 6. GB (2) 1973, F (2) 1973, GB (2) 1974. 1973 Kangaroo tour. Points – nil.
WALKER Andrew (Sydney City): Tests 1. PNG (1) 1996. Points – nil.
WALKER Bruce (Manly-Warringah): 1978 Kangaroo tour.
WALSH Ian (Eugowra, St George): Tests 25. GB (3) 1959, F (3) 1959, NZ (2) 1961, GB (3) 1962, NZ (3) 1963, SA (1) 1963, GB (3) 1963, F (1) 1963, F (1) 1964, NZ (2) 1965, GB (3) 1966. 1959-60 Kangaroo tour, 1961 NZ tour, 1963-64 Kangaroo tour, 1965 NZ tour. Points – nil.
WALSH Pat (Newcastle): Tests 3. GB (3) 1908. 1908-09 Kangaroo tour. Points – nil.
WALTERS Elwyn (South Sydney, Sydney Easts): Tests 12. NZ (2) 1969, GB (2) 1970, NZ (2) 1972, GB (3) 1973, F (2) 1973, GB (1) 1974. 1967-68 Kangaroo tour, 1969 NZ tour, 1970, 1972 World Cups, 1973 Kangaroo tour. One try – 3 points.
WALTERS Kerrod (Brisbane Broncos): Tests 8. N7 (3) 1989, F (1) 1990, NZ (1) 1990, GB (1) 1990, PNG (2) 1991. 1989 NZ tour, 1990 Kangaroo tour, 1991 PNG tour, 1992 World Cup. One try – four points.
WALTERS Kevin (Brisbane Broncos): Tests 9. PNG (2) 1991, GB (3) 1992, PNG (1) 1992, NZ (3) 1993. 1990 Kangaroo tour, 1991 PNG tour, 1992 World Cup, 1993 NZ tour, 1994 Kangaroo tour. Points – nil.
WALTERS Steve (Canberra): Tests 15. NZ (3) 1991, GB (3) 1992, PNG (1) 1992, NZ (3) 1993, F (1) 1994, GB (3) 1994, F (1) 1994 (f). 1991 PNG tour, 1992 World Cup, 1993 NZ tour, 1994 Kangaroo tour. Four tries – 16 points.
WARD Dennis (Manly-Warringah, Newcastle): Tests 2. NZ (2) 1969. 1969 NZ tour, 1972 World Cup, 1973 Kangaroo tour. Points – nil.

AUSTRALIAN INTERNATIONALS 1908–1997 **297**

WARD Laurie (Newcastle, North Sydney): Tests 10. NZ (3) 1935, NZ (2) 1937, GB (3), F(2) 1938. 1935 NZ tour, 1937-38 Kangaroo tour. Points – nil.
WATKINS Jack "Bluey" (Sydney Easts): Tests 7. GB (1) 1914, NZ (4) 1919, GB (2) 1921. 1919 NZ tour, 1921-22 Kangaroo tour. One try – 3 points.
WATSON Alex (Brisbane Wests): Tests 14. GB (3) 1954, F (3) 1955, NZ (3) 1956, GB (3) 1956, F (2) 1956. 1953 NZ tour, 1954 World Cup, 1956-57 Kangaroo tour, 1957 World Cup. Four tries – 12 points.
WATSON George (Brisbane): Tests 1. NZ (1) 1908. Points – nil.
WATT George (Sydney Easts): Tests 3. GB (3) 1946. Points – nil.
WATT Horrie (Balmain): Tests 3. GB (3) 1924. Points – nil.
WEARING Benny (South Sydney): Tests 1. GB (1) 1928. Two tries, three goals – 12 points.
WEIER Lloyd (North Sydney): Tests 3. NZ (2) 1965, GB (1) 1966. 1965 NZ tour. One try – 3 points.
WEISS Col (Bundaberg): Tests 3. NZ (1) 1969, GB (2) 1970. 1969 NZ tour. Points – nil.
WEISSEL Eric (Temora): Tests 8. GB (2) 1928, GB (3) 1929, GB (3) 1932. 1929-30 Kangaroo tour. One try, 15 goals – 33 points.
WELLINGTON Gary (Burdekin): 1965 NZ tour.
WELLS Harry (Wollongong, Sydney Wests): Tests 21. GB (1) 1952, F (1) 1953, NZ (3) 1953, GB (1) 1954, F (2) 1955, GB (2) 1958, NZ (3) 1959, GB (3) 1959, F (3) 1959, F (2) 1960. 1952-53 Kangaroo tour, 1953 NZ tour, 1954, 1957 World Cups, 1959-60 Kangaroo tour, 1960 World Cup. Eight tries – 24 points.
WESTAWAY Roy (Brisbane Valleys): Tests 2. GB (2) 1946. Points – nil.
WHITE Noel (Kurri Kurri): Tests 1. GB (1) 1946. Points – nil.
WHITTLE Gordon (Toowoomba): 1935 NZ tour, 1937-38 Kangaroo tour.
WHY Jack (South Sydney): Tests 2. GB (2) 1933. 1933-34 Kangaroo tour. Points – nil.
WILLEY Ron (Canterbury-Bankstown): 1952-53 Kangaroo tour.
WILLIAMS Bert (Bombala): Tests 3. GB (2) 1937, F (1) 1938. 1937-38 Kangaroo tour. Points – nil.
WILLIAMS Percy (South Sydney): Tests 4. NZ (2) 1937, GB (2) 1937. 1937-38 Kangaroo tour. Two goals – 4 points.
WILLIAMS Robert (Sydney Easts): Tests 2. GB (2) 1911. 1911-12 Kangaroo tour. Points – nil.
WILLIAMSON Lionel (Innisfail, Newtown): Tests 5. NZ (1) 1971, GB (2) 1973, F (1) 1973, GB (1) 1974. 1968, 1970 World Cups, 1971 NZ tour, 1973 Kangaroo tour. One try – 3 points.
WILLOUGHBY Gordon (Manly-Warringah): Tests 2. F (1) 1951, NZ (1) 1952. One try – 3 points.
WILSON Graham (Newtown): Tests 3. F (2) 1963, F (1) 1964. 1963-64 Kangaroo tour. One try – 3 points.
WILSON Joe (Ipswich): Tests 3. GB (3) 1932. One try – 3 points.
WILSON Billy (St George, North Sydney): Tests 10. NZ (3) 1959, GB (3) 1959, F (2) 1959, NZ (2) 1963. 1959-60 Kangaroo tour. Points – nil.
WISHART Rod (Illawarra): Tests 17. NZ (2) 1991, PNG (2) 1991, GB (2) 1992, GB (2) 1994, F (1) 1994 (f), NZ (3) 1995, E (2) 1995, NZ (1) 1995 (w), FJ (1) 1996, PNG (1) 1996. 1991 PNG tour, 1994 Kangaroo tour, 1995 World Cup. Thirteen tries, 43 goals – 138 points.
WITTENBERG John (Theodore, St George): Tests 6. GB (2) 1966, NZ (2) 1969, GB (2) 1970. 1968 World Cup, 1969 NZ tour. Points – nil.
WOODHEAD Charlie (North Brisbane): Tests 4. NZ (2) 1909, GB (2) 1910. Five tries – 15 points.
WOODWARD Frank (New Zealand): 1911-12 Kangaroo tour.
WOOLLEY Fred (Balmain): Tests 2. NZ (2) 1909. Points – nil.
WRIGHT David (Brisbane Brothers): 1975 World Series.
WYNN Graeme (St George): 1980 NZ tour.
WYNN Peter (Parramatta): Tests 3. NZ (3) 1985. 1985 NZ tour. Points – nil.
YAKICH Nick (Manly-Warringah): 1965 NZ tour.
YORK Colin (Queanbeyan): Tests 2. GB (2) 1928. Points – nil.
YOUNG Craig (St George): Tests 20. NZ (1) 1978, GB (3) 1978, F (2) 1978, GB (3) 1979, NZ (2) 1980, F (1) 1981, NZ (2) 1982, GB (2) 1982, F (2) 1982. PNG (1) 1982, GB (1) 1984. 1978 Kangaroo tour, 1980 NZ tour, 1982 Kangaroo tour. One try – 3 points.

1998 PREMIERSHIP DRAW

Round 1 — March 13, 14, 15
Brisbane	v Manly	ANZ Stadium
Canterbury	v Canberra	Belmore SG
Parramatta	v Penrith	Parramatta Stadium
Balmain	v Gold Coast	Leichhardt Oval
Adelaide	v North Qld	Adelaide Oval
Norths	v Newcastle	North Sydney Oval
Cronulla	v Sydney City	Shark Park
St George	v Wests	Kogarah Oval
Illawarra	v Melbourne	WIN Stadium
Auckland	v Souths	Ericsson Stadium

Round 2 — March 20, 21, 22
Canterbury	v Brisbane	Belmore SG
Penrith	v Canberra	Penrith FS
Gold Coast	v Parramatta	Carrara Stadium
North Qld	v Balmain	Cowboys Stadium
Manly	v Adelaide	Brookvale Oval
Sydney City	v Norths	SFS
St George	v Cronulla	Kogarah Oval
Wests	v Melbourne	Campbelltown SG
Souths	v Illawarra	SFS
Newcastle	v Auckland	Marathon Stadium

Round 3 — March 27, 28, 29
Brisbane	v Penrith	ANZ Stadium
Canberra	v Gold Coast	TBA
Parramatta	v North Qld	Parramatta Stadium
Balmain	v Manly	Leichhardt Oval
Adelaide	v Canterbury	Adelaide Oval
Norths	v St George	North Sydney Oval
Cronulla	v Melbourne	Shark Park
Wests	v Souths	Campbelltown SG
Illawarra	v Newcastle	WIN Stadium
Auckland	v Sydney City	Ericsson Stadium

Round 4 — April 3, 4, 5
Gold Coast	v Brisbane	Carrara Stadium
North Qld	v Canberra	Cowboys Stadium
Manly	v Parramatta	Brookvale Oval
Canterbury	v Balmain	Belmore SG
Penrith	v Adelaide	Penrith FS
Melbourne	v Norths	Olympic Park
Souths	v Cronulla	SFS
Newcastle	v Wests	Marathon Stadium
Sydney City	v Illawarra	SFS
St George	v Auckland	Kogarah Oval

Round 5 — April 10, 11, 12
Brisbane	v North Qld	ANZ Stadium
Canberra	v Manly	Bruce Stadium
Parramatta	v Canterbury	Parramatta Stadium
Balmain	v Penrith	Leichhardt Oval
Adelaide	v Gold Coast	Adelaide Oval
Norths	v Souths	North Sydney Oval
Newcastle	v Cronulla	Marathon Stadium
Wests	v Sydney City	Campbelltown SG
Illawarra	v St George	WIN Stadium
Auckland	v Melbourne	Ericsson Stadium

Round 6 — April 17, 18, 19
Manly	v Brisbane	Brookvale Oval
Norths	v Auckland	North Sydney Oval
North Qld	v Newcastle	Cowboys Stadium
Sydney City	v Adelaide	SFS
Cronulla	v Balmain	Shark Park
Canterbury	v Gold Coast	Belmore SG
Canberra	v Illawarra	Bruce Stadium
Parramatta	v Melbourne	Parramatta Stadium
Penrith	v St George	Penrith FS
Souths	v Wests	SFS

ANZAC TEST MATCH — Friday, April 24
Australia	v New Zealand	TBA

Round 7 — April 25, 26
Brisbane	v Norths	ANZ Stadium
Manly	v Souths	Brookvale Oval
Auckland	v Newcastle	Ericsson Stadium
North Qld	v Sydney City	Cowboys Stadium
Adelaide	v Cronulla	Adelaide Oval
Balmain	v Canterbury	Leichhardt Oval
Gold Coast	v Canberra	Carrara Stadium
Illawarra	v Parramatta	WIN Stadium
Melbourne	v Penrith	Olympic Park
Wests	v St George	Campbelltown SG

Round 8 — May 1, 2, 3
Newcastle	v Brisbane	Marathon Stadium
Norths	v Manly	North Sydney Oval
Sydney City	v Auckland	SFS
Cronulla	v North Qld	Shark Park
Canterbury	v Adelaide	Belmore SG
Canberra	v Balmain	Bruce Stadium
Parramatta	v Gold Coast	Parramatta Stadium
Penrith	v Illawarra	Penrith FS
Melbourne	v Wests	Olympic Park
St George	v Souths	Kogarah Oval

Round 9 — May 8, 9, 10
Brisbane	v Sydney City	ANZ Stadium
Manly	v Newcastle	Brookvale Oval
Souths	v Norths	SFS
Auckland	v Cronulla	Ericsson Stadium
North Qld	v Canterbury	Cowboys Stadium
Adelaide	v Canberra	Adelaide Oval
Balmain	v Parramatta	Leichhardt Oval
Gold Coast	v Penrith	Carrara Stadium
Illawarra	v Wests	WIN Stadium
Melbourne	v St George	Olympic Park

Round 10 — May 15, 16, 17
Cronulla	v Brisbane	Shark Park
Sydney City	v Manly	SFS
Newcastle	v Norths	Marathon Stadium
Souths	v Melbourne	SFS
Canterbury	v Auckland	Belmore SG
Canberra	v North Qld	Bruce Stadium
Parramatta	v Adelaide	Parramatta Stadium
Penrith	v Balmain	Penrith FS
Wests	v Gold Coast	Campbelltown SG
St George	v Illawarra	Kogarah Oval

State of Origin — Game 1 — Friday, May 22
NSW	v Queensland	SFS

Round 11 — May 23, 24
Brisbane	v Canterbury	ANZ Stadium
Manly	v Cronulla	Brookvale Oval
Norths	v Sydney City	North Sydney Oval
Newcastle	v Souths	Marathon Stadium
Auckland	v Canberra	Ericsson Stadium
North Qld	v Parramatta	Cowboys Stadium
Adelaide	v Penrith	Adelaide Oval
Balmain	v Wests	Leichhardt Oval
Gold Coast	v St George	Carrara Stadium
Melbourne	v Illawarra	Olympic Park

Round 12 — May 29, 30, 31
Canberra	v Brisbane	Bruce Stadium
Canterbury	v Manly	Belmore SG
Cronulla	v Norths	Shark Park
Sydney City	v Newcastle	SFS
Illawarra	v Souths	WIN Stadium
Parramatta	v Auckland	Parramatta Stadium
Penrith	v North Qld	Penrith FS
Wests	v Adelaide	Campbelltown SG
St George	v Balmain	Kogarah Oval
Melbourne	v Gold Coast	Olympic Park

State of Origin — Game 2 — Friday, June 5
Queensland v NSW — Suncorp Stadium

Round 13 — June 6, 7
Brisbane v Parramatta — ANZ Stadium
Manly v Canberra — Brookvale Oval
Canterbury v Norths — Belmore SG
Cronulla v Newcastle — Shark Park
Souths v Sydney City — SFS
Auckland v Penrith — Ericsson Stadium
North Qld v Wests — Cowboys Stadium
Adelaide v St George — Adelaide Oval
Balmain v Melbourne — Leichhardt Oval
Gold Coast v Illawarra — Carrara Stadium

Round 14 — June 12, 13, 14
Penrith v Brisbane — Penrith FS
Parramatta v Manly — Parramatta Stadium
Norths v Canberra — North Sydney Oval
Newcastle v Canterbury — Marathon Stadium
Sydney City v Cronulla — SFS
Souths v Gold Coast — SFS
Wests v Auckland — Campbelltown SG
St George v North Qld — Kogarah Oval
Melbourne v Adelaide — Olympic Park
Illawarra v Balmain — WIN Stadium

State of Origin — Game 3 — Friday, June 19
Queensland v NSW — Suncorp Stadium

Round 15 — June 20, 21
Brisbane v Wests — ANZ Stadium
Manly v Penrith — Brookvale Oval
Parramatta v Norths — Parramatta Stadium
Canberra v Newcastle — Bruce Stadium
Canterbury v Sydney City — Belmore SG
Cronulla v Souths — Shark Park
Auckland v St George — Ericsson Stadium
North Qld v Melbourne — Cowboys Stadium
Adelaide v Illawarra — Adelaide Oval
Gold Coast v Balmain — Carrara Stadium

Round 16 — June 26, 27, 28
St George v Brisbane — Kogarah Oval
Wests v Manly — Campbelltown SG
Norths v Penrith — North Sydney Oval
Newcastle v Parramatta — Marathon Stadium
Sydney City v Canberra — SFS
Cronulla v Canterbury — Shark Park
Melbourne v Auckland — Olympic Park
Illawarra v North Qld — WIN Stadium
Gold Coast v Adelaide — Carrara Stadium
Balmain v Souths — Leichhardt Oval

Round 17 — July 3, 4, 5
Brisbane v Melbourne — ANZ Stadium
Manly v St George — Brookvale Oval
Norths v Wests — North Sydney Oval
Penrith v Newcastle — Penrith FS
Sydney City v Parramatta — SFS
Canberra v Cronulla — Bruce Stadium
Souths v Canterbury — SFS
Auckland v Illawarra — Ericsson Stadium
North Qld v Gold Coast — Cowboys Stadium
Adelaide v Balmain — Adelaide Oval

Round 18 — July 10, 11, 12
Illawarra v Brisbane — WIN Stadium
Melbourne v Manly — Olympic Park
St George v Norths — Kogarah Oval
Wests v Newcastle — Campbelltown SG
Penrith v Sydney City — Penrith FS
Parramatta v Cronulla — Parramatta Stadium
Canberra v Canterbury — Bruce Stadium
Souths v Adelaide — SFS
Gold Coast v Auckland — Carrara Stadium
Balmain v North Qld — Leichhardt Oval

Round 19 — July 17, 18, 19
Brisbane v Gold Coast — ANZ Stadium
Manly v Illawarra — Brookvale Oval
Norths v Melbourne — North Sydney Oval
Newcastle v St George — Marathon Stadium
Sydney City v Wests — SFS
Cronulla v Penrith — Shark Park
Canterbury v Parramatta — Belmore SG
Canberra v Souths — Bruce Stadium
Auckland v Balmain — Ericsson Stadium
North Qld v Adelaide — Cowboys Stadium

Round 20 — July 24, 25, 26
Balmain v Brisbane — Leichhardt Oval
Gold Coast v Manly — Carrara Stadium
Illawarra v Norths — WIN Stadium
Melbourne v Newcastle — Olympic Park
St George v Sydney City — Kogarah Oval
Wests v Cronulla — Campbelltown SG
Penrith v Canterbury — Penrith FS
Parramatta v Canberra — Parramatta Stadium
North Qld v Souths — Cowboys Stadium
Adelaide v Auckland — Adelaide Oval

Round 21 — July 31; August 1, 2
Brisbane v Adelaide — ANZ Stadium
Manly v Balmain — Brookvale Oval
Gold Coast v Norths — Carrara Stadium
Newcastle v Illawarra — Marathon Stadium
Sydney City v Melbourne — SFS
Cronulla v St George — Shark Park
Canterbury v Wests — Belmore SG
Canberra v Penrith — Bruce Stadium
Souths v Parramatta — SFS
Auckland v North Qld — Ericsson Stadium

Round 22 — August 7, 8, 9
North Qld v Brisbane — Cowboys Stadium
Adelaide v Manly — Adelaide Oval
Norths v Balmain — North Sydney Oval
Newcastle v Gold Coast — Marathon Stadium
Illawarra v Sydney City — WIN Stadium
Melbourne v Cronulla — Olympic Park
St George v Canterbury — Kogarah Oval
Wests v Canberra — Campbelltown SG
Penrith v Parramatta — Penrith FS
Souths v Auckland — SFS

Round 23 — August 14, 15, 16
Brisbane v Auckland — ANZ Stadium
Manly v North Qld — Brookvale Oval
Adelaide v Norths — Adelaide Oval
Balmain v Newcastle — Leichhardt Oval
Sydney City v Gold Coast — SFS
Cronulla v Illawarra — Shark Park
Canterbury v Melbourne — Belmore SG
Canberra v St George — Bruce Stadium
Parramatta v Wests — Parramatta Stadium
Penrith v Souths — Penrith FS

Round 24 — August 21, 22, 23
Souths v Brisbane — SFS
Auckland v Manly — Ericsson Stadium
Norths v North Qld — North Sydney Oval
Newcastle v Adelaide — Marathon Stadium
Balmain v Sydney City — Leichhardt Oval
Gold Coast v Cronulla — Carrara Stadium
Illawarra v Canterbury — WIN Stadium
Melbourne v Canberra — Olympic Park
St George v Parramatta — Kogarah Oval
Wests v Penrith — Campbelltown SG

Final Series
Week One — August 28–30
Week Two — September 4–6
Week Three — September 12–13
Week Four — September 19–20

GRAND FINAL September 27

Draw is subject to change.